EXPERIENCE, ENVIRONMENT, AND HUMAN POTENTIALS

EXPERIENCE, ENVIRONMENT, AND HUMAN POTENTIALS

HERBERT L. LEFF
University of Vermont

New York
OXFORD UNIVERSITY PRESS
1978

Library of Congress Cataloging in Publication Data

Leff, Herbert L   1944-
    Experience, environment, and human potentials.

    Includes bibliographical references and indexes.
    1.   Environmental psychology.   2.   Self-actualization
(Psychology)   I.   Title.
BF353.L43   301.31   76-57478
ISBN 0-19-502254-8
ISBN 0-19-502255-6 pbk.

on, environmental studies, futuristics, utopian thinking,
behavioral geography, environmental design, social policy,
eld that touches directly on questions involving our major
ronmental problems and what we can do both to alleviate
ild a more humane, ecologically viable future.

nts

ke to thank my wife, Ellen, for her tireless and insightful
nce throughout the years of work on this book. In addi-
ke to express deep appreciation to William Halpin, Vice
ford University Press, and Oxford's editorial staff for an
lly working relationship, and to the following reviewers
elpful comments and suggestions at various stages of the
velopment: Irwin Altman, Saul Cohen, Kenneth Craik,
and Robert Sommer. Many friends, colleagues, and stu-
rous to mention individually here, also contributed stimu-
uragement along the way. And special thanks are due
terle, Leslie Weiger, Llynda Cobb, and Kimberly Nelson
typing of the manuscript. Finally, I would like to ac-
aid of my son, Jacob, who at the age of three began
it wings on the chapters." I'm still not sure exactly what
but he was definitely a source of inspiration.

H. L. L.

To my parents, Rachel and Samuel Leff

mental educati
social change,
and any other f
social and envi
them and to bu

Acknowledgme

First, I would l
editorial assista
tion, I would li
President of Ox
open and frien
for their very h
manuscript's de
Brewster Smith
dents, too nume
lation and enc
Hildegarde Bols
for their expert
knowledge the
urging me to "p
he had in mind,

Burlington, Vt.
May, 1977

PREFACE

My main goal in this book h
enhancement of human exp
as possible to theory and res
Most centrally, I have tried
bility for a more fulfilling, m
way of life. At times such a
contrast between things as
despite the critical tone of
is that we human beings ge
experience and environmen

In addition, this is a te
with an extensive range of
of interrelations between
However, this book also t
cial-action approach to iss
any single academic discip
the desirability of suggest
in major sociocultural inst
and orientation, the cent
mental, social, and cogn
theories, and findings p
should also be of interest
will prove of value to st

CONTENTS

EXPERIENCE, ENVIRONMENT, AND HUMAN POTENTIALS

1
INTRODUCTION

EXPERIENCE

EXPERIENCE AND BEHAVIOR

SYSTEMS THINKING

ENVIRONMENTAL PSYCHOLOGY

MAIN THEMES
1. Intrinsic Motivation
2. Self-Directed Cognition
3. Pro-Life Values
4. Ecological Consciousness
5. Life-Enhancing Environmental Design
6. Designing and Moving Toward "Utopia"

NOTES

EXPERIENCE

Experience is conscious awareness. Perceiving, remembering, imagining, thinking, and feeling, insofar as they involve awareness, are processes of *experiencing*. In dreamless sleep, we are not experiencing; when wide awake, we are. To define "experience" other than by pointing out instances of it is an impossible task, like the conundrum of explaining what a particular color looks like to someone who has been blind from birth. Although the current scientific belief is that experience arises only through the functioning of a living nervous system, let us for the moment skirt the philosophical problems of mind/body relations and how you can ever know whether "minds" other than your own exist or what is going on in them. Let us assume that human beings (and presumably other animals with similar nervous systems) do experience—that is, are consciously aware—and can, at least in the case of people, readily communicate with each other about many aspects of their experience. Armed with this assumption and, I trust, an intuitive understanding of what it means to experience, we can proceed to examine why experience is a topic worth our consideration.

Anything that makes your life pleasant or unpleasant does so only because it affects your experience. The joys of climbing a tree, giving toys to children, or spinning out wild daydreams obviously arise from what you are aware of when you do them and how this makes you feel. (The torture of breaking an arm as you fall out of the tree also derives from your experience, but we might as well stick to pleasant examples at the start.) The quality of your life over the long haul may be conceived of as a weighted composite of all your experiences. Each of us no doubt has different ways of weighting experience—some giving special impor tance to moments of intense joy, others to enduring feelings of moral o intellectual excellence, and so forth—but it seems obvious that the de gree to which one finds one's life valuable, pleasant, or worthwhile rests inextricably on characteristics of one's experience.

Indeed, it makes no sense to speak of finding something pleasant or valuable in the absence of conscious awareness. Computers and thermo stats, for example, may be goal-oriented in varying degrees, make use of feedback from their environments, and (in the case of computers) sometimes engage in actual decision-making behavior; but they will be neither happy nor sad, regardless of what happens to them or to their environments or goals. Something that does not experience cannot care about anything or feel concern, and can thus regard nothing as valuable or worthwhile. Some non-conscious things can behave, discriminate among alternatives, and even choose, but none can be bothered or elated by anything that happens. Only conscious creatures have this ability, and I submit that everything that is important is important solely insofar as it does impinge or might impinge in some way on the experience of the creature it is important to. Turning this around, if you want to gauge the importance of anything to you, find out how it does affect or might affect your experience.

EXPERIENCE AND BEHAVIOR

Before turning to the interrelations of experience and environment, let us briefly consider the following question: If experience is so inherently important, why has so much emphasis in psychology and related disciplines been placed on overt *behavior?* That is, why have the explanation, prediction, and control of the observable actions of people often been treated as the ultimate goals of psychology and the social sciences? Aside from simple curiosity about the things people do, two likely reasons are that, first of all, overt behavior, as opposed to inner experience, is easier to study (except when psychologists study themselves); and second, the study of overt behavior makes psychology seem more like physics or biology. In addition, only a person's overt behavior can have a direct effect on *another* person's experience (excluding telepathy, if it occurs). This last point is important, because if you are interested in predicting or controlling another person for *your* benefit—that is, to improve the quality of your experience—it is that person's *behavior* you are likely to be most concerned about. It is possible that people who support or conduct psychological or social research may at times be motivated by such selfish concerns; but aside from research in areas such as advertising and military defense, there is little reason to suspect deliberate Machiavellian motives.

Unfortunately, however, there may be an even more insidious reason underlying the emphasis on behavior in the "behavioral" sciences. It is no secret that ours is a highly utilitarian and materialistic culture, devoted to growth in the production and consumption of goods and services. In such a cultural context it makes distressingly good sense for psychology to focus on the prediction and control of overt behavior; the production and consumption of goods and services occur only through overt behavior. Our value system, religions, and educational establishments also stress hard work, productivity, achievement, and acquisition —very behavioral goals, you must agree. Happiness, enjoying your work, and so on, are not ignored, to be sure, but the hierarchy of importance is clear: the main goal of education is performance, not interest or joy in understanding; the main goal within most occupations is to move up the ladder of success, not to enjoy the work; the main goal of psychology and the social sciences is to find out how people behave and what determines their behavior, not what that behavior feels like or whether people could enjoy life more doing something else.[1]

But this is not to say that behavior is unimportant for the quality of experience, and certainly not that psychology should eschew studying overt behavior (indeed, unless psychologists study only themselves they have no choice but to obtain their raw data by studying the behavior of others). In addition to its essential role in biological survival, behavior is obviously important for the quality of experience. Human environmental influences ranging from park landscaping to radioactive pollution—each the result of all sorts of overt behavior—provide unlimited examples. On a personal level, the relation between behavior and experience is even more intimate. What a person does overtly usually registers in some fairly direct way on that person's experience, and also yields indirect effects produced by the reactions of other people or the environment. Kicking your dog may ease your frustration—and give rise to the experience of a bitten ankle.

The important underlying questions are *why* we study behavior, *what behavior* we study, and *what use* we make of the information we obtain. To the first question I would answer that it is important to understand the determinants of behavior *because* behavior can have such important direct and indirect influences on the quality of experience. To the second, behavior that can help us understand or increase the enjoyability of our experience should be studied with special alacrity. Finally, the information obtained should be used to help us understand experience better and to enable people to increase the immediate and long-range enjoyability of their experience. The behavioral sciences cannot escape value considerations such as these, for the questions chosen for study automatically embody decisions about what is important to know. Research, theory, and the choice of questions also produce effects that can eventually affect everyone's experience. A crucial question for behavioral science thus becomes whether it will concentrate on behavioral variables as *ends* to be studied for their own sake or as *means* to gain greater understanding of how to improve the quality of experience.

SYSTEMS THINKING

Now we turn to the issue of how environment and experience are interrelated. A flippant answer is "quite intimately," but as thinkers such as Dewey (1958), Watts (1966), and Tomkins (1962) have argued, the relation between nature or "the world" and conscious awareness is far more intimate than our dualistic language implies. It makes sense, for example, to think of consciousness as a process of nature becoming aware of itself, although this may at first seem an odd way of talking. The underlying idea is that conscious organisms such as human beings are part of nature. We are in a sense mere extensions of our environment. This way of thinking can be developed on different levels, ranging from the poetically mystical to the analogically mechanical, but somewhere in the middle lies an application of *systems* thinking. This approach stresses examination of the intricate interrelations among interacting elements, as opposed to a more linear causal analysis that strives to isolate simple relations between small sets of variables. Experience, for example, arises and operates within an enormously complex system of biological, behavioral, social, cultural, and environmental events. Although it is presently a hopeless task to try to fully understand the operation of this total system, it is possible to consider at least the outlines of some of the interrelations involving diverse elements and processes.

To take a concrete example, consider the way two carloads of people, one of linear thinkers and one of systems thinkers, might experience a traffic jam. The linear thinkers would probably see the congestion as the unfortunate consequence of too many cars using a too-narrow road. If they are apathetic, their inclination might be to treat the unpleasantness of recurrent traffic jams by taking mind-numbing drugs, in much the same way that advertisers have urged victims of city smog to use eyewash regularly. However, if inclined toward intervention, they might think that widening the road would be a good idea. After they succeeded at this, they would probably recommend building additional roads when the widened one became packed with cars again. They might also recognize the need for more parking places and gas stations. If their city continued to spread across the countryside, so that many services and businesses (perhaps including their own place of work) became harder to reach from their new suburban homes (to which they would have moved when displaced by one of the new roads), the consistently linear thinkers would undoubtedly recommend still more and bigger roads. We shall return to these people shortly, but first let's take a look at the occupants of the "systems" car.

The systems thinkers would probably see the traffic jam as only one symptom of the malfunctioning of the transportation system. They would quickly discount the solutions proposed by the linear thinkers (except perhaps the mind-numbing drugs, if all else failed). It would be obvious to them that building more roads and other automobile services would prove self-defeating in the long run. Such "solutions" lead to problems not contemplated by the linear thinkers: urban sprawl, atrophy of public transportation, and the resulting need to use more automobiles more often (see, for example, Leavitt, 1970; Stone, 1971). Positive feedback operates: traffic congestion leads to solutions that eventually generate more automobile use, which increases traffic congestion. The systems approach would view the traffic jams, smog, accidents, and so on, as signals that we should do less of the same (negative feedback)—that we should stop encouraging the use of cars and look for alternative ways for people to get around. The functioning of transportation systems would be examined in relation to other social practices. Questions like these would be asked: What are the economic and political decision-making processes that have led to and that maintain the current dominance of the automobile? What are the influences that affect these decisions (for example, special-interest groups, effects of decisions on the economic well-being and careers of decision makers, results of attitude polls)? What are the determinants of dominant American attitudes concerning transportation (for example, the role of advertising, the competitive economic system, the long tradition of violence, the view of nature as adversary, the emphasis on personal achievement and individualism)? What essential functions are served by the current transportation system and what possible alternative systems could fulfill these functions? Is it possible to design a feasible system of transportation that would be comfortable and efficient and allow for the construction of a more pleasant human environment than we have now? If so, what changes in *other* systems (economic, political, land-use, city-planning, family-planning, educational, etc.) might be necessary to change the transportation system? Considering the way these systems function and interrelate, what actions would be most helpful in getting the ball rolling?

This example of the "linear" and "systems" approaches is intended to give only a feeling for the difference between two ways of thinking about people/environment relations. The example might also make us ask how such different ways of thinking could arise and function within our culture. What might lead one person to view a traffic jam as a simple inconvenience to be corrected by a wider road, and another person to experience it as a sign that something is wrong with the society? Approaching this question from an informal systems perspective, we can note that people come to think in given ways because of a huge number of *interacting* factors, including the structure of their language; the beliefs of their parents, teachers, and peers; the things they are rewarded and punished for expressing; their intelligence and ability to imagine new things; feedback about the usefulness of a particular way of thinking; their willingness to tolerate uncertainty and to depart from the views of other people; the way they were brought up as children; the things they have read; and so on for an obviously long list.

The whole network of beliefs and values engendered by these variables may affect the way a person experiences traffic jams. To see the congestion as a symptom of a complex social problem and to envision the massive benefits and efforts that might attend significant change could be exhilarating to a person who valued public spaces and believed that collective action was possible. The experience might even lead such a person to join with others to effect some of the envisioned changes. For a person who believed in competitive individualism as the most desirable way of life, however, visions of the systemic changes required for enhancing the general quality of life might seem incomprehensible or subversive. And for a person who believed that cooperative action was inconsistent with human nature, utopian systems thinking could seem futile. As indicated above, these varied orientations toward public values and collective behavior would depend on many social, psychological, and environmental forces. The important point is that a person's habitual way of thinking arises in a very complex context; to help people deal with problems more constructively, it may be necessary to consider many interacting aspects of that context.

This example, obviously, has been far from a formal systems analysis, replete with diagrams, detailed feedback loops, discussions of energy exchange and information flow, and so on.[2] While more detailed analyses will be presented in later chapters, the main application of systems thinking will be to consider the *contexts* in which psychological processes or suggested social and environmental changes might occur; the *interrelations* among the various psychological, social, and environmental variables considered; and the *ramifications* and long-term effects of introducing new processes based on these variables into the people/environment system.

ENVIRONMENTAL PSYCHOLOGY

The whole field of environmental psychology can in fact be defined as the study of the interrelations between psychological and environmental variables. Psychological variables include characteristics of mental or behavioral events. Although they are interrelated, representative categories of psychological events are thinking, perceiving, feeling, imagining, manipulating, locomoting, and communicating. Similarly, the environment, the total physical surroundings that impinge on an organism, can be analyzed in terms of categories such as complexity, similarity to past surroundings of the organism, degree and type of human influence present, and the number and type of other organisms present. Interactions between human beings and their environments of course generate some of the most important variables in environmental psychology. Included among these variables are the meanings attached to environments, patterns of social behavior linked to special types of environments, and processes of modifying and designing environments. Such variables embody the interrelations of culture—socially mediated patterns of thought, feeling, action, and technology—and environment. It is in this context that processes of experience function.

MAIN THEMES

In examining the interrelations of environment and experience, this book applies research and theory in cognitive, motivational, social, and environmental psychology, together with an informal systems approach, to the issue of how people can increase the enjoyability of their experience. Thus, rather than concentrating exclusively on how and why people normally function in the world as it presently is, this book explores questions that relate as well to the implications of theory, research, and observations for how people and their environments *could* function in ways that would produce more enjoyable experience. Improvement in the quality of human experience will no doubt arise only if certain special biological, psychological, behavioral, social, cultural, and environmental conditions are met. Our main focus will be to explore some of the contributions that psychology might make toward understanding what these conditions are, how they interrelate, and how people might behave, think, and work with each other and their environments to improve experience for everyone.

This exploration of human possibilities in relation to the environment is developed through the following six themes, pursued, in order, in Chapters 2 through 7:

1. Intrinsic Motivation

Many of our social institutions seem to operate with a truncated and jaundiced view of human motivation. For example, all too often it is assumed that workers or students must be coerced into productive behavior. There are actually many sources of satisfaction or "reinforcement" that can lead to a given pattern of overt behavior, but the way this behavior is experienced by the person engaging in it—and the implications for his or her later behavior—may be very different for different types of reinforcement. It is especially important to consider the difference between sources of reinforcement deriving from behavior satisfying in itself and reinforcement that is extrinsically linked to behavior (for example, reading out of interest versus reading for a good grade). There are in fact many sources of intrinsic satisfaction that are being grossly ignored in our society. The prerequisites for opening up these sources of intrinsic motivation involve changes in our views of human nature and in our educational and economic systems, but the potential benefits include increased human happiness and a rejuvenated and less lethal pattern of relating to the environment.

2. Self-Directed Cognition

Environmental experience arises in part from active mental processes of construction and interpretation. Similarly, *affect*—the emotional or feeling tone of experience—is partially based on active cognitive processes. Since many of these underlying mental processes can be influenced by conscious decisions, it may be possible for people to exert considerable control over the quality of their experience. Even slight twists in our patterns of thinking and perceiving can lead to substantial changes in our experience of aesthetic qualities in environments, our awareness of ecological interrelations and environmental problems, and our sense of possibilities for better environmental designs.

For example, deciding to view your surroundings as a collection of abstract colored forms can greatly intensify your visual experience, and vividly imagining design improvements in a place can alert you to environmental problems and possible solutions as well as help you feel creative. The better we understand the interrelations between the way we process information (our "cognitive sets") and the nature of our experience, the more freedom we can obtain to have the kinds of experience that we value. Surprisingly, this has been a realm of human potential only sparingly explored by recent psychological research. Nevertheless, there is strong reason to believe that through education people could be helped to a new joy in environmental experience, a new awareness of the possibilities and problems of human influence on the environment, and a new appreciation of their own interrelatedness with each other and with the ecosystem.

3. Pro-Life Values

There are many possible systems of human *values*—conceptions of what is desirable. Analyses and critiques of American values (for example, Slater, 1970, 1974; Mumford, 1970; Means, 1969; Rokeach, 1973) have pointed to serious problems in our dominant value system. This is true both for values relating to the treatment of human beings and for values involving the uses of technology as it affects the environment. There are, fortunately, other possible value systems—systems that would have more benign consequences for the environment and for human beings. For instance, in place of currently prevalent orientations toward competitive individualism, dominance over nature, and unquestioning obeisance to technology and growth, it would be possible to emphasize cooperation, an "ecological conscience," a more rational ordering and differentiation of means and ends, and other considerations that would tend to enhance life rather than threaten it. In short, we could move from an "anti-life" value system that virtually ignores the quality of experience to a "pro-life" value system that considers it preeminently important.

Here again it is necessary to consider the interrelations among social institutions, psychological processes, and characteristics of the physical environment. All of these interact in the determination and functioning of value systems. Clearly, effecting a change in values—even for the purpose of enhancing the quality of life—is likely to be a tremendously complicated and slow process. Nonetheless, current theory and research in the development of human cognition and character, together with increasing efforts in the areas of values clarification and "moral education," hold promise that human beings have the potential, and perhaps even naturally tend, to develop a pro-life value orientation.

4. Ecological Consciousness

When a system of values is considered in combination with a corresponding cognitive and motivational orientation toward the world, we can speak of a particular *consciousness*. This is in the sense of "Puritan consciousness," "masculine consciousness," Reich's (1970) trichotomy of "Consciousness I, II, and III," and so forth. The critical one for our purposes can be dubbed "ecological consciousness." With this concept, many of the ideas about potentials inherent in human motivation, cognition, and alternative values can be integrated and related to environmental experience and action. As I use the term, ecological consciousness is a way of thinking and feeling characterized by (1) a sense of self as part of a larger holistic system, (2) an understanding and awareness of the ecological processes within this system, (3) a high ability to enjoy and appreciate things in themselves (that is, without concern for their usefulness), (4) a pro-life value system, and (5) a creatively cooperative motivational orientation toward people and other living things.

This may sound like a big order. Since it would mean nothing less than a revolution in American consciousness, it is. Nevertheless, we can strive to understand what conditions may hinder it or give rise to it. Indeed, given the potential inherent in human motivational and cognitive processes and the continuing development of the environmental movement, ecological consciousness could be emerging as a powerful force. It may be that the social theorist Philip Slater (1974) is correct in his contention that the old way of life (the old consciousness) has pushed environmental degradation so far that a kind of massive corrective feedback process is setting in; perhaps we are at last being pushed into ecological consciousness. Perhaps—but at the very least, we can strive to discern and aid whatever social forces might help bring about the revolution in consciousness described above.

5. Life-Enhancing Environmental Design

Our current patterns of environmental design and modification obviously leave a bit to be desired. In addition to pollution and various dangerous and oppressive aspects of our constructed environment, we also endure the egregious squandering of both resources and opportunities. These problems seem linked to our society's value system and to the various social institutions that operate in consonance with that system. However, by using a special eight-part scheme for analyzing and evaluating the affective quality of experience (a "theory of happiness," if you will), it is possible to suggest at least a few general guidelines for moving toward more optimal environmental design. This eight-part scheme is first presented in Chapter 3 (on cognitive potentials) and is used there to evaluate how different cognitive sets (patterns of thinking) might affect the overall quality of our experience. These same criteria, however, appear equally applicable to evaluating the experiential effects of environmental designs—and even cultural designs (see next theme). In any event, this theory of happiness points to potentials for considerably more fulfilling patterns of environmental design and influence than those we currently impose—or allow to be imposed— upon ourselves.

6. Designing and Moving Toward "Utopia"

As noted above, the same set of criteria used to evaluate experiential effects of patterns of thinking and patterns of environmental design can also be used as guidelines for assessing whole cultures. More to the point for examining human potentials, these criteria can be used as guides to evaluating or even designing "utopian" visions—designs for the best achievable human societies. The first part of this theme is thus that (1) a utopian social system would optimize all of the components in the theory of happiness scheme, (2) such a system would fulfill certain associated structural requirements (including an ecomonic and political system based on equality and cooperation; a high level of resources and ecologically sound practices; socialization for ecological consciousness and full social participation; and societal commitment to pro-life rationality, diversity, and experimentation), and (3) it is possible to devise workable social designs that would function in this way.

The second part of this theme, moreover, is that there are possible lines of action that hold out hope for moving us in such a utopian direction. It is one thing to explore relations between psychological processes and characteristics of society and the physical environment, or to examine human potentials and utopian schemes; it is something else to be able to *do* anything to change the status quo constructively. This is nonetheless the direction I hope we can pursue. To this end, I have offered suggestions for possible tactics at various points throughout the book and have presented a more concentrated compendium of change strategies in Chapter 7. Although these suggestions contain no magic formula for producing a better world, let alone utopia, there *are* a lot of things that could be tried.

Let us turn first to an examination of certain basic—but often overlooked or undervalued—aspects of human motivation. These reveal some of the most important positive human potentials and also suggest the feasibility and value of certain changes in social practices, cultural norms, and people/environment relations.

NOTES

1. Also compare Csikszentmihalyi (1975).
2. Good introductions to systems theory include Parsegian (1973), Emery (1969), and Miller (1971). In the environmental realm, works by Meadows et al. (1972), Forrester (1972), Jacobs (1961), Theobald (1972), and Bateson (1972) provide varied examples of applied systems thinking, both formal and informal. Also see the journal *Fields Within Fields* (published by the World Institute Council, New York).

2
MOTIVATION AND ENVIRONMENT

CONTINGENCIES OF REINFORCEMENT

INTRINSIC VERSUS EXTRINSIC REINFORCEMENT
  Experience of "Locus of Causality"
  Intrinsic + Extrinsic Reinforcement = ?
  Social and Environmental Implications

SOURCES OF INTRINSIC REINFORCEMENT
  Arousal
  Effectance Motivation
  The Origin/Pawn Concept
  Some Social and Environmental Implications

A HIERARCHY OF MOTIVATIONS?
  Maslow's Hierarchy
  Self-Actualization
  Evidence
  Environmental Implications

VIEWS OF HUMAN NATURE
  Theory X and Theory Y
  Evidence
  Environmental Consequences

ALTERNATIVE NORMS OF EQUITY
  Equity Research
  Equity and Motivation
  "Equity 1" versus "Equity 2"
  Equity, Society, and Environment
  Toward Equity 2: A Few Practical Considerations

NOTES

Questions of what moves people and other organisms to act, what our underlying needs or desires are, and what produces feelings of pleasure or displeasure have long constituted critical issues in psychology. The following discussion explores selected theoretical and empirical work in this field of motivation and attempts to trace some of the implications for the possible enhancement of social institutions, people/environment relations, and the quality of human experience. As should become apparent, a dominant theme running through the discussion is that human motivational potentials, if developed and utilized in an appropriate sociocultural environment, could enable us to live considerably more enjoyable and ecologically sound lives than most of us currently do.

CONTINGENCIES OF REINFORCEMENT

A central concept in the psychology of motivation is the notion of *reinforcement*. Although the idea of reinforcement may be associated with concepts such as pleasure, feelings, and relief of tensions, the trend in psychology consistently has been to define reinforcement in empirical and behavioral terms.[1] Turning to B. F. Skinner (for example, 1953, 1969, 1974) as our key source, we find that reinforcement is conceptualized in terms of impact on the likelihood that a response will be repeated. Specifically, reinforcement refers to any consequence of a response that increases the probability that the response will recur under similar initial conditions. According to Skinner (1953, pp. 72–73), "the only way to tell whether or not a given event is reinforcing to a given organism under given circumstances is to make a direct test. We observe the frequency of a selected response, then make an event contingent upon it and observe any change in frequency. If there is a change, we classify the event as reinforcing to the organism under the existing conditions." Skinner goes on to acknowledge that this concept of reinforcement leads to a circular statement if the claim is made that an event increases the likelihood of a given response *because* the event is reinforcing. Nevertheless, such a purely empirical notion of reinforcement does prove useful in practice. This is because reinforcers for one type of behavior can usually be used to modify the probability of recurrence of other types of behavior.

Unfortunately, little attention has been paid to the experiential (and even behavioral) effects of different *types* of reinforcers. One exception is Skinner's distinction between positive and negative reinforcers. The former are conditions or stimuli that reinforce an act when the act leads to their *presence;* the latter, to conditions or stimuli that reinforce when the act leads to their *removal.* Skinner labels the modification of behavior by negative reinforcement "aversive control," and refers to "punishment" as the presentation of a negative reinforcer or the removal of a positive reinforcer. People generally enjoy life more when their behavior is influenced by positive reinforcement rather than either punishment or negative reinforcement, but Skinner (1971) notes that positive reinforcements can sometimes subvert pressures for valuable social or personal change, as in the case of ancient Rome's bread and circuses. (Skinner, by the way, views punishment as both ineffective and offensive.) Although these distinctions are important, there are also subtle but significant differences among positive reinforcers themselves. These differences will serve as a point of departure for much of the later discussion in this chapter. First, let us take a closer look at Skinner's central motivational concept and some of its environmental implications.

Skinner (1969, p. 7) defines *contingencies of reinforcement* as the interrelations among "(1) the occasion upon which a response occurs, (2) the response itself, and (3) the reinforcing consequences." Contingencies of reinforcement thus involve the conditions and consequences of a given type of behavior. According to Skinner, such contingencies ultimately account for all behavior. Although this proposition has been debated at length (see, for example, Wann, 1964; Chomsky, 1959; Skinner, 1974), contingencies of reinforcement are undoubtedly a critical consideration for both behavior and experience. Certainly all goal-directed behavior can be discussed in terms of the conditions and consequences of given actions. If you have enjoyed walking through a park on your way to school in the past, you will be likely to take that path again in the future. If something is pleasant only under certain conditions, such as sunbathing in warm, sunny weather, the behavior will tend to occur only under these conditions. More complicated situations arise when given behaviors result in pleasant consequences only some of the time, as in gambling, conducting scientific experiments, or voting for political candidates. As Skinner—and common observation—have shown, intermittent reinforcement can be very powerful in maintaining and even intensifying given behavior patterns.

The important point for us to consider is that anlysis in terms of contingencies of reinforcement can reveal interactions between the functioning of social and environmental systems and the behavior and experience of the participating human beings. Our system of laws, for example, provides a codified statement of contingencies of reinforcement (here taken to include punishments as well as rewards) for innumerable categories of behavior. Ranging from which side of the street to drive on to how many months of separation are required for a divorce, laws spell out what we should do under given circumstances and what will happen to us if we don't do it. Those who make or enforce the laws thus have enormous power over the behavior of nearly everyone in the society. And those who influence the people who make or enforce the laws have enormous power over the behavior of nearly everyone in the society.

It is here essential to realize the interrelations of the economic, political, and legal systems in determining the contingencies of reinforcement imposed by social institutions. Since money constitutes our society's most important "generalized reinforcer," the distribution of wealth corresponds closely to the distribution of power—power to control the contingencies of reinforcement. One interesting aspect of the system is that groups with the greatest wealth also have the greatest influence on the people who make decisions governing the distribution and use of wealth (for example, tax laws and decisions concerning the use of public funds). Thus the shape of the legal, social, and physical environment—and the attendant contingencies of reinforcement—are disproportionately influenced by people with vested economic and political interests. As John Kenneth Galbraith (1973) makes clear, it is this situation that has led to an oversupply of deodorants, weapons, cars, roads, and pollution and to an undersupply of good housing, parks, public transportation, and health care. The most harrowing consideration in all this is that to a large extent the salience of reinforcers and even the needs that people seem to feel (and thus what things constitute reinforcers) are also under the manipulative control of the economic and political power structure. Advertising, political priorities, and national purposes, combined with the lack of readily available alternatives, create an atmosphere in which certain things are deemed good and other things—of potentially greater value—are ignored. Thus, possessing sleek cars and no body smells and sending men to the moon may come to seem more important than creating a pleasant public environment and manufacturing fewer carcinogens.

Contingencies of reinforcement can also be viewed in terms of feedback loops in people/environment relations. Many actions have immediate consequences for experience and behavior, as in the case of letting garbage pile up in one's house or planting grass in the yard. Behavior toward the environment may also elicit short-term social feedback, as in the case of being fined for littering. Unfortunately, some of the more serious consequences of human impact on the environment involve delayed effects that become manifest only after long periods of time. Eutrophication of lakes, deterioration of urban centers, growth of strip developments, and artificial changes in the earth's climate are usually very slow processes that occur without immediate or obvious links to the human behaviors that eventually produce them. Perhaps most damage to environmental quality can even be viewed as a side effect of behavior intended for other purposes. Obtaining money and having plenty of cheap electric power, for example, are short-term goals we can all understand. Unfortunately, it is easy to ignore the long-term effects of how we go about obtaining money or producing the cheap electric power, especially if the unpleasant effects occur elsewhere or to someone else. As Skinner has often advised, one of humankind's chief tasks is to bring its behavior more under the influence of these long-term reinforcement contingencies.

Of course, it is no easy task to adjust behavior to long-term reinforcement contingencies. People know that lung cancer is unpleasant, but what's a far-off year or two of suffering and a premature demise in comparison with the immediately available addictive pleasures or withdrawal problems of cigarette smoking? If each puff were accompanied by a sharp pain in the chest, quitting would be much easier, even without the threat of terminal illness. It appears that long-term considerations introduce an unwonted strain into our cognitive/motivational system. As human beings we are tuned to react to more immediate links between behavior and its effects (compare Bateson, 1972, as well as Skinner's works). There are at least two approaches to increasing the present behavioral effects of long-term contingencies of reinforcement: (1) provide socially mediated sanctions or reinforcements of a more immediate nature, such as fines or praise, to induce behavior that has long-term benefits and to prevent behavior that has long-term negative consequences; (2) educate people to think in terms of long-term, ecologically oriented systems functioning.

Obviously, if even the first approach is to be instituted intelligently, *some* people must understand and care about the long-term consequences of their behavior and that of others. Furthermore, to obtain broad social acceptance of sanctions and reinforcements for ecologically valuable behavior, it would probably be necessary for a great many people to learn to see the world from a far-sighted ecological perspective. Thus, even a Skinnerian approach (of sorts) leads ultimately to a recognition of the interaction of cognitive processes and what constitutes effective long-range contingencies of reinforcement. When we come to understand that a given behavior will eventually have an effect that will be important to us, we can thus be motivated to induce or inhibit the behavior in question.

INTRINSIC VERSUS EXTRINSIC REINFORCEMENT

Our discussion thus far has concentrated on the relation between contingencies of reinforcement and patterns of behavior. Let us now turn to a consideration of the nature of different types of reinforcers. Although a particular type of behavior can be induced by any of a variety of reinforcers, the experiences arising from the various combinations of behavior and reinforcer may differ considerably, as may subtle aspects of the behavior itself. The overt behavior of picking up trash may look much the same if done for pay or if done voluntarily as part of a clean-up campaign, but the experiences of the workers are likely to be different. Unfortunately, in many aspects of our economic and educational systems, a very important distinction between types of reinforcers is overlooked. This is the distinction between reinforcement deriving from the behavior itself or some inherent consequence of the behavior, and reinforcement that is artificially linked to the behavior through the actions of other people or social institutions.

Note that there are actually three kinds of reinforcement involved, the distinctions being based on the relation of the reinforcer to the act that it reinforces. The first we might label *pure intrinsic* reinforcement, which arises when an act is itself the source of satisfaction. Examples might include eating an ice cream cone, looking at a majestic mountain range, swinging on a swing, or reading a book for pleasure. We shall examine the nature of intrinsic reinforcement in detail later in this chapter. The second type of reinforcement may be labelled *consequentially intrinsic*. In this case an act is reinforced by some *consequence* that is intrinsically linked to the act. For example, wearing eyeglasses to see better, chopping wood for a fire, reading a book for information, and crossing a road to get to the other side are all acts performed for consequences that arise "naturally" from the behavior involved. Acts performed for long-term consequences, such as exercising to maintain a healthy heart or recycling paper to help maintain virgin forests, are also examples of this type of intrinsically motivated behavior. Finally, reinforcement that is provided by the "artificial" mediation of other people or of institutions may be labelled *pure extrinsic*. Examples include reading a book in order to obtain a good grade, chopping wood for money, participating in a psychology experiment for course credit, and recycling paper to win votes as an "eco-candidate."[2]

For the moment, let us lump the two types of intrinsic reinforcement together and inquire into the relations between intrinsic and extrinsic motivation. Again, note that many specific types of behavior—for example, reading a book—can be induced by either intrinsic or extrinsic reinforcement. Issues to consider as we contrast the two kinds of motivation include (a) what experiential effects the different types of motivation may have; (b) possible motivational effects arising when both types of reinforcement are present for the same behavior; and (c) the interactions between these different bases for reinforcement and the functioning of social and people/environment relations.

Experience of "Locus of Causality"

Richard deCharms (1968) has presented a slightly different distinction between intrinsic and extrinsic motivation. According to his view, people are intrinsically motivated when they perceive themselves to be the "locus of causality" for their behavior and extrinsically motivated when they perceive the locus of causality to be external. Thus if you feel you are doing something simply because it is what you want to do, you are intrinsically motivated; if you feel you are doing something because some external force is reinforcing you for doing it, you are extrinsically motivated. This can easily be turned around to fit the above formulation, however. If you do something because the act or some inherent consequence is itself satisfying, you will tend to feel that you are the locus of causality—that you are behaving in precisely the way you want to. If, on the other hand, you do something in order to obtain a reward (or avoid a punishment) administered by someone else, you will tend to feel that the locus of causality lies "outside"—that you are doing not what you want to do but what someone else wants you to do. Thus, aside from the obvious consideration that intrinsically reinforced acts will tend to be more inherently pleasant than extrinsically reinforced behavior, they will also tend to be experienced as more self-generated.

Intrinsic + Extrinsic Reinforcement = ?

At first blush, one might think that combining intrinsic and extrinsic re-inforcements for the same behavior would strengthen a person's tend-ency to engage in the behavior and also to enjoy it. In many cases this may be true, but deCharms's (1968) analysis and some recent research cast considerable doubt on the wisdom of adding extrinsic reinforce-ment to behavior that is already intrinsically satisfying. DeCharms based his argument on a finding by Harlow et al. (1950) that monkeys who were originally motivated to take a puzzle apart "for the fun of it" seemed to lose interest in the activity after first being reinforced with a raisin and then having the raisin reward omitted. From this experiment and a study by Weick (1964)—which showed that subjects seemed to enjoy an experimental task more when they knew they would *not* re-ceive credit for the experiment—deCharms reasoned that people (as well as monkeys) can often derive greater satisfaction from performing a task solely for its inherent pleasure than for this pleasure plus some extraneous reward. According to deCharms's theory (to be discussed in more detail below), the reason for this phenomenon is that performing an act for intrinsic reasons leads a person to feel more like an "Origin," while performing an act for extrinsic reinforcement leads a person to feel more like a "Pawn" (that is, pushed to perform the act by the ex-trinsic control of the outside source of reinforcement). In addition, deCharms noted that Harlow's monkeys tended to attack the puzzle less efficiently when the raisin was given as a reward, indicating that an ex-trinsic reward may tend to take one's attention off the intrinsic sources of satisfaction involved in the behavior itself.

Recent experiments by Edward Deci (1975), Mark Lepper et al. (1973), and several others (see, for example, Notz, 1975), add credibil-ity to deCharms's contention that extrinsic reinforcement can decrease intrinsic motivation. Deci has conducted experiments similar to Har-low's, but using humans instead of monkeys and reinforcers such as money instead of raisins. Although the findings were sometimes of mar-ginal statistical significance, there was a consistent tendency for subjects implications for education are especially far-reaching, given the nearly ubiquitous use of extrinsic reinforcers such as grades, gold stars, praise, and token economies (used in behavior modification programs). As Lepper et al. (1973) and Deci (1975) are careful to point out, extrinsic reinforcement *does* have value for encouraging wanted behavior when initial intrinsic interest is lacking or when skill must be developed in order to enjoy a given type of behavior. However, the point remains that using extrinsic reinforcement seems to short-circuit the process of deciding to engage in a given activity because that activity seems worth doing either for itself or for its "natural" consequences. Especially in an educational context, one might expect that every effort should be made to help people *understand* the value of engaging in particular behaviors rather than simply relying on "shaping" their behavior with whatever seems to be the most efficient system of extrinsic reinforcers. The long-range consequences for self-esteem, understanding, the ability to make intelligent choices in a changing environment, and the realization of personal values (not to mention a happier school experience and a happier life) should make such efforts on behalf of understanding—as opposed to shaping—worth whatever costs and changes in the system are involved.

The implications for people/environment relations may be equally profound. Insofar as possible, it would seem that care for and improvement of the environment should be based on intrinsic motivation. Intrinsic motivation requires no monitoring for the administration of rewards and sanctions, relies on inherent rather than socially mediated feedback processes, enhances self-esteem and a sense of personal responsibility, and should arise naturally from an understanding and appreciation of ecological processes and long-term effects. Extrinsic reinforcement in the form of law enforcement and other social sanctions will doubtless also be necessary in any society of human beings, but the structure of these reinforcement contingencies should be based on a deeper understanding of sources of intrinsic satisfaction and ecological interrelations. As Garrett Hardin (1968) argued in his essay on "the tragedy of the commons," individual motivation may prove a very shaky basis for environmentally sound policy; even a few selfish people or organizations can easily disrupt a delicately balanced system.[3] So the argument is not to eliminate socially determined reinforcement contingencies, but rather to enlighten them and to rely on intrinsic motivation wherever possible. The remainder of this chapter will examine some

to decrease spontaneous puzzle-solving activity following i
the extrinsic incentive (relative to their activity before the in
of the incentive and/or relative to the behavior of control grc
offered extrinsic incentives). Furthermore, an especially strik
by Lepper et al. (1973) found clear evidence that nursery-sc
dren decreased their use of artistic play materials following a
mental manipulation in which they were offered and given
Player Award" for engaging in the same type of activity. Ne
control group, who were simply asked to draw with the mate
given no award, nor a second experimental group, who we
awards unexpectedly after they drew, showed any decrease
drawing activity. Other research, such as that reviewed by Notz
has also clearly supported deCharms's hypothesis that extrins
forcement can interfere with intrinsic motivation.

How are these effects of extrinsic reinforcement to be explaine
(1975) sees the source of the effects mainly as deCharms did—e
reinforcement leads to a decreased sense of self-determinati
hence of intrinsic satisfaction. Lepper et al. (1973) and Nisbi
Valins (1972) also discuss the effects of "overly sufficient justifi
in terms of the attributions people make about their behavior. T
you find yourself doing something after being offered an extrin
ward for doing it, you may think that you are not really interes
the activity for its own sake. Also, you might think that if someor
feels it is necessary to offer a reward for doing a given task, the
must lack sufficient attractiveness to be performed without the re
According to such "attribution theory" explanations, even c
quentially intrinsic reinforcement could conceivably decrease pur
trinsic satisfaction. For example, viewing vacations as rests for the
pose of refreshing oneself for more work could perhaps lead to decre
enjoyment of the intrinsic pleasures of leisure during retiren
In addition, the type of reinforcement that one concentrates on (tha
intrinsic pleasures of the act or rewarding consequences) may influe
the salience of intrinsic sources of satisfaction when the extrinsic r
forcements are no longer available.

Social and Environmental Implications

There is thus considerable evidence that extrinsic reinforcement can
least under some circumstances interfere with intrinsic motivation. T

psychological bases for intrinsic reinforcement, explore some of the changes in our views of human nature and in our economic and value systems that would facilitate reliance on intrinsic motivation, and discuss further the relevance of all this for our environment and experience.

SOURCES OF INTRINSIC REINFORCEMENT

What produces pleasant or reinforcing experiences for human beings? Obvious answers include reducing any unpleasant state (such as hunger, pain, anxiety, or boredom), enhancing self-esteem, perceiving beautiful or interesting stimuli, becoming sexually aroused and gratified, loving and feeling loved, feeling capable, and so on for an indeterminately long list. Two key issues involved in answering this question are (1) whether there are any processes or dimensions common to all reinforcing experiences, and (2) the relation of sources of human satisfaction to conceptions of human nature. Although it may well be fruitless to look for some universal characteristic of reinforcement, we shall begin by examining a body of theory and research that points to arousal level as especially important in mediating pleasantness. The discussion will then proceed to a consideration of human motives for self-direction and being an effective causal agent. In addition to examining the implications for people/environment relations, we shall also explore the relevance of this work for Abraham Maslow's "humanistic" conception of motivation and for alternative conceptions of human nature.

Arousal

Recent developments in motivational psychology and experimental aesthetics have increasingly emphasized the importance of *levels of arousal* in human motivation and preference for stimuli. Concepts such as "arousal" or "psychological complexity" refer basically to the degree of activation or excitement in the organism. Physiologically, this corresponds to the complexity and the degree of activity in the nervous system. Indices of high arousal include, for example, higher-frequency and lower-amplitude brain waves (that is, greater desynchronization in the electrical activity of the brain), increased muscle tension, increased electrical conductance of the skin, and dilated pupils (see Berlyne, 1967, 1971; Kahneman, 1973). Phenomenologically, higher arousal corresponds to feelings of greater excitement, alertness, and activation. This concept is important because a substantial body of research and theory indicates that achieving an "optimal level of arousal" is a major source of intrinsic reinforcement (as well as a critical factor in optimal performance of tasks).[4]

D. E. Berlyne (for example, 1971), an eminent investigator of arousal processes, has built an impressive theoretical edifice that assigns the central role in mediating the affective tone of experience to arousal level. Berlyne's model utilizes the neurophysiological theory of Olds and Olds (1965), according to which *hedonic tone*—the pleasantness or unpleasantness of experience—is controlled by the relations among three systems in the brain. The *primary reward system* yields pleasant experiences the more it is activated. The *aversion system* produces unpleasant experience when it is activated and also inhibits the primary reward system (thus adding insult to injury, so to speak). Finally, the *secondary reward system* inhibits the aversion system and thus produces positive hedonic experiences indirectly by releasing the primary reward system from the inhibitory influence of the aversion system. According to Berlyne's theory and review of the evidence, the functioning of all three of these systems is intimately related to the organism's arousal level. An increase in arousal is held to be concomitant with an increase in activation of both the primary reward system and the aversion system, and a decrease in arousal is in theory concomitant with activation of the secondary reward system. Furthermore, activation of the aversion system is thought to require higher levels of arousal than activation of the primary reward system. Thus, as arousal increases from a very low level, first the primary reward system becomes activated, reaching its peak at some moderate level of arousal. If arousal continues to increase, the aversion system becomes increasingly activated, inhibiting the primary reward system and also producing an increasingly unpleasant experience through its own functioning. Phenomenologically, the sequence would be as follows: as arousal increases, the organism's experience becomes more pleasant up to a maximum at some moderate level of arousal, then becomes less pleasant as arousal continues to increase, passing the point of indifference and becoming increasingly unpleasant as arousal continues to rise. On the other hand, when arousal decreases from high levels—as when hunger is satisfied or a fear-producing stimulus is removed—a somewhat different process is envisioned. As arousal decreases, the secondary reward system is activated, producing a pleasant experience indirectly by inhibiting the aversion system and thus releasing the primary reward system from inhibition.

Berlyne's central idea is that there are two basic mechanisms for producing pleasant experiences. Arousal can increase to a moderate level or arousal can decrease from high levels. Although the model as it stands does not seem to account very well for the unpleasantness of boredom from very low arousal, there is a substantial body of empirical evidence that organisms with complex nervous systems do seek moderate levels of arousal. For example, Fiske and Maddi (1961), Walker (1964), Lester (1968), Weisler and McCall (1976), deCharms (1968), Berlyne (1971), Berlyne and Madsen (1973), and Smets (1973) present an impressive array of research that seems to establish that animals ranging from rats to humans find moderately arousing changes in stimulation to be reinforcing.

Furthermore, work in sensory deprivation (see, for example, Zubek, 1969) has clearly shown that people find very low levels of stimulation to be unpleasant after even a few hours. This work has been especially important in dispelling the notion that mere satisfaction of survival needs—such as for food, water, warmth, and rest—would lead to a satisfying existence. The sensory deprivation findings, together with the data on optimal arousal levels, have also helped to remold psychological thinking about the basic nature of motivation. No longer can organisms be viewed as striving only to reduce "drives," to eliminate the unpleasant inner signals that some organic process is out of balance. People and other animals seek more out of life than the correction of tissue deficits. The nature of the other things we seek, as will be seen, has important implications for our ability to count on each other to be creative and productive even without threats to our survival needs or promises of extrinsic reinforcements.

First, what are the sources of changes in arousal? Berlyne (1971) has classified them into three categories: (1) "psychophysical variables," consisting of characteristics such as the intensity or quality (for example, color hue, sound pitch) of physical stimuli; (2) "ecological variables," involving the meaning or significance that an event or stimulus has for the organism's survival or well-being; (3) "collative variables," which are properties deriving from processes of comparison. This last category includes variables such as complexity, novelty, surprisingness, incongruity, and ambiguity. Berlyne views such collative variables as central in aesthetic experience, and most of the work (aside from sensory deprivation research) on the reinforcement value of arousal has concentrated on this class of stimulus variables. Research by Berlyne (1971), Munsinger and Kessen (1964), and Smets (1973), for example, has established that moderately complex abstract stimuli tend to be judged as more pleasant than either extremely simple or extremely complex stimuli (although recent work by Kaplan and Wendt [1972], and Wohlwill [1973, 1976], points to interactions with *content* whenever real environments are considered—see below).

One obvious implication for relations between environment and experience would appear to be that environments that help people approach or maintain optimal levels of arousal should be most pleasing. However, as in so many cases in psychology, a principle can be misleading if it is viewed in isolation from other considerations. Berlyne's theory, for example, seems to posit that the "arousal potential" of a stimulus or event is the primary—if not the sole—determinant of its pleasingness. However, it seems entirely plausible that different events or stimuli might lead to comparable or even identical levels of arousal and yet produce experiences of greatly differing pleasantness. This might occur, for example, because of the meaning or interpretation of the events or stimuli or even of the experienced arousal itself (see the discussion of cognitive theories of emotion in Chapter 3). It is at least conceivable that two environments, such as a particular park and a particular slum, might elicit very similar overall levels of arousal for a given observer based on the net effects of the psychophysical, ecological, and collative properties of each place. Nonetheless it would seem that the experience of one environment might be pleasant and the experience of the other unpleasant because of the meaning or interpretation of the particular place or of the arousal experienced.

Indeed, recent research in judgments of environmental preference has at least indicated that the meaning or content of a scene can be as important as its complexity in determining how pleasant it is judged. An early study by Wohlwill (1968) did seem to indicate that ratings of the pleasantness of environmental scenes followed an inverted-U–shaped function of their complexity. However, later studies by Kaplan and Wendt (1972; Kaplan et al., 1972) and Wohlwill (1973, 1976) clearly revealed a tendency for natural scenes to be judged as more pleasant than highly human-influenced urban scenes, independent of the judged complexity of the scenes (although *within* sets of urban or natural scenes, complexity was related to preference). Although this research in

itself does not rule out the possibility that arousal processes were ultimately responsible for the pattern of preference ratings, it is nonetheless consistent with the thesis that meaning or interpretation can operate as an independent (or interacting) determinant of environmental
pleasantness. Given the full range of determinants of arousal postulated
by Berlyne and other arousal theorists—and the inherent vagueness of
the concept of arousal itself—it is difficult to obtain a clear reading of
the relation between arousal potential per se and other possible determinants of pleasantness. We shall address this issue further in Chapter
3, but let us now simply surmise that contributing to an optimal level of
arousal is an important, but not all-important, factor in the perceived
pleasantness of environments.[5]

We might also consider that simplicity, consistency, and coherence
are satisfying in important ways to human beings. Not only do people
seek to lower unusually high levels of arousal and seek out moderate
arousal through complex or novel or surprising stimuli (typical examples include magic shows, difficult puzzles, and scary amusement-park
rides), but they also seek the resolution of inconsistencies, ambiguities,
and doubts. Berlyne attempts to deal with this side of motivation
through arousal-reduction processes and the "secondary reward system"
in his model. Theories of cognitive consistency, such as Leon Festinger's
(1957, 1964) notion of "cognitive dissonance," similarly seem to rely on
a tension-reduction model for seeking consistency. However, it may also
be that simplicity, coherence, and elegance have a more direct capacity
for producing pleasurable experience, perhaps in much the same way
that the meaningful content of a scene can.

Aesthetic experience, for example, appears to involve more than
simple processes of change in arousal level. Hans and Shulamith Kreitler
(1972) have presented the view that, in addition to processes of tension
and relief, the enhancement of one's "cognitive orientation"—one's understanding and conceptualizing of the world—constitutes a primary source
of aesthetic satisfaction in experiencing works of art. Similarly, Rudolf
Arnheim's (1954) masterful analysis of the psychology of visual art indicates that subtle cognitive processes may be essential to aesthetic
pleasure. According to his theory, the enjoyment of a work of art derives
substantially from *appreciating* the skillful and creative use of form to
express meaning. These two aesthetic theories stand in some contrast
to the more unidimensional view put forth by Berlyne (1971), with its
heavy emphasis on arousal potential as the main (if not the exclusive)

determinant of aesthetic enjoyment. Perhaps one insight to be derived from the thought of these different theorists is that intrinsic aesthetic pleasures may involve both approaching optimal levels of arousal and appreciating the meaning, content, and form of what is perceived.

Effectance Motivation

Robert White (1959, 1960) placed people's tendency to seek optimal levels of arousal in a broader theoretical framework. He noted that human beings, along with other higher animals, derive satisfaction both from being stimulated in an interesting way and from manipulating elements of the environment. Citing phenomena ranging from exploratory behavior in rats and monkeys to the play of human children, White built a powerful argument that in the absence of strong physiological needs, higher animals are motivated to explore and manipulate their environments actively. The overall tendency of such behavior, he pointed out, is to yield higher levels of *competence* in dealing with the environment. Motivation to explore and to manipulate would seemingly be especially important for organisms such as human beings, who are born with few instinctive patterns of behavior but who have nervous systems capable of very complex learning. White labelled this type of motivation "effectance," and argued persuasively that the urge to explore, manipulate, and make interesting changes in the environment could not be derived from more basic drives such as hunger or the desire to reduce fear. In fact, as White and others have noted, exploratory, manipulative, and playful behaviors are most likely to occur under conditions of relative safety and low drive arousal.

Just as there appears to be an inverted-U–shaped relation between the arousal value of a stimulus and its pleasantness, a long-standing psychological principle holds that the level of motivation, activation, or arousal bears an inverted-U relation to performance on any given task (see Yerkes and Dodson, 1908; Hebb, 1955; Fiske and Maddi, 1961; Kahneman, 1973). That is, performance on a task will improve with motivation or arousal up to some optimum level and then drop off as arousal increases further. Moreover, the optimal level of arousal for complex tasks will usually be lower than that for simple tasks. Experience from everyday life readily demonstrates the plausibility of these relations. One's performance on a school test will tend to be poor if one is sleepy or only slightly motivated to do well. With a moderate increase in arousal and motivation, one's performance will tend to improve; but with very high excitement or anxiety (as might be produced by extremely high motivation), one's performance on the test will probably worsen. A similar pattern holds for performing complex motor activities, such as surgery or drawing. Compare this with the relation between arousal level and performance on simpler tasks, such as running a race, mopping a floor, or chopping wood. Although relatively high levels of arousal or motivation will lead to optimal performance on such tasks, even here excessive arousal is possible. At extremely high levels one might "freeze" in panic or at least lose a needed degree of muscular control (stumble out of the running blocks, chop off one's foot, etc.).[6]

White's theory of effectance motivation refers to this relationship between arousal and performance in its evolutionary argument that higher animals should be motivated to seek stimulation, to explore, and to manipulate primarily when they are safe and organically satisfied. It is under precisely such conditions of moderately low arousal that they should best be able to learn complex skills and acquire information about the intricacies of their environments. Such skills and information would in turn have survival value at other times, as when escape from danger was necessary or food difficult to obtain.

White has also argued that effectance motivation extends far down the evolutionary scale and that even in human beings, its clearest and purest manifestations may be in the play of children. Nonetheless, if this aspect of human motivation is so firmly grounded in the processes of biological evolution, we might reasonably expect it to account for a fair proportion of adult behavior as well. Effectance motivation may be evidenced in such diverse behavior as mountain climbing, amateur sports of all types, do-it-yourself carpentry and home improvement, pleasure driving, reading newspapers and magazines, volunteer political activities, gourmet cooking, and nearly any hobby (see Csikszentmihalyi, 1975). It may also play a large role in people's tendency to introduce substantial modifications into their environment: damming rivers, building bridges, generating nuclear power, landscaping countrysides, depositing flags on the moon, and so on.

Recall that there are two components to effectance motivation: reinforcement from interesting stimuli and reinforcement from the ability to manipulate. The first component involves the search for optimal levels of arousal and relates most clearly to exploration, the preference for moderately complex stimuli, aesthetic appreciation, curiosity, and so on. The second component, motivation to be effective in making changes in the environment or to feel "in control," may also be theoretically related to optimal levels of arousal. Obviously, the more control over the environment one has, the easier it is for one to regulate one's level of arousal. Indeed, the very act of manipulating or making changes may itself be a source of arousal. However, this second motivational component of effectance may conceivably constitute a source of human satisfaction (and behavior) somewhat independent of arousal regulation per se. Let us now turn to a theory that posits the feeling of "personal causation" (as deCharms terms it) as itself a primary source of intrinsic reinforcement.

The Origin/Pawn Concept

Richard deCharms (1968, 1971, 1976) has carried White's position a step further by arguing that human beings' primary motivation (other than survival) is "to be effective in causing changes in [their] environment." Theorists such as White and Skinner agree that organisms can be reinforced by producing feedback from the environment by their own efforts, but deCharms argues that this source of reinforcement is a basic component of human nature. DeCharms further distinguishes between "Origins"—people who are consciously self-directing in accordance with a realistic conception of themselves and their goals—and "Pawns," or people who feel at the mercy of forces outside themselves. The dichotomy is of course intended as a bipolar continuum, but the closer one is to the Origin pole, the happier and better-functioning one should be.

DeCharms has conducted two types of research based on his concepts. In the first study, laboratory experiments demonstrated that people enjoyed building Tinkertoy models more when the people determined the design of their models than when they were directed by the experimenter (although the subjects often thought the prescribed—Pawn—model was a better product than their own—Origin—model; see deCharms, 1968). Although these experiments provide only meager support for so important a concept (and even failed to show any substantial behavioral differences in subjects' choice of materials for the two types of models), they seem in accord with many real-life experiences. Doing something in a way that *you* choose does often seem more pleasant than doing it according to external directions. Self-direction almost certainly affords a greater feeling of creativity, a greater feeling of responsibility, and a heightened ability to identify with the activity and any final product. In addition, recent research in the area of "reactance"—a concept proposed by Brehm (1966) to refer to a human propensity to feel displeasure and to rebel whenever freedom of choice is arbitrarily restricted—has indicated that restriction of freedom of choice is indeed unpleasant and that people will strive to restore it through various means (see also Wicklund, 1974).

The second phase of deCharms's research (1971, 1976) involved an extensive investigation of the effects of an "Origin training program" in an urban school district. This research included a two-step process in which a group of teachers were first trained in the Origin/Pawn concept and participated in the development of exercises for use with their students (note that this research process itself treats the teachers as Origins rather than Pawns, as would have been the case had they simply been told how to train their students). In the second step of the research, the participating teachers actually carried out the Origin training program with their students. The program consisted mainly of four basic classroom units: (1) introspective exercises to help students gain self-insight and clarify their goals and values; (2) story-writing exercises designed to stimulate achievement imagery (adapted from techniques developed by David McClelland—for example, 1965—to induce people to higher levels of achievement motivation); (3) a spelling game designed to teach the advantages of moderate risk-taking (an important trait of people with high achievement motivation and an important aid to success, apparently); and (4) a special "Origin manual" with exercises stressing the setting of realistic personal goals and evaluating progress toward them. The children were also introduced to the Origin/Pawn distinction through discussions and experiences designed to make the concept clear. The overall effort was to help the students understand their individual abilities and limitations, choose realistic goals, take constructive action toward those goals, and obtain useful feedback about the effects of their efforts. Thus, the idea was not merely to get the students to *feel* that they were self-directing but actually to help them become more effective and self-directed problem-solvers. The resulting experiences of success would presumably lead them to have greater feelings of self-direction and self-esteem, to feel more like Origins.

This research project was apparently very successful. Compared with control groups, the children exposed to the Origin training procedures evidenced higher achievement motivation, more realistic goal setting, higher Origin feelings (as measured by a projective test), improved academic achievement, and reduced absences and tardiness. That these effects were obtained in schools of lower-income black children may be especially significant, since these are precisely the children who seem to have the most difficulty feeling like Origins or following the behavior patterns that are associated with people of high achievement motivation. Julian Rotter (1966), in his work on the assessment of feelings of internal versus external locus of control, also noted the tendency for lower-class black youths to feel externally controlled. Unfortunately, however, this feeling may reflect the bitter realities of our society more than any personality deficit in the children; and it will take more than an Origin training program to overcome the barriers in the social and economic system that lower-class people of all colors face. Nevertheless, deCharms's work could serve as an inspiration to social scientists and lay people alike. People *do* derive satisfaction and thrive when they are treated as Origins and allowed control over what they do and what is done to them.

Some Social and Environmental Implications

Before proceeding to the environmental implications of this research on effectance and the Origin/Pawn concept, let us dip briefly into an issue of general social relevance. To what extent does our society, and especially its educational system, encourage people to become Origins or to rely on effectance motivation? Educational critics such as Henry (1964), Holt (1964), Leonard (1968), Farber (1969), and Silberman (1970), have lambasted the prevailing educational system for stultifying and inhibiting the creative development, self-expression, and curiosity of our children. That more than a few people survive to criticize the system and make original contributions may be more a testimony to human resilience than to the wisdom of the system that "educated" them. Hard and fast evidence on these points is scanty, but Silberman's (1970) massive review is most impressive in both its indictment of current educational practices and its demonstration of promise in alternative "open classroom" approaches that rely on children's capacity for self-directed learning.

Just how stultifying and even dehumanizing the educational system is is difficult to gauge precisely. A few years ago some of my students were inspired by deCharms's ideas to perform an informal study. They asked people of varying ages (preschool, various elementary grade levels, high school, college, and post-college) to choose whether to draw a picture freehand or to trace a little cartoon. As I recall their results, 90 percent of the preschoolers chose to draw freehand as compared with only 35 percent of the post-collegians, with a nearly linear drop-off for the ages in between. Does this mean that an initial joy and confidence in artistic self-expression is slowly eroded by formal education? There are many alternative explanations, and I offer this result only as an anecdote. Its real importance probably lies not in whether it "proves" anything but rather in the way it seems to square with the experiences most of us have had. School often *does* stultify intrinsic motivation, instill obedience, and suppress creativity and sensitivity. In later discussions we shall pursue this problem further; suffice it to say now that we all do seem to possess the potential, based on our underlying motivational system, to thrive in a far freer social atmosphere than we typically encounter.

That human beings are motivated to change their environments, to seek optimal levels of stimulation and arousal, and to be self-determining has several implications for interactions between people and their environment. Since our discussion has so far considered these intrinsic sources of reinforcement favorably, let us begin by noting some of their potentially *negative* consequences.

1. If unenlightened by ecological values and understanding, human efforts to make changes in the environment and to feel "in control" can easily lead to dysfunctions in ecosystems and to various other forms of environmental deterioration. Garrett Hardin (1972) has noted that as technology increases in sophistication and potency and as populations using advanced technology increase in size, human power to modify the environment increases. Modifications of the environment on a small scale may be absorbed by the ecosystem without damage; modifications on a *large* scale may not be absorbed harmlessly. One dammed river or nuclear power plant may make little difference in the total scheme of things, but a vastly changed hydrological pattern or a world-wide change in air temperature from thermal pollution may make a catastrophic difference. Automobiles may allow their owners greater feelings of autonomy than any system of public transportation could provide, but the consequences of an overpopulated society's relying heavily on private cars can destroy other sources of human satisfaction (including good health and open space, for example). National or even world-wide efforts at efficacy may similarly produce environmental degradation or

squander resources. Detonating super-potent thermonuclear bombs and thrusting huge rockets moonward may give many people a sense of humanity's power, but consider the possible costs in higher cancer and birth-defect rates and in the diversion of human effort and natural resources from less spectacular—but more humane and ecologically desirable—uses. This is of course getting to be an old story, and doubtless effectance motivation plays only a partial role. But it is worth remembering that virtually any human motive can be channeled for good or ill, depending on how benign or enlightened the social system is.

2. The motivations to feel efficacious in making changes in the environment and to be "self-determining" would seem to favor an individualistic or competitive orientation. Again, in the absence of highly developed technology or huge populations, such orientations might detract from the quality of life for many people but would not necessarily do irremediable damage to ecological balances. Unfortunately, in our current world, individualistic ("selfish") and competitive orientations can lead to policies favoring short-range personal or national gains that may have devastating long-range consequences. The catalogue of environmental horror stories in the spate of recent books on the environment amply documents the possibilities.[7] Interestingly, McClelland (1961) found a clear tendency for countries in which achievement themes were emphasized in the early part of this century to demonstrate relatively high levels of per capita use of electric power in recent times. McClelland's conclusion, not surprisingly, was that a high need for achievement seems to lead to industrial development. This in itself is not necessarily bad, but the knowledge that the industrialized nations produce most of the pollution in the world should at least give us pause in our headlong rush to stimulate ourselves to even greater "productivity." Concentration on achievement, individual accomplishment, and control may dull our sensitivity to the intricate *interdependencies* we have with each other and the physical environment.

3. Our culture and the psychological theories that it spawns tend to adopt an individualistic and culturally *masculine* orientation toward human functioning. As Brewster Smith (1973) acknowledged, concepts such as self-determination, being an Origin, self-actualization, and achievement have a vaguely masculine ring (see also Kasten, 1972). They also have a decidedly individualistic tone. Can it be that *machismo* is alive and well in American psychology? We shall return to this issue, but let us note here that just as an academic emphasis on overt behavior

might be based on the cultural stress on production and consumption, so an emphasis on individualism in the analysis of human motivation might be based on a cultural preoccupation with personal achievement and male dominance. Of course, the times may be changing: there is continuing pressure for sexual equality, and our environmental and social problems may be slowly sensitizing us to the advantages of collective action. But right now—in the mid-seventies—the decision-making power structure is about as masculine and individualistic as ever (readers in doubt may compare Galbraith, 1973, and their newspapers). To the degree that psychological theories of human potential reflect and reinforce this prevailing cultural pattern, they may fail to promote such ecologically positive values as cooperation, concern for the welfare of future generations, environmental beauty, and sympathy for other living things. Need I point out that in our culture such values have a decidedly feminine tone?

Now for the *positive* environmental implications:

4. Within a cultural system that favored cooperation and ecological understanding and values, the propensity of humanity to seek efficacy in making environmental changes might prove valuable in creating a more pleasant life for everyone. Modifying the environment is not necessarily harmful. René Dubos (1972a, 1973a,b), for example, has presented a convincing case for valuing intelligent remolding of the environment in accordance with human values and ecological good sense—as opposed to the more purist ecological ethic of leaving nature untouched at nearly any cost. The point, to follow Ian McHarg's (1969) similar position, is to design *with* nature. Human motivation can be channeled in a number of ways by education, social and economic influences of all sorts, and the values of the culture in which people live. That human beings seem to derive pleasure from being able to make interesting things happen in the environment is in itself cause for neither joy nor alarm. But this implies that there exists a driving force for adapting the environment in any number of ways to our needs and desires. Combined with growth in our understanding of the complex systems in which we function, such motivation could mean that we would derive great satisfaction from engaging in efforts to humanize the environment while taking long-term ecological effects into account. Indeed, if we really want to be efficacious in the fullest sense—which would mean making changes that would facilitate our long-range survival, health, and psychological well-being—this is exactly what we should most enjoy doing.

5. Effectance motivation and the satisfactions for individuals of being Origins offer a rationale for society to relinquish much of its reliance on extrinsic reinforcement. This issue will be explored further below, but let us note a few points here. If people would derive satisfaction from performing given tasks because of the chance to create, manipulate, make interesting things happen, satisfy curiosity, or boost their sense of being Origins, why use payment or some other extrinsic incentive to get them to do the tasks? (As discussed earlier, it may even be that such extrinsic incentives ultimately serve to decrease the inherent satisfaction in the tasks.) For example, some economists admit that it is unnecessary to pay executives exorbitant salaries to get them to do jobs they manifestly enjoy (see, for instance, Galbraith, 1973). Galbraith indeed goes on to note that our society has evolved the ironic practice of providing the highest material incentives for the most desirable jobs and the lowest incentives for the least desirable ones. The types of human motivation we have been discussing imply that people should not have to be forced to learn by threats and prizes, nor should they have to be lured to work at meaningful and exciting jobs by huge amounts of money. Furthermore, as White (1959) and several others have persuasively argued (see below), people are not basically lazy or opposed to striving. Although extrinsic reinforcements will doubtless always be necessary for performing dull, stressful, or ostensibly meaningless work, it would seem that we could profit from a reexamination of the way our society allows resources and reinforcements to be distributed. It may be possible to obtain current or higher levels of performance in all vital areas of human endeavor while providing a higher quality of life for virtually everyone. The greater flexibility in the use of material resources that would be possible if intrinsic sources of motivation were fully utilized could well yield a far more pleasant environment than that possible under our current system of using vast resources for individual extrinsic reinforcement.

6. It may be possible to adapt educational programs similar to deCharms's Origin training procedures and McClelland's achievement motivation training to include attention to ecological values and understanding. For example, new units could presumably be added to deCharms's training program in which understanding one's relation to the ecosystem would be stressed or in which the interdependence of people in achieving collective self-determination would be better appreciated. Lower-class black children, women, and other low-power groups

in our society, it would seem, might ultimately gain more control over their lives from training in collective action and problem-solving skills than from training only in individualistic skills. Widespread "collective-Origin" training, especially if combined with environmental education, might well help the public to institute more humane and environmentally sound use of our resources.

7. These theories of motivation also indicate that environmental design processes should allow people to have more say in determining the shape of their world. Advocates such as Sommer (1972), Goodman (1971), and Halprin (1969) have stressed the value of user participation in design decisions. All three of these writers have noted the pride people take in designing and building their own spaces, public or private. Such observations obviously fit the model of effectance motivation. It makes sense from this perspective that people would derive great satisfaction from helping to shape their own environments. Rather than focusing on questions of "good" and "bad" design as a characteristic of the finished product, it might be motivationally more meaningful to distinguish between designs that people participate in and feel they can modify and those that they feel are thrust upon them by outside forces. The motivational theories under consideration would also suggest that changeable and malleable environmental designs might satisfy both the need for optimal arousal and the need for being able to make environmental changes.

8. Finally, a look at the nature of human motivation suggests that art and aesthetics are more important than is commonly believed in our society. Aesthetic pleasures may be subtle and nonessential to biological survival, but the creation and appreciation of beauty is certainly one of the best ways to fulfill our need to experience and produce interesting effects in the environment. Our culture's masculine bias (aesthetics has traditionally been regarded as a predominantly feminine domain) and its emphasis on behavior as opposed to inner experience may help account for the neglect of aesthetics. But why is enjoying life not viewed as "practical"?

A HIERARCHY OF MOTIVATIONS?

White's theory of effectance motivation and deCharms's notions about fundamental human motives both embody a two-level hierarchy. Each theorist holds that the motive to produce interesting changes in the environment emerges only when physiological or survival needs are not pressing. This of course makes perfect biological sense: survival first, any other pleasures second. The person who developed the notion of a motivational hierarchy most fully, however, was Abraham Maslow (for example, 1970), and it is to his ideas that we now turn.

Maslow's Hierarchy

The central idea in this part of Maslow's work is that human motives are arranged in a five-level hierarchy. Lower needs must be more or less satisfied before higher needs can emerge. The proposed hierarchy of needs, in order of priority or "prepotency," is as follows: (1) *physiological needs*—needs to maintain various organic balances or homeostatic bodily conditions, as in the case of the need for air, food, or warmth; (2) *safety needs*—needs for security, order, freedom from fear and anxiety, and stability (in many ways safety needs seem to correspond to freedom from excessive levels of arousal arising from uncertainty or threat of harm); (3) *belongingness and love needs*—needs for friends, companionship, and intimate relations with other human beings; (4) *esteem needs*—a combination of needs for accomplishment, self-respect, independence, and the esteem of other people; (5) *need for self-actualization*—the desire to realize one's potential as a human being, assuming Maslow's positive conception of human nature (to be discussed below). Maslow (1963, 1970) also discussed needs for knowledge, understanding, and beauty, but in this discussion these will be subsumed under the self-actualization level of the hierarchy.

There are several points to note in Maslow's theory:

1. The first four levels of motivation are regarded as ."deficiency" (D) needs, while the self-actualization level embodies the realm of "Being" (B) needs or what Maslow (for example, 1971) has also labelled "meta-motivation." The distinction is basically that unsatisfied D-needs leave you dead, sick, or unhappy (satisfied D-needs leave you yearning for the goals at the next level of the hierarchy); striving to gratify B-needs, on the other hand, is itself a fulfilling process, dependent on an initial high level of deficiency need satisfaction. Satisfaction of D-needs is thus a selfish process, bringing at best only a low level of happiness and

serving mainly to remove feelings of deficiency. Only in the B-realm do people enjoy life to the fullest and experience the joys and creativity of which they are ultimately capable.

2. According to Maslow, all of the needs are "instinctoid," meaning that they are inherent in human nature. If lower needs are satisfied, the higher needs will tend to emerge, regardless of culture or individual personality. However, cultural practices or special personal circumstances (such as severe or prolonged deprivation of needs at the lower levels of the hierarchy) may inhibit or even prevent the emergence of higher needs.

3. The higher needs are hypothesized to be less imperious or subjectively urgent but to provide more profound happiness when gratified than the lower needs. In addition, the theory obviously holds that pursuit and gratification of the higher needs have more preconditions than is the case for the lower needs. Finally, Maslow posits that striving to fulfill the higher needs leads to both greater individuality and heightened social concern than does seeking to satisfy the lower needs (for example, compare looking for food with looking for friendship or social esteem).

4. In Maslow's view, gratification of a particular need level does not have to be complete for the higher need levels to be activated; it is a matter of degree. As physiological and safety needs become less urgent, needs for companionship and self-esteem become more significant. A higher need may also come to take precedence over a lower need. People may risk safety in the interest of love or renounce food in the interest of self-esteem. Although there may be some exceptions, Maslow argues that for most people, the higher needs can *first* emerge in full force only after the more basic needs have been satisfied. Once this has occurred, the motivational power of the higher needs may be sufficient to override the push of lower needs.

Self-Actualization

Let us turn now to an examination of the highest level of Maslow's hierarchy, the motivations involved in "self-actualization." This concept is not unique to Maslow (compare Goldstein, 1939; see also, for example, G. W. Allport, 1955; Rogers, 1961), but his is probably the best developed of self-actualization theories. According to Maslow, self-actualizing people tend to possess such qualities as accurate, nonstereotyped, and appreciative perception of people and things; acceptance of themselves, other people, and nature; a concern for problems outside themselves and for philosophical issues; a need for privacy and a strong tendency to be autonomous; a highly developed ability to appreciate everyday experiences; and a high frequency of "peak experiences"—moments of overwhelming joy or profound experiences of unity and understanding (as in mystical experience). They also tend to have a sense of identification with and sympathy for other human beings; deep love relations with intimates; nonprejudiced and "democratic" character structure; highly developed ethical feelings; a philosophical, unhostile sense of humor; and high creativeness (see Maslow, 1970). In addition, self-actualizers are held to pursue the B-values in the course of their meta-motivation. These consist of truth, goodness, beauty, unity, aliveness, uniqueness, perfection, necessity, completion, justice, order, simplicity, richness (comprehensiveness), effortlessness, playfulness, self-sufficiency, and meaningfulness (Maslow, 1971, pp. 318–319). People whom Maslow judged to be self-actualizers also had a few faults, including occasional ruthlessness or impoliteness; but the important point is that Maslow viewed the qualities of self-actualization to be potentials inherent in human nature and representative of the way people would tend to be if their D-needs (the first four levels of the hierarchy) were gratified.

It seems to me that the essential characteristics of self-actualization according to Maslow are (1) being an Origin in deCharms's sense (a person who is an effective problem solver, has high self-understanding, and is self-directing); (2) being creative in the sense of taking fresh perspectives as well as producing novel things or ideas that are also interesting, pleasing, or useful; (3) perceiving primarily in terms of "B-cognition," Maslow's term for disinterested, appreciative, aesthetic, insightful perception (to be discussed further in later chapters; see also Maslow, 1963, 1968, 1971); and (4) relating to other people in a loving, sympathetic, and highly ethical manner. Maslow (1971) has also distinguished between ordinary or pragmatic self-actualizers, who tend to be creative in their work but have only moderate peak experiences, and "transcenders," who seek greater understanding and more profound levels of B-cognition and who have more peak experiences.

Evidence

The research evidence bearing on Maslow's theories is far from definitive. In their extensive review of theory and research on motivation, Cofer and Appley (1964) noted some indirect support for the preemptive motivational power of severely frustrated physiological or safety needs. However, they could point to no clear empirical evidence for the hierarchical functioning of the higher needs in Maslow's hierarchy. More recent reviews by Korman (1974) and Graham and Balloun (1973) have similarly turned up only sparse and inconclusive research bearing on Maslow's hierarchy (although Graham and Balloun's own study was consistent with Maslow's notions).[8] Given the dearth of convincing evidence, these reviewers note how remarkable it is that Maslow's notion of a motivational hierarchy enjoys fairly widespread appeal within psychology.

However, the work of Frederick Herzberg and his colleagues (Herzberg et al., 1959; Herzberg, 1966) can be interpreted as providing support for a central aspect of Maslow's theory. Herzberg conducted and inspired several studies of job satisfaction and dissatisfaction in a variety of work settings. The basic methodology involved obtaining and coding reports from people concerning times when they felt especially good or especially bad about their jobs. These studies have very consistently revealed two separate groups of factors—one group relating to feelings of satisfaction and the other to feelings of dissatisfaction. The factors leading to satisfaction with one's work include achievement, recognition, responsibility, advancement, the possibility for growth, and the work itself. These Herzberg interpreted as relating to the inherent quality of the job and to human motivation for growth and self-actualization. The factors leading to dissatisfaction include working conditions, company policy and administration, interpersonal relations with supervisors and fellow workers, the effects of the job on one's personal life, and status, security, and salary. Herzberg interpreted these as relating to the *context* of the job and to human needs for sustenance, security, and creature comforts. This research indicated that satisfaction of these latter needs did not in itself lead to happiness with the job, although dissatisfaction with the job tended to be based on *not* having them satisfied. Conversely, not having growth needs satisfied did not in itself seem to result in job dissatisfaction, although these needs were intimately involved in experiences of great satisfaction with the job.

Although Herzberg did not posit a hierarchy of needs, his findings bear a close resemblance to Maslow's distinction between qualities of B-needs and D-needs. Satisfaction of deficiency needs will keep one from being miserable but will not bring happiness. Unmet higher needs will usually cause less distress than is the case for D-needs, but real joy in life supposedly comes through fulfillment of the B-needs. Furthermore, a case could be made that salary, security, working conditions, relations with fellow workers, and status correspond roughly to the first four levels of Maslow's hierarchy; while achievement, joy in the work itself, and possibilities for growth correspond to the self-actualization level. Of course, the match is not perfect. Recognition and advancement, for example, would seem to belong at the esteem level of the hierarchy; and many aspects of Maslow's concept of self-actualization are not included. What is more serious, Herzberg does not view the evidence as indicating that the growth needs emerge automatically when the lower, "hygiene" needs (as he calls them) are satisfied. Rather, he believes that special circumstances and opportunities are probably required to elicit motivations for personal growth and accomplishment. The important consideration, however, is that the research of Herzberg and his colleagues provides clear evidence that the so-called growth motives do exist and that the higher reaches of human happiness seem to require fulfillment of needs along the whole range of Maslow's proposed hierarchy.[9]

For a critique of Maslow's concept of self-actualization, we can turn to a cogent analysis by Brewster Smith (1973). Along with others (for example, Cofer and Appley, 1964; or Maslow himself, 1970), Smith notes the loose methodology with which Maslow simply picked out acquaintances and historical and public figures whom he felt were self-actualizers. Although over fifty people were chosen, there is no reason to view the sample as representative of anything other than Maslow's own personal view of what a self-actualizer is like. Maslow's conclusions about the characteristics of self-actualizers can thus be criticized as circular or question-begging. What is more serious from Smith's point of view, Maslow's theory attempts to tie what Smith agrees are very desirable human qualities to a "pseudo-biologistic" psychology. Maslow's claim was that the need hierarchy, including the ultimate tendency to seek self-actualization in the positive sense, was more or less "wired in" to humanity's biological structure (he thought of needs as instinctoid). Smith argues with some plausibility that through most of human evolutionary history people were of necessity functioning at the level of deficiency needs: how then could the Being needs of self-actualization arise from evolutionary processes? Smith's conclusion is that "human nature" has many potentials, ranging from the brutal to the more sublime sort that both he and Maslow *like*. Rather than positing the sublime possibilities as biologically inherent in a human "essence," Smith holds that we should view human possibilities and motivational propensities as primarily influenced by human culture and values. What people become, according to this view, is more a question of value decisions, education, and politics than of biology.

Overall, however, Maslow's postulation of a motivational hierarchy seems to make good sense in terms of the human tendency never to be completely satisfied. In Maslow's apt phrase (1965), there are "low grumbles, high grumbles, and metagrumbles" (corresponding to the need hierarchy, of course), but there are always grumbles. As psychology advances, it is at least becoming clearer and clearer that human beings are active, striving creatures. When the basic life support systems are all in order, people are not then permanently satisfied, content to bask in a state of homeostatic bliss. For good or ill, they continue to strive for new goals, including varying levels of arousal; satisfaction of curiosity; feelings of control over self and environment; and love, esteem, and self-expression. In theory, it may be possible to relate all of these emergent motivations to different ways of satisfying the tendency of the nervous system to seek particular types and levels of activation when survival itself is not being threatened. The story may also be more complex than that, with the content of our beliefs about ourselves and the world playing a much larger role in higher-level motives (see Korman, 1974).

The importance of Maslow's contribution probably lies not so much in any revelation of some underlying inborn human essence as in, first, its emphasis on studying human possibilities for psychological *health*, joyous and enlightening experiences, and the emergent nature of many aspects of motivation; and second, its contention that only when certain basic needs are satisfied do people have a real chance to approach these "farther reaches of human nature." That such happy outcomes are not guaranteed by biological essence but rather depend on interactions within complex people/environment systems may simply mean that it is more difficult to approach utopia than Maslow hoped.

Environmental Implications

Let us now examine a few possible environmental implications of this theory of need hierarchies and self-actualization:

1. Perhaps the most important implication is that basic needs must be met for higher levels of motivation to have a chance to emerge. If people are constantly harassed by unsatisfied needs for food, warmth, or safety from criminals or creditors, it is unlikely that they will be much concerned with environmental beauty or with long-term threats to the global ecosystem. Nor will they be likely to care about growth in ecological understanding and appreciation, designing with nature, or creating a happier society. They will be overwhelmingly concerned with eking out a sufficient supply of basic necessities to stay alive and safe; and beyond that, they will probably seek pleasures untutored by broad concerns for society or the environment. It is only when the basic needs are satisfied that people can be moved by aesthetic, cognitive, and humanitarian sources of reinforcement. Consider that the environmental movement has primarily blossomed among the affluent and educated (see McEvoy, 1972; Morrison et al., 1972), that complex cognitive tasks such as systems thinking require low anxiety and brains undamaged by nutritional deficiencies, and that appreciation of beauty is much easier with a full stomach and a liberal education.

A society or environment that makes it difficult for even a minority of its human residents to satisfy their basic needs does two things at least. It chokes off the chance for such people to enjoy the higher levels of human satisfaction, and it produces a group of people who are neither equipped nor motivated to prevent long-term ecological harm or to produce a more benign society for all. Satisfying basic needs thus can liberate types of motivation that can have long-range utility for human happiness. This means that using threats to basic needs as a source of extrinsic motivation for "productive work" may lead to a tragic waste of human resources.

2. Assuming no biologically given human essence, however, mere satisfaction of basic needs will probably be insufficient to produce the millennium of self-actualization motives. Consideration of the total cultural/

environmental system is required. As deCharms (1971) noted, Origins are made, not born. Indeed, his educational procedures for helping people gain more control over their lives were carefully developed with an eye toward the reinforcement contingencies involved for both the teachers and the students. Full stomachs, safe streets, loving friends, and high self-esteem are thus not alone in being prerequisites for concern with environmental quality and ecological well-being. Special educational procedures and revised patterns of social decision making (as in how resources are used) will also be necessary.

3. People who actually are self-actualizing in Maslow's sense would almost certainly create a more benign environment than ordinary mortals have so far managed. Their concern with peak experiences, understanding, feelings of unity with nature, cooperation with other people, aesthetic enjoyment, and so forth, would lead them to a high level of environmental awareness and intelligent action. Also, the closer people come to being self-actualizing, the more relying on their intrinsic sources of satisfaction would lead to environmentally and socially beneficial behavior. Someone seeking truth and beauty is more likely to build a pleasant world than someone after food, love, or status symbols. Furthermore, people at the self-actualization level would be more able to enjoy the fruits of social and environmental creativity.

4. Even in a society that satisfied basic needs at the physiological and safety levels, motivational trouble could arise for people/environment relations at the level of self-esteem. In our society, for example, self-esteem rests to a large extent on competitive success, especially for people who occupy important decision-making positions. As argued earlier, a competitive, individualistic orientation can have nasty environmental consequences when it operates in conjunction with a highly developed technology. A competitive and individualistic social structure can inhibit the cooperation, coordination, and concern with long-range consequences needed for creating and preserving a healthy and pleasant public environment.

However, self-esteem can be based on personal qualities other than competitive success. Alternatives might include cooperating with other people, having peak experiences, or simply being a human being. Self-esteem is determined by what a particular culture holds to be valuable, and the self-assertive version of this need is played down in cultures that stress cooperation among people and with nature. As Margaret Mead (1937) concluded after surveying a wide range of cultures differing in competitive versus cooperative orientation, competitive cultures tend to stress individual initiative, individual use of property, a single scale of success, and strong ego development. Cooperative cultures, in contrast, have much weaker emphases on individual interpersonal power or advancement in status and provide a high degree of security for all members.

It is important to keep in mind that competition entails both winners and losers, but *everyone* can win in a cooperative system. If self-esteem is based on competitive success, some people (perhaps most) are bound to suffer some loss or at least threat to their self-esteem. By blocking this need, competition can thus presumably inhibit the development of self-actualization motives as well as reduce the quality of experience for all but the "winners." When one considers further that competitive systems are less open than cooperative ones to coordination, the exchange of information, and actions in the long-range interest of the total population (see Deutsch, 1973), it should be clear that ecological values will have the best chance to be realized in a cooperative culture.

Drawing on a series of lectures given in 1941 by Ruth Benedict (Maslow, 1965, 1971; Benedict, 1970), Maslow incorporated the concept of "synergy" in much of his thinking about social and cultural processes. The concept of synergy, as developed by Benedict, refers to the degree to which the reinforcements within a culture function so that individuals benefit the group through the same actions that satisfy them personally. Cultures with high synergy tend to be cooperative and have low levels of internal aggression. There is a *correspondence of interests* among the members (many social psychological theorists indeed define cooperation as a situation of correspondent interests or mutually facilitative goals— see Thibaut and Kelley, 1959). Maslow himself studied the Blackfoot Indians, a cultural group of apparently high synergy. Among these people, esteem was accorded the person who gave away wealth or shared possessions freely (as opposed to the dominant American practice of according highest esteem to the persons or families who acquire and keep the most wealth for the longest time). The synergy is represented by the correspondence between satisfaction for the giver in high social (and self-) esteem and satisfaction for other members of the culture in meeting needs for food, clothing, transportation, and so on. Contingencies of reinforcement within a culture can channel even the "higher" human motives, including needs for social acceptance and self-esteem, into contributions to the total social welfare or into aggressively competitive behavior. Especially as growth occurs in technology, concentrations of surplus wealth, and population, we should pay attention to the long-range consequences of the direction our culture chooses.

VIEWS OF HUMAN NATURE

Our assumptions about "human nature"—about the qualities, motives, and patterns of behavior to be expected from people—can obviously play a large role in how social institutions and practices function. If you view people as dishonest and lazy, you will tend to treat them differently than if you view them as trustworthy and eager to work. In his extensive study of people's philosophies of human nature, Lawrence Wrightsman (1974, 1977) has proposed six central dimensions for characterizing a person's views about other people. These include trustworthiness versus untrustworthiness, strength of will and rationality versus lack of will power and irrationality, altruism versus selfishness, independence versus conformity to group pressures, complexity versus simplicity, and variability versus similarity. The first four dimensions relate to substantive qualities and can be characterized as differentiating "favorable" views of human nature from "unfavorable" ones. The last two dimensions refer to the complexity and degree of interpersonal differentiation in one's view of human nature and individual differences.

Wrightsman and others have conducted extensive research with a test developed to measure a person's beliefs on each of these dimensions. Although the results certainly do not reveal the full role that views of human nature play in social institutions, several interesting findings have emerged. For example, women tend to have more favorable and more complex views of human nature than do men; one's evaluations of individuals tend to reflect one's general views of human nature; during the turbulent 1960s there was apparently a decline in many college students' views of human rationality, trustworthiness, altruism, and resistance to conformity; and, although it appears to be very difficult to produce substantial and lasting changes in a person's view of human nature, certain encounter-group experiences can lead to a more favorable view (see Wrightsman, 1974).

Theory X and Theory Y

The great importance of a society's dominant assumptions about human nature lies in the potential effects on how people are treated by economic, educational, and political institutions. Douglas McGregor (1960), for example, has differentiated two opposing views of human nature that can greatly influence the conduct of industrial organizations. According to *Theory X*, people are regarded as having an aversion to work, requiring coercion to contribute to the organization's goals, and desiring direction and the avoidance of responsibility. *Theory Y*, in contrast, holds that people can enjoy working, will exercise self-direction when committed to goals, and become committed as a function of the goal's potential for satisfying their needs for achievement and self-actualization. Additionally, according to Theory Y, people can learn to want responsibility, generally have the "capacity to exercise a relatively high degree of imagination, ingenuity, and creativity in the solution of organizational problems," and thus have many creative potentials that are being inadequately realized in their jobs.

As Wrightsman (1974) has pointed out in relation to this and other work in organizational psychology, the assumptions managers make about human nature can determine the way an organization is set up. The contingencies of reinforcement thus generated can in turn serve to produce something of a self-fulfilling prophecy. If workers (or students) are treated as if they must be coerced in order to work and are constantly regarded as potentially dishonest and unreliable, they may come to feel and act accordingly. Indeed, as we have seen, piling extrinsic reinforcements on top of intrinsically satisfying activities can have the effect of deadening the original interest. What may be even worse in industrial or educational settings, if managers or teachers assume that their subordinates are irresponsible or need coercion, they may forego the effort of trying to discover the workers' or students' intrinsic interests or ideas. They may also forego trying to create situations in which the workers or students are encouraged to understand and participate in the choice of goals and the means for reaching them.

The Theory Y approach at least opens the way for people to find and pursue points of communality involving their own interests and those of the organizations for which they work. As McGregor (1960) very effectively argued, this approach can also serve to enhance the performance and experience of everyone involved in an organization. When one considers that the basic idea is to replace an *adversary* relationship (as is typically produced by Theory X management or teaching) with a cooperative, problem-solving approach (Theory Y), it makes good sense that beneficial results should follow.[10] The opportunity for higher levels of "synergy" is created by acting on the assumption that people will take an interest in the welfare of institutions with which they are interdependent.

In his presidential address to the American Psychological Association, George Miller (1969) advocated broad dissemination of a view of human nature similar to McGregor's Theory Y. Miller argued that the view of people as totally controllable by manipulations of extrinsic reinforcement (including punishments) could have very damaging social consequences and could even become a self-fulfilling prophecy. Citing developments in psychology following the line of McGregor (1960) and White (1959), Miller went on to observe that a more active and self-motivated view of human nature is emerging in present-day psychology—a view that could have positive consequences for humanizing industry, education, and the general welfare of our society. Miller's main contention was that by "giving psychology away," by helping and teaching people to solve their problems using this more recent and positive conception of human possibilities, psychologists can help to establish a new view of human motivational potential. The prevailing legacies of pessimism derived from Freudian psychoanalysis and of reliance on extrinsic control derived from oversimplified reinforcement theories could thus be ameliorated by the understanding of human desires for effectance, interesting and meaningful work, aesthetic pleasures, responsibility, social participation, and sense of creativity.

Evidence

As should be apparent from the previous discussions, there is a dearth of hard evidence for some of the more sweeping assertions in this positive view of human potentials. (If one looks carefully, though, one observes that there is frequently a dearth of hard evidence for sweeping assertions in any of the behavioral sciences.) However, as we have seen, there is certainly substantial support for the idea that arousal processes play a large role in aesthetic experience and in task performance. Theorists such as White, deCharms, and Brehm have also developed potent arguments and accumulated much empirical evidence that people do indeed gain satisfaction from feeling competent, in control, and free to choose for themselves. Furthermore, evidence from settings as diverse as industrial organizations (for example, McGregor, 1960; Herzberg, 1966) and open classrooms (for example, Nyquist and Hawes, 1972; Rogers, 1969; Silberman, 1970) demonstrates that people can indeed function very productively and happily under conditions where intrinsic sources of satisfaction are stressed. It is also clear from Maslow's somewhat anecdotal research and from everyday observation that people will under some conditions strive for "self-actualization" pleasures such as peak experiences, creative insights, a pleasant public environment, and justice for other people.

Perhaps the main point, however, is not to prove that these "positive" human tendencies are inherent in our nature or independent of reinforcement contingencies that could be externally manipulated. It has been acknowledged by many (even Maslow) that unpleasant traits can be brought out as easily as the synergistic ones, given appropriate external circumstances. People can apparently be trained to be vicious killers *or* loving pacifists, depending on their culture or even subculture. Rather, the main point is that viewing the positive side of "human nature" as a possibility on which to base an organization, educational system, or society may be a crucial and necessary step toward helping humanity to realize a happy and cooperative existence. Miller (1969) was indeed not so much arguing that one view of human nature was *truer* than the other, but rather that either view could *come* to accurately reflect the way people function.

Thus, if we assume the need for extrinsic controls, this may lead to situations in which extrinsic controls are necessary. One often finds, for example, that youths trained in a repressive school system find it difficult to adjust to a "free school" system at first. They don't know what they are interested in or want to do if no one tells them. Perhaps it is a testimony to human resilience that after a period of "laziness" most such students come to thrive under the greater freedom. On the other hand, if we begin by assuming that people can function very effectively and productively in the pursuit of intrinsic satisfactions such as effectance, then we will be more prone to create a social system that makes use of intrinsic motivation. Socially mediated contingencies of reinforcement (such as the opportunity to choose one's own goals, Origin training, ready satisfaction of survival and security needs, and praise for sharing) would favor socially valuable behavior that would nonetheless derive mainly from intrinsic satisfactions. Since the evidence indicates that this is indeed a possible basis for a viable and productive society, we should have much to gain in human happiness by shifting our predominant assumptions toward those of Theory Y.

Environmental Consequences

The consequences of such a shift for human interactions with the environment could be very beneficial. For example, Theory Y assumptions of more widespread ingenuity and desire for creative responsibility could lead to greater involvement of the public in environmental goal-setting and decision making. This of course would have to be a *system* effect. The idea is that in the *context* of a society that followed Theory Y assumptions in the functioning of educational, economic, and political institutions, most people would desire and receive an opportunity for greater involvement in decisions affecting the design and functioning of their collective and private environments. This in turn would lead to (and be supported by) greater feelings of public ownership and responsibility for the society's environment and resources. That many people are currently unconcerned or shirk responsibility does not so much argue against the Theory Y view of human potentials as illustrate the extent to which our society has failed to provide opportunities for people to experience their own individual and collective effectiveness. What can one expect in the way of social concern and zeal when the educational system typically stifles creative efforts, the industrial system largely assumes people work only for money, and the political system is most amenable to influence from only the very rich or powerful?[11]

It is thus necessary to consider ways in which the society could favor both revised assumptions about human possibilities *and* positive action to reinforce the development of Theory Y qualities such as creativity, responsibility, and intrinsic satisfaction from socially useful work. Both the social and physical environments can help in this endeavor. For example, the educational system can obviously play a key role in facilitating growth in effectance motivation, the appreciation and creation of beauty, and understanding of the interdependence of people with each other and their environments. As will be discussed in more detail later in this chapter, the economic system can also be a critical force in aiding the realization of Theory Y potentials. A more egalitarian distribution of resources and the enhancement of personal security, for example, could aid the development of self-actualization motives. Such changes might additionally require and entail transformations in political decision making. A populace aroused to its own intrinsic needs would seemingly be most congruent with a political structure that placed the public welfare ahead of special dispensations for elite segments of the population.

Modifications of the physical environment might also aid the development of effectance, responsibility, cooperation, and qualities of self-actualization. Simply participating in environmental design projects can apparently stimulate some of these motives by providing rich and unusual experiences.[12] In addition, experiencing pleasant environments—whether or not one helps to design or construct them—may help to alert people to the potential enjoyment of visiting or living in attractive and interesting places. If one has never experienced a beautiful, exciting, and safe city or park, for example, it might be unlikely that one would strive to have such environments created. More fundamentally, only if people have the opportunity to experience beauty and have sufficient security and education to appreciate it will this aesthetic level of human motivation have a chance to develop.

Finally, one can observe even in the work of such humanistically oriented psychological theorists as Maslow, Rogers, McGregor, and Miller (in his APA address) a tendency to focus predominantly on individualistically oriented motives. Wrightsman's dimensions of philosophies of human nature do include altruism versus selfishness, but even here the main emphasis is on views of the nature of individual motivation. Similarly, both Theory X and Theory Y concern the purported nature of the individual's motivation, considered more or less independently of the social and environmental system as a whole. The key ideas in the theories of White, deCharms, Maslow, McGregor, Rogers, G. W. Allport, and many other psychologists concerned with human potentials involve striving for *personal* competence, *self*-actualization, *self*-determination, and similar self-oriented concepts of *individual* growth. In itself there is nothing wrong with this as a positive human value; certainly the experience of *individuals* is the ultimate touchstone for determining what is valuable. As noted earlier, however, the highly individualistic bias of even the humanistic views of human nature may imply insufficient concern with the interdependence of people with each other and the rest of the ecosystem.[13]

As Skinner (1953) observed, the concept of self-determination may have its uses for helping people appreciate their own worth and powers, but in the literal sense no one can be viewed as the ultimate origin of his or her behavior. In Skinner's words (p. 449):

> When the individual is strengthened as a measure of counter-control [for example, against political oppression], we may, as in democratic philosophies, think of him as a starting point. Actually, however, we are not justified in assigning to anyone or anything the role of prime mover. Although it is necessary that science confine itself to selected segments in a continuous series of events, it is to the whole series that any interpretation must eventually apply.

(It is interesting that Alan Watts, 1963, approvingly quoted this same passage as equivalent in tone and meaning to the "purest mysticism.") The importance of Skinner's lucid observation is that the entire system of interrelations between the individual and the world must be taken into account even when speaking of "self-determination." Recall that people were taught to become Origins by special *social* training.

The underlying problem of how we can come to think of ourselves as an integral part of a larger system (as opposed to separate atomistic egos struggling to become "self-actualized" through dint of will power) will be examined more fully in Chapter 5. Let us at this point simply take note of a pragmatic consideration. Just as Miller (1969) argued that a mechanistic view of human nature might lead to oppressive social practices, so one might contend that any individualistic focus—regardless of its humanistic quality—is inadequate to lead us to optimal long-term patterns of relating to each other and to the environment. Broad dissemination of a view of human nature that stresses individual striving, satisfaction from personal accomplishment and responsibility, and joy in pursuing intrinsic interests may indeed help to counter coercive techniques of behavior control that can stifle creativity and pleasure. But preoccupation with this "agentic" view (see Bakan, 1966; May, 1969) may fail to provide sufficient orientation toward interpersonal coordination, ecological values (see Chapters 4 and 5), and long-term societal cooperation and planning. One should also consider that in our society, pervaded for so long by an ethic of competition, even humanistic values are easily perverted to provide a basis for invidious comparisons between people (for example, one-upmanship on the "human potentials" circuit concerning who is more self-actualized, or even using the degree of personal fulfillment as a criterion for competitive success in the scramble for jobs or promotions). It is essential to bear in mind that individual creativity and happiness arise only in interaction with complex social/environmental systems. Concentration on the nature of such systems and such interactions may yield a better basis for promoting long-term human welfare than a more direct focus on even the most positive aspects of individual motivation.

Indeed, Skinner (1953) argued that the total culture is central in understanding human behavior and potential; and environmental psychologists, such as Barker (1968), Altman (1973), and Ittelson et al. (1974), increasingly stress the theme that the total system of people *and* environment should become the focus of psychological analysis. Thinking in terms of cultural or people/environment system "actualization" may thus prove a better long-term strategy for optimizing human experience than will any individualistic focus. For the moment, however, let me simply borrow from Philip Slater's (1974) iconoclastic analysis and apt phrases to raise the following question: A lifelong quest for personal growth and self-actualization may bring us closer to being a "race of psychic behemoths," but is it the best path to "attunement" with each other and the world around us?

ALTERNATIVE NORMS OF EQUITY

Views of human nature and motivation have an effect on the rules within a society concerning the distribution of resources among its members. Such rules about what is "fair" or "just" in the distribution of rewards and costs constitute norms of "distributive justice" or "equity." Social psychological theorists such as Thibaut and Kelley (1959), Homans (1961), Blau (1964), Adams (1965), and Walster et al. (1973) have explored these concepts in relation to a variety of processes of social exchange, ranging from payment for work to the exchange of affection in romantic relationships. As we shall see, the cultural norms and assumptions that underlie judgments of equity or fairness in exchange and distribution interact in important ways with different types of human motivation, with different economic systems, and with the resulting people/environment relations. Equity norms thus can provide a key to understanding processes within the social system that deeply affect the quality of both environment and experience.

Equity Research

Recent research and theory concerning equity processes have focused on how people in our society function within the existing equity norms. Investigations usually proceed from the conception of "equity" as a situation in which the participants feel that they are getting the "outcomes" they deserve based on contributions or other "inputs." In general, according to recent equity theory (see, for example, Adams, 1965; Walster et al., 1973), a social exchange or distribution process is viewed as equitable when people who compare themselves with each other (such as workers in the same factory) find that the *ratio* between the outcomes and inputs is the same for each person. Thus, participants would believe equity exists if people who have higher inputs (such as effort, seniority, age, education, skill, and social position) receive outcomes (such as money, office furnishings, praise, and power) proportionately higher than those with lower inputs. All of the exchange theorists postulate that people will find departures from conditions of equity to be unpleasant and will strive to restore at least the feeling of equity. J. Stacey Adams (1965), for example, details research pertaining to many techniques for restoring equity, ranging from attempting to alter one's own or others' actual outcomes or inputs to distorting one's perception of the situation. Indeed, an especially provocative series of studies by Melvin Lerner (for example, 1970; see also Lerner, 1975) indicates that the tendency to maintain belief in a "just world" is so great in our culture that people will derogate an apparently innocent victim of a misfortune under the presumption that everyone gets what she or he "deserves."

Most of the research and theory concerning equity has simply assumed the current cultural norms of equity as *the* norms of equity and proceeded to examine how people act to maintain or restore equity or how the existing norms interact with other aspects of behavior. Although this work is certainly very important, it has generally failed to take account of a crucial consideration: there are other potential norms of equity.[14] It is not an immutable characteristic of human beings that they will regard level of age, effort, skill, knowledge, education, social position, hereditary right, or competitive success as inputs entitling a person to a greater or lesser share of the society's goods and services. Even within our society, a major change is underway: being white or male is beginning to be seen as no longer a higher input than being black or female. Furthermore, it seems evident that the most rational criterion for a society to use in differential distribution of goods and services would be to accord wealth in proportion to actual contribution to the social welfare (perhaps with some weighting according to the desirability or difficulty of the tasks involved). This is far from our own society's principles of distribution. For example, do executives of companies that produce pollution and manufacture unsafe (and perhaps unnecessary) goods really make fifty or a hundred times the beneficial social contribution of people who collect garbage, grow food, or work on outdoor sculptures?

Equity and Motivation

More fundamentally, however, we may question the systemic value of linking the distribution of goods and services so pervasively to the performance of work, socially useful or otherwise. To argue that people will not "produce" unless rewarded differentially by extrinsic reinforcers such as money, social standing, or threats to their survival is to fall back on a Theory X conception of human nature. There is at least enough evidence from the work on arousal, effectance, innovative procedures in education and industry, and the functioning of other cultures (including communal subcultures in our society; see Chapter 7) to argue that this view is not warranted. As we have seen, there are many sources of motivation in addition to survival, safety, or obtaining goods and services. Striving for competence, interesting stimulation, the friendship and respect of others, self-esteem, feelings of unity with nature, and creative expression are potential human motives of great social value. However, such higher motives are apparently contingent on satisfaction of more basic human needs for survival, safety, and some degree of comfort. This would seem to argue strongly for a more even distribution of vital goods and services. Again, it is not that the Theory Y motives will automatically arise if basic needs are satisfied; education and special socially mediated reinforcement contingencies would also be required. Rather, it is simply that there *are* potential intrinsic motives for productivity and creativity on which society could rely—provided that basic needs are satisfied.

"Equity 1" versus "Equity 2"

The implication of this argument is that alternative equity norms and the concomitant social systems for distributing vital goods and services could make a critical difference in whether members of a society live happy, creative, and cooperative lives or anxious, stifling, and competitive ones. Let us christen as *Equity 1* any norm that holds that goods and services should be distributed in accordance with individual differences in performance, skill, intelligence, sex, race, social status, effort, or any other basis for discrimination among people. The label *Equity 2* may then be applied to a norm that holds that each member of a society should have access to vital goods and services, regardless of the member's individual contribution or status. In effect, simply being a human being or a member of the society would be viewed as a preemptive input, entitling the person to an equal share of the society's life-sustaining and life-enhancing resources. By the same token, however, an Equity 2 system would call for the equal distribution of the *costs* entailed for the maintenance and well-being of the society. For example, unpleasant work needed for the welfare of everyone would be viewed as justly shared by everyone.[15]

Note that each type of equity norm is merely an ideal, referring to the set of assumptions and expectations that members of a given culture hold concerning what a person "should" legitimately receive and contribute. In actual practice, deviations from the ideal would of course occur. Such would be the case, for example, in an Equity 1 system calling for distributions in accordance with individual effort or social contribution but falling into an actual pattern of rewards determined by social power or family heritage. Or in an Equity 2 system some people might manage to accumulate differentially high wealth or fail to contribute to the work necessary for maintaining the society. Furthermore, a given society might operate under a mixture of equity norms, as in the case of providing grudging aid to indigent families while stressing competitive success as the only path to respectability and wealth.

Equity, Society, and Environment

Equity norms of course operate within a broader sociocultural context of interacting institutional patterns. Any viable social system will function to maintain itself, and thus we might reasonably expect to find congruence between the dominant norms of equity and other aspects of a culture. Our society, for example, certainly espouses Equity 1 in its dominant norms for how wealth should be distributed. That is, people are viewed as "deserving" differential wealth in accordance with their individual performance, education, skill, competitive success, sex, race, intelligence, or a variety of other achievements or traits. Such norms are perfectly in accord with an economic system that employs material reinforcements as a primary mechanism to get people to work. Other social institutions also operate in support of Equity 1 orientations. For example, educational practices (such as competitive grading, awarding of prizes and memberships in honor societies, and in general, the primary emphasis on extrinsic and coercive techniques of motivation) combine with commercial advertising and numerous other social pressures to prepare people to be eagerly and aggressively acquisitive and to respond submissively to people of higher status. These conditions lead people to expect that they should not enjoy work and should do it only if they receive extrinsic remunerations. Although there are of course exceptions, this is basically the old Theory X story. There can be little doubt that our educational and economic socialization prepares us to function under its assumptions.

Unfortunately, such a system encourages rampant individualism, competition, and insecurity. Each member of the society must struggle in competition with others to meet basic needs and to achieve a measure of status or social respect. People are encouraged to view each other as potential threats and to adopt an egocentric perspective toward the use and distribution of material resources. Since work is so inextricably associated with extrinsic rewards, people come to believe that humans are inherently lazy and will engage in socially productive activities only *for* extrinsic rewards. Theory X views of human nature and Equity 1 norms of distribution thus mutually reinforce each other. As we have seen, the concomitant cultural patterns of individualism and competition may have deleterious environmental consequences of many sorts. Indeed, Garrett Hardin's (1968, 1972) problem of the "commons" may be loosely interpreted as the tendency under Equity 1 systems for individuals or corporations to pursue private gain at public cost—as by polluting or squandering resources. Such a process is encouraged by a social system that views great concentrations of wealth as legitimate and even deserved.

Recently, several ecologically oriented economists, including Robert Theobald (1972), John Galbraith (1973), and Herman Daly (1971, 1973), have advocated a shift toward an Equity 2 system for affluent societies. Their arguments vary somewhat, but one main theme seems to be that technology and plentiful resources have made it possible to provide a decent standard of living for all participants in advanced societies, although difficult to provide full employment. Our society may indeed be *overproducing* in certain segments of the economy, as in the case of cars and roads. In any event, it is no longer necessary—if it ever was—to press people into higher and higher levels of basically superfluous production and consumption. More important, there are limits to certain types of ecnomic growth; and economic growth has traditionally served as the main means for the economic advancement of the poor.[16] If growth is approaching such limits, a decent life for many people will be possible only if wealth is redistributed. These economists thus call for institution of procedures such as relatively high guaranteed minimum incomes and reform in taxation to distribute wealth more evenly. Their suggestions also include greater attention to the use of public funds for the pursuit of the public welfare (see especially Galbraith, 1973).

There are many ramifications to the changes such economists propose. For example, shifting toward Equity 2 norms of distribution would orient people toward eliminating all unnecessary unpleasant work and toward spreading the burden of what remained more thinly and equally through the population. This by itself would drastically improve the quality of life for many people. In addition, a slowing in the competitive massing of wealth and profit would reduce such parasitic activities as advertising and designing for obsolescence. Since necessary work would be shared by all, the social and personal reinforcement would lie in decreasing the total amount of work needed. Hence, there would be more motivation to create long-lasting products of high quality and to pool accurate information about product functioning. There should also be a reduction in the overall level of conflict as social class differences, economic oppression, economic sources of prejudice (see Allport, 1954), and levels of frustration and anxiety all declined.

Increased leisure time, the widespread satisfaction of basic needs, and the release from many of the current pressures of economic rat races would also create the opportunity for greater interest in beauty, environmental design, and harmonious functioning with nature. As

noted in the discussion of Maslow's hierarchy, many economically deprived people in our society are unconcerned with issues of environmental quality or ecological values. They are too worried about decent
food, safe housing, or keeping their jobs to be concerned with ugliness,
pollution, or possible ecological catastrophes. An Equity 2 system would
be especially valuable for enhancing the lives of these people and for
engaging their ecological concern and constructive input.

In addition, an Equity 2 system would give people little opportunity
or motivation to amass great personal wealth at the cost of damage to
the collective welfare. Growth in personal wealth would require growth
in collective wealth, and damage to others would become damage to
onself. In this way Equity 2 functioning could lead to greater synergy in
the society and help to eliminate Hardin's problem of the commons.
Where private gain and public gain are recognized as completely interdependent, there can be little incentive to pursue one at the cost of the
other.

This may sound a bit utopian, and it is. However, establishing an
Equity 2 system and reaping the benefits in terms of cooperation, improved environmental quality, and a happier existence for most people is
not impossible. Consider first that our society already espouses Equity 2
ideals in many areas. For example, the power to vote is supposed to be
equally distributed without regard to individual differences (although
it is chastening to recall the struggle of women and poor black people to
be brought into the fold of "one man, one vote"). Similarly, all members
of the society are ideally held to deserve an equal share of basic education, legal counsel if accused of a crime, and police and fire protection.
In practice things do not always work out that way, but at least we
could anticipate some indignation at the suggestion that business executives or real estate owners should be given extra votes or that people
should be accorded fire protection in correspondence with their grades
in school.

It is admittedly a large step from these norms to the position that all
members of a society deserve an equal share of the life-sustaining and
life-enhancing wealth. Nevertheless, some societies have approached
Equity 2 norms in the distribution of goods and services. In addition
to many small "primitive" groups such as the Blackfoot Indians studied
by Maslow, even some large nations such as China and (to a lesser degree) the Scandinavian countries seem to have approached Equity 2
norms. These societies appear to have been successful in greatly re-

ducing abject poverty and its consequences in human suffering. We might note also that within our own culture certain items presumed to be of unique and sublime value, such as some great works of art and some beautiful natural areas, are considered too valuable to be owned by any single person or group. They therefore are regarded as rightfully shared by all. It is at least conceivable that such an attitude could be extended to a much wider range of resources, especially when it is recognized that these resources—for example, food, energy, land, and medical care—can be viewed as finite and of unique value for improving the quality of life.

However, to understand how an Equity 2 system of distribution could work—how a society could function with vitality when goods and services are freely shared rather than used as extrinsic motivators for productive effort—several other factors must be taken into account. It must first be noted that in a fundamental sense even an Equity 2 system *does* use goods and services as extrinsic motivators. Under Equity 2 goods and services can be viewed as consequentially intrinsic reinforcement: making a contribution to the productivity of the society increases the total wealth, which in turn is passed on to everyone, including oneself. If thoroughly understood and appreciated, this aspect of Equity 2 can serve as at least one source of motivation for productive work.[17] In addition, insofar as it proves necessary, added extrinsic rewards can be offered for especially unpleasant work that is difficult or inefficient to distribute equally. With planning and social understanding, such mild use of differential extrinsic rewards need not interfere with the basic principle of the Equity 2 norm—that all members of the society deserve to share the collective wealth without regard to individual differences.

For people to function optimally under such a norm, they would have to be educated in ways that bring out and develop intrinsic interests, lead them to value cooperation, and encourage them to think in terms of long-range interrelations and systems functioning. Just as our current social institutions and practices prepare people to function under Equity 1 assumptions, a different system of education, entertainment, advertising, and child rearing could create equally good preparation for functioning under Equity 2 assumptions about what people deserve. It is probably true that a system of education and socialization based on cooperation, intrinsic interests, systems thinking, and a Theory Y conception of human nature would be more difficult to establish than our current practices have been. However, the idea that people might need special preparation to function effectively under Equity 2 bears a resemblance to our culturally popular notion that a certain type and level of education is necessary for democracy to work. Perhaps education for Equity 2 is simply the next level up.

Fortunately, as we have seen in earlier discussions, human beings seem to have the underlying motivational potential to function effectively in educational and economic systems that hold to a Theory Y view of human nature. Indeed, one of the chief advantages of more nearly equal distribution of wealth or the provision of "basic economic security" (see Theobald, 1972) is that the opportunity would thereby be created for people to satisfy motives for esteem, creativity, feeling effective, and so on. Whether or not Maslow is correct that such motives would *automatically* arise if basic needs were satisfied, there can be little doubt that these are potential human motives and that the satisfaction of basic needs can facilitate their emergence. The catch may simply be that enlightened educational and work environments will also be needed to make Theory Y a truly self-fulfilling prophecy.

A fully functioning Equity 2 system would involve more than these humanizing changes in the educational and economic systems, however. A high material standard of living—and a high quality of life—under Equity 2 distribution would require intelligent and concerted planning in the areas of population level and resource use. Such concerns are also important in preserving the quality of life in Equity 1 systems, but uneven distribution of wealth often overrides and clouds the relations of population size and resource use to the prevailing quality of life. If all members of a society shared the wealth in accordance with Equity 2, the total number of members and the use made of available resources would be more readily discerned as issues of important public relevance. Similarly, the importance of the government's genuine concern for the public welfare would be magnified under Equity 2 distribution. The underlying principle is basically that in a society whose members share outcomes equally, anything that affects the prosperity of the society will have a relatively equal and universal impact on all. Such is not necessarily the case in an Equity 1 system, where changes in net social wealth will often have a substantial effect on only a small segment of the members. Equity 2 involves a more obvious interdependence among *all* members, and hence would both require and favor a more socially responsible system of governmental decision making. This would be especially true if the previously discussed educational system were in operation.

People who are oriented toward cooperation, intrinsic interests and motivation, systems thinking, and self-actualization are unlikely to create or tolerate any but a government oriented toward the public.

This discussion of Equity 2 systems has admittedly been in terms of their ideal or potential functioning. However, the research and theory discussed earlier in the chapter clearly indicate that people have the potential to thrive in this type of society. Indeed, a good argument can be made that existing societies that approach Equity 2 operation tend to provide a better quality of life in relation to their resource base than do existing Equity 1 societies. This seems to be most clearly evident with respect to the elimination of extreme poverty, the delivery of health care, and the treatment and design of the public environment (one need only compare Sweden or Norway with the United States, for example). Nonetheless, all existing cultures have their problems, ecological and otherwise. Equity 2 systems as envisioned here would simply be more likely to provide a favorable *context* for ecologically sound practices and the enhancement of life than systems based on Equity 1 norms.

Although societies with minimal resources might remain tied to concerns for collective survival, safety, and reasonable comfort, the various system changes under Equity 2 in affluent societies could generate new levels of human understanding, appreciation, and capability for improving the world. Thus, as the quality of life and the security of the whole population were enhanced, more people could become involved in the enjoyment and creation of beauty and in the quest to discover new ways to improve the quality of life. Even now, in our affluent but primarily Equity-1-based society, many people engage in this type of life to some extent. The tragedy is that it is being denied to so many others.

Toward Equity 2: A Few Practical Considerations

1. There is of course some risk that an Equity 2 system would allow for laziness and living off the fat of the land. Especially if the society had long functioned under Equity 1 norms or if its system of education and social expectations failed to generate universal feelings of collective responsibility, some people might live an easy life without work while others toiled to produce the goods. That this happens now under Equity 1 is perhaps beside the point. (I am thinking of the super-rich in so many countries who can enjoy their lives of fun and leisure only because

others work to produce their income, saddle their horses, set their tables, and clean up their mansions. Consult Daly, 1971, for an economist's enlightening view on this.) There is indeed *some* risk under Equity 2 systems, as even successful communes have discovered. Pragmatically, however, the damage produced by a few freeloaders in a society of relatively equalized wealth would be far less than that produced by the concentration of power in the hands of the selfishly super-rich spawned by Equity 1 distribution. It is the active pursuit of wealth, not "laziness," that leads people to wreak large-scale havoc on air, water, and beauty. And if the Equity 2 system were fully functional according to the Theory Y pattern of education, socialization, work environments, and so on, there would be few "lazy" or socially irresponsible people anyway.

(As a reasonable last resort, or as an expedient initial procedure, some minimal contribution could simply be required of every capable person. This has the added advantage of allowing the amount of work expected of each person to be adjusted in accordance with the pleasantness of the tasks. Rather than providing higher material rewards for doing especially difficult or unpleasant jobs, this arrangement would allow the people who did them to spend less time working than people who performed more pleasant work. Such in fact is the system that was suggested by Skinner in *Walden Two* and that has actually been employed in at least one very successful American commune. See Chapter 7.)

2. How does a society shift from an Equity 1 to an Equity 2 system? This is certainly a most difficult problem. Although it will be discussed more fully in the final chapter, a few brief observations may be offered here.

a. Increasing public awareness of alternative ways for the total social system to function may be important in creating pressures for changes in the system. As more and more people begin to think in terms of the *interrelations* among environmental, economic, political, military, health, and educational problems, the chance for concerted political and social action should increase. It is interesting to note that concern with each of these areas considered *separately* has apparently grown in recent years, as witnessed by the rapidly growing number of books on each of these topics. The integrative pressures of dealing with environmental problems may provide just the catalyst to help many "intellectuals," at least, to perform the needed synthesis in terms of looking to alternative societal systems.

b. The growth of the "counterculture" and the resurgence of communes may betoken a new ethic of cooperation, sharing, and living in harmony with nature.[18] As a causal factor, this movement may be slight at present; but if taken as a symptom, it may indicate the presence of an underlying "structural conduciveness" (see Smelser, 1963) for social changes in the direction of Equity 2. There are also a few signs, ranging from relatively egalitarian rhetoric by many politicians (especially liberal Democrats) to the appearance of popular books such as those by Herbert Gans (1973) and Barry Commoner (1971, 1976), that the desire for real economic change is growing among a large segment of the population.

c. Seemingly small changes, such as modifications in laws pertaining to campaign contributions, can have an important impact on the functioning of our societal system. Thus, if the political influence of rich individuals and huge corporations were substantially reduced by new campaign laws, more politicians might be elected who reflected the true public interest. Resulting improvements would presumably occur in areas such as health care, education, transportation, and environmental quality—not to mention public feelings of greater involvement and decision-making power. These effects might in turn encourage more concern with cooperation, improved community life, and a more nearly equal distribution of wealth (at least to the extent of truly progressive taxation and intelligent use of public funds for the public good). Similarly, modifications in advertising, news coverage, educational curricula and grading practices, public involvement in land-use planning, and the employment of women can conceivably have ramifying effects that may move us in the direction of Equity 2 norms. None of this answers the question of what we can *do* to promote such change, but consideration of system interdependencies seems a good place to begin the search.

3. Finally, there are many different ways in which Equity 2 could be applied. As noted, the ideal of distribution of wealth without regard to individual contribution might in practice need to be tempered to some extent, even if everyone were oriented toward cooperation, creative effectance, and communal self-actualization. Furthermore, equal distribution of wealth can mean many different things. Everyone can simply be given an equal share of all resources, which is perhaps the ultimate version of the guaranteed income idea. Or more realistically (and beneficially), the society could combine some base level of guaranteed individual income (dependent on the total productivity of the society) with

the collective use of remaining resources to improve public services and environments. Indeed, by distributing wealth in such forms as high-quality public parks, transportation, health maintenance services, entertainment, education, and housing, it might be possible to provide a much more pleasant life than people acting individually could achieve with the same collective resources.

Turning briefly to the *scale* of applying Equity 2 norms, we must note obvious differences in equal distribution of resources within a family, a community, a nation, and the world. Our discussion has mainly focused on the level of the community or the nation ("society"). Equity 2 within families is probably fairly common and relatively easy to achieve, but on a world-wide scale there would obviously be very difficult problems resulting from national differences in population, resources, political practices, religions, and so on. I shall make no attempt to deal with these issues here, except to bring up two considerations. First, environmental problems frequently raise international and even global issues. Successfully dealing with ecological issues on a long-range basis may well involve rethinking questions of world-wide distribution of goods and services as well as seeking greater international cooperation (see Falk, 1972, for an excellent discussion of the global ramifications of ecological concerns). Second, if it is true that realization of human potential for creativity and happiness on a national scale would be facilitated by change toward an Equity 2 system, the same effects should obtain for the entire human race. There would be tremendous problems in bringing this about, but we may hope that they are not insurmountable.[19]

In later chapters we shall return to problems of broad change in people/environment relations. These discussions will also examine specific suggestions for promoting human welfare and the realization of ecological values. The next chapter will help provide a framework for psychological input to such considerations by examining the basic cognitive and emotional processes involved in experiencing the environment.

NOTES

1. References to experience have been made occasionally, as when Thorndike (1913) or Boring (1950) used such terms as "satisfying" or "pleasure" in presenting formulations of the "Law of Effect" (essentially, behaviors with pleas-

ant consequences tend to be repeated). However, even where such subjective terms are employed, an attempt is usually made to define them in reference to overt behaviors such as approach or avoidance. For recent, divergent treatments of the concept of reinforcement, compare the experientially toned discussions in Berlyne and Madsen (1973) with the more purely behavioristic orientation of those in Glaser (1971).

2. The distinction between "consequentially intrinsic" and "pure extrinsic" reinforcement, it must be noted, is pragmatically useful but probably inapplicable from the perspective of the total system. The consequences of an action that are socially mediated are in a sense intrinsically linked to the act itself. When the act is viewed as part of a total interacting system including the physical and social environments, the socially mediated consequences of the act can be considered to be as intrinsically linked to the act as any other consequences following from the act. This is apparent under the assumption that human behavior is determined by the same overall set of natural "laws" that operate throughout the total system. Furthermore, the distinction between "pure intrinsic" and "consequentially intrinsic" reinforcement may break down in relation to satisfaction deriving from feelings of success or competence obtained from performing a particular act. However, since such feelings of competence are so intimately linked to the actual performance of the act (and could not be obtained without performing the act), it seems justifiable to consider acts performed in order to feel competent as intrinsically motivated.

3. Hardin derived the term "tragedy of the commons" from the situation in which individuals who graze their individually owned cattle on collectively owned pasture land might each be motivated to increase the size of his or her own herd, thus eventually overgrazing the jointly owned "commons." The "tragedy" derives from what Hardin regarded as the inexorable logic of each individual's selfishly based but apparently rational decision to keep adding cattle: each additional animal would bring considerable gain to its owner relative to the cost suffered by the owner from the additional overgrazing caused by the animal. The aggregate effect produced by all commons users (or even by only some, for that matter) could eventually be detrimental to everyone, however. Hardin of course noted the similarity of the tragedy of the commons to the motivations that can lead to human overpopulation and pollution of our shared environment. His solution was "mutual coercion mutually agreed upon," as in the case of democratically instituted laws and taxes.

4. Some representative accounts of research and theory in the area of arousal include Fiske and Maddi (1961), Walker (1964), Fowler (1965, 1971), deCharms (1968), Lester (1968), Berlyne (for example, 1960, 1967, 1971; Day and Berlyne, 1971; Berlyne and Madsen, 1973), and Mehrabian and Russell (1974). It should be noted that the notion of an "optimal level of arousal" must be considered in relation to factors such as mood states, diurnal cycles of sleep-wakefulness, task demands, adaptation levels, and a variety of personality variables (see, for example, Fiske and Maddi, 1961; Eysenck, 1973; Helson, 1973).

5. A recent research program by Mehrabian and Russell (1974) provides evidence that—at least for imagined situations—the arousal value of a situation interacts with the degree to which the situation leads one to feel dominant. Thus, one's preference for situations in which one feels dominant increases sharply with the increasing arousal value of the situation (such as riding a powerful motorcycle); but one's preference for situations over which one feels little or no control decreases sharply with the increasing arousal value of the situation (al-

though these situations, such as getting caught in a downpour or witnessing a serious wreck, seem to be confounded with the unpleasant *meaning* of the events).

6. One explanation for the inverted-U relationship between arousal level and task performance involves the effects of arousal on attention. As formulated by Easterbrook (1959), the theory holds that high levels of arousal cause a restriction of attention so that cues needed for successfully performing complex tasks can be ignored. Kahneman (1973) has reviewed a wide range of evidence and reformulated the theory to reach the conclusion that high arousal both narrows attention and increases the difficulty of controlling attention. Very low arousal, according to Kahneman's review, can interfere with adopting a "task set" and lead to inadequate use of feedback and to consequent poor adjustment to task demands.

7. A few telling examples of such books include *Moment in the Sun* (Rienow and Rienow, 1967), *The Dying Generations* (Harney and Disch, 1971), *This Endangered Planet* (Falk, 1972), *Our Plundered Planet* (Osborn, 1948), *Blueprint for Survival* (Goldsmith et al., 1972), *On the Shred of a Cloud* (Edberg, 1969), and *The Closing Circle* (Commoner, 1971). *The Limits to Growth* (Meadows et al., 1972), *Man and the Environment* (Jackson, 1973), *Population, Resources, Environment* (Erhlich and Erhlich, 1970), and *Man's Impact on the Global Environment* (SCEP, 1970) are a few less poetically titled, but equally telling, examples. For an exceptionally comprehensive and well-reasoned text covering the whole field of environmental studies, see *Living in the Environment* (Miller, 1975). Additionally, a browse through the ecology section of any large bookstore will reveal the range of environmental atrocities we have to contend with, both in the present and in the foreseeable future.

8. Some additional research support for Maslow's hierarchy is provided by Aronoff (1967) and by Cantril's (1965) massive cross-cultural study of "human concerns" (see also Rokeach, 1973). However, see M. B. Smith (1977) for a critical discussion of Maslow's basic motivational theory. (Smith argues, for example, that the theory is "inappropriately biological" and inadequately treats such basic aspects of human motivation as effectance and various prosocial motives, such as concern for one's family.)

9. It should be acknowledged that the overall research evidence on job satisfaction/dissatisfaction is mixed in its support of Herzberg's specific theory and findings. However, Martin Wolf (1970) has indicated in his review and interpretation of an extensive range of research in this area that the preponderance of the evidence affirms the existence of growth motives and does suggest that they are more important determinants of job satisfaction than are context factors. Wolf also concludes that the overall evidence is basically consistent with Maslow's motivational-hierarchy theory.

10. Compare the discussion of Argyris and Schön's work in Chapter 7.

11. On the interrelations among the very rich and powerful in the worlds of corporate business, large public and private institutions, the military, and the various branches of government, see, for example, Mills (1956), Domhoff (1967, 1970), and Galbraith (1973). (See also Chapter 7, footnote 8; and consult Dye and Zeigler, 1975, for a somewhat more pluralistic view of the operation of elites in America.)

12. Goodman (1971), Halprin (1969), and Sommer (1972) offer at least anecdotal evidence for this. A personal communication from John Anderson, an architect,

also recounted a case in Philadelphia in which a whole neighborhood seemed awakened to a new community spirit of self-help and improvement by the experience of planning and constructing its own recreation area (with the assistance of Anderson and his class of architecture students).

13. Also see Slater (1974) and Smith (1977) for similar criticisms.

14. Some psychologists *are* beginning to take account of this consideration, as evidenced by several of the contributions to Lerner (1975); see also note 15.

15. The distinction I have drawn between Equity 1 and Equity 2 corresponds closely to what has been labelled an "equity" versus an "equality" norm (see, for example, Gans, 1973; Walster and Walster, 1975; Sampson, 1975; Deutsch, 1975). My own preference for sticking with alternative "equity" labels arises from my desire to emphasize the idea of basic differences in the ways *fairness* itself can be conceived. Even verbal distinctions between "equity" and "equality" might lead people to the conclusion that equality is somehow not "equitable" (fair), *whatever* the underlying norm. Equity 2, it should be clear, is not to be identified with charity or with a departure from fair distribution, but rather with a basic change in the way "fair distribution" might itself be culturally defined. My argument for the potential value of such a change, however, is not based on metaphysical or even ethical precepts—nor on mere personal preference—but on certain potential contributions that an Equity 2 norm could make to widespread human (and overall ecological) well-being. However, for a philosophical derivation and defense of a very sophisticated Equity 2 norm based firmly on the concept of "fairness," see Rawls (1971). (Rawls's basic idea is briefly discussed in Chapter 7.)

16. There has been much continuing debate over the inevitability of any stringent limits to economic growth, in the sense of continued expansion in the gross national products of countries on this planet. *The Limits to Growth* (Meadows et al., 1972), for example, has served as the focus of much heated debate (see Cole et al., 1973; Oltmans, 1974). I can make no attempt to resolve such far-reaching and complex issues here, but the following observations seem pertinent: (1) We do inhabit a finite system; limitless material growth in any ultimate sense is obviously impossible. (2) The typical argument of the materialistic optimist runs that technology has saved us so far and that we can count on economic forces and human ingenuity to see us through in the future as well (see, for example, Solow, 1973; Beckmann, 1973). This argument, and futurists' predictions of innovations such as virtually limitless nuclear power, at best merely indicate that it may not be utterly impossible for us to continue to grow as we have in the past. However, a very wide and impressive range of ecological evidence (see note 7) implies that basing economic and environmental policy decisions on such speculations and hopes may be a very poor bet. To illustrate a bit fancifully: if in exactly thirty years we could make a machine to get rid of waste heat, but our ecosystem collapsed from thermal pollution in twenty-nine, how much good would our machine do us? (3) Finally, as Daly (1971) noted, increased production in *affluent* societies often serves only to meet artificial needs, exacerbate environmental problems, promote planned obsolescence, and expand work time. In many ways material growth beyond a certain point may thus actually lower the quality of life.

17. Indeed, this principle seems to have worked out well in at least some small communes, such as Twin Oaks in Virginia (Kinkade, 1973; Kanter, 1972) and many Israeli kibbutzim (Criden and Gelb, 1974). Developments in contempo-

rary China also seem to offer promise that such enlightened collective self-interest can operate on a large scale when Equity 2 norms are widely held. (See Chapter 7 for a more detailed discussion.)

18. See, for example, Roszak (1969), Reich (1970), Hedgepeth and Stock (1970), Kanter (1972), Melville (1972), and the discussion in Chapter 7.

19. For examples of pessimistic prognoses concerning the likelihood of utopian transformations, see Heilbroner (1974) and Dye and Zeigler (1975). Such works generally argue (plausibly, I might add) that existing and past patterns of social, economic, and political behavior raise serious doubts that human beings and societies will be able to transcend their tendencies toward selfishness, short-sightedness, authoritarianism, and so forth. However, as I hope this book argues convincingly, certain human psychological and social potentials do indeed hold out realistic hope that we can achieve a much more utopian existence for ourselves—meaning the inhabitants of the entire planet—and our progeny.

3
COGNITION, AFFECT, AND ENVIRONMENT

INTRODUCTION

Cognition refers to the psychological processes whereby human beings or other organisms obtain, store, use, and operate on information. (The term *information* will be used in the somewhat nebulous sense of "whatever is processed by the nervous system" or "all mental content, both conscious and nonconscious.") To put it in everyday language, cognitive processes are involved in perceiving, remembering, daydreaming, dreaming, problem solving, contemplating, judging, deciding, imagining, and virtually any other mental activity. Cognition is thus intimately related to experience (and to behavior). The ways in which we process information are central considerations in the content and the emotional tone of our experience, the style and effectiveness of our adaptation to the environment, and the potential enhancement of each of these domains.

In this chapter we shall explore some of the interrelations among environment, cognition, and experience (with a little behavior thrown in). Part One presents some basic notions concerning mental processes, especially with respect to environmental perception and interpretation. Part Two explains how we can consciously direct our cognitive processes in ways that enhance the quality of our environmental experience. And the appendix briefly examines the psychological processes involved in the conceptualization ("mental mapping") of large-scale environments.

The most essential sections for understanding the rest of the book include the basic introduction to the model of environment/experience/behavior interrelations (pp. 86–101), the account of an associated eight-component theoretical scheme for evaluating the experiential effects of cognitive processes and environmental input (pp. 116–131), and at least the gist of the material presented in Part Two (pp. 132–190). However, the appendix, the remaining sections of Part One, and the details of Part Two should also be of interest to readers who are concerned with the underlying processes relating environmental cognition to affective response—or who are especially interested in using their own mental powers to increase their aesthetic sensitivity, general environmental awareness, and creativity. Furthermore, the more difficult sections of Part One should be clarified by the discussion in Part Two.

In following the discussion throughout this chapter, it might be helpful to keep in mind a few key cognitive goals that have special importance for people/environment relations. The following are examples of general goals that I find especially exciting, although you may be able to think of others that are more specifically relevant to your interests.

Real over Psychological Adaptation

In this environmentally concerned era it is increasingly recognized that people can readily become habituated to a wide variety of environmental degradations. Robert Sommer (1972) and René Dubos (for example, 1965, 1968, 1972b) have eloquently pointed to the perils of habituation to noise, smog, barren and ugly cityscapes, crowding, and other forms of visual and functional pollution. Sommer additionally observes that people can adapt even to the apocalyptic warnings of environmental scientists. What is more, he notes that adaptation to environmental problems or warnings seems to follow the Weber-Fechner principle in psychophysics, according to which the "just noticeable difference" in a particular type of stimulation increases in proportion to increases in the amount of the given stimulation. Not only will people adapt to a particular level of pollution (or warning); as the level creeps upward, it will take larger and larger increments even to be noticed as a change. Well, so goes the theory; but whether or not such an insidious relationship holds for all types of environmental problems, there can be little doubt that *psychological adaptation* (habituation, getting used to things, deadening of awareness) is a potentially serious block to ecologically enlightened public action. Furthermore, psychological adaptation also can reduce the joys of experiencing pleasant things as one gets used to them.

Let us contrast this form of adaptation with what may be labelled *real adaptation.* By this term I mean taking effective psychological and/or physical action to improve the quality of both the environment and the experience of it. Psychological adaptation relieves one's stress (and reduces one's pleasure) by an inner deadening process, but real adaptation can serve to alleviate the external problem causing the stress—or to enliven one's experience of the world.

Joseph Sonnenfeld (1966) and Joachim Wohlwill (1974) have made a related distinction between "adaptation" (habituation or psychological adaptation) and "adjustment" (making a change in the environment). When the distinction is couched in this form, it is not always clear which is preferable. Sometimes it is better to habituate or adapt rather than modify the environment in ways that may have long-term harmful effects (consider the overuse of heating and air conditioning, for example). At other times, as in the case of pollution, it is certainly better to adjust the environmental influences. The distinction between psychological and real adaptation is a bit more subtle. Psychological adaptation occurs any time one becomes so habituated to a given type of stimulation that it becomes less noticeable. Real adaptation is more akin to intelligent, far-sighted behavior and includes any effort to improve the quality of experience both immediately and over the long term. When an unpleasant situation is genuinely impossible to change, real adaptation might consist simply of allowing oneself to become habituated or to adapt psychologically. In pleasant situations or when improvement is possible, however, real adaptation would include deliberately sharpening one's awareness or deliberately making changes in the environment. A central consideration in the environmental application of cognitive psychology might thus be finding cognitive processes that would facilitate gaining greater control over our psychological adaptation and enhancing our general ability for real adaptation. Indeed, the following goals could also be construed as aspects of real adaptation, in the broadest sense of the term.

Control of Affect

Affect is a psychological term for the inner experience of an emotion or feeling. The term *emotion*, by contrast, is used to refer to the *combination* of experiential, behavioral, and physiological processes involved in states such as anger, fear, and joy. Thus, the whole syndrome of flushed face, rapidly beating heart, aggressive actions, and inner feelings of irritation and hostility would characterize the emotion we label as "anger." The *affective* quality of anger would consist simply of the experiential feelings of hostility and irritation. It should also be noted that feelings that would not normally be classified as full-fledged emotions may still qualify as affects. Thus, the aesthetic pleasure experienced in a beautiful environment, the unpleasant feelings stimulated by polluted or ugly settings, or the feelings generated by imagining environmental changes are all affects even though they might not necessarily be considered emotions.

If, as was argued in the first chapter, the quality of life and the importance of anything to us derive from the nature of our experience, this is by definition because of the *affective tone* of the experience. Removing emotions and feelings of pleasure and displeasure would quite literally take all of the joy, desire, and satisfaction out of life (as well as the misery and disappointment, of course). There is nothing more important than affective tone, for it is this that makes it possible for anything to seem important or valuable. The very concept of "value" involves the notion that one state of affairs can be more satisfying—that is, yield more positive affect—than another. (As we shall see, though, this is not to argue for a value system stressing egocentric hedonism. On the contrary, to improve life it seems far preferable to think in terms of long-term optimization of everyone's affective experience.)

As will be discussed later, the affective quality of experience arises from complex interactions involving cognition, physiological processes, and environmental input. Active processes of interpretation and imagination thus can enter integrally into the arousal or direction of affects. Since we can consciously control our processes of interpretation and imagination to a considerable extent, we thus possess the potential to exert self-direction over much of the affective quality of our lives. Although our concern in this chapter focuses mainly on cognitive techniques for enriching and enlivening environmental experience, we shall see that self-regulation of cognitive processes can also be used to alleviate pain, to short-circuit unwanted stress reactions, to increase interest, to improve self-esteem, and presumably to do all sorts of other wondrous things.

Promotion of Ecological Consciousness

For a final example of a cognitive goal bearing on more pleasant experience and improved human/environment relations, let us briefly consider the notion of *ecological consciousness*. A full explication will have to wait until after the discussions in this and the following chapter, but you might recall from the sketch in Chapter 1 that ecological consciousness is a way of thinking and feeling characterized by all of the following: a sense of self as part of a larger holistic system; an understanding and awareness of the ecological processes within this system; a high ability to enjoy and appreciate things in themselves; a "pro-life" value system; and a creatively cooperative motivational orientation toward people and other living things. Obviously, the way in which individuals process information is deeply involved in whether they are moving toward this admittedly idealistic pattern of thinking and feeling. It is my hope that the theory, research, and suggestions to be discussed here and in the next two chapters will contribute to our understanding of how ecological consciousness might be promoted.

Part one
A Model of Environment/Experience/ Behavior Interrelations

The "model of the mind" developed in the pages that follow is intended mainly to provide us with a coherent framework for dealing with environmental cognition and to provide a basis for proposing new cognitive techniques for enhancing experience and increasing self-direction. Although this model will be used in a fairly pointed way—to help discover how to enhance the quality of experience—it is based on a wide range of recent research and theory in cognitive psychology. Unfortunately, cognitive psychology is far from a definitive conception of how the human mind works. As a glance through virtually any of the rapidly growing number of journal articles, symposium proceedings, and textbooks on cognition will reveal, there are many competing theories for how memory, attention, perception, imagination, linguistic processes, and so on, operate. The conception presented here is intended insofar as possible to integrate, or at least to be consistent with, many of these disparate theories concerning the processes of human cognition.[1] But the model should certainly be considered only a general framework, not a full-fledged theory.

The essence of the view espoused by this model and by most current cognitive theories is that human information processing is *active*. Our conscious experience, whether it derives mainly from perceptual environmental input, from memories, or from imagination, seems frequently to involve complex processes of concept formation, hypothesis testing, abstracting, problem solving, the activation and interlinking of frames of reference, and other active mental operations. The details of exactly what processes operate, when they operate, and how they interrelate are still partially (and sometimes wholly) conjectural. But the overall nature of human information processing, at least as envisioned by most contemporary cognitive theorists, suggests that we should be able to exert considerable self-direction over the quality and content of our experience by performing appropriate cognitive operations.

As a prelude to the detailed presentation of the model, let us first briefly consider what seems to me the most central concept for understanding the active and self-controllable nature of human information processing: "Plans."

PLANS

Much of the rationale and even scientific respectability for conceiving of cognition as an active and multilevel process has come from analogy with information processing by electronic computers. Earlier qualms about homunculi in the head who would be needed to perform cognitive control operations have dissolved in the light of computer programs that can execute complex multilevel information processing, including rudimentary pattern recognition and fairly sophisticated problem solving.[2] In the case of computers, in usual contrast to humans, scientists know the underlying information processes for such complex operations because these processes have been programmed by the scientists themselves. This sort of omniscience has built up confidence that human information processing can at least be partially understood by analogy with the concept of a computer program (although not necessarily with the specific operations or physical hardware of existing computers).

This analogic view of human functioning received one of its clearest and most sweeping developments some years ago by George Miller, Eugene Galanter, and Karl Pribram (1960) in their book *Plans and the Structure of Behavior*. Far from picturing humans in a mechanistic way, Miller and his associates were attempting to develop an alternative to the simplistic reflex-arc, stimulus-response, black-box, conditioning models of yore. They in effect were trying to peer into the "black box" of the mind and figure out the underlying processes by which people regulate their own behavior. As one might guess from the title of their book, their attention was devoted to the concept of *Plans*. Their formal definition of a Plan is "*any hierarchical process in the organism that can control the order in which a sequence of operations is to be performed*" (p. 16). In effect, a Plan is comparable to a computer program and may be conceptualized basically as a set of internal instructions to perform given types of operations under given conditions. Most simply, a Plan is a procedure for doing something. Virtually all goal-directed behavior and information processing thus operate according to conscious or nonconscious Plans.[3] We tie shoes according to a Plan (first put on the shoe, then cross the laces, then . . .), hammer nails according to a Plan (find a nail; find a hammer; place the nail in the wood; lift the hammer; hit the nail; check to see if the nail is up; if it is up, lift the hammer and hit it again; if it is down, quit), memorize poems according to Plans, solve problems according to Plans, and, as we shall explore in some depth, perceive and conceptualize environments according to Plans. The chief type of Plan to be discussed in this chapter will be procedures for performing mental operations. Such Plans will be referred to as *cognitive sets*.

Before proceeding to the discussion of cognition, however, we should note two other points concerning the above theory. First, the basic unit of analysis for how Plans operate is called a "Test-Operate-Test-Exit," or "TOTE," sequence. The basic notion is that all Plans or goal-directed behavior can be conceived of as organized in terms of tests to determine whether a sought-after state has been reached and of operations to try to reach that state if the test is negative. A TOTE is thus a process of cycling between testing, operating, and retesting. The final exit (always to another Plan or set of TOTE units as long as the organism is alive and consciously functioning) occurs only when the test indicates that the goal has been reached or when the cycling process is stopped by a higher-level Plan.

To take an example relevant to later discussions, in attempting to execute the Plan (cognitive set) to imagine changes that would make a specific environment more pleasant, the following sequence might occur: (1) You perform an implicit test to determine if you have thought up suitable imagined changes. (2) If the test is negative, you perform various mental operations to try to generate suitable imagined changes (for example, you might look for things in the scene that could be improved, try to remember similar but more pleasant environments, or try to figure out better ways to meet the human needs served in the given environment). (3) You again test to see if you have devised imagined changes that measure up to your internal standards for suitability. If the test is negative, you try more mental operations to generate better imagined changes, and continue testing. When the test is finally positive—when you are finally satisfied with your imagined changes—or when you decide the task should be interrupted for some more pressing or fruitful activity, you (4) exit. This last step simply means that you begin executing another Plan, characterized by a different master TOTE unit.

Note that this is a highly simplified description of what goes on when a Plan is being carried out. As described above, a Plan as complex as imagining how to improve an environment would presumably involve numerous subplans, such as figuring out what bothers you about the environment, searching your memory for possible alternative environmental features, and so on. In addition, such subplans in turn can be conceived of as organized in TOTE structures of their own, each with its own tests (for example, "Have I located all the things that bother me about this environment?") and operations (for example, evaluating more items in the environment). Any Plan, being hierarchical, will have subplans and usually sub-subplans. Another way to say this is that the operate, or perhaps even the test, phase of a Plan's master TOTE unit will have subsidiary TOTE units of its own; and these "sub-TOTEs" may themselves contain still lower-level TOTE units. This whole approach may of course seem a bit artificial, overly complicated, obvious, or all of the above. But it does provide a convenient framework for discussing any type of goal-directed behavior and for dealing with the relations between a goal and the operations used in attempting to reach it. Furthermore, as we shall see, the TOTE concept is also useful for exploring the relations among cognitive processes, values, and overt behavior.

The second major point in the theory of Miller and his associates is that Plans can themselves be treated as information. Thus, Plans can be stored in memory, as when a person learns how to perform some new behavior or mental operation. To facilitate such learning, Plans are often represented symbolically: a description of the procedure for carrying out an activity is commonly used to communicate the Plan from one person to other people. Instruction books for fixing washing machines or for engaging in Zen meditation are examples of such public communication of Plans. Moreover, Plans can be generated or modified by other Plans. This is where the action is for discovering cognitive techniques that would help people gain greater self-direction of their experience. Miller and his associates (1960) have illustrated some of the possibilities for self-regulation of one's information processing in their account of Plans for generating more effective ways of remembering and problem solving. Our concentration in the ensuing discussions on environment and cognition will extend this approach to the realm of special Plans (cognitive sets) for enhancing perceptual experience and for increasing one's comprehension and critical awareness of environmental design, ecological interrelations, and possibilities for improving human well-being.

AN OVERVIEW OF THE MODEL

One derivation from the thinking of Miller and his associates is that human beings and other organisms are indeed active creatures, constantly forming and executing Plans of one sort or another (although many of the component processes may occur outside awareness). The model represented by Figure 1 and its later elaborations is meant to extend this view to the whole domain of environment/experience/behavior interrelations and to provide a framework for discussing the Plans that are—or that could come to be—involved in generating our experience and conception of the world.

Figure 1 provides a basic sketch of the main components in this model. As the discussion and the later figures elaborate on this sketch, it might help to keep the following points in mind: (1) The model is entirely schematic, and its main features are meant to correspond only to cognitive processes or to determinants and consequences of information processing; location or form in the model is not necessarily intended to mirror the location or form of possible underlying neurophysiological structures or processes. (2) The arrows represent the flow of information, control, or influence. Functionally, there is substantial overlap among these three concepts when they are considered within a system of psychological processes, and I would prefer to live with the resulting ambiguities than to attempt any further specification for particular arrows. (3) The diagram is meant to depict a dynamic process occurring over time. The subprocesses are open to influence from their own previous execution, as in the case of habituation or fatigue of sensory receptors as a result of repeated stimulation. Similarly, complex psychological operations, such as those represented under "cognitive-set processes," can impinge on their own functioning over time.

Although this model will provide a framework for our discussion of all types of cognition, it is perhaps easiest to explain the components by focusing first on perception. Let us use vision as an example. Light from the environment impinges on the retinas of the eyes (*sensory reception*), which respond to the pattern of light stimulation with spe-

Figure 1. A simple model of environment/experience/behavior interrelations.

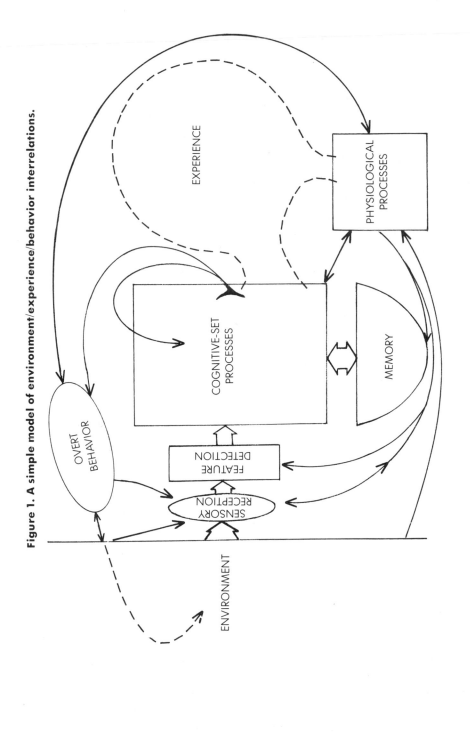

cially coded patterns of neural messages to the brain. The total pattern of information received from the eyes provides information about certain structural features of the environment (*feature detection*). At a minimum, these features include colors, lines, angles, contours, various types of movement, and textural qualities; but some perceptual theorists argue that the sensory systems directly "pick up" (or "resonate to") information about the entire three-dimensional configuration of surrounding surfaces and environmental "layouts."[4]

This information about features or perhaps whole configurational layouts serves as environmental input to the person's higher-level mental operations or *cognitive-set processes*. Cognitive sets may be briefly defined as Plans for selecting and processing information, and will be discussed in much greater detail below. Although many of these operations are performed at a nonconscious level, *experience* or conscious awareness may be said to arise from—or perhaps correspond to—certain cognitive-set operations. (Experience is of course also intertwined with *physiological processes* such as arousal.) While there is some question about how much complex higher-level processing is necessary to generate the basic visual configurations that enter awareness, it seems clear that the meanings, interpretations, and affective impact embodied in experience are the result of processes of interpreting the basic visual input. These interpretive or cognitive-set processes in turn are interrelated with aspects of long-term *memory*, such as semantic networks, assumptions about how the environment is structured, and memories of other scenes.

Overt behavior of course constitutes the active outgoing link between an organism and its surrounding environment. To the extent that behavior is goal-directed, it also forms part of the "operate" phase of some Plan or other (hence the arrow in Figure 1 from cognitive-set processes to overt behavior). It is also clearly intertwined with all sorts of internal physiological processes. In addition, as James Gibson (1966) and other investigators of perception have shown, we and our perceptual systems are very active in obtaining information from the environment. Body, head, and eye movements, for example, all play key roles in sensory exploration and the reception of environmental information. (The sensory effect of this sort of operation is represented in Figure 1 by the arrow from overt behavior to sensory reception.) And, of course, overt behavior can have both immediate and long-term effects in the environment. In Figure 1, the feedback arising from these effects is represented respectively by the solid and dashed arrows emanating from the overt behavior oval.[5]

Before proceeding to a detailed examination of certain key aspects of the model, let us run through the diagram using a simple perceptual example. Imagine you are looking at a tree. Light reflected from the tree as you walk around it enters your eyes and provides information about the visual features and three-dimensional configuration of the tree (sensory reception and feature detection). If things stopped here, you might be aware that you saw something, but you wouldn't know what it was. In normal, everyday perception this feature-analyzed information is automatically related to information stored in memory. The type of Plan directing this process might be characterized as a nonconscious cognitive set to see environmental objects in terms of their usual or generic classifications. Thus, your conscious experience will simply be "seeing a tree."

If you try to classify the tree as to type, however, the process may become considerably more active and consciously controlled. A cognitive set to figure out the tree's biological classification might entail carefully studying its leaves and bark, searching your memory for information about what types of trees grow in the area, forming and testing specific hypotheses, and so on. Other examples of possible deliberate cognitive sets would be concentrating on the aesthetic qualities of the tree's limbs, comparing the difficulty of climbing this tree with that of trees you have known in the past, or even imagining what it would feel like to *be* the tree. Cognitive sets for interpreting visual information can thus entail various types of imagination and remembering as well as just "looking." Whichever way you look at the tree, however, your final perceptual experience of the tree will tend to be influenced by your learned networks of linguistic (semantic) codes for dealing with trees, your assumptions about how trees normally look, your personal tendencies to see such things as trees in complex or in simple ways, your immediate goals, how awake or aroused you are, and so on. Such factors represent interactions of cognitive sets, memory, and physiological processes.

Clearly, then, your experiential, physiological, and overt behavioral responses to the tree can be shaped by the way you look at it. Concentrating on the shape of the limbs may give you aesthetic pleasure or perhaps make you feel dizzy; comparing this tree with others you have observed over many years may involve the same basic visual information as contemplating the limb patterns but yield a very different emotional tone (for example, nostalgia). Finally, the action (if any) you take toward the tree will interact with your cognitive set and perceptual experience. Depending on that set and experience, you might be tempted to paint a picture of the tree, climb it, or chop it down (all overt behaviors). I'll leave it to your imagination to run through the feedback processes that would be involved in each of these varied actions.

It is neither possible nor necessary in this book to describe the internal operations of each component of the model in detail. However, the cognitive-set processes depicted in the model play the central role in our potentials to exert direct mental influence on the quality of our experience (environmental and otherwise). Hence, let us look more closely at what is involved in the operation and control of cognitive sets and at how .these processes relate to the other aspects of the model.

COGNITIVE-SET PROCESSES

The term *cognitive set* will be used to mean a Plan to select specific types of information for processing and/or to perform specific mental operations on information being processed.[6] This definition is of course very broad; it covers virtually all higher-level mental processes for handling information. However, its central role in our model highlights the active, goal-oriented, and potentially self-directed nature of human cognition. The cognitive sets of most interest to us will be consciously controllable Plans for selecting and operating on information of special relevance to the physical environment or to people/environment relations. These will be referred to as *environmental cognitive sets* (in contrast to, for example, cognitive sets to select or operate on information about dreams or crossword puzzles). Imagining environmental improvements and the different ways of viewing a tree have already provided us with a few examples; many more will be given in the discussions that follow (see especially Part Two of this chapter).

Figure 2 presents one way of envisioning cognitive-set processes. This model incorporates the notion that each cognitive set is a Plan consisting of nested or hierarchically structured TOTE units. Furthermore, the diagram's indefinitely large "repertoire of cognitive sets" is meant to convey the idea that each of us has the potential for processing information according to any of a virtually unlimited number of different Plans.

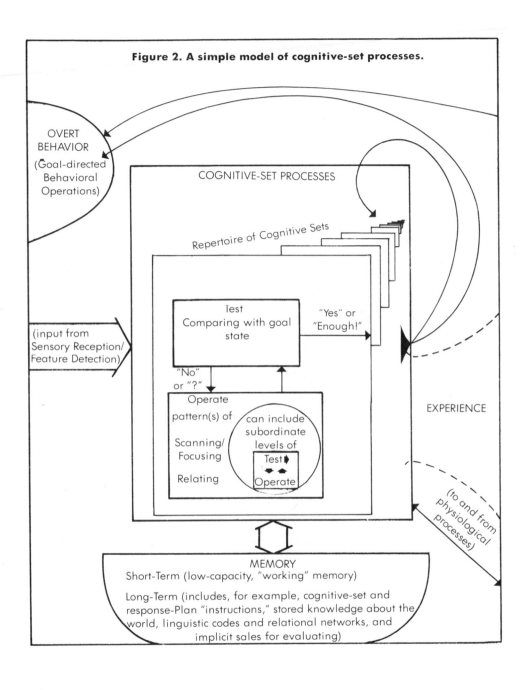

Figure 2. A simple model of cognitive-set processes.

To make a culinary analogy, a cognitive set can be thought of as something like a recipe; both specify what ingredients to search out and what to do with them. Just as a good cook can use different recipes calling for various cooking ingredients (Plans to *select*) or giving different ways to prepare the same ingredients (Plans to *process*), so each of us has a repertoire of cognitive sets not unlike the cook's repertoire of recipes.

In any case, the diagram depicts potential Plans for selecting and processing information as if they were discrete entities in the cognitive-set processes box. Strictly speaking, of course, one's *potential* cognitive sets are stored in memory as representations of instructions or else exist only as possibilities that one could either learn from the environment (for example, as instructions in an experiment or a book) or that one could create on one's own. Furthermore, it is often impossible to specify whether a person is using a single complex cognitive set or is using several separate but interlinked Plans for processing information. These quibbles aside, the diagram reminds us that although only one or a few complex sets would ever actually be activated at any given time, there are always many possible Plans for selecting and processing information. Also, as indicated by the arrow that leaves and re-enters the cognitive-set processes box, "executive control" can pass from one cognitive set to another. A simple example of this occurs when you shift from concentrating on determining the meaning of a question to concentrating on figuring out the answer. As Miller and his associates (1960) pointed out, we are always executing one Plan or another; when a Plan is completed, interrupted, or abandoned—or calls for carrying out another one—we shift to a different Plan. (Note that, at least when we are awake, we are always processing information. The recipe analogy would thus hold only if the cook were always cooking something or other.)

Let us now look more closely at the nature of cognitive-set *processes*. As noted, any cognitive set can be represented as a hierarchically structured TOTE unit. This simply means that cognitive sets, like all other Plans, can be conceptualized as goal-directed and as including subordinate plans—"subsets," if you will. The basic idea is that in selecting or processing information you are trying to achieve a certain goal, such as constructing a meaningful image, solving a problem, answering a question, or whatever. Although you may not be aware of some of your goals or of the operations that go into seeking them, it should be clear that virtually any higher-level mental activity can be couched in terms of testing to determine whether a given state has been achieved and of operating (searching, remembering, classifying, hypothesis-testing, imagining, and so on) in an effort to achieve it. As indicated in Figure 2 and as mentioned in our earlier example of the set to imagine improvements in an environment, these subordinate operations can themselves be considered as subplans, complete with TOTEs of their own.

The sections to follow will briefly examine the specific types of mental operations that seem to be involved in our execution of cognitive sets—that is, in the way we think, perceive, remember, decide, judge, and so forth. Basically, my model posits that all the relevant mental processes fall under the general headings of *scanning/focusing* and *relating*. But I certainly do not wish to make any claims for the unique value of this way of conceptualizing cognitive operations. This scheme is merely one useful way to think about how cognitive sets seem to function.

Mental Elements

I use the term *mental element* with some trepidation, as it seems to imply some sort of naive, atomistic view of how our minds work. But as the ensuing discussions of scanning/focusing and relating will demonstrate, some such term must be used if discussing those cognitive processes is to be possible; and "mental element" is probably as good as any. Basically, this term will be used to apply to any item of information that one can think about, perceive, or otherwise process as a discrete unit. According to George Miller's (1956) famous paper on "the magical number seven, plus or minus two," most of us can consciously process no more than seven or so "chunks" of information at one time—although with practice and a good coding system, each chunk can contain a fairly large amount of actual information (compare, for example, seven letters versus seven words). However, rather than pursue the impossible task of trying to pin down an acceptable account of the underlying nature of mental elements, let us just take note of a few general categories into which such denizens of the mind might fall.

Based on common sense, introspection, and contemporary research and theory in the field of cognitive psychology, a list of general categories of mental elements could be drawn up including entries such as the following: concepts, images, beliefs, propositions, expectations, sensory input (at least as feature- or layout-analyzed), representations (symbols and certain combinations of symbols), memories of specific events, and schemas. This list is doubtless far from exhaustive; and, depending on the cognitive theorist consulted, some—or perhaps even all— of these categories might be seen as overlapping or nonexistent. Again, I am not asserting the psychological, physical, or metaphysical validity of either the notion of mental element or of the above list of caetgories. My purpose is purely pragmatic: to enable us to discuss cognitive processes in a way that they can be related to experience. I am also going to assume that all the terms in the above list—except one—make reasonable intuitive sense. Let's take a moment to examine this term, since it and its synonyms seem to loom ever larger in academic cognitive psychology.

The mystery term is, of course, *schema*. (The traditional plural is "schemata," but I prefer the simpler form "schemas.") Like most key terms in cognitive psychology, "schema" has been used in many ways. Rather than wade through a multitude of formal definitions, however, let us simply use the word to mean a conceptual framework or frame of reference that can guide the interpretation of new information.[7] Although "schema" is admittedly a vague concept (sometimes difficult, in fact, to distinguish from "concept" itself), the importance of schemas or frames of reference should be apparent from the following example: Your experience and behavior would be very different if your interpretation of the sound of a civil-defense siren were guided by your schema for "equipment testing" or "practice drill" than if it were guided by your schema for "nuclear attack." (As another example, the model we are now examining could be considered a schema—a conceptual framework—for thinking about environment/experience/behavior interrelations.)

Thus armed with this sketchy but explicit look at schemas and other mental elements, let us proceed to an examination of the chief types of cognitive processes included in the overall model.

Scanning/Focusing

One very simple way to think about cognitive processes is to start with the notion that anything going on in one's head is a form of *activation*. Thus, when a person attends to sensory input, that input might be said to be activated. If you look for red objects around you, before long all red things will seem almost to jump out at you: a certain kind of sensory input and a Plan for selecting it have been activated. Try to remember your mother's maiden name, and if you succeed, a mental representation of that name (probably along with various other images) will have been activated. If you imagine a nuclear holocaust, particular processes of image construction and the resulting gruesome images will be activated. And so on. Obviously, this is a very simple way of thinking about thinking, but let's see if we can use it to understand scanning and focusing.

In everyday language, *focusing* means concentrating on something. Here its meaning will be slightly expanded to include any discrete act of mental activation. That is, focusing is the activation of one mental element or the simultaneous activation of more than one discrete mental element. Since activation is not necessarily conscious, it is thus also possible to speak of either conscious or nonconscious focusing. However, the important consideration for our purposes is that controlling focusing means deliberately directing (1) what type of information or mental element is activated (for example, a special type of sensory input or a particular memory), (2) the amount of information activated at one time (for example, several mental elements or only one), and (3) the intensity of activation. ("Intensity," as used here, corresponds metaphorically to physical amplitude and would presumably be a joint function of the number of mental elements simultaneously activated, one's arousal level, and the amount of "mental effort" or "processing capacity" devoted to the specific activation [see Kahneman, 1973].)

Scanning is basically multiple focusing—the successive activation of more than one mental element or simultaneous group of elements, usually as part of a search or survey through available information. This mental operation can be rapid or slow, wide-ranging or restricted, and systematic or haphazard. One might also consider Paul Wachtel's (1967) metaphorical distinction between focusing as the width of the attentional "beam" (and, I would add, as the intensity and direction of the beam) and scanning as the extent (and way) that this beam moves around the informational field. Although perceptual scanning often entails the execution of overt response Plans, such as goal-directed eye or body movements, the underlying notion is that scanning is primarily a mental process. It is perhaps best thought of as any process of information search or sampling, whether directed toward sensory input or toward information stored in memory.

The operations of scanning/focusing are obviously inherent in all information processing, whether conscious or nonconscious. Hence, scanning/focusing should be considered more as a dimension of mental activity than as an independent process. Any of the processes of "relating" discussed in the next section could thus be characterized by different types of scanning/focusing. The consideration of most importance for the use of cognitive sets to increase the enjoyment of life is that it is relatively easy for most people to exert some control over this dimension of cognition. To broaden your "beam of attentional focus," for instance, you can make an effort to integrate more elements or information into your focal awareness. Such a process could be important in promoting systems thinking and ecological consciousness. Or you might be able to achieve aesthetic experiences by focusing narrowly and intensely on especially pleasing or interesting details in your surroundings. Similarly, we seem to have the ability to regulate scanning by conscious decisions to vary the rate and extent of surveying available information. Indeed, deliberately trying out a variety of different interpretations of the same environmental information could itself be viewed as a kind of higher-level scanning of different schemas or cognitive sets. As Part Two will illustrate, such processes of self-directed scanning of diverse interpretations can be important for enhancing creativity and for expanding one's repertoire of cognitive sets.

Relating

Most higher-level mental activity includes more than simple activation of separate mental elements or even scanning through a number of such elements. Our cognitive lives generally involve the activation not only of discrete images, representations, "thoughts," and so on, but also the forming of relationships, associations, combinations, comparisons, and transformations involving such elements. *Relating* is any mental operation that combines, links, or transforms one mental element—or pattern of activation—to another. Included are such processes as associating, combining, organizing, categorizing, interpreting, understanding, comparing, evaluating, encoding, translating, representing, and transforming.

Let us now take a closer look at these operations that relate mental elements to one another. It should be borne in mind that these various processes are presumed to be integral to what is normally referred to as perceiving, remembering, imagining, deciding, "thinking," and so on. As noted in the above definition of "relating," the characteristic that runs through the following apparently disparate cognitive operations is that each of them combines or links mental elements or transforms one mental element to another. The main reason for singling out these processes is. that, together with the scanning/focusing dimension, they collectively form the building blocks of all our cognitive sets. Thus, understanding such subprocesses may help us gain insight into both how we normally process information and how we might do so in new ways.

Associating, combining, and organizing.   Perhaps the simplest type of relating is the concurrent or successive activation of two or more linked mental elements. This we might call *associating*. Thinking of two physical objects in juxtaposition or responding to a word association test provide examples. *Combining*—or perhaps we should say "fusing"—is a more intricate associative operation, in which a new mental element is generated. An example would be forming the image of a centaur by borrowing elements from two disparate schemas ("man" and "horse"). As we shall consider later, forming unusual combinations is a key aspect in much creative thinking, including creative environmental design. The third process, *organizing*, consists of creating internal orderings or groupings of any set of activated mental elements. An example would be arranging topics into an outline. Of special relevance to environmental and aesthetic experience is the process of perceptual organizing, the creation of mental groupings among perceptual elements. The Gestalt psychologists (for example, Koffka, 1935; Katz, 1950), for instance, have posited certain principles of perceptual organization. According to the Gestalt theory, perceptual elements (dots, lines, and so on) that are close to one another, similar to one another, or moving in the same way, will tend to be grouped together in perceptual experience. On a more complex level, aesthetic qualities of visual rhythms and other types of patterns often appear to hinge on subtle forms of perceptual organizing (see the discussion of aesthetically oriented cognitive sets later in this chapter).

Although in many cases the "organization" seems to be virtually immanent in either the environment or the nervous system, it is possible to learn to reorganize perceptual experience and to do so deliberately. Even in the case of Gestalt principles, it is possible with deliberate effort to shift the way elements appear to be grouped (see Katz, 1950; or just try it with a set of dots or lines). It is similarly possible to deliberately reverse many figure-ground relationships, as in the case of learning to notice the shape of the "negative" or empty space surrounding or enclosed by physical objects such as trees, sculptures, or buildings. The ability of human beings to learn cognitive sets that lead to new and richer perceptual organization is also illustrated by the success of art and music students in learning to perceive intricate structure in paintings and musical compositions, as well as by the wide range of other forms of human perceptual learning (see E. Gibson, 1969).

Categorizing, interpreting, and understanding. Operations such as these can be viewed as a higher-level kind of combining or associating. To put it colloquially, it is here that schemas really "do their thing." When you understand, interpret, or classify environmental stimuli, for instance, you are presumably activating associational or schematic networks stored in your memory and in some sense applying them to the new information. These processes often seem automatic, as when you recognize a specific configuration of surfaces as your childhood home and feel a surge of nostalgia at the memories aroused. The processes seem more active in other cases, as, for example, if you struggle to figure out what a blurred photograph depicts (see Bruner and Potter, 1964) or try to master a difficult passage in philosophy or poetry. The essentially active nature of comprehension is also illustrated by the role that context plays in the way we interpret most new information (see, for example, Klatzky, 1975; Lindsay and Norman, 1977).

Again, though, the central consideration for enhancing experience is that we can deliberately vary the schemas or frames of reference that we apply in interpreting input. (An example to be discussed later is to interpret inanimate objects as if they were living creatures, thus linking into a whole new schematic network for construing one's environment.) Furthermore, learning new information and acquiring new conceptual schemes is something we can control. Studying ecology, for example, helps us to interpret everyday events in new and richer ways, perhaps finding intricate levels of biological meaning where previously we perceived nothing but smelly fumes or nameless plants.

Comparing and evaluating. *Comparing* is essentially any operation of relating mental elements by seeking to detect similarities and differences among them. As Figure 2 indicates, such a process is inherent in the test phase of any cognitive set. Comparing is in fact a pervasive mental operation that plays a key role in processes such as generalizing, recognizing patterns, and all forms of judging. Indeed, *evaluating* may be considered simply a form of comparing in which the item to be evaluated, or some abstracted dimension of that item (for example, color, usefulness, beauty), is placed on an internal scale of judgment. Such judgmental or evaluative placement presumably involves at least an implicit comparison of the evaluated item or dimension with the ordered elements that make up the internal scale.[8]

Obviously, the internal judgmental scales on which we evaluate environmental (and other) items vary widely in the specificity of judged dimensions, the width of scale categories, the nature of the endpoints or anchors, and so on. To cite just one example of differing types of environmental evaluations, Kenneth Craik (for example, Craik and Zube, 1975) has distinguished between "preferential judgments" of environments (placement on one's general personal scale of liking) and "comparative appraisal" (placement on a scale based on comparison with a specific type of standard). According to Craik, the first type of judgment is simply one of "subjective appreciation" and tends to elicit more diversity of opinion than does comparative appraisal. Thus, it is more likely that people will agree on the degree to which a particular shopping center is relatively good or bad compared with other shopping centers (a comparative appraisal) than on how much they like or dislike it as an aspect of their environment (a preferential judgment). As will be discussed later in this chapter, the self-direction of the extent and type of evaluative mental processing can have a marked effect both on aesthetic appreciation and on the awareness of environmental problems.

Encoding, translating, and representing. *Encoding* or *translating* is the process of systematically changing information from one form into another. The obvious example is of course translating from one language to another—systematically relating one form of verbal expression to another. However, it is also possible to translate from one sensory modality into another, as in forming a visual image of an unseen object explored by touch (see Gibson, 1966). And, obviously, people can translate or encode perceptual information into words or other symbols.

Another common term for referring to these and similar mental operations is *representing*. Jerome Bruner (1964, 1966), for example, described three modes of forming representations of concepts or environmental information: enactive, iconic, and symbolic. Enactive representation is encoding in terms of Plans for performing actions. An example would be thinking of a city in terms of the operations (types of movements) needed to get to various places in it. Iconic representation is encoding through images, as in thinking of a city in terms of its skyline. Symbolic representation is encoding in words or other abstract markers used to stand for something else. Thinking of a city in terms of a verbal description or label, such as "Fun City," provides a simple example. (See also Appleyard, 1973.) Furthermore, the whole domain of cognitive or mental "mapping" (see extended discussion in Appendix) can be considered in terms of how people encode or represent environmental information for the purposes of navigation or orientation.

However, for our purposes, a most important consideration is that how we encode or represent environmental input can have a marked effect on the quality of our experience and on the degree of our environmental awareness. An extreme form of this consideration is represented by Benjamin Whorf's (1956) thesis that one's language determines the way one perceives the world. Although it now seems likely that cultural differences in language have only a negligible effect on the basic perceptual processing of sensory input, it does appear that language and related cultural patterns can have a marked impact on what is easy to express or remember and on the aspects of the environment to which most attention is paid (see, for example, Tajfel, 1969; Cole and Scribner, 1974). To give a familiar example, Eskimos have many different words for snow, which enables them to express fine distinctions very efficiently and perhaps encourages them to notice these distinctions.

But aside from differences among languages, it is important to consider that symbolic encoding in itself presents both advantages and hazards for the enrichment of experience. Certainly the use of language and other systems of symbols has extended human information processing and cultural development in innumerable and spectacular ways. Symbolic encoding also makes possible the communication and enhancement of experience in ways that would otherwise be impossible. The use of words to express and point out fine distinctions and to aid in discerning abstract dimensions provides obvious examples of this. Nonetheless, excessive symbolic interpretation of perceptual information can impoverish one's experience of the environment. As Ernest Schachtel (1959) and others have long argued, the concepts, schemas, and words through which we filter our perceptions can deaden us to many of the joys and insights inherent in close attention to "pure" perceptual content. Also, the recent research on the differing functions of the right and left hemispheres of the brain, the resurgence of psychologists' interest in mental imagery, and the various impassioned pleas to give visual thinking the same cultural status now accorded only verbal thinking all point toward potential gains from becoming more flexible in how we encode environmental input.[9]

Transforming. Perhaps the most complex and sophisticated form of relating is *transforming.* This can be defined as any mental operation that changes a mental element in some systematic way (thus relating the original pattern of activation to the new, transformed one). As used in this sense, "transforming" would apply exclusively to operations of the imagination (although at times, as in the case of hallucinations, the resulting experience might be confused with veridical perception). A simple example would be the "mental rotation" of one's mental image of a physical object (see, for example, Shepard, 1975). Although the notion of transforming probably cannot be totally distinguished from certain forms of combining or translating, a few further examples of transformational operations would be the following: imagining any type of physical change in a perceived, remembered, or imagined object or environment; applying rules of grammar, logic, or mathematics to systematically change symbolically represented propositions; and embellishing perceptual images through imagination.

This last item, imaginational embellishment, seems especially prominent in much of our everyday environmental experience. For instance, when parts of objects are blocked from our view, we are easily able to fill in the missing information. As Rudolf Arnheim (1969) observed, we often seem virtually to *see* the typewriter in the closed typewriter case—a transformational operation we might call "mental X-raying." Similarly, Edward Hall (1966) pointed out that the mountain one has climbed never looks quite the same again when viewed from afar (perhaps "mental zooming in"). And of course children are generally very adept at imbuing toys and other environmental objects with imaginary qualities and actions. In all such cases, people embellish the immediate sensory information through processes of imaginational transformation. Obviously, many other processes, such as combining and categorizing, are also usually involved. But systematic transformative operations clearly play a major role both in "pure" imagination and in everyday perceptual embellishment. Indeed, there is considerable evidence that imagination and perception share common processing mechanisms (see, for example, Segal, 1971b, 1972; Neisser, 1970).

One can also use transformational operations deliberately to produce pleasant internal experiences or even to heighten one's awareness of environmental problems and possibilities. Cognitive sets involving self-directed imaginational transformations can also be helpful in increasing a sense of interrelatedness with other people and with the ecosystem, thus promoting ecological consciousness. But these are issues for later discussion.

Interrelations among operations.   It should be clear that the various forms of relating that have been pigeonholed under the above headings are in fact highly interconnected. The processes of associating, combining, organizing, categorizing, interpreting, understanding, comparing, evaluating, encoding, translating, representing, and transforming—not to mention scanning/focusing—are distinguishable for analytical purposes. But they are all intimately intertwined in most of our complex mental activities, such as perceiving, imagining, problem solving, deciding, questioning, and so on. The purpose of making these distinctions is simply to give us some handles to help us grasp the explicit programming of our actual and potential cognitive sets.

In the overview of the model and in the extended discussion of cognitive-set processes, we have already touched briefly on the other components of the model. Little more need be said here concerning the relatively automatic processes of sensory reception and feature (or layout) detection. However, before embarking on a tour of the model's account of experience, let us pause for the following short considerations of memory, physiological processes, behavior, and environment.

MEMORY

We have already considered some of the interrelations between memory and active cognitive-set processes. Only a few additional comments will be offered at this point. First, it should be noted that although Figure 2 depicts memory as including short-term and long-term components, current memory theorists are divided on just how memory is structured. There do appear to be definite functional differences in various types of memory processes. Such processes range all the way from the sensory "iconic" storage that may last only a fraction of a second (see, for example, Sakitt, 1976), through short-term processes that seem to hold a very limited amount of information for a period of several seconds, to various types of long-term storage that seem capable of maintaining a vast quantity of information for decades. The issue among memory theorists is not whether there are such functional differences, but rather whether there are separate memory storage systems or simply varying types or "depths" or "degrees of elaboration" of the processes that store information.[10] Even though Figure 2 indicates separate terms for short-term and long-term memory, no special theoretical stance is intended on the issue of separate structures versus differing processes.

However the information gets into memory and is stored there, the contents of long-term memory are of great importance to the way in which cognitive sets operate. As discussed earlier and as indicated in Figure 2, a human being's memory comes to include all of the following (at least): some sort of access to a wide variety of Plans for processing information and for making overt goal-directed responses; networks of schemas; linguistic and other symbolic codes; implicit (and explicit) ordered scales for making various types of judgments; tidbits of general knowledge; and tidbits of specific or "episodic" knowledge about particular events.[11] In addition, our ability to retrieve and use this stored information betokens a massive interlinking organization within memory (see especially Norman et al., 1975). The exact form in which this information is entered and stored and exactly how it is organized and retrieved (activated) are still moot issues. Whatever the final answers, a crucial consideration for the enhancement of one's own experience is that it is possible to use, add to, and in many cases modify this information by deliberately employing particular cognitive sets. It might also be noted that according to the model, all effects of memory must be mediated by cognitive-set processes, although these processes in many cases would of course be nonconscious (see Neisser, 1967, and Bartlett, 1932).

PHYSIOLOGICAL PROCESSES

Everything we have been considering presumably involves neurophysiological processes; that is, it can be assumed that all information processing in human beings is directly mediated by activity in the nervous system. At the current stage of knowledge, this may not yield any very specific insights, but at least it indicates that many activities in the nervous system are involved in the processing of information. There is also much evidence that subtle cognitive operations can influence arousal levels, which in turn can affect receptor, feature-detection, and cognitive-set operations. The bundle of brain tissue known as the ascending reticular activating system (ARAS), for example, seems to have profound influence over the functioning (for example, arousal level) of the cerebral cortex—traditionally considered the primary site for our higher mental activity. However, the cortex also has *outgoing* connections with numerous other parts of the brain, including the ARAS (see, for example, Dixon, 1971; Mountcastle, 1974). Very complex feedback loops thus exist, and what happens in one part of the brain has repercussions in other parts.

Thus, cognitive processes (in or out of awareness) can influence "noncognitive" physiological processes and vice versa. Fascinating examples can be gleaned from recent research on biofeedback control, whereby people learn to consciously control bodily responses ranging from skin temperature to the electrical activity of the brain.[12] Even more spectacular feats of conscious control over bodily processes seem possible through disciplines such as Yoga, which do not rely on elaborate electronic devices for feedback about biological states. Thus, in addition to conscious modulation of information processing through cognitive sets, people may be able to enhance their experience by deliberately controlling certain physiological processes. At the very least, learning to reach states of relaxed attentiveness (apparently related to particular patterns of electrical activity of the brain) may facilitate performing certain valued cognitive operations, such as creative imagination or appreciative, nonevaluative perception.

As indicated in the model, environmental input can also affect physiological processes, which in turn can affect cognitive operations and the tone of experience. For example, stimulation of receptors (as by intense sounds or light) can increase arousal in the central nervous system even without cognitive processing of the stimulation. This is represented in the model (see Figure 1) by the arrow from sensory reception directly to physiological processes, and would be illustrated by being waked up by a loud sound or a bright light. An example of an even more direct environmental effect on neurophysiological functioning is provided by the apparent influence of air ionization on mood states and biological processes. Increased negative ionization, produced by phenomena such as falling water, seems to facilitate feelings of well-being and even certain healing processes. Increased positive ionization, such as that produced by many atmospheric pollutants, seems to induce tension, anxiety, and respiratory congestion (see Krueger, 1969; McHarg, 1969, p. 195; Beal, 1974). Also, our biological rhythms, such as monthly hormone cycles or diurnal cycles of arousal, appear to be tuned to cyclical changes in the geophysical environment. These biorhythms respond to environmental input, such as cycles of light and darkness, independently of cognitive interpretation of such input (see, for example, Luce, 1971).

Since physiological processes are a major factor in the quality—as well as the continuance—of our experience, it may be helpful to note that there are at least three ways to exert deliberate influence over our physiological functioning. (1) How we interpret environmental and bodily information can have an impact on physiological processes. This impact is represented in the model by the arrow from cognitive-set processes to physiological processes. It is illustrated by Richard Lazarus's research showing that both physiological and psychological stress reactions to films depicting human mutilation could be significantly reduced by inducing viewers to use certain cognitive sets. (These sets involved either intellectualization of the content, as by viewing the happenings as a social scientist would, or denial of suffering, as by thinking of the film as play-acted.)[13] (2) We can learn techniques of more or less direct physiological control by the use of biofeedback training or the practice of Eastern disciplines such as Yoga. Such processes would be represented in the model by feedback loops involving virtually all of the processes represented, but this approach will not be examined here. (3) We can deliberately modify the environment so that it will influence our physiological processes in ways that we wish. Environmental modification currently seems to be the way in which people have the biggest influence on their biological functioning. Positive examples include growth in medical and hospital care, obtaining more nutritious food, and architectural design for better health. Negative examples include pollution, resource depletion, crowding, and certain forms of food processing. Deliberate modification of the environment for the sake of better functioning is by far the most complicated of the three paths. It involves not only the interrelation of all the components represented in the model but also the coordination of social, cultural, and environmental processes. Such considerations transcend the individualistic focus of this chapter on cognition but will be taken up in the remainder of the book.

OVERT BEHAVIOR

Overt behavior of course includes all our physical actions, ranging from random muscle twitches to highly complex and goal-directed acts of communication or skilled performance. One might therefore think of overt behavior as the "environmental output" of the organism. I have argued that American psychology—in keeping with our culture's performance/achievement/production/consumption orientation—has tended to overemphasize the study of overt behavior as an end in itself. But it should be clear that human actions are indeed of paramount importance as *means* for affecting the quality of experience. Furthermore, it should be clear that an account of overt behavior would in effect be an account of *all* that the behavioral or social sciences have to offer. Hence, the following remarks are intended only to highlight a few points of special relevance to the model and to later discussions.

According to the model, overt behavior is influenced by the environment, by physiological processes, and by cognitive-set processes. Clearly, the environment (see the next section) virtually always limits and otherwise interacts with our behavior. Much of what we do is of course designed to make some sort of change in the world around us and thus depends on the nature of the environment. But this sort of environmental effect on behavioral patterns is largely *mediated* by information processing. *Direct* effects of the environment on behavior would appear mostly limited to the influence of physical forces, such as gravity, wind, temperature, and so on. However, as just discussed in reference to physiological processes, the environment can have many direct influences on our biological functioning; and overt behavior is in turn pervasively influenced by physiological variables, such as arousal level or state of health. Indeed, when it comes to muscle twitches, sweating, sneezing, and the like, it is hard to separate overt behavior from physiological processes.

The main concern for our purposes, however, is the relation between overt behavior and cognitive-set processes. First, all feedback operations linking goal-directed behavior and the environment are presumably mediated by some sort of information processing, although much of this processing occurs at a nonconscious level. Just think of any physical activity, such as riding a bicycle. Although your body is indeed in direct contact with the environment, virtually all your movements are guided by information processes such as interpreting sensory input and deciding that various mental and physical operations be performed. Even if we define a *response Plan* (or response set) as a Plan for performing overt behavioral acts, it is clear that any such Plan must include *cognitive* sets to test whether goal states are being reached. These cognitive sets may in many cases be rudimentary or even nonconscious, but the performance of any goal-directed action must at some level direct our attention to the processing of information relevant to that action. The total response Plan for riding a bicycle, for example, will usually include cognitive sets for noticing obstacles, testing for bodily feedback indicating imminent loss of balance, checking on progress toward one's destination, and so forth. Although usually conducted nonconsciously or at a very low level of awareness, unusual or dangerous situations can bring such information processing into conscious attention.

In addition to noting the role of cognitive sets in the test phases of response Plans, we should also consider that Plans for selecting and processing information can generate overt behavioral operations. This occurs at a very simple level when, for instance, you move your eyes to scan for new visual input during a search for certain types of information (for example, looking for all red objects in a room or trying to comprehend a passage in a book). But most important, all of our decisions about what behavior to perform are essentially guided by Plans for selecting and processing information. Consider first that a *goal* corresponds to the comparison standard employed in the test phase of a Plan. Having a goal thus involves in part the activation of a cognitive set to test whether the world or oneself is in a particular state (that is, the "goal state"). This much has already been noted in reference to the role of cognitive sets in the execution of response Plans. However, *the active selection of Plans* is itself the function of a type of cognitive set—namely, a cognitive set to evaluate the relative merit of different goals or of courses of action. All of our deliberately chosen goal-directed behavior, whether mental or physical, could thus be said to arise in part from the operation of cognitive sets to evaluate alternative Plans. Indeed, our *values* can be viewed as the criteria used in the tests of our highest-level Plans for selecting or evaluating other Plans.

That last point and related issues will be taken up more fully in the next chapter. However, we may note here that the actual response Plans a person chooses will generally be the result of complex interactions involving such cognitive operations as the formation and evaluation of Plans and the assessment of immediate environmental contingencies. Thus, the way we think can very much affect the way we behave, and we might therefore find it easier at times to affect our behavior by first working on the way we think.

ENVIRONMENT

In Chapter 1, the environment was referred to as the total physical surroundings that impinge on an organism. Broadly conceived, in the case of human beings and any other gregarious or symbol-using organisms, such physical impingements often carry information of social significance. Thus, in the widest sense, and as intended in the model (see especially Figure 3), the environment includes *everything* that impinges on us as physical, social, and psychological beings. The full issue of the environment's multidimensionality and of the nature of behavior/environment interactions will be taken up in later chapters. Only a brief comment need be made here.

As noted in Figure 3 (p. 117), the environment can be conceptualized in terms of physical/social "content," "structure," and "dynamic properties." *Content* refers to all the actual things or ongoing events that are present, such as particular people, activities, buildings, vegetation, weather conditions, media messages, and so on. *Structure* refers to the degree of diversity and complexity of these things, the way they are located or organized relative to each other, and other abstract dimensions of the total array of content. *Dynamic properties* refer to the *process* or cause/effect aspects of content and structure (as exemplified, say, by both natural and human-made laws). Such dynamic aspects of the social/physical environment contribute to contingencies of reinforcement (the conditions and consequences for given types of behavior; see Chapter 2). As Chapter 6 will discuss, there are other ways of thinking analytically about the environment. This simple three-factor scheme is offered to help us explore the interrelations of environmental variables, cognitive-set processes, experience, and behavior.

EXPERIENCE

Conscious awareness may seem rather passive and epiphenomenal as it is represented in the model. Considerable activity seems to go into its generation, but it has an ambiguous position in relation to influences on these input operations. To consider *interrelations* among experience, cognitive-set operations, physiological processes, behavior, and the environment again seems to bring us to the verge of the mind/body problem and the question of conscious "will power"—philosophical issues I would here prefer to avoid because they seem to me virtually impossible to resolve (especially in a limited space).[14] This is of course a bit embarrassing in a book with "experience" in the title and even more so in a model designed in large measure to account for cognitive processes underlying experience. However, if we can put aside the big philosophical questions for the moment, we can make the following observations based on the relations depicted in the model.

1. There is overlap between experience and some cognitive-set processes. That is, we *are aware* of the formation and execution of some Plans for selecting and processing information. Indeed, George Mandler (1975) has theorized that consciousness serves the following "adaptive functions": (a) It facilitates decisions among alternative Plans, as when we imagine various possible consequences of different actions. (b) Consciousness allows us to modify our Plans deliberately. (c) It aids in the retrieval of information from long-term memory (as when one asks oneself guiding questions). (d) It enables us to perform complex operations of encoding and representing new information, to devise and use special mnemonic procedures (for example, making up rhymes to help remember something), and to use remembered solutions to old problems to deal with current problems. (Consciousness is thus also crucial in the interpersonal communication of ideas.) (e) Finally, consciousness serves a "troubleshooting" function whereby normally or temporarily nonconscious operations are brought into conscious awareness for "repair work" or for more careful processing. (An example of this is provided by the earlier observation that unusual or dangerous situations might increase one's conscious attention to normally nonconscious aspects of bicycle riding.) Overall, Mandler's view suggests that conscious

awareness is important for many aspects of deciding, planning, remembering, communicating, and other types of activity that require reflection, concentration, and the consideration of alternatives.

In a basic sense, then, increasing one's control over cognitive and behavioral operations (and over experience itself) may involve expanding the overlap between conscious awareness and the cognitive sets that guide information processing. The more we are aware of what we are doing, the more potential control we can have over it. There is of course still a missing link—something like desire, will, or intention (not to mention ability)—but the best point of view may be simply to avoid the dichotomy between experience and those cognitive-set processes "of" which we are aware. It is perhaps most accurate to say that under conditions of conscious self-direction of information processing, carrying out one's cognitive set *is* the experience.[15]

2. Our conscious awareness of the environment arises in large measure from processes of which we are not usually aware, although sometimes we can extend our awareness of such processes. James Gibson (1950), for example, intimated this in his distinction between the "visual field" and the "visual world." The visual field is the actual view conveyed by a single fixation of the eye, while the visual world is the normal experience of the surrounding environment. By careful practice and effort, according to Gibson, we can learn to experience the visual fields on which our visual world is based. One technique is to close one eye and pay careful attention to the visual configuration (independent of the meaning of objects) conveyed by a prolonged fixation of the open eye. This is apparently similar to what some painters do as they attempt to duplicate a scene on canvas. The important consideration, however, is that we are normally not aware of the basic input out of which we build the visual world of our everyday experience. Perceptual experience is the result of a very complex process; and although we may be able to influence many of the operations involved, even when we exert substantial conscious control we may not be fully aware of the underlying means by which our "commands" (Plans) are executed. Thus, you can decide to see clouds as animal shapes, but exactly *how* do you manage to see animals in the clouds?

3. Finally, the affective or emotional tone of experience seems, according to much current theory and research, to be the result of interactions involving both physiological processes and various cognitive operations, such as the interpretation of environmental and physiological

events.[16] We need not go into the details of the theories, experiments, and clinical observations that form the basis for the view that affect is the result of interactions between cognitive and physiological processes. However, a few general comments will be helpful for understanding the "integrative and evaluative scheme" to be presented shortly. The main idea is that specific affects or emotions arise from (a) one's physiological state (especially one's level of arousal but probably more specific physiological processes as well, although that is a point of debate among theorists); (b) one's interpretation of what the state of arousal or other bodily feedback signifies (for example, a given state of inner excitement might be interpreted as either joy or anger); and (c) one's interpretation of external events, inner imagery, and the overall situation.

Clearly, all three of these factors interact. The interpretation of environmental input can affect physiological processes, as was noted earlier in reference to Lazarus's research on reactions to stressful films. Also, the affective state aroused by a given physiological state and its interpretation can color one's interpretation of environmental events. For instance, misreading one's premenstrual tension as a sign of anger may lead to interpreting a mild criticism from one's husband as a nasty insult. The resulting quarrel may in turn provide new environmental stimuli that can be interpreted in ways that further increase physiological arousal and tension (which then can contribute to an even higher level of inner feelings viewed as anger).

One implication of this view of the generation of affect is that deliberate selection of certain types of cognitive sets can be a path to enhancing the affective quality of experience. That is, by carefully choosing your Plans for the selection and processing of information, you can influence your interpretations and awareness of the world around you and presumably also of your bodily states. In addition, cognitive techniques can be used to influence physiological processes themselves and to map out behavioral strategies that will have environmental impacts with pleasant affective consequences. Furthermore, you can use imagination and other mental operations to directly generate experiential states that have a given type of affective tone (see, for example, the work of Jerome L. Singer, 1966, 1970, 1973, 1974, 1975).

Many examples of how cognitive-set processes might thus enable one to enhance one's environmental experience will be explored in the second part of this chapter. First, however, let us consider the following integrative and evaluative scheme. This scheme is essential to the full model of environment/experience/behavior interrelations and will later provide a central framework for suggesting goals in the design of the physical and social environment as well as the design of cognitive sets.

AN INTEGRATIVE AND EVALUATIVE SCHEME

This section introduces the eight components in a theoretical scheme for evaluating the affective impact of cognitive processes and environmental input. Most of these components relate specifically to how processes of thought and perception can influence the affective tone of experience. Also included, however, are components that apply to patterns of behavior and to considerations of long-term ecological and humanistic values. Figure 3 elaborates our model to include all of these components as well as summary embellishments of the various parts of the model so far discussed. This model will be referred to later in this chapter to aid in assessing the potential experiential and behavioral effects of different cognitive sets. In later chapters the same central scheme of eight components—Complexity, Composition, Comprehension, Comparison, Competence, Complications, Comportment, and Compatibility—will be applied in discussions of environmental and social design. The main purpose of these explorations will be to examine how we can use our powers of mind and behavior to bring about transactions with our total environment that are more pleasant and ecologically sound.

The idea underlying the components listed under *experience* in Figure 3 is that affective tone arises directly from the combined action of these six overlapping and interrelated aspects of conscious experience. The seventh and eighth components, Comportment and Compatibility, represent a different level of analysis, applying to behavior and to long-term consequences for the quality of experience. We shall now examine each component in turn. Again, though, it should be remembered that the eight elements in the scheme overlap, interrelate, and have been formulated primarily as an analytic convenience for integrating and summarizing the relations among cognition, affect, and the environment. (That all the components begin with "comp" is in part an actual coincidence, helped along only in the later stages of the scheme's growth and evolution. Although the normal meanings of these eight words strike me as appropriate for the ideas represented, the alliteration may

Figure 3. A slightly less simple model of environment/experience/behavior interrelations.

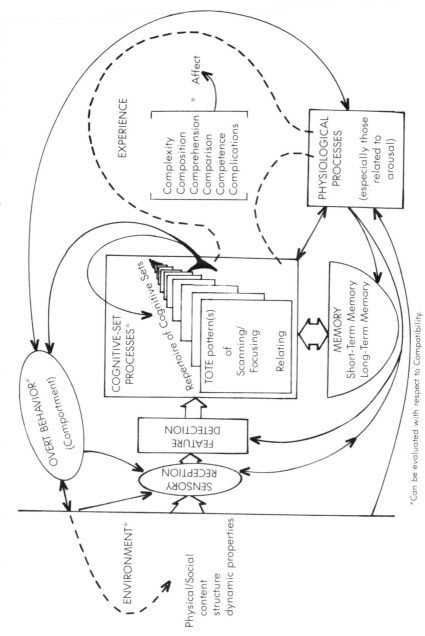

*Can be evaluated with respect to Compatibility.

serve as a reminder that each term refers to a component in this integrative and evaluative scheme.)

Complexity

Complexity will be our shorthand term for the arousal potential—in effect the level or degree—of the complexity, intensity, novelty, and other
structural aspects of an ongoing experience (compare Berlyne's "collative" and "psychophysical" variables, discussed in Chapter 2).[17] Our discussion in Chapter 2 concerning arousal processes as an important factor
in intrinsic motivation briefly reviewed some of the relevant theory and
research relating to the role of Complexity as a determinant (or concomitant) of arousal. As noted in that discussion, moderate levels of
arousal—often induced by moderate levels of Complexity—usually produce the most pleasant affective tone.[18] Very high Complexity tends to
be associated with informational or stimulus overload and thus to be unpleasant. Very low Complexity tends to seem boring and unpleasant. Of
course, factors such as personality, mood, and biorhythms will help determine specific optimal levels of Complexity for a given person at a
given time.

   This structural aspect of experience appears to be of central importance in affective tone and aesthetic experience. The old formula of
"unity in variety" has long served as a pithy synopsis of one key to
beauty (see, for example, Dewey, 1934; Platt, 1961). Indeed, as discussed in Chapter 2, Berlyne (1971) has built a psychological theory of
aesthetics around the idea that aesthetic pleasure derives from shifts toward optimal arousal levels, largely as a function of the collative properties of beautiful stimuli. Although it is easy to dispute such a unidimensional view, there is abundant evidence that the structural aspects
of arousal potential are very important in determining stimulus preference and affective response generally (again, see Chapter 2). Examples
of such Complexity effects in everyday life might include the pleasant
excitement of being at a carnival or hiking through varied terrain, the
boredom of working at a repetitive task or living in drab surroundings,
and the unpleasant tension often created by rushing crowds or by overly
garish surroundings. Note, however, that Complexity as conceptualized
here is a quality of the *experience* and not merely of the stimulus or
situation. Indeed, the Complexity of ongoing experience can be affected

by purely mental processes, as in the case of daydreaming, or by the cognitive set one uses in processing environmental information.

Composition

Composition refers to the content, meaning, and significance of ongoing experience. Like Complexity, Composition can influence one's arousal level, as is illustrated by such Compositional factors as Berlyne's "ecological variables" (the meaning or significance that an environmental event or stimulus has for one's well-being). As discussed earlier in this chapter, one's interpretation of a given environmental stimulus or situation is obviously important in determining whether the experienced content, meaning, and significance bode ill or well for one's needs and desires. Considerations of meaning, indeed, seem as important as arousal level per se in determining the affective tone of experience. As pointed out in Chapter 2, some aesthetics theorists (for example, Arnheim, 1954; Kreitler and Kreitler, 1972) clearly imply that factors of meaning and content can be important in aesthetic experience independent of their role in influencing arousal level. It is certainly conceivable that cognitive factors of meaning and interpretation can influence emotions by means other than the modifying of arousal level. Our example in Chapter 2 was of two environments, a particular park and a particular slum, that might elicit nearly identical levels of overall arousal and yet produce oppositely toned affective experiences because of the meaning associated with each. The research by Kaplan and Wendt (1972) and by Wohlwill (1973, 1976) on preferences for natural versus urban scenes is at least consistent with this possibility, as is common sense.

We have also noted that there is considerable evidence that how one interprets a given feeling of physiological arousal helps to determine the emotion experienced. Similarly, one's imagery and the attributions one makes about the causes of one's behavior or of environmental events also illustrate Compositional variables that can influence one's affective state. Imagining beautiful scenes or attributing a stream's discoloration to natural runoff should make you feel better than imagining possible catastrophes or attributing the stream's color to industrial pollution (see Lowenthal, 1972). As in the case of Complexity, however, past research on how Compositional variables influence affect has tended to focus on variations in environmental stimuli or situations rather than on how people process information. In Part Two we shall explore in some depth how mere changes in cognitive set can modify the experienced content, meaning, and significance of a given environment or situation.

Comprehension

The degree to which an experience involves a sense of understanding, clarity, or insight constitutes *Comprehension*, the third aspect of experience having affective potency. In the environmental realm, understanding and having a clear impression of your surroundings are obviously important to your ability to function effectively and to your general sense of well-being. Kevin Lynch (1960) and Stephen Carr (1967), for example, have noted the great importance of clearly comprehending one's environment for purposes of navigation and flexibility in the execution of diverse Plans. Stephen Kaplan's (1973) functionalist theory of human cognition also points to the possible evolutionary basis (that is, survival value) for positive affect arising from cognitive clarity. As mentioned in Chapter 2, Hans and Shulamith Kreitler's (1972) theory of aesthetics similarly stresses the role of enhancement of "cognitive orientation" (one's way of understanding and conceptualizing the world) in aesthetic appreciation. According to this view, great art contributes not only to pleasant patterns of tension and relief but also gives satisfaction by enhancing one's sense of understanding and insight.

Comprehension is obviously related to Complexity and Composition. For example, extremely complex experiences are likely to prove difficult to comprehend, and understanding would seem to be a direct function of experienced content and meaning. Nonetheless, positing Comprehension as an analytically distinct aspect of experience seems useful and appropriate. Consider, for instance, the case of gaining an insight into environmental pollution—for example, becoming aware of some hitherto unknown link between auto exhaust and damage to attractive plants or garden-grown food. The content, meaning, significance, and perhaps even complexity or intensity of such an experience might all produce feelings of unpleasantness. However, the sense of greater understanding and ecological insight charaterizing the experience might yield at least a modicum of positive affect. Human beings can apparently derive *some* satisfaction simply from increasing their cognitive grasp of what is going on around them. Such satisfaction, of course, may not be sufficient to override displeasure induced by negative influences on Composition or Complexity; but as Albert Camus (1955) argued in *The Myth of Sisyphus,* understanding even a crushing truth can be a prelude to happiness.

Finally, let us note that comprehension and insight can be facilitated in a number of ways. Environments can be designed for clarity and ease of understanding. Education, the mass media, and other forms of communication can also be used to enhance Comprehension by passing along and clarifying information. And, of most importance to our later discussion, a promising path to enriched insight into interrelations, problems, and possibilities in one's environment may lie in the systematic control of one's own cognitive sets.

Comparison

Before defining "Comparison," it is necessary to consider the meaning and environmental significance of the following concepts:

Adaptation level and comparison level. Dispositional factors of considerable importance in determining a person's affective response to environments are the individual's "adaptation levels" for various aspects of the environment. An *adaptation level* (AL) is a person's point of subjective neutrality for making judgments along a given dimension. For example, in the case of judgments along the dimension of "weight," stimuli above the person's AL will seem "heavy" and those below will seem "light." According to Harry Helson (for example, 1964), the originator of adaptation-level theory, an AL is a joint function of (1) the "focal" stimuli that are being judged, (2) surrounding or "background" stimuli, and (3) "residual" stimuli arising from past experiences that have influenced the person's inner standards relevant to the given judgment. Thus, a person's ALs can shift with new surroundings, changes in the salience of various memory information, or even shifts in imagined stimuli.

Adaptation levels are of great importance in determining both judgmental and affective response to environments. For instance, Joachim Wohlwill and Imre Kohn (1973, 1976; Wohlwill, 1974) have provided empirical evidence that adaptation levels arising from past residential experience can influence migrants' judgments of a new city. Wohlwill and Kohn found, for example, that people who had recently migrated from rural areas or small towns to a medium-sized city tended to judge it as larger, more polluted, noisier, and more crowded than did recent migrants from large metropolitan areas. (Interestingly, such AL effects were not evident in judgments of the very extreme case of New York City.) Other examples of probable AL effects on environmental judgments can be gleaned from anthropological observations, such as those by Edward Hall (1959, 1966) concerning cultural differences in reactions to social and spatial situations. For example, Hall has noted that the Japanese, who have traditionally concentrated home activities and furnishings in the center of their rooms, tend to view American rooms (with their bare centers) as less cluttered than Americans would judge them to be. Similarly, Germans, according to Hall, are accustomed to heavy doors and furniture, and hence tend to judge American walls, doors, and furniture to be flimsier than Americans are likely to regard them.

As noted, however, ALs can also have an impact on affective response to environments. Common examples are provided by gradual acclimatization to extreme weather conditions, to pollution, to higher levels of inflation, or to beautiful new environments. As one's AL shifts toward the current level of environmental stimulation on the given dimension, the intensity of associated affective response will usually drop. Conversely, stimulation that departs greatly from one's AL will tend to elicit a relatively strong affect. Examples might include a dramatic decrease in air pollution or a move back to a drab environment after one has gotten used to a beautiful new one. Research in environmental psychology has also demonstrated the influence of ALs on affect. One example is provided by Wohlwill and Kohn's findings of AL influences on the presumably affectively relevant dimensions of urban pollution, noise, and crowding. Also, Joseph Sonnenfeld (1967) and Peter Gould (1966; Gould and White, 1974) have uncovered some evidence that people tend to like their home regions more than outsiders do, especially in the case of regions that fail to fulfill stereotypes of desirable places to live. That familiarity may thus serve to decrease contempt is of course consistent with AL theory.

However, as our previous consideration of arousal processes has indicated, departures from adaptation levels can also be a source of pleasant affect—as long as the deviations are not too severe and as long as they do not carry unpleasant information. The variety entailed in moving to a new city may itself be a source of pleasure, provided the new place is not so different from one's old home that adjustment becomes a serious problem and that the move does not involve adversities such as a drop in one's standard of living.

The concept of adaptation level was originally proposed by Helson to deal mainly with psychophysical judgments (subjective estimates of physical quantities such as weight or brightness). Although Helson himself (for example, 1964, 1973) has argued that his theory extends to social and affective judgments as well, the social psychologists John Thibaut and Harold Kelley (1959) have provided an especially lucid application of adaptation-level notions to individuals' judgments of personal satisfaction and dissatisfaction. One of Thibaut and Kelley's key concepts is the "comparison level." A *comparison level* (CL) is an individual's point of subjective neutrality (adaptation level, basically) for judging the satisfactoriness or attractiveness of something. If we think of the pleasing and the displeasing consequences (that is, the "rewards" and "costs") obtained from something as the "outcomes" that it yields, then a person's comparison level for a particular type of thing would correspond to the level of outcomes that the person would regard as neutral—as neither good nor bad. Something—say, a blind date or a vacation—yielding net outcomes better than your CL (for dates or vacations) would seem attractive or good. If the outcomes averaged below your relevant CL, the judged item would seem unsatisfactory or bad.

Although Thibaut and Kelley were concerned mainly with interpersonal relationships, their concepts apply equally well to "relationships" between a person and an institution, task, or place. For example, a person well acquainted with the amenities of certain European cities might form a relatively high CL for cities and thus feel dissatisfied with many American cities. On the other hand, someone with a high need for excitement but who had previously resided only in a quiet small town might find experiences in the same American cities to be very much above his or her CL.

There is an intriguing aspect of Thibaut and Kelley's theory that helps to differentiate it from a straight application of Helson's adaptation-level notions. Thibaut and Kelley (1959) posit that a person's CL is determined by "some modal or average value of all outcomes known to the person (by virtue of personal or vicarious experience), *each outcome weighted by its salience*" (p. 81, italics added). An actual or potential outcome will be salient largely to the extent that it seems relevant to the judgment or relationship at hand and has been frequently experienced or is easy to call to mind. (One might compare Tversky and Kahneman's

[1973] notion of subjective "availability" [see Chapter 5].) In addition to incorporating traditional adaptation-level concepts, Thibaut and Kelley hypothesize that the salience of a particular outcome will also be determined by the degree to which the person feels that receiving the outcome is under his or her control and by the overall subjective probability of obtaining the outcome (see also Upshaw, 1969). Thus, outcomes that an individual feels able to control or that seem likely to occur will have higher salience in determining the individual's CL than will outcomes perceived as uncontrolled or unlikely.

It should be clear from all these considerations that changes in patterns of interpretation and imagination, as well as in actual outcomes, can produce substantial shifts in CLs. This conclusion can have important implications for human/environment relations. For instance, vivid alternatives for existing environmental designs and strong feelings of personal or collective power to achieve them may be essential ingredients in raising people's CLs for environmental quality. (Note that this in effect would mean higher standards for environmental quality.) Such a process might be facilitated by deliberate and frequent efforts to imagine how the public environment could be enhanced and to devise feasible personal or collective actions for effecting the improvements. The probable rise in CL produced by such cognitive sets would increase temporary dissatisfaction, to be sure; but as Kelley and Thibaut (1969) intimate, perceiving one's outcomes to be below CL spurs one to search for corrective information. On a widespread scale, this process could presumably serve as a goad to collective social action. We must become dissatisfied with our plight before we will do anything about it, and it appears that the belief that we *can* do something about it—combined with a clear vision of better alternatives—helps us to raise our CLs and become dissatisfied with our plight. Sometimes, then, a little negative affect, so long as it is not accompanied by feelings of helplessness, can lead to a better environment and a happier life in the long run.[19]

Now, finally, we can return to *Comparison.* This component refers to the way that an experience relates to or changes one's adaptation or comparison levels. Obviously, outcomes or stimuli that fall substantially above or below these internal standards will tend to elicit strong positive or negative affect. As one gets used to a situation, however, there is a tendency for one's relevant adaptation or comparison levels to be drawn in the direction of the experience—that is, for CLs to rise for pleasant situations and to fall for unpleasant ones. The result is a flattening of affective response to a given situation over time. This is of course an aspect of what was earlier labelled "psychological adaptation." Although such affective habituation may supply a welcome relief from some unpleasant feelings (as in the case of psychologically adapting to a bad marriage or a drab environment), such creeping desensitization can reduce one's potential for a more pleasant life in at least two ways. First, one may fail to notice or care about problems that can be corrected. This would be illustrated by habituation (psychological adaptation) to forms of pollution that may have harmful long-term consequences but that could be ameliorated by concerted public action (real adaptation). Such action would presumably be more likely if people didn't habituate easily and if their CLs didn't shift downward with duration of exposure to the pollution. Second, we may miss much of the potential beauty in environmental experience by psychologically adapting to pleasant surroundings and stimuli and by having our CLs creep upward when we live in desirable locations.

However, it is possible to prevent or reverse these shifts in one's CL or adaptation level by such means as deliberately exposing oneself to new surroundings (as in taking a trip through a slum or to a foreign land of great beauty) or even by vividly and frequently imagining changes in one's actual situation (pleasant changes to raise one's CL, unpleasant changes to lower it). The cognitive processes underlying both psychological adaptation and the techniques that can counter it can be characterized as operations of explicit or implicit *comparing*. (Obviously, the affective or judgmental effects arising from one's current CL or AL also involve at least implicit comparison or evaluation operations.) In the case of habituation and the automatic shift of CL toward one's current level of outcomes, a repeatedly experienced situation gradually becomes the standard with which new input is compared. In effect, one virtually comes to compare one's current situation with past replicas of itself. To break this process of affective deadening it is necessary to change the standard of comparison or, in Thibaut and Kelley's (1959) terms, to increase the salience of outcomes other than those one is currently receiving. As we shall see, in addition to such techniques as taking a trip or making use of one's imagination, it is also possible to "shake up" one's environmental adaptation and comparison levels by learning to evaluate and perceive one's surroundings in new ways.

Competence

Competence refers to the degree to which an experience involves feelings of control or of personal effectiveness. Chapter 2 discussed the motivational role of such concepts as effectance (R. White, 1959), the Origin/Pawn distinction (deCharms, 1968, 1971, 1976), and reactance (Brehm, 1966; Wicklund, 1974). These theoretical notions—and the research on which they are based and to which they have given rise—serve to illustrate the affective potency of feelings of competence and freedom of choice. Although Comprehension would appear to be a significant ingredient in Competence, the two aspects of experience are conceptually distinct. Comprehension applies only to one's sense of understanding and insight, while Competence applies to one's feelings of personal control and effectiveness. Even though understanding often contributes to personal effectiveness, it is obviously possible to have a sense of either without the other.

In reference to people/environment transactions, one influence of Competence on affect can be illustrated by the satisfaction people generally obtain by being able to modify their environments in accordance with their own wishes. For example, feelings of effectiveness and control play an obvious role in the pleasures of building one's own campfire or neighborhood park and in the delights of living in a responsive and malleable environment. Even very minor freedoms and personal influences, such as choosing the paint for one's dormitory room, can improve the quality of environmental experience. Also, as Chapter 6 will discuss, research in areas such as crowding and noise pollution indicates that a sense of personal control over environmental irritants can help reduce subjective annoyance and other ill effects.

In addition to the good feelings created by experiences of potency in modifying the physical environment, however, people can derive satisfaction by increasing their sense of control over their ways of processing information and over the resulting quality of their experience. The mushrooming interest in meditation, consciousness expansion, and psychedelic drugs attests to the pleasures of producing changes in one's state of consciousness. It is also possible to exert direct cognitive influence over the quality of one's perceptual and imaginational experience. Cognitive techniques that increase one's self-regulation of the Complexity, Composition, Comprehension, and Comparison aspects of experience should thus also enhance one's sense of "experiential" competence, thereby adding another source of positive affect.

Complications

Complications refers mainly to the strain or difficulty experienced in carrying out a particular set of cognitive operations or in interacting with a particular environment. This component is included in our analysis primarily to take account of the negative feelings people may experience when they attempt to think, perceive, or act in ways that otherwise would have positive effects on their experience but that are too difficult or too out of keeping with their cognitive style for them to execute comfortably. One example to be discussed later in this chapter concerns the cognitive set to see the world as a collection of abstract forms. For people who can perform the requisite cognitive operations easily, the resulting experiences may be aesthetically pleasant; but for many people this set is so difficult to execute that the dominant affect is one of strain. Similarly, some environments are beautiful to behold but too difficult to interact with to be very enjoyable. Not too fanciful examples of this might be living in a house designed like an abstract sculpture or hiking through the Rocky Mountains as a novice.

As later discussions will treat in more depth, human cognitive limitations may also render otherwise very valuable forms of systems thinking too difficult for most of us to perform comfortably. Such limitations could introduce serious complications into any hope for widespread ecological consciousness. The evidence is not yet decisive on this point, so we can still hope that appropriate educational procedures (and perhaps new contingencies of reinforcement) will greatly widen human cognitive vistas. Just as aesthetic appreciation or athletic skills can be taught and improved with practice—rendering difficult or stressful operations pleasant and fulfilling—so it would seem that cognitive skills of ecological thinking and awareness might also be learnable. It is perhaps most productive, indeed, to treat most sources of high Complications more as challenging problems to be solved than as insurmountable obstacles to be bemoaned.

Comportment

Comportment refers to any pattern of behavior or action arising from an experience. This component obviously differs from the others we have been considering, since it does not directly involve the quality of experience per se. Indirectly, however, patterns of behavior are very important for mediating cognitive and environmental effects on the affective quality of experience. The consideration of Comportment is also needed for a complete evaluation of the long-term experiential and environmental effects of a cognitive set or of a cultural or environmental design. The basic notion is first that a given way of thinking or a given environmental design can influence the Complexity, Composition, Comprehension, Comparison, Competence, and Complications aspects of experience. These in turn may lead to particular patterns of behavior (Comportment) that can produce results either immediately or eventually affecting the various components of experience. This sort of feedback loop is of course represented in our model, keeping in mind the "overlap" between cognitive-set processes and experience.

Compatibility

Basically, *Compatibility* refers to the degree of consistency with a value orientation stressing cooperation, human happiness, and ecological concerns. This component is included in the scheme to take account of the long-range experiential consequences of thinking, behaving, or designing in particular ways. A given way of thinking, behaving, or designing may yield short-term satisfaction for some individuals by giving them experiences having pleasant Composition, optimal Complexity, high Competence, and so on, but still wreak biological or psychological havoc on other people or at a later time. Obviously, individuals could derive all sorts of satisfactions from activities such as building private homes in national parks, driving a hundred miles an hour through city streets, or making a fortune by selling unsafe or polluting items. But think of the consequences.

The first seven components can probably account for the immediate affective tone of an individual's ongoing experience. However, if used alone as a guide for the evaluation of new ways of thinking, perceiving, or designing, these seven components obviously would not be sufficient to guard against patterns of thought or behavior that might have consequences leading to unhappiness and environmental degradation. Although the concept of Compatibility involves a definite set of values, these values are based on the consideration that long-term and widespread human happiness will probably be contingent on certain patterns of thought and behavior. If the world's population now and in the future is to have a chance to realize human potentials for positive affect, it would seem that ecological, cooperative, and happiness-oriented values will have to guide our thought and action much more than they have in the past. This argument will be more fully developed in later chapters.

Summary Tables

The following two tables are intended to present a compact overview of the eight components we have been considering. Table 1 presents brief definitions and examples of how each component can contribute to positive or negative affect. Table 2 presents examples of how each of the first seven components could contribute to either high or low Compatibility. In comparing the examples in these two tables, it should be noted that some processes might lead to short-term positive affect but nonetheless be low in Compatibility, while other processes might arouse negative affect but be high in Compatibility. However, in the long run, high-Compatibility processes should result in more overall positive affect than low-Compatibility processes. Finally, it should be emphasized again that all eight components are interrelated. As later discussions will attempt to clarify, the overall quality of experience arises from their interactions and combined effect.

This integrative scheme has consisted of eight components considered as contributing to the affective quality of experience. The scheme thus constitutes an incipient theory of happiness and has been presented here both as a summary of cognitive and environmental influences on affect and as a framework for evaluating cognitive sets and environmental designs. We shall tackle the issue of environmental (and cultural) design in Chapters 6 and 7, but let us turn now to an examination of how consciously controllable Plans for processing environmental information can be used to enrich life and increase environmental awareness.

TABLE 1 EIGHT COMPONENTS LINKING COGNITION, ENVIRONMENT, AND AFFECT

Component	Definition	Example of Positive Influence on Affect	Example of Negative Influence on Affect
Complexity	arousal potential of structural aspects of experience	approaching optimal arousal level by noticing details when bored or ignoring them if overstimulated	being bombarded by too intense or complex stimulation (e.g., "future shock"); sensory deprivation
Composition	content, meaning, and significance of experience	imagining beautiful scene or happy situation; interpreting stressful film via intellectualization; interpreting felt arousal as euphoria	imagining threat to cherished value; interpreting stressful film as if you were victim; interpreting felt arousal as anger
Comprehension	sense of understanding, clarity, or insight involved in experience	having clear and accurate mental map; insight into a problem	feeling lost; inability to figure out what something is
Comparison	way in which experience relates to or changes adaptation or comparison levels	breaking habituation to pleasant scene; lowering CL for environmental quality; receiving outcomes above CL	habituating to pleasant scene; increasing CL for environmental quality; receiving outcomes below CL
Competence	feelings of control or effectiveness involved in experience	sense of personal control over one's experience or environment (e.g., feeling able to control noise)	feelings of helplessness (e.g., feeling unable to control interactions with others)
Complications	experienced difficulty of particular cognitive or behavioral operation being attempted	finding it easy to intellectualize content of stressful film, to imagine something pleasant, or to appreciate art	finding it difficult to imagine something pleasant, appreciate art, or intellectualize content of stressful film
Comportment	pattern of behavior arising from an experience	creating something beautiful; leaving a bad situation	destroying something beautiful; creating something unpleasant
Compatibility	consistency with cooperative, ecological, and happiness-oriented values	high Compatibility should lead to long-term positive affect (see Table 2)	low Compatibility, if widespread, could lead to ecological disasters, wars, and other catastrophes (see Table 2)

TABLE 2   EXAMPLES OF HIGH AND LOW COMPATIBILITY
FOR OTHER COMPONENTS

Component	Example of High Compatibility	Example of Low Compatibility
Complexity	approaching optimal arousal level via means that favor environmental quality (e.g., public art, wilderness appreciation)	approaching optimal arousal via means that degrade environment or harm other people (e.g., pyromania, enjoying the excitement of war)
Composition	interpreting scenes in terms of ecological interrelations	interpreting scenes in terms of how much money one can make for oneself
Comprehension	gaining insight into ecological relations and problems; understanding the needs of other people	failure to understand environmental consequences of own actions; insight into how to achieve own ends when these are incompatible with environmental values or with needs of other people
Comparison	increasing CL for environmental quality; reducing psychological adaptations to correctible environmental problems	habituating to environmental problems that could be corrected; lowering CL for environmental quality
Competence	feeling capable of achieving beneficial social change via cooperative, collective action	feeling capable of getting own way at cost of others' happiness; feelings of competence deriving from making or contemplating unwise environmental changes
Complications	finding it easy to think ecologically; finding it difficult to make own atom bomb	finding it difficult to think in systems terms or to consider wide range of alternative coping strategies
Comportment	creating something beautiful *and* ecologically sound; joining organizations working to enhance the public environment	destroying beauty; disrupting ecological balances; voting according to private gain rather than society's well-being

Part two
Enhancing Environmental Experience

SELF-DIRECTION OF COGNITIVE SETS

As the foregoing discussion has suggested, deliberately activating certain types of cognitive sets—at least now and then—can aid in enhancing your environmental awareness and appreciation, your creativity, and perhaps even your general happiness. In a way this is no more than saying that the way you think can make a big difference in what you are aware of and how you feel. Nonetheless, filling in the details is far from a trivial task. In view of the potential importance of self-direction of one's Plans for information processing, it is indeed curious that comparatively little research has been devoted to helping people gain such control or to pinpointing connections between specific types of cognitive sets and the types of experiences they evoke. A suspicion I share with W. Lambert Gardiner (1973) and probably many humanistic psychologists is that the mainstream of American behavioral science has traditionally been concerned more with learning how to control other people than with discovering ways to help people direct their own lives and experience. Considering our society's emphasis on efficient production, overt performance, and obedience, it is not surprising that the search for techniques to aid in the self-directed enhancement of experience has been slighted.

Fortunately, there are signs that this situation may be changing. Burgeoning popular and academic activity in areas such as consciousness alteration and expansion, biofeedback, meditation, imagery and imagination, creativity, and even aesthetics all point to an intensifying concern with self-directed experience.[20] It is true that much of this interest has an egocentric or individualistic focus and therefore does not necessarily rank very high in Compatibility. But at least we seem to be moving toward a recognition that the quality of experience is intrinsically important and that people can exert some direct influence over it by the way they process information.

Examples of research on the active use of cognitive sets to enhance experience are provided by Richard Lazarus's work on the use of intellectualization and denial sets to reduce stress (discussed in Part One) and by Jerome L. Singer's (1966–1975) research and theory concerning the positive uses of imagery. Singer's work is especially intriguing for its analyses of how the cognitive-set processes involved in daydreaming, fantasy, imaginative play, and psychotherapeutic imagery techniques can all be used to enrich the affective quality of experience. Thus, day-dreaming can be deliberately used to relieve boredom; playful fantasies can be enjoyable activities in themselves; and, properly employed, imagination can function to enhance one's awareness of one's problems and of alternatives for constructive action. Similarly, theorists and practitioners such as Robert Masters and Jean Houston (1972), Aaron Beck (1967), and Maxwell Maltz (1960) have advocated the use of imagination exercises for such purposes as consciousness expansion, relief of depression-producing fantasizing (note that imagery is a two-edged sword!), and enhancement of one's self-image and resulting behavior patterns.

Psychological research has even demonstrated that cognitive-set processes can play a role in reducing the unpleasantness of pain. This emerges very clearly in the work of Ronald Melzack (1961, 1973) and Theodore Barber and his associates (1974). Melzack, for example, has adduced a wide array of evidence indicating that the experience of pain, even in the presence of severe bodily damage, is affected by both physiological and cognitive factors. For instance, soldiers whose battle injuries meant relief from the battle itself have often reported not being especially bothered by pain, whereas car accident victims with similar types of injuries are much more likely to find themselves in agony (in part, according to Melzack, because they view these injuries as catastrophic occurrences—unlike the view of the wounded soldiers; see also Beecher, 1959). Barber's work on hypnosis and related phenomena has also revealed the potential role of cognitive factors in the experience of pain. Apparently, with or without hypnotic induction, many people can relieve their own pain by such techniques as imagining that the afflicted bodily area is numb, distracting their attention with unrelated imagery, or carefully attending to the sensations involved without thinking of these as "pain."

However, our main concern for the remainder of this chapter will be to examine specific types of cognitive sets for enhancing the overall quality of environmental experience. As a preface to this discussion, let us briefly consider where cognitive sets come from. The following headings are meant to represent a rough sampling of the main types of sources of our everyday Plans for selecting and processing information. They are also important to an understanding of individuals' opportunity and ability to exert self-direction over their cognitive sets.

Cognitive styles and other "personality dispositions." These in fact pertain more to the way a person executes cognitive sets and what cognitive sets the person selects than where the sets come from. But cognitive styles and certain other "dispositional variables" are of great importance for whether a person will be able or willing to make use of given environmental cognitive sets.

A *cognitive style* can be defined as any relatively pervasive aspect of the way a person selects or processes information. Examples would be tendencies to level versus sharpen perceptual details, to tolerate versus resist ambiguity, to perceive objects as possessing expressive (physiognomic) character versus perceive more "literally," to use complex versus simple schemes for encoding and interpreting, and to scan broadly versus narrowly.[21] At least some dimensions of cognitive style can probably be brought under conscious control, but many seem to be underlying dispositions that operate outside awareness. These could probably be changed only by special training, if they could be changed at all (see Kogan, 1971).

Dimensions of cognitive style such as those mentioned above clearly have important implications for the specific environmental cognitive sets that an individual could use or find enjoyable. For instance, someone with a low tolerance for ambiguity presumably would resist using a cognitive set that introduced multiple subjective meanings or that radically changed the usual interpretations placed on everyday objects. Furthermore, cognitive styles and related cognitive abilities will obviously affect the *way* any given cognitive set is performed. Thus, someone who habitually uses complex schemes or who scans broadly would execute a cognitive set to imagine environmental improvements very differently than would a person who used simple interpretive schemes or who scanned narrowly. Indeed, virtually all of the various mental abilities subsumed under the concept of intelligence could similarly be considered as basic aspects of cognitive style; but we need not here go into their pervasive interactions with cognitive-set processes.

Other personality dimensions of importance for a person's choice and execution of environmental cognitive sets would include what Kenneth Craik (1976) and George McKechnie (for example, 1974, 1977) have labelled "environmental dispositions." For instance, McKechnie's carefully developed psychological test, the Environmental Response Inventory, gives indices of a respondent's standings on the following environmental dispositions: *pastoralism* (positive orientation toward the natural environment), *urbanism* (enjoyment of city life), *environmental adaptation* ("man over nature" value orientation), *antiquarianism* (preference for the old and traditional), *stimulus seeking* (enjoying and seeking high levels of complexity, novelty, etc.), *environmental trust* (trust versus fear of challenging or dangerous environments), *mechanical orientation* (interest in technological and functional processes), and *need for privacy*. McKechnie's research indicates that these dimensions characterize reasonably stable personality differences in how people feel about the environment.[22] Brian Little (1976) has also pointed out the importance of whether a person is typically oriented toward *things* or toward *persons* (or toward neither or both).

Certainly, these and other relatively stable environmental dispositions are important in mediating how an individual perceives, thinks about, and responds to different environments and situations. As Craik (1976) emphasized, however, there is always a person/environment *interaction* to be considered; so-called personality dispositions must always be considered in relation to situational demands and to particular social/environmental contexts (see also Mischel, 1968, 1969; Caplan and Nelson, 1973).

Goals, tasks, and roles.   Turning now to these key *instigators* of specific cognitive sets, we might note again that any goal will induce a cognitive set to select and process information relevant to its achievement. Whenever you are trying to do something, you will tend to seek out information that will help you do it and to think about this information in a way that you believe will help you reach your goal. This is obvious, but it highlights what may be the single most important source of our everyday cognitive sets. Furthermore, this form of set induction happens fairly automatically, and we usually do not make a conscious effort to choose goals simply for the purpose of inducing particular types of cognitive sets. You go to the grocery store to buy food, not to make yourself activate the cognitive sets needed to navigate to the supermarket or to make decisions about what purchases to make. It might indeed be an interesting exercise first to think of many of your everyday cognitive sets and then to identify the types of situations or *tasks* (goal-directed behavior) that could induce you to activate these sets. (It might be an even more interesting exercise to think up new and interesting cognitive sets and then figure out tasks that would call for them.)

Roles can be loosely defined as the patterns of behavior associated with specific social positions (for example, student, date, gardener, husband, patient, environmental lawyer).[23] Role enactment, the carrying out of the pattern of behavior associated with a social position, involves being guided by a specific network of goals and tasks, often including the overriding task of simply behaving appropriately for the given role. The demands of such tasks and goals are common sources of our everyday Plans for selecting and processing information. Derrick Sewell (1971), for instance, found that a sample of Canadian engineers concerned with water resources problems tended to conceive of water pollution and its solution in technological and economic terms. This contrasted with the tendency of Canadian public health officials to view water pollution as a health problem calling for better regulations and stricter enforcement of water quality standards. Mary Barker (1974) similarly uncovered systematic differences in the way samples of senior students in training for different professional fields thought about the problem of air pollution. (For example, law students seemed most prone to synthesize information and take a multidisciplinary approach, while Barker's sample of economics seniors tended to be much less flexible and multidisciplinary in their thinking—although this finding should be replicated before being generalized!) Indeed, Jerome Bruner (1962, p. 147) has noted the psychological effects of occupational roles in the following terms: "In time one develops what the French have long called *une deformation professionelle,* a set of habits and outlooks to match the requirements of the job." The same could be said for virtually any long-term role, and even momentary roles tend to induce concomitant momentary cognitive sets.

Education. In addition to inducing specific cognitive sets through the direct imposition of various tasks, formal educational procedures transmit culturally approved patterns of thought in numerous other ways. Any *question,* for instance, can be translated as an instruction for how to process information. Simply turn the question into a command: for example, "Why does ice melt?" = "Figure out the reasons that ice melts." All questions, then, represent implicit mental tasks. Attempting to answer any one of the many questions posed by standard educational practices will thus induce a corresponding cognitive set, even if the question is not directly imposed as part of an exam or other assigned task.

Furthermore, the *knowledge* gained as one becomes educated is itself a subtle inducer of cognitive sets. As noted earlier in relation to processes of categorizing/interpreting/understanding, gaining knowledge of ecology can help one use new and more intricate cognitive sets for thinking about biological processes in one's everyday surroundings. And on the grand scale of the history of science, we might note with Thomas Kuhn (1970) that formal educational procedures and textbooks generally pass along the prevailing "paradigms" within the various sciences taught. Although Kuhn acknowledged using the term in different ways, we can regard a *paradigm* as essentially a guiding scheme that induces particular cognitive sets for thinking about issues within a given scientific (or other) discipline. Forming a successful new paradigm, as when Einstein's conceptions displaced the Newtonian paradigm in physics, can thus be an act of consummate creativity. Most of us, however, continue to think about things, scientific and otherwise, within the conceptual frameworks we have been taught.

An additional educational procedure for inducing cognitive sets is of course *direct instruction* in how to process information. Examples of this approach can be found wherever students are taught specific procedures for analyzing or classifying material or solving problems within a given subject area. Thus, teaching people exactly how to analyze paintings, classify trees, or solve mathematical problems are examples of direct instruction in cognitive sets. My impression, however, is that most such cognitive-set instruction is conducted in highly task-oriented contexts, with the main emphasis on imparting knowledge or skill at answering questions rather than on helping people become more aware of their own powers to direct their cognitive sets per se.

The setting. As a final example of the sources of our everyday environmental cognitive sets, let us briefly consider that the environmental setting itself can stimulate a particular way of thinking. As we shall explore in Chapter 6, the total combination of the physical environment and associated patterns of expected social behavior tends to shape the way people behave—and the roles they adopt—in most public places. Such influence over behavior patterns will of course be accompanied by the induction of corresponding cognitive sets. For instance, one will tend to think about religious subjects at a church service, just as one will tend to behave in a "reverent" way there. As Donald Norman (for example, 1976) has put it, our thinking is both "data-driven" and "conceptually-driven"; that is, schemas can be activated both by information entering from the environment and by deliberate mental processes. Thus, you might *decide* to think about some nonreligious topic while in church, but the situation would tend to call forth schemas relevant to religion. Similarly, some environments or settings probably elicit reveries and other imaginational cognitive sets, while others tend to induce more direct attention to the immediate physical surroundings (compare, for instance, sylvan lakes with bustling shopping centers).

Keeping this consideration in mind, and also remembering that there is always an interaction between *how* one processes environmental information and *what* the environmental information is that one is processing (that is, the content, structure, and dynamic properties of the given environment), let us examine some special cognitive sets designed specifically to enrich environmental experience.

SPECIAL ENVIRONMENTAL COGNITIVE SETS

In this section, guidelines for more than three dozen special environmental cognitive sets will be presented. Although the guidelines are presented as instructions, these cognitive sets are likely to be most beneficial when an individual adopts them voluntarily to achieve a desired state of experience or other valued outcome. That is, viewing a cognitive set as an imposed "lesson" may be a good way to *lessen* its value. The whole point of using alternative environmental cognitive sets is to enliven one's immediate experience and one's degree of understanding and creativity in dealing with environmental problems and possibilities. It is only if you *want* to do such things, however, that it makes any sense to deliberately try to process environmental information in the ways suggested by the guidelines offered below.

Perhaps no one has better captured the spirit of such an effort at the self-direction of experience than Ross Parmenter (1968) in his book *The Awakened Eye*. This highly anecdotal, autobiographical account tellingly conveys the excitement, pleasure, and awakening of interest that can accompany a *self-directed* odyssey into the world of experience-enhancing cognitive sets. However, as Parmenter and others have pointed out, there are many cultural blocks to such an endeavor. Even in such a rudimentary matter as attending very closely to one's everyday surroundings, especially for the pure enjoyment that can be derived from such "general observation," Parmenter (p. 127) points out "that our culture does not value it, that our schools do not teach it, and that our mores disapprove of it." Intently experiencing some common, ordinary object or scene for an hour or two is not considered normal recreation (although passively attending to images flickering for hours on end on a TV screen is).

As we have seen before, our culture simply fails to place a high value on the quality of experience per se. This goes a long way toward explaining our relative neglect of aesthetics (in virtually all senses of the term), fantasy and daydreaming as valued activities, and indeed most of the other ingredients for creativity (see, for example, Wallach, 1971; Arnheim, 1969; Stein, 1974). The general "pragmatic" emphasis on efficiency, performance, and massive production, not to mention the resulting need for obedient workers, clearly militates against a widespread concern with perceiving and thinking about the environment in ways such as those we are about to consider.

Nonetheless, if these cognitive sets are to be used effectively, the spirit or attitude or frame of mind with which they are approached is far more important than whether the exact "instructions" are followed. It is difficult to convey that frame of mind in a few words; perhaps an entire book such as Parmenter's is needed to get the message across. But, simply put, the important considerations seem to be that you be open and curious about the experiential effects of using different cognitive sets; that you actively desire to enhance your aesthetic experience, environmental awareness, and creativity; and that you be sufficiently committed to such goals that you will exert the mental effort needed to invent or try new cognitive sets. Furthermore, as a result of this sort of curiosity, openness, desire, and commitment, your approach to the whole process of trying out new Plans for thinking and perceiving should be playful and flexible. After all, the whole point is for you, through your own self-directed cognitive processes, to enhance your own experience in ways that you consider desirable. Whether you do this by trying other people's suggestions for new cognitive sets or by inventing your own, the process is inherently under your control and should be intrinsically motivated. In short, it should be *fun.*

With that happy thought in mind, let me offer just two additional comments. First, as other people who have written about such "mental exercises" have indicated, it is important to recognize that many of the most enjoyable and worthwhile things in life take not only the right frame of mind, but also practice and preparation.[24] Thus, some cognitive sets may indeed be easy and enjoyable and clearly beneficial even the first time you try them; but others will be difficult (produce a high level of Complications) at first, even though with a little effort and time they may have much to offer as ways of thinking or perceiving. Here again it is important to be flexible, to vary your approach, and to try to ease into a complex or difficult way of thinking by small steps. Where possible in the guidelines below, I have offered a few suggestions for doing this. Second, however, it is good (common) sense to try to regulate your mode of information processing according to your mood. For instance, executing a cognitive set that produces high arousal might be very enjoyable if you are bored but may be overstimulating if you are anxious or tired. Again, *flexibility* is the key word.

The following guidelines for special-purpose environmental cognitive sets were devised in conjunction with a research program that I have been directing over the past several years. The primary purpose of this program has been the discovery of self-controllable cognitive sets that are enjoyable and interesting to use and that, at least taken collectively, would facilitate enhancement of all eight components in the scheme linking cognition, environment, and affect (that is, Complexity, Composition, Comprehension, Comparison, Competence, Complications, Comportment, and Compatibility). The initial research, conducted in partnership with my colleagues Lawrence Gordon and James Ferguson, included a number of experiments designed to explore various experiential and judgmental effects of five special environmental cognitive sets (Leff et al., 1974). The next phase of the project consisted mainly of a longitudinal experiment, conducted with Lawrence Gordon, in which the range and number of cognitive sets under consideration were considerably expanded.[25] The cognitive sets discussed below have been drawn primarily from this latter study.

The underlying idea is to make use of a wide range of cognitive sets and to interrelate them into a richer and more environmentally alerting way of experiencing one's surroundings. For purposes of clarity and ease of assimilation, however, the set instructions (guidelines) are presented here in four separate groups. Even though the primary purpose of the cognitive sets differs from group to group, in many cases there is substantial overlap; given sets can involve more than one type of purpose. The four main groupings are as follows: (1) cognitive sets designed primarily to enhance aesthetic experience of environments; (2) cognitive sets designed primarily to deepen awareness and understanding of how environmental components interrelate with each other; (3) cognitive sets designed mainly to facilitate the exercise or development of creativity in perceiving one's surroundings; (4) cognitive sets designed primarily to increase awareness both of environmental problems and of the possibilities for improving environments. Where appropriate, the discussion will also mention research findings relevant to particular cognitive sets and include other comments that may be of help should you wish to use these Plans for thinking and perceiving.

Enhancing Aesthetic Experience

According to the British aesthetician Harold Osborne (1970), the key to aesthetic experience or appreciation is *percipience*. By this Osborne meant a mode of experience in which one centers attention on the object of perception without engaging in any conceptualizing, analysis, imaginational embellishment, or virtually any other type of relating. As Osborne put it, pure aesthetic experience is based on a kind of *contemplation* or complete absorption in the perceived object or environment as of interest purely for its appearance, not for what it means, signifies, or could be used for. As he acknowledged, the full richness of aesthetic experiences may well derive also from mental operations of analysis and other forms of relating; but these are viewed only as providing a basis for—or as deriving from—enriched percipience or pure "here and now" contemplation, not as in themselves aspects of experiential appreciation.

Actually, the consistency among diverse writers on the nature and aesthetic value of this type of experience is truly impressive. Abraham Maslow's (1968) notion of "Being-cognition" (B-cognition), for instance, involves a total focusing on the object of perception and a suspension of processes of comparing and evaluating. Furthermore, in B-cognition, perception is focused on the "endness" of the object—a thing is seen independent of all human needs and purposes, as an end in itself; and the object is not "rubricized" or categorized. Similarly, Ernest Schachtel (1959) has written of "allocentric" perception as perceiving the object "in its suchness, without any labeling, naming, classifying, thinking of possible similarities, relations to other objects, etc." (p. 179). For Schachtel this form of perception involves openness, receptivity, and a "full turning toward the object." According to him, allocentric perceiving arises from an attitude of intense interest and can lead to far richer experience than our usual ("autocentric") mode of perception, in which our main concern is with the relevance of the object to our personal needs. As a final example, this time from an artist, Frederick Franck (1973) in *The Zen of Seeing* defines true *seeing* or contemplating in terms of nonlabeling, nonevaluating, total focusing on the object seen. Here again we encounter the idea of viewing something as of interest for itself rather than for what it means, signifies, is worth, or can do for you.

It would be easy to go on listing writers in the areas of aesthetic and environmental appreciation who have expressed similar ideas about the essence of aesthetic appreciation.[26] True, there are other theories about the basis for such experience; and the writers cited, as well as such experts in the psychology of art as Arnheim (1954, 1974) and the Kreitlers (1972), have acknowledged that processes of relating are certainly involved in the production of full aesthetic experience. The *meaning* of a work of art, or the associations called up by certain types of environments, can clearly enhance our appreciation of them. However, as perhaps best argued by Osborne (1970), the immediate aesthetic experience of a given object (or environment) rests primarily on attending wholly to that object as of interest in itself. This Osborne called viewing the object as "opaque"—as opposed to seeing "through" the object to some related meaning that it conveys. Thus, the meaning of a word, if fully and contemplatively attended to as somehow an end in itself, might yield an aesthetic experience; but for the word itself to do so would require attending to the sight or sound of the word as a form that is of interest in its own right—something that might happen, for instance, in contemplating the calligraphy in a fancy sign or in listening to a language you do not understand. (Of course, it is possible that both the "vehicle" and the meaning conveyed might be appreciated as noncategorized ends-in-themselves. Perhaps this is the essence of appreciating poetry and even of appreciating nature.)

The following guidelines for six aesthetically oriented cognitive sets are attempts to codify certain mental procedures that should facilitate such object-centered, receptive, appreciative perception. However, as Osborne (1970) has discussed in depth, percipience or appreciation is a *skill*. It takes considerable practice to become adept at it. Becoming adept, though, can reward us both with the enhanced Complexity, Composition, and Comprehension involved in aesthetic experiences and with the heightened Competence that accompanies the successful exercise of any skill. Furthermore, even with high skill in allocentric perception or B-cognition, continued object-centered examination and contemplation will tend to yield deeper and more rewarding aesthetic experience; beauty may not jump out at you with the first percipient glance. However, Osborne also cautioned that not all objects have the inherent complexity and organization to yield high and deepening aesthetic experiences when aesthetically contemplated. Percipience may thus breed discrimination—and even frustration, if the environment is bad.

The following six cognitive sets are listed in a special order that should be clear from the comments. As developed for consistency and clarity in the research, the guidelines (instructions) for each set refer to *the scene*. This phrase applies simply to whatever object or environment one is attending to while using the cognitive set; in general, "the scene" means your immediate surroundings. Finally, each cognitive set has been affectionately labelled with a three- or four-letter code name for easy reference.

COL: SEEING THE COLORS IN THE SCENE.   The idea is to focus on really *seeing* the colors and fine shadings of color around you. Avoid thinking of the names of the colors; just concentrate on the pure visual experience of the colors or shades you can see. Try to notice as many different colors as possible, but feel free to carefully explore and linger on any color areas you find especially interesting or pleasing.

Comments.   The type of aesthetic experience that this cognitive set can produce was very clearly expressed by a participant in the longitudinal experiment. In one phase of this study, subjects in a special randomly chosen group made visits to several pre-assigned locations around Burlington, Vermont. While at a given "scene," each of these subjects successively engaged four sets of her or his choosing from among the lists presented in this chapter. Immediately after executing a given set, the subject would rate it for enjoyability, interestingness, and difficulty, and write a brief description of the experience induced by the set. Some people, as one might expect in a situation defined as an *experiment*, seemed to treat many of these cognitive sets as an imposed task; but others genuinely seemed to "get into" the sets they chose. The following description of a COL experience appears to be of this latter type (the scene in this case was the person's own dormitory room):

> I noticed that within a couple [of] basic hues present in my room, an infinite variety of shades, tones, etc., are present. This really intrigued me. I noticed how the light sources affected the colors and the shadows that were formed. I thought about the incredible use of color, etc., in prints of paintings that are on the walls of my room. I noticed that there were so many different colors in my room that I overlooked.

Interestingly, COL was the most frequently chosen of all the cognitive sets presented in this chapter—although overall it was rated as only moderately interesting and enjoyable, about the same as control subjects rated their normal way of viewing the same scenes. It was rated as one of the *easier* sets to execute, however. This is very important, since one of COL's most valuable purposes may well be to serve as a stepping stone to the execution of the following *key* cognitive set for perceiving beauty in the pure physical forms around you.

ASF: SEEING THE SCENE AS A COLLECTION OF COLORED ABSTRACT FORMS. The idea *is to see the scene as "meaningless" colored, textured, three-dimensional shapes rather than as everyday objects.* It is very important to forget about what the objects actually *are,* to suspend your usual everyday categorization of things. Instead simply dwell on the immediate visual experience of colors, shapes, lines, textures, patterns of light and shade, repetitions of similar forms, etc. As you do this, relax and just let the experience sink in.

One purpose of focusing your attention in this way is to experience your surroundings more intensely and to perceive elements of beauty that might otherwise go unnoticed. In opening yourself up to this sort of visual experience, it is very important to become absorbed in the sensory experience itself—*without labeling or even consciously evaluating what you're looking at.* You should view everything in the surroundings as abstract ("meaningless") forms. If you find this difficult to do, here are some techniques that seem to help:

1. Try concentrating just on colors or just on shapes (but without naming them). Let the "pure visual experience" of the colors or shapes around you fill your consciousness. If you relax and focus just on colors

or shapes, your inner mental verbalization and labeling will automatically stop.

2. Do not try to repress thinking of words or evaluating things; just concentrating on the visual experience will automatically squelch mental verbalizing.

3. At first, you might find it easiest to see single objects at fairly close range as "abstract forms." With a little practice, you should be able to extend this way of seeing to include anything you like. In the early phases, though, contemplating a single object (such as a tree trunk, telephone booth, or a patch of ground) for an extended period of time should help give you a good feeling for what it is like to "see the world as a collection of colored abstract forms."

4. As you progress in your ability to see things "abstractly"—to become absorbed in the pure visual experience of your surroundings—you might try attending to patterns or configurations of different shapes, textures, or colors. Other visual elements of interest might include reflections, shadow patterns, subtle variations in color hue and brightness, depth, the shape of space between and around objects, and any other aspects of the visual environment that you find interesting or pleasant to experience.

5. In addition to focusing on interesting or pleasing *details* in your surroundings, you should also focus on *broad expanses* of the environment. Viewing the whole scene as an abstract "composition," you may discover interesting patterns of forms or colors and perhaps experience a new sense of visual unity.

6. You might also try to experience sounds, smells, and touch feelings as abstract sensations, without thinking of their usual meanings.

Comments.   It should be apparent that ASF (for "abstract sensory focusing") embodies many of the characteristics imputed by Osborne to "percipience," by Schachtel to "allocentric perception," by Maslow to "B-cognition," and by Franck to "seeing." As some of the following cognitive-set guidelines and commentaries will imply, there may well be more to those concepts—and of course to aesthetic experience—than simply experiencing the world "abstractly." But it is surprising just how closely ASF squares with the kind of information processing described by the writers mentioned. Indeed, this way of looking at one's surroundings is often recommended in aesthetic education as a way of sharpening one's observation and appreciation of details and of visual elements (see, for example, Linderman and Herberholz, 1969). Many writers on consciousness expansion have similarly suggested that abstract sensory focusing on objects or environments can be intensely pleasant and "mind expanding."[27] And Steve Van Matre (1974) and Annie Dillard (1974) have offered ASF-type suggestions for increasing one's percipience and enjoyment in natural settings.

What all of these suggestions have in common is the idea that it is aesthetically interesting and enjoyable to focus intensely on one's environmental sensory input without relating this information to information in long-term memory (such as language codes, schemas, scales of judgment, and so on). ASF, then, is a cognitive set to scan and focus on environmental input intensely but not to perform the usual relating operations (associating, categorizing, evaluating, transforming, and so on). The only relating called for is a kind of external relating or perceptual organizing involving immediately perceived elements, as in picking out patterns of similar shapes or contemplating sensory relations among different colors (harmony, gradation of tones, contrasts, and the like).

The pleasantness of this sort of experience could derive from several sources. In our earlier research (Leff et al., 1974), for instance, my colleagues and I found that an ASF-type set led viewers to rate most of the presented environmental scenes as more complex than these scenes were rated when viewed normally. In view of the importance attributed to complexity and similar determinants of arousal level by many aesthetics theorists (see Chapter 2), an increase in subjective complexity could well make the experience of viewing an ordinary or boring scene more interesting, exciting, and pleasant. Also, the greater awareness of details induced by abstract sensory focusing can contribute to a heightened sense of comprehending the environment. And, to quote from the 1974 article:

> Perceiving abstractly should rather profoundly change the composition of the perceptual experience, since functional significance will be replaced by abstract sensory qualities. In addition, new elements, patterns, and relationships between elements may be noticed for the first time. Under some circumstances the apparent unity of the scene may be affected, since all elements are now being viewed along common dimensions (rather than differentiated by function or material). In theory, the pleasingness of at least many normally "ugly" or neutral scenes should be increased by viewing them as abstract configurations. Finally, the intense

perceptual experience engendered by this set should prove very useful in decreasing habituation to familiar surroundings. (Leff et al., 1974, p. 408)

In addition to these potentially beneficial effects on Complexity, Composition, Comprehension, and Comparison, the self-direction of the ASF process can also enhance Competence by giving one a sense of greater control over one's perceptual experience. The research evidence, however, does indicate some problems with respect to Complications. Also, as Maslow (1968) discussed with reference to B-cognition in general, there are potentially serious problems relating to Comportment and Compatibility; but let us consider those problems later.

With respect to Complications, my colleagues and I have found that for many people ASF is a very difficult cognitive set to execute. Most of us are so wedded to our usual highly verbal, relational modes of thinking that we find it difficult to shut off our inner talking and musing and classifying. We find it difficult to "just perceive." Many subjects thus cannot focus abstractly when they first try. Overall, only about 30 percent of the people who were instructed to use ASF in our experiments found it more enjoyable than their normal way of viewing scenes; and only slightly over 20 percent reported a significant increase in the judged pleasantness of scenes viewed under ASF instructions. Indeed, even people who report that the experiences induced by this set are extremely enjoyable often indicate that it is difficult to perceive in this way.

Having experimented with this set for several years myself, I can understand this difficulty. One source of complications may be a low tolerance for ambiguity, since successfully seeing the world as abstract forms might be upsetting to the person who likes to see things as clearly categorized and stable in meaning. Also, research on selective attention (for example, Treisman, 1969; Kahneman, 1973) has revealed the difficulty of focusing exclusively on only *some* aspects of a stimulus. It is hard to ignore related aspects. Although this work often pertains to highly linked aspects such as shape and color, it is clear that with words at least, it is very hard to ignore meaning while considering physical form (unless one repeats the word over and over again). In any case, it can indeed be a difficult task to concentrate on the abstract sensory qualities of an object without thinking about the classifications or functional meanings of the object. And the comparatively low value that our culture places on aesthetic experience and perceptual awareness certainly does not help to promote the requisite mental skills for abstract sensory focusing.

Since this type of cognitive set has been so widely suggested by those concerned with promoting environmental awareness and aesthetic experiences, discovering how to overcome such difficulties could be of benefit to many people. At this stage, I have no definite answers to offer; but a few examples from my own experience may prove helpful. First, I have found that focusing on colors is a relatively easy way to jolt my perception into an ASF mode. Starting with shapes or textures does not seem to work as well, perhaps because these seem less immediately "given" than do colors and hence require more sustained mental effort to notice or figure out. Also, colors encompass everything in one's visual field, and nuances and changes in color serve to delineate shapes and textures. Second, quite by accident I discovered that deliberately looking for scenes that would make photographic configurations that other people could easily see as abstract forms induced a very pleasant and easily continued ASF set for *me*. As indicated below in the discussions of the two "photographic" cognitive sets, SNP and FOT, this technique does not even require a camera. Drawing or painting scenes is also often recommended to induce ASF, although concern with the quality of one's artwork can easily distract from one's pure visual appreciation of the object (see Franck, 1973). Third, certain types of photographs seem to help some people gain a better understanding of what an ASF experience is like. Slides or other photographs of everyday objects such as sewer gratings, rusty fences, or telephone booths often seem to convey an impression of abstract art and thus get the point across better than the actual objects.

Finally, I would urge you to go back over the full ASF guidelines, take the "tips" section to heart (including trying senses other than vision!), and really give it a try. Perhaps the most important single consideration is simply to be receptive to finding pleasure in the intense experience of colors, forms, patterns, sounds, and so on. I have met at least one person, a creative architect, who claims that this is his normal (and very pleasurable) way of looking at the world around him. As noted, many of our experimental subjects found ASF extremely interesting and enjoyable; and this cognitive set has induced something very close to what Maslow calls "peak experiences" for me on several occasions. One might even compare descriptions of certain drug-induced experiences (for example, Huxley, 1956). But ASF requires no external aids, and can enhance Competence as well as the other experiential components in our scheme.

SNP: RAPIDLY SWITCHING YOUR VISUAL FOCUS FROM ONE POINT TO ANOTHER IN THE SCENE AND FORMING A VIVID IMPRESSION OF EACH VIEW.   The idea is to think of your mind as a camera and to view the world around you as a set of photographs taken very quickly. Each photograph should be of a different view or aspect of the scene. Don't linger on any one aspect; simply take a mental photograph of it and then switch to another. The important thing is to form rapid, but very vivid, visual impressions of everything you can in the scene.

Comments.   Although comparatively few of the subjects in the longitudinal experiment chose to use this set, those who did were uniformly enthusiastic about it. They rated it as very interesting, enjoyable, and easy to do. SNP seemed to result in a multitude of clear, vivid, and diverse visual impressions. This set might thus be an easy way to induce an ASF-type experience, since with very rapid shifts of intense visual focus there is simply no time to verbalize or perform other types of relating operations. The evidence does not indicate that all people respond with abstract visual focusing, but my own and others' personal experience suggests that if the shifts are rapid enough and the focus intense enough, this may be a good priming set for ASF and other modes of aesthetic experience. Also, like ASF and most of the other sets under discussion, SNP is easily adapted to apply to any sense modality. You might even try switching back and forth among different senses or intensely attending in more than one modality simultaneously.

EST: SEEING EVERYTHING IN THE SCENE AS PERFECT EXACTLY THE WAY IT IS. The idea is to experience everything in the scene as perfect and unimprovable just as it is.

Comments.   This was not one of the more frequently chosen or highly rated ways of viewing the scenes, perhaps because it tended to strike experimental participants as fraudulent or difficult. Those who did enjoy it, however, tended to speak of an enhanced sense of orderliness (for example, "the clothes on the floor belonged there"). The intent behind this set, however, is to directly induce what Maslow viewed as part of the essence of B-cognition and "B-love": appreciating something just for what it is in itself—in effect, regarding it as perfect and not needing change. EST was meant to achieve this experiential effect directly, but the other sets in this section may at times do the same thing indirectly.

FBN: FINDING BEAUTY IN EVERYTHING YOU NOTICE IN THE SCENE.   The idea is to try to find at least *some* aspect of whatever you notice that you can consider beautiful or pleasant to experience. Even things that you might normally consider ugly or nondescript usually have some detail or sensory quality (color, feel, shape, etc.) that is aesthetically interesting or pleasant. Or some of the things in the scene might be "beautiful" because of meanings or associations attached to them. Or you might look at the scene as if it were a painting or a set of sculptures. Just try to see beauty everywhere you possibly can.

Comments.   As one might guess, most subjects who chose this set found it to be enjoyable and interesting. However, this set is perhaps best employed either as an underlying goal in using such sets as COL or ASF or as a framework for employing other special techniques for actually finding beauty in things around you. For instance, the architect Steen Rasmussen (1962) gives some excellent advice in his book *Experiencing Architecture* for just how to go about finding more beauty in the human-made structures around you (the good ones anyway). A few of his suggestions, for example, are to attend to the softness or hardness of materials, to use *all* of your senses to actively experience architectural structures, to try to see architecture "physiognomically" (for example, to see buildings as soaring upward, straining outward, or as being ominous, kind, and so on), to think of buildings as having been hollowed out of solid blocks, to look for rhythmic patterns in building elements such as window arrays, and to attend to the interaction of texture with patterns of lighting.

As the guidelines are stated, however, FBN clearly can involve perceiving *meaning* and performing other cognitive operations of relating. There are many ways to find pleasure in the experience of one's surroundings. In discussing "topophilia," or one's affective response to an environment, Yi-Fu Tuan (1974) has pointed to such diverse sources of positive environmental affect as pleasant physical contact, visual experience, familiarity, and special meanings such as those involved in patriotism or childhood memories. While not all such sources of pleasant affect would be classified as aesthetic, it would be hard to argue that all experiences of beauty are based purely on seeing things abstractly.

A set such as FBN thus opens the way to shifting across various levels of information processing, sometimes finding beauty through intense concentration, for example, on pure form or sound, and sometimes relying more on the "beauty" of the meanings or associations themselves. In this regard, I might also mention UVL, a cognitive set related to both FBN and EST but which I have not yet explored in research. It consists basically of first assuming that each thing you notice is "one of a kind" and has some unique or special value, and then trying to figure out what that value might be. The pliability, softness, and other qualities of an ordinary towel, for instance, can take on new significance if you for a moment pretend that it is the only such object in existence. Note, however, that even when one concentrates on meanings, an aesthetic mode of experience would require appreciating these meanings as of interest in themselves, not simply as paths to fulfilling practical needs.

FOT: LOOKING FOR VIEWS IN THE SCENE THAT WOULD MAKE INTERESTING OR PERSONALLY MEANINGFUL PHOTOGRAPHS.   The idea is to pretend that you have only a few pictures left to take with a camera and you want to capture the most interesting or personally meaningful images in the scene that you can.

Comments.   Like FBN this is a very open-ended cognitive set. Some people may look for relational meanings, while others may be inclined to concentrate on abstract forms. Both types of responses emerged from our longitudinal subjects, and it is interesting to note that this was one of the most widely chosen and highly rated of the cognitive sets under examination. As hinted earlier, a good pathway to easier abstract sensory focusing may arise if FOT is taken to mean "find views that would make photographs which would be easy and interesting to view abstractly." Indeed, any number of cognitive sets might be generated by simply setting up different criteria to be used in searching out interesting or personally meaningful images. Thus, one might look for especially vivid images to depict pollution, carelessness, cooperation, or whatever, instead of searching only for those high in "beauty." The restriction of being able to select only a *few* pictures, however, seems to be important for generating discrimination and close observation.

Concluding comments. As mentioned with reference to ASF, certain problems might arise from cognitive sets that can make normally ugly or unpleasant things seem beautiful—or perhaps even that render them subjectively neutral. Would, for example, the widespread use of abstract sensory focusing lead people to "stop even minimally noticing environmental problems in favor of soporific basking in the abstract beauty of smog-shrouded slum buildings" (Leff et al., 1974, p. 441)? Abraham Maslow (1968), as noted, has raised similar questions concerning B-cognition in general. He acknowledged that if carried to an extreme, this disinterested, sometimes ecstatic mode of processing environmental information could stultify action, annihilate responsible behavior, cause "undiscriminating acceptance," and lead to "over-aestheticism" and the disregard of values concerned with morality and practicality.

Thus, no matter how pleasant the effects of sets such as ASF, FBN, and FOT might be on the Complexity, Composition, Comprehension, Comparison, and Competence of one's immediate experience, possible effects on Comportment (namely, doing nothing) might rank very low in Compatibility. That is, aesthetic experiences in the wrong context might prove counter to widespread and long-term human happiness and to ecological well-being. Indeed, even cognitive sets that simply reduce stress reactions may be very low in Compatibility if used in certain circumstances. In discussing his work on using denial or intellectualization to "short-circuit" the usual stress produced by watching filmed mutilation, Richard Lazarus (1968) acknowledged that turning off such stress reactions is not necessarily good in all situations. In his words: "Perhaps the capacity to be emotionally aroused or disturbed . . . , as well as the flexibility to turn such reactions off, should be regarded as desirable human qualities" (p. 231). Such considerations would apply *a fortiori* to replacing concern and agitation with aesthetic pleasure when viewing, say, sites of Nazi concentration camps or nuclear explosions.

Agreed, then, there are dangers in overindulgence in the potential pleasures derivable from cognitive sets that can enhance aesthetic experience. There are, nonetheless, several considerations that might allay our concern and also perhaps guide us to avoid the dangers, while still allowing us to reap the not inconsiderable rewards that such sets have to bestow:

1. The problems of overindulgence apply to virtually *any* source of pleasure. Eating, basking in the sun, meditating, engaging in sexual

activity, and even doing meaningful work all help to illustrate the common-sense principle of doing things in *moderation* and when *appropriate*. Basically, the idea is not to sacrifice all other values in the service of one single value.

2. Maslow (1968) reported that the people he selected as self-actualizers (see previous chapter) were indeed good at *both* Being-cognition and deficiency-cognition. That is, these abnormally "healthy" and creative individuals were good at thinking in practical terms and in meeting their various deficiency needs as well as in achieving peak experiences and appreciating things as ends in themselves. Full human development would seem to entail not only a high level of ability in various forms of B- *and* D-cognition but also the sense to know which is most appropriate (highest in Compatibility?) in a given situation.

3. Our evidence (Leff et al., 1974) indicates that sets such as ASF are probably good preparatory sets for imagining how to improve a given environment. Viewing a scene intensely and as of interest for its pure physical form could well alert one to aspects of the scene's content and structure that might otherwise have gone unnoticed. And, as noted earlier, only certain types of environments or objects are capable of producing a high level of aesthetic pleasure when viewed abstractly or with percipience (Osborne, 1970). Indeed, many of our subjects have reported that sets such as ASF, COL, and EST have led them to notice pollution, lack of harmony, and other flaws in the way human beings have shaped many environments.

4. Finally, as my colleagues and I pointed out in our 1974 article (p. 441), "learning to enhance perceptual experience through one's own cognitive processes should stimulate concern with improving all determinants of that experience, both internal and external." By that we meant that becoming adroit in the use of cognitive sets such as those presented in this section can (a) alert people that experiencing their everyday surroundings *can* be enjoyable as an end in itself (see Parmenter, 1968); (b) reveal that some environments are much more enjoyable than others when experienced in this intense, object-focused way (see point 3); (c) facilitate interest in trying out other types of special environmental cognitive sets, some of which may be very effective in increasing awareness of environmental problems and possibilities; and thus, (d) have the overall effect of heightening concern with producing an environment that is truly enjoyable to experience, whatever one's cognitive set.

Deepening Environmental Understanding

The whole area of environmental education is of course concerned with just this goal of expanding and deepening people's insight into what is going on in their surroundings and into human/environment interrelations. (The topic of environmental education per se will be discussed in Chapter 5.) The following cognitive-set guidelines are thus intended primarily as *examples* of mental procedures that can enhance our comprehension of our everyday surroundings and of how we influence and are influenced by those surroundings. Indeed, each of these lists of suggested cognitive sets is probably of most value simply as a spur to thinking up your own new patterns of thought and perception.

Thinking about your surroundings according to the guidelines suggested in this section—or according to similar Plans that you might devise yourself or encounter in environmental education—may be viewed as having at least the following four benefits to offer: (1) to activate knowledge that you have accumulated about environmental and social matters and to incorporate it into your ongoing awareness of your immediate surroundings—in short, to help you experientially relate what you know to what you encounter; (2) to stimulate your curiosity for finding out more about environmental content and processes and about people/environment interrelations; (3) to prepare you for more effectively figuring out changes that would improve the environment and people's interrelations with it (including each other); and (4) to thereby enhance the Comprehension aspect of your experience and to facilitate greater cognitive and overt behavioral competence in dealing with the environment.

Since the "comments" are more limited in this section than in the last, it may prove helpful to read the guidelines presented here with the cognitive set to see how each of these special ways of thinking could indeed facilitate all of the above four goals. As noted earlier, any cognitive set can be executed in a perfunctory way or can be used enthusiastically and creatively as a guide to new, interesting experiences.

IOF: SHIFTING BETWEEN THINKING ABOUT WHAT IS GOING ON INSIDE THE THINGS IN THE SCENE AND JUST NOTICING THEIR OUTSIDE APPEARANCE. The idea is to shift between contemplating what the things in the scene (buildings, various objects, animals, plants, etc.) are like on the *inside* (or what is happening inside them) and just looking at their *outside* features and relations to other things in the vicinity.

Comments. As one of our subjects pointed out, it is also interesting when you are using this set to attend to the relationships between what is going on inside and what happens outside. (IOF, by the way, received the highest average enjoyability rating of the eleven main sets presented in this section.)

COM: FIGURING OUT WHAT THE HUMAN CONSTRUCTIONS AND OTHER HUMAN INFLUENCES IN THE SCENE "COMMUNICATE" TO PEOPLE. The idea is to ask yourself what types of "messages" are being communicated by the human constructions or other human influences in the scene. What types of behavior or feelings are elicited by the specific design or layout of a building, room, façade, street, lawn, or any other human influence in the scene? What "impressions" do you think particular materials, interior designs, window displays, and so on, are intended to create on passers-by or users of places in the scene? What *un*intended messages are being communicated by the human influences around you? How do you think the physical layout and design of things in the scene help to "shape" people's behavior in the scene?

VAL: FIGURING OUT THE VALUES OR GOALS REPRESENTED BY THE HUMAN-MADE OBJECTS AND OTHER HUMAN INFLUENCES IN THE SCENE. The idea is to figure out what values or goals would lead people to construct or influence the scene in the ways that they have.

Comments. This and the preceding cognitive set are similar in that both direct attention to the motives behind human influences on the environment. However, COM is both broader and shallower than VAL: broader because it orients one toward virtually all of the ways that the human-made environment directly influences people's feelings and behavior (see the discussion in Chapter 6); but shallower because COM's emphasis is more on the impact of the environment on immediate behavior and impressions, while VAL involves an attempt to delve into the probable underlying value structure of the people—or the culture—that constructed or otherwise influenced the given environment. COM might thus be viewed as a good preliminary cognitive set to try before attempting VAL (or many of the other sets presented below).

It is also interesting, as our longitudinal subjects demonstrated in their reports, to apply sets such as VAL and COM not only to "other people's" environmental influences but also to the places *you* have had a hand in shaping.

FTN: FIGURING OUT WHAT HUMAN PURPOSES OR NEEDS ARE SATISFIED BY THE VARIOUS THINGS IN THE SCENE.   The idea is to figure out for as many things in the scene as you can just what human desires, needs, purposes, or goals are being met and how they are being met.

COO: FINDING POINTS OF COOPERATION OR CONFLICT IN THE SCENE.   The idea is to think about how the people and other things in the scene may be thought of as helping each other or hindering each other. To take a simple example, a house and its owners in a sense "cooperate" with each other when the owners take care of the house (paint it, put on new roof, etc.) and the house shelters the owners. Or, cars "cooperate" with riders when transporting them to desired locations, but "conflict" with pedestrians. Or, a sewer drain may be regarded as "cooperating" with the street by draining off excess water. See how many types of conflict and cooperation you can find in the scene.

ENE: THINKING OF HOW THE THINGS IN THE SCENE RELATE TO ENERGY.   The idea is to think about how the various things in the scene (animals, plants, people, buildings, vehicles, utensils, etc.) can or do relate to energy (heat, light, electricity, gravity, etc.). Try to figure out ways that each thing in the scene is or could be a *source* of energy, a *user* of energy, a *transmitter* of energy, or a *storer* of energy.

Comment.   Note that the *form* of this guideline for a cognitive set can be readily adapted to generate a virtually unlimited number of ideas for cognitive sets. Just fill in the blank in the phrase "thinking of how the things in the scene relate to —————." Substitutions such as "money," "health," "crime," "natural hazards," "opportunities for children's play," and just about any other noun or noun phrase will do the trick of suggesting a cognitive set. Of course, not all such sets would necessarily have a lot of potential for deepening your environmental understanding; but it is surprising how many probably would. (The next set is itself another example, although it was actually formulated in a much more roundabout manner.)

HES: THINKING OF HOW THE HUMAN-MADE ITEMS AND OTHER HUMAN INFLU-
ENCES IN THE SCENE RELATE TO "NATURE." The idea is to think about how
the various human artifacts and influences in the scene relate to nonhuman aspects of "nature." For example, how do the human constructions and activities in the scene affect various natural cycles, the local
climate, nearby water and air, local plants and animals, and so on (e.g.,
a house may heat up the air around it, provide food for termites, etc.)?
Similarly, how does nature affect the human-made items and the human activities in the scene (e.g., the house may be shaded by a tree,
chilled by the wind, etc.)? Also, think about what natural materials go
into making up the human influences in the scene. Try to notice as many
ways that humans have influenced the scene as you can, and try to figure out as many interrelations with nature as possible.

Comment. It is interesting to compare the rather prosaic examples
mentioned in the above guidelines with the following self-report from
an experimental participant who used this suggested cognitive set in a
creative and rather philosophical manner (the scene in this case was a
mixed-use street bordering the university campus):

> Thought of all the natural laws that applied to man-made things—all
> the laws of physics that applied to the fact that the buildings are stand-
> ing—the basic Buddhist law of impermanence and how all was also de-
> caying—then the natural progression of man which evolved to incorporate
> sciences and higher learning which created all these buildings and the
> hospital—saw the scene in the sense that all that happens and is, is nature.

WLL: SEEING THINGS IN THE SCENE IN TERMS OF THEIR PROBABLE PAST HIS-
TORIES AND PROBABLE FUTURES. The idea is to think of the probable past
and the probable future of the various things in the scene that you notice. For example, as you look at a car you might think of the sources of
the raw materials, the manufacturing processes, the shipment to a
dealer, the sale, the places the car has since gone, its current movement,
and alternative future possibilities for this car. Try to get a feeling for
the "temporal depth" of things around you; try to think of every "thing"
as in fact an "event" taking place and changing over a period of time.

Comments. The basic idea for the above cognitive-set guidelines was
suggested by Buryl Payne (1973) in his book *Getting There Without
Drugs.* His notion was to see every "thing" as in fact a sort of pathway

through a four-dimensional space/time continuum—as a "world line," in his terminology. To extend this way of thinking about yourself, other people, and the rest of the world around you, Payne also suggested seeing things (including all facets of one's environment) in terms of their interrelations as these have occurred and probably will occur over time. I formulated some specific cognitive-set guidelines to get at this idea, although preliminary studies indicated that the set was too difficult for inclusion in the longitudinal experiment. Nonetheless, here is one way to extend thinking of things as "world lines" to thinking in terms of full "world fields":

WFF: SEEING THE SCENE IN TERMS OF INTERRELATIONS AND INTERDEPEND-ENCIES.   The idea is to think of how the diverse items in the scene relate to each other, affect each other, and—in whatever sense—"depend" on each other. To extend this way of looking at the scene, think also about the past histories and probable futures of the various things in the scene; in doing this, consider the vast and complex interrelations of things in the scene with people and things *not* present in the scene. Try to get an intuitive, experiential "feel" for the way diverse things are intertwined over time.

Aside from highlighting philosophical considerations about general interdependence and flux, however, cognitive sets such as WLL and WFF can help us to alert ourselves to the environmental ramifications of our life styles and to our interdependencies with common objects. Such sets can stimulate insight into ecological considerations involving the use (or waste) of natural resources, the sources of pollution, the need to consider future disposal of even beloved objects (for example, cars), and—perhaps most important—the wide range of possibilities or options for the future. Also, as Kevin Lynch (1972) has delightfully illustrated in his book *What Time Is This Place?*, there is intrinsic satisfaction as well as practical gain to be had from simply being tuned in to the temporal depth of one's surroundings. Environments vary in how fully and clearly they communicate the past and the planned part of the future; but the more we attempt to decipher such cues and relate our own historical and futurological knowledge, the more we will be able to pick up what temporal cues the environment provides and the more our Comprehension and Composition will be enhanced.

The cognitive sets discussed thus far in this section have applied primarily to achieving a better objective grasp of what is going on in the environment, including content, structure, and (especially) dynamic properties; but these sets have not called for deliberate evaluation of whether these objects, events, qualities, and interrelations seem good or bad. Even in using such sets as VAL (figuring out the values that would lead people to influence the environment as they have), the primary objective was simply to gain greater insight, not necessarily to make any value judgments yourself. The next two cognitive sets do encourage such judgments, but it may be a good idea to view a scene while using some (or all) of the preceding types of sets before making any deliberate evaluations.

NBG: NOTICING SOCIAL, ENVIRONMENTAL, AND AESTHETIC ASPECTS˙ OF THE SCENE THAT SEEM ESPECIALLY BAD AND THAT SEEM ESPECIALLY GOOD.   The idea is to pick out whatever social, environmental, and aesthetic "problems" you can find in the scene, and also to pick out whatever social, environmental, and aesthetic "strong points" you can find in the scene. (Try to figure out as many problems and as many strong points as possible.)

Comment.   As hinted by the parenthetical statement, this cognitive set can be treated as a kind of mental game, much like the set induced by puzzle pictures that are supposed to contain hidden figures. In the case of NBG, then, you might try thinking of a scene as containing a number of hidden (nonobvious) social, environmental, and aesthetic bad aspects and good aspects (according to your own personal standards of bad and good): your job, should you decide to accept it, is to find as *many* of them as possible.

EHW: FIGURING OUT HOW THE THINGS AND ACTIVITIES IN THE SCENE AFFECT HUMAN WELL-BEING.   The idea is to think of how the various things and activities you notice in the scene affect human well-being or happiness (both in the short run *and* in the long run). Key considerations might be whether each thing or activity has a positive or a negative effect on health, safety, recreation, convenience, and so on. In short, try to figure out the present and future effects on anything you deem important for people's well-being.

Comments. In contrast to the previous set, NBG, according to which you are simply to look out for things that strike you as especially good or especially bad, this set starts from the other end and involves actively figuring out the effects on human well-being of the various things and activities in the scene. Of course, EHW could thus serve as almost an algorithm (foolproof problem-solving technique) for actually finding the good and the bad aspects of the scene—provided you could examine everything in or going on in the scene. In fact, though, this set does involve a more searching, analytical, and future-projective orientation than does NBG. In addition, as indicated by the directive to consider general human well-being and by the specific examples of criteria, EHW is meant to entail a concern with determining the degree of Compatibility evidenced by an environment. (See Chapters 6 and 7 for detailed discussions of how Compatibility applies to physical/social environments.)

TEC: THINKING OF HOW YOU DO OR MIGHT AFFECT THIS SCENE OR WHAT HAPPENS IN IT, AND THINKING OF HOW THIS SCENE OR WHAT HAPPENS IN IT DOES OR MIGHT AFFECT YOU. The idea is to try to think of all the ways—even very small ways—in which you affect or are affected by the scene or events in it. Consider how your life actually affects the scene now (e.g., what are the effects of just being there or walking through it? do you ever take *anything* from the scene or leave *anything* there? do *any* of the things you do outside this scene have *any* effects inside the scene?). Also think about how things that you probably *will* do in the course of your life could affect this scene (again, even in very small ways as well as larger ones). Similarly, consider how the scene or things and events in it do or might affect *you*—whether in small or large ways. In short, try to get a feeling for *all* ties that now exist or might come to exist between you and this scene.

Comments. In the introduction to this section on deepening environmental awareness, four main goals were mentioned for the set guidelines. Included were incorporating environmental and social knowledge into your immediate experience of your surroundings, stimulating your environmental curiosity, preparing you to figure out improvements in environments and people/environment relations, and thereby enhancing the Comprehension and Competence aspects of your environmental experience. While each of the other cognitive sets considered in this section has indeed been proposed for the purpose of contributing to these goals, this concluding one, TEC, most directly addresses the issue of your own personal involvement with your surroundings. Thus, if you are tireless and devoted enough to engage in the thoroughgoing environmental analysis suggested by the other sets, TEC would seem a good way to try to tie it all together, make it personally relevant, and maybe even stimulate yourself to take action. But wait! If you are *that* tireless and devoted, you should certainly continue on through at least the remaining two groups of sets in order to be as creative, imaginative, and ecologically conscious as possible in choosing your goals and your actions.

Using and Boosting Creativity

The cognitive sets outlined in this section are not really intended in themselves to be especially effective for improving your choice of environmental actions. But they should help limber up your thinking and perhaps put you in the appropriately playful frame of mind for using the somewhat more serious environmental cognitive sets presented in the next section. An additional, extended list of techniques for being more creative is also presented there.

Before turning to these creativity sets—which the longitudinal subjects, incidentally, generally reported to be a lot of fun—let us first briefly consider the general nature of what it means to be creative. The following four overlapping characteristics may not be exhaustive, but they do seem to capture much of the flavor of what is usually meant by "creativity" both in everyday language and in much of the academic literature:[28]

1. Coming up with *unusual* (and good) ideas—this is what seems to be meant by being "original" or "innovative"

2. Having high *fluency* of ideas—that is, being able to generate and express a large number of ideas (especially if most of them are unusual and good)

3. Being very *flexible* in one's thinking—that is, having the ability and inclination to take many different points of view when considering an issue or problem, to shift one's focus easily, to think in a variety of verbal and nonverbal modes, to be open to unlikely possibilities and unusual approaches, and so forth

4. Making unusual *connections* between normally disparate ideas or frames of reference; coming up with unusual (but good) *combinations* or syntheses. (This point deserves a special comment since it forms the heart of Arthur Koestler's (1964) impressive theory of creativity. Koestler's central idea is that creativity—whether in humor, science, or art—derives from mental acts of "bisociation." This he defined as "the perceiving of a situation or idea . . . in two self-consistent but habitually incompatible frames of reference" (p. 35). Puns and metaphors provide examples of bisociation in the use of language: a word or phrase is simultaneously interpreted in two normally incompatible frames of reference. One of Koestler's examples in the realm of technological invention is the printing press, which he argued was derived from bisociating the frames of reference or "associative contexts" relating to wine presses and relating to document seals. Examples of cognitive sets that may facilitate such bisociative thinking will be offered both in this section and in the special creativity techniques presented in the next section.)

Critics of our culture concerned with creativity have often leveled the charge that our society, through its educational and value systems, discourages the full flowering of most people's creative potential. Michael Wallach (1971), for instance, in his account of the "intelligence/creativity controversy" chided modern technological societies for disproportionately stressing such "intelligence" skills as analyzing, organizing, and abstracting, while giving short shrift to creativity-enhancing skills such as synthesizing, fantasizing (and otherwise using one's imagination), and increasing one's "ideational fluency." Similarly, Paul Torrance (for example, 1971; Torrance and Myers, 1970) has spent an active career trying to find ways to increase creativity in the classroom. It is sad that empirical evidence in fact supports the common criticism that creativity tends to be downplayed and undervalued in common educational practice (see, for example, Stein, 1974). Indeed, as will be discussed in the next chapter, there is evidence that in our society at large, people tend to rank personal traits pertaining to rationality and creativity as less important than many other types of personal characteristics (Rokeach, 1973).

So, as in the case of encouraging greater aesthetic appreciation and sensitivity, it is easy to encounter cultural blocks in the area of facilitating creativity. Nonetheless, the following cognitive-set guidelines—designed to help boost or at least activate creative ways of experiencing one's surroundings—have so far been fairly successful, judging by the responses of many of our subjects. Most of these cognitive sets seem at least enjoyable and interesting; presumably they readily have direct positive effects on Complexity and Composition, and perhaps on Comprehension and Competence as well. Also, when asked to generate new cognitive sets on their own, people in my experiments and classes have tended to be most creative in coming up with original sets similar to the ones in this section (as opposed to sets similar to those in the other sections). I urge you to give it a try yourself right after reading over the following guidelines.

IWX: IDENTIFYING WITH (IMAGINING THAT YOU ARE) THE OBJECTS IN THE SCENE.   The idea is to try to feel that you *are* each thing that you notice in your surroundings. As you look at a tree or a house or a truck, imagine that you are that tree or house or truck. Think of how it might feel to be each thing you notice. (If possible, also try to imagine that you are the *whole scene.*)

Comments.   The act of "empathic identification" with nonhuman or even nonliving things appears to be a potent device for stimulating more creative ways of thinking. Paul Torrance (1971) has used this as a mental exercise for creativity education, and the developers of the powerful group creativity procedure called "synectics," William Gordon (1961, 1973) and George Prince (1970), have found that this type of cognitive set—which they call "personal analogy"—is a useful device for facilitating creative group problem solving. Gordon (1973), however, has pointed out that there are degrees of such mental identification, ranging from superficial role playing to full kinesthetic and emotional identification. A person operating at a superficial level might only think of the immediate facts of the object's situation (for example, "as a rock, I rest flat on the ground and am hard and solid," or, "if I were that tree, I would be very tall and sway in the wind"). Gordon has argued that only full empathic identification with an object, both emotionally and kinesthetically, helps boost creativity. The following selections from one experimental subject's report of using IWX come close to illustrating this higher-level type of identification:

> I am the third tree in the row. . . . Sometimes I get really thirsty and the rain tastes good. . . . some kid came by and tugged at one of my

branches and ripped off some of my leaves. Well, it hurt. . . . I am a piece of dirt. Everyday, all day I get walked on. . . . It's really no fun being dirt. All that ever happens is, I get ground in. Occasionally I get picked up on a sneaker or something but those times are few and far between. . . . This is the whole scene speaking. These two specimens speak as though they get abused all the time. Well, maybe the dirt does, but usually people are pretty good to me overall. Sometimes the trees or dirt complain to me (I am the actual brain of the scene) but I never hear the grass complain and they would certainly have cause to. . . .

The following two cognitive sets also call for the use of empathic identification, and at times may be even better than deliberate IWX for stimulating this way of thinking. (Note, however, that the set to *identify* with objects or especially with whole scenes may, over time, be a good way to stimulate a feeling of kinship with your surroundings. This is important for ecological consciousness as well as for creativity per se.)

ALV: SEEING EVERYTHING AROUND YOU AS IF IT WERE ALIVE.   The idea is to see every object in your surroundings as if it were a living creature that is aware of what is going on around it and has feelings. As you wish, you may either imagine that these "creatures" are able to move about anytime they feel like it or you may think of "sedentary" objects (such as buildings) as creatures that exist on a very slow time scale (so that their "movements" would be as imperceptible as those of a clock's hour hand).

Comments.   This cognitive set has received the highest overall ratings for combined enjoyability and interestingness of any cognitive set I have studied empirically (including nearly all the sets in this chapter). All experimental participants who have used it thus far have liked it. When I first formulated the above guidelines, however, I did not anticipate such popularity for this set. In fact, I thought that many people would find this way of viewing things to be disturbing or even frightening. After all, animate beings need to *eat*, and a living creature as big as a house or a cloud might find *us* to be tasty tidbits. Also, might it not be disconcerting to think of the sidewalk or your armchair as alive and possibly scheming? Clearly, this set seemed to suggest a science-fiction nightmare. But experimental participants who chose to give ALV a try took a very different, and much more playful, approach. I find their way of seeing things as alive much more fun and creative than the way I originally had in mind. Let me illustrate with a few quotations from different subjects' reports (based on different outdoor locations):

> When I did this, I imagined what the objects might say if they were alive. Cook [a big university science building] was a deep baritone. The library would be very intelligent sounding. . . . The lights were speed freaks buzzing away. The grass and roadways were musical.

> There is a lot of wind today so things are moving. Like the telephone wires are jiggling around, they seem to be nervous. . . . The trees are writhing with rage. The road is dependable. It would rather get up and walk away but it is aware of its duty.

> . . . The sidewalks would be a type of creature capable of carrying you wherever you'd like to go. The houses would be a relatively stable creature and people would be parasites to them. Cars would be mean creatures—always running around trying to go faster . . .

> I could imagine the trees getting up and tiptoeing across the street on their roots. Also I could see them weeping if someone hit them, or when their leaves fall off. The houses are different. They can't move but they see everything that goes on. Their windows are eyes and their doors are mouths, but they can't say anything; they can only see.

More than most of the other sets we have so far considered, ALV involves imaginational transformations of environmental information. Indeed, this set can perhaps serve as a model for generating many other entertaining (and creativity-enhancing) ways of viewing environments. All you need do is think of types of imaginable transformations of what environmental objects are or are composed of. Here are some examples suggested by students who were asked to devise new cognitive sets similar to the ones in this section:

Viewing all things as edible.

Thinking of all objects as changed drastically in weight.

Looking at everything as if it were a transportation device.

Seeing everything as if it had a personality. (This is perhaps a better statement of the way most people have actually interpreted the ALV guidelines.)

Viewing everything as artificial. (This reversal of ALV was devised by a student who taught nature study. He found it to be a provocative set for awakening people's appreciation of organic complexity, leading to such musings as, "I wonder how they ever got an engine small enough to power that thing that looks like a mosquito.")

WRT: SEEING THE SCENE AS SOME REALLY DIFFERENT BEING OR CREATURE WOULD. The idea is to let your imagination go and see the scene as if you were a particular type of animal (cat, caterpillar, walking fish, etc.), inanimate object suddenly come to life, creature from another world with very different senses, or any other wild thing you can think of.

Comments. Unlike IWX, in which you identify with the various things *in* the scene, the point here is to identify with one type of creature or thing (not necessarily present in the scene) and then look at everything as you think that being would. Again, this proved to be interesting and enjoyable for most of the subjects who tried it. Perhaps the following excerpts from different reports will show why and also illustrate WRT's potential for stimulating playful and creative environmental experience.

> I'm a dead, tired, old sneaker and I hate this scene. Too much concrete. It wears out my sole. The cracks and upheaves in the sidewalk are terrible, I'm constantly bumping my nose. My poor nose is getting all worn and raw. The playground is hell. I'm getting jumped on, pushed off, and scraped on every side. Sometimes I go on the grass, but that's getting worn thin too. The uphill climb and steps means that I'm always getting bent and squished up in the middle. Ick. [This seems an excellent example of full empathic identification, by the way.]

> As another creature I became something from another planet. I imagined that the cars were the living part and didn't even notice the people. The cars became everything in the scene; the lights told the cars what to do and the cars made all the decisions. Once in a while the cars would eat a person. I wondered if the cars would be afraid of me if they noticed me. I wondered why they all just seemed to be so busy without really serving any purpose.

> I viewed the scene as a dog might have. . . . I got sort of frightened—all the cars, etc. Really scary and dangerous. Smelt some strange odor running by—must be gas. Oh—an interesting mate stands across the street with his master . . . there's plenty of things on which I could relieve myself—posts, etc. Oh yum—someone dropped some pieces of popcorn . . .

> I am an ant . . . it was hard for me to notice the stores, etc. What I mainly saw was dirty sidewalks with large obstructions (pieces of chewing gum) on them. I saw a lot of different types of shoes walk by—some were nice, others not so nice because they almost trampled me.

To quote from another "ant":

> . . . then from the cars (I still don't know if they're alive) come these funny sounds. It's sort of like the sounds humans make when they blow their nose, only a lot louder. I suppose it's the car blowing its nose . . . [This may be seen as a "bisociation" of the frames of reference applying to car exhausts and to human exhausts.]

It should also be clear from these varied examples that WRT is not a specific cognitive set but rather a *family* of different cognitive sets. The specific type of creature or thing chosen for your excursion in "wild role taking" determines the exact set used. Indeed, as suggested for the next set, it might be interesting to try several versions (wild roles) with a single scene.

SVL: SEEING THE SCENE AS IF YOU HELD DIFFERENT VALUE SYSTEMS. The idea is to think of different value systems and to view the scene "through" each one. For example, how would you look at this scene if money were the only thing that really mattered to you, or if beauty were the most important thing in your life? You might also try formulating more complex value systems, and be sure to view the scene (in succession) according to several different and incompatible value orientations.

Comment. Obviously, this is also a family of sets, or what we might call a "set-generating set." You might find it especially interesting to try SVL or some variation of it after reading the next chapter, which explores specific aspects of current and possible value systems that have special environmental relevance.

USE: FIGURING OUT NEW USES FOR THE THINGS IN THE SCENE. The idea is to imagine possible alternative uses for the things around you. For example, a door may also be used to circulate air, a road can be used as a tennis court, a car as a playhouse for children. Try to think of as many alternative uses as possible for each thing you notice.

Comments. This set is based on a commonly used creativity test in which scores are based on the number of unusual uses an individual can think up for a common object, such as a brick.[29] The set guidelines for

USE of course encourage you to consider as many objects as possible and to think up many alternative uses for each of them (or for the scene as a whole for that matter, but that would get us into the next section of sets). I might also note that in a recent seminar on creative thinking, my students vividly demonstrated that thinking up alternative uses is much more fun when done in small cooperative groups than when attempted alone. Although this point has not yet been explored in systematic research, many types of cognitive sets may be more enjoyable when shared with other people.

LIN: SEEING RANDOM PAIRS OF OBJECTS AS FORMING A SINGLE FUNCTIONAL UNIT.   The idea is to pick pairs of objects in the scene and to figure out some real or imaginary way in which these objects might be functionally related to each other. For example, you might pick a car and a telephone pole and think of the pole as providing a marker for a parking space or for the side of the road or as providing a tiny line of shade for the car's steering wheel on a hot day. Another example might be linking a cloud and a puddle by seeing the puddle as a "work of art" whose purpose is to reflect the image of the cloud.

Comment.   Although a rather difficult set to execute, LIN has the potential to facilitate bisociations and other types of creative combinations.

SIM: SEEING THINGS IN THE SCENE AS IF THEY WERE SOMETHING ELSE.   The idea is to see objects as if they were something else that they remind you of, perhaps transformed in scale. For example, from an airplane you might see a lake as a piece of a giant jigsaw puzzle, or on the ground you might see a street lamp as a big coatrack or telephone wires as parts of a spider web.

Comments.   Unlike the others, this set was not included as an option for subjects in the longitudinal study. The above guidelines are based on a set suggested by Ross Parmenter (1968), who also supplied the example of seeing lakes as puzzle pieces. As Parmenter presented the idea, it seems best simply to let the similes hit you rather than trying to force them. It is certainly more fun that way, but it may be difficult for many people to think of such visual similes without some practice. However, this whole way of thinking metaphorically may have some very important implications for boosting creativity, in addition to just being fun. William Gordon (1973), for instance, has persuasively argued that metaphorical thinking is the key to creativity. Instead of waiting for similes, analogies, or metaphors to hit you, however, he suggests techniques such as deliberately asking how two subject areas can be related. (For instance, what geological phenomena are like social revolutions?) The general idea behind SIM can easily be extended to this sort of deliberate "force fitting" of one frame of reference with another, which should of course also bring to mind Koestler's notion of bisociation.

Also, I should not leave the topic of metaphorical thinking without at least mentioning Gaston Bachelard's (1964) fascinating work on "the poetics of space." He points out, for instance, how the cellar can be considered the "dark entity" (id?) of the house, and he noted how he could lull himself to sleep amid the noise of Paris by thinking of the city as a "clamorous sea." Perhaps a set suggested by one of our research participants both captures the spirit of Bachelard's approach and offers an intriguing extension of SIM: the set to think of poetic imagery to express what you perceive in your surroundings.

QSN: THINKING OF QUESTIONS ABOUT THE SCENE OR THINGS IN IT.   The idea is to deliberately formulate questions that you would genuinely be interested in knowing the answers to. You might also try taking a guess at what the answers are, but the main point here is just to think of as many interesting questions about the scene as you can.

Comments.   My original interest in this type of set arose in the context of trying to find cognitive sets that would enhance interest in academic subject matter. A preliminary experiment did in fact indicate (although not quite significantly) that what seem to be two of the main cognitive sets induced by traditional educational procedures—namely, the student set to remember content and the teacher set to evaluate people's performance—were inferior to other cognitive sets in their ability to arouse interest in the topic of a group discussion. One of these others was the set to think of questions suggested by the discussion. I do not wish to make any claims for the conclusiveness or generalizability of that research result. However, it does seem a plausible hypothesis that thinking of questions suggested by one's surroundings could stimulate curiosity and the relating of environmental information to one's own interests. It could also facilitate "lateral thinking" (de Bono, 1970) in one's encounters with a specific environment. (The basic idea of lateral thinking is to try many different approaches rather than just one "vertical" line of thought. Thus, one point of QSN is to think of a number of diverse questions.) In addition, QSN can quickly suggest many new sets; all you need do is try to answer the questions you formulate.[30]

Here are some questions from a single experimental subject at a residential scene:

> Why are the houses so close? Why aren't there more trees and shrubs? Why is there so much traffic? Where does this road go? What is the income of the people that live here? Why do some people take such good care of their houses and why do others neglect them so? What type of people live here? Why can't people park their cars in their driveways? What would happen if there was a big fire in the area? Where are all the people today? What would happen if this area turned commercial?

NNA: NOTICING THINGS YOU WOULD NOT NORMALLY BE AWARE OF. The idea is to focus on whatever aspects of the scene you would not normally notice.

Comments.   This set is also intended to facilitate lateral thinking. Making an effort to notice things you would normally overlook can obviously help rechannel your thinking in diverse ways and provide new entry points for operations of relating. This might prove helpful—as indeed might all of the sets in this section—as preparation for more creatively imagining improvements in your surroundings, the topic of the next section.

In closing, here are the reported NNA experiences of two experimental participants:

> First started to look at the tops of the buildings . . . found them to be pretty interesting . . . noticed the pointed objects and really got off on them . . . found the tops of the buildings, in many cases, more interesting than the rest . . . then I noticed the curb . . . was very battered and weathered . . . also noticed how the telephone poles and wires reminded me of a nerve system branching out to all the houses. [Complete transcript; ellipses in the original.]

> The vast amount of different types of cars. What is going on in the rooms above the stores. The variety of noises. Different markings on the road. Time left on parking meters. The amount of old people compared to young. What people are talking about. License plates on cars. The amount of taxis driving by.

Increasing Awareness of Problems and Possibilities

All of the environmental cognitive sets previously discussed are intended to be interesting and valuable in their own right; but from the perspective of improving actual physical/social environments, they can be regarded mainly as preparation for the kind of mental activity discussed in this section. Here our focus shifts from Plans for promoting new kinds of environmental experience per se to Plans for figuring out how to *change* our surroundings. Indeed, it is surprising and a bit disconcerting that so little psychological research has thus far been concerned with understanding or improving how people go about imagining changes in their environments.[31] Because our early research indicated that imagining environmental improvements was both enjoyable and useful in alerting people to environmental problems and possibilities, my colleague Lawrence Gordon and I have concentrated our efforts on exploring this type of cognitive set further. The following guidelines, together with the preceding ones, are intended as an example of a program of cognitive sets that, if made use of, might gradually help people become more insightfully and creatively oriented toward enhancing their surroundings.

IMG: IMAGINING CHANGES IN THE SCENE THAT WOULD MAKE IT A MORE PLEASANT PLACE.   The idea is to imagine as *vividly as you can* what changes you would like made in this environment in order to make it more pleasant. These changes should all be things that could conceivably be brought about by human endeavor, but the changes may be as sweeping and "impractical" as you like. Be sure to form a clear mental image of what the changed scene would be, and feel free to imagine various alternative sets of changes that would make the scene more pleasant.

Comments.   This is the basic or core set for all the sets to follow. The guidelines above are a slightly modified version of the IMG set reported in Leff et al. (1974). That research included a series of ten experiments involving IMG. To quote from the synopsis of that report, my colleagues and I found that imagining improvements in a scene "decreases the judged pleasantness of the actual scene; increases both awareness of environmental problems and the individual's sense of perceptual control; is relatively easy, enjoyable, and interesting (both absolutely and compared to 'normal' viewing); and is more effectively, easily, and enjoyably activated when occurring later in a series of different cognitive sets than when occurring earlier." Furthermore, we found strong evidence that "the more intensely this cognitive set is engaged, the more enjoyable and interesting it seems to be."

Our more recent research casts some doubt on whether IMG is easy for people to use and also on whether it is especially effective for increasing people's sense of perceptual control. It now appears as well that people may tend to get tired of imagining environmental changes—at least when they are "forced" to imagine changes repeatedly as part of a longitudinal experiment. However, participants in our recent research have shown a continued tendency to find IMG at least initially enjoyable and interesting. More important, in a follow-up study several months after the main longitudinal experiment, over 60 percent of the subjects who had had extended practice in using IMG reported using it on their own as a result of their earlier experimental participation. Furthermore, over 25 percent of the follow-up subjects who had had only one or two earlier experimental exposures to IMG also reported using it on their own as a result of their prior participation.[32]

Given that at least under some circumstances IMG constitutes an enjoyable and interesting way of thinking about one's surroundings, it is interesting to analyze this set in terms of the integrative scheme presented at the end of the first part of this chapter. As noted, one purpose of that eight-component scheme is to account for links between cognitive sets and the affective quality of experience. Very briefly, IMG's enjoyability and interestingness may derive from the following effects on the five main experiential components: (1) enhanced Complexity arising from the intricacy of the mental operations themselves (including virtually all of those discussed under "relating" in Part One) and from the novelty or complexity of the imagined environmental changes; (2) positive effects on Composition produced by envisioning pleasant scenes (but note that IMG tends to increase awareness of faults in the actual scene); (3) enhancement of Comprehension deriving from increased awareness of environmental problems and possibilities; (4) increased Competence based both on feelings of creativity in generating the images of changes and possibly on heightened feelings of perceptual and affective control; and (5) positive impact on Comparison by provision of imagined outcomes well above one's CL for environments (although this may of course raise one's CL, leading to further dissatisfaction with the actual scene).

Although our subjects' anecdotal reports have tended to bear out these speculations (and in fact led to some of them), there are obviously some potential problems. As noted already, using IMG will tend to lead you to judge the actual scene as less pleasant, thus inducing seemingly negative effects on both Composition and Comparison. (With respect to long-term Comportment and Compatibility, however, such effects might actually be positive.) Perhaps most important, if you cannot think of a way to *achieve* the imagined changes, IMG can lead to frustration and even to decreased feelings of competence. Furthermore, our recent evidence indicates that IMG and related sets are more difficult (produce a higher level of Complications) than our initial research had indicated. And finally, if taken in their simple form, the IMG guidelines could encourage people to imagine—and to try to achieve—all sorts of ecologically harmful (but personally pleasant) environmental changes. As we shall see, the later sets in this section, while perhaps still high in Complications, are designed to direct one's attention in ways that can help avoid potential negative effects on Competence, Comportment, and Compatibility.

Nonetheless, IMG, even in its simple form, has in general been relatively popular with our experimental participants. Their tendency to use it after an experiment certainly points to this conclusion, as do most of the initial enjoyability and interestingness ratings of this set. The possible environmental significance of the popularity of IMG is underscored by the following two considerations: (1) In our earlier research (Leff et al., 1974), subjects reported that their awareness of environmental problems was raised by two other cognitive sets as well as by IMG. These two other sets were earlier versions of VAL (the set to figure out the values represented by human-made environmental influences) and NBG (EVL: the set to evaluate whether the human influences in the scene were pleasant or unpleasant). However, of the three sets, only IMG was rated as both more enjoyable and more interesting than normal viewing. Since noticing environmental problems presumably tends to make environments seem less pleasant, it is especially significant that any set that achieves this effect can *itself* be enjoyable. (2) In the earlier research, our only evidence that IMG actually did increase awareness of environmental problems was first of all that subjects reported that it did, and also that scenes were rated as less pleasant after being viewed under IMG than after being viewed normally. Our later experiments have clearly shown that subjects actually remember more negative human influences on a scene after viewing it with the IMG set than after viewing it normally. In addition, ratings of subjects' reports of what they were thinking about while observing a scene indicate substantially more mentions of human-made environmental problems under IMG than under normal viewing.

But sets such as IMG are important for more than merely providing a pleasant experience while alerting us to environmental problems. Cognitive sets to imagine changes in our surroundings are perhaps most valuable as ways of generating ideas (and actions) for improving the environment. To facilitate increased creativity (and enjoyment) in using *any* IMG-type set, the following list of "techniques for being more creative" was formulated.[33] This list can of course be supplemented by the cognitive-set guidelines in the previous section, and, like those guidelines, is intended to promote the four characteristics of creativity mentioned at the beginning of that section.

TECHNIQUES FOR BEING MORE CREATIVE

1. Think of the things that help you to be creative.
   For example, many people find that their creativity is boosted by
   being playful
   relaxing
   being confident
   trying to be absurd
   feeling independent
   not straining
   not worrying about criticism
   nonverbal thinking
   becoming immersed in the problem
   thinking up lots of different ideas ("solutions")
   looking at the problem from different points of view . . .
   What other things can you think of that have been especially helpful to *your* creativity?
2. Break your usual assumptions!
   Try to think of *unusual* things.
   For example, in imagining how to improve a scene, you might think of unusual locations for buildings or activities, come up with un-

usual shapes for things, figure out ways to use materials in new ways (paper or water as a building material, for example). Also try to recognize your assumptions and be ready to break them. (Do floors really *have* to be flat? Do homes and businesses *have* to be in separate buildings?)

3. Ask yourself lots of "What if . . . ?" questions and follow through on figuring out potential implications.

For example, "What if all the houses were built on stilts?"

"What if everybody had the same amount of wealth?"

"What if the population were one tenth what it is?"

Think of the implications of such questions and try to use these implications to generate new ideas for change.

4. Try to think of unusual combinations of things.

Take any two things at random and try to think of something that would in some sense "combine" them. A car and a house might make you think of a trailer. A suitcase and a door could yield a new idea for a "portable door." A lamp and a sidewalk might combine to form a luminous walkway.

5. Think of how different types of people might imagine improving the scene.

Some examples: geologist, chemist, sociologist, city planner, architect, lawyer, doctor, historian, biologist, economist, land developer, painter, sculptor, criminal, blind person, little child, slightly older child, garbage collector, out-of-town visitor . . .

(To be a bit wilder, you might imagine how a dog, a tree, or even the wind would probably imagine pleasant changes.) The idea is to "get outside of yourself," to think from other perspectives.

6. Try to form especially vivid images of the changes. Make these images as detailed as you can. Be flexible and manipulate *images* in your mind in addition to thinking in words.

Also, use all of your senses for figuring out and imagining changes. What types of changes in sounds, smells, and touch sensations would improve the scene?

7. Think of analogous situations: What are some similar types of scenes that are more pleasant than this one? (E.g., if you're at a shopping center, try to think of a nicer shopping place you once visited.) Or analyze the scene into functional or physical components and try

to think of more pleasant examples of each type of component (e.g., a more pleasant place where goods are exchanged, a more pleasant type of place to walk).

One especially good analogy technique is to think of situations in nature that are similar to the design problem. For example, new ideas for house design might be generated by thinking of how various animals shelter themselves.

8. Alternate between analyzing what's "wrong" with the scene (and how to solve these *problems*), and analyzing what human purposes are served in the scene. Figuring out how to improve meeting these *underlying purposes* may help you imagine changes even in scenes that at first may seem unimprovable.

For example, a beautiful residential neighborhood may have no obvious "problems," but you may be able to think of even better ways to satisfy human needs (purposes) such as recreation, getting together with friends, transportation, and so on.

9. Try to imagine more than one set of improvements in the scene.
The first attempts may help clear out cliché changes (e.g., "tear everything down and put in grass and trees"), and later images may thus be more creative and original. However, rather than criticizing your early images, try to build on them—look for what is positive and useful for forming more pleasing and creative changes. Try to think of as *many* improvements as you can.

10. Try to think of ways that improve both how the scene looks and how well the scene meets human needs (i.e., consider *both* aesthetic and "practical" aspects).

11. Break the problem into smaller problems.
If you find it hard to think of changes for the whole scene, try focusing on one part at a time. How could you make one part of the scene serve multiple functions? How could you improve the transportation system in the scene? What human activities would you like to see added to the scene? And so on.

12. Imagine you could make absolutely any type of change you wanted in the scene (even changes that would not appear to be humanly feasible, such as changing the season or moving the whole scene to a mountaintop or another planet). Then figure out what *specific aspects* of such changes appeal to you (e.g., colorfulness, beautiful views, friendliness of people, or whatever). Finally, try to figure

out ways that the scene actually could be changed to make it *more like* your initial wilder image.

The idea here is to let your imagination go and think of places or times you like most; then use this as a *guide* for imagining specific, humanly possible changes. As an example, you might wish the season were changed from winter to summer. What exactly is it you like about summer? How could some of these *elements* be added to the scene even in winter?

13. Examine your own personal criteria ("values") of most importance for improving the scene. Really think about, examine, and question these criteria or values; make sure they are really important to you. Then deliberately apply them one at a time (and all together at the end) in imagining how you would like to see the scene improved.

14. Now think about alternative sets of criteria (guiding values) for imagining changes. Especially consider what types of changes *people who live or work in the scene* (or who own parts of the scene) would consider pleasant. Compare these changes with those *outsiders* (perhaps including *you*) would consider pleasant changes. After thinking about this, can you think of any *basic* values common to all or most people that could be used to guide imagined changes that would be pleasant to virtually all the people affected by the scene? Vividly imagine changes guided by these values.

15. What is the total *range* of changes you can imagine—*from the most to the least feasible; the most pleasant to the most unpleasant?*

Summary of Creativity Techniques:
1. Think of things that help you be creative.
2. Break your assumptions; think of *unusual* things.
3. Ask "What if . . . ?"
4. Think of unusual combinations.
5. Take on different roles; imagine how other people would think.
6. Think in vivid nonverbal images; use all your senses.
7. Think of analogous problems and solutions; use nature as a source.
8. Imagine improvements via problems *and* purposes.
9. Imagine lots of different types of changes.
10. Consider *both* aesthetics and "practical" needs.
11. Break the problem into subproblems.

12. Use your wildest images as a guide for feasible changes; work backwards from "ideal" to "feasible" changes.
13. Examine your personal criteria (values) for positive change.
14. Consider alternative criteria and try to find "universal" values.
15. What ranges of changes can you imagine?

Comments. In two separate experiments, randomly chosen subjects were asked to use these creativity techniques while imagining environmental changes according to the IMG guidelines previously presented. In each experiment, and across a variety of actual environments, the imagined changes reported by subjects given the creativity techniques were rated as of significantly higher quality than imagined changes reported by subjects who had only the IMG guidelines.[34] The creativity techniques seemed not only to provoke more ideas for change, but also to help free people from focusing just on correcting what they perceived as problems with a scene. People using the creativity techniques appeared much more likely than other IMG subjects to think in terms of *positive possibilities*, not mere amelioration. Thus, these techniques may be especially helpful for imagining how to improve environments that have few apparent problems. (With minor alterations, the techniques should also prove applicable to virtually any type of mental designing, such as imagining better social institutions, play activities, or even cognitive sets.)

No subjects were supplied with our raters' specific criteria for judging the quality of imagined changes. However, taking these criteria into account when using IMG-type cognitive sets might supplement the actual creativity techniques. Indeed, Donald Johnson (1972) has presented a strong case that creativity is greatly helped by a clear understanding of the criteria that will be used to evaluate one's ideas or solutions. Nonetheless, psychological research usually avoids revealing such criteria to minimize "biasing" of subjects' responses. Here are the criteria that were used by our raters in judging the quality of IMG performance: (1) *Creativity:* originality, innovativeness, unusualness. (2) *Ecological sophistication:* showing attention to ecological interrelations and implications; attention to ramifications and prerequisites for changes. (3) *Complexity, Detail, and Sweepingness:* complexity, detail, and sweepingness (amount of scene changed and radicalness of the change) in the reported imagined changes. (4) *Other indicators of high quality:* suggested changes that increase efficiency, involve multiple uses of the same spaces or constructions, improve both aesthetics and the functional aspects of the scene, give people more collective control over their environments, reflect potentials provided by the surrounding environment, or take account of existing needs met by the scene or that would have to be met in the changed scene.

The guidelines for various IMG-type cognitive sets presented below, together with the creativity techniques (and, indeed, all the other sets discussed in this chapter), are collectively meant to provoke high-quality imagined environmental changes as defined by the above criteria. The difficulty level of these cognitive sets tends to build, culminating in IMG-E, the most complex cognitive set I have attempted to study experimentally and one that actually incorporates many of the others. Again, though, it should be kept in mind that gaining facility with new cognitive sets is a kind of skill acquisition. What seems difficult, even impossible, at first, may become almost second nature when practiced by easy stages. All of this chapter's cognitive-set guidelines and aids to creativity (most of which are themselves simply other cognitive sets) are thus intended to be cumulative and mutually reinforcing.

IMG-V: IMAGINING CHANGES IN THE SCENE THAT WOULD MAKE IT A LESS PLEASANT PLACE, AND THEN IMAGINING CHANGES IN THE SCENE THAT WOULD MAKE IT A MORE PLEASANT PLACE.   The idea is first to imagine as *vividly as you can* changes you would *not* like made in this environment. After you have gotten a clear image of what the changed scene would be like, switch and imagine as *vividly as you can* changes you would *like* to have made in this environment. (Both the negative and the positive changes should be things that could conceivably be prevented or brought about by human endeavor. Be sure to form clear mental images of each type of change, and feel free to imagine various alternative sets of changes that would make the scene less pleasant or more pleasant.)

Comments.   Our research has repeatedly yielded indications that people are less mentally taxed and may even be spontaneously more "creative" when imagining *negative* changes than when trying to think of positive ones. However, they clearly find it less enjoyable to imagine negative changes than to imagine improvements. The intent of this particular dual set is to give one a heightened sense of possible environmental dangers as well as positive possibilities, to provide a wider overall perspective in considering what can happen to environments over time (compare set WLL and creativity technique 15), and to stimulate suggestions for improvements based on avoiding the imagined dangers.

IMG-R: IMAGINING CHANGES IN THE SCENE THAT YOU THINK WOULD APPEAL TO PEOPLE OCCUPYING PARTICULAR ROLES.   The idea is to imagine the sorts of changes that would appeal to various types of people (e.g., occupants of different professions, people with various types of handicaps, old people, children, etc.). To extend this way of thinking, you might also try imagining changes that would appeal to nonhuman creatures, such as pets, insects, and so on.

Comment.   The guidelines for IMG-R are of course simply an alternate statement of creativity technique 5; but this is a good technique to emphasize both as fun in itself (IMG-R was one of the more popular IMG sets) and as special preparation for the next four sets, each of which is used most effectively when one takes a variety of role perspectives.

IMG-S: IMAGINING CHANGES IN THE SOCIAL PROCESSES OR INSTITUTIONS IN THE SCENE THAT WOULD MAKE LIFE MORE PLEASANT FOR THE PEOPLE AFFECTED BY THESE PROCESSES OR INSTITUTIONS.   The idea is first to figure out what social processes or institutions are present in the scene (e.g., processes of play, talking, buying, etc., may be occurring; and institutions such as schools, businesses, courts, etc., may be present). Then try to think of ways to change these processes or institutions so that life would be improved for the people involved or affected. Try to get a vivid image of what the scene would be like (and what life for the affected people would be like) if your imagined changes actually occurred.

PPR: THINKING OF HOW PUBLICLY OWNED THINGS IN THE SCENE COULD BE USED FOR PRIVATE PURPOSES AND PRIVATELY OWNED THINGS COULD BE USED FOR PUBLIC PURPOSES.   The idea is to think of what the scene would be like if the buildings or land areas (or other things, such as vehicles) were reversed in public vs. private ownership. To what uses might the privately owned buildings, cars, lots, etc., be put if they were owned by the whole community? Conversely, how might the publicly owned parks, governmental buildings, streets, etc., be used if they were privately owned by individuals or corporations? One good approach is to ask yourself what the scene would be like if *everything* in it were publicly owned; then switch and ask what it would be like if *everything* in it were privately owned.

STN: IMAGINING WHAT THIS SCENE WOULD BE LIKE IF THE SOCIETY WERE CHANGED.   The idea is to imagine what this scene would be like if our society were changed in fundamental ways. For example, what would the scene probably be like if our economic system were completely socialistic, or if we lived in a military dictatorship? Other possibilities might include imagining how the scene would be changed if our monogamous nuclear family system were replaced by group marriages of eight to ten people, or if our material wealth were multiplied (or reduced) by a factor of ten. *Also try to imagine what* this *scene would be like if our society were transformed into your vision of the best imaginable type of society* (i.e., your version of "utopia").

IMG-C: FIGURING OUT WHAT NEEDS OR PURPOSES ARE SERVED BY THE HUMAN INFLUENCES IN THIS SCENE; THEN IMAGINING WHAT THE SCENE WOULD LOOK LIKE (HOW IT COULD BE IMPROVED) SO THAT EACH OF THESE NEEDS OR PURPOSES WOULD BE FULFILLED IN A WAY THAT WOULD IMPROVE THE QUALITY OF LIFE FOR PEOPLE WHO LIVE IN OR NEARBY THE SCENE, VISIT THE SCENE, OR WHO LIVE IN THE SURROUNDING COMMUNITY.   In short, while taking into account the general functions served by or in this scene, *imagine as vividly as you can* how the scene could be made more pleasant for the whole community.

Comments.   The sets IMG-S, PPR, STN, and IMG-C all involve a more explicitly nonegocentric approach to imagining environmental changes than does the basic IMG set. These last four cognitive sets also entail more direct consideration of social as well as physical changes in the environment. Although these sets tend to be difficult to execute, many of our experimental subjects rated them among the most interesting and enjoyable of the sets under investigation. I might add parenthetically, however, that my impression is that in following virtually any of the cognitive-set guidelines presented here, it seems more interesting and productive for people to generate their own specific ways of carrying out the general set operations, rather than simply using the specific examples mentioned in the guidelines.

Up to now, each set has involved imagining only the content of different types of changes. The next two sets finally turn to a preliminary consideration of how changes might be achieved.

LTA: ENVISIONING HOW THIS SCENE MIGHT BE CHANGED IN THE FUTURE AS A RESULT OF SPECIFIC ACTIONS THAT YOU COULD TAKE NOW.   The idea is to envision *as clearly as you can* what this scene would probably be like in the future (say, any time between tomorrow and twenty years from now) as a result of specific actions you could take now. For example, imagine that you planted a pine seedling today. There would likely be a small pine tree in the scene several years later. Your action might also inspire other people to plant seedlings. This might in turn heighten their sense of community and collective power and lead them to make other improvements in the scene. Another example might be that you could point out a problem or make a suggestion to people who have power over the scene. This might result in substantial changes over time. In short, try to think of small actions (either inside *or* outside the scene) that might have powerful long-term effects on the pleasantness of this scene, and try to get a vivid image of what the scene would then be like.

IMG-A: IMAGINING CHANGES IN THE SCENE THAT WOULD MAKE IT A MORE PLEASANT PLACE, AND FIGURING OUT SPECIFIC ACTIONS THAT YOU AND OTHER PEOPLE COULD ENGAGE IN THAT WOULD HELP BRING ABOUT THESE CHANGES. The idea is to imagine as *vividly as you can* what changes you would like made in this environment in order to make it more pleasant, *and* to get clearly in mind specific, feasible things that you and others could do that would facilitate such beneficial changes. These changes may be as sweeping and "impractical" as you like, and you should try to get a clear mental image of how the scene would look when changed. Also try to generate a clear conception or image of possible actions that you and other people could take (beginning right now) either to produce the full changes you imagine or at least to make some smaller changes that would make the scene *more like* the way you imagined it changed.

Comments.   LTA and IMG-A are virtually complements of each other. LTA involves the attempt to think of actions first and then trace out their eventual consequences, while IMG-A entails starting with the goals and trying to work back to specific actions that might achieve them. Whichever approach one tries, the task of thinking up effective actions is extremely difficult. In our research this was evidenced not only by subjects' high difficulty ratings of these two sets, but even more so by the paucity of actual suggestions for effective action. This was especially telling in comparison with the generally creative and prolific variety of desired changes that these same people (each familiar with the creativity techniques) were able to generate. As we shall have occasion to consider again, actually achieving desirable social and environmental change may be very difficult indeed. Nevertheless, a good beginning would seem to be to think about what we really want and to integrate this process of imagining goals with an intensive effort to figure out feasible and effective means. The above two cognitive sets and the "grand finale" coming up next certainly do not in themselves provide any answers, but they may help us to ask the right questions.

IMG-E: IMAGINING CHANGES THAT WOULD MAKE THE SCENE MORE PLEASANT, WHILE TAKING ACCOUNT OF THE PRESENT FUNCTIONS OF THINGS IN THE SCENE, THE RAMIFICATIONS AND LONG-TERM EFFECTS OF YOUR IMAGINED CHANGES, PREREQUISITES AND SIDE EFFECTS OF YOUR CHANGES, AND SPECIFIC ACTIONS THAT YOU COULD TAKE TO MAKE THE SCENE MORE LIKE THE WAY YOU IMAGINE IT CHANGED.   The idea is to consider *all* of the following guidelines as you imagine changes that would make the scene a more pleasant place:

1. Try to figure out what human needs or purposes are being served in the scene. You might call this the "functions" of the things in the scene (a function = the serving of some need or purpose). For example, you might think of the function of telephone poles and wires as conveying electricity into the scene and as conveying information (telephone conversations, cable TV signals, etc.) between this scene and the surrounding world. You might also ask yourself, in this example, what human needs or purposes are served by the electricity and information. Similarly, try to figure out both the "surface" functions and the deeper needs and purposes associated with other human influences in the scene (buildings, vehicles, etc.).

2. In imagining changes that would make the scene more pleasant, think of: (a) which of these functions (and the underlying needs and purposes) are really necessary or beneficial to the quality of life for people affected by the scene; (b) how the underlying needs or purposes might be better met to make life more pleasant; (c) what other functions might be *added* to the scene so that life could be made more pleasant for people who live or work in the scene or who visit the scene (or

who are otherwise affected by the things in this scene); (d) which functions you think should be eliminated altogether in order to make life more pleasant (but note that if a truly necessary function were eliminated in *this* scene in order to make it a more pleasant place, such a function would still have to be met somewhere else—be sure to include in your imagined changes how this might be done).

3. Ramifications of your imagined changes: Think of how your imagined changes would affect the whole community over time. Try to think of changes that would have beneficial long-term effects as well as providing more immediate improvement.

4. Prerequisites for changes: Also be sure to consider what would be required in order to *produce* your imagined changes. What changes in social values, institutions, and patterns of behavior might be necessary in order to achieve the changes you envision? What additional modifications in the physical environment would be required to achieve your changes? Finally, what would be the immediate and longer-term effects of these social and environmental prerequisites? See if you can figure out ways to achieve your desired imagined improvements that would in themselves have beneficial side effects (or at least no harmful side effects).

5. Last, but not least, WHAT ACTIONS WOULD BE REQUIRED FOR PRODUCING THE CHANGES YOU IMAGINE? What might be a series of steps *leading in the direction of your imagined changes?* Especially, what are some things *you* could do that would be heading in the right direction? These might include changing the physical environment directly, trying to change other people's minds in ways that would facilitate relevant actions, or contributing in some way to ongoing social efforts. The key point is to figure out anything that you and other people could actually *do* (beginning now or in the near future) that would help make the scene at least a little more like the way you would like it to be.

In summary:

As you imagine how to make the scene more pleasant: (1) take account of the "functions" of the things in the scene; (2) consider the ramifications and long-term effects of your imagined changes; (3) figure out what needs to be done (both socially and environmentally) for these changes to occur, and take account of any side effects of these prerequisites; and (4) think of specific, feasible actions that you and others could take to help bring about your imagined changes or at least to make the scene *more like* the way you imagine it changed.

Comments.   IMG-E is of course not so much a single cognitive set as a program of interlinked cognitive sets. Carrying out this program in a thoroughgoing way even for a relatively small, circumscribed location such as a single residential street is a mammoth undertaking. It is perhaps easiest to start with specific aspects of a scene, such as transportation, recreation, and so on, and work on these subcomponents one by one before tackling the whole integrated scene. However, the world *is* integrated. That of course should become especially evident to anyone who diligently used IMG-E. In 1974, my colleagues and I wrote that

> . . . our interest in the set to imagine changes in the environment originated from an attempt to devise a cognitive set that would promote "ecological awareness" in the sense of appreciating the interrelatedness of human influences, life processes, and enjoyment of environments. While the particular set [IMG] which we have been studying is probably too simple to produce the full appreciation of ecological interconnections, we believe that it and similar imaginational processes may be very useful in making the interrelations and ramifying effects of human influences more salient. (Leff et al., 1974, p. 407)

Although not simple in any absolute sense, IMG-E, even combined with the collection of all the other cognitive sets discussed so far, is doubtless still too simple to engender a full flowering of ecological consciousness (see Chapter 5). If nothing else, certain types of knowledge and cognitive skills would also be needed. My hope is that, taken together, this whole collection of cognitive sets can act as a catalyst for the active use of such knowledge and skills and for the generation of new environmental sets and experiences that will move us a bit closer to ecological consciousness.

Designing Your Own Cognitive Sets

"Normal" cognitive sets.   There is obviously a lot of variety in the way different people, or even the same person over time, will process environmental information. Because of the self-consciousness and special "demand characteristics" introduced by participation in psychological research, a person's "normal" way of viewing scenes is probably the

most difficult type of cognitive set of all to study experimentally. Nevertheless, based on many interviews and on hundreds of self-reports by people who were asked to view many different types of environments "as you usually look at your surroundings when you are taking a walk or waiting around," certain very tentative conclusions can be drawn:

1. It is rare for people to make a deliberate effort to direct their cognitive sets for perceiving or interpreting their everyday surroundings.

2. A predominant orientation seems to be to "just notice things," usually involving a brief classification of what is being noticed (for example, "there's a dog") and either not much further mental processing or else one or more of the following operations: (a) activation of associations to the things noticed, either based on personal memories or on generic associations (for example, thinking of one's own experiences in similar scenes or thinking of the types of activities that generally occur in the scene); (b) formulation of questions about what is noticed; and (c) evaluations of what is noticed (for example, "I would like to live here," or "what a rotten neighborhood").

3. There is a tendency to pick up (nondeliberately) the mood or ambience of a place (compare Ittelson, 1973b). Thus, people seem specially tuned to react to such qualities as rusticity, busyness, poverty, wealth, sunshine, and so on.

4. People's normal perceptual experience tends to be highly toned by their momentary mood and often by salient goals, anticipations, or unfinished tasks that loom in their immediate lives. Such factors often provoke virtual daydreams in addition to coloring the selection and interpretation of information from the immediate surroundings.

5. The depth of processing immediate environmental information—and the degree of curiosity, number of associations, and extent of noticing details—seems linked to how enjoyable a person finds her or his normal way of viewing, although such a relation could well be mediated by mood in many cases. Alternatively, a feeling of placid relaxation, with a "wandering mind," also tends to be experienced as pleasant.

6. There is often much apparently spontaneous variety in a person's normal thoughts, perceptions, and (presumably) momentary cognitive sets, even at a single location.

7. People in our experiments often tended to view scenes much more closely and attentively than they would "normally." This was indicated both by direct self-reports and by a surprisingly strong tendency for people in the longitudinal control group (who were asked only to view

scenes normally) to report greatly enhanced awareness of their surroundings as a result of their experimental participation. (Lynch and
Rivkin, 1959, reported a similar finding obtained by simply having people tape record what they noticed during "a walk around the block.")

In brief, then, normal environmental information processing seems
characterized by a free-floating, nondeliberate mélange of cognitive sets
such as briefly noticing and classifying environmental content, associating personally or generically meaningful material to this content,
interpreting environmental information in terms of salient goals and
moods, evaluating what is noticed, and formulating questions suggested
by environmental content. Of course, that list of example sets is far from
complete and it is certainly not meant to imply that *all* such sets would
be used on any given occasion. Depending on one's mood, task, education, companions, and so forth, one might activate virtually any type
of cognitive set as one's momentary "normal" way of perceiving or
thinking. Some people indeed normally appear to view their surroundings using some of the cognitive sets we have been discussing, including
ASF and IMG, for example. But based on the research information I
have been able to gather, it is very rare for individuals to make a systematic and deliberate effort to direct their own cognitive sets for the
purpose of enriching their experience and environmental awareness. To
appropriate the previously cited quotation from Parmenter (1968), "our
culture does not value it, our schools do not teach it, and our mores disapprove of it." I'm not so sure about the mores parts, but clearly there
is little emphasis in our culture on the deliberate self-direction of environmental cognitive sets.

Designing new sets.   This brings us to the question of exactly how people could gain greater facility in creating, choosing, and activating new
cognitive sets. Presumably, one's normal cognitive sets will tend to feel
the most natural, require the least effort, and thus introduce the least
overall strain (that is, such sets will produce lower levels of Complications than will most other sets). This alone is enough to keep many
people from trying new cognitive sets. Perhaps a more serious block to
the use of new sets such as the ones discussed in this chapter, however,
is that they are likely to be attempted, if at all, as part of some assigned
task. That is, people are likely to encounter such sets only as part of an
educational lesson (usually an imposed task) or as instructions in a psychological experiment (ditto). This is unfortunate, since the underlying

idea is to help people become more able to direct their own experience and awareness, rather than having their thinking directed by an outside source. The whole point is to help all of us expand our repertoire of experience-enhancing cognitive sets—to develop and master information-processing Plans that help to optimize Complexity, Composition, Comprehension, Comparison, and Competence—and to do so with minimal increase in Complications and with positive implications for overall Comportment and Compatibility.

So in choosing or designing a new cognitive set, I would advise taking each of the eight components in the integrative/evaluative scheme into account; try to find sets that optimize all of them if possible, but at least "balance" the sets you actually use so that the net effect will be positive. (For example, too much ASF without any IMG could stultify your concern for humanity; but overdoing *any* single type of set will tend to have negative consequences.) The key words are *variety, flexibility,* and *appropriateness.* Indeed, one of my all-time favorite sets (in principle, at least) is this:

FAS: TRYING TO FIGURE OUT THE MOST INTERESTING OR ENJOYABLE WAY TO LOOK AT THE SCENE.   The idea is to try to think of the most pleasant or interesting way to think about *this* scene. Here you should ask yourself what the best "match" would be between the content of the scene and the various ways you might look at scenes.

FAS is just one type of cognitive set for choosing a cognitive set. Any type of criterion could be substituted for "interesting or enjoyable" to create a new set for finding a set. The most complete one I can think of would be that mentioned in the previous paragraph—the set to design or choose a set that would optimize all eight components in the scheme linking cognition, affect, behavior, and environment.

To conclude, let me suggest some additional aids for designing your own new cognitive sets. First of all, it might help to use the creativity techniques as aids to imagining (devising) innovative sets. As stated earlier, most of those fifteen techniques can be adapted to apply to virtually *any* type of design problem. Second, you might think of your own special interests and try to figure out cognitive sets that would help you relate those interests to your surroundings in ways that would make these surroundings more meaningful to you. An example of such a set was QSN—the set to think of intriguing questions—but you can doubtless create more specific sets for relating your own interests to your surroundings. Third, you can simply start with a variety of personally meaningful roles, subjects, tasks, or general purposes and use each one (or combinations of them) to generate new cognitive sets. Such sets often arise spontaneously, as when a TV news program on violence sensitizes viewers to previously ignored instances, effects, and causes of violence (that is, induces a "violence set"). The world can indeed be viewed in terms of any particular role, subject, task, or purpose: each way of thinking constitutes a new cognitive set, and at least some of these will probably have something special to offer you. Fourth, you can use the four groups of cognitive sets presented in this chapter as sample lists to which you can add your own cognitive sets for enhancing aesthetic experience, deepening environmental understanding, boosting and using creativity, and promoting awareness of environmental problems and possibilities. This in fact is a procedure I have used successfully both in research and teaching. Many people who have never thought about it before can generate impressive cognitive sets in just a few minutes after reading only the "headline" part of the cognitive set guidelines discussed in this chapter.

Furthermore, it can obviously add to your cognitive and experiential repertoire to exchange information with other people about the actual experiences engendered by various cognitive sets. It should also be enlightening and productive to join with other people in developing new cognitive sets cooperatively. And in trying to execute complex sets such as IMG-E, a group effort can make the process easier and more enjoyable for all participants.

Finally, you might try combining cognitive sets into coherent programs of sets. That is what IMG-E does, of course; and you may be able to think of other combinations that can help you fuse your knowledge or interests with your ongoing experience, have more fun using your senses, move toward ecological consciousness, or reach whatever other cognitive and experiential goals appeal to you.

Note on Cognitive Set and Social Change

Social change is a topic discussed in later chapters, but it might be helpful to emphasize a related consideration here. The widespread use of some of the cognitive sets discussed, especially those of the IMG type, might go a long way toward shaking up people's CLs (comparison levels) for environments. This effect on Comparison could increase dissatisfaction with environmental deterioration and increase the demand for environmental improvement. Especially if people could also successfully use the associated cognitive sets that involve trying to figure out how to achieve change, some real societal effects might be brought about by this way of thinking. However, here it seems particularly important for people to think and act *collaboratively*. Each of us imagining changes alone will not produce change; concerted, cooperative group efforts are needed. Toward this end, it would seem that the schools offer a good opportunity for collective experience in using new environmental cognitive sets. Such educational innovations constitute one of my chief hopes for awakening both enriched experience and greater collaborative environmental concern and competence. But as yet it is only a hope.

The next chapter extends considerations of motivation and cognition to the broader realm of attitudes and values, central factors in mediating personal and social decision making. The environmental and social implications, especially of value systems, are profoundly important. However, to avoid repetition, only brief elaborations are offered for the relations of cognitive-set processes to that material. It may therefore prove useful to keep in mind the discussion in this chapter—and many of the specific sets mentioned—as you read the next chapter (and the rest of the book). Virtually everything we think, we think "through" a cognitive set.

Appendix
"Mental Mapping"

CONCEPTION OF LARGE SCALE ENVIRONMENTS

The central issues to be considered in this appendix are the ways people conceive of large-scale geographical environments such as cities; the role of physical features and structure versus the role of meaning and association in such environmental conceptualization; and the developmental processes involved in the mental representation of geographical environments. Such representations of the environment are called by different names, such as "cognitive maps" or "spatial representations," but my favorite is the simple phrase "mental maps."[35] This term should be interpreted very metaphorically, however, since the way people normally represent environments to themselves, or even the internal guides they use for navigation, may not be much like a cartographer's version of a map. As Roger Downs and David Stea (1973a) point out, the important consideration is that one's internal representation of the environment seems to *function* as something like a mental map (especially when one actually knows enough about a place not to get hopelessly lost).

Let us briefly examine some of the research and theory dealing with these inner geographical representations. Following the tidy scheme suggested by Kevin Lynch (1960; see also Seamon, 1972), the discussion will focus first on how environmental form interrelates with the apparent structural properties of individuals' mental maps. After that, we shall consider the role of environmental meaning in mental maps.

Mental Maps: Structure

Probably the most widely known figure in the recent history of research on mental maps is Kevin Lynch. His original exploratory study, *The Image of the City* (1960), continues to be the most prominent landmark in a growing series of related studies. The great value of Lynch's book lies not only in what it reveals about mental maps of cities, but also in its vivid concern for how cities and whole metropolitan regions might be designed to provide clearer, more interesting impressions and thereby lead to more enjoyable environmental experiences (see also Lynch, 1976). This, however, is a topic for Chapter 6.

The research that Lynch conducted involved asking a relatively small number of predominantly middle-class residents of Boston, Jersey City, and Los Angeles about their inner representations of the central areas of their cities. His interviews assessed the respondent's city image by asking for a sketch map of the central city area, a verbal list of the city elements thought to be most distinctive, directions for making specific trips within the city, and a few other items concerning orientation and affective response to the city. (In Boston, other assessments were also made, such as recognition tests for photographs and requests for directions from a large number of passers-by.)

The collective images of the three cities were compared with corresponding representations derived from assessments of each city center by a trained observer. These assessments were made in terms of the five elements Lynch held to be essential in city images: paths, edges, districts, nodes, and landmarks. Briefly, *paths* are conduits of movement, such as streets. *Edges* are linear boundaries, such as walls or shorelines. *Districts* are distinctive areas of the city, such as Beacon Hill in Boston or Chinatown in San Francisco. *Nodes* are basically junctions that can be entered, such as major intersections of streets. Finally, *landmarks* are external points of reference, such as tall buildings or even distinctive doorknobs. Lynch classified his subjects' responses according to these five categories, and found reasonably good agreement between the collective city images and the presumably accurate representations provided by the trained observers. This correspondence was taken to indicate that the actual physical structure of cities is more or less represented in residents' mental maps.

Since most adult residents of a city do manage to find their way around without undue difficulty, this finding should not be surprising. However, Lynch also uncovered certain systematic distortions in people's images of their cities. For example, the respondents tended to picture networks of paths as more perpendicular and straight than they actually were. To quote Lynch (1960, p. 87):

> The image itself was not a precise, miniaturized model of reality, reduced in scale and consistently abstracted. As a purposive simplification, it was made by reducing, eliminating, or even adding elements to reality, by fusion and distortion, by relating and structuring the parts. It was

sufficient, perhaps better, for its purpose if rearanged, distorted, "il-logical."

Lynch concluded that although people's mental maps may be distorted, they nonetheless maintain a "topological invariance with respect to reality." The "map" might be stretched and twisted relative to the actual city form, but it was "rarely torn and sewn back together in another order."

A related analysis of distortions in mental maps has been offered by Roger Downs and David Stea (1973a). They pointed out that cognitive maps of geographical areas tend to omit areas, distort distance and direction, rely on "schematizations" or conventional symbols that may oversimplify geographical representations, and also contain "augmentation" or embellishment with items not actually present in the environment (see also Appleyard, 1973). For example, Lynch found an egregious case of incompleteness in the consistent tendency of his Boston respondents to omit a particular section of the city in their representations. Research on distance distortions is illustrated by the work of Ronald Briggs (1973, 1976), David Stea (1969), and David Canter and Stephen Tagg (1975). Common distortions seem to include relative overestimation of distances toward the city center (Briggs, 1973, 1976; but compare Lee, 1970) and biasing of intercity distance estimates in accordance with such factors as the attractiveness of the destination relative to the starting point (Stea, 1969; Cadwallader, 1976). Canter and Tagg (1975) have conducted a series of studies that indicates a general tendency for people to overestimate distances within cities, especially if the city has a complex and confusing structure.

Another common distortion in subjective scale is the tendency to exaggerate the size of one's own city, state, or country relative to outlying places. This has been humorously illustrated by Wallingford's maps of the New Yorker's and Bostonian's views of the United States (see, for example, Gould and White, 1974). Thomas Saarinen's (1973) cross-cultural comparisons of students' sketch maps of the world have provided research evidence that people do tend to represent their own countries and adjacent areas as disproportionately large. Furthermore, there is evidence, according to Robert Beck and Denis Wood (1976), that people tend to overestimate the size of especially liked areas within liked environments and of especially disliked areas in disliked environments. Beck and Wood report that their evidence also indicates the converse: people tend to underestimate the size of liked areas within disliked environments and of disliked areas in liked environments.

These various distortions in mental maps can be conceived of as resulting from corresponding biases in the way information about the large-scale environment is processed. Our normal cognitive-set and memory processes may conceptualize geographical regions (such as cities) as simplified geometrically, altered in scale as a function of familiarity or emotional association, conforming to preconceived categories or expectations, and so on. However, as will be discussed below, drawing conclusions about basic cognitive processes on the basis of such responses as freehand sketch maps can be a tricky undertaking. At least some of the apparent distortions in mental mapping may in fact merely result from inadequacies in people's *response Plans* for drawing maps or reporting their environmental images and conceptions. Nevertheless, there can be little doubt that human information processing involves intricate processes of construction and transformation (see Part One of this chapter). It would indeed be surprising if we did *not* introduce substantial distortion into our cognitive representations of environments as complex and amorphous as cities.

Turning back to Lynch's work, we might note that merely becoming familiar with his scheme for classifying city features can serve to heighten one's sensitivity to city and town content and structure. Such categories as path, edge, node, landmark, and district, especially when enhanced by an understanding of the richness of Lynch's conceptualization, can in effect serve as a new encoding system for interpreting the physical structure of urban environments. This was apparently the orientation adopted by the trained observers on Lynch's staff, for example. As Lynch and Rivkin (1959) observed, merely reporting what one sees on a walk can greatly intensify and enliven one's environmental experience. Perhaps familiarity and practice with classification schemes for environmental features can further enhance environmental experience, if one is thereby enabled to perceive the structure and interrelations in one's surroundings with greater clarity and interest.

Lynch (1960) also pointed out that his five-element scheme can be applied on different scales, ranging from one's immediate surroundings to vast geographical regions. Thus, an unusual doorknob may be a "landmark" in the interior of a large building, the building a landmark within the city, and the whole city a landmark in the context of a cross-country plane flight. Such considerations are obvious when made salient, but the process of making them salient may for many people constitute a relatively new, but easily grasped, environmental cognitive set. To the extent that it enlivens and clarifies environmental images and helps one navigate, using such a set may be an easy way to enhance one's environmental experience.

Since Lynch's original study, many related investigations have been carried out to determine the structure of people's mental maps of a variety of geographical entities. For example, Florence Ladd (1970) and Terence Lee (1968, 1973) have studied urban residents' images of their neighborhoods; Donald Appleyard (for example, 1969, 1970, 1973), Robert Beck and Denis Wood (1976; Wood, 1973), Derk de Jonge (1962), and Peter Orleans (1973), to name only a few, have investigated residents' and visitors' images of cities in several parts of the world; Thomas Saarinen (1973) has explored mental maps of the whole planet; and Peter Gould and Rodney White (1974) have examined collective patterns of information, ignorance, learning, and preference concerning different areas of nations. Although the research to date has by no means laid bare the underlying structure of mental maps, it has revealed probable dimensions of accuracy and distortion (discussed above). Deeper insights will doubtless be forthcoming in the near future.

However, Denis Wood's (1973) very provocative (and memorably unorthodox) dissertation deserves special mention for its critical treatment of much of the earlier work. Wood especially questioned the validity of using free sketch mapping as a technique for getting at respondents' real cognitive representations of the geographical environment. The typical approach had been to ask people to draw freehand maps on a blank sheet of paper, with little or no instruction about how to proceed. Wood very plausibly observed that such a task may introduce spurious distortions and incompleteness if the maps drawn are taken as adequate representations of the underlying mental maps.

For example, uninstructed and unpracticed respondents may not know how to draw or represent many of the things they know about a given environment. There also appears to be a tendency in sketch mapping to create inadvertent scale distortions by leaving too little room on the page for later entries and by a curious momentum generated in drawing a street line without first placing a terminal point on the paper. Certainly many of us have had the experience of trying to sketch a map giving directions to a friend only to realize that the resulting mess was far from what we knew to be the actual layout of streets, landmarks, and other environmental features.

Whether Wood is correct in his belief that data collected by free sketch maps are very nearly worthless, he has at least sounded a clear warning that conclusions about anything more than how people *draw* maps should be very carefully drawn. Indeed, Peter Orleans (1973) and Kevin Lynch (1960) have noted that sketch maps and verbal interview responses often show little correspondence in indicating what individual respondents actually know about their cities. Orleans even suggests using partially completed outline maps as a way of obtaining more veridical insight into people's environmental images of large areas.

Wood's solution, however, was to instruct his subjects in the use of a special mapping "language" called *Environmental A*. The basic technique is to begin a map with a small circle or dot representing the center of the area to be mapped, then add a second dot representing some prominent point at a known distance from the center (the placement of this second point thus setting the scale for the rest of the map), then connect the two points with a line indicating the path between them, and proceed by adding other known points at proper relative distances and connecting points with lines representing known paths. Subjects are also encouraged to label the points, to number the order in which lines are drawn, and to use question marks to indicate uncertainty (and thereby also relieve anxiety).

After this base map is completed, sheets of tracing paper serve as overlays on which special generic symbols of *Environmental A* are used by the respondent to label points, lines, and areas. These symbols indicate particular types of buildings, vegetation, or other geographic features ("points"); different types of streets, edges, or rows of similar structures ("lines"); and regions such as parks or industrial districts ("areas"). In addition, *Environmental A* contains a group of attribute symbols for indicating social and physical characteristics (such as "bumpy," "crowded," "high-class") and for indicating one's own affective responses (such as "sadness," "loved it," "relaxing").

Although learning the procedure does require some special preparation by the respondents, Wood's technique presents some definite advantages over free sketch mapping. First, it makes possible ready comparison between different individuals' maps, since all respondents use the same basic procedure and symbols to indicate their images of a place. (There is of course also the potential problem that a scheme is in fact being imposed on their conceptualization, but *Environmental A* seems reasonably broad and close to everyday terminology for thinking about environments.) Second, it encourages a fuller representation of what respondents actually know about a place, while also helping them to avoid most of the common problems people face in drawing freehand maps. Third, and perhaps most important, familiarity and practice with a mapping language such as *Environmental A* may, over time, help people form clearer and richer images of their environments. This may constitute something of a methodological drawback for longitudinal studies of how people normally learn to orient themselves within a large-scale environment, but it offers promise as an aid to geographical education and to stimulating environmental interest. In any case, Wood's (1973) research with high school students on a tour of European cities led him to conclude that this approach both is superior to the use of free sketch maps for revealing the underlying structure of mental maps, and is also of considerable potential value to the participating subjects themselves.

Another main conclusion from this research was that cognition of new environments develops first in terms of points, then lines, and finally areas. This pattern, obtained in Wood's study in which subjects learned about a foreign city in the course of a few days, seems mirrored in Peter Gould's (1973; Gould and White, 1974) research concerning Swedish children's knowledge of their country. Children at about seven years of age knew only a few major cities and separated small areas (points); slightly older children added linkages between the points (lines); thirteen-year-olds were able to fill in much more information about whole regions (areas).

Before pursuing the larger issues involved in such developmental aspects of mental mapping, let us briefly leave the subject of cognizing environmental structure and take a look at the role of environmental *meaning* in relation to mental maps.

Mental Maps: Meaning

Here again, I find myself in some sympathy with Wood's (1973) critical perspective on much earlier research. As he noted, the attention of many theorists and researchers seems to have been riveted primarily on the purely cognitive and structural aspects of environmental conceptualization. Questions about people's knowledge of location and environmental structure have predominated while questions about the role of affective response and social meaning have been relatively neglected. A similar argument has been made by Richard Jones (1968) concerning a dominant trend in the applications of psychology to education (especially applications deriving from the work of Jerome Bruner and Jean Piaget). According to Jones, far too little attention has been given the *affective* or emotional side of life in our mad scramble to sharpen little minds. But there is hope. Just as affective, humanistic, value-oriented education has sprung to life in recent years,[36] there appears to be increasing interest in affective, meaning-oriented, and evaluative responses to the large-scale physical environment.

In fairness to Lynch (1960), it should be emphasized that he viewed environmental images as analyzable in terms of the three components of identity, structure, and meaning. His work deliberately concentrated on the relation of physical features to the ways in which people's environmental images seemed to identify and structure urban surroundings; his main effort was to discover what physical features and layouts yielded the greatest "imageability" or "legibility" in city form. Lynch's analysis, however, reveals a deep concern for what physical forms lead to environmental enjoyment as well as to clear cognition. This is illustrated in his observations on the affective quality associated with various urban forms (such as the pleasant quality of broad vistas), the enhanced emotional intensity of living in a city of special character (Florence, for example), the annoyance produced by confusing intersections, and the potential enhancement of human experience to be obtained by a heightened "sense of place."

Nevertheless, Lynch did concentrate on the role of physical form in the image, largely ignoring the social *meanings* of these physical forms. A study by James Harrison and William Howard (1972) illustrates how a modification of Lynch's techniques can reveal that social meaning indeed plays as important a role as physical form in residents' mental maps of urban areas. Harrison and Howard's procedure was first to obtain sketch maps and then to ask the respondents to indicate what they felt to be the most distinctive features and to tell why these features had been drawn. (The subjects were forty-four residents of a municipality in the Denver area.) Analysis of the responses indicated that social and personal meanings, such as the cultural functions or personal associations of a given feature, were nearly as important as location and physical appearance in determining what was included on the sketch maps.

Harrison and Howard concluded that such structural elements as paths, nodes, landmarks, edges, and districts may require considerations of social and personal meaning to account for particular inclusions in people's mental maps.

Many other investigators and theorists have also observed or speculated on the role of social meaning and personal association in determining the structure and content of environmental images. Wood (1973), for example, found that the *Environmental A* symbols for affective response and functional attributions were used with increasing frequency as the respondents became more familiar with each foreign city. Appleyard (1969, 1970) also found that attributes of "use" and "significance," as well as "form" and "visibility," contributed to the mental maps of residents of a new Venezuelan city (Ciudad Guayana). An example of how form and meaning can be interrelated in both environmental structure and residents' images is provided by David Stea and Denis Wood (1971) in their study of residents' mental maps of four Mexican cities. Stea and Wood used the term *opportunity surface* to refer to the mental map one forms when one considers the various locations that offer opportunities to engage in a particular activity. For example, if you are thinking of going out to eat, your opportunity surface will probably consist of a mental map of the various available restaurants. In the terms of our model, having a goal to engage in a particular activity will generate a cognitive set to select information from memory concerning places appropriate to the activity. Processes of integrating and interpreting this information give rise to the subjective opportunity surface for the given activity. An illustration of Stea and Wood's findings was that San Cristobal las Casas was an especially "lucid" city, since it tended to promote high congruity between the "orientation surface" and the opportunity surfaces. That is, locations likely to serve as goal destinations also tended to stand out structurally and thus to be easy to find and to incorporate in mental maps.

Numerous other examples of research concerning social or personal meaning could of course be cited, and much further research and theory will be forthcoming. For instance, nearly any study using bipolar adjective pairs (the "semantic differential" technique) is likely to qualify.[37] Also, some of the most interesting accounts of the role of meaning in cognition of the large-scale environment have derived more from historical, impressionistic, and anecdotal analyses than from quantitative research. A few impressive examples include Anselm Strauss's (1961) observations in *Images of the American City,* David Lowenthal's impressions of people's responses to the American and British landscapes (Lowenthal, 1968; Lowenthal and Prince, 1965, 1976), and Yi-Fu Tuan's (1974) and Roderick Nash's (1973) studies of the varied historical and cultural meanings with which natural and constructed environments have been viewed.

DEVELOPMENTAL PROCESSES IN ENVIRONMENTAL COGNITION

To conclude, we shall now briefly examine some of the changes that occur in environmental cognition as children mature or as people become familiar with a new place. Roger Hart and Gary Moore (1973) have provided an excellent review and interpretation of theory and research on these topics.[38] Relying mainly on the perspective provided by the work of Jean Piaget (for example, Piaget and Inhelder, 1967) and Heinz Werner and his colleagues (for example, Werner and Kaplan, 1963), Hart and Moore derived several conclusions concerning the development of spatial cognition in children.

Two essential features of such cognitive growth are deemed to be (1) increasing differentiation and abstractness in cognitive representations of the environment, illustrated in part by a progressive shift from enactive to iconic to symbolic modes of representation and by Piaget's developmental stages (sensory-motor, preoperational, concrete-operational, and formal-operational; see also Flavell, 1963, 1977); and (2) increasing ability to conceive of the environment from different topographical perspectives. The latter is illustrated by a·shift from an *egocentric* (spatial reference possible only with respect to one's own bodily position) to a *fixed* (spatial reference possible with respect to some fixed object or direction) to a *coordinated* system of reference (spatial reference possible with respect to a system of polar coordinates, such as the cardinal directions of east-west and north-south). In the terms of the cognition model, these trends represent progressive increases in the complexity and sophistication of (usually nonconscious) cognitive styles and sets for organizing and interpreting environmental information.

In addition, Hart and Moore posited that, as adults or children become familiar with a new place, their "topographical representations" or mental maps will tend to shift from a *route* to a *survey* orientation. That is, the new place will first usually be conceived of in terms of paths from point to point, but newcomers will gradually tend to form mental maps embodying an awareness of broad areas and interrelations. This "micro-genetic" developmental principle seems in basic accord with Wood's (1973) finding that his summer tour subjects seemed to become familiar with new cities first in terms of points, then lines, and finally areas. As discussed above, Gould (1973; Gould and White, 1974) found that Swedish children displayed a similar pattern of growth in areal knowledge with increasing age. However, it should also be noted that David Stea and James Blaut (1973; Blaut, 1969) have discovered that children as young as three to five years of age can interpret features (and at least some areas) on black and white aerial photographs without any special training or prior exposure to such photographs. Stea and Blaut interpreted their work in terms of a theory that play with toys or miniature models gives children practice in the three essentials of mapping: the use of a vertical perspective, reduction in scale, and the use of symbols. Their work at least indicates that very young children may be able to learn some type of survey perspective.

To conclude with an aside, there seems to be an analogy between the distinction between route and survey maps and a point made by Gregory Bateson (1972) concerning the human propensity to think in linear rather than systems terms. Linear thinking can be represented graphically by drawing directed lines from one point to another to indicate a literal "chain of thought." Systems thinking, on the other hand, requires representation of the interrelations and contexts of the various points. The analogy may not be perfect, but there is a suggestive similarity between being limited in one's mental maps to considerations of routes or links between otherwise unrelated points and being limited in one's thoughts to considerations of linear causal connections between isolated events. Similarly, one might detect a correspondence between mental maps that encompass whole areas and picture the interrelations among the various points and paths, and patterns of thought that take into account interrelations among diverse events and embody an understanding of the way the whole "system" operates.

NOTES

1. See the various references cited in the following discussion and notes.
2. See, for example, Raphael (1976), Feigenbaum and Feldman (1963), Apter (1970), and Newell and Simon (1972).

3. Miller et al. use the capitalization to denote the special "hierarchical" aspect of most behavioral and mental control processes covered by the term *Plans*. This simply means that most of our actions, whether overt behaviors or mental operations, can be regarded as organized or directed in a series of nested levels, much as in a topic outline. Generally, specificity of operation increases as one descends levels in the hierarchy. Another way of expressing the hierarchical nature of Plans is simply to say that a Plan contains subplans. Thus, even a simple act, such as mailing a letter, may be considered as having a hierarchical structure operating according to a Plan with subplans (and even sub-subplans):

> Mailing a Letter
>> Opening the mailbox
>>> reaching out your hand
>>> grasping the lid handle (extending the fingers, closing the fingers, and so on)
>>> pulling back the lid
>> Dropping in the letter
>>> raising the letter over the opening
>>> releasing your grip on the letter
>> Closing the mailbox

4. The "resonance" or layout-detection view has been proposed by James Gibson (for example, 1966), and has apparently gathered some support over the years (see, for example, Weimer and Palermo, 1974; also compare Neisser, 1976). For an interesting neurophysiological theory on the nature of feature detection and related processes, consult Konorski (1967); see L. Kaufman (1974), Lindsay and Norman (1977), and Haber and Hershenson (1973) for general accounts of research on visual feature detection.

5. Feedback from behavioral interactions with the environment also seems to play an important role in shaping our perceptual interpretations of the physical environment and even in allowing normal perceptual development to occur. See especially the work of the "transactionalists" (for example, Ittelson, 1960, 1962; Kilpatrick, 1961) and also Richard Held's (1965) work on *reafference*—the sensory, or "afferent," feedback correlated with the perceiver's self-produced movements.

6. To borrow from a footnote in Leff et al. (1974, p. 443): "This definition of cognitive 'set' departs somewhat from many past usages of the term. As Gibson (1941) noted in his critical review, the term 'set' has enjoyed numerous meanings in psychological research, ranging from various types of expectation to cognitive or behavioral perseveration. Allport (1955) has also discussed the concept of 'set' at length, pointing to a predisposition to perceive or respond according to a specific expectancy or intention as a central characteristic. Uznadze (1966) in his extensive work on 'set' seemed to conceive of it as a kind of psychological inertia resulting from a series of similar experiences. Nevertheless, we know of no less ambiguous or misleading term for our concept."

7. For recent accounts of the concept of "schema" and closely related notions such as "frame" or "prototype," see Norman et al. (1975), Neisser (1976), Stotland and Canon (1972), Minsky (1975), Goffman (1974), and Klatzky (1975). The definition I am using is perhaps closest to those explicitly presented by Norman et al. and by Minsky.

8. For thorough examinations of the psychology of judgment, see Eiser and Stroebe (1972) and Upshaw (1969).

9. On the apparent differentiation of the right hemisphere for spatial and "intuitive" information processing and the left hemisphere for linguistic and "analytic" modes of information processing, see, for example, Ornstein (1972). Recent theory and research on imagery are illustrated by Hebb (1968), Richardson (1969), Segal (1971a), Sheehan (1972), Pylyshyn (1973), Singer (1966–1975), and Paivio (1971; this is also a good source for some of the distinctions between verbal and imagerial thinking. See also the *Journal of Mental Imagery* (published by Brandon House, New York, beginning in 1977). Arguments for more attention to visual thinking in our culture may be found in Arnheim (1969), McKim (1972), and Parmenter (1968). Finally, it should be noted that although Bruner (1964, 1966; Bruner et al., 1966) emphasized symbolic encoding, he also discussed the value of enactive and iconic representation in areas such as motor skills and aesthetic activities. He additionally pointed out the importance of facility in all three modes of representation (see also Rusch, 1970; Bissell et al., 1971).

10. See, for instance, Klatzky (1975), Norman (1976), Norman and Bobrow (1976), and Restle (1974).

11. See the references cited in note 10.

12. See, for example, Ornstein (1972), Payne (1973), Brown (1974), the *Aldine Annuals on Biofeedback and Self-Control* (Chicago: Aldine, beginning in 1970), and the journal *Biofeedback and Self-Regulation* (New York: Plenum, beginning in 1976).

13. See Lazarus (1966, 1968) and Lazarus et al. (1970). Also compare related work by Stotland (1969; Stotland et al., 1971) and especially by Holmes and Houston (1974). The latter study found evidence that cognitive sets could decrease stress reactions even to personal—as opposed to vicarious (or "empathic")—threats.

14. For a stimulating discussion of the mind/body problem and certain related issues, see Globus et al. (1976). I should also point out, in case it isn't obvious, that "experience" is encased in dotted lines in the model diagrams to express the ambiguity involved in trying to relate it to the other components. It may, indeed, be best thought of as either emergent from or partially identical with the components of cognitive-set processes and physiological processes. Hence, also, there are no arrows directly to or from the dotted enclosure representing experience.

15. One might also compare Miller et al.'s (1960) contention that an "intention" is simply "the unfinished part of a Plan that is being executed" (p. 68). Miller et al. also theorize that "an 'effort of will' seems to be in large measure a kind of emphatic inner speech," and they consider "this inner shouting" as in a sense the person's actual controlling Plan at the time (p. 71). In addition, though, see William James (1890) for a fascinating discussion of topics such as "will" and "attention." James's brilliant introspective and phenomenological analyses, while not necessarily correct, sound surprisingly contemporary at times.

16. See, for example, Schachter and Singer (1962), Schachter (1964, 1970, 1971), Beck (1967), London and Nisbett (1974), E. Jones et al. (1972), Arnold (1970), Mandler (1975), and Lazarus (1966, 1968, 1975).

17. This use of the term "Complexity" is similar to Edward Walker's (1964, 1973) notion of "psychological complexity." For Walker this meant the degree of complexity of a "psychological event" and was conceptualized in basically the same way as arousal level. My usage is perhaps more restricted, since "Complexity"

    refers only to the arousal potential of the structural aspects of experience and does not include reference to aspects of the *meaning* of an experience that may also influence arousal (see the discussion of "Composition").

18. However, see Wohlwill (1976) for a research review indicating that at least in the environmental realm, the actual empirical evidence is far from conclusive on this question (although much of the difficulty appears to be based on methodological problems rather than on the emergence of clearly contradictory findings).

19. We might also consider here the interrelated notions of "reference groups," "social comparison processes," "rising expectations," and "relative deprivation." The key idea for our purposes is that people become dissatisfied more as a function of the disparity between what they expect (or think they deserve) and what they actually receive than as a function of the absolute level of their outcomes. Revolutions, it seems, are most likely to arise when things improve enough to whet people's appetites—but not enough to satisfy them. (See Pettigrew, 1967, for a fine summary of the basic concepts.)

20. On "consciousness expansion" and meditation, see, for instance, Ornstein (1972), Naranjo and Ornstein (1971), Lewis and Streitfeld (1970), Otto and Mann (1968), Masters and Houston (1966, 1972), Robbins and Fisher (1972), A. Smith (1975), Lilly (1972), Pelletier and Garfield (1976), Gustaitis (1969), Tart (1972, 1975) and J. White (1972, 1974a), to mention only a few of the many studies available. References for the other items mentioned (imagery, biofeedback, and so on) are provided elsewhere in this chapter.

21. For extended treatments of the interrelations between personality and styles of information processing, see discussions by Klein (1970), Kelly (1955), Gardner (1966), McGhie (1969), Eriksen and Eriksen (1972), Schroder et al. (1967), Kagan and Kogan (1970), and Kogan (1971).

22. For other examples of recently developed tests for assessing environmental dispositions and attitudes, see R. Kaplan (1973), Winkel et al. (1969), Mehrabian and Russell (1974), and Maloney and Ward (1973; Maloney et al., 1975).

23. For a thorough review of role theory, see Sarbin and Allen (1968). For discussions of the importance of roles as determinants of how people construe or interpret their environments, see Craik (1969), Wapner et al. (1973), Kaplan et al. (1976), and Tuan (1974).

24. See, for instance, Payne (1973), Cook and Davitz (1975), de Mille (1973), and many of the later references on creativity.

25. Since this experiment is frequently referred to, a few additional comments concerning its design may be helpful. A total of eighty-six University of Vermont undergraduates, randomly drawn from a larger pool of volunteers from an introductory psychology class, completed the central "longitudinal field phase." This consisted of visiting seven assigned locations on or near the campus. These visits were systematically spaced over a four-week period. The eighty-six field participants were randomly divided into four groups, each of which visited the same seven locations but had different instructions on how to view the "scenes." Members of Group 1 were always asked to view the locations as they normally would when taking a walk or waiting around. Members of Group 2 were always asked to imagine changes that would make the scenes more pleasant. The other two groups received different instructions during each of the four weeks, as follows: (a) During the first week, Groups 3 and 4 were given the same instructions as Group 2. (b) For the second week, Groups 3 and 4 were given a list of techniques for being more creative (presented in this chapter) to use while

imagining changes that would make the scenes more pleasant. (c) During the third and fourth weeks, members of Group 3 were asked to use cognitive sets from the last list presented in this chapter, while Group 4 members were asked to use sets of their choice from all of the lists presented. The chief dependent variables in the field phase consisted of various ratings and judgments made by the participants concerning the scenes and sets and of various content analyses and ratings (made by our staff) of the participants' reports of their experiences during the visits. (The experiment included much more, and I would like to express appreciation to the National Institute of Mental Health for supporting this project through Research Grant PHS R01 21736-02.)

26. Just to mention a few in the environmental realm, see R. A. and C. M. Smith (1970), Van Matre (1974), and Dillard (1974).
27. See, for instance, Payne (1973), Lewis and Streitfeld (1970), Brooks (1974), Cook and Davitz (1975), and Gunther (1968).
28. See Adams (1974), Arieti (1976), Barron (1968), de Bono (1969, 1970, 1971), W. Gordon (1961, 1973), Guilford (1967), D. M. Johnson (1972), Koberg and Bagnall (1974), Koestler (1964), Maier (1970), McKim (1972), Prince (1970), Stein (1974, 1975), Torrance (1971, 1974), and Wallach (1971). (Also see Polya, 1957, and Wickelgren, 1974, for some related ideas on good techniques of problem solving.) This is of course only a small portion of the literature on creativity, but I believe it is representative of both the diversity and the surprising degree of underlying agreement to be found.
29. The original version of this test was devised by J. P. Guilford (see, for example, Guilford, 1967). Paul Torrance (1974) has developed a modified version (his "Unusual Uses" test), along with several other tests—each of which can itself be used to suggest creativity-oriented cognitive sets (for example, "Guess Consequences," "Guess Causes," and "Just Suppose"). Torrance's main scoring criteria are also worth noting as potential guides to using such sets more creatively: *fluency* (number of relevant ideas), *originality* (rarity or unusualness of each idea), *flexibility* (variety of types of ideas), and *elaboration* (degree of embellishment of each idea).
30. For an excellent and provocative discussion of questions and their potential for stimulating creative thinking, see Torrance and Myers (1970). Their focus is on the creative use of questions in classroom situations, but their analysis and examples of different *types* of questions can easily be extended to the way one thinks about the everyday environment—or to the manner in which one uses QSN.
31. Much of the work on techniques for increasing creativity certainly relates to this (for example, Gordon's and Prince's work in synectics, and Torrance's and de Bono's efforts in creativity education—see the previous section). However, actual research on the issue of imagining environmental improvements appears, as of now, surprisingly sparse in environmental psychology. See Baird et al. (1972), Eisemon (1975), and Zerner and Hubka (1972) for examples of such research; and see Sanoff (1975, 1976) for an illustrative relevant program in environmental-design education (see also Chapter 5). Also, Moore (1970, Section 9) offers some intriguing theoretical discussions by designers on psychological models of environmental designing.
32. Only two out of fifty-five subjects who had never been given IMG instructions reported imagining environmental improvements as a result of their earlier research participation.
33. This list is based on a distillation of much of the literature on creative thinking

that was referred to in the previous section (see especially note 28) and on the experiences of my colleagues and myself. (I would also like to acknowledge the substantial contributions of our research assistant Michael Cote.)

34. All ratings were of course done by raters who were unaware of each subject's actual instructions, and a special rank-ordering rating procedure that yielded very high inter-rater reliabilities for this type of task was used. Furthermore, the ratings indicated that instructing subjects specifically to "try to be as *creative* as possible" had no effect unless accompanied by the actual list of creativity techniques.

35. Representative reviews of the theory and research in various aspects of environmental perception and conceptualization are provided by Craik (1970, 1973), Kameron (1973), S. Lee (1975), Saarinen (1969, 1974, 1976), Seamon (1972), and Stea (1974). Mental mapping and related phenomena represent a continuing theme of major interest in the fields of environmental psychology and behavioral geography, as is amply illustrated by these reviews, several books (for example, Lowenthal, 1967; Ittelson, 1973a; Downs and Stea, 1973b; Gould and White, 1974; Moore and Golledge, 1976), and the substantial space that has been devoted to studies of environmental conceptualization in the journal *Environment and Behavior.*

36. In addition to Jones (1968), see, for example, Brown (1971), Castillo (1974), Borton (1970), Rossiter (1976), Weinstein and Fantini (1970), Howe and Howe (1975), and the discussion in Chapters 4 and 5.

37. The "semantic differential" is essentially a rating technique whereby something is evaluated on a number of short rating scales, each labelled or "anchored" by a bipolar adjective pair (for example, "good:___:___:___:___:___:bad"). This technique has been used in a very wide range of psychological research, and regardless of what is being rated (people, words, environments, and so on), three dimensions tend to underlie the ratings: an *evaluation* factor (good-bad), a *potency* factor (strong-weak), and an *activity* factor (active-passive)—see, for example, Osgood et al. (1957), Snider and Osgood (1969), and Heise (1969). Studies of environments do, however, often seem to disclose more or fewer than three dimensions. As Hershberger (1972) argued, the factors that emerge may be as much a function of the bipolar word pairs given to respondents as of the environments rated or the raters' actual way of thinking about them. (For representative examples of the use of this technique see Lowenthal and Riel, 1972; Calvin et al., 1972.) Another interesting approach to assessing the meaning of environments to people has been developed by Harrison and Sarre (1971, 1975), who have adapted George Kelly's (1955) Role Construct Repertory Test for use in environmental evaluations (see also Moore and Golledge, 1976). There is no need to go into the details here, but the basic idea is to enable respondents to generate their own personally meaningful and salient bipolar constructs to use in making ratings.

38. See also Siegel and White (1975), G. T. Moore (1974), and Moore and Golledge (1976).

4
ATTITUDES, VALUES, AND ENVIRONMENT

If there is one consistent thread in popular appraisals of purported environmental crises, it is probably that the ultimate solution involves a change in people's attitudes or values. Conversely, these same psychological entities are often held somehow responsible for the various environmental and social messes we find ourselves in or approaching. In the discussion that follows we shall explore some of the ways in which attitudes and values relate to environmental issues and to the overall quality of life. Specifically, we shall address these questions: (1) What do the terms *attitude* and *value* mean, and how do these concepts relate to the motivational and cognitive material so far discussed? (2) What are some existing patterns of attitudes and values that have special importance for people/environment relations? (3) How are these attitude and value patterns formed and maintained? (4) Are there alternative patterns of values and attitudes that, if widely held, would facilitate ecological well-being and the enrichment of human experience? (5) If, after a thorough analysis, we want to shift our own (or other people's) attitudes or values in a specific direction, how might we do this and what value implications would the different techniques of change themselves have?

If you'll take a look back at Theme 3 (Pro-Life Values) at the end of Chapter 1, you will be reminded that this chapter is going to present a case for some substantial changes in the way we orient ourselves toward each other and our environment. However, let us begin gently with a few definitions and an examination of how the central concepts relate to material discussed earlier.

DEFINITIONS AND RELATIONS

Attitudes

As one can easily gather by reading virtually any of the steadily increasing number of books and articles on "attitude," there are many definitions of this term.[1] Rather than wade through a long list of these here, let us simply agree to use the word *attitude* to mean an organized set of affectively toned beliefs that predisposes one to have positive or negative feelings and action tendencies toward the object of these beliefs.[2] This definition is close enough to the mainstream of usages in social psychology to allow us to proceed without undue risk of misleading ourselves.

210

Now, what does this definition really mean? First of all, it means that "attitude" is an exceedingly vague concept. It is a nebulous organization of a special kind of beliefs about some object. A belief is presumably some sort of internal representation of the way things are (according to the representer). Notice that while most of a person's beliefs would in some sense be stored in that person's memory, they are probably not stored as explicit propositions. Rather, our beliefs are probably best thought of as implicit in the various relationships among concepts and other items stored in our memories.

To be part of an attitude, the activation of a belief should be associated with either a positive or a negative affective state. Having such an affectively toned belief should also increase the probability that we will engage in behavior that is either for or against the object of the belief. (The object of a belief can of course be anything a person thinks about. One can thus have attitudes about *anything*.) For example, a person's attitude toward trees might include the set of beliefs that trees provide needed oxygen, give shade, cool the surrounding air in warm weather, are great for climbing, are being brutally murdered when chopped down, and so on for many other, let us say, "positive" beliefs about trees. For this person, thinking such thoughts (activating these beliefs) will tend to arouse concomitant emotions such as affection for trees or hatred of loggers. Indeed, this set of beliefs has already tapped at least two attitudes—a positive constellation of beliefs about trees and a coordinate negative one about people who cut them down. A person with this set of beliefs would also presumably be likely to engage in "pro-tree" behavior *if* such behavior did not conflict with his or her other attitudes or with situational constraints.

The qualification represented by that little "if" is helpful in clarifying the relationship between attitudes and behavior. It has become a commonplace observation in psychology that self-report measures of attitudes often fail to correspond with a person's actual behavior toward the attitudinal objects. People will say one thing about what they believe and feel, but often behave in some apparently inconsistent way in particular situations. Thus, someone with an averred negative attitude toward loggers may turn out to be extremely polite and friendly when faced with a live, hulking lumberjack. Does this mean, as some would argue, that people are less than honest when they answer attitude questionnaires or that the whole attitude concept is functionally useless for predicting or understanding behavior? Or should we follow attitude researchers such as Milton Rokeach (1968), Harry Triandis (1971), and Herbert Kelman (1974) in their view that overt behavior should be viewed as the result of a complex interaction of factors, only one of which is the person's attitude toward the object of behavior? Other factors would include the person's attitude toward the whole situation in which the behavior occurs (including, for example, her or his attitude toward applicable rules of etiquette and toward the behavior itself), any other cognitions the person may have about the various contingencies of reinforcement operating in the situation, and the person's ability to engage in various alternative types of behavior. You should be able to think of some vivid examples applying to people with negative attitudes toward lumberjacks!

Thus, although much research has clearly indicated no clear, simple correspondence between single attitudes and particular patterns of behavior, it is still possible to preserve a belief in attitudes as "causes" of behavior. That is, constellations of affectively toned beliefs about some object or category of objects can obviously be among the total set of factors that influence how a person behaves. It is also interesting to note that how people *behave* can apparently affect their attitudes (see Kelman, 1974, for an excellent and brief discussion of this).

Values

As hard as it may be to believe, "value" is probably an even vaguer concept than "attitude" in the realm of the behavioral sciences. As in the case of attitudes, it is easy to find numerous definitions of "value." However, we can draw on excellent discussions by three social scientists to help clarify this concept. Clyde Kluckhohn (1951), Robin Williams (1971), and Milton Rokeach (1973)—anthropologist, sociologist, and psychologist, respectively—all seem to agree in conceiving of *values* as conceptions of the desirable that help to guide decision making. The rub in this definition is of course the word "desirable," and any student of axiology (the philosophy of values) should be able to list philosophical treatises going back three thousand years that have struggled to define this concept. Although by no means a final solution, let us settle for now with the observation that considering something to be desirable at least means that it should be possible to provide a culturally or personally acceptable justification for desiring it. In short, one will not feel guilty about desiring something consistent with one's own or one's culture's underlying values.

Rokeach (1973) emphasizes the distinction between *instrumental* values and *terminal* values. The former refers to "desirable modes of conduct" and the latter to "desirable end-states of existence." Later we shall consider some of Rokeach's specific examples of each type of value, but for the moment let us just note that he postulates that although an individual may have thousands of attitudes, each of us presumably has only a few dozen or so values. The reason for this is that one can have an attitude about virtually any object or class of objects, whereas each person has a very limited number of central criteria for judging the desirability of modes of behavior or "end-states of existence." Furthermore, according to Rokeach, a person's values are at least implicitly organized into a hierarchical *value system*. According to this view, each of us has a more or less stable rank ordering of his or her values. When values conflict, the one highest in the hierarchy will tend to win and serve as the final guide for making the decision at issue.

Two other distinctions of some importance concern explicit versus implicit values and asserted versus operative values (see Kluckhohn, 1951). *Explicit* values are those that people are consciously and overtly aware of, while *implicit* values are criteria of the desirable that are used in making decisions but that are not usually recognized as such. In the way these terms are used here, note that both explicit and implicit values function in actual decision making. *Asserted* values, on the other hand, simply refer to the values people claim to hold. They may or may not be accurate or honest reflections of the individual's actual criteria for determining desirability. *Operative* values are the real criteria of desirability that are in fact used for making decisions. Patterns of persistent striving by individuals or institutions, patterns of actual choices, and patterns of approval or disapproval all seem, according to Kluckhohn (1951), to be good indices of underlying operative values. What people or institutions assert to be their values may of course differ considerably from the criteria that really determine their choices, their effort, and even what they actually and overtly approve and disapprove of. Which is just to say that hypocrisy or self-deception can be alive and well just about anywhere people talk about their values.

This view of values as criteria for what is to be considered as desirable should also make clear that virtually all human enterprises involve the explicit or implicit operation of values. There is thus no such thing as "value-free" science or news reporting or textbook writing. *All* goal-directed human activities involve decisions about what is desirable and choices among alternative content and ways of doing things. Even science, which may claim a relatively "neutral" value such as "truth" as its only criterion of the desirable, ends up operating according to many other directive values. As noted in the first chapter, the very questions scientists choose to address reflect underlying values concerning what is important. In fact, in most information-handling areas (science, news reporting, and textbook writing, for example) it is possible to appear to be quite neutral and "objective" (valuing only truth?) in treating any particular content and yet to be following the direction of many values other than truth in the choice of the content to be explored. Peter Sandman (1974) indeed has convincingly pointed this out with respect to news coverage (see later section on the mass media), and Barry Commoner (1966) has made a related case with respect to science. Values influence not only *how* we deal with issues but also *which* issues we choose to deal with. Of course, when it comes to using the information gathered or reported, the role of values is readily acknowledged. The point I wish to emphasize here is that values play a role in virtually *all* human goal-directed activities; but whether by design or oversight, this role is often not acknowledged. At times an attempt is even made to deny its existence.

Relations to Motivation and Cognition

Since by definition attitudes and values involve affectively toned beliefs and conceptions of what is desirable, they should relate in many important ways to human motivation. For instance, human needs will tend to be reflected in people's specific attitudes and values, and attitudes and values may themselves sometimes create desires or needs. Values especially should be related to patterns of striving, since what we deem desirable presumably lies at the core of our decisions about what to do or seek. Again, though, in analyzing what people actually do, it is essential to bear in mind that any determining role of attitudes or values will be a function of *interactions* among different values, attitudes, abilities, situational demands, and so on. Just to take one example, what people believe to be feasible for them to achieve will interact with their beliefs about desirability (their values) in determining what they actually decide to do. This is an important point to keep in mind when seeking to persuade individuals to change their behavior. Often it is not a change in attitudes or values that is required, but only a shift in people's conceptions of what is really possible. Indeed, our society's inability to move more rapidly toward an Equity 2/Theory Y social structure is probably due as much to ignorance of human potentials as it is to an underlying value system at variance with the goal of human happiness.

Attitudes and values also relate to motivation by helping to define what an individual will find reinforcing. One charge often leveled against advertising, for instance, is that it evokes unnecessary or even harmful "needs" (motivations) by creating positive attitudes toward environmentally harmful products. Similarly, but more benignly, educational procedures that help people clarify their values may lead to new patterns of striving as the individuals gain insight into what is really important to them. We shall take up such points in more depth later in this chapter, although it should be reiterated here that attitudes and values *follow* as well as influence needs and other motivational tendencies. Recall, for example, that according to Maslow's motivational hierarchy the Being values associated with self-actualization (for instance, truth, beauty, justice) are posited to arise *after* the person has had more basic deficiency needs satisfied. If this view is correct, it may be very difficult simply to persuade or educate people to change their values; a change to environmentally beneficial values might first require helping people satisfy their needs for food, shelter, safety, and so on.

This by no means exhausts the interrelations between attitudes, values, and motivation, but it exemplifies some of the links to the theme of human motivational potential discussed in Chapter 2. Let us now turn briefly to some ways in which attitudes and values relate to the cognitive processes discussed in the previous chapter.

We might first note that because attitudes and values are usually enduring aspects of a person's functioning, they must be at least implicitly contained in the content of his or her long-term memory. I say "implicitly" because attitudes and values both involve beliefs; and, as Karl Scheibe (1970) has pointed out, beliefs seem to take form as a function of interactions between the person and a situation that calls forth a specific type of information processing. Thus, you may not realize that you "believe" a particular thing until you are asked a question or face some problem that elicits the specific belief as your answer. The question or problem may activate processes of scanning and relating various items and networks in memory that you had never consciously put together before. Indeed, attitude questionnaires may in some cases virtually create the attitudes that are being measured. Many respondents may simply never have thought about some issues until faced with the questions about their attitudes. Furthermore, a person can have inconsistent attitudes or values without being aware of the inconsistencies. Different situations may call forth varying beliefs or values, and the inconsistencies may never be consciously juxtaposed. For instance, if you do not have a firmly entrenched attitude about trees to begin with, thinking about building your house may lead you to think of them as nothing but a source of lumber; but contemplating a mountain hike may lead you to think of trees as valuable mainly as an aesthetic delight.

This example also illustrates some of the relations between one's cognitive sets and one's attitudes and values. Namely, particular Plans for processing information can accentuate or even create particular attitudes and values; and, conversely, holding particular attitudes or values can evoke particular cognitive sets. Let us look at each side of this coin in turn. First, the influence of cognitive sets on attitudes and values can arise in at least the following two ways. First of all, your ways of selecting and processing information will obviously influence the *conception* you build up of what the world is like. Such conceptions, as in the case of coming to think of trees as either mainly sources of lumber or mainly sources of aesthetic delight, play clear roles in generating constellations of affectively toned beliefs (attitudes) predisposing one to "pro" or "anti" action. Your conception of the world can also influence your values by accentuating specific relationships or affecting the salience of particular consequences. For example, you might come to value environmental beauty more if you frequently activate a cognitive set to notice things that give people pleasure but do not cause long-term harm.

A second way that cognitive sets may influence attitudes and values is that certain cognitive sets may lead to experiences that directly change your *affective response* to various aspects of the world. Imagining pleasant environmental changes (IMG), for example, can evoke anger and concern by sensitizing you to ugliness or environmental problems in places that previously seemed neutral; or sets such as seeing the world as abstract forms (ASF) may elicit pleasant aesthetic experiences, resulting in a more positive attitude about a previously neutral or even negative area. On a deeper level, activating such cognitive sets might lead, over time, to changes in one's basic values by stimulating realization of one's own potentials or of the joys and costs inherent in certain types of experience or environments.

Equally important, of course, is the consideration that attitudes and values influence cognitive sets. Certainly one's beliefs and feelings about various aspects of the world and one's conceptions of what is desirable will be central factors in determining how one selects and interprets information both from the environment and from one's memory. This can often be vividly illustrated in ambiguous situations, as Hastorf and Cantril (1954) found in their study of how fans of opposing football teams diverged in interpreting controversial happenings in a particular game. In the environmental realm, one might reflect on how ghetto activists are likely to emphasize the economic and social problems of inner-city living, while many environmentalists might see inner-city problems of air pollution, crowding, and traffic congestion as especially troublesome. Indeed, just as we all tend toward heightened awareness of information pertaining to our areas of special interest, we also tend to select and specially process information that relates to our strongly held attitudes.

Since values are such a central component in the selection of Plans both for overt behavior and for information processing, it is clear that they too will be reflected in everyday activities and cognitive sets. If, for example, seeking truth is a person's most basic criterion for judging desirability, that person's pattern of thought and activity will probably be somewhat different from what it would be if contributing to the world's beauty were the central criterion. In the former case the individual would probably tend to interpret events in terms of their implications for discovery (much as professional experimental psychologists tend to discuss every human event in terms of the research it suggests). If beauty were the prime value, the person would be more likely to interpret things and events in terms of aesthetic effects and implications. This is of course just to say that values point to what is important to a person, and what is important to someone will help determine what that person seeks out and thinks about—that is, *how* the processes of scanning/focusing and relating are carried out. More technically, we might say that values are the common dimensions running through a person's highest-level "tests"—the tests in the guiding Plans for selecting other Plans or for making judgments of desirability.

Again, this brief discussion is certainly far from exhausting the interrelations between attitudes, values, and cognition; but it illustrates a few of the intricate ties. We now turn to an examination of some specific attitudes and values and the problems they help to cause.

VALUES, ATTITUDES, AND ENVIRONMENTAL PROBLEMS

Problems

You have heard it before, but unfortunately it is still true: American cities tend to be crowded blends of asphalt, cars, impersonality, poor (or no) planning, dehumanizing bureaucracy, crime, grime, decaying slums, juxtaposed wealth and poverty, putrid air, misanthropic buildings, and nondescript suburbs. True, the package usually also includes museums, theatres, schools, restaurants, excitement, fantastic variety, and other attractions; but virtually everyone acknowledges that the problems are all too real. To the urban ills must be added our society's relatively poor showing among other rich nations in providing good health care and housing for the poorer members of the society (see, for example, Harrington, 1971). We are also plagued with acknowledged problems of planned obsolescence in consumer goods, rapid depletion of vital natural resources, a seeming inability to recycle or even decontaminate our wastes, a propensity to create ever more (and increasingly more dangerous) wastes, a knack for defiling even our own dwindling natural spaces, instability in our close interpersonal relations, high anxiety as a national trait, high rates of drug addiction, a prison system that incarcerates but does not prevent or rehabilitate, a disregard for old people that is at times almost unbelievable in a human society, a degree of interpersonal and international violence that seems to know few bounds, and a capacity for domestic and foreign oppression that seems all too much in keeping with our ability to drain vast quantities of the world's resources and to spew forth pollution with no apparent thought for other peoples now or in the future.

Well, this may seem an unnecessarily bleak picture; but the point is that we do have very serious environmental and social problems. The issue I wish to raise in this section is whether these diverse problems may arise in part from certain of our dominant attitudes and values. Values would seem to be necessarily important in how a society operates, since they are by definition involved in the higher-level tests or goals that guide the overall pattern of living. Attitudes likewise can be expected to have at least some behavioral manifestations, although in general I have less confidence in attributing basic causal importance to attitudes, since they may arise from the value system and also may often follow rather than precede behavior. Nevertheless, it would seem a worthwhile endeavor to explore the possible roles of both attitudes and values in generating our various problems.

We shall also inquire into the possible role of existing attitudes and values in facilitating or inhibiting viable solutions to the problems. Are the things we believe and value likely to encourage or even allow us to deal effectively with problems after we recognize them as problems? As a further step, we can also ask whether our current attitudes and values will facilitate or inhibit any long-term improvement in the quality of the environment and of our lives beyond the mere solution of problems. That is, will those values we now hold dear help us or hinder us in seeking a truly better life?

As must by now be apparent, I am going to argue that elements in our current value/attitude system have indeed been involved in the development of our environmental and social problems. Unfortunately, these same elements in our values and outlook seem likely to inhibit any lasting solution to these problems; there is even more reason to believe that these elements will decrease our chances of creating as satisfying a life as is possible for human beings on this planet. Before proceeding, I would simply like to add two cautionary (and defensive) notes: (1) My argument must necessarily be based more on theory and impressionistic social analyses than on "hard" data; it is thus intended to be more suggestive than conclusive. (2) Variables such as attitudes and values must themselves be viewed as part of a broader sociocultural system if their purported causal role is to be understood; they are merely elements in an interlocking network of factors.

Let us now consider some of the aspects of America's dominant attitude/value system that may reasonably be construed as contributing to our problems. We shall then look at the probable genesis of these attitudes and values and will conclude the chapter with an extended look at an alternative value system and how it might become our own.

What Are the Offending Attitudes and Values?

Some Environmental Attitudes and Values

Let us first examine some specifically environmental attitudes and values that may be getting us into ecological difficulties. For example, the geographer David Lowenthal (1968; Lowenthal and Prince, 1976) has argued that Americans tend to mainly value idealized and isolated features in the environment. According to Lowenthal, such *featurism* takes the form of sacrificing appreciation and concern for the total everyday environment—for the actual and near at hand—in favor of remote or spectacular individual environmental elements. Thus in America we find nostalgia for an idealized past (here and there preserved in individual historical monuments, sites, and simulations), a willingness to tolerate perpetually scarred cityscapes as we build the "glorious future," and a concentration on individual buildings with little thought about the aggregate effects of our motley creations or the context in which the individual structures reside. We also observe a tendency to gloat over remote scenic sights (the distant mountain, the city skyline across the river) but to neglect the ugliness and squalor nearby, and even a bent toward isolating particular natural spots or views as the only scenic goals of nature visits rather than appreciating the whole continuous experience.

Although this American leaning toward featurism might in itself account for much of our neglect of the aesthetic and other aspects of the environment, it is perhaps a small factor compared with some of our other environmental attitudes and values. Especially important would seem to be what Paul Shepard (1967) has labelled *nature hating*. There are at least three forms this orientation takes: an anti-organic bias, a view of nature as a hierarchy with humans at the top, and a disposition to regard nature as merely a collection of resources to be used according to human whim. Let's look at each of these in turn. (See also Shepard, 1969.)

Anti-organic bias.   Nature in the raw—which also means *us* as organic entities—involves "all those squirting, palpitating, secretory, carnivorous convulsions of life" (Shepard, 1967, p. 214). We are in fact an intimate part of this web of life, but our cultural biases can lead us to view such organicity with disfavor. Our religious heritage often tends to deny and denigrate our animal nature. We also seem to have a special disdain for "dirt" and what often borders on an irrational fear and disgust concerning "germs" and anything having to do with several vital bodily processes. Again in the words of Shepard (1967, p. 214): "The holy war against swamps, fens, heaths, deserts, jungles, snakes, leopards, spiders, brush, weeds, bacteria, fungi, worms, and all the other ecological equivalents of the cell's organs of catabolism is the fanatic scorn for organic nature coupled with a fixation on the runny blemishes and the awful odors to which we, as mammals, are so sensitive and so attracted."

The most important problem here, as with virtually all of our other problematic attitudes and values, is a failure to recognize our *interrelations* with our environment. We somehow seem to have developed the idea that we are separate from nature even to the point of thinking of our bodies as *things* rather than as *us*. Moreover, to the extent that we come to view nature not only as separate but also as "dirty" and even disgusting, we may be inclined to treat it—and ultimately ourselves— rather harshly.

Hierarchical orientation.   Even if we felt no scorn or disgust for organic processes and substances, we would very likely face environmental problems arising from our tendency to view nature as a hierarchy with human beings at the top. Indeed, we manage to go much further than that in our hierarchical thinking, since we are also adept at ordering individuals and groups hierarchically, with lopsided distributions of basic life needs and embellishments as a result; but that is a matter for later discussion. With reference to nature, our hierarchical thinking again keeps us from recognizing our interdependence with the rest of nature. It thus helps predispose us to linear thinking about how the environment can and should be treated. After all, if nature is a hierarchy rather than an interlocking network of equally essential components, then the "higher-ups" should indeed have dominion over the lower reaches of the hierarchy. This view readily leads to the cavalier assumption that we function far more independently than we actually do. The whole notion of "mastery over nature" would indeed seem to spring from such an orientation. It is true, as René Dubos (1972a, 1973b) and Ian McHarg (1969) argue, that *modifying* nature to be more in accord with our wishes is not necessarily bad and can often be both ecologically sound and humanly beneficial. However, the notion of totally *mastering* nature seems to be the sort of self-aggrandizing and self-deceptive fantasy that can lead to profound ecological errors.

Although there seems to be general agreement that we in the West have traditionally tended to think of nature hierarchically and to believe that we can and should "master" it, there is some debate as to the cultural source of this view. Both Paul Shepard (1967) and especially Lynn White, Jr. (1967, 1973) see religion (particularly Christianity) as a major culprit. However, White's (1967) famous—some might say notorious—paper, "The Historical Roots of Our Ecologic Crisis," has provoked much criticism as well as much facile agreement. His thesis was basically that our religions' traditional emphasis on humankind's having dominion over the earth has been taken to heart and interpreted almost literally. (He also offers a religious solution, which will be discussed in Chapter 5.)

This thesis has been challenged by a number of critics (Dubos, 1972a; Moncrief, 1970; and Passmore, 1974, to name only some). The main negative arguments hinge on the presence of "stewardship" themes in Christianity and on the observation that non-Christian cultures have also wreaked environmental havoc. It is certainly easy to find both historical and modern examples of this second point. Yi-Fu Tuan's (1968) brief historical review of Chinese treatment of the environment (especially forests) clearly shows a disregard for many ecological considerations and values, despite the expression of such values in Chinese philosophy and art. And it is apparent, as indicated by continuing news reports (see also Passmore, 1974) that Japan, despite its Buddhist tradition, its tea ceremonies, its neat homes and gardens, and its moon watching ceremonies, manages to produce some of the worst air and water pollution in the world (and at this writing refuses to join an international agreement to abate the slaughter of endangered species of whales).

However, perhaps the critical thing is not to determine whether our high-handed approach to the rest of nature rests on some single element of our culture (such as religion) or even whether our "mastery" orientation by itself will lead to ecological crises. Rather, the most important considerations appear to be that we do indeed have such a hierarchical approach, and that this hierarchical thinking inhibits our awareness of our interdependence with the environment, thus increasing the likelihood that we will produce ecological disturbances.

"Resourcism." Finally, Shepard (1967) has pointed out that we have a tendency to think of nature as simply a collection of resources to be used. Even conservationists often take this view of both living and nonliving aspects of the environment. Such an orientation is especially distasteful to Shepard, since, according to him, it "poses as a virtue" while still destroying the world. Again, the underlying problem is one of failing to recognize interrelations and thus coming to rely on linear thinking where more profound insight is called for. In a sense, viewing the rest of nature as only a collection of resources to be used is simply a consequence of the hierarchical mastery orientation our culture has taken toward the environment. If nature is a hierarchy, and we are at the top, why not just use the lower parts as we wish?

Before proceeding to a look at more general aspects of our culture's attitude/value system, two other points about our environmental attitudes and values should be mentioned. First, although the discussion to this point implies that we hold a rather negative view of nature, this obviously is not entirely true. In fact, as Roderick Nash (1973) has documented generally and as Leo Marx (1964) has pointed out in relation to literature, Americans have shifted historically from an initial view of nature as something to be feared and conquered (in frontier days, for example) to a more ambivalent orientation. Both in our literature and in our daily transactions with the environment, the ambivalence is apparent. On the one hand, we value nature "in itself"—often in a very romantic and idealized form, it is true, but nonetheless as something good. On the other hand, we want to master it, to have it under our control. We also want to use it and tend to view it simply as a resource for satisfying our material or perhaps recreational needs. All in all, this represents a fairly clear shift from our society's initial hostile attitudes toward nature and the wilderness. Unfortunately, however, even ambivalence produces problems, especially when at the policy level our worship of technological and material growth usually outweighs our devotion to natural processes. Thus, a park may occasionally win out over a dam, but with our current attitudes and values, we are unlikely as a society to choose a more pleasant environment over a more "productive" one, even if that productivity threatens to have long-term ill effects.

Second, in the public mind environmental issues have been separated from social issues. This prevailing separation of environmental and social issues is itself one of our problems as a society. Many writers have of course pointed to the interconnections, but along with our tendency to think in hierarchies we also tend to compartmentalize. The result is that we see our problems as separate when in fact they may all be interrelated. As we turn to the following examination of some general features of our attitude/value system, the connection between environmental and social problems should become clearer.

Some Underlying Values and Attitudes

It would be incorrect to argue that the environmental attitudes and values so far mentioned are in themselves responsible for our ecological problems. They are involved in the generation and perpetuation of these troubles, but they are at worst only part of the source. As mentioned earlier, more than attitudes and values must be considered when the cause or cure for environmental and social problems is sought. Nevertheless, attitudes and especially values are certainly important *factors* in behavior. However, we must look beyond purely environmental attitudes and values if we are to grasp the role of attitudes and values in the genesis of environmental—and social—problems.

The following aspects of our dominant value system seem to me to be the main culprits:

1. Individualism and competition
2. A negative view of human nature
3. Hierarchical thinking in human as well as environmental relations
4. Material accumulation and "growth" as dominant evaluative criteria
5. A general tendency to treat means as if they were ends
6. A tendency to accept violence as reasonable
7. A relatively short-term future time orientation

The following sections will examine and criticize each in turn and point out some important interrelations among them.

1. INDIVIDUALISM AND COMPETITION

A dominant, if not all-pervasive, theme in American culture is that each individual (or at least each nuclear family) should be self-reliant and self-supporting. Being dependent on other people is considered bad;

being independent, good. What is more, one is typically considered a *better person* if one has successfully outstripped other individuals in some area of competitive striving, especially if the success entails fame or fortune (preferably both). This general orientation is exemplified in American education, economics, politics, entertainment, and sports, and in numerous related aspects of everyday life.

It is actually somewhat difficult to prove this point with conventional social science research (see below), but let's briefly examine our everyday experience. From the early grades, our schools typically encourage individualism and competition through a variety of techniques: grading on a curve to promote frantic competition or just regular grading of individual performance to promote individualism; emphasis on individual homework assignments and *individual* performance in general; special awards and honors given on an individual basis; history lessons that stress individual achievements (such as having to learn the names of inventors—as if each one had worked all alone and thought everything up out of the blue); individual teachers acting alone with individual jurisdiction over their classes; spelling bees where each individual vies for the ultimate championship. That list can easily be expanded. Then there's economics: just listen to your local junior chamber of commerce, or read any traditional economics textbook or consider how welfare recipients are degraded. Sports? Although there is teamwork in some sports, the dominant orientation—from the problem of making the team to begin with, to inter-team rivalry, to the big differences in pay for different members of the same professional team—seems clearly competitive and individualistic. In politics there is the special irony that the person who is elected is viewed as the *winner,* the vanquisher of the opponents (note the way our political system almost universally thrives on actual and metaphorical conflict—usually of the highly combative, win-or-lose variety). I say "irony" because the elected official is supposed to be a public servant, and yet we normally treat political victory as a great prize and a personal victory for the winner, much like a victory in sports. This brings to mind the zero-sum parlor games most of us play as children: in a zero-sum game, what one side wins all other sides lose.

It would be easy to go on listing examples of how competition and an orientation toward individualistic achievement and self-sufficiency play prevalent roles in American life. (Indeed, in Chapter 2 it was noted that even the humanistic side of American psychology sometimes reflects this theme.) However, let us instead look more deeply into what competition and individualism mean and also examine a few examples of social-science analysis of their role in the American value system.

Competition is basically a pattern of interpersonal or intergroup interaction that involves incompatible goals by the different participants. In effect, what one person (or group) wants conflicts with what the other person(s) or group wants. As Morton Deutsch (1973) put it, in competition between two parties, an increase in the probability of goal attainment by one party decreases the chances of goal attainment by the other party.

Individualism, on the other hand, is a somewhat more complex and perhaps nebulous concept. As used in this discussion, it essentially means a personal or cultural value system in which primary value is placed on individual accomplishment, self-reliance, and independence. In its extreme form, individualism involves placing primary value on aggrandizement of oneself without concomitant concern for the well-being of others, especially if others' interests conflict with one's own. Proponents of such a position are easy to find in our society, and they often attempt to bolster their position with rationales drawing on our dominant Equity 1 norms for distributing resources. (One might compare writers such as Ayn Rand, members of the right wing of American politics, capitalistic economists, and so on.) Philip Slater (1974) insightfully noted a concise literary example of this self-aggrandizing orientation in his analysis of the popular novel *Jonathan Livingston Seagull* (Bach, 1970). In this, as in many other works of popular fiction and film, a key consideration is that the hero can, does, and should "do it alone." *That* is the essence of individualism.

It is obviously a risky business to attempt to demonstrate anything in the social sciences by simply alluding to "our" experience or citing instances from everyday life. Indeed, someone could probably even make a case that we in fact live in a cooperative, communal society by selectively presenting aspects of our culture (for example, the emphasis on team sports, early childhood training for sharing, the norm of Equity 2 within families, community spirit and social helping after catastrophes, and so on). These, of course, do represent less individualistic and competitive features of our culture—which, after all, is not purely individualistic or competitive. However, if one looks to the everyday functioning of our main social institutions, and especially if this functioning is compared with that of certain other societies (for example, China or the kibbutzim in Israel), there does seem to be a reasonably objective basis for the claim that individualism and competition form relatively dominant themes in our lives. This is especially evident at the level of fundamental operative values—those criteria of the desirable that are actually applied in decision making and in evaluating people and events.

Thoroughgoing empirical studies of values are still relatively rare at this writing, and those that have been carried out have sufficient methodological flaws not to qualify as "proof" for any sweeping claims about value systems. However, the results of cross-cultural survey studies by Triandis (1972), Cantril (1965), Kluckhohn and Strodtbeck (1961), Rokeach (1973), and Morris (1956) generally support the view that individualism and competition (especially individualism) are prominent American values.

Perhaps as convincing as a spate of hard data, however, are the impressionistic analyses of our culture by various social scientists and other presumably astute social observers. I have found the books by the anthropologist Francis Hsu (1970) and the sociologist Philip Slater (1970, 1974) especially provocative, but many others could be cited. In *The Pursuit of Loneliness,* for example, Slater (1970) argued that American culture stresses competition, uninvolvement, and independence. He also pointed out, however, that the opposites of these—community, engagement, and dependence—appear to be ambivalently desired at some implicit level by most people in our society, and that indeed such values are often stressed for very young children before the reverse system of individualistic values is imposed. In his follow-up book, *Earthwalk,* Slater (1974) forcefully continued his analysis and critique of American culture, this time clearly laying the blame for our "trashing" of the environment on our drive for self-aggrandizing individualism. In both of these books Slater has presented a wealth of observations, metaphors, and explanations centering on the theme that our cultural emphasis on individualism and other values that disconnect us from each other and from environmental feedback loops (for example, values such as courage and perseverance) are at the root of our social and environmental ills. There are many points where it is easy to disagree with Slater, and many others where the lack of hard evidence should certainly give pause to any facile acceptance of his indictments or hypotheses; but he seems to me to have succeeded very well in laying bare much of the cultural core that plagues us with personal anxieties and with social and environmental deterioration.

Francis Hsu (1970), in his comparison of American and Chinese culture, similarly expresses concern about the ill effects of our version of individualism. Hsu characterizes American culture as mainly devoted to individualistic self-reliance, which he sees as resulting in a widespread lack of interpersonal security. The contrast with the emphasis given by traditional Chinese culture to interpersonal networks is helpful in seeing where our own individualism fits in the broader context of cultural possibilities. Although Hsu finds both problems and advantages in each culture's dominant orientation, his overall analysis of American culture appears to be quite consistent with Slater's. Each of these social theorists—one an anthropologist originally from China and the other a native American sociologist—clearly sees attention to individual success and a resulting neglect and instability of interpersonal relationships as key ingredients in the American way.

Numerous other social commentators could of course be cited and discussed. Some (for example, Goodwin, 1974; Reich, 1970) stress alienation and bureaucratic domination more than do Slater and Hsu. Others (for example, Williams, 1970) take a less critical stance and attempt to assess a wider range of values. Still others (for example, Parkes, 1948; Passmore, 1974) concentrate on value elements in our past that often seem to offer hope for dealing with present-day difficulties (for example, a stress on community and on utopian striving). However, through most such commentaries, if not indeed through all, seem to run the observations that our current culture involves a fragmented and fragmenting value system, that individual achievement and success and self-reliance are primary cultural values, and that competition is inextricably involved in our ways of doing things and of gaining self-esteem. If these observations are accurate—if individualism and competition lie at the core of our value system—what implications does this have for our interpersonal and environmental relations?

Critique of Individualism and Competition

Obviously, I think something is wrong with individualism and competition. Specifically, I think that a social system or culture that holds individual competitive success as a terminal value (as something that is inherently good or desirable) is less likely than some alternative system to produce widespread human happiness. When combined with other values, such as materialism and technological control over things and people, I also believe that the individualistic or competitive system is likely to produce—and to be unable to solve—various social and environmental problems. Before tackling my precise reasons for these beliefs, however, let us take a look at an important distinction and at the bright side of individualism and competition.

A distinction.   *Individualism* must be carefully distinguished from *individuality.* The former term is being used here to refer to value systems that place primary emphasis on individuals' being independent, self-reliant, and self-aggrandizing. This orientation will be criticized primarily because of its positive relation to competition and its negative relation to cooperation. *Individuality,* on the other hand, will be used to refer to individuals' differentiation from each other on the basis of personal tastes, styles, experiences, and so on. It is not, in short, going to be argued that people should be *alike.* Nor will it be argued that we should turn into conformists, doing things we don't want to do just because other people do them or want us to do them. It should indeed be obvious that individualists in the sense of those seeking self-aggrandizement can themselves be very much like each other and can even be among the most abject conformists (each conforming to social pressures for individual achievement, for example). Individualism and individuality are two separate dimensions. Although it is true that some individual differences must be stressed in order for self-aggrandizement to be a primary value (individualism), it is also quite possible for a cooperative, nonindividualistic system to value individual differences (individuality).

Furthermore, in any value system in which human happiness is central, it would obviously be essential to use the quality of experience of each *individual* as a touchstone for making value choices. Experience is an "individual" thing, since it presumably arises only in connection with the functioning of an individual's nervous system. The difference between a value system that stresses general happiness and an individualistic value system is that the former encourages everyone to use the quality of *every* person's (individual) experience as the central criterion for making decisions, while the individualistic system at best encourages each person only to use the quality of her or his *own* experience as the central criterion. In its extreme form, this is the difference between each person's being important to everyone else and each person's being important to virtually no one else.

Positive aspects of competition and individualism.   Since individualism and competition seem so intertwined in our culture (indeed, we might better refer to this aspect of our culture as "competitive individualism"), they will be treated as a single orientation in what follows. First, let us note several aspects that seem genuinely beneficial.

1. *Arousal value.* Competition and conflict are often very exciting and interesting. They can add spice to an otherwise dull existence, perk up play, and even provide thrilling and exhilarating diversion. Anyone who has followed a World Series can certainly appreciate this point. The questions I would raise, however, are (a) is *competition* really essential to this interest and arousal value—or would perhaps elements of uncertainty, skilled performance, action, tradition, and perhaps a few other ingredients be sufficient—and (b) are there costs (such as someone's having to lose) that adulterate the apparent pleasure more than we think? Nevertheless, the arousal value (contribution to Complexity) of competition cannot be denied.

2. *Aid to competence.* A more telling point for many defenders of competition would probably be that it sharpens people's skills and promotes human achievement. I would not deny that competition (and individualism) can in fact be a path to competence and achievement. It can even do this on a broad scale, for both the winners and the losers. Competing with each other can of course motivate people to strive, to gain skills, and to accomplish things. As in the case of its arousal value, however, we can at least ask if there are alternative, noncompetitive sources of human motivation that could lead to equivalent development of necessary or beneficial personal skills. We might also ask if competitive and individualistic motivation might have the side effect of inhibiting the development of certain types of skills (facility in the domains of interpersonal cooperation, collective efforts, group problem solving, and so on). Nevertheless, it cannot be denied that competition can indeed serve as one way to generate motivation for developing skills and achievements.

3. *Necessity.* Perhaps most important, it is probably impossible for people to interact without at times finding themselves at odds over goals. No matter how much we might desire to cooperate and help each other, there will doubtless always be disagreements and incompatible desires. There is thus probably no way to design or socialize competition and conflict completely out of existence. Nor would it be desirable, since conflict of some sort would seem to be essential in the develop-

ment of new ideas and in higher syntheses of initially incompatible ideas or orientations. The critical consideration is whether the arousal and resolution of conflict (competition, in the case of conflicts of goals) occur in a competitive or cooperative *context*. That is, the important question is not whether there is competition in the system, but whether the system itself is based on a competitive or a cooperative value structure.

Negative aspects of competition and individualism.   The following criticisms of competitive individualism should therefore be taken as applying to the orientation of self-aggrandizement and competitive success mainly insofar as it represents the *dominant* theme of a cultural value system. As argued above, this does unfortunately appear to be the case for our society.

1. *Failure to take account of actual interdependencies.* As in the case of the various types of nature hating, competition and individualism (considered as guiding social principles) are associated with a lack of insight into our true relation to each other and to the biosphere. Instead of realizing the intricate levels of interdependence that actually intertwine the fates of people and other living things, competitive individualism encourages the illusion of independence and self-sufficiency. Furthermore, we are thus encouraged to ignore the needs of other people as each of us strives for his or her (usually his) individual "success." This can have the ironic consequence of eventually alienating other people, perhaps even one's own family, and thereby reducing one's own real sources of satisfaction in life. In the broader societal arena, striving to amass individual or national wealth and power without recognizing interdependencies with nature and other nations can lead to wars, environmental deterioration, and inefficiency in improving the long-term quality of life. Notice, for example, that pushing for economic conditions that favor one's financial advance may reduce the quality of the environment necessary for one's own health and happiness, not to mention other people's. Since competitive individualism rests on incorrect premises about one's interdependence with others and with the ecosystem, it easily leads to decisions that have deleterious ramifications that can ultimately affect everyone.

2. *Lack of coordination.* Morton Deutsch (1973) has presented theoretical reasons and empirical evidence that competition tends to lead to (a) distorted or truncated communication; (b) perceiving other people

(competitors) as malevolent; (c) hostile interpersonal attitudes and behavior; and (d) the use of coercive strategies in the resolution of conflicts and disagreements. Obviously, people or groups that relate to one another in these ways are likely to have difficulties in dealing with collective problems. Indeed, if each person (or country) is pursuing narrowly and egocentrically defined interests, there is little chance of mutual coordination of efforts except perhaps in dire emergencies (and even then, a competitive individualistic orientation could be conducive to panic rather than constructive efforts—see Brown, 1965). The sad truth is that many of our current and impending problems require *social* decision making and concerted *collective* action. The welfare of the society, and indeed of the world, in areas such as health, transportation, the quality of urban environments, arms control, food quantity and quality, and so on, will most certainly require coordination and some degree of mutual concern. In short, our present system is spinning off social and environmental problems that will only be amenable to solution through cooperative effort. Competitive individualism (and its societal cousin, nationalism) is not preparing us for that effort.

3. *Reduced tendency to seek higher-order goals.* In addition to both generating our problems and making it difficult to solve them, competitive individualism keeps us from focusing on goals and techniques that would open new paths to the enhancement of all our lives. Thus, it is one thing to worry about getting rid of the smog or "cleaning up" the environment, but quite another to contemplate building truly beautiful and joyful communities or turning the whole world into a joyful community. Such goals may even sound unreasonably unrealistic. But would they seem so far out of reach in a country (or a world) in which people cared about each other's welfare and took a genuinely cooperative stance in all aspects of everyday life?

R. E. Walton and R. B. McKersie (1965), for example, have distinguished between "distributive" and "integrative" bargaining. The former is the usual win/lose type of interaction we associate with strikes and used-car negotiations. The latter, however, is actually creative group problem solving. In integrative bargaining the negotiators try to explore new paths of joint behavior that transcend egocentric disputes and that involve open and complete communication. Thus, integrative bargainers seek not just to decide how to split up the pie, but to discover a bigger or better pie to split up. It is only when we transcend the idea of *winning* and focus instead on *figuring out* what is really best for everyone that we can hope to realize our best possibilities.

One qualification that should be noted here, however, is that competition might in fact be cooperatively chosen as an appropriate technique for achieving given collective (cooperative) purposes. For example, some problems might be most efficiently solved at times by setting up competing teams of people (or even competing individuals) to work on them. Again, the important consideration is not whether there is competition in the system, but whether competitive or cooperative processes are directing the system's functioning. It is only if cooperation guides system functioning that seeking and realizing mutual superordinate goals seems a likely possibility.

4. *Necessity of losers.* In a competitive system some participants must lose in order for others to win. Because success is defined in large part as doing better than other people, it is simply impossible for everyone to be successful. This is especially true in a system such as ours that recognizes relatively few paths to self-esteem. Material acquisition, outstanding performance of some skill, or being especially well-endowed with some culturally favored physical trait are key examples. In any case, the emphasis is clearly on being better than other people in at least some respect. Since only one person can ultimately be the *best* at anything, an intensely internalized competitive orientation can make even the better people feel inadequate if they feel impelled to compare themselves with the best. Moreover, since one's standing and even livelihood can easily depend on one's competitive performance, the general level of anxiety will tend to be high in any system that operates according to competitive individualism. People cannot count on each other for mutual support or aid. One need only think of workers vying with each other for promotions, students competing for grades, companies competing for bigger shares of the market. (An alternative, cooperative approach would allow much more attention to such activities as the creation of safe and pleasant working conditions controlled by the workers themselves; the creation of exciting and pleasant learning environments where students helped each other to learn and to develop interests; and the pooling and coordination of industrial efforts to serve the real needs of humankind.) As it stands now, our system produces many more losers than winners, but in a cooperative system that focused on improving the overall quality of life, virtually everyone could "win."

5. *Inefficiency*. Deutsch (1973) also pointed out that competition will tend to be inefficient since it promotes duplication of effort as people compete to accomplish the same thing. One obvious example of this is the international space race, whereby the United States and Russia have managed to squander an obvious opportunity to conserve human and environmental resources by joining in space exploration rather than competing in it. The underlying principle is of course that cooperation is best for dealing with problems that require joint efforts and open communication for optimally creative and efficient solutions. It would seem that a world steadily being bombarded by an ever-increasing number of complex large-scale problems would be much better off with concerted efforts rather than patchwork competitive duplication.

Interpretive summary.   If competition and individualism do indeed lead to disregarding our social and ecological interdependencies, to lack of coordination, to overlooking superordinate goals, to anxiety and low-ered self-esteem over losing, and to inefficiency in dealing with complex shared problems, what is the overall effect? Clearly, we should expect to see environmental and social problems of major proportions develop in a social system dominated by competition and individualism. This will be true all the way from the neighborhood level to the international scene, and the problems will be exacerbated as technological power and population increase. The underlying reason is built into the operation of individualistic functioning: If people or groups are selfishly pursuing their own goals in competition with or disregard of each other, they will tend to miss the opportunities for intelligent collective action designed to further their common welfare. The "tragedy of the commons" (Hardin, 1968, 1972) arises from individualistic pursuit of ends without regard for long-term collective welfare and without an understanding of ecological interrelations. Translated into the terms of current crises, this means that by acting separately we manage to achieve what none of us really wants and we fail to achieve what we all would really like if we only thought about it and worked together. Instead of polluted air and water, scarred landscapes, unsafe and ob-solescent consumer goods, squandered resources, vast inequities in the distribution of wealth and health, and so on, we could have a reasonably pleasant world. But from an early age we in this society and in the West generally are trained to be blind to our collective well-being. We think in terms of individual success rather than group success, winning rather than collective growth and harmony, being "independent" rather than making the most of our inescapable interdependence.

Thus, industrialists in many countries can defile, pollute, destroy, and kill (at least indirectly) in the pursuit of accepted "social values." A social system that sets up individualistic aggrandizement and accumulation as the highest good will easily open itself up to environmental degradation. Ironically, those who reduce the quality of other people's lives in the pursuit of individualistic goals may end up having the quality of their own lives diminished by others in pursuit of similar ends. The industrialists can themselves end up sick from their own or other industrialists' pollution. The manufacturer of profitable but unsafe cars may end up injured in a car wreck. But the big losers are the poorer people—often the basic workers who carry out essential production or housekeeping tasks—and very possibly also future generations.

So I hope it does not sound like a gross exaggeration to claim that the competitive individualism at the base of our value system is probably our single worst problem. But, alas, it is not our only one.

2. A NEGATIVE VIEW OF HUMAN NATURE

As pointed out in Chapter 2, our social institutions seem largely to be based on a Theory X conception of human motivation. Our highly individualistic and competitive value system, combined with the dominant Equity 1 norms of distribution and attendant reliance on extrinsic reinforcers, tends to push such a view of human nature in the direction of becoming a self-fulfilling prophecy. We expect very little of each other, and we get just that. There is no need to repeat the argument here, but recall that in Chapter 2 a case was presented for considerable hope in human capacity for creative and productive functioning according to Theory Y conceptions of motivation. Furthermore, it was argued that basic changes in our economic and educational systems could greatly facilitate actual social and individual functioning according to this more positive view of human nature. Finally, it was argued that such a change would allow us to produce a far more pleasant environment—and life. The first step, it would seem, is for us to recognize that our view of human nature as untrustworthy and uncreative is not accurate. Our social systems may currently be making it so, but if we begin to open our eyes to human possibilities we might cease to perpetuate this form of "psychological pollution."

3. HIERARCHICAL THINKING

This aspect of our value system was discussed earlier in relation to environmental attitudes, but it actually applies very generally to our dominant ways of processing all types of information, social as well as environmental. In brief, a pervasive cognitive set in this culture is to interpret things or people as forming hierarchies (see, for example, Bookchin, 1973; Ecology Action East, 1973). However, it should be noted that hierarchical thinking—viewing items as forming a rank ordering of priority or importance—is certainly not inherently harmful. Indeed, this way of thinking is obviously essential in making decisions; value systems inherently entail the use of hierarchies. Problems can arise, however, when we unnecessarily apply hierarchical notions to items that are in fact interdependent with each other (such as human beings and the rest of nature) and when we force people into unnecessary rank orderings and invidious comparisons.

For example, our culture's tendencies to encourage interpersonal domination, social classes, vastly unequal distribution of wealth, status seeking based on defeating other people, and the various other spin-offs of competitive individualism are all supported by our readiness to view *people* as forming hierarchies. This sometimes takes such extreme and unfair forms that we even rebel against it, as in the case of slavery or racial and sexual prejudice. Nevertheless, needless hierarchical thinking and the patterns of domination that accompany it are all too apparent in our everyday lives. For instance, school principals are viewed as genuinely "more important" (valuable?) than teachers, who are in turn regarded as more important than students (who outrank janitors sometimes). If you think about it, though, all these people or roles are necessary for the school to function. Similarly, we blindly accept hierarchical organization—and resulting differentials in power, wealth, and privilege —in factories, stores, civil services, professions, and so on. But note that in terms of immediate necessity for maintaining the smooth functioning of any of these systems, the *lower* positions in many of our everyday hierarchies turn out to be more essential than some of the higher ones. Even short strikes by garbage collectors or transportation workers probably foul up the works much more than would a similar walkout by bank vice-presidents or advertising executives. (And everyone has

heard the "joke" that secretaries actually run universities and corporations.)

My point is not that our social or environmental hierarchies should be
reversed—that the lower parts are really more important than the higher
ones—but simply that we often deal with systems of mutually essential
interdependent parts as if we were confronting only a linear arrangement. Our tendency to view and treat the parts as forming a hierarchy
of importance (value) is in this sense a gross distortion of the nature of
these systems. This type of inaccuracy in both the social and environmental realms can easily lead to various forms of unfair, cruel, and unwise treatment of nature and of each other. It also easily gets in the
way of the cooperative, collective behavior and mutual concern that we
as a society will need to deal effectively with our environmental and
social problems.

4. MATERIALISM

To compound the problems created by our individualistic and hierarchical orientations toward each other, our society tends to use material
success and growth as dominant values. It is of course commonplace to
find diatribes against "technology" and "technocracy" (for example,
Ellul, 1964; Roszak, 1969; Slater, 1974; Mumford, 1970), and we do
seem fascinated with gadgetry. On a more basic level, we seem oriented
toward the acquisition of *things*. Individuals' self-esteem frequently
appears indelibly linked to their material wealth. Indeed, there is the
common question, "How much is he (she) *worth?*" There is also our
widely acknowledged near worship of the gross national product
(GNP). This kind of criticism is old hat, but it is important to consider
one more point: materialism, when combined with competitive individualism and a high level of technology, can easily equal environmental crisis. Our emphasis on private ownership of wealth and property
clearly leads to much needless duplication and over-use of resources.
We are loath to share things, and as a result, our form of materialism
has a particularly virulent effect on the state of the public environment.
We use vast quantities of resources so that every individual can have a
car or whatever. We use material goods as signs of personal success,
again leading to accumulations that drain resources and are themselves
under-used. What would happen were we to look around for other

types of things to value, such as each other and the quality of our collective environment?

5. TREATING MEANS AS ENDS

Aside from the negative effects of competition and individualism per se, the most environmentally harmful aspect of our value system is probably our tendency to regard things such as those included in Lewis Mumford's (1970) "pentagon of power"—power, productivity, profit, property, and publicity—as intrinsically good rather than as merely possible contributors to the quality of human experience. In the words of René Dubos (1972a, p. 233), "the demonic force in our life is not technology per se, but our propensity to consider means as ends." It is not that people or institutions, if pressed, could not muster some deeper justification for their pursuit of wealth or feats of technology. It is rather that so many of our personal and especially societal decisions seem to be based on *unquestioned* assumptions about what is really good for us. This leads us to act as if we regarded many things to be ends in themselves, when a deeper questioning and understanding might have led us to see these things as only potential means to more satisfying states of being.

Our apparent pursuit of technology for technology's sake is probably the most notorious example in the environmental realm. This devotion to technology can itself be broken into several subareas, each of which seems to reveal at least misplaced values. Thus, we evidence an almost paranoid concern with ever-increasing levels of overkill in weapons technology, as if developing every possible new means of destruction were indeed an end in itself. In the realm of "peaceful" technology, we leaped into the space race with an outpouring of treasure that is almost unbelievable in view of our toleration of poverty, environmental deterioration, and relative paucity of research in areas such as preventive medicine and clean energy sources. Even the defense of the space program by some environmentalists that it has yielded the pictures of "Spaceship Earth" has a hollow ring when one considers that much cheaper unmanned flights could have accomplished that. Similarly, in the "private sector," we nonchalantly tolerate profit-oriented (rather than public-service-oriented) research and development policies by corporations. Technology in the service of technology, technology in the service of international games of threat or status, technology in the service of profit: all this seems fine with us. Technology *could* be used in the service of human welfare (see Papanek, 1971, for example), but we do not seem inclined as a society (or world, for that matter) to direct it concertedly to that end.

Our most serious problem in getting our means and ends straight seems to be that we do not adequately inquire into the consequences of our alternative choices or even consider an appropriate range of options open to us. Thus we treat our car-centered transportation system as if it were virtually an end in itself, rather than giving due attention to possible alternative means of getting people around. We treat private rights to land ownership as if they were beyond question rather than asking what the effect is on the overall quality of life for all the members of the society and what effects alternative systems of collective ownership might have. We treat competitive success as if it were an unquestionable good rather than thinking of it only as a possible means to motivation and self-esteem—to be questioned and compared with other possible means.

Another way to put all this is that we tend to be too superficial and uncritical in our operative value system. We accept the status quo as if it really were the best of all possible worlds. Unfortunately, this sort of irrationality and restriction of vision permeates many aspects and levels of our society. Our schools, for instance, have traditionally treated learning and "discipline" as ends. If instead such goals were viewed only as possible *means* to enhancing life, they would more readily be compared with alternatives such as creativity, skill at developing personal interests, skill at questioning the status quo, ability to cooperate with other people to effect beneficial social change, and so on. However, the actual goals of our schools mainly involve producing people who will perform well at work that is extrinsically motivated. This may fit students well for existing social and economic conditions, but it is functionally the same thing as treating preservation of the status quo as an intrinsic good.

Yet another illustration of how we elevate means to the status of ends is provided by our tendency to seek justification for virtually anything by appeal to some effect on economics or productivity. We generally tend to accept saving money or developing strong bodies as the right sort of justification for, say, a purchase or a new playground. But why can't we recognize that simply enjoying something may itself be adequate justification? As Robert Sommer (1972, p. 130) put it, "good experiences should be made an end in themselves"; we should not have to justify beauty or comfort or fun by appeal to criteria such as learning or performance.

Ultimately, it is the quality of experience, and only the quality of experience, that is *intrinsically* valuable (a point to be expanded later on). If this point is accepted, rationality would require that we use enhancement of the quality of experience (presumably for everyone and over both the short and long run) as the underlying criterion for how to use our resources and live our lives. Can anyone doubt that we have failed to do this?

6. ACCEPTANCE OF VIOLENCE

That America has historically been a relatively violent society, and continues to be one, has been clearly documented in the massive study directed by H. D. Graham and T. R. Gurr (1969). To sense the current cultural toleration of violence, however, one need only tune in evening television. There may not be much actual blood in evidence, but violent deeds are pervasively splattered all over the screen. We in the United States carefully censor any explicit sex (*love*-making) but expose ourselves and our children to a steady stream of murder and mayhem. Could this have the effect of inuring us to the violence on the streets and on the highways—as well as to violence perpetrated by us in foreign lands?

Unfortunately, in our culture violence is indeed acceptable in more than just dramatizations. Sports such as boxing and football glorify real violence of a "mild" sort, while some kinds of hunting and our profligate profusion of guns demonstrate an even more active acceptance of willful destruction of life. And of course our foreign policy in Vietnam involved a degree of needless aggression that is still almost beyond belief. Vietnam also revealed in raw form our willingness to engage in "ecocide"—deliberate, massive destruction of ecological systems.

All this is not to say that we regard violence itself as good. We do seem to get a kick out of watching it, true; but the problem is probably more that we all too easily look to violence as an acceptable or reasonable means for reaching our ends (which of course usually involve acquiring more material wealth or power). It is this facile acceptance that seems so insidious. It is hard to be sure of this point, but it might even be that our willingness to allow hundreds of thousands of people to be maimed or killed each year in automobile wrecks is a partial reflection of our unwillingness to regard violence as unacceptable. Similarly, our abusive treatment of forests, air, and water is at least consistent with our acceptance of violence generally. Again, I am not arguing that we are therefore sadistic, but only that our failure to reject violence as a suitable means allows us to do a good job of simulating sadism.

7. SHORT-TERM TIME ORIENTATION

Finally, our value system generally fails to look very far into the future. That is, in making decisions, we as a society typically consider only effects that occur within a short period of time (usually not more than twenty years or so, and generally far less). Florence Kluckhohn and Fred Strodtbeck (1961), for example, posited that all cultures must deal with at least five basic questions as part of their "value orientation." These questions concern human relations with nature (over, subjugated to, or in harmony with nature); human interpersonal relations (individualistic, collateral, or lineal); human nature (good, evil, or mixed; mutable or immutable); favored type of activity (doing, being, or "being-in-becoming"); and time orientation (past, present, or future). The dominant traditional American value orientation, according to Kluckhohn and Strodtbeck, has involved mastery over nature, individualistic interpersonal relations, a view of human nature as evil but mutable, a stress on doing, and a future time orientation. Their scheme, however, fails to distinguish between short- and long-term future time orientations, and this could be a most important consideration where ecological problems are concerned.

Jorgen Randers and Donella Meadows (1973) argue that our current value system tends to concern only the welfare of people alive today, at best, and to assign essentially no value to any effects occurring more than about twenty years in the future. It is almost as if we thought the world were going to end in less than twenty years. This tendency to consider only short-run outcomes is illustrated on the individual level by activities such as smoking, and on the broad social/environmental level by profligate use of nonrenewable resources and the ready use of pesticides and other chemicals that provide potential long-term harm but short-term gains. Other illustrations can be gleaned from our tendency to build houses meant to last only one generation and to readily accept consumer goods with obsolescence built in. It is to be hoped that our various environmental crises and our increasing understanding of the nature of ecological problems will shift our time perspective to a longer-term orientation. We might thus not only improve the quality of life for future generations but actually improve our own lives as well.

Interrelations Among These Value Elements

It would be nice if the troublemaking components in our value system somehow cancelled each other out, but it seems more likely that they actually reinforce each other. This should not be surprising, since they constitute a value *system*. Competitive individualism, a negative view of human nature, hierarchical thinking, materialism, treating means as ends, accepting violence, and taking a short-term perspective all fit together. They also cohere with our "featurist" way of relating to the physical environment and with the various forms of "nature hating" discussed earlier. What all of these value elements have in common is a truncation and distortion of our interrelatedness with each other and with nature. This value system embodies a blindness to the welfare of other people and other living things; and it embodies a concomitant blindness to the fact that the welfare of *other* people and other living things ultimately affects one's own welfare.

Pure selfishness might not be such a problem if it were truly intelligent, enlightened selfishness and if everyone were informed and bright enough to see all the implications for different types of action—*and* if everyone had roughly equal power in societal decision making. Under such circumstances, whether people started out focused on their own or on others' happiness might make little difference in the type of society that they would eventually choose. Even highly egocentric individuals—if intelligent, rational, concerned with happiness, and faced with equally powerful and egocentric peers—would very likely conclude that each person would actually have the best chance to be happy in a social system that was based on cooperation, concern for ecologically sound life styles, stress on intrinsic motivation for everyone, and other "means" values related to increasing the quality of life. However, before considering a value system that would explicitly favor happiness and ecological well-being, let us look briefly at some of the social and cultural processes that maintain our current pattern of values.

How Are Our Values Formed and Maintained?

The following analysis is meant to be suggestive rather than exhaustive or definitive, but it does seem likely that the main sources of our value system are family socialization practices, dominant educational procedures, prevalent practices in the mass media, and similar patterns in the operation of other major social institutions. We shall look at each of these in turn.

The Family

Based on cross-cultural comparisons and a thoroughgoing study of socialization practices, Urie Bronfenbrenner (1970) has argued that the contemporary American family has given up much of its socializing influence to schools, television, and the child's peer group. Although this may be true, the American nuclear family still represents home base for young children at least, and parents still represent enormously important models and socializing influences in the early lives of their children. Slater (1970, 1974), for example, has offered some pointed criticisms of the nuclear family as a main source of our individualistic value system. According to his view, children (especially males) raised in American nuclear families tend to form very strong early dependencies on their mothers for emotional satisfaction and relatively weak attachments to adults other than their parents. The resulting "steep gradient of affection," according to Slater, is the precursor of all sorts of "disconnector" values involving willingness to postpone gratification in the pursuit of virtually unattainable symbolic goals (such as everincreasing status, power, or wealth).

Slater's view perhaps relies a little too heavily on the Freudian concept of the Oedipus complex, but the underlying point seems to be that the nuclear family situation focuses the child's affection on one or two adults at the expense of a more diffused pattern of affection and identification. Somehow this seems to serve as a kind of emotional model for later single-minded goal orientation. Also involved, at least for middleclass families (see, for example, Hess, 1970), would be the guilt motivation produced by love withdrawal as a disciplinary technique and what Slater has termed the "Spockian challenge" to mothers to raise little prodigies. It is easy to see (although not necessarily easy to prove) that the hothouse emotional atmosphere created by the steep gradient of affection, combined with a maternal emphasis on early achievement, can set the stage for a highly individualistic and competitive value system.

However, one need not buy the "depth" analysis of parent-child relations offered by theorists like Slater to see how family socialization passes along basic cultural values. The behavior of parents and indeed the structure of the nuclear family itself provide the child with models for what is culturally appropriate. For example, each nuclear family (especially in the middle class) is expected to "make it alone." In addition, each family typically has or strives for its own private house or apartment. This insular physical arrangement alone is usually sufficient to orient young children rather exclusively toward their own parents as the only adults they can really count on and to set a model for "independence." Furthermore, within the family there are many factors working to pass along dominant American value orientations. For instance, as Hsu (1970) pointed out, U.S. families typically attach great importance to privacy and exclusivity of possessions even inside the home. (He contrasted this with the much more open and sharing atmosphere of the traditional Chinese home, for example.) And Slater (1970, 1974) observed that our families provide a ready model for hierarchical structure and "social climbing." The children are in effect the lower class and the parents the upper, complete with all the usual differentials in deference, privilege, and power.

Add to all this the likely role of sibling rivalry in setting an early pattern of competitive individualism, the possibility that physical punishment models violence, and the consideration that materialism is reflected in everything from Christmas presents to the tooth fairy. Even though child-rearing practices usually differ across social classes (again, see Hess, 1970), and even though some families apparently manage to instill values leading children later to desire radical social change (see Keniston, 1968), the fact remains that common practices of family socialization and the very insularity of the nuclear family support our existing value structure.

Education

Traditional educational practices also pass on and bolster the value system we have been examining. Listed below are just a few of the ways in which the schools help to form or support environmental attitudes and our social values.

With respect to environmental attitudes, we can begin by taking a look at Mark Terry's (1971) delightful little book *Teaching for Survival*. He pointed out that there is usually a hidden curriculum that passes on environmental messages even in the absence of a formal program in environmental education. Some of his examples, drawn from his own experience, are (pp. 7–8):

"Any amount of garbage is all right, just don't litter."
"The Asians won't starve, as long as I eat everything on my plate and we harvest the sea."
"Man has always had problems, and he'll always be able to solve them through science and industry."
"Wildlife is a precious, but unnecessary, resource."
"Hydroelectric dams bring nothing but good: power, irrigation, recreation."
"Standard of living is based on annual income and purchasing power."
"Driving to school is approved if I am licensed, permitted by my parents, and safe."
"The history of man is the history of his growing mastery over nature."

In a similar vein, James Swan (1972a) insightfully noted that the apparently extraneous content of many school subjects often serves to support status-quo attitudes and values. For example, math problems often stress things like compound interest rates, speeds of cars, stock market prices, and so on. Lately, we have also begun to become aware of how elementary-school texts help to spread sexism and other types of hierarchical thinking. And our history lessons have long glorified wars and violent exploits. To the extent that positive views of material accumulation, environmentally deleterious transportation systems, the "conquest" of nature, a competitive economic system, and so on, actually represent threats to environmental well-being, the schools are certainly doing their part.

As Terry (1971) noted, the hidden environmental curriculum is present in more than the subject matter of regular lessons. Like other public institutions, the schools are often guilty of hypocrisy even when they try to teach sound environmental attitudes. Witness the waste of resources (for example, paper), the ready use of cars, the poorly designed and under-used buildings, and so on. Schools and individual teachers are *models* to the students, after all. They are also creatures of our culture, and they are likely thereby to express dominant values and practices.

Finally, on the topic of environmental attitudes promulgated by our educational system, we should consider that emphasis is pervasively placed on *verbal* thinking and that art and aesthetics are typically given low priorities (see Arnheim, 1969). This may be especially unfortunate from an environmental perspective. An emphasis on verbal information processing is of course in keeping with the primary attention given to performance and productivity, especially in the scholastic realm (tests, and so on). However, to help people gain a greater appreciation of sensory delights in the environment, other types of information processing skills need to be fostered. As implied in the previous chapter, helping children to develop facility in various nonverbal cognitive sets can greatly boost their appreciation of environmental beauty as well as of environmental problems and possibilities. To the extent the schools belittle or even stifle aesthetic and nonverbal (for example, imaginational) concerns, they help to choke off much potential creativity, environmental appreciation, and ecological awareness. (One indication of the damage being done can be gleaned from Rokeach's [1973] finding that "a world of beauty" tends to be ranked very low in the average value hierarchy of Americans.)

On the more general level of social values, it is even clearer that traditional education helps to instill the orientations we discussed earlier. Competitive individualism certainly permeates our educational system in everything from grades to sports. Several examples were listed earlier, such as competitive, individualistic grading and the use of special individual awards as motivators. That list could obviously be extended, but anyone reading this book is likely to be intimately familiar with the way our education favors competition and individualism.

The schools also seem to operate according to a relatively negative view of human nature. Reliance on extrinsic reinforcers and the various devices used to forestall or catch cheating implies a rather unhopeful—and psychologically uninformed—view of human nature. (Jerry Farber [1969] even reports the case of a professor who made college students answer examinations on forms encased in special paper bags!) Theory X lives on in the schools without a doubt.

Hierarchical thinking is of course endemic in most academic institutions. Distinctions of academic rank and the bureaucratic structure of school administrations drive this point home even to teachers. Students, of course, learn quickly to distinguish ranks among each other on the basis of considerations such as grades and class level. They also learn to respect the various levels of authority in the institution. Indeed, Robert Dreeben (1971) has argued that one of the basic functions of the school has been to prepare children to behave with proper deference in situations of "superordination" (for example, doctor-patient relations, police commands, and so on). Again, we might note that the subject matter itself often emphasizes hierarchical thinking rather than making interdependencies the focus.

Bald materialism is perhaps less directly inculcated by the schools, since they are supposed to value the life of intellect more than mere accumulation of wealth. However, as George Leonard (1968) noted, "eager acquisition" is one of the key lessons imparted by our educational system (*getting* good grades, awards, status, and so on). Furthermore, the curriculum usually contains enough implicit praise of wealth to make it clear that this *is* a central value in our society.

Perhaps more critical is the role of the schools in fostering our confusion of means with ends. The content of instruction may lead students to conclude, for example, that technological advance and a growing gross national product are good in themselves. Additionally, the *process* of traditional education often yields object lessons in treating means as ends. Performance and productivity are apparently valued as if good irrespective of their consequences for the quality of experience. And of course grades usually end up being regarded as ends by the students. However, as will be discussed later in this chapter, the new movement toward "values clarification" as part of the curriculum may provide a powerful antidote to this perpetuation of confusion of means and ends.

With respect to violence, school probably contributes less directly to a positive orientation than it does for the other major value components we have been considering. However, the emphasis on war in many history texts probably helps to legitimize this form of human aggression and also to habituate us to its presence and potential "usefulness." Indirectly, the animosities stirred by interscholastic sports and other forms of competition may at least increase students' tendencies to aggression. A famous social psychological study by Muzafer Sherif and his coworkers (Sherif et al., 1961) indeed showed that just setting up separate, competing groups in a boys' camp could lead to at least mild forms of intergroup violence. Nonetheless, it is hard to blame the schools for this particular aspect of our culture.

Finally, our tendency to take a short-term future time orientation is helped along at least by the *omission* of any effort to educate people to take a longer-term perspective. The recent advent of a growing academic interest in futuristics, the study of possible and probable long-term future conditions of society, may well help to counteract this, just as values clarification may be aiding us to get our means and ends straight. The schools now perpetuate the culture; but, as we shall see, they also offer what is probably our best single hope for long-term change.

The Mass Media

Newspapers, magazines, radio, billboards, movies, and especially television play an obviously large role in conveying information and entertainment to all of us. It is hard to prove that they thereby help to form our values and attitudes, but it is plausible that they do. Advertising, the lifeblood of many of the mass media, has especially come in for attack as a culprit in stimulating ecologically unsound desires and values. It has been argued (see, for example, Willard Miller, 1972) that advertising creates new and often "false" needs (craving for newness, wanting shirts that are "whiter than white," thirsting for more powerful automobiles, and so on). The maverick advertising executive Jerry Manders (1971) has also come down hard on traditional advertising for helping to promote a growth mentality with all its attendant environmental dangers. (Manders has also helped to popularize the word *ecopornography* to refer to advertising that tries to con the public into thinking that certain companies or products are really benefiting the environment when they are not.) Perhaps equally serious is the way many ostensibly pro-environment ad campaigns attempt to make it seem that things like pollution are the responsibility of "each individual" rather than corporations or other institutions (see, for example, Gale, 1972). On other levels, it is also clear that advertising helps to maintain and exacerbate our general individualism, materialism, status-seeking hierarchical thinking, confusion of means and ends, and short-term time perspective.

However, it is not through ads alone that the mass media help to form and perpetuate our value system. The content of both the news and entertainment purveyed by the media often do the job very well by themselves. The content of news and entertainment helps to establish accepted cultural patterns and models (for example, heroes) and to define or accentuate what is to be considered reinforcing. In this way, for example, TV programs can help legitimize or even inculcate a *machismo* ethic, violence, competitive individualism, hierarchical thinking about people or nature, materialism, a short-term time perspective, and so on. Note that once a value pattern is established in the society, it is not surprising that the mass media would reflect it. Nevertheless, this reflection also serves as a form of socialization and education for the young. What is becomes what continues to be.

One curious point in this age of concern over bias in news reporting is that not only the entertainment offered through the media reflects dominant cultural values, but the news does also. Peter Sandman (1974), for example, has pointed out that the media tend to follow the status quo in setting standards for objectivity. "Objective" reporting becomes reporting that orders priorities on the basis of current dominant values. In Sandman's (1974, p. 239) words, since our institutions "are dominated by white, upper-middle-class, Establishment interests . . . an objective concept of news turns out to be a white, upper-middle-class, Establishment picture of what is happening and what is important." It is thus, Sandman notes, "that the objective media pay more attention to a beach-destroying oil spill than to the impact of pesticides on migrant farm workers, or of strip mines on the Appalachian poor."

Other Social Institutions

It is impossible to pin the blame for the problem-generating aspects of our value system on any single social institution or practice. We have very briefly explored how the family, the educational system, and the mass media help to promote and perpetuate competitive individualism, materialism, confusion of means and ends, and so on. However, it is important to consider that our value system is expressed by nearly every aspect of our culture. Each institution in a sense simply reflects and furthers the practices of the others. Our dominant religion talks about sharing and love, but emphasizes individual salvation as the ultimate goal and reward (see Max Weber, 1958, on the underlying materialism of the "Protestant Ethic"). Our economic system makes no bones about competitive achievement as the main criterion for success, and of course materialism lies at the root of most commercial products as well as practices. Even our courts operate in large measure according to competitive interactions between conflicting lawyers, with a very clear win/lose setup in the handling of legal disputes. As noted earlier, politicians also vie with one another for *winning* elections. Talk of being a "public servant" is clearly just empty rhetoric, and political victory is openly treated as a personal triumph for the elected official.

The point is that nearly all our social contingencies of reinforcement involve extrinsic rewards or punishments that usually depend on winning out over other people in some way. We are steadily and pervasively being shaped to compete with one another; to look out for our own interests rather than our collective well-being; to view each other as untrustworthy (as indeed people often *are* when they work mainly for extrinsic satisfaction); to rank one another and to be anxious about our own status; to be concerned with material accumulation; to treat behavior and material things as if they were ends in themselves rather than means to improving the quality of experience; to accept official violence as justified; to look only to the short-term consequences of our actions; and to treat the rest of nature as if it were nothing but a collection of resources for us to squander or pollute as we like. Some of this is changing, perhaps, but the traditional pattern of cultural support for our traditional values is still evident in practically every facet of our society.

TOWARD A PRO-LIFE VALUE SYSTEM

Two common links between our value system and both our social and environmental problems would appear to be, first, inadequate consideration given to the long-term quality of experience as a criterion in major societal decisions, and second, inadequate recognition of our various social and environmental interdependencies. In other words, our values place little emphasis on experience as an end and also take little account of interdependence in choosing means. We treat the GNP or personal status as if it were good in itself, irrespective of its impact on experience; at the same time we think and behave as if we were independent rather than ineluctably embedded in complex biosocial systems. Is there an alternative value system that would help guide us to make more benign and reality-based decisions? Presented in the section below is a sketch of what elements such a system might include. The concluding section tries to point out some of the techniques for change that might facilitate the growth of this "pro-life" orientation.

Pro-Life Values

I have borrowed the phrase *pro-life* from A. S. Neill (1960), who defined it as equalling "fun, games, love, interesting work, hobbies, laughter, music, dance, consideration for others, and faith in men." ("Anti-life," according to Neill, "equals duty, obedience, profit, and power" and is "pro-authority, pro-church religion, pro-repression, pro-oppression, or at least subservient to these.") The concept of a pro-life value system will be used a bit more abstractly in this discussion, but the spirit in which Neill used the term is at the heart of what I am talking about. Namely, a pro-life value system is one that is based on the notion that the most important single value or criterion for making decisions is the generation and maintenance of the most enjoyable possible quality of experience for all sentient creatures. There is no way to define "the most enjoyable quality of experience" unambiguously (and unambivalently), but it is possible to use goals such as minimizing suffering and maximizing the opportunity for lasting widespread happiness as criteria in making major social decisions. Let us explore some of the implications.

Priorities and Ecological Conscience

While it is not necessary or desirable to use hierarchical thinking about all relations among people or with nature, the very concept of a value system entails priorities and therefore hierarchies. In the case of pro-life values, there are at least two hierarchies of importance. The first concerns deciding *whose* experience should take precedence if conflicts occur. As an overall guideline, John Cobb's (1973) idea of ranking by capacity for experiencing seems to make some sense. According to Cobb's view (and mine), all value is ultimately grounded in "feeling"; it would make little sense to speak of anything as valuable if there were no beings that could experience varying degrees of affect. Cobb points out, however, that organisms differ greatly in their capacity for feeling. Humans generally have far greater capacity than paramecia, for instance. There is of course the obvious danger in this view of falling into a kind of elitism either in favor of the human species as a whole or in favor of certain classes of persons (for example, do very intelligent people have a higher capacity for experience than less intelligent ones?). However, general ranking by capacity for experience, if kept general, at least saves us from the impossible position of having to give equal priority to *all* forms of life. As John Passmore (1974) has persuasively argued, this extreme view would make human action and even survival almost impossible.

The important point in the pro-life orientation (which, by the way, as used here has nothing to do with anti-abortionism) is that the experience of all sentient creatures will at least be considered in making decisions. While human happiness and well-being will presumably be ranked ahead of that of poisonous snakes, gratuitous cruelty to "lower" animals would be deemed a clear violation of pro-life values. Even such activities as using animals in scientific research would have to be reexamined from the perspective of the effects on the animals' experience and the likelihood that the research would actually improve the quality of human experience. However, as Passmore (1974) argued with respect to both future generations of humans and existing nonhuman forms of life, this concern with the quality of experience for other sentient creatures would ultimately have to be based on *caring* about what they experienced. In short, although we might be forced to cast those we affect into some sort of hierarchy of importance, we would be deciding and acting from the perspective of caring about their experience and welfare. We would value positive experience as a good thing in itself, even though at times we would have to choose between two instances of this good.

What we have just been considering can form the basis for much that goes under the heading of "ecological conscience."[3] The naturalist Aldo Leopold (1949), for example, argued for a "land ethic" that would accord a respect to the natural environment that would be similar to that we now reserve for people. (He also pointed out that we used to treat some people—slaves—as we now treat the land.) A lawyer, Christopher Stone (1974), has even argued that natural objects and areas should have legal standing so that they could be defended in court independently of their usefulness to human plaintiffs. It seems true, as Passmore (1974) has argued, that this sort of thing can be carried to unrealistic extremes if it is held that humans and nature form a unified community of mutual *concern;* we might care about nature, but nature doesn't "care" about us. Nevertheless, an ecological ethic would be an important derivative of a pro-life value system and would be likely to have beneficial consequences for human as well as natural well-being.

For instance, concern for the welfare of natural areas and of living creatures would make us more cautious in interfering with natural processes. We would thus be less likely to make grievous errors in modifying ecosystems, and we would thereby contribute to our own well-being at the same time. This, in essence, seems to be Stone's (1974) key argument for what would appear to be the rather extreme step of giving natural objects legal standing. By not having constantly to prove direct damage to humans, we could then use the courts more easily as a path to preventing ecologically unsound decisions. Of course, we might occasionally also slow up "progress," but there is already ample evidence that we have tended to behave with ecological stupidity.

Furthermore, a pro-life ecological conscience would probably enhance our enjoyment of nature and of each other. We would be more likely to view other living things as ends in themselves—as experiencers.[4] In essence, this type of value system would facilitate B-cognition with respect both to other people and to nonhuman sentient creatures. Such a shift in our dominant cognitive sets for thinking about the rest of the living world could add enormously to the quality of our own immediate experience.

Priorities and Getting Our Means and Ends Straight

The first hierarchy of pro-life values basically concerned ranking possibly conflicting ends—namely, whose experience was to be regarded as taking precedence. We shall return to this issue in the discussion of problems concerning pro-life values, below. However, there is another hierarchy of considerable importance. This concerns the ranking of means and ends. As Cobb (1973) and Dewey (1939) have pointed out, there is nothing that can be considered as good irrespective of how it is achieved or that could never be considered as a means to some other end. However, as Cobb did note, only the quality of feeling (experience) can rationally be considered as actually containing intrinsic value. Anything other than an aspect of experience can be valuable only on the basis of some contribution to the quality of experience. According to this view, for example, money would never be considered as an intrinsic good but at best only as a means to producing conditions that would yield a higher quality of experience. Similarly, learning, productivity, power, fame, status, material acquisitions, and even longevity would not be intrinsic goods but only possible means to the improvement of experience. Two key problems in our society are, first, that we often allow means such as these to be treated as if they were ends— that is, as criteria that do not need further justification for their pursuit or maximization—and second, that we fail to examine the underlying states and processes that would really be most likely to produce continuing high levels of happiness for everyone. I submit that one reason we make these errors is that as a society we fail to treat everyone's continuing happiness as the most important end.

Although we do aver that happiness (or at least the opportunity to seek happiness) is a value, our basic orientation, as analyzed earlier in this chapter, seems to rank individual competitive success in certain defined domains (especially acquiring wealth and power) as the main "social" good. We act as if the one value we cannot question is the preservation of conditions under which people *must* compete with each other for resources and status. From the perspective of pro-life values and of a positive view of human nature, our society's orientation is insane.

Since that was a strong statement, let's look at the sort of instrumental (means) values that would probably stand out in a pro-life society. That is, what kinds of things would a society that regarded broad-scale, continuing (and increasing) happiness as its main goal be likely to view as desirable means or subgoals? Since I do not know of any purely pro-life society uncontaminated by extraneous values (such as glorification of the state or obeisance to nonrational religious beliefs or taboos), the following list is not based on a real-life model. However, some existing societies and some enclaves within existing societies (such as certain communes) come much closer to espousing these values than do others. Also, note that this list of contributing values for a pro-life orientation is meant to be suggestive rather than exhaustive.

1. *Health and physical well-being.* A pro-life society would give high priority to the health of *all* its citizens. Rather than developing a health care system that artificially restricted the number of doctors and concentrated on quality treatment for the rich while the poor suffered, it

would give more attention to preventive medicine and would devote a high proportion of its material and human resources to ensuring good health for as many people as possible. Furthermore, health would never take a back seat to profit making and status seeking. For example, no transportation system that mercilessly killed and maimed would be tolerated when alternative systems of far greater safety were feasible. People would never drive themselves and each other to ulcers and heart attacks in the pursuit of competitive success. Social and economic practices would be sought and adopted that allowed for relaxation, low levels of anxiety, minimal overwork, healthful food based on careful analysis of nutritional needs rather than on profit seeking, and so on. Money-motivated activities that threatened public health, such as using shoddy pollution controls in industry or attempting to foster addiction to known carcinogens (for example, cigarettes), would seem as unacceptable as the deliberate poisoning of another person to obtain an early inheritance. Many other examples could be given, but it should be clear that happiness requires health as one of its most important prerequisites; and widespread long-term health requires an ordering of priorities far different from that of our society's current operating values.

2. *Reliance on intrinsic motivation.*   As pointed out in Chapter 2, when people are motivated by intrinsic reinforcement they are more likely to be happy than when they are subjected to predominantly extrinsic reinforcement. This is in part because intrinsic reinforcement allows each person to choose activities that are personally satisfying, while extrinsic reinforcement constantly forces the person to do another's bidding. Even a totally pro-life society would doubtless have to utilize extrinsic reinforcers for some purposes (for example, attracting people to necessary but universally disliked jobs). However, as argued in Chapter 2, there is substantial reason to believe that a society could function productively under an Equity 2 system of distribution that relied very heavily on intrinsic motivation for much of the necessary and beneficial work. Furthermore, education and other socialization processes in a pro-life society would presumably avoid resorting to extrinsic reinforcements such as grades, gold stars, or spankings. Instead, every effort would be made to devise situations and procedures whereby children would be treated as Origins and learning would be an enjoyable, intrinsically motivated activity.

3. *Enhancement of sources of intrinsic satisfaction.*   A central priority for any society truly devoted to enhancing the quality of experience would be the cultivation of both collective and individual sources of intrinsic satisfaction. Aesthetics, for instance, would be a central rather than a peripheral concern. Although beauty would undoubtedly take second place to survival and health, the public environment would not be allowed to deteriorate in the interest of material accumulation for a few individuals. Tax incentives would never be provided for the maintenance of slums rather than their improvement, for example. Indeed, the criteria for design decisions would very likely be oriented toward creation of a total environment that would be genuinely enjoyable. Costs (in the sense of trade-offs with other uses of resources, such as health care), ecological soundness, and other considerations relevant to long-term welfare would of course also be important criteria. But the process of making decisions about the design of the environment would be focused on the improvement of the quality of experience of everyone affected rather than on the maximization of wealth for a small segment of the population.

Similarly, consumer goods would be designed to be as useful, long-lasting, reliable, and happiness-increasing as possible. Planned obsolescence, deliberately shoddy products, environmental contamination, and anything else that decreased the usefulness and intrinsic satisfaction derivable from an item would be anathema to producers and consumers alike (because both groups would value the quality of everyone's experience). The key test in product design would be, "Will this product, considering its costs and likely side effects, enhance life?" The test would not be, "Will this make us lots of money, and can we get away with it?" (Conversely, work and working conditions would be devised as much as possible so that people could derive intrinsic satisfaction and exert personal and collective control.)

4. *Enhancement of skills for increasing intrinsic satisfaction.*   A pro-life society would also presumably give high priority to helping its citizens become capable of higher levels of enjoying life. Along with valuing a healthful and beautiful environment for everyone rather than conditions that allowed only a minority to live in luxury, pro-life values would create an educational system that would do far more than prepare people to work. At least equal emphasis would be placed on increasing people's ability to enjoy their lives. For instance, according to

Neill (1960), *interest* is the royal road to happiness. Schools that operated according to intrinsic motivation would necessarily have to rely on interest, but a pro-life system would also tend far more than an extrinsic one to find ways to help people learn how to develop and pursue interests. (This is a skill our current school system does not often foster.) Considerable attention might be given, for example, to introducing cognitive sets that would help people enhance their aesthetic appreciation or gain insight into the nature and sources of their personal feelings. Furthermore, pro-life education would encourage skill at intrinsically satisfying activities that simultaneously boost individuals' abilities to help other people. Creative problem solving, diverse forms of artistic endeavor, facility at seeing interdependencies, and skill at working cooperatively with others are a few examples.

5. *Cooperation.* Listed below are a few reasons why cooperation would very likely be a major instrumental value of any pro-life system.

a. *Competition creates losers and an atmosphere of anxiety.* When competition serves as the guiding principle for distribution of life-enhancing (or even sustaining) resources and for self-esteem, the anxiety and other ill effects even for eventual winners make for an amazingly anti-life system. In contrast, cooperation at least makes it possible for everyone to "win"—to be valued as a contributing member of a mutually concerned and achieving group.

b. As Deutsch (1973) pointed out, *a cooperative system allows for much greater efficiency* than a competitive one. This is the case because in a cooperative system duplication of effort can be greatly reduced (people are not competing with each other to do the same thing, and individuals can more readily identify with the success of the group as their own success), and information flows much more freely and honestly (people are not afraid of having their ideas stolen, for example). Moreover, many tasks (such as solving environmental problems of international scope) simply require cooperative, collective efforts.

c. *Cooperation is itself a source of pleasant affect.* For example, in a truly cooperative setting participants are by definition trying to further mutual goals, and this sort of support increases feelings of belonging and security. Furthermore, cooperative interaction and mutual effort, because of greater efficiency and free sharing of information, are likely to increase participants' sense of competence and comprehension. Additionally, as Deutsch (1973) also pointed out, cooperation enhances mutual liking and positive interpersonal attitudes. It generally feels better to like people and be liked by them than to experience the mutual animosity that competition tends to spawn.

Furthermore, given that we are interdependent, it makes more sense to recognize that we affect one another and to make the most of this interdependence rather than to deny it and opt for competitive individualism. A society that sought to improve the quality of everyone's experience would be evidencing a high level of insight and rationality. Consequently, it would probably realize that cooperative relations are a more happiness-producing way of being interdependent than are competitive relations. Just to take one example, Hardin's "tragedy of the commons" and indeed all "Prisoners' Dilemma" situations (which tempt each participant to act selfishly, even though mutual cooperation yields a higher joint outcome than does mutual competition) would tend to dissolve in a pro-life society. Even aside from issues of pure rationality, a group of people who valued each other's welfare would be unlikely to find reward in activity that yielded personal benefit but hurt other people. Damage to other people would be felt as damage to oneself.

Finally, as an aside, let me pass along Slater's (1974) important observation that relations of cooperative mutuality neither eliminate individuality nor result in conformity. Rather, cooperating individuals both influence and are influenced by each other. This is the typical situation in a group working on a common task or decision, for instance, and it can produce an extremely pleasant and creative atmosphere (compare, for example, synectics groups as described by Gordon, 1961, and Prince, 1970; see also D. and R. Johnson, 1975).

6. *Minimal unpleasant conditions.* A pro-life society would obviously work to reduce unpleasantness to a minimum. It is hard to say exactly what trade-off might be allowed between the suffering of some people or other living things and the concomitant enjoyment of others (as in the case of some medical research, for example). However, it is my guess that people who valued a high level of positive experience for all sentient creatures, even ranked along some hierarchy of "capacity for experience," would give extra weight to preventing suffering whenever a benefit for some would produce suffering for others. In any case, it seems clear that keeping unpleasantness at a minimum is essential for keeping happiness at a maximum (aside from the possibly invalid argu-

ment that some unpleasantness is always necessary so that we can appreciate the good times).

As one example, a priority under a pro-life value system would probably be to minimize the amount of unpleasant work. In contrast to the "Protestant Ethic" with its stress on the value of work per se (usually the more unpleasant, the better), pro-life notions of work would be that it is merely a means and that it should always be as enjoyable as possible. Also, whatever unpleasant work could not be eliminated or taken over by machines would tend either to be shared equally or to be extrinsically rewarded in proportion to its unpleasantness. (A far cry from our current pattern of giving the most disagreeable work to a low-paid minority of the people!) As another example, a pro-life society would not make the lives of prisoners miserable when more humane methods of crime prevention and rehabilitation were possible (see, for example, Li, 1973; Sommer, 1976). Indeed, pro-life values would dictate that *no one* would be sentenced to an insufferable environment.

7. *Freedom, individuality, and diversity.* Along with stressing cooperation and community, a society truly interested in maximizing happiness would give high priority to maintaining sufficient diversity to provide freedom of choice and to give different types of people opportunities to find intrinsic satisfaction. This would not only benefit individuals who happened to deviate sharply from the norm; it would also increase the potential for creative innovations that could benefit the whole society. In any case, a high degree of choice, diversity, and individual expression is doubtless necessary for human fulfillment.

Alas, however, as social analysts such as Goodwin (1974) and Slater (1974) have pointed out, it is not possible to maximize everything that is good. Community and mutual concern will in some ways conflict with individual freedom and diversity. This problem is inherently unsolvable; *any* value system will involve some such conflicts. A pro-life society would probably deal with the conflict between freedom and community by actively seeking out creative and humane compromises. Perhaps for some individuals the best situation might even be a competitive and individualistic enclave within the society, just as we now have some cooperative communes in the midst of our generally competitive culture. However, competitive individualism (or any system stressing individual aggrandizement without equal attention to everyone's welfare) ultimately tends to reduce both general well-being and the diversity of opportunity for people to lead fulfilling lives. If my analysis of its role in producing ecological problems is correct, such individualism may even reduce the long-term probability of survival. So even if there should turn out to be a trade-off in some aspects of individual freedom, it would very likely be a small sacrifice in comparison with the benefits. Finally, though, it should be mentioned that a pro-life system would ideally maintain a high degree of flexibility in its structure—both to yield to successive generations the joys of shaping their own well-being and to increase the chances of developing new ways to enhance the quality of experience.

You can probably come up with many more goals that a pro-life value system would generate. So rather than continue this list, let me conclude by noting that this type of value system would entail deliberate reflection on the implications of any course of action or of any state of the world for the quality of experience. To the degree that such reflection was rational and based on accurate information, a pro-life society could reasonably be expected to produce as high a level of happiness (long-term positive affect) as could be achieved. Of course, a good case can be made that such a society would simply be a *rational* society, since it would clearly distinguish means and ends and would have the best interests of all its members as the central criterion in its decision making. That it would also be cooperative and ecologically sound in its practices, create an intrinsically satisfying environment, and express concern for both future generations and nonhuman sentient creatures seems very likely. Such a position would result from a rational recognition of interdependencies and from the basic value of optimizing experience wherever it occurs. All this is of course what was described in Chapter 3 as Compatibility.

Possible Problems

Even a partially anti-life culture such as ours manages to inculcate and at least to outwardly espouse many pro-life values and attitudes (see the next section). However, as is the case with most utopian visions, the ideal society I have been describing may sound too good ever to exist in reality. We in the United States, for example, pride ourselves on pragmatic realism. But is this tendency to debunk utopian visions as "unrealistic" in fact just a self-serving rationalization by a system trying to maintain the status quo? I doubt that the feasibility of a pro-life society can be convincingly demonstrated by words alone, but before turning to some preliminary guidelines for how pro-life values might·be adopted, let us briefly examine some probable objections to the notion of basing a value system on the optimization of the quality of experience.

Necessity of compromise.   As noted earlier, one of the main problems for any coherent value system is the resolution of conflicts between incompatible "goods" or between alternative combinations of good and bad effects. Notice how in trying to optimize the quality of experience we are likely, for instance, to face conflicts between short- versus long-term effects, our own versus others' happiness, the welfare of present generations versus the needs of future generations, human versus non-human welfare, and so on.

There are probably no simple ways to deal with such conflicts. As indicated earlier, pro-life decision-making strategies would probably strive first of all to minimize suffering, and to seek optimal compromises where other conflicts were concerned. This would be a new, but probably very fruitful, set of problems for people to work on. However, it seems pointless to try to work out all the decisions that *might* be needed to handle these abstract problems. The important difference between pro-life and non–pro-life decision making is that the former deliberately gives priority to the quality of experience as the guiding criterion for making choices and resolving conflicts; other value systems use different criteria and therefore have less chance of optimizing experience, since that is not what they are trying to do.

Differing definitions of "quality."   Perhaps the most serious problem that might be raised concerning pro-life values is that people and cultures have widely differing and presumably conflicting definitions of what constitutes a high quality of experience. This is of course really a variation of the previous problem concerning the necessity of compromise, but it does seem especially important for a value system based on something as apparently nebulous and unquantifiable as "happiness." Indeed, I have already alluded to the likely incompatibility between certain values in a happiness-oriented social system (for example, cooperation, equality, and mutual concern versus individual freedom). Let us first take up the issue of differing definitions of happiness.

While there are certainly great differences in what different individuals and cultural groups find satisfying, many of these differences are not incompatible and could all be present in a suitably diverse pro-life system (for example, eating fish versus eating meat; meditating versus having orgies; living in round houses versus living in square ones). Some life styles would of course be less expensive or more popular than others, but it should be possible to allocate "fair shares" of resources to satisfy a wide variety of tastes. This would be the case especially if people realized the underlying benefits of integrative bargaining and cooperation in making decisions about resource use.

There is, however, a more basic issue at stake. There seem in fact to be cultural and individual "universals." The anthropologist Clyde Kluckhohn (1951), for example, observed that there are some values that appear to be "givens in human life." According to Kluckhohn, these arise from "the fundamental biological similarities of all human beings" and from "the circumstance that human existence is invariably a social existence." Some of the purported cultural universals Kluckhohn listed were reciprocity, truth, beauty (albeit all varyingly defined by different cultures), and a rejection of suffering as good in itself. Given that virtually all human beings do indeed possess the same basic nervous system structure, have the same essential biological needs, and mature in a social and language-using community, it is not unreasonable to expect that we all share the same basic structural requirements and potentials for happiness.

Indeed, the model of environment/experience/behavior interrelations discussed in the previous chapter implies exactly that. The experiential components of Complexity, Composition, Comprehension, Comparison, Competence, and Complications are intended to represent *universal* aspects of experience that contribute directly to the substantive and affective quality of experience. As our understanding of the nature and interrelations of these aspects increases, we should in effect gain insight into the nature and sources of human happiness. While it is not certain at present, such understanding would probably enable us to design social and physical environments that could enhance virtually everyone's happiness. Furthermore, psychologists such as Abraham Maslow (for example, 1970) and Lawrence Kohlberg (for example, 1969) have argued that all humans tend toward common higher-level desires and even common ethical precepts (favoring justice and human welfare; see below) when their basic needs are satisfied and they have been exposed to education for rational examination of values. Hadley Cantril (1965) has also detected among a broad sample of societies what appears to be a common hierarchy of desires. Fulfillment at one level seems to call forth a higher level of wishes, generally consistent with Maslow's conception of a hierarchy of needs shared by all people. Overall, it would seem that as human society advances culturally and educationally, common or at least compatible conclusions about collective happiness would be reached.

Getting There

How Far Do We Have To Go?

The discussion of our society's operative value system concentrated on what appear to be its trouble-causing aspects. Competitive individualism, lack of faith in intrinsic motivation, materialism, pervasively hierarchical thinking, treating means as ends, acceptance of violence, and a short-term time perspective all were criticized as ingredients helping to produce our environmental and social problems. However, there are other components in our dominant value system that can at least partially mitigate these ill effects. What is perhaps more significant, these other components can also serve as corrective criteria for recognizing our value problems. That is, inconsistencies between various aspects of our value system, if recognized and resolved, may help us to change our values in a pro-life direction.

For example, as Robert Parkes (1948) pointed out in his historical analysis of "the American experience," the United States has long-standing traditions of valuing utopianism, freedom *and* equality, self-assurance, optimism, honesty, generosity, idealism, and adaptability. Of course, Parkes also argued that these have gone along with values of acquisitiveness, conquering nature, dominating others, materialism, private property, nationalism, and, obviously, a lack of unity of values. Indeed, this last problem of a lack of unity and coherence in our value system has been cited as a major problem by analysts as diverse as Parkes (1948), Williams (1970), and Goodwin (1974). There are simply many diverse strands in our values. It is to be hoped, then, that we can use such values as equality, justice, honesty, generosity, and the pursuit of happiness to critically evaluate our other values (materialistic acquisition, competitive individualism, and so on).

That several recent popular American books have criticized our value system from a broadly pro-life social and environmental perspective (for example, Slater, 1970, 1974; Reich, 1970; Means, 1969; Goodwin, 1974; Falk, 1972; Mumford, 1970) indicates that forces *within* our value system are beginning to produce some negative assessments of our headlong rush into social and environmental deterioration. For the remainder of this chapter we shall examine a few possible ways to spread and deepen this re-evaluation of our values. Since the discussion of techniques for both psychological and social change will be continued and broadened in the next chapter and in the final chapter, our focus here will be on procedures concerned specifically with changing values and attitudes.

Traditional Approaches to Changing Attitudes

The "attitude change" literature in social psychology is enormous.[5] Questions and techniques cover such diverse issues as how to construct persuasive communications (present a two-sided or one-sided case? draw conclusions or leave that to the audience? deviate only a little from what the audience believes or present a very divergent position? try to excite high, low, or moderate fear of what will happen if the listener does not do what you suggest?[6] and on and on); whether to give the "target" of your attitude change attempt a high or a low extrinsic incentive (for example, more or less money) for expressing or doing something counter to his or her original attitude; and whether attitudes are changed more readily by direct communications or by those the listener thinks she or he is merely "overhearing." These and numerous similar questions (is repetition of a message enough to produce acceptance? over the long run, does it matter if you hear it from a high-prestige source or a nobody? and so on) are of obvious interest to advertisers, politicians, and other people who—who what? The answer would seem to be "who want to *manipulate* people into changing their attitudes in a specific direction."

As at least a few psychologists (for example, Rokeach, 1973; Argyris, 1975) have begun to point out, much of the research in social psychology in general and in attitude change in particular has focused on questions of unilateral interpersonal manipulation and has typically used deceptive and manipulative techniques to pursue this study. Argyris (1975) has labelled this approach a "Model 1" design as opposed to a more cooperative, open-information approach ("Model 2"). This distinction will be explored further in Chapter 7, but for now we can note that traditional attitude change research seems to have been exploring questions related primarily to indoctrinative and manipulative techniques for changing other people's attitudes. That the results of such work will probably be of most use to advertisers and propagandists should not be lost on the reader.

Of course, there still remains the question of the actual effectiveness of these manipulative strategies for changing attitudes (and presumably behavior). Certainly the often artificial conditions and other methodological problems attending laboratory research on attitude change may give even advertisers pause in applying the results to real-life situations. However, even with all the caveats and qualifications concerning complex interactions involved in attitude change (see, for example, McGuire, 1969), progress in this area of research will doubtless yield increasingly effective techniques for getting people to change their attitudes whether they want to or not.

Nevertheless, there is reason to believe that trying to change specific attitudes would not be especially effective in solving our underlying social and environmental problems, or in moving us any sizable distance toward a pro-life orientation. Our problems are just too deeply intertwined with our operative *value system*. To take one example, manipulative communications (say, advertising) over the mass media might conceivably shift public attitudes on relatively superficial aspects of conservation or pollution abatement, such as the acceptability of lower room temperatures in winter or the nastiness of littering. However, deeper sources of environmental deterioration, such as our orientation toward ever-increasing material acquisition and our toleration of both poverty and corporate devotion to power and profit, are unlikely to be attacked or changed without a re-examination of our basic values. Thus, not only are the manipulative aspects of most efforts at attitude change inadequate to produce a more insightful and rational populace; the very topics most amenable to such efforts are typically not basic or important enough to produce fundamental cultural change. Even the few pro-life advertising campaigns that are mounted generally fail to touch underlying processes of thought or to challenge deep-seated cultural biases.[7]

Furthermore, as Milton Rokeach (1968, 1973) has argued, people tend to change their attitudes or values through the process of resolving inconsistencies (say, between attitudes and values or between values and self-concepts). Since values are presumably more basic or "central" elements in a person's cognitive system than are attitudes, a change in an attitude will tend to be unstable if there is any inconsistency between the person's new attitude and her or his continuing values.

All in all, then, traditional (manipulative) approaches to changing attitudes seem not only out of keeping with the cooperative spirit of pro-life values but are also probably inadequate to further the sorts of far-reaching changes in orientation that seem needed to deal with our social and environmental problems. Let us therefore turn to what appears to be a much more basic level of consideration and examine recently developed techniques for educating people to be clearer and more rational about their values.

Values Clarification and Change

In the words of Brewster Smith (1969, p. 184), here's how to shift someone's values through basically educational approaches:

> If you want to persuade someone to value something as you do, you can follow one of at least two strategies (assuming that physical or social coercion is ruled out, which historically has unfortunately not been the case): You can, first, try to open his eyes to new ways of seeing things—increase the range of possibilities of which he is aware, create the conditions for differentiations and restructurings in his experience from which it is possible (not necessary) that, seeing things like yourself, he may come to value them likewise. Or, second, you can give him evidence that the position he takes on a particular value has consequences for other values to which he is also committed.

Milton Rokeach (1968, 1971, 1973) is a major proponent of the second of these two approaches. In his research on value change, Rokeach has been chiefly concerned with exploring how people respond to having inconsistencies in their values pointed out to them. In a major study using this technique, Rokeach (1971, 1973) first had college students rank-order a standard list of either twelve or eighteen "terminal values." As it turned out, most students ranked *freedom* well ahead of *equality*. Rokeach's value-change procedure was basically to point out to experimental subjects that ranking freedom well ahead of equality seems to imply that one desires freedom for onself but not necessarily for other people. Although perhaps less purely educative in execution than one might wish, this research has suggested the potential power of even simple experimentation with individuals' awareness of interrelations among their own values. For one thing, subjects subjected to the above "insight" did evidence an upward shift in their ranking of equality on the list of terminal values (an effect that was undiminished even three months later). Also, subjects who showed this upward shift in ranking of equality also tended to evidence various attitude changes (especially in racial attitudes) that were consistent with their new value position. Finally, the value change was significantly associated with behavioral effects, such as willingness to join the NAACP.

In a related study, one of Rokeach's students (see Rokeach, 1973, p. 308) simply pointed out to subjects that "young people and better educated people tend to rank *a world of beauty* higher than the general public ranks it." As a result of this simple (and truthful) message, these subjects showed not only an upward shift in their ranking of this value but also changes (presumably positive) "in attitude toward various ecological issues, such as attitude toward highway beautification programs, the banning of nonreturnable bottles, and the banning of automobiles from cities."

It is easy to quarrel with some aspects of Rokeach's methodology (although would-be critics ought to consider Rokeach's well-thought-out defense in his 1973 book), but his results are nonetheless basically consistent with his underlying theory. First, the apparent value changes seemed to arise from subjects' realizing a discrepancy between their self-concepts (or perhaps "self-ideals" would be more accurate) and their actual value rankings. Specifically, most of the subjects would presumably like to think of themselves as unselfish, and hence would not consider it in keeping with their self-concepts to rank values in a way that implied they were in fact selfish. Similarly, finding out that people similar to oneself (for example, other young and well-educated people) tended to rank a particular value (for example, beauty) higher than did a less respected out-group ("the general public") would make a high ranking for that value seem consistent with one's view of oneself.

Notice, though, that if this interpretation is correct and if this process of value change is to have benefit for advancing our society toward pro-life values, we must make an important assumption (as Rokeach seems to do). We must assume that the values that go into making up our ideal self-concepts are basically pro-life, even if our own or our society's operative values for making everyday decisions are not. For instance, only if someone genuinely regarded being unselfish and cooperative as better than being selfish and competitive could we hope to change this person's values by pointing out that her or his value ranking implied selfishness or competitiveness. Perhaps Rokeach's results, tentative as they are, can at least provide some hope that the values contributing to our *self-ideals* are relatively inconsistent with many of our actual operative values.

A second point of consistency between Rokeach's theory and his results is of course the tendency for the experimentally induced value changes to be accompanied by corresponding attitudinal and behavioral changes. This is in accord with the hierarchy of beliefs that he hypothesizes. According to Rokeach (1973), one's cognitions or beliefs can be rank-ordered according to how central or important they are in one's life. In general, cognitions about oneself will be most central, followed by one's beliefs about what states of being are most desirable (that is, one's "terminal value system"), followed by one's instrumental values, attitudes, cognitions about one's own behavior, and so on all the way down to "cognitions about behavior of nonsocial objects" at the bottom. The important consideration is that inconsistencies between beliefs at different levels of the hierarchy will tend to produce change in the less central or important beliefs. While Rokeach's research certainly does not prove this (and indeed, some attitude theorists would doubtless dispute some of the specific orderings), his results are consistent with the main structure of his hierarchy and with the thesis that value change will ramify to produce attitude and behavioral change as well. The research results of the "world of beauty" value-change study reveal obvious environmental implications for this type of ramification.

However, from the broader perspective of current work on values clarification and moral education, Rokeach's style of relying on simple experimental manipulations such as pointing out inconsistencies or citing the values of a respected group may seem simplistic or even manipulative. Recent work by several educators and psychologists seems to carry the spirit Rokeach apparently had in mind a step further; it focuses on the development of a general training program in how to be more rational and "mature" in dealing with value issues.

There are at least two main approaches centering on educational efforts to improve people's ability to deal with value questions. One of these, *values clarification,* has been developed mainly by educators (for example, L. Raths et al., 1966; S. Simon et al., 1972) and focuses on helping people to gain insight into their values, to explore alternatives, to think about consequences, and to take an active stand (behave) in accordance with their self-determined values. These educators have devised numerous exercises and other techniques to help students clarify their values through exploring value alternatives, examining relations between values and actual behavior, thinking about effects of various values and behaviors, exploring their real feelings, and so on. Thus, in addition to helping people realize value inconsistencies, this approach also involves Smith's other technique for changing values: opening a person "to new ways of seeing things," increasing the person's awareness of possibilities, and creating "conditions for differentiations and restructurings" in the person's experience. To the degree that pro-life values really do reflect what people would find most satisfying if they just stopped to think about it carefully, values clarification could be a powerful, nonindoctrinative and nonmanipulative path to a more pro-life orientation.

However, it may not be as simple as that. As Anne Colby (1975) points out in her constructively critical review, values clarification has so far focused primarily on helping students clarify what they already value. Such self-knowledge encouraged from a position of ethical relativism on the part of the teacher may be inadequate by itself to elevate the students' "maturity" of moral reasoning. To speak of maturity in ethical reasoning presumes that just as children advance through identifiable and presumably universal stages in logical reasoning (compare Piaget's work; see, for example, Flavell, 1963, 1977), a similar maturational hierarchy can be isolated for styles of reasoning about value problems. Piaget (1932; Hoffman, 1970) himself held such a position, positing the sequential stages of "heteronomous" moral thinking (for example, accepting established rules as absolute) and "autonomous" moral thinking (independent ethical reasoning based on considerations such as reciprocity, situational demands, and human needs and intentions).

Lawrence Kohlberg (for example, 1969, 1973), however, is the outstanding current proponent of the theory that moral reasoning progresses through a series of universal stages. Over the years, Kohlberg has continued to evolve his theory about the exact number and nature of these stages; but the core notion is that *with appropriate education* all people would progress from egocentric hedonism through successive initial stages of (1) orientation to punishment and obedience, (2) viewing instrumental satisfaction of one's own needs as a basis for morality,

(3) orientation toward being a socially acceptable "good boy/nice girl," and (4) total acceptance of existing laws as defining what is right, to the "postconventional" stages of reasoning about moral issues by reference to philosophical principles of social contract, individual conscience, or (at Stage 6) presumably universal ethical principles of justice and human welfare. (Note that these various stages may be thought of as progressively more sophisticated and social-justice–oriented cognitive sets for dealing with information in moral decision making.)

Unfortunately, the evidence for Kohlberg's theory is by no means overwhelming, especially with respect to the posited invariance and universality of the upper stages of this particular hierarchy. (For a very critical review, see Kurtines and Greif, 1974; but their conclusions should also be looked at critically.) However, as in the case of Maslow's hierarchy, there seems a bit more evidence that people do indeed tend to progress sequentially through the lower stages as a function of maturation and socialization.

For our current purposes, though, the most important aspect of Kohlberg's work is the emphasis he and his colleagues have placed on finding educational techniques that help people progress in their level of moral reasoning (see, for example, Kohlberg and Turiel, 1971). Their most apparently successful procedure so far has included the use of challenging moral dilemmas and the exposure of students to a level of moral reasoning just one step above their current stage of thinking. The existing research indicates that people have difficulty even understanding moral reasoning more than one stage higher than their own dominant stage, but that they do tend to find reasoning at stages higher than their own more acceptable than reasoning at lower levels.[8] We might note that *if* Kohlberg is correct about the nature of Stage 6 (reaching decisions about issues involving moral values by reasoning from principles of universal justice and welfare), and *if* most people would really tend to reach this level of moral reasoning (and learn to act on it) by being exposed to an educational program that facilitated progressively higher levels of moral reasoning, *then* this sort of educational program could conceivably bring about a world of people who genuinely cared about each other's welfare. Assuming that the long-term quality of experience is the main component in "welfare," this would be a pro-life world.

But, again, is it really so simple? At present, there is not enough evidence to say whether such an educational program would actually produce Stage-6 thinkers of the type Kohlberg envisions. (Presently, for example, Kohlberg's evidence indicates that the dominant level of moral reasoning in the United States seems to be in the middle, "conventional" stages—"good boy/nice girl" and "law and order" thinking; there are so few people who consistently operate at Stage 6 that it is difficult even to study it.) Indeed, serious doubts can be raised on philosophical grounds as to whether Kohlberg's notion of postconventional moral reasoning is likely to be universal. In a recent book, Robert Hall and John Davis (1975), a philosopher and an educational psychologist, have raised such questions about Kohlberg's content orientation for defining the highest levels of moral reasoning. They have also proposed an educational program that follows Kohlberg's general approach but, according to Hall and Davis, avoids some of the potential pitfalls implicit in Kohlberg's assumptions.

Very simply, Hall and Davis base their program on the idea that moral judgments (ideally) involve decisions based on principled commitment, such that the principles take priority over other motives or reasons, are supposed "to apply impartially to all," and interlock with the person's overall set of social and personal ideals (Hall and Davis, 1975, p. 59). This definition seems to represent an ideal picture of just the sort of principled moral reasoning that Kohlberg envisions at the top of his hierarchy and that the proponents of values clarification ultimately have in mind. Hall and Davis's educational program involves a combination of case study material (moral dilemmas to be discussed by the students, perhaps with exemplary reasoning and Socratic questioning by the teacher); analysis of moral concepts via group discussion; and various exercises involving role-playing, games, and simulations (all designed to help the students advance in their ability to see implications, understand other people's points of view, and otherwise increase their empathy and rationality).

It should be noted that all of these approaches to values clarification and "moral education" explicitly eschew (even forbid) value *indoctrination.* Each approach claims only to be concerned to help individuals improve the logical quality of their reasoning about matters of values or ethics. Even Kohlberg's specific assumptions about the presumed content of the higher stages is intended only as a prediction about the conclusions people would come to on their own if they actually reached the stage of reasoning according to universal principles. (Nonetheless, a philosophical stickler could point out that each of these educational programs is at least based on—and is promoting—the value of *rationality,* often rather explicitly defined according to the educator's own criteria.)

But what does all this have to do with people/environment relations? If you have followed the argument in this and the second chapter, you will know that the answer to that question must involve long-term systemic effects. Helping people gain more insight into their values and to be more rational in considering consequences of choices, logical relations between values, and so on, can be expected to have important, but not necessarily direct, effects on environmental experience and behavior. Indeed, it could have important effects on all experience and behavior. Here are several points that should be considered:

First, if the ideas presented in the previous chapter concerning the determinants of the affective quality of experience are sound, greater self-insight and rationality should lead people to recognize the importance of such determinants (that is, Complexity, Composition, Comprehension, and so on, and the conditions that enhance each of them). Even the simpler forms of values clarification could thus alert people to potential sources of satisfaction they might otherwise overlook. Such insight could be especially important in the realm of aesthetics and environmental design, for example. As people began to realize the satisfactions obtainable from enhanced levels of Complexity, Composition, Comprehension, and Competence, for instance, they might become much more concerned with obtaining and preserving environmental diversity, beauty, personal and collective control over human-made aspects of private and public environments, and so on. In addition, gaining insight into sources of intrinsic satisfaction should help people realize the value of greater reliance on intrinsic rather than extrinsic motivation. The environmental and social implications of this could be profound, as the discussion in Chapter 2 intimated.

Second, an educational program that awakened concern with long-range consequences of choices and actions *and* that encouraged empathy with other people would seem very likely to open the way to a more cooperative and pro-life value system. I would of course argue (in much the way that Kohlberg or Kluckhohn probably would) that a pro-life value orientation—a primary concern with the overall quality of experience for all people and other sentient creatures—is in a way "immanent" in a truly rational understanding of one's options and embeddedness in the world. Unemcumbered by indoctrinative socialization (but equipped with an educated ability to reason and an awareness of how the world functions), people would seem to have a natural tendency to seek higher states of happiness. Rational insight should lead them to see that even if only their own happiness were of real concern to them, the inextricable interdependence of people with each other and with nature points to a cooperative orientation as most likely to produce individual as well as collective happiness over the long run. (That is, even "selfishness"—as long as it is enlightened selfishness—might lead to a cooperative, pro-life society. The important thing is for the enlightenment to be widespread.) And can there be any doubt that a pro-life society would design *with* nature?

Third, another way to put these points is that education for rational decision making should help people stop treating means as ends. Our blind worship of technology, material accumulation, and status might be softened considerably if people were encouraged early on to take a close, rational look at what they really find satisfying and at what the long-term implications are for themselves and others. In this emphasis on rationality, however, we might also note that one of Rokeach's (1973) most chilling findings was that his sample of the United States' population as a whole tended to rank the instrumental values of being *imaginative, logical,* and *intellectual* very near or at the bottom of his total list of eighteen instrumental values. These were the only three instrumental values explicitly related to rational or creative thinking, and they were ranked well below such values as being *ambitious, courageous,* and *clean.* Perhaps we need more rationality just to recognize the value of rationality!

Finally, to approach the higher forms of ecological conscience and intrinsic concern for the quality of other people's experience may require a shift up the sort of hierarchy that Kohlberg proposes. It is hard to say whether rationality and values clarification alone would do the trick. After all, one's view of what is "rational" might depend on one's moral and logical "maturity." Achieving widespread and genuine concern for the welfare of other human beings and the rest of the living world probably does require something like Kohlberg's or Hall and Davis's educational programs. However, since these programs are not content-oriented, we are still left with the question of whether growth in the level of moral thinking, combined with an increased understanding of social and ecological interrelations, would be sufficient to produce a shift toward an ecological conscience. I think that they would, and that any value-change strategy that did not include attention to such cognitive growth would probably involve indoctrination or other techniques that might defeat the end because of the means used.

Toward a Systemic Approach

There are of course many other paths to attitude and value change besides the traditional attitude change approaches and the more educative models of values clarification and change just discussed. More communal patterns of child rearing, for example, might help extend feelings of identification and interdependence beyond the immediate nuclear family. This could flatten Slater's hypothesized steep gradient of affection with its presumed promotion of disconnector values (see the earlier section on the family as a source of our values), and also set up a socialization pattern in which cooperative interaction with a broad range of people might come to be valued above competitive individualism.

Technological innovations themselves might also produce value changes in a pro-life direction. For example, increased leisure time and increased satisfaction of basic needs as a result of some types of automation could yield greater attention to intrinsic satisfaction, cooperative play activities, environmental beauty, and pleasant interpersonal relations. Such effects, however, would probably be contingent on other changes in the society, such as a lessening of our puritanical devotion to work as good in itself.

Even advertising may inadvertently contribute to such a pro-life orientation, it turns out. If we can trust Charles Reich's (1970) analysis, for instance, ads that emphasize the carefree joys of youth or that vividly depict vacations and other types of recreation might help to legitimize enjoyment as an essential value. (Interestingly, Slater [1974] makes a related point about advertising's effect on ecological values. Even instances of companies' falsely advertising that they are doing something good for the environment, according to Slater's argument, help to establish in the public mind the belief that industries will and *should* be ecologically sound in their practices.)

Additionally, the schools can do much more than merely expose children to new values-clarification and moral-education curricula. Indeed, as Hall and Davis (1975) argued, such curricula will probably only be optimally meaningful and effective in a school atmosphere of mutual trust and cooperation. Such an atmosphere in itself would of course model and contribute to a pro-life orientation. Furthermore, as is discussed elsewhere in this book, educational curricula could facilitate growth in various aspects of systems thinking, creativity, aesthetic appreciation, ecological and social awareness, and other skills that would contribute to understanding the benefits of a pro-life style of living. All considered, change in the educational system would seem a particularly appropriate place to begin if one wanted to encourage a shift to pro-life values. The schools are, after all, the only societal institutions specifically charged with the pursuit and training of rationality and awareness.

In the long run, though, it will certainly take support from a variety of social and cultural forces to produce and maintain pro-life values on a broad scale. A shift toward Equity 2, for one thing, would seem to be both a necessary prerequisite and a probable result (which means that a pro-life system might be hard to produce, but would be likely to maintain itself if achieved). Distribution of resources according to Equity 2 norms, as argued in Chapter 2, would require just the sort of changes in other societal institutions that would encourage a cooperative, rational, environmentally sound pattern of behavior in all aspects of life. Additionally, if the basic needs of all people in the society were met, everyone would be better able to *appreciate* the pleasures offered by the B-cognitive mode that would characterize a pro-life orientation. People who are worried about where their next meal is coming from or whether their life or status is safe are not very likely to think in terms of overall human/environmental welfare or even to consider the personal long-term consequences of their own actions.

In conclusion, then, I have argued that solving our existing and imminent environmental problems—not to mention realizing our potential for a vastly more pleasant environment—will require a major shift in our dominant criteria for making basic decisions. These criteria are our "values." This problem seems especially acute at the level of our institutional operative values—those criteria that guide our actual collective behavior. The resulting social and environmental problems lie not so much in any malevolence in our intentions, but rather in a basic irrationality in our criteria. This irrationality—perhaps best represented by the various ways in which we treat means as if they were ends and by our tendency to compete when cooperation could be so much more pleasant and efficient—arises in part from our failure to recognize our interdependencies with nature and with each other and from our tendency to neglect long-term consequences of our actions. The "cure," I would argue, is to adopt a new set of procedures and criteria for our decisions, especially our broad-scale decisions affecting the social and physical environment in which we live. These procedures and criteria have been summarized under the heading "pro-life values," and include emphasis on the quality of experience as the chief *end* and on such items as health, cooperation, and attention to sources of widespread intrinsic satisfaction as the chief *means*. To shift from our current muddled value system with its somewhat irrational decision making to one that would improve the quality of our experience over the long term will probably require wide-ranging changes in many of our institutions and cultural practices, but education seems like a good place to start.

In this chapter we have been considering only some of the psychological changes needed to enhance life. Chapter 2 examined potentials in the area of motivation, and Chapter 3 expanded this to include possibilities offered by various ways of processing information. In a sense, this chapter has partially integrated these two domains, since values can be interpreted as components in cognitive sets for making decisions (or judgments) about what is desirable—and these judgments in turn affect (or reflect) our motivations. However, there is a more broad-based and holistic way of integrating what we have been considering up to now. That is the concept of "ecological consciousness," which will be presented in the next chapter. Along with this notion, we shall also take a closer look at the systemic approach to changing attitudes, values, cognitive sets, and motivation.

NOTES

1. See, for example, McGuire (1969), Insko (1967), Fishbein and Ajzen (1975), or virtually any recent introductory textbook in social psychology.
2. This definition draws heavily on the views of Rokeach (1968) and Triandis (1971).
3. See, for example, the anthologies edited by Disch (1970) and Barbour (1972, 1973).
4. At least this would apply to "higher" animals. However, some people would probably argue that even plants may experience (see, for example, John White, 1974b). Such a belief might in fact have ecologically beneficial consequences.
5. See, for example, Cohen (1964), McGuire (1969), Triandis (1971), Suedfeld

(1971), Fishbein and Ajzen (1975), the various volumes of *Advances in Experimental Social Psychology* (so far edited by Leonard Berkowitz and published by Academic Press), and virtually any of the general textbooks or journals in the field of social psychology.

6. The issue of fear-arousing communications may of course have special significance for changing certain environmental attitudes and behavior patterns. The research on fear arousal as an approach to attitude change, however, has so far been rather inconclusive (see Higbee, 1969, for a good review). The preponderance of the evidence seems to indicate that high threat (fear arousal) is more effective than low threat, but the research is actually riddled with contradictions and *numerous* qualifications on this point (the main theorists in this area seem to agree that there is actually an inverted-U relation between fear arousal and attitude change). Also, it does seem that more change is produced when the fear-producing message includes how to avoid the threat, but this seems to hold regardless of how much fear the message is intended to arouse. Whatever new insights this line of research produces, however, at least three considerations might be borne in mind: (1) This is often a highly manipulative and counter-rational approach. (2) People may adapt to fear-arousing communications just as they do to actual dangers and annoyances (see Sommer, 1972, and our earlier discussion of psychological adaptation). (3) As James Swan (1974, 1975) has argued, reliance on fear (and guilt) as motives for change may be counter-productive (as in the "boy who cried wolf" effect) and demoralizing. I would certainly agree with Swan that a better approach is to help people expand their awareness of the positive *benefits* brought by ecologically sound living. One might thus arouse hope rather than fear; this would be a stimulant for change that reflects pro-life values.

7. One noteworthy example is the many antismoking ads that appeared *along with* cigarette ads during their last days on television. In a fascinating piece of journalism, Thomas Whiteside (1974) has alluded to some of the negative effects this campaign seemed to have on cigarette sales. According to Whiteside's view, the juxtaposition of the basically rational and health-oriented appeal of the anti-smoking ads and the crassness of the cigarette ads heightened the effect of the former.

8. Also see Keasey (1975).

5
ECOLOGICAL CONSCIOUSNESS

WHAT IS IT?

A *consciousness*, according to my terminology, is a constellation or syndrome of interrelated cognitive sets, values, and resulting motives and action tendencies. It may be thought of as a person's general cognitive, valuational, and motivational orientation toward the world. Since this concept in abstract form may be even more nebulous than "attitude" and "value," let's quickly examine some postulated examples of consciousnesses. The ones that most readily spring to my mind are those offered by Charles Reich (1970) in *The Greening of America*. Admittedly, Reich has been sharply criticized by many people for "oversimplifying," among other things (see, for example, Nobile, 1971). But his notions of Consciousness I, II, and III do indeed seem to describe syndromes of interrelated cognitive sets, values, and resulting motives and action tendencies. To risk oversimplifying even Reich's presentation, Consciousness I corresponds to the traditional American orientation of rugged individualism, competition, defining social problems in terms of individual responsibility, and (it seems to me) extremely linear thinking. Consciousness II represents a more recent cognitive/valuational/motivational syndrome and applies mainly to the "organization man" mentality, with emphasis on conformity, other-directedness, bureaucratic and technocratic thinking, and the view that centralized regulation and external control are the best paths to solving social problems. Finally, Consciousness III applies to a mentality (perhaps best represented by some "hippies") stressing "the absolute worth of every human being," honesty with oneself and others, community (of the do-your-own-thing type), creativity, self-expression, enjoying nature (and life in general), and liberated awareness.

It would be possible, and perhaps interesting and instructive, to break Reich's three Consciousnesses into plausible cognitive, valuational, and motivational/behavioral components. The same could of course be done for any other candidates for the title of a "consciousness"—say, masculine consciousness, Puritan consciousness, or even true versus false consciousness (see Marcuse, 1964, 1972, on the last). However, let us for the moment resist that temptation and instead consider the main topic of this chapter, *ecological consciousness*.

This notion is put forth here as a specific *ideal* cognitive, valuational, and motivational orientation toward the world. Ecological consciousness thus represents more a goal to strive for than a particular pattern of psychological functioning that we can readily investigate. Keeping in mind that this is thus also only a suggested goal, here are the chief components as I conceive of them: (1) *ecological systems thinking,* including a sense of self as part of a larger system and a high level of ecological understanding and awareness; (2) *a high ability to enjoy and apprepicate things in themselves* (that is, high levels of B-cognition and even B-love); (3) *a pro-life value system,* including an ecological conscience and the other aspects discussed in Chapter 4; and (4) *a synergistic orientation* in interactions with one's social/physical environment—that is, an interdependent, communal, creatively cooperative pattern of relating to people and other aspects of nature.

Let us briefly examine each of these in turn.

Ecological Systems Thinking

As pointed out in the first chapter, "systems thinking" as used in this book applies predominantly to the informal variety. Synonyms might be "holistic thinking," "nonlinear thinking," or any other terms that connote active consideration of interrelationships, total contexts, radical alternatives, and long-range ramifications. Such thinking takes seriously the ecological maxim that everything is connected to everything else. Presumably, some exposure to the formal side of systems thinking (systems analysis) helps to foster an intuitive "feel" for the operation of interconnected processes and complex feedback relations. In discussing ecological systems thinking here, my focus is primarily on this intuitive feel itself—that is, on the general style of thinking that emphasizes interrelations and larger contexts—rather than on the formal analyses that might contribute to it. As indicated above, there would appear to be at least two components to this way of thinking about and experiencing the world: an expanded, holistic sense of self and a high degree of ecological understanding and awareness.

Sense of Self as Part of Larger System

For some analytical, pictorial, or even experiential purposes, we might want to consider ourselves as somehow separate from our environments. Indeed, the graphic representations of my "model of the mind" in Chapter 3 contain a sharp demarcation between the environment and the cognitive/experiential/physiological/behavioral processes presumably within or "of" the organism (person). However, as the figure titles indicate, the overall model actually pertains to environment/experience/behavior interrelations. It has been frequently pointed out by environmental psychologists and others concerned with environmental matters that each of us is an integral part of a complex web of interlinking processes.[1] Our experience, cognitive processes, and overt behavior arise from and can be understood only in relation to the environment. It is often hard to experience this intuitively, although perhaps not so hard to grasp it analytically; but the whole world, including ourselves, is a unified system.

Although he drew heavily on various Eastern religious and philosophical disciplines, perhaps no Western writer has better conveyed the intuitive feel of being at one with this system (all of nature) than did Alan Watts (for example, 1966, 1961, 1958a,b). His basic theme was that in a fundamental sense you *are* the universe—or, in one of his phrases, "the world is your body." An interesting facet of Watts's presentation is that one need not assimilate Eastern mysticism to understand—or agree with—the essential message. For, as Watts and numerous others have argued, each of us is generated by, and totally interdependent with, the physical/social world. We may have the illusion of being atomistic, independent egos, but fundamentally we are organic outgrowths of our physical and social environments, not detached and independent entities. This should be obvious the moment you stop to think of your dependency on your total physical/social context (*you* are of course part of this "context") for your bodily sustenance, your various social/mental skills such as language, and even your concepts and feelings about your "self."[2]

As Andras Angyal (1941) has pointed out, we are all integral parts of the biosphere, but our usual linear "causal" mode of thinking leads us to treat entities and events (such as ourselves) as separate from one another: we then look for causal connections between isolated events. With "system thinking," on the other hand, Angyal observed that we would seek rather to understand the "superordinate system" to which apparently disparate entities and events belong and through which they are connected. As noted, this latter mode of thinking may be difficult to internalize, but it seems to offer the key to an active awareness and appreciation of our essential unity with each other and the rest of nature.

Ecological Understanding and Awareness

Besides an intuitive appreciation of one's own underlying "identity" (or at least integral connection) with the biosphere, ecological systems thinking would involve both an understanding of ecological processes and a continuing awareness of how these processes operate in one's own life and surroundings. Thus, you could know a lot about ecological processes and still fail to use cognitive sets that would actively relate this knowledge to your ongoing environmental experiences. Conversely, you might try to attend to ecological processes in your environment, but such a cognitive set might well prove impossible or misleading if you did not understand ecological principles. Hence, both ecological knowledge and the activation of cognitive sets that used such knowledge effectively and experientially (see the discussion in Chapter 3) would be essential for what we might call *ecological awareness*. Also implicit in this, of course, is the idea that a thoroughgoing and active application of ecological understanding would entail a high degree of at least informal systems thinking. As a look through virtually any text on ecology will amply demonstrate, systems thinking seems an essential part of this discipline.

B-Cognition

Maslow's concept of Being-cognition and related notions such as Schachtel's allocentric perception have already been discussed in Chapter 3 in connection with cognitive sets for enhancing aesthetic experience. Such modes of cognition that involve appreciation of things in themselves are also important for ecological consciousness. As pointed out in Chapter 3, there are potential dangers in nonevaluative fascination with the "being" of things; even Maslow (1969) observed that B-cognition, if carried to an extreme, might lead to inaction and irresponsibility. Clearly, *total* object-centered appreciative contemplation is not what is intended by the concept of ecological consciousness. Rather, people should ideally possess a high ability to enjoy this mode of experiencing when it is appropriate. The idea is thus to be able to break away from pure "deficiency" (D-) cognition, as Maslow referred to cognitive sets that are mainly concerned with relating information to practical human purposes or deficiency needs (see Chapter 2). And B-cognition

286 Experience, Environment, and Human Potentials

need not be purely aesthetic in Osborne's (1970) sense of "percipience" or in the sense of most of the aesthetically oriented cognitive sets discussed in Chapter 3. One indeed can appreciate even the *functions* of human-made objects as interesting in themselves (that is, independent of their relation to one's own deficiency needs).

Perhaps of most relevance to the farther reaches of ecological consciousness is B-cognition and its associated B-love for entities, processes, and interrelationships that occur within the ecosystem—including human as well as nonhuman aspects. The key may well be simply to be *interested* in nature, in people, and in their interrelations. (Note: We might think of *interest* as involving curiosity about the area of interest; enjoyment of gathering or contemplating information about the area; non–self-conscious (self-transcending) involvement when considering the area or engaging in tasks related to it; and a predisposition to activate cognitive sets relating to the area of interest.[3] Clearly, being "interested" in something would thus be likely to lead one to "B-cognize" it.)

Pro-Life Value System

There is no need to repeat the discussion from the preceding chapter, but the following two points are worth brief reiteration. First, it was argued that a pro-life value system, because of its concern with the quality of experience for all sentient creatures, would entail an ecological conscience. That is, living things would be viewed as ends in themselves and their welfare would be considered intrinsically important— not important solely because one's own welfare is intimately involved. In addition to helping us avoid ecological mistakes (and interspecies crimes), such an orientation would also probably facilitate and accompany ecological systems thinking and B-cognition. Indeed, the underlying spirit of ecological conscience is perhaps best summed up by Paul Yambert's (1975, p. 181) term *ecocentric*—meaning "concerned with or focused primarily upon the welfare of the ecosystem as a whole" (see also O'Riordan, 1976).

Second, the supporting (means) values in a pro-life orientation would be based on an understanding of the determinants of the quality of experience as well as on insight into the basic interdependence of people with each other and the rest of their environment. The examples of such values suggested in Chapter 4 included (1) health and physical well-being; (2) reliance on intrinsic motivation; (3) enhancement of sources of intrinsic satisfaction; (4) enhancement of skills for increasing intrinsic satisfaction; (5) cooperation; (6) minimal unpleasant conditions; and (7) freedom, individuality, and diversity. It was of course also noted that any value system, pro-life ones included, would doubtless involve internal conflicts if one tried to maximize all the things deemed good. Solutions to such internal value conflicts are not necessarily easy or transparent. But, we might note here, a high level of ecological systems thinking, B-cognition, and internalized concern for the welfare of all sentient creatures would probably facilitate coming up with creative and effective resolutions to such conflicts within a pro-life value system. At the moment, I fear that such a confluence of these elements of ecological consciousness is so rare in our culture that we have little familiarity with what actually could be done.

Synergistic Motivational/Behavioral Orientation

Given the other components of ecological consciousness, it would seem reasonable to expect that such a pattern of values and cognitive sets would be accompanied by an interdependent, communal, cooperative pattern of relating to other people and, indeed, to other aspects of nature. In Chapter 2, the concept of *synergy* was discussed in reference to cultures that evidence high internal cooperation and correspondence of interests among members. "Synergy" means "combined action," and "synergistic" can be used as a synonym for "cooperative." However, this term, when applied to human action or thinking, also carries connotations of creative integration, recognized interdependence, and doing good for all parties concerned. More than does simple cooperation, synergistic action implies seeking creative, higher-level syntheses to resolve conflicts (as opposed to settling for simple compromises) and having concern for the well-being of the whole ecosystem in addition to one's fellow humans (also see Esser, 1974).

Thus, in addition to *thinking* ecologically and systemically, *experiencing* in a B-cognitive mode, and *valuing* "ecocentrically," a person high in ecological consciousness would also be genuinely motivated—and thus would tend to *behave*—in creatively cooperative, and even altruistic, ways. At the very least, ecological consciousness would entail motivation to take account of the interpersonal and environmental effects of one's actions from a pro-life value perspective. One would thus presumably try to do such things as "design with nature" (McHarg, 1969), master the way humanity relates to the rest of nature rather than "master nature" itself (Leiss, 1974), and in general *share* power, wealth, information, and whatever else would enrich life for all people (and other creatures).

Admittedly, such an open, cooperative, and altruistic orientation could be somewhat foolhardy in a world populated by those with a more egocentric—and less enlightened—consciousness. However, if a pattern of *eco*centric consciousness were widespread, it might be foolish *not* to think and feel in ways that would lead you to be oriented cooperatively and even altruistically. (I am predicating that remark on the idea that the cognitive/affective aspects of ecological consciousness are simply much more fulfilling and enjoyable—as well as more sane in the long run—than, say, linear thinking, exclusive D-cognition, egocentric values, and a competitive orientation toward other people.) In any event, the picture I have so far painted of ecological consciousness is much more likely to be criticized for being unrealistic than for depicting an unpleasant or otherwise undesirable cognitive, valuational, and motivational orientation toward the world. Before writing it off as unrealistic, however, consider my arguments in the rest of this chapter. The discussion will focus in turn on (1) some indications about how far along toward ecological consciousness we might already be; (2) some of the likely problems for reaching it; and (3) some possible ways to facilitate it.

HOW FAR ALONG ARE WE?

A consciousness can probably be regarded as applicable to a whole society as well as to individuals—although, as Harold and Margaret Sprout (1965) have aptly pointed out, psychological concepts are strictly applicable only to individuals or perhaps to interacting groups of individuals, not to whole nations. Attributing characteristics such as aggression (or a type of consciousness) to a country as a whole may obscure the responsibility of *particular* people for what goes on in the world. Nevertheless, we can at least say that a given society at a given time may reflect a given type of consciousness in its social institutions and decision making. As argued in Chapter 4, societies can apparently be characterized by their dominant operative value systems. It seems a reasonable extension to characterize societies also in terms of the modes of information processing and motivational/behavioral orientations evidenced by key decision makers or by average citizens. This is of course what Reich (1970) was attempting to do with his impressionistic historical survey of different American consciousnesses.

So, allowing for some likelihood of oversimplification and even a danger of reification, let us pose the following compound question: How much ecological consciousness does our society evidence, and are we moving toward more of it? On the optimistic side, it is possible to find several proponents of the idea that whether or not we are now high in something like ecological consciousness, we are moving in that direction. For instance, Philip Slater (1974) optimistically argues that pro-life "social eversion" processes are pushing us toward increased "attunement" with each other and our physical environment.[4] George Leonard (1972), even in the title of his book *The Transformation: A Guide to the Inevitable Changes in Humankind*, implies that we are heading toward a type of consciousness that he describes as featuring heightened awareness, joy, and a sense of oneness with nature. F. E. Emery and E. L. Trist (1973) predict that the emerging "post-industrial" culture will be characterized by pro-life values, collaborative social and institutional relations, and ecologically enlightened planning and decision making. George Lodge (1975) foresees the imminent growth of "a new American ideology" consisting of a stress on "communitarianism," Equity-2–type "rights of membership," "community need," the "state as planner and coordinator," and ecologically enlightened "holistic" thinking. And, of course, Reich's (1970) optimistic view of Consciousness III sweeping the country might apply here as well (notwithstanding its rather individualistic tone).

Is there any evidence for all these optimistic predictions? My impression is that most of the evidence is anecdotal or impressionistic, and that the little research evidence available—such as the results of the value surveys discussed in Chapter 4 or the failure of psychologists to find many people at the higher levels of moral or ego development (see the next section)—is not particularly encouraging. Even on an impressionistic level, such problems as the national and international distribution of wealth, continuing world dissension, and global pollution must certainly give anyone pause in proclaiming a new age of ecological consciousness.

On the hopeful side, though, there are a number of recent social developments—"movements," if you will—that may indicate some trends toward heightened social and ecological consciousness. A few examples would be the continuing civil rights movement, the women's liberation movement, growing public interest in consciousness expansion, increasing academic interest in systems analysis and general systems theory, the growth of various forms of environmental and humanistic education, the resurgence of cooperative intentional communities (communes), increasingly positive attitudes toward China (not to mention continuing interest in Eastern philosophies), and of course the environmental movement itself. Since most of the other topics are discussed elsewhere in this book, and since it seems in many ways most directly relevant to the issue of public ecological consciousness, the environmental movement will here be singled out for a closer look.

Apparently beginning in the 1960s a rapid growth in public concern about the environment became manifest, at least in highly industrialized Western nations such as the United States. As many observers have pointed out, the movement seemed to peak in popular interest around 1970 and seems to have declined and leveled off over the past few years.[5] However, David Sills (1975) has cited evidence that there are probably five to ten million members of environmental organizations in the United States; and a good case can be made that the environmental movement has already helped to change corporate, governmental, legal, and individual decision making in "pro-environment" directions.[6] As Denton Morrison and his associates (1972) have argued, the environmental movement seems to be shifting from a purely "participation" strategy of education and voluntaristic urging to an increasingly "power" strategy of seeking legal and institutional coercion (regulation). However, they also pointed out that both internal and external conflicts are emerging for those concerned with environmental quality. To see how all this may actually bear on ecological consciousness, let us take a closer look at what seem to be the underlying ideological positions encompassed by the environmental movement.

One common distinction is that between the preservationist side of environmentalism and the utilitarian contingent (see, for example, Sills, 1975; Morrison et al., 1972). The preservationist position represents the more extreme form of "nature loving": the goal is to preserve natural areas and avoid human influence (interference) as much as possible. The utilitarian approach, on the other hand, is more concerned with conservation and the "wise use" of resources. Even within each of these orientations, however, there is much diversity in goals and means. Disregarding these distinctions for the moment, my impression is that two central aspects of the environmental movement have been a concern for a safe, "clean," and pleasant environment—usually meaning, at a minimum, the absence of various forms of pollution—and a concern for the preservation of at least some natural areas.

Beyond this, Sills (1975) has cited critics of the environmental movement as giving the following characterizations of environmentalists: they are *alarmists* about such matters as "ecocatastrophes," hopeless depletion of essential and nonrenewable natural resources, insufficient future food supply, overpopulation, and all sorts of pollution; *pessimists* (perhaps even misanthropes) about humankind's ability to influence nature benignly; *nature worshipers* who tend to idealize nature, ignore beneficial human interventions, and give too low a priority to the needs of people (as opposed, say, to other endangered species); *superficial analysts,* concerned mainly with cosmetic issues (for example, "green-up" campaigns); and *elitists,* heedless of the costs to the poor at home and abroad for instituting antipollution or "no-growth" policies. More is included in Sills's account, but this list should indicate the flavor and variety of critical characterizations of environmentalism.

Such criticisms do seem to have elements of truth. Some environmentalists' alarms will doubtless turn out to be false. Some extreme condemnations of humankind, such as regarding humanity as a "cancer" on the earth, do have the ring of pessimism and perhaps even misanthropy about them. And even as staunch an environmentalist as René Dubos (for example, 1972a, 1973a,b) has faulted overzealous idealization of nature and rejection of human intervention—not because technology is good in itself or because humans can "conquer nature," but because designing *with* nature *for* a better life can "humanize the earth" in a pro-life way (as in the case of the British countryside at its best, for instance). Finally, and perhaps most seriously for impugning the ecological consciousness of the movement, many of those associated with environmentalism have in fact evidenced a superficial and, perhaps inadvertently, an elitist orientation.[7] One might ask, to follow the polemics of an ardent humanitarian critic such as Richard Neuhaus (1971), whether it is evidence of ecological consciousness to ignore the plight of the urban poor in favor of concern with oil on the beaches of a suburban resort or to devote oneself to preserving a bird sanctuary while doing nothing to alleviate the suffering of millions of people adversely affected by one's own society's economic practices.

It seems likely, to answer that rhetorical question, that true ecological consciousness would in principle entail striving for goals that would somehow both alleviate human suffering and provide higher-level pro-life amenities. As we shall consider shortly, such goals—and the cultural transformations they would involve—may not always be within the practical grasp of particular individuals or even of single social movements. But before pursuing that issue, I would like to stress two other considerations: First, it does seem important in striving to solve environmental problems, or in otherwise trying to improve the environment, to consider overall implications and ramifications of both the ends and the means (compare cognitive set IMG-E in Chapter 3). Thus, striving to "clean up the environment" or even to preserve wilderness, *if done without attending to the ramifications of the means used,* could actually turn out to lower the overall quality of life—say, by inadvertently raising the taxes paid by the poor.

And perhaps even more important, it seems to me, environmentalists and others striving to enhance life should avoid the trap of accepting narrow and status-quo–maintaining definitions of problems or alternatives. Thus, many potential conflicts between "environmental" and other pro-life goals can be resolved at a higher level of systems thinking. For instance, viewed from a systems perspective, an apparently irreconcilable conflict between curtailing pollution versus maintaining jobs or between devoting public funds to help the poor versus using them to preserve a wilderness area might be seen as pointing to the need for substantial revisions in our economic system. With some rethinking we may find that it is possible to have jobs *and* a beautiful environment (indeed, maintaining and producing a beautiful environment can make jobs), to eliminate poverty *and* pollution, and to similarly resolve many of the other false dilemmas promulgated by people with limited vision or with vested interests in the status quo.

Finally, we may return to the question of whether an individual environmentalist or even the entire environmental movement can be reasonably expected to tackle the gargantuan issues of pro-life cultural transformation. As a practical question of strategies for social change, the answer is probably no. Effective change tactics, environmental or otherwise, often seem to hinge on seeking limited and well-defined ("reachable") goals.⁸ However, if only for the sake of their own ecological consciousness, it might be beneficial for all environmentalists to actively consider the larger systemic alternatives as well as more immediately reachable goals. Actually, my impression is that most dedicated environmentalists *are* inclined to do this. Environmental issues, perhaps more than many purely "social" ones, tend to expose the underlying shortcomings of our basic economic and societal decision-making systems. As a result, just *studying* environmental problems can be extremely consciousness-raising and radicalizing (see the discussion of environmental education later in this chapter).

Furthermore, it is unfair to blame the environmental movement for failing to strive to change everything that needs changing or to achieve everything that pro-life values might dictate. One might as well fault the civil rights movement for failing to consider pollution or wilderness preservation, or the women's liberation movement for not being concerned with the plight of American Indians or the injustices of our foreign economic policies. The point, ultimately, is that all of our basically pro-life movements perhaps need to broaden their goals or at least the way in which they conceptualize the problems and possible solutions. Each movement has tapped part of an essentially interrelated network of problems. To correct the root causes of any one of these problems, I believe, will be to treat the root causes of all of them. What I am referring to, of course, is the need for change in the underlying operative values and in many of the basic institutions of our society—and the world, for that matter. Systemic change of that magnitude would require a high level of both ecological consciousness and cooperative coordination for virtually all of our pro-life social movements. We're clearly not there yet, but we may well be slowly heading in that direction.

WHAT MIGHT BE BLOCKING US?

Whether or not we are heading *toward* ecological consciousness, it would be difficult to argue that we have already arrived. Worse, there is reason to believe that even if we want—and actively strive—to attain this pattern of thinking, valuing, and behaving, the path may be strewn with hurdles and perhaps even blocks. In looking at this somewhat pessimistic side of the problem, though, it might be comforting to bear in mind that ecological consciousness can probably come in varying degrees. It might be possible to reap some of its fruits even if only certain key decision makers attained a high degree of ecological consciousness or if a society as a whole evidenced only a moderate—but pervasive—level of it.

Even given that hopeful thought, there would appear to be some serious blocks (or at least hurdles) to reaching ecological consciousness as conceptualized in this discussion. Let us first take the four main components in turn and look briefly at some primarily cultural factors that may hinder their realization. Following that, we can examine what may be the more serious problem of possibly inherent limitations on normal human psychological capacities. The hope, of course, is that the latter kind of hindrance is really itself a cultural problem or at least can be overcome by appropriate educational or other cultural means.

Possible Cultural Blocks

George Leonard (1972) has argued that just as some subcultures of beggars in various parts of the world deliberately maim their children as a kind of "gift" to help them be successful beggars, our own culture may be seen as bestowing a similar type of gift in the form of "neurosis/disease/discontent." This gift, according to Leonard, involves such things as implicitly socializing people to have dulled senses and feelings and to have a "dis-ease"–producing drive for success.[9] As I argued in Chapter 4, our culture does seem to prepare people for competitive individualism, materialism, hierarchical thinking, confusion of means and ends, a short-term time perspective, and so on. This list is easily extended, but let's do it in relation to the specific components of ecological consciousness.

Blocks to Ecological Systems Thinking

Holistic sense of self. The first aspect of ecological systems thinking was posited to be thinking of oneself as part of a larger system. As suggested by the work of Alan Watts (for example, 1958a,b) and other writers on Eastern philosophy, it may be much easier for members of many non-Western cultures than for Westerners to gain this feeling of being one with the world around us. Even Gregory Bateson (1972), whose writings strike me as inspirational invitations to systems thinking, claimed that he experienced difficulty in *not* thinking of himself as separate from his "context." (However, he may have viewed this problem as more or less innate to human "purposive" thinking rather than due simply to culturally ingrained patterns of thought. As he pointed out, human beings tend to think in *"arcs* of circuits" rather than in *whole* circuits. Nevertheless, his seeming confidence that we can learn to think "cybernetically" implies at least that culture could help to produce a sense of self as an integral part of nature's circuits.) Our culture's emphasis on competitive individualism—or even on individualistic growth or on being an Origin, if interpreted literally—could certainly contribute to this type of difficulty. What I am suggesting is that we may need new categories of thought (schemas) for considering human motivation, personality, and potentials—categories that take more explicit account of contextual effects and of the idea that all human behavior (Origin as well as Pawn) occurs only as part of circuits or networks.

Ecological understanding and awareness.   This may actually be an area in which our culture is starting to *facilitate* ecological consciousness. Certainly most writing on environmental issues and most scientific analyses in ecology seem currently to emanate from the West. This may even be an example of Slater's "social eversion" process. The power of science, for so long in the service of linear thinking, is finally being turned on issues the scientific investigation of which forces a degree of systems thinking. And, as will be discussed later in this chapter, environmental education programs are now often being explicitly designed to foster virtually all of the components I have attributed to ecological consciousness. So, despite such blocks to systems thinking as traditional compartmented, linear-thinking education and scientific investigation, there is reason to hope that ecological understanding and awareness, at least, are beginning to get a cultural boost.

Blocks to B-Cognition

Our culture certainly has had a bleak tradition of failing to value appreciative, nonevaluative perception and the contemplation of the "being" of things. As we have seen, aesthetic experience, nonverbal thinking, and even the affective quality of life in general have been low on the totem pole of American concerns. Performance, achievement, production, material wealth, competitive success, a *machismo* ethic, and so on, all militate against placid appreciation and aesthetic sensitivity—not to mention empathic identification and unselfish (B-) love. However, the growth of interest in consciousness expansion, meditation, sensitivity training, and other "turn on" phenomena (even some drugs) may portend a genuine awakening of B-cognitive awareness in many people. Let us hope that they will see fit to pass *this* sort of gift along to other people who cannot currently afford it (meaning that the predominantly well-off people who can afford to study consciousness expansion might consider equalizing the wealth and other good things needed for *all* people to advance up Maslow's hierarchy to the point where B-cognition can become a world-wide passion).

Blocks to Pro-Life Values and Synergistic Behavior

Culturally based impediments to pro-life values and to synergistic motivational/behavioral orientations have been at least implicitly covered in Chapters 2 and 4. Thus our discussion here can be brief. To put it baldly: Is it going to be easy for anyone to place the highest priority on the well-being of all people (not to mention other sentient creatures) and to behave in an open and creatively cooperative way in a society in which (1) a Theory X conception of human motivation prevails, reflected in the often self-fulfilling prophecy that people are untrustworthy and in the indiscriminate use of extrinsic motivation at home, at school, and at work (and often even at play); (2) one of the main things that is extrinsically reinforced is doing better than other people or otherwise defeating them; (3) another thing that is reinforced is accumulating material wealth as an end in itself (or as an indication of status), even if this hurts other people; (4) wealth and power are very unequally distributed; (5) such unequal distribution is supported by a highly competitive Equity 1 norm; and (6) violence is a commonly accepted "solution" to problems ranging from socializing children to settling international conflicts—and is often glorified even in entertainment, sports, history lessons, and relations to other species? Unfortunately, this list could go on.

Possible Innate Blocks

For those of us who hope that ecological consciousness might be attained on a broad scale as a result of cultural transformations, it is certainly a nightmarish thought that this attainment might be blocked by *innate* limitations or biases in human psychological functioning. Even more than the topics of the previous section, however, consideration of whether psychological hindrances are innate—genetically built in—is a highly speculative matter. Thus, some ethologists (for example, Lorenz, 1966) have argued by analogy with other animals that people are probably innately aggressive—thus implying that pro-life values and synergistic motivation and behavior might be difficult to attain. But the logic of such arguments is easily criticized (see, for example, Montagu, 1968; Scherer et al., 1975); and, in fact, a case can even be made that humans are probably innately prone to cooperation.[10] Similar problems are likely to arise for virtually any argument that imputes innate psychological dispositions to humankind. Reasoning by analogy to other species is very precarious when applied to human psychological or behavioral functioning; and there are very few universals that hold for all human cultures. Furthermore, *even if* we have genetically built-in predispositions to a particular kind of psychological functioning, human adaptability seems to know few bounds when cultural innovations are taken into account. Hence even an "innate" block to ecological consciousness might be overcome by educational or other cultural adjustments.

Nevertheless, there are some disturbing considerations that we should take into account in thinking about the feasibility of widespread ecological consciousness. The two that seem most serious concern possible limitations on widespread capacity for cognitive and moral development and for rationality and systems thinking.

Cognitive and Moral Development

Psychologists who have attempted to study the upper reaches of human potentials for pro-life development tend to come up with very few living examples. Maslow (1970) could find few self-actualizers and indicated that only "older people" even had a real crack at it. Less impressionistically, investigators of moral development, such as Lawrence Kohlberg (see Chapter 4), seem to have a very hard time finding individuals in any culture who reason at the highest postulated stages of human moral thinking (for example, Kohlberg's stage of philosophically based moral reasoning that stresses principles of justice and universal human welfare). Similarly, Jane Loevinger (1976) has pointed out the difficulty of finding people at the top levels of "ego development"—not surprisingly, since this integrative concept incorporates a Kohlberg-type hierarchy and relates not only to moral development but also to cognitive and interpersonal growth. Since ecological consciousness would certainly require very high moral and general ego development, there can be little doubt that a search for current representatives would yield similar results.

The frightening thought, of course, is that this dearth of representatives of the highest stages of moral, cognitive, and interpersonal development is not merely due to inadequacies in child rearing, education, or other aspects of culture. It is possible that for many—even most—of us, inherent cognitive or motivational limitations mean that these high stages simply are not part of our human potentials. *That* would be an innate block to give us nightmares.

But fortunately, the small number of residents at a given psychological destination is not sufficient evidence that the rest of us can't get there. We should indeed be encouraged by the very fact that *some* people make it to these top stages of moral or ego development and that, as Loevinger (1976) pointed out, there is so much similarity among various conceptions of the stages.[11] Clearly, prerequisites for ecological consciousness, such as high integrative complexity in moral reasoning and other cognitive processes, high capacity for synergistic human relations, and high capacity for B-cognition, are all within the range of actual traits displayed by members of the human species.

The crucial issue may be whether it is possible to develop educational and other cultural techniques that can overcome low levels of genetically endowed cognitive and motivational capacity and thus help most, if not all, people reach the stages of moral, cognitive, and interpersonal development now attained by so few. As indicated in Chapter 4, educational procedures are being developed that may well help people raise their level of moral and value reasoning. Loevinger's (1976) work also provides an indication that similar programs may be possible for full ego development, although further research is clearly needed. As in the case of deCharms's work on Origin training, however, most of the attempts at moral and ego-development education have thus far been aimed at moving people up a notch or two at the lower levels of the proposed hierarchies. And, as Augusto Blasi (in Loevinger, 1976) noted, the procedures that work at one stage may be ineffective if applied at another. Nevertheless, we may be on the threshold of a new age of psychological education. As we shall see later in this chapter, emerging suggestions for environmental, synergistic, and confluent education may, if applied intelligently and widely, reveal that fears about innate limitations in human capacities for ecological consciousness are unfounded.

Before settling into a mood of complacent optimism, however—or at least before embarking full-steam on a search for pathways to ecological consciousness—let us turn to the second disturbing consideration: the possibility of innate limitations on human capacity for rationality and systems thinking. Rather than attempt to treat this issue in an abstract and general way, I shall simply try to illustrate the potential problems— and some possible solutions—by focusing on a relevant specific area of human/environment interaction.

Rationality and Systems Thinking: Illustrations from
Responses to Natural Hazards

Ironically, considering the emphasis in environmental studies on human-made problems, hints of limitations on our species' rationality and systems-thinking ability (at least when dealing with environmental contingencies) are perhaps most clearly revealed with respect to so-called natural hazards. For many years now, an international group of researchers have been examining patterns of people's perception and response to such hazards as floods, hurricanes, droughts, volcanoes, earthquakes, avalanches, and other natural occurrences that disrupt and threaten human life.[12]

Before looking specifically at the implications for blocks to ecological consciousness, we might gain some perspective by first very briefly examining some general psychological and sociological conclusions thus far yielded by this research. Perhaps chief among the psychological findings (see, for example, Ian Burton, 1972) is that people commonly respond to the uncertainty of natural hazards by (1) cognitively "eliminating the hazard"—as by denying the existence of the threat or denying the possibility of recurrence—or by (2) cognitively "eliminating the uncertainty"—as by believing in a highly predictable pattern of recurrence, such as "floods come every five years," or by "transferring uncertainty to a higher power," such as viewing the events as "in the hands of God" or in the care of "the government." Another very important point summarized by Burton (1972) is that survivors of disasters very often return to the same hazardous site to live. Some explanations for what in many cases appears to be irrational behavior are that (1) the hazardous site usually holds some particular attraction for its residents, such as physical attractiveness, sentimental attachment, or economic advantages not readily available elsewhere; (2) as noted, many people employ what appears to be defensive reappraisal (see Lazarus, 1966) to eliminate the sense of threat even after they have experienced a natural catastrophe; and (3) social and governmental practices often virtually force people back to the same hazardous sites, as in cases where relief payments are available only to people who rebuild in their original location.

Burton (1972) has also summarized the various classes of adjustment alternatives potentially open to hazard zone occupants. These include affecting the cause (for example, changing hydrological patterns to prevent floods), modifying the hazard (for example, stabilizing soil in earthquake areas), modifying the potential for loss (for example, establishing early warning systems for hurricanes), adjusting to losses (for example, spreading the losses by public relief and insurance—although, as many of the hazard researchers note, such procedures may serve to encourage occupancy of hazard zones and inhibit local action to avert damage), planning for losses (for example, using voluntary insurance), and bearing the losses (biting the bullet?).

Presumably, this large-scale program of research will continue and reveal much additional information of value in forming policy dealing with natural hazards. However, the implications for ecological consciousness are perhaps most evident in a paper by Paul Slovic, Howard Kunreuther, and Gilbert White (1974), entitled "Decision Processes, Rationality, and Adjustment to Natural Hazards." This paper reviews and synthesizes a range of research findings that seem of very great—and possibly grave—importance not only for understanding human reactions to natural hazards but also for appreciating human cognitive limitations generally. These apparent limitations, if they prove to be biologically inherent, may indicate that some fairly radical changes will soon be needed in our methods of social decision making if we are to avoid potentially catastrophic mistakes. At the very least, the existing evidence implies that achieving societal ecological consciousness will require a substantial increase in the rationality of our collective thinking.

The paper by Slovic and his associates first distinguishes between (1) decision-making procedures that attempt to reach an optimal decision or to "maximize expected utility [net gain]" and (2) decision making based on "bounded rationality." The latter procedure attempts only to reach a satisfactory—not necessarily an optimal—decision. Herbert Simon (for example, 1956) has termed such a goal "satisficing," and it seems to be more characteristic of human decision making than is the optimizing approach. However, as Slovic and his colleagues very cogently argue, human decision making under bounded rationality appears to involve cognitive limitations that can lead to totally inadequate coping strategies in dealing with many natural hazards or other uncertain events posing threats to human well-being. The three main limitations seem to be (1) the tendency to consider only a very limited range of alternatives; (2) the tendency to perceive risks inaccurately and to deny uncertainty; and (3) the tendency to respond primarily to crises. Let us examine each of these in turn.

Restricted consideration of alternatives. It should not come as a shock that most individuals have difficulty integrating numerous interacting factors in different ways so as to generate a wide range of viable alternatives. To appreciate the possibility and feasibility of many types of alternative coping strategies often requires a fairly high degree of systems thinking and a willingness to tolerate substantial changes in the status quo. Truly effective long-range solutions to problems of natural hazards as well as to human-made environmental and social problems may involve transformations in the economic, educational, and political systems. Such systemic transformations are frequently ignored as possible options, in part because of human cognitive limitations and in part because of social and cultural restrictions on what people allow themselves and others to think about. As Slovic and his colleagues point out, this tendency to consider only a very limited range of options is not restricted to individuals. For example, they cite research by Cyert and March (1963) and by Lindblom (1964) that suggests that business and governmental organizations tend to change policy by introducing only minimal deviations from existing policies. Responses by such institutions are based mainly on short-term feedback, and corrective actions are taken mainly in response to crises.

In addition, various research findings in human perception and problem solving (see, for example, Posner, 1973) suggest that once a person (or culture?) adopts a given conceptual framework for dealing with a class of problems, change to a different framework is extremely difficult. If insurance, safety measures, and technological changes become the dominant ways for handling traffic accidents or catastrophic floods, shifting to a new life style or new pattern of residence may never even be thought of as possible alternative solutions. Since sweeping changes usually (1) involve many different dimensions that must be considered simultaneously, (2) require a more thorough understanding of complex problems than most of us can muster (at least intuitively—see following paragraphs), and (3) tend to run counter both to a culture's dominant patterns of thought and to powerful vested interests within the culture, it is even less shocking that most individuals have difficulty considering a wide range of alternative coping strategies for dealing with complex problems.

Distortions in the perception of risk and probability.   We have already taken note of the conclusions of Ian Burton and his colleagues concerning distortions in residents' perceptions of the likelihood that natural disasters will affect them. Many potential flood victims, for example, either deny the existence of the hazard altogether or distort the likelihood of recurrence by mistakenly believing that floods occur at regular intervals. Such distortions, of course, may serve the obvious function of preserving some degree of psychological comfort in the face of uncertain threats. (Jackson and Mukerjee, 1974, have even found that San Franciscans often refused to be interviewed about their views on earthquakes; those who would talk tended to think the hazard was small.) Indeed, it is a common observation that the *uncertainty* of when an unpleasant event will occur is itself a source of stress and unpleasant affect. Nonetheless, Slovic and his associates present a wide range of evidence to indicate that more than mere comfort seeking is probably involved in such misperceptions of the risk of natural hazards.

There is convincing evidence that most people are simply not very good at handling many types of information involving probabilities. Amos Tversky and Daniel Kahneman (1971, 1973, 1974; Kahneman and Tversky, 1972), for instance, have conducted numerous experiments indicating systematic biases in the functioning of people's estimates of probabilities. Their work has even revealed that research psychologists, who are generally well aware of statistical principles, tend to overgeneralize from very small samples when making intuitive estimates of what further research will disclose. Tversky and Kahneman have also found substantial support for their hypothesis that the "availability" (ease of calling to mind) of instances of an event plays a major role in determining one's estimate of the probability of instances of that event. Thus, subjects in one experiment were found to think that more words begin with "k" than have "k" in the third letter position. The opposite is actually true, but people presumably find it easier to think of words beginning with "k" than of words having "k" as the third letter and hence err in gauging the relative frequencies. This apparent tendency to judge probability by subjective availability does not always lead to error and does not always present a serious problem when it does. For events of high visibility and frequency it may even lead to accurate estimates. However, in the case of natural (and other) hazards, the role of availability may lead to serious distortions, such as overestimating the future risk of recently experienced hazards and underestimating the risk of hazards not made salient by recent experience.

Research on human adjustment to future earthquake hazards (see Jackson and Mukerjee, 1974), for instance, indicates that preparatory adjustments were most likely to be made by people who had had relatively intense experiences with earthquakes. Similarly, research on reactions to flood danger (for example, Kates, 1962) has also identified a tendency for people to give undue weight to their recent experience in planning future adjustments. For everyday examples, however, one need only consider with Tversky and Kahneman (1973) that the subjective probability of being involved in an auto accident or even a thermonuclear war seems to rise precipitously when one actually witnesses a car wreck or a vivid cinematic depiction of an accidental war. To darken the picture of human information processing even further, Tversky and Kahneman also posit (with some supporting evidence) that people may frequently form mistaken judgments of the *relationship* between two variables as a function of the ease of calling to mind instances of such association. This, as well as work cited by Slovic and his associates (1974), points to possible limitations in people's ability to detect true correlations or potential causal relations among events.

Slovic and his associates also found that people have difficulty perceiving random events *as* random; tend to underestimate the range within which events are likely to fall, leading perhaps to overconfidence in considering potential hazards; commonly err in making judgments of correlation and causality because of incorrect expectations and preconceived hypotheses; and often fail to integrate available information properly when making decisions involving risk, thus reaching decisions that are inconsistent with their own underlying values.

Crisis-oriented responses.   The foregoing limitations and biases in human information processing should make it easy to understand why people would tend to change or adjust primarily in response to actual crisis situations. Events such as a recent flood, storm, earthquake, accident, or war have very high subjective availability and thus arouse concern for their recurrence. In addition, responding only to crises fits the linear, status-quo–oriented mode of thinking and coping discussed in relation to the restricted consideration of alternatives. A crisis orientation relieves the cognitive strain and uncertainty that would be involved in attempts at long-range planning and also serves vested interests by tending to preserve the status quo. However, this *is* an effective coping strategy under some circumstances. As Slovic and his associates (1974, p. 201) put it, short-term, crisis-oriented strategies can work well "in static environments where the same decision is made repeatedly and the consequences of a poor decision are not too disastrous." The trouble, of course, is that many environmental hazards—natural and otherwise—are either insidious, slowly growing problems with no obvious crises but only gradual deterioration (one might think of population growth, urban blight, and coastal erosion, for example) or involve crises with disastrous consequences (nuclear war, some forms of pollution and resource depletion, and so on).

Optimism, pessimism, and possible solutions.   On the side of optimism, we can begin by repeating that human bounded rationality, even with all its limitations, has thus far allowed us to "muddle through." At least the species has not *yet* made an obviously fatal mistake. More optimistically, it would appear possible to use our growing knowledge of human information-processing biases to help ourselves correct for these biases and thus make more effective long-range decisions. We might be able to utilize the availability bias, for example, to boost concern for non-obvious, distant, or uncertain risks by producing and exposing ourselves to films or other graphic depictions of potential hazards.

Of course, as other research on natural hazards seems to imply (for example, Jackson and Mukerjee, 1974), more may be involved than correcting for low subjective availability resulting from lack of images or information. People's emotionally based defense mechanisms must also be taken into account. But at least as our understanding of the relevant cognitive processes increases, we may be able to design corrective stimuli or educational procedures to enlighten each other about potential dangers and coping strategies. It may also turn out that the discussion by Slovic and his associates (1974) is actually overstated in its imputation of more or less inherent limitations and irremediable biases to human beings' probabilistic thinking. With appropriate techniques of education we may be able to change our intuitions about probabilistic information, just as we now use education to teach people to think of the earth as round or to enjoy classical music.

There are other optimistic considerations, but let us turn briefly to the pessimistic side. Slovic, Kunreuther, and White have presented a fairly grim picture of people's ability to intuitively handle probabilistic information and hence of their ability to make long-range rational decisions about many complex problems. They acknowledge that this conclusion may seem at odds with the confidence many (if not most) people feel about their intuitive abilities to deal with such information. After all, human beings *are* good at processing sensory information (especially in visual and auditory modalities), and in general our evolution has provided us with highly adaptable perceptual-motor potentials. However, this may mislead us into overestimating our other cognitive abilities. Also, Slovic and his colleagues note, we are very adept at finding rationalizations for our failure to make wise decisions. Indeed, we often receive little feedback about the effects of our decisions or operate with such vague criteria that "we can't tell how poorly we are actually doing" (p. 199). And of course if a mistake isn't fatal or disabling, we can take corrective measures as we move from crisis to crisis. All told, it thus seems easy enough for us to delude ourselves into thinking that we are more capable than we are.

Consider as well the ideas of environmental psychologist Stephen Kaplan (1973) about the information-processing side of human nature. According to Kaplan, human beings have been shaped by evolutionary processes to have "a bias toward action," "to jump to conclusions," to have a low tolerance for ambiguity, to be "quick to perceive and quick to decide," and to tend toward oversimplification, prejudice, and "going off half-cocked" (p. 77). Acknowledging that these and other considerations do not present an especially attractive picture of our species, Kaplan argues that human history itself presents a rather sordid panorama.

Keep in mind, however, that whatever our limitations, we human beings are extraordinarily adaptable. Kaplan (1973), for example, goes on to point out that we are "eager to learn, to explore, and to act," and that we seek and create order. He also sees some hope that we will realize the complexity, delicacy, and interdependence of our social and environmental systems before it is too late. For Slovic, Kunreuther, and White (1974), the answer seems to lie in a two-fold approach. First, we should use our knowledge of normal human information processing to (1) inform people of potentially distorting biases in the way they process information (thus promoting self-correction if all goes well); (2) design simulations to help people gain the informational equivalent of having coped with real hazards; (3) otherwise increase the awareness (subjective availability) of potential hazards and of a broader range of alternative coping strategies; and (4) utilize public policy, such as insurance programs that deliberately encourage innovations in coping, to increase awareness and open new options. Such tactics might free us from what Robert Kates (1976) has aptly termed "the prison of experience."

The second approach of Slovic and his associates for dealing with problems that have major societal importance is labelled "decision analysis." This amounts essentially to formal systems analysis applied to decision making under conditions of uncertainty. Using computer technology it is possible to treat decision problems in terms of numerous interacting dimensions and to attempt to optimize outcomes across many social and environmental values. (It is also apparently useful in many cases to combine certain types of human probability estimates with computer information processing—see, for example, Peterson, 1973.) Of course, life usually requires compromise even in attempts to optimize, and Slovic and his colleagues admit that formal decision analyses can commit dangerous oversimplifications or be used to justify policies arrived at on grounds other than the public good. As they suggest, however, such techniques of sophisticated quantitative analysis may be the only truly effective means for us to transcend any inherent information-processing limitations and biases we have.

Before we turn over all our major environmental and social decisions to teams of computer technologists and to computers themselves, however, we might at least strive for a broadly based ecological consciousness. That would make us better able to monitor what's going on at the upper decision-making levels and provide a pool of enlightened decision makers. Ideally, those enlightened decision makers would of course be virtually all of us—with computers and other technological aids being used solely to help us achieve our own collectively chosen (and presumably pro-life) ends. To conclude this chapter, let us therefore turn to a consideration of some possible ways to overcome whatever blocks there are and to encourage ecological consciousness on a wide scale.

HOW COULD WE GET THERE?

Encouraging the widespread development of ecological consciousness would obviously be a complex undertaking, probably involving all major institutions of our culture. The following discussion attempts to point out just a few of the more hopeful possibilities.

Education

In keeping with my own (perhaps overly optimistic) hope that education offers the most promising path to effecting long-term pro-life changes in our consciousness and in our society, this path will receive the most attention. To justify this emphasis, I would point out that education is the cultural institution in our society most directly concerned with potential direct influences on *all* the components of ecological consciousness. But rather than divide my discussion in terms of influences on the individual elements of ecological consciousness, I shall simply concentrate on several encouraging developments in the content and procedures of education: environmental education, synergistic education, confluent education, and the summary idea of educational reconstructionism.

Environmental Education

Perhaps one of the most important fruits of the environmental movement has been the growing interest in developing and incorporating programs in environmental education at virtually all levels of the educational system.[13] Although some forms of environmental education have been accused of being superficial and insufficiently revolutionary (Agne and Nash, 1974, 1976), the study of environmental issues in fact shows signs of being one of the most potentially radicalizing and transformative forces at work in education today. Let me support that statement with a few observations from the literature on environmental education and from the underlying logic of environmental studies itself.

First, two dominant themes of books on environmental education such as those by Mark Terry (1971), James Swan and William Stapp (1974), and Noel McInnis and Don Albrecht (1975) are the following: (1) Environmental education should aim to increase not only environmental knowledge and awareness but also ecological systems thinking, ecological conscience and other aspects of a pro-life value system, and the motivation and ability to take action in accord with all this. (2) Procedures for effectively accomplishing those aims should include (a) training for problem solving and using active inquiry methods; (b) organizing the total curriculum in as interdisciplinary a fashion as possible; (c) incorporating values clarification as an integral consideration in teaching; (d) encouraging student participation in decision making (that is, sharing power with students); (e) making environmental issues and concerns pervasive throughout the educational curriculum (both horizontally across subject areas and vertically across grade levels); (f) using cooperative goal structures for students (see the following section on synergistic education); (g) making use of the whole community and helping students to relate environmental studies to actual local environmental, political, and social issues; and (h) involving students (and teachers) in action projects that include striving for pro-life changes both in the school and in the broader community.

Throughout such a program in environmental education there would clearly run an emphasis on social as well as purely "environmental" concern. The stress would be both on the interrelatedness of environmental and social problems and on the need for carefully considered collaborative action to make life better for the whole community. As Terry (1971) pointed out, achieving even small environmental successes from such an educational approach would serve as a possibly inspiring (and newsworthy?) example to the world outside the school and also help the participants—students and teachers—gain an enhanced sense of competence. Also, as is apparent to most people who have tried, attempting to make pro-life changes in one's social/physical surroundings can be a radicalizing ("consciousness-raising") experience whether one succeeds or not.

That last comment can also serve to introduce my second major reason for viewing environmental education as a potent force for encouraging ecological consciousness. Namely, our environmental problems are by nature deeply intertwined with our cultural institutions, our operative values, and hence our *other* problems (poverty, anxiety, and so on —see Chapters 2 and 4). I thus concur with Paul Shepard and Daniel

McKinley (1969) that ecology—especially as treated in environmental studies—really is "the subversive science." Whether our concern is with avoiding ecocatastrophes or simply with realizing hopes for a better (happier) life for everyone, the study of environmental problems, more than just about anything else I can imagine, should alert us to the interrelatedness of all things.

I should emphasize that we need not dwell on environmental *dangers* in order to stimulate environmental concern or a sense of interrelatedness. As James Swan (1974, 1975) has argued, *hope* for surroundings to which we can relate more joyously is preferable to fear or guilt as a way of eliciting ecological conscience and consciousness.[14] Environmental education, like advertising or political campaigns, can probably take either tack; but I wholeheartedly agree with Swan's sentiment that the positive approach is in the long run far more powerful and far less manipulative. Indeed, one of my main hopes for educational applications of the special cognitive sets discussed in Chapter 3 is that such sets would stimulate visions of a more pro-life environment and ideas for how to turn them into reality.

Finally, we might note that various types of outdoor nature study can certainly contribute to enhanced environmental sensitivity and to the development of greater concern for environmental values. Even being exposed to a brief field experience in nature appreciation (or "interpretation") while visiting a national park can be an awakening experience for many city-bound people. As Freeman Tilden (1967) has instructed the instructors, the idea is *provocation* rather than instruction: park visitors should be aided to arrive at an original experience that enriches their ability to appreciate nature. An excellent and more extended program of such provocation is described by Steve Van Matre (1974), who has developed programs of nature experience complete with special cognitive sets and planned field trips. These are designed to increase ecological understanding, nature awareness and appreciation, feelings of harmony (both with other people and with nature), and even a sense of unity with nature. Perhaps someday such programs will be incorporated as a standard part of the curriculum throughout our educational system. As George Leveson (1971, p. 161) has observed from his experience as a geologist, it is the combination of "detailed physical contact and continued theoretical and philosophic contemplation" that leads to "deep intimacy" between person and natural environment.

Synergistic Education

In keeping with our earlier use of the term "synergistic," let us define *synergistic education* as an educational approach that combines emphasis on cooperation at all levels of human activity with concern for seeking creative syntheses. As detailed in Chapter 4, educational procedures in the United States have traditionally tended to promote competitive individualism. And, as noted in Chapter 3, our educational system has not typically favored creative thinking, cooperative or otherwise. Thus, our traditional patterns of education have hardly been synergistic. Nevertheless, a number of recent developments may give us some hope for the future.

For example, the book *Learning Together and Alone* by David and Roger Johnson (1975) has presented a generally very well-reasoned and well-documented case for the advantages of a cooperative "goal structure" over either a competitive or an individualistic one. According to the Johnsons and their evidence, designing educational tasks and environments so that students will be encouraged to work cooperatively yields beneficial effects not only on the development of various interpersonal skills (communication, role taking, and so on) and feelings toward oneself and other people, but also on creativity, problem-solving ability, mastery of complex subject matter, attitudes toward education, and indeed virtually every aspect of ego development. (Also compare the discussion in Chapter 4 of cooperation versus competition and individualism.)

That is quite a claim for cooperation, but the Johnsons support it not just with research evidence but also with many excellent suggestions for facilitating cooperative behavior in ways that will contribute to these beneficial effects. You don't, in short, just say, "Hey, let's everybody cooperate!" and then sit back and wait for miracles to happen. The Johnsons point out that effective cooperation involves skills in areas such as interpersonal communication, building and maintaining trust, and resolving controversies constructively and creatively. To teach these or other skills, they recommend careful attention to (1) making sure students thoroughly understand the nature of the skill and its benefits; (2) giving the students a chance to use the skill successfully; (3) encouraging perseverance·in the use of the skill; (4) giving clear feedback on performance; and (5) encouraging the frequent use of the skill and establishing an atmosphere that supports the use of the skill. (These tips on teaching people skills indeed seem appropriate to virtually every facet of environmental education, education in special cognitive sets, and just about any other educational approach for aiding the development of ecological consciousness.) Furthermore, the Johnsons point out that inducing cooperation involves setting up group goals, encouraging sharing and a division of labor, rewarding the whole group collectively, and setting up a physical arrangement that facilitates friendly interpersonal behavior.

If teachers were to take such suggestions to heart—and the Johnsons argue that teachers as well as students would enjoy and profit from education much more if they did—we might well face the makings of a major cultural transformation. That is, students would be gaining both the cognitive and interpersonal skills and attitudes needed to prepare them for synergistic relations with others at the same time that they learned the subject matter of the curriculum. And, fortunately, the Johnsons are certainly not alone in their call for such changes in educational procedures. Indeed, many writers on education suggest not only the encouragement of cooperation among students, but also the greater sharing of power *with* students (see, for example, T. Gordon, 1974).

Furthermore, more and more people are now working on educational procedures for enhancing the skills needed for cooperation and for creativity. A preeminent example of the former is Chris Argyris's research on training for "Model 2" behavior, which involves open collaboration and the sharing of decision-making power as well as information (see Chapter 7). For training in cooperative approaches to creativity, the work of William Gordon (1961, 1973) and George Prince (1970) on "synectics" provides insight into what can be done. This approach, already mentioned in Chapter 3, involves the "joining together of different and apparently irrelevant elements" and "the integration of diverse individuals into a problem-stating, problem-solving group" (Gordon, 1961, p. 3). It would take us too far afield to go into the details, but briefly, synectics as a creativity-inducing procedure basically involves special group techniques for generating analogies to problems, building constructively on other group members' ideas (see especially Prince, 1970; and compare Maier, 1970), and combining "different and apparently irrelevant elements" to come up with creative syntheses. Judging by the fees that corporations seem willing to pay for synectics training (see Stein, 1975), and by the inventions cited by Gordon and Prince, this approach *is* effective. Fortunately, some of these procedures are now being passed along to teachers and schoolchildren as well as industrialists (Gordon, 1973).

The next step after stimulating creativity and cooperation within the classroom would seem to be extending this synergistic orientation to the world outside the school. Indeed, to facilitate true ecological consciousness, it strikes me that nothing less than education for *world-wide* cooperation will do. For instance, David Conrad (1976), an educationist deeply concerned with promoting both ecological consciousness and world-mindedness, has suggested that in addition to stressing internal cooperation and community involvement, "education for transformation" should also concentrate on the issues of world poverty, global environmental problems, international social and economic justice, peace studies, alternative models of "world order," the nature of other cultures, and other studies that could prepare people to seek and enjoy "world citizenship" (see also Brameld, 1965, 1976; Boyer, 1975). Even creative cooperation and altruism, if limited to an in-group, can fall far short of ecological consciousness. Synergistic education, when going full force, would necessarily be global in its focus.

Confluent Education

Confluent education, according to those who regularly use the term, such as George Brown (1971) and Gloria Castillo (1974), is education that helps to integrate affective and cognitive domains. Included would thus be education to expand self-awareness, promote values clarification, clarify feelings, experience new feelings, enhance aesthetic sensitivity and expression, enhance the ability to fantasize and otherwise use imagination, relate more openly and authentically to other people, explore the feelings aroused by ideas and the ideas aroused by feelings, and so on. Insofar as this sort of approach to education actively encourages cooperation and creativity, it of course would overlap with synergistic education. But the lesson I wish to draw from the recent trend toward "confluence" and the closely related ideas of humanistic and affective education is that growth in self-understanding and in cognitive/affective integration and awareness may in itself be a potent force for enhancing ego development, B-cognition, and pro-life values. Confluent education, by including values clarification and awareness exercises as basic elements in the curriculum, and by legitimizing the affective side of experience as an important educational consideration, clearly holds potential for helping students raise the level of their moral and value reasoning (see Chapter 4) and helping students become more interested in the quality of their experience and more aware of what determines that quality for themselves and others.[15]

In Sum: Education for Reconstruction

In the terminology of the educational philosopher Theodore Brameld (for example, 1965, 1971), the position I have been advocating is a "reconstructionist" view of education. That is, my argument (and Brameld's) is that education best serves the long-term interests of humankind not by preparing us to perpetuate the culture as it is—or even to make minor adjustments in it—but by preparing us to cooperatively reconstruct or transform our culture and the world into a more pro-life form. Of course, for our society this would also mean a reconstruction of education itself. As I have attempted to show in my brief examination of environmental education, synergistic education, and confluent education, this transformation of education, society, and consciousness is precisely the promise—if not in every case the actual goal—inherent in these educational developments.

Child Rearing

As in the case of education, some suggestions for new directions in parent/child relations may contribute to the development of at least some of the components in ecological consciousness. Examples of these promising suggestions include the work of Thomas Gordon (1975, 1976) on "parent effectiveness training," research such as that by Ervin Staub (1975) on raising children to take altruistic or "prosocial" orientations, ideas such as those put forth by Philip Slater (1970, 1974) and implied by Bruno Bettelheim (1969) on the advantages of collective child rearing, and various urgings to parents to help their children appreciate nature and otherwise enjoy B-cognition (for example, Carson, 1956). Let us look very briefly at each of these.

Gordon's work on parent effectiveness training will be discussed in Chapter 7, but his basic idea is that an open and collaborative—and consultative or helping—relation with one's children will, in the long run, produce the best results for both children and parents. According to Gordon, treating children more or less as equals, actively listening to their problems and encouraging the children themselves to deal with them, and working cooperatively with children to resolve parent/child conflicts in a mutual problem-solving approach (rather than using power tactics) will help both children and parents to become more creative, cooperative, loving, and happy. Obviously, this represents a highly synergistic approach to child rearing.

Another synergistic approach is exemplified by Staub's (1975) suggestions for rearing children to be prosocial. Of most importance, according to him, is "a warm, affectionate, nurturant relationship between the parent and the child" (p. 115). Beyond that, he also draws on psychological research evidence to suggest that parents (1) themselves model altruistic or prosocial, cooperative behavior; (2) make sure the child actually engages in prosocial behavior (even if this requires using extrinsic reinforcement); (3) set up situations in which prosocial behavior is likely, as by giving the child responsibility for taking care of pets or younger children; (4) get the child to teach other children to be prosocial; and (5) reason with the child in ways that induce cognitive sets to attend to other people's feelings and to interpret that information empathically (say, by orienting the child to mentally take the roles of other people).

We have already examined Slater's views on the hazards of child rearing in a tightly encapsulated nuclear family (see Chapter 4), but it might be reiterated here that the presence of a group of cooperating adults, all of whom help in the raising of their children, might well facilitate a more cooperative and generally synergistic orientation in the children. The evidence from child rearing in Israeli kibbutzim (for example, Bettelheim, 1969; see Chapter 7), which rely on a collective approach, seems to bear this out. For American society, however, a less radical shift might well suffice. For instance, Uri Bronfenbrenner (1970) has suggested that some synergistic benefits would be gained simply from involving children more in the adult life of the community—as by parents' taking their children around with them more and by a general increase in adults' contacts with children other than their own.

Finally, in addition to modeling prosocial or synergistic behavior, parents can also set an example for ecological systems thinking, B-cognition, and an ecological conscience. Rachel Carson (1956), for instance, in her delightful book *A Sense of Wonder*, has given many simple but potentially effective suggestions for how adults can help children as well as themselves to appreciate and enjoy nature. (For example, when out on a clear night try asking yourself and your children how you would react if you could see the stars but once in your lifetime.) Actively involving both yourself and your children in exploring the world in a B-cognitive mode should certainly be an enjoyable and consciousness-raising experience all around. And it might help to counteract Parmenter's (1968) complaint that contemplative observation is discouraged by our culture, schools, and mores. Similarly, parental displays of active, pro-life concern for the environmental ramifications of their purchases and patterns of behavior might well rub off on their children. Just as Kenneth Keniston (1968) has found that highly socially conscious youth tend to reflect their parents' value system, so we might expect the same to hold for full ecological consciousness.

Political Processes

It may seem odd to think of political processes as a path to ecological consciousness, but if interpreted broadly and conducted in the right context, political discussion and decision making could be an invaluable stimulant to ecological systems thinking, pro-life values, and synergistic behavior. For instance, on the level of "political socialization" of children, researchers Judith Torney and Robert Hess (1971) have pointed out the value and possibility of exposing children in school to (1) examples of social or political conflicts that are resolved by creatively cooperative (synergistic) procedures, (2) *non*-conflict models of international relations, and (3) possibilities for citizen action other than voting and violence. Torney and Hess also suggested that children might be encouraged to be more flexible and sophisticated in their political thinking by such educational techniques as carefully constructed role-playing situations and the use of "curriculum material which presents an optimum step above the student's current level of thought" (p. 500; also compare Kohlberg and Turiel, 1971, and the discussion of moral education in Chapter 4).

However, on the broader level of the functioning of the whole society, political processes could be utilized or restructured in ways that would facilitate ecological consciousness in adults as well as children. The most important thing would be to increase people's involvement in decision making in *each* of the major institutions that directly affect their lives. It is certainly true that many people would rather not have to spend a lot of time in group meetings making political decisions (see Dahl, 1970; Partridge, 1971); but, as was argued in Chapter 2, it is also true that people want to have some feeling of control over their lives. To come by this feeling of control in a non–self-deluding fashion, individuals must actually have some say in important social decisions. For instance, corporations run by the workers themselves, or schools in which students shared equal power with teachers and administrators, could go a long way toward providing people with opportunities for truly meaningful input into institutional decisions that directly affect their lives.

If such opportunities were built into our basic institutional structures (including not only the school and factory, but also institutions such as the family), even our existing political system might function in a more synergistic fashion and with much broader participation. As political analysts such as Robert Dahl (1970) have argued, direct participatory democracy on a national scale appears to be an impossible dream, but open participation and collective self-determination *can* be achieved on the level of local (say, small-city–wide) and institutional decision making. The need, in short, is to democratize as many levels of political, social, and economic functioning as possible. Every inroad made in democratizing the family, school, factory, town, or whatever, should help spread and deepen the feeling that we can collectively and cooperatively determine our fates.[16]

However, for such collective determination to truly promote a pro-life, synergistic orientation, the ideal would seem to be the seeking of collective agreement (*consensus*) on important decisions rather than settling for something like the majority rule of traditional democracy. As David and Frank Johnson (1975) have cogently argued, the process of reaching consensus not only maximizes overall commitment and satisfaction with the decision, but also develops group creativity and problem-solving skills and makes the best use of group resources. But, as they also point out, reaching a meaningful consensus takes time and skill: (1) people must communicate clearly and logically and be prone to *listen* to each other; (2) they must support only positions they genuinely agree with; (3) they must eschew conflict-reducing cop-outs such as settling for the majority position or for unimaginative compromises; (4) differences of opinion, diversity of ideas, and participation by everyone present must be actively sought out; and (5) conflicts must be resolved not by a win/lose orientation but by a careful questioning of basic assumptions and a search for better alternatives and higher-level, creative syntheses.[17]

Clearly, reaching consensus by these rules could be a demanding process, perhaps only to be used by small groups and only for important issues. Nevertheless, it might be possible to design a political system in which programs or sets of goals generated by consensus at the local level could serve as input for higher-level consensus groups made up of representatives of these lower levels. For example, one such system might be based on virtually all people periodically meeting in small neighborhood or organizational groups for the purpose of reaching some initial consensus on important local, national, or even global issues. Such consensual positions could then be represented in second-level consensus groups made up of either randomly or consensually chosen representatives from each of the initial groups. And this process could continue, in a pyramidal or "Chinese-boxes" fashion (to borrow Dahl's, 1970, expression), through as many levels as necessary to encompass a whole institution, community, or nation—or even the world. The members of the highest-level consensus group in the institution, community, or whatever, would thus represent views passed up from groups originally involving all members. These highest-level groups could be responsible for reaching consensual decisions (presumably in a public forum, such as televised meetings) that would constitute or guide actual social policies.[18]

Unrealistic? Well, perhaps. But such a process would not only *be* synergistic; it might well *stimulate* synergistic thought and behavior by people involved in it. The initial consensus meetings would, if run according to the guidelines suggested by David and Frank Johnson, both give new meaning to "citizen participation" and encourage cooperative, creative approaches to pressing social (and environmental) problems. Consensus meetings on political matters would also expose many people to higher levels of moral and political thinking—a procedure, we have seen, suggested by both moral-development and political-socialization researchers as a prime educational device for raising people's level of moral or political reasoning. In any case, if people could gain widespread practice in reaching consensual group decisions—in their homes, schools, workplaces, political meetings, and wherever else possible—the gains for ecological consciousness could be substantial.

Economic Processes

Objectives such as control of workplaces by the workers clearly involve both political (collective governance and decision-making) processes and more purely economic ones. As is often pointed out, the important consideration for political or even ecological well-being may not be so much whether the state in some sense owns the means of production, but who precisely it is that determines what is to be produced and how.[19] The ideal situation might be what Staughton Lynd (1971) has termed "participatory socialism"—collective ownership combined with decentralized, cooperative control.

Leaving aside these issues of political/economic decision-making procedures, the actual distribution of material and service resources is clearly crucial for the widespread development of ecological consciousness. It was argued in Chapter 2, for instance, that certain basic needs must probably be satisfied before people will be able to develop concern for B-cognition and other aspects of self-actualization. One need not accept Maslow's theory of a biologically built-in hierarchy to agree that a certain level of material well-being, education, and other amenities seems very helpful for developing the perspectives, sensitivities, and concerns characteristic of ecological consciousness. As noted earlier, the environmental movement itself has found most support among the wealthier individuals within the wealthier nations. Furthermore, as argued in Chapter 2, one of the main advantages of an Equity 2 norm of distribution would be that cooperation and other aspects of synergistic behavior would be encouraged on a broad scale—in contrast to our competitive economic system's tendency to create a competitive spirit throughout the society (see Deutsch, 1975). Taking all this into account, it seems a likely bet that if ecological consciousness is to be widely shared, so must the wealth be.

Mass Media

As noted in the previous chapter, media such as television and newspapers generally seem to be more in the service of the status quo than of pro-life cultural transformation. But there are some exceptions. It was also pointed out, for instance (citing Slater and Reich), that even advertising can promote pro-life values, albeit often inadvertently, by helping to legitimize concern with environmental matters and with the quality of one's experience. Of course, the media could do much more than they now do, inadvertently or otherwise. Peter Sandman (1974), for example, has argued that it would help the environmental cause if the media passed along more information such as the following: basic principles of ecology; suggestions for effective environmental actions; advance warnings of likely environmental problems; and accounts of precisely who is to blame for various environmental degradations. As Sandman detailed, there are currently many forces, such as economic pressures, that prevent the media from doing these things on a consistent basis. If these pressures could be removed, or counterpressures applied, there could of course be benefits for ecological consciousness.

However, more broadly conceived, existing media can do much to further certain components in ecological consciousness. For instance, Tom Bender (1973) has provided an exciting list of what he calls *trans-formers*—for example, films and records that convey ecological information, stimulate B-cognition, or induce a sense of oneness with nature. Listening to a record of the eerie beauty of whale "songs" can be a moving and consciousness-raising experience (especially if one is familiar with research and theory on whales and dolphins such as that by Lilly, 1967, or Bateson, 1972). Similarly, *art*, which we might subsume under the heading of "media," can obviously help enrich our ability for B-cognition. Just to cite one example, Kenneth Clark (1949) pointed out how impressionistic paintings have "enlarged our range of vision," guiding many people to enhanced experiences of color and to appreciation of the effects of different kinds of light. Art, according to Gregory Bateson (1972), can also have much more profound benefits for stimulating ecological consciousness, such as helping us overcome the limited linear focus spawned by our "purposive thinking." As Maslow (1968, 1970) pointed out, the feelings of unity and transcendent B-cognition characteristic of peak experiences are often induced by paintings, music, or poetry. Reversing the low priority our culture gives to art might thus pay off by facilitating ecological consciousness as well as just making life more enjoyable.[20]

Religion

As mentioned in the previous chapter, some people—Lynn White, Jr. (1967, 1973) probably preeminent among them—have argued that our environmental problems stem largely from the Judeo-Christian view that humanity has a divine sanction to "dominate nature." That earlier discussion also pointed out that this argument can be challenged on a number of grounds; but let us briefly consider here White's (1967) suggestion for an alternative religious solution, again drawn from the Judeo-Christian heritage. White advocated adopting Saint Francis of Assisi as "a patron saint for ecologists" and in general substituting the Franciscan notion of the sacredness of all of nature for the more traditional Judeo-Christian concept that human beings are something special, with a divinely given right to lord it over the lower animals. This suggestion, like White's analysis of the underlying problem, has of course not gone unchallenged. René Dubos (for example, 1972a, 1973a) has proposed still another religious position derived from the Christian tradition. For Dubos, it is not Saint Francis's "passive worship" of nature that we should take as our model, but rather the "creative intervention" and "stewardship" themes espoused by Saint Benedict.[21]

Also, on the topic of religion, it was already noted earlier that certain Eastern philosophical and religious positions, such as Zen Buddhism (for example, Watts, 1958b; Herrigel, 1953), often help instill a sense of oneness with the universe and teach the value of the "intuitive" side of ecological systems thinking. I have reservations about the wholesale adoption of Eastern thinking, however, largely because I suspect that in undiluted form it can lead to passive acceptance of the world as it is. But whether or not that suspicion is justified, there can be little doubt that an infusion of Eastern ideas of oneness and harmony with nature has given us, and will probably continue to give us, a boost toward ecological consciousness.

To Continue Toward a Systemic Approach

Chapter 4 ended on the idea that there are in fact many paths to pro-life attitude and value change, and the implication was that *all* of them are needed in the end. Similarly, the development of full ecological consciousness—which, after all, is but an extension of the idea of pro-life values—would ultimately require a transformation of many aspects of our culture. It would probably be overly optimistic to believe that this transformation is going to happen any time soon. Does this mean that it is hopelessly naive to go on and on about the wonders of ecological consciousness and about the possible pathways to it? From the point of view of short-term pessimistic practicality, it probably is naive or worse. But from the point of view of long-term human potentials, and perhaps even from the point of view of relatively short-term optimistic practicality, thinking about the possibilities for high-Compatibility types of human consciousness is a perfectly rational—and a potentially very important—thing to do. For if we *can* have some control over our destiny, it is only by thinking about our possibilities and trying to figure out how to realize the ones we want that we are likely to optimize our future. Furthermore, every little bit of ecological systems thinking (and other ecological-consciousness components) we can gain should make it easier to figure out systemic pathways to gaining more, either for ourselves or for future generations.

We shall return to the subject of broad cultural transformation—and how to achieve it—in Chapter 7, but first let us shift gears a bit and examine the actualities and possibilities of environmental design.

NOTES

1. See, for example, Altman (1973), Ittelson et al. (1974), Barker (1968), Craik (1976), and Simon (1969). Simon indeed argues that the apparent complexity of behavior, whether that of ants, computers, or humans, "is largely a reflection of the complexity of the environment" to which the ant, computer programmer, or human was attempting to adapt. Also consult the journal *Fields Within Fields* (published by the World Institute Council, New York).
2. On the issue of situational determination of one's self-concept, see, for instance, James (1890), G. H. Mead (1934), Gergen (1971), and Schneider (1976). The research evidence does indicate considerable flexibility in a person's self-concept, perhaps thus offering some indication that shifting to a view of oneself as an integral part of the environment is not so far out of reach after all. (Also compare Ittelson et al.'s [1976] observation that people commonly *do* more or less identify with cherished objects, personal belongings, and even locations. It is perhaps a large step from this sort of thing to considering the "environment as self," but Ittelson and his colleagues suggest that this may indeed be "a further developmental step" for mature adults.)
3. This conception of "interest" is adapted from Leff (1972).
4. Slater (1974) uses the term *social eversion* to apply to processes "whereby the intensification of some social form leads directly to its opposite" (p. 129). Slater sees certain recent trends, such as increasing pollution and linearly derived scientific accomplishments, as slowly pushing us toward ecological consciousness—and hence toward a reversal of the original trends.
5. See, for example, Sills (1975), Albrecht (1976), and Morrison et al. (1972).

6. See, for instance, Albrecht (1976), Caldwell (1971, 1975), Robertson and Lewallen (1975), Fanning (1975), and O'Riordan (1976).

7. As noted in Chapter 2, concern about environmental issues has tended to be highest among the affluent and highly educated (see, for example, McEvoy, 1972; Tognacci et al., 1972). However, as Morrison et al. (1972) pointed out, social movements often evidence a "participation paradox" whereby "those persons who are objectively most deprived of the goals that social movements seek are not, in general, those who initiate and provide the early support for the movements" (p. 270). A main reason for this, Morrison et al. argued, is that expectations, and hence demands, tend to be higher for those who have made some gains than for the continuously deprived. We might also note that a certain degree of education and perhaps basic need satisfaction may be necessary for the development of higher levels of moral reasoning and concern for social justice (see Chapters 2 and 4).

8. See, for instance, Alinsky (1971), Robertson and Lewallen (1975), Sommer (1974), and the discussion of strategies for change in Chapter 7.

9. Compare Slater's (1974) "disconnector" values discussed in Chapter 4, and see also Putney and Putney (1964) and Henry (1963).

10. See, for instance, Montagu (1950, 1965); also compare Wilson (1975). But note that I am not trying to argue that humans are innately cooperative any more than that they are innately aggressive. (My own guess is that if either orientation is in some sense genetically built in, then both are—again, compare Wilson, 1975.)

11. See also Jahoda (1958) for an overview of common elements in conceptions of "positive mental health" (generally similar, as one might guess, to Maslow's ideas on self-actualization).

12. See, for instance, G. White (1974), Mitchell (1974), Kates (1976), Burton (1972), and Burton et al. (1978).

13. See, for example, Terry (1971), Swan and Stapp (1974), McInnis and Albrecht (1975), and the *Journal of Environmental Education* (published by Heldref Publications, Washington, D.C.).

14. Also see Chapter 4, note 6.

15. In addition to Brown (1971), Castillo (1974), and the references for values clarification mentioned in Chapter 4, a small sample of other relevant work on affective, humanistic, and confluent education includes Borton (1970), Weinstein and Fantini (1970), Rossiter (1976), Hawley and Hawley (1975), Howe and Howe (1975), Jones (1968), Rubin (1973), de Mille (1973), and Leonard (1968). Also, the work of deCharms (1971, 1976) discussed in Chapter 2 is consistent with the confluent approach (and note that Origin training could be extended to help people become aware of their potential for *collective*, cooperative "Originship" in addition to the more individualistic variety represented by the initial program). Furthermore, innovative, humanistic work in art education (for example, Lowenfeld and Brittain, 1970) confluently integrates training in cognitive and affective sensitivity, as in fact do many of the forward-looking efforts in environmental education (discussed earlier) and in design education (for example, Sanoff, 1975, 1976; Rowland, 1964–1966; Papanek, 1971).

16. For general discussions of the merits and possibilities of "participatory democracy" in a broad range of political and economic institutions, see Pateman (1970) and Benello and Roussopolos (1971). (Both of these works seem especially good at countering the prevailing pessimism among many political-science theorists concerning the potentials for "the common person" to participate mean-

ingfully and democratically in collective government. As Carole Pateman documents, there is considerable evidence that increased participation, even at the lower levels of industrial self-management, contributes to the individual's ability and motivation for *further* participation. She also notes that political apathy and authoritarianism seem linked to low socioeconomic status, and are thus probably not inherent in human nature.) For some other arguments for greater participation by the general citizenry in social and environmental decision making, see Raskin (1971), Etzioni (1968), A. M. Lee (1973), Linville and Davis (1976), Stavrianos (1976), and the discussion in Chapter 7. Finally, though, we might note with Schattschneider (1960, p. 140) that ultimately "the power of the people in a democracy depends on the *importance* of the decisions made by the electorate, not on the *number* of decisions they make."

17. This list of "rules" is adapted from D. and F. Johnson's (1975, pp. 60–61) list of "basic guidelines for consensual decision making." Additional advice for reaching creative consensual decisions might be gleaned from the creativity techniques and associated references discussed in Chapter 3. (One especially valuable additional guideline might be to focus on—and try to build on—the *good* aspects of others' ideas, rather than to take a predominantly critical orientation toward them. This not only seems to boost one's own creativity [compare Stein, 1974], but should also facilitate positive interpersonal relations. [See also Prince, 1970.])

18. Obviously, such a plan would need considerable elaboration if it were to be a serious contender as a design for workable governmental structure. I shall make no attempt to do that here, except to add the following two considerations: (1) It would of course be possible to maintain any number of intermediate levels of local self-government (say, as we have now in the United States with our electoral system), each level having jurisdiction over decisions primarily relating to its functioning (compare Dahl, 1970) but making these decisions according to the procedure of hierarchical consensus groups. (2) It would also be possible and advisable to maintain feedback systems so that citizens could protest higher-level decisions with which they disagreed and suggest possible resolutions for disagreements or problems faced by higher-level consensus groups. Thus, in addition to placing higher-level consensus meetings in a public forum, some system of two-way communication might be instituted (compare Schiller, 1973); and perhaps major high-level policies should have to be approved (or not protested) by some large proportion of the population.

19. See, for example, Dahl (1970), Raskin (1971), Pateman (1970), Stavrianos (1976), and Russell (1966). An at least equally important consideration, of course, is *what values* guide the decision makers, whoever they are (compare Taylor, 1972; Schumacher, 1973).

20. Robert Sommer (1975) has also discussed the value of *collaborative* forms of art, such as community murals, for stimulating synergistic behavior (as by giving practice in reaching consensus and working cooperatively with others on a creative project).

21. See also Glacken (1967) for a thorough historical treatment of Western religious views on nature.

6
ENVIRONMENT AND DESIGN

ENVIRONMENT AND BEHAVIOR

According to the environmental sociologist William Michelson (1970, p. 168), there is a (previously) unwritten rule that a chapter such as this must contain the following quotation from Winston Churchill: "We shape our buildings, and afterwards our buildings shape us." If you have read very much about environmental design, you doubtless recognized those words. Of course, Churchill's dictum is at best only part of the story, but it does set the mood for a discussion of the interrelations of the built environment and human behavior. In this chapter we focus on the issues of (1) environmental influences on behavior and experience; (2) ways in which we are short-changing ourselves (and worse) by poor environmental design; and (3) pro-life environmental design criteria and examples. As usual, the main underlying theme is that we human beings *do* have the potential to lead more fulfilling lives—in this case, through better environmental design.

The Environment: A Many-Dimensioned Thing

As Rudolf Moos (for example, 1973, 1976) has vigorously argued, the human "environment" actually includes more than the purely physical or "ecological" dimensions that are most prominent in fields such as architectural and environmental psychology (narrowly defined). Additional environmental dimensions, according to Moos, are those pertaining to organizational structure, "behavior settings" (see below), characteristics of the inhabitants, "psychosocial characteristics and organizational climate" (see also Insel and Moos, 1974), and variables related to the reinforcement contingencies or other functional aspects of the environment. Perhaps we should call all this the "social/physical environment" to distinguish it from narrower usages of the word "environment." Terminology aside, just considering Moos's list should immediately remind us that the human environment consists of intertwined and multileveled social and physical dimensions. Nevertheless, we can't get away from it: the "environment" that fields such as environmental education, environmental studies, environmental psychology, and so forth, are focused on *is* the physical environment—meaning buildings and other artifacts, grass and trees, pollution, and all the rest of our material surroundings. For the "environmental" disciplines, our interrelations with this physical environment figure prominently even when social variables are examined. (In the next chapter, however, the broader view of the environment will be pursued in reference to "utopian" criteria and to effective techniques for social and environmental change.)

Let us now examine some of the specific ways in which the total environment—but especially the physical environment—meshes with human behavior.

Environment/Behavior Congruence

In our discussion of ecological consciousness, the emphasis was on thinking about the environment in terms of *processes* or dynamic interrelationships occurring over time. Roger Barker (for example, 1968), perhaps more than any other psychologist, has developed a conceptual system and methodological techniques for analyzing the human environment in a process-oriented framework. His key concept is the *behavior setting*, which he defines in part (1968, p. 18) as "one or more standing patterns of behavior-and-milieu, with the milieu circumjacent [surrounding] and synomorphic [similar in structure] to the behavior." Roughly translated, this means that a behavior setting is an environmental unit consisting of the *combination* of a physical place and the types of behavior that occur there during a particular type of social activity. Examples of a behavior setting would include a store (when it is open for business), a basketball game, a doctor's office, and virtually any public or institutional activity that involves a delimitable pattern of behavior and that occurs (and perhaps recurs) in a bounded time and place.

For our current purposes the important consideration is that in a behavior setting the physical setting ("milieu") and the "standing pattern of behavior" are *synomorphic* or "similar in structure." Thus, in a traditional classroom, the seats are arranged in rows facing the front of the room, which in turn is equipped with blackboards and other paraphernalia for presenting information. This physical structure is specifically suited to the type of activity that typically occurs there when the classroom is part of an actual behavior setting (such as a psychology class taught by the lecture method). Of course, if one wished to conduct the class via small-group discussions, this physical setting might no longer be so synomorphic, especially if the chairs were bolted to the floor.

But now a crucial question may be raised: Exactly how does this congruence or synomorphy between physical structure and behavior arise? It will be impossible to present a complete answer to this question, but we can briefly touch on some of the main ways in which behavior and environment influence each other.

For example, Barker (1968) listed the following (overlapping) sources of "behavior-milieu synomorphy":

physical forces (for example, streets and sidewalks often tend to channel movement; some spatial arrangements tend to be "sociofugal" and force people apart, while other arrangements, such as chairs facing each other, are "sociopetal" and promote human relationship—see Osmond, 1957; Sommer, 1969)

social forces (for example, the teacher's authority can be used to induce appropriate behavior by students)

physiological processes (for example, cold temperatures produce brisk but stiff movements; this factor seems hard to distinguish from "physical forces," however)

physiognomic perception (that is, "picking up" the mood suggested by a setting, as when open spaces call forth free, exuberant movement; or when the behavior of other people in a setting, such as a carnival or funeral, elicits feelings leading to similar behavior by newcomers)·

learning (for example, parents may overtly teach children to be quiet at a concert)

selection by persons (that is, self-selection by participants who want to be in a particular type of behavior setting and are therefore especially likely to behave appropriately)

selection by behavior settings (for example, a course may have entrance requirements; people who behave inappropriately may be expelled from a setting)

influence of behavior on the milieu (for example, pedestrians may wear a path across a field; people can deliberately modify the milieu to fit their behavior—that is, design their environment)

To pursue our discussion of environment/behavior interrelations, however, it seems helpful also to interject a scheme proposed by Allan Wicker (1972). In his paper "Processes Which Mediate Behavior-Environment Congruence," Wicker proposed that environments, considered as behavior settings, influence behavior through operant learning, observational and instructional learning, maintenance mechanisms within the behavior setting, and processes of selection. The following headings may be considered mainly a transformation and combination of Barker's and Wicker's typologies.

Physical Contingencies of Reinforcement

The physical structure of the environment can readily influence behavior by providing patterns of reward and punishment for particular types of action. Although she may well not consider herself a Skinnerian behaviorist, Jane Jacobs (1961) seems a consummate master of analyzing the city as a kind of giant "Skinner box." Although we shall consider aspects of her work in greater detail later, a few examples will show what I mean. To rephrase Jacobs's analysis of city streets, for instance, a high diversity of behavior settings (shops, theaters, restaurants, and so on) will provide numerous rewards for people to be out and active at all hours of the waking day. The presence of so many people will, in turn, discourage crime by increasing the probability of interference, witnesses, and other factors inimical to unpunished malefaction (also see Newman, 1973; Freedman, 1975). To take another example from Jacobs's implicit insights into operant learning, widening a sidewalk will tend to reinforce pedestrian use (especially if the widening is accompanied by amenities, such as small trees or attractive benches) but will reduce the reward value of driving a car down the resultingly narrowed roadway.

Similar examples of how contingencies of reinforcement can arise from physical structure can be gleaned from much of the work on proxemics or the study of how people use space.[1] For instance, Osmond's (1957, 1966) and Sommer's (1969, 1974) observations on spatial features that bring people together or push them apart can readily be couched in operant terms. Intimate, friendly discussions (or arguments) are easier to conduct, and are consequently more reinforcing, if the participants are facing each other at relatively close range than if they are seated back to back or several yards apart. It should be noted, however, that such effects of space on behavior are often mediated by culture. As Edward Hall (1974) has pointed out, even the sociopetal/sociofugal distinction seems to be culturally influenced, as in Hall's example of certain villages in Lebanon and Syria where casual conversations are carried on by people sitting across the room from each other. For these villagers, many of our "colder" waiting rooms might actually reinforce communication.

Obviously, it would be easy to go on listing examples of how physical structure, at least in interaction with cultural variables, yields contingencies of reinforcement that influence behavior. Some cases in point are hard chairs that discourage lingering in a bar or an airport waiting room (Sommer, 1969, 1974), intricate or unusual buildings that reinforce lingering as opposed to more ordinary "functional" ones that have no such effect (McRae, 1972), and the implicit contingencies of reinforcement in the natural environment that help to guide the good "fit" evidenced by so-called "primitive" architecture (Rapoport, 1969; Rudofsky, 1964). Clearly, if we want to lead more enlightened lives and to realize pro-life environmental potentials, we should pay close attention to the reinforcement contingencies present in the natural environment and to those we build into our artifacts.

Social Contingencies of Reinforcement

Here of course we encounter many aspects of what might be called *environmental socialization*—how people are trained, cajoled, and even forced into appropriate behavior within specified environments. To the degree that we do think of the environment as encompassing the total social/physical matrix of our surroundings, these social forces are also of course involved in shaping virtually *all* of our behavior, environmental and otherwise. To avoid grappling with all of sociology and social psychology, however, let us concentrate on social forces that lead people to use and relate to their physical surroundings in specific ways.

For example, from a sociological and anthropological perspective, we might note that different social classes and cultural groups use the same types of space in very different ways. We have noted Hall's (1974) example of cultural determinants of whether a particular spatial arrangement will push people apart or together, and many more cross-cultural differences in the use of space can be gleaned from Hall's writings (especially 1959, 1966). Closer to home, there is substantial concurrence among various sociological observers that lower-class urban residents use neighborhood space in a very different way than do middle-class urban and suburban residents.[2] For the urban lower class, the neighborhood streets immediately surrounding their homes seem to function as an extension of their residences and as a shared, but personally relevant, territory for life and recreation. Members of the middle class, on the other hand, tend to display far less "localism" in their use of space, viewing the home as less interconnected with the immediate neighborhood and spreading their social and recreational lives over a much more dispersed territory than do lower-class urban residents. Presumably, the social reinforcements provided by family and friends help mold children of different classes into continuation of the respective behavioral patterns.

On the level of specific behavior settings, we have already noted (in Barker's list of forces) that authority and other social forces can shape behavior to meet behavior-setting demands. Barker (1968) has also proposed that participants in behavior settings can use at least two types of "maintenance mechanisms" for eliminating deviant behavior. One is *deviation-countering*, which consists of getting the offender to correct the deviant behavior. Examples would be direct instruction and social pressure. The other mechanism is *vetoing* or expulsion (for example, throwing a rowdy drunk out of a bar, or disbarring a lawyer who always behaved contemptibly in courtrooms).

There are also many other levels on which social reinforcement contingencies regulate behavior and the use of environments. Laws and police power obviously play a role in setting limits to what is acceptable environmental behavior, ranging from how people drive to how loudly families quarrel. Socially determined economic costs and benefits constitute another major area of socially mediated reinforcement contingencies, as in the case of travel costs or the price and benefits of admission to a country club. Reinforcements are also regulated through social acceptance and blame, illustrated both by the "deviation-countering" mechanisms within specific behavior settings and by the reactions of others to culturally appropriate or inappropriate behavior (for example, approaching other people in our culture too closely in casual conversation will tend to evoke a nonverbal rebuke). To risk belaboring the obvious with one further point, note also that specific types of places can set the tone for the range of behaviors that will be reinforced or at least tolerated by other people. As Goffman (1963) observed, for instance, parks seem to allow a loosening of standards for acceptable behavior.

Cognitive Forces

Information provided by the environment constitutes a major "cognitive force" in matching behavior and milieu. For instance, as Wicker (1972) pointed out, a prime force in shaping behavior to behavior-setting specifications is simply observation of what other people do. The old saw about "When in Rome . . ." often captures the spirit of one's approach in a new place, especially if one is alone or in the minority. Also, signs and other forms of instruction play a large role in creating and regulating the Plans people form. As Barker suggested with his posited environmental force of "physiognomic perception," however, signs do not necessarily have to be verbal. Indeed, investigators of nonverbal behavior such as Ruesch and Kees (1964) have been quick to point out how environments "communicate" all sorts of messages to people (also see set COM in Chapter 3). One need only think of banks designed to tell you how safe or friendly they are (see Raskin, 1974), stores that announce their chicness or cheapness by their façade, or even park paths that tell you to keep off the grass by an attractive little ridge or moat rather than an authoritarian sign (Cullen, 1961).

Barker's notions of self-selection and selection by the behavior setting also fit under "cognitive forces," and have been developed by Wicker in relation to Thibaut and Kelley's (1959) theory of comparison levels (see Chapter 3). Decisions to enter or to admit someone else to a particular setting can obviously be conceptualized in terms of comparison processes. Such cognitively mediated selection is thus a factor in determining exposure to the other congruence-increasing forces that we have considered.

Design

As Barker intimated by his synomorphy-producing category of "influence of behavior on the milieu," a major force for congruence between behavior and environment is human modification of the environment. When such modification is deliberate, we are talking about environmental *design*.[3] Architecture, landscaping, industrial design, and even deliberate destruction would fall into this category. Barker's example of wearing a path might be considered as a borderline case; but for the most part, human modification of the physical environment can be seen as deliberately promoting some sort of increased congruence between at least some types of behavior and the environmental setting for that behavior. Of course, the behavior may in many cases not be desired by the people actually having to engage in it (as in the case of a war-torn environment or a traditional school classroom), even though it may help to satisfy the goals of someone else (the attacker or teacher). As we shall explore below, much of the criticism of existing human influences on the environment—and much of the humanistic or pro-life thought about how to improve these influences—rests on considerations of the match between the attributes of an environment and the goals and needs of the actual users of that environment. Improving the quality of an environment often involves two processes: increasing the resources or amenities available *and* increasing the environmental control exerted by the actual users.

A Systemic Overview

To the degree that Churchill's dictum ("We shape our buildings . . .") implies architectural determinism, it is easily criticized. As environmental sociologists and anthropologists (for example, Gutman, 1972; Michelson, 1970; Rapoport, 1969) are wont to point out, buildings and other physical environmental features do not *determine* behavior except in extreme instances (such as when a safe falls on someone or cold temperatures cause "freezing behavior"). Using Moos's (1975, 1976) analysis, we might note that the physical environment can cause stress, limit behavior, select organisms, release human abilities and actions, and stimulate and challenge us. It is, though, only one set of forces working on us. Forces of culture, subculture, social class, and other social relationships seem to play an even greater role in shaping human behavior and even in influencing satisfaction with one's total environment (see, for example, Gutman and Westergaard, 1974).

However, Churchill did say that *we* shape our buildings, not that the environment shapes them. This insight concurs with the observations of astute behavioral scientists and architects (for example, Rapoport, 1969; Raskin, 1974), who have noted that architecture is shaped at least as much by sociocultural (including political and economic) forces as by simple environmental demands. We shall examine this issue in more detail later on when looking into the social and cultural sources of our current patterns of environmental design. For now, let us simply note that the built environment may be taken more as a symptom or expression of underlying social forces than as either a response to the natural environment or as a cause of social behavior.

Perhaps a better way to put this is simply that the physical environment is part of a vast interacting system of social and physical components, none of which is a pure cause or pure effect. Our habits of mind and the readiness with which we can point to elements of the physical environment perhaps push us toward simplistic linear thinking about environmental matters. But the world is a messy network of many levels, relationships, and processes. It is not easily understood and certainly not easily described. Nevertheless, let us continue our quest for insight into the way things are, why they are that way, and what they might become. In keeping with the human potentials orientation of this book, we shall first examine psychological aspects of certain negative ways human beings have influenced the physical environment and then turn to criteria for improving it.

THE ENVIRONMENT STRIKES BACK

Human-Induced Environmental Stressors

This section will examine some of the ways that human modification of the environment induces stress, with special attention to the social and psychological factors intertwined with this type of environmental influence and its effects. As an introduction, let us look briefly at the nature of stress itself.

Definition of stress. Searching discussions of stress are provided by Appley and Trumbull (1967), Cofer and Appley (1964), McGrath (1970), and Lazarus (1966). This literature makes clear that the term "stress" can be used in a variety of ways. It may refer to (1) the stimuli or situations that arouse certain patterns of reaction in the organism; (2) these patterns of reaction themselves (defined in terms of physiological responses, behavioral or performance responses, affective states, or combinations of these); (3) transactions involving both the environmental situation and the organism's interpretation and response to the situation; or (4), as Lazarus (1966) prefers, the whole area of study represented by these varied usages.

One major distinction is especially important. Both Cofer and Appley (1964) and Lazarus (1966) distinguish between physiological or *systemic* stress and *psychological* stress. The first type refers mainly to the "General Adaptation Syndrome" proposed by Hans Selye (for example, 1956). This consists of a complex pattern of physiological reactions, including the three basic phases of "alarm reaction," "resistance," and "exhaustion." Selye noted that the same general physiological pattern may be seen in response to virtually any intense stressor (inducer of stress). "Psychological stress," on the other hand, refers to a state in which one appraises a situation as threatening to produce a level of harm or frustration that will severely tax or even exceed one's coping abilities. Obviously, psychological stress may involve or lead to physiological stress reactions. However, psychological stress is a somewhat broader concept, applying to any transaction between a person and the environment such that the person perceives a threat that seems very difficult or impossible to avoid or cope with.

Overload. As we shall see in examining sources of stress in modern urban life, an important factor seems to be the overloading of individuals with information, sensory stimulation, or multiple task demands. However, a more general meaning of "overload" can apply to all forms of stress. As is made clear in the discussions by Appley and Trumbull (1967), Cofer and Appley (1964), Lazarus (1966), McGrath (1970), and others, a key condition for stress seems to be the actual or believed inability to readily cope with an actual or believed threat to one's well-being. In a sense, then, virtually all threats could be viewed as a kind of overload of the organism's coping or defensive system. Common stressors such as extreme temperatures, difficult task demands, sleep deprivation, uncontrollable noise, bureaucratic red tape, and physical accidents or diseases all seem to have this quality of overloading or straining the individual's coping capabilities. Perhaps even such apparently anomalous stressors as sensory deprivation (see discussion in Chapter 2) can be regarded as overloading (that is, exceeding) the organism's capacity to deal with strange situations or with severe deviations from optimal levels of environmental arousal.

Delayed effects. As noted in the discussion of contingencies of reinforcement in Chapter 2, one of the chief difficulties presented by environmental problems is that the harmful consequences arising from human impingements on the environment often seem to follow long after the actual "insult" is registered. Years or even decades may pass before the diseases induced by chemically polluted water or air become manifest; the building and transportation-system decisions that eventually produce urban blight are made long before the actual deterioration sets in; the effects of genetic damage from radioactivity do not show up until the next generation.

Lazarus (1966) has indeed distinguished between the process of psychological *stress*, which he sees as a state produced by the appraisal that harm is on the way, and *confrontation,* or the actual encounter with the harm. Much of the literature on stress tends to lump these two conditions together, but it might prove enlightening to keep the distinction in mind when environmental problems that have delayed effects are considered. Perhaps the difficulty is that people do not experience sufficient anticipatory stress in the contemplation of long-term problems. Or perhaps many people simply tend to opt for what Lazarus calls "defensive reappraisal" (for example, denial) when they encounter information that they or their descendants will someday have to confront severe harm created by the unwise actions they are presently engaging in. However, as Lazarus also notes, individuals' education, sophistication, and beliefs help determine their processes of appraising potential threats and the appropriate coping strategies. It may thus be that our educational system has failed to induce what may turn out to be a much needed and in fact healthy level of stress concerning long-term problems.

Let us now look briefly at a few of the potentially harmful stressors that human influence has introduced into the physical environment.

Pollution

Pollution is dirtying or contamination. In reference to environmental matters, pollution is usually discussed in terms of the medium fouled, be it air, water, land, or the phenomenological worlds of sight, sound, and so on. The list of known pollutants seems to be growing constantly and includes such diverse dirtying agents as a wide range of noxious gases and particulate matter in the air; bacteria, viruses, oil, floating debris, and potentially carcinogenic chemicals in the water; another wide range of chemicals on land; a plethora of annoying sounds, smells, and sights in our sensory environment; and special delights, such as pesticides and radioactive wastes, that can pollute just about anything. (For a list of a few of the many books that detail the world's pollution problems, see Chapter 2, note 7.) In keeping with common usage, we may leave the definition of "pollution" a bit vague, meaning anything that adulterates, contaminates, dirties, or creates annoyance or irritation by its presence.

Of course, some types of pollution can produce bodily damage and physiological stress irrespective of how people interpret their presence.

Very loud sounds, for example, can cause hearing loss and considerable discomfort; even disruptive sounds of lower intensity, if experienced over a long period of time, may have deleterious effects on psychological and physiological functioning.[4] It is also easy to demonstrate that certain types of polluted air are irritating to human eyes and respiratory systems.[5] Similarly, it is becoming increasingly well known that bacteria-contaminated water can make you sick, that water or food containing certain chemicals may in the long run make you *very* sick, and that technological "advances" have steadily greater power to play havoc with all sorts of delicate biological systems (some of which are our bodies). All of this can happen in spite of what we believe, perceive, or try to tell each other.

It is perhaps more questionable whether visual "pollution" in the form of flashing neon lights, discordant strip developments, bland or outrageous colors, treeless vistas of asphalt, and so on, can similarly do us in regardless of how we interpret what we see. One may indeed feel appalled by Peter Blake's (1964) photo-essay on America, see a sinister message in Maslow and Mintz's (1956) experimental findings that subjects rated pictures of others as more negative when the ratings were made in an ugly room than in nicer rooms, or side with architect Richard Neutra's (1969) theory that poorly designed artificial environments can cause physiological or psychological stress by violating human needs and tolerances for certain types of stimulation. Even so, the evidence that these "softer" forms of pollution are inherently harmful to your health does not yet seem firm.

For the purposes of examining the psychological effects of pollution, however, an illustrative and important issue concerns the role of cognition and culture in mediating the impact of environmental pollutants.

Cognition, culture, and pollution.   Samuel Klausner (1971) has presented an especially enlightening discussion of how cognitive and cultural factors can influence the psychological stress induced by pollutants such as dirt and low-intensity noise. As Klausner points out, different cultures or different subcultural groups can have very different views of what constitutes filth. What appears intolerably filthy to some people may be regarded as an acceptable way of life to others. City dwellers, for example, may have a hard time getting used to the smells around a farm. Western visitors to the huts of certain nonindustrial peoples may experience similar difficulties, while the residents sense nothing amiss.

Klausner's discussion also points out that being bothered by dirt (as defined by one's culture) may hinge on whether the dirty area is conceived of as an extension of oneself. Klausner's sex-role example is that men may care more for the cleanness of their cars, while women worry more about their kitchens. (One might hope that *that* will change and both will worry more about the cleanness of the kitchen!)

It might also be noted, to cite an insight of one of my students, that people will tolerate conditions of filth and other forms of pollution in the neighborhood where they *work* that they would never abide near where they *live*. This seems to be true even though the people may spend more waking time at their place of work. It is, of course, quite in keeping with Klausner's point linking concern for cleanness with a feeling of identity with the environment in question. Unfortunately, this bodes ill for city centers where more and more people work and visit, but fewer and fewer live.

Noise provides Klausner's other main example of how cognitive and social factors can mediate pollution impact. Although, as noted, very intense noise can be bothersome or damaging regardless of how it is interpreted by the listener (victim), the stressfulness of lower-intensity sound may depend to a considerable extent on how it is interpreted. For example, a bulldozer's sounds might be music to the ears of the developer whose land is being readied for yet another fast-food drive-in. The nearby homeowners, on the other hand, may hear approaching doom in the same snorting machine. As Klausner points out, a sound's meaning, origin, and relevance to one's ongoing activities will play major roles in determining the sound's annoyance value. (Klausner also cites work by others indicating that unexpectedness, interference, inappropriateness, intermittency, and reverberation tend to make sounds more annoying.)

An important consideration raised in Klausner's discussion and strongly supported by experimental studies by David Glass and Jerome E. Singer (1972, 1973) is that self-generated sound is generally much more tolerable than sound generated by other people. Certainly numerous examples should readily spring to mind, from the sounds of your own versus another's voice singing in the shower to the difference between *your* exploding firecracker and someone else's. Glass and Singer's experimental work actually extends this point to the conclusion that the mere predictability as well as the felt controllability of loud, intermittent sounds helps to reduce their harmful effects.

It should be made clear, however, that unlike Klausner, Glass and Singer were not so much concerned with whether the sound was annoying or disturbing while it was occurring as in what the behavioral aftereffects were.[6] Their findings were that noise perceived as uncontrollable or unpredictable—as compared with noise perceived as controllable or predictable—tended to result in negative postexposure effects on such measures as performance on a proofreading task and number of attempts at solving puzzles. Glass and Singer interpreted these effects as resulting in part from stress induced by feelings of helplessness to influence one's environment. At the very least, their work seems to demonstrate the power of cognitive factors, such as predictability and a sense of control, to temper the adverse effects of intermittent noise. Since Glass and Singer (1972) found similar effects for reactions to electric shock and even uncovered some supporting evidence in the realm of social stressors (such as "bureaucratic" harassment), it is a plausible hypothesis that similar cognitive factors could influence the psychological and behavioral impact of other forms of pollution.

In the realm of "visual pollution," the geographer David Lowenthal (1968, 1972) has also discussed the mediating influence of cognitive and cultural factors. For example, Lowenthal pointed out that visitors will often perceive places in a way very different from that of residents. Quoting from William James's essay "On a Certain Blindness in Human Beings," Lowenthal cited James's initial revulsion at seeing what appeared to him to be squalid, denuded little clearings in the North Carolina mountains. James quickly realized, however, that the farmers who had made the clearings saw not squalor and scalped forest land but "personal victory" and symbols of successful struggle. Lowenthal (1972) also recounted his own experience in a tropical country in which he perceived an otherwise pleasant area of greenery as "tawdry" because it was strewn with litter. However, the residents seemed to see nothing amiss, for to them paper and cans belonged among the flowers and grass. It is also true, as Lowenthal noted, that what may be litter to one culture or social class may be useful building material to another.

Two other important observations made by Lowenthal (1972) are that (1) there seems to be an increasing tendency to regard human constructions or environmental influences as bad and untouched nature as good; but (2) an exception to this may be seen in our positive view of ancient or historical "litter" (*old* ruins are often cherished). These points illustrate the powerful role that interpretive operations such as categorization, evaluation, and imaginational embellishment can play in shaping our affective response to the visual environment. As Lowenthal illustrated by historical and current examples, people tend to react positively or negatively to a landscape depending on whether they see the features in the scene as derived from nature alone or as reflecting human influence. A discolored stream may be seen as hideous if human pollution is believed to provide the strange hue, but a very different reaction will very likely be elicited if natural runoff from spring rains is imagined as the source of discoloration. And, of course, ugly strip developments may be seen by some people as glorious signs of economic progress, especially if the viewers happen to own a piece of the action.

Danger and Oppression

Aside from the vast variety of contaminants and irritants that "advanced" societies have managed to inject into the environment, there is a somewhat ironic collection of stressors that have been introduced as side effects mainly of certain transportation modes and certain architectural policies. Let us turn first to transportation.

The automobile and its effects.   The ill effects of the automobile and its associated industries are almost unbelievable in their scope and severity.[7] In the mid 1970s in the United States, well over 50,000 people per year are killed and many times more are severely injured, cities are shrouded in smog, billions of dollars are lost in property damage and medical costs, urban land that would be valuable for parks and other humane uses is sacrificed to parking and roadways, urban sprawl is encouraged and even necessitated, vast quantities of irreplaceable fossil fuel and other natural resources are consumed unnecessarily, transportation for the young and poor is made needlessly difficult (but also necessary because of the sprawl), and life is made less pleasant for all people who like to walk or play in outdoor urban areas. These are just a sample of the ill effects of the mass and uncontrolled profusion of the automobile in America. All in all, it is hard to imagine a greater single source of stress and unpleasantness for people who live in cities. As Jane Jacobs (1961) argued, automobiles *erode* cities.

All this is not to say that automobiles have no redeeming human value. As even such a severe critic of "autocracy" as Kenneth Schneider (1971) admits, cars can be fun and can provide freedom and mobility in sparsely populated regions. However, when the use of automobiles becomes a *necessity* and when the resulting uncurbed use leads to the Pandora's box of troubles listed in the above paragraph, much of the fun is taken out of both driving and urban life (and traffic jams weren't even mentioned!). Automobility run amuck does in effect seem to follow a kind of Gresham's law, with the bad uses driving out the good: parking lots pushing out parks, the highway/automobile industrial complex pushing out public transit development, highways pushing out (usually poor) people's communities, smog pushing out clean air, even wrecks pushing out life. Yes, there are psychologically and perhaps even socially beneficial effects of cars—increased feelings of power and competence and freedom, opportunities for relative privacy, the basis for interesting car-centered hobbies, and of course the opportunity for travel. But, as is usual in the case of harmful addictions, there are other ways to achieve such benefits with much less dire side effects—ways that would call for shifts in our operative values, increased rationality in social decision making, and probably considerable redistribution of power and wealth.

"Hard" architecture.   Robert Sommer (1974) used this term to refer to buildings and other environmental constructions that are oppressive, dehumanizing, impermeable to their surroundings, difficult to alter, oriented toward internal status differentials among users, promotive of "passive adjustment and psychological withdrawal," based on distrust of occupants, and typically drab, uniform, and impersonal in design. Common examples of such structures are traditional prisons, office buildings, zoos, airports, and college classrooms (and often dormitories). A central characteristic of hard architecture is that it is unresponsive to users—people are prohibited from personalizing or adjusting these spaces and in effect have no personal or collective control over them. As we shall see in more detail later, a very common theme among commentators on environmental design is that much more attention should be paid to designing environments that are responsive to users and their needs.

   Is the unyielding quality of hard environments a source of stress? Work such as that by Glass and Singer (1972) on the stress-reducing benefits of feelings of potential personal control over disturbing stimuli indicates that unresponsive and intimidating environments might contribute to stress by increasing general feelings of helplessness. However, as Sommer (1969, 1972, 1974) has repeatedly argued, it is perhaps not necessary to demonstrate that an environment produces physiological or psychological harm or that it decreases performance in order to argue that it is a bad environment. It should be enough to show that the environment is unpleasant or falls short of what could easily be done to improve the quality of life for its users.

As Sommer (1974) has also noted, hard architecture is often used by a group with high power to oppress a lower-power group. He pointed out, for instance, that bureaucracies find it quite all right to impose drabness on workers or students but tend to prohibit personalization of space by these people, because that would allow "imposing" their taste on others! In addition, according to Sommer, hard environments tend to lead to numbness to one's surroundings. Softening, even through such simple means as putting flowers in a parking space or painting a mural on a wall, can greatly boost environmental awareness by producing a sharp contrast with the surrounding hardness. Perhaps somewhat cynically (although I share his suspicion), Sommer speculated that "softening" is often opposed by Establishment powers precisely because of its potential for increasing people's awareness of their oppression. Certainly, the pecuniary motivation of much hard architecture should not be overlooked (for example, hard airport waiting areas designed to drive passengers into the expensive gift shops and restaurants). The important consideration, however, is simply that hardened spaces are unpleasant and discourage both community and environmental awareness. Whether or not real "stress" can be proved, decrement in the quality of life is itself a reason for personal and public concern.

Crowding

Although not, strictly speaking, a question of design, the exponential growth of the world's population does seem to present a potentially overwhelming human-made threat to human well-being and possibly even to human survival. One need only refer to the dire scenarios of Paul Ehrlich (1968, 1969) or Donella Meadows and her associates (1972) or look to the already present world food shortages to sense the dangers inherent in an overextended population. As many spokespersons for the Third World have argued, the problem is at least in part actually one of distribution (see, for example, Neuhaus, 1971). There might be enough food or other natural resources to support a world-wide population of a given level *if* everything were equally distributed, but lopsided distributions may greatly lower the total size of a viable population. Nevertheless, the problem persists that even under conditions of maximal production and use and of equal distribution, the more people there are (past a given point needed for efficient production), the less there is for each person.

However, there may be other dangers inherent in large or dense populations. Of particular relevance to environmental design is whether the very presence of other people can introduce psychological stress independent of the broader issues of dividing up resources (other than space per se). Experimental work with rats (for example, Calhoun, 1966, 1971; Marsden, 1972) and a field study of overpopulated deer (Christian et al., 1960), for example, have indicated that higher-than-normal densities can wreak havoc on the social and sexual lives—and even the very existence—of our fellow mammals. If overcrowded rats develop sexual, aggressive, and parental aberrations sufficient to threaten their survival or well-being, and if overcrowded deer die of internal physiological stress reactions even in the presence of sufficient food, do we face a similar fate in our clogged cities? As may be gathered from the debate over whether human beings are innately aggressive (see, for example, Lorenz, 1966; Montagu, 1968), the justifiability of reasoning about humans by analogy with "lower" animals is an inherently tricky business and one that becomes especially questionable in the behavioral and psychological realm.

It is of course easy to point to the social degradation and depredations common in many areas of urban high density (especially ghettos). However, it is surprising just how little hard evidence exists that crowding people together—in and of itself—causes social, psychological, or physiological problems. Several good recent reviews of the literature on crowding concur in finding no firm scientific support for a simple causal relation between physical variables of density and social or psychological problems.[8] It is of course even possible to think of special situations—such as sports events or orgies—where a measure of "crowding" might be highly desirable. Many writers (for example, Jacobs, 1961; Whyte, 1968) also argue that relatively high density is essential for urban vitality. Nevertheless, common sense and experience at least point to high interpersonal densities as a potential factor that in interaction with other factors can bring humans to grief. Jonathan Freedman (1975), for example, has found experimental evidence that density increases the intensity of affective response, so that higher densities might increase the felt pleasantness of friendly situations but have the opposite effect in unfriendly circumstances.

In their excellent paper on crowding, Steven Zlutnick and Irwin Altman (1972) presented an impressive comprehensive scheme for considering the various factors that may lead to adverse effects from high density. This scheme suggests how complex the problem of "crowding" really is. Basically, Zlutnick and Altman held that crowding (as a long-term stressful situation) involves (1) high densities both inside and outside of residences; (2) low levels of resources; (3) having to live under such conditions for a long period of time; (4) difficulty in controlling interactions with other people in the environment; and (5) the presence of such psychological factors as an adaptation level tuned to lower densities, lack of social skills, an introverted personality disposition, or other personal factors that increase the difficulty of adjusting to other people. (Additionally, Altman, 1975, has pointed out that as in the case of Glass and Singer's findings on the effects of noise, ill effects from crowding may arise over time as the result of strain produced by the coping processes themselves.)

It should be clear from this scheme that "density" and "crowding" are two distinct concepts, a point also brought out by Daniel Stokols (1972) in his differentiation between *density* as a purely physical condition and *crowding* as "a motivational state directed toward the alleviation of perceived restriction and infringement." Amos Rapoport (1975) similarly related crowding to negative affect aroused by high *perceived* density. Thus, except for extreme conditions such as being crushed or suffocated by a crowd, the stressful effects of high density seem to involve a cognitive appraisal that the presence of other people is frustrating one's goals or limiting one's freedom.[9]

Returning to Zlutnick and Altman's scheme, we may note first that most of the research studies on crowding have been unable to take account of all the mentioned factors. For example, widely cited experiments by Griffitt and Veitch (1971) and by Freedman and his colleagues (for example, Freedman et al., 1971, 1972) focused on the effects of density on variables such as task performance, aggressiveness, and evaluation of strangers.[10] However, density was manipulated only for relatively short periods of time inside laboratory rooms. Factors such as extended duration and inadequate resources (as would be true for living in a crowded ghetto) could not readily be taken into account in the experimental setting, and thus the results are of limited utility.

On the other hand, studies of correlations between factors such as urban densities and the rates of crime or mental illness generally fail to establish firm causal links between density per se and the associated social and psychological problems. This is because possible alternative causal factors such as nutrition, education, and economic status are usually associated with high population density, making causal inference from correlational findings very difficult. A study by Galle and his associates (1972), however, has provided tentative support for a relation between the density measure of persons per room of residence and various signs of social pathology. Even these investigators, though, caution against causal interpretation of their findings because of the nature of the statistical operations involved in the study (see also Fischer et al., 1975).

Let us turn now to the issue of controlling interactions with others and to the psychological factors in Zlutnick and Altman's scheme. A seminal paper ("The Experience of Living in Cities") by the social psychologist Stanley Milgram (1970) has proposed that the large size, high density, and heterogeneity of urban populations yield social inputs that tend to overload the processing capacity of the average city dweller. According to Milgram, potential adaptations to this stressful situation include responses such as (1) paying less attention to each input; (2) ignoring low-priority inputs; (3) shifts in patterns of transaction so that other people have to do more of the processing; (4) blocking off reception of inputs (as by taking one's phone off the hook); (5) allowing only superficial involvement with other people; and (6) interposing institutions between the individual and potential social demands (Milgram's example is the welfare agency as a means of cutting down on street mendicants). In sum, such "adaptive" mechanisms can lead to a brusque and cold interpersonal style, a lack of concern for other people's feelings, an atrophied sense of social responsibility, an unwillingness to help others, and a high degree of alienation and "deindividuation" (compare Zimbardo, 1970). Milgram even reported a study clearly revealing a tendency for residents of small towns to be more helpful to strangers in need than were urban residents.

However, Milgram (1970) also discussed differences in the "atmospheres" of great cities such as London, Rome, and Paris. Although the specific points he brought out do not bear specifically on the issues of crowding, it is important to recognize the role of culture and personal experience in mediating response to crowding. Observations by the anthropologist Edward Hall (1966) are especially enlightening on the power of culture in shaping people's response to density, the presence of other people, and the use of space generally. For example, Hall has pointed out that the Japanese often seem to prefer situations, such as sleeping together in groups on the floor, that would strike Americans as an invasion of privacy. Similarly, Hall noted, Arabs seem to lack "any concept of a private zone outside the body" (p. 157). This and other adjustments allow Arabs to tolerate much closer physical contact with nonintimate others than would be acceptable for most Westerners. In sharp contrast, Hall observed that Germans may feel intolerably "invaded" in situations that Americans or English would consider quite acceptable. In terms of Zlutnick and Altman's scheme, each of these cultures has evolved different techniques for controlling interactions— or the psychological impact of interactions—with other people in the environment. As Hall (1959, 1966) anecdotally detailed, contact between members of different cultures often leads to problems because the individuals fail to interpret each other's behavior in the appropriate cultural context (for example, the Arab's close approach seems aggressive to the American, while the American's withdrawal seems unfriendly to the Arab).

Hall's cross-cultural perspective also serves to illustrate Aristide Esser's (1972, 1973) observation that the experience of crowding is in part often generated by unfamiliar social encounters or by a failure to find a common social definition with other people involved in a given situation (also exemplified by the intruder on an intimate couple or by the person who wants to talk business at a party). As mentioned in Chapter 3, Hall's examples also highlight the role of culturally induced adaptation levels in influencing people's response to social or environmental stimuli. However, Wohlwill and Kohn's work (see Chapter 3) demonstrates that, even independent of gross cultural differences, individuals' residential background (urban versus small-town or rural) can influence their perception of the degree of crowding in a new urban situation.

Perhaps the key lesson to be derived from these cultural and psychological considerations is that people may be able to learn new ways of thinking about and relating to other people so as to reduce the stress sometimes associated with crowded living. We might, for instance, attempt to understand and incorporate some of the Japanese or Arab modes of evaluating and responding to the close presence of other people. Or we might follow Zlutnick and Altman's (1972) suggestion to find new ways of subtly using the environment to gain more control over interaction with others. Research such as that by J. A. Desor (1972) might provide leads on architectural design, for example. (Desor found that the density level for perceived crowding was higher in model rooms that were rectangular rather than square or that contained partitions rather than being open. He theorized that the rectangular or partitioned physical structures reduced the degree to which occupants seemed to impinge on each other.) Freedman (1975) has also suggested techniques such as increasing the number of rooms per housing unit and outfitting high-density apartment buildings with convenient communal areas that encourage friendly contact.

The theory, research, and observation by writers such as Hall, Zlutnick and Altman, Milgram, Esser, and Freedman also point to many possibilities for psychological regulation of stress stemming from the presence of other people. With the appropriate cognitive sets for perceiving and thinking about our fellow human beings, we may well be able to restore a sense of freedom and reduce the unpleasant impingements we often feel in dense situations. Perhaps. But Zlutnick and Altman's total scheme should force us to consider the multidimensional aspects of the problem of crowding, especially as these involve the inadequacy of resources and the inability of people to extricate themselves from situations of high density.

Before closing this brief overview of crowding, the contribution of Roger Barker and his colleagues in "ecological psychology" should also be mentioned. Much of this group's work has concerned the experiential and behavioral effects of the level of "manning" in behavior settings. The basic idea is that any behavior setting has both a certain minimum number of roles that must be filled if it is to function and also a certain maximum capacity for participants. According to Barker, there is also some optimal number of participants for any given behavior setting. The ecological psychologists' theory and research indicate that the social and psychological dynamics are very different for behavior settings (or clusters of behavior settings, as in institutions or towns) that have fewer than the optimal number of available participants (are "undermanned") versus those that have at least the optimal number of participants.[11]

According to both the theory and at least suggestive research findings in environments ranging from high schools to whole towns, a shortage of people relative to the number of roles needed by the available behavior settings leads to such effects as increased participation of individuals in a variety of behavior settings, more responsibility per person, decreased use of vetoing (expulsion) for deviant or inadequate behavior, greater use of deviation-countering (instruction, and so on), and higher difficulty and importance of role activities. In short, if there are relatively few people to do a variety of things, each person is likely to do (and be expected to do) many things, to have relatively high responsibility, and to be needed (and therefore accepted). When there are too many people for the available roles, on the other hand, the opposite conditions are likely to prevail: variety and responsibility of roles per person will tend to be lower, expulsion rather than correction will be a more likely response to deviant or inadequate behavior, and so on.

Thus, if people in fact lead happier, more fulfilling lives under conditions of relatively high responsibility and involvement in communal undertakings (see, for example, the evidence presented in Chapter 2—especially the work on work satisfaction by Herzberg and his associates), there may be a subtle deleterious effect of high population levels. That is, if there are too many people for the number of available positions in behavior settings, or even just if the number of central positions is low relative to the number of people, many people will be left out and tolerance of any failure will be very low. When sufficient material resources are available, however, there is no inherent reason that a larger absolute number of people must result in the deleterious effects of "overmanning." As Robert Bechtel (1975) has observed, the advantages of "undermanning" can be achieved by simply increasing the responsibility of participants. Presumably, this can be done by techniques such as decentralization, increasing the total number of behavior settings, using democratic decision-making processes, and distributing power and wealth relatively equally.[12]

"Future Shock"

For a final example of human-produced environmental stress, we may turn very briefly to Alvin Toffler's (1970) intriguing concept of *future shock*—the stress reaction produced by too much rapid change in one's environment. Toffler theorized that the combinaiton of accelerating diversity, transience, and novelty in technologically advanced societies produces sensory, informational, and decisional overload for the people living in these societies. Rapid turnovers in material possessions, places of residence, marriage partners, friends, and many aspects of the technological and architectural environments all serve to make severe demands on individuals who have to deal with such change.

Citing work by the physicians Thomas Holmes and Richard Rahe, Toffler (1970) even presented evidence that individuals who have recently undergone substantial changes in their lives are more likely to become physically ill than those with more stable existences. (However, affectively negative changes—such as the death of a spouse— tended to receive the highest "impact" ratings in gauging life changes. It is therefore difficult to tell from this research whether change per se or some interaction between change and the unpleasantness of the experience increased the chance of illness.) Toffler perhaps laid too much blame on the normal "orienting response" (the physiological adjustments involved in attending to interesting or novel stimuli) as a primary culprit in stressful reactions to change. However, he presented plausible hypotheses that repeated *startle* responses and full-fledged physiological stress reactions could be responsible for the debilitating effects of too much environmental change. Severe demands on people's information-processing capacity, decision making, and planning would also certainly appear to have high stress potential.

Toffler's position is of course similar to Milgram's (1970) overload theory of city living (see above). Indeed, many of the mechanisms for adjusting to urban social overload might be employed to avoid being overwhelmed by environmental change. For possible amelioration of future shock, Toffler himself (1970) recommended such measures as deliberately ignoring unwanted or overloading stimulation, establishing "personal stability zones" of routine or sameness in one's life, and learning to think and plan more intelligently about one's future (for example, by deliberately trying to regulate the total amount of change one opts for in a given period of time). On a broader social scale, Toffler advised that the society make a far greater effort to choose goals of technological development democratically and collectively, taking into account the long-range systemic effects of alternative types of development.

So that the citizenry will be able to participate insightfully in such decision making on both a personal and a societal level, Toffler and many others (see, for example, Toffler, 1974) have urged that the schools "educate for the future." In place of traditional approaches, education should emphasize such skills as creative imagination, making choices in keeping with one's self-consciously explored values, facility in relating to diverse types of people, and learning how to learn. Thus, although our cognitive limitations and our culture's uncontrolled ingenuity may set the stage for future shock, we may yet be able to educate ourselves to make the social and cognitive adjustments essential for alleviating the problem.

Squandered Opportunities

In addition to the outright "insults" to ourselves that we have designed or allowed to be introduced into the environment, the negative side of human environmental influence includes a substantial measure of misapplied technology and wasted resources (including both materials and design efforts). Indeed, Victor Papanek (1971), a most humane and socially concerned designer, has issued a profound critique of the whole design profession. Papanek argues that rather than showing concern for real human needs, prevalent practices in American industrial design—and other kinds of environmental design—have tended to be guided by a fast-buck mentality. The array of frills, unsafe designs, and cosmetic designs—as well as the unmitigated waste of materials and talent—that Papanek points to would be astounding were it not for its familiarity. What does seem astounding is Papanek's discussion of how much lower the cost of many of our everyday gadgets could be and of how much more could be done by designers to benefit people throughout the world. We shall deal with Papanek's ideas in more detail in the section on environmental potentials, but let it suffice for the moment to note with him that design efforts in our society have shown little concern for the needs of the poor, the underdeveloped world, the handicapped, or the average consumer; nor has sufficient design attention ever been given to areas such as medical equipment, teaching aids, industrial safety equipment, nonpolluting transportation, and even housing. According to Papanek's analysis, the chief criterion for design problems and design decisions seems to have been optimizing profit for the producer, not amenity for humankind or even for the average American consumer.

Papanek is certainly not alone in his misgivings about the direction of modern American design efforts. The use of our vast resources for all too often tawdry, ugly, dehumanizing, and wasteful purposes has been pointedly reviewed by critics such as Peter Blake (1964), Stephen Kurtz (1973), Robert Sommer (1974), Victor Gruen (1966), Lewis Mumford (1970), and Jane Jacobs (1961). Each of these writers has somewhat different bones to pick, it is true; but concerned observers of our public environments agree that we are wasting our very real potential for creating pleasant surroundings. When these criticisms are contrasted with examples of *good* design (see, for example, Von Eckardt, 1967; Halprin, 1972; and the later sections of this chapter), the magnitude of our wasted opportunities takes on an almost surrealistic quality, it is so unbelievable. For instance, to compare an average American suburban development with the Finnish "new town" of Tapiola (see, for example, von Hertzen and Spreiregen, 1973) or even with good examples of "cluster development" (clustering of houses to provide communal open space; see Whyte, 1968) may come as a veritable shock to those who passively accept our suburbs as the true American Dream. And even a casual perusal of Bernard Rudofsky's (1969) *Streets for People* should convince the average American that we have a woefully myopic vision of what a street is or could be.

In closing, it should be acknowledged that some of these criticisms can probably be written off as mere conflicts of tastes. Certainly, not everyone would enjoy the specific types of environments that would appeal to me or to any of the particular critics and commentators just cited. But that is not the issue. We have wasted our opportunities in allowing a kind of uniformity—and many would say a mediocre uniformity—to be imposed across the whole country and to insinuate itself into most aspects of consumer-products design. There is little choice in America relative to what there so easily could be. We do not have the choice, for example, of deciding whether to live in a "garden city" or a conventional suburb—there are thousands of conventional suburbs, but hardly any garden cities. Nor can we readily choose whether to ride on a pleasant public transit line or use a car—the public transit is either unpleasant or unavailable. Similarly, we cannot readily choose to purchase cheap and attractive modular housing, to live in a place designed for pleasant walking or bicycle riding as the main modes of getting around, to buy nonpolluting cars, to work in "soft" buildings, or to live in clustered housing with shared open space. Our so-called diversity and choice tend rather to be limited to alternative models of the same thing, none of which are usually designed with a full slate of pro-life values or with community concern in mind.

Let us now turn to a glimpse of why we have introduced unnecessary stress and botched so much of our opportunity for amenity and real choice.

Sources of Our Environmental Design Shortcomings

My concern in the first part of this chapter has been the negative aspects of what we are doing to ourselves through our environment. Before taking a necessarily cursory look at the probable sources of these problems, I should acknowledge that America's contributions to environmental design have not all been negative. Lawrence Halprin's (1972) pleasing pictures of urban environments do include examples from American cities, for instance; and Jane Jacobs (1961) did derive her examples of city vitality from American urban neighborhoods. Perhaps more important, many technological innovations with great potential for helping the entire world have indeed arisen from our culture (see, for example, Papanek, 1971; Fuller, 1969). And perhaps even more important, many sophisticated and humane proposals for improved environmental design certainly have originated in our society (see last part of this chapter). Nevertheless, it is easy to point to everyday examples of how we have failed to make pro-life use of our resources, and hard to think of instances where we could be said to have realized our human potentials. Why?

Our Underlying Value System

In Chapter 4 an effort was made to detail some features of modern American operative values that might partially account for the various environmental and social problems we face. It was pointed out, for example, that our cavalier and anthropocentric attitude toward the rest of nature, combined with such value orientations as gross materialism and competitive individualism, seem implicated in the generation of pollution, the waste of resources, and other environmental problems. Furthermore, these same cultural biases—along with distrust of human nature, unnecessary hierarchical ordering of people, confusion of means and ends, acceptance of violence, and a short-term time orientation—probably help to engender social problems such as poverty, crime, insecurity, and so on. My concern at this point is to ask whether these features of our value system also contribute to the other environmental design failings outlined in this chapter.

For example, both Robert Sommer (1974) and Alexander Tzonis (1972) have linked oppressive environments to the social oppression of one group by another. Hard architecture, as noted above, seems to involve distrust of human nature (this is especially evident in prisons and many college dormitories). An equally serious problem pointed out by Sommer is that hard bureaucratic architecture is often designed around status differences, with attendant limitations on community and personal contact (not to mention much lower levels of amenity for those of low status). This, to me, is a clear expression of the fruits of our competitive, hierarchical value orientation and our devotion to Equity 1 norms of distribution. Indeed, competitive individualism is especially problematic for handling practically any type of communal environmental coordination. We thus easily settle for far less in individualistic suburban housing than we could readily obtain by intelligent collective planning and the use of techniques such as house clustering that retains open space. If, as Victor Gruen (1966) has declared, we seek good private environments (and certainly only some of our private environments are good) but "criminally neglect" public ones, the absence of public amenity can vitiate the lives of even the rich. Clearly, our heritage of individualism makes concerted planning for a truly pleasant communal environment very difficult. This heritage also allows us to tolerate poverty and the terrible environments often associated with it.

Our tendencies to treat means (such as cars) as if they were ends, to accept violence, and to focus on only the relatively short-term future also help to explain many design failures, with the triumph of car-centered urban sprawl just one example. Indeed, when these aspects of our value system are considered along with materialism and competition, the picture becomes very clear, helping to account for planned obsolescence, cosmetic design, building for profit rather than people, design for lucrative trivia, and so on (see especially Papanek, 1971). The irony is that in this scramble for personal (and corporate) wealth and "success" without regard to the resulting quality of life, even the winners get a relatively low return: too many human needs and potentials are being ignored.

Let us now take a more specific look at the framework within which design decisions are made in our society.

The Sociocultural Context of Designing

Capitalism, private property, and the profit motive. It is becoming a commonplace criticism of profit seeking and other aspects of capitalistic economics that they set the stage for environmental problems ranging from ugliness (for example, Blake, 1964) to urban deterioration, environmental pollution, and energy waste (for example, Bookchin, 1974; Commoner, 1971, 1976). This problem would seem to be an expression of the difficulties engendered by competitive individualism and materialism—the primary difficulty being that when private profit becomes the chief criterion for design decisions, considerations of general human welfare tend to be forgotten. It is easily argued, for example, that it is the *profitability* of things such as slums (for example, Raskin, 1974), marginally safe and definitely annoying overhead extra-high-voltage power lines (Young, 1973), many forms of hard architecture (Sommer, 1974), and all sorts of material waste and pollution that makes these conditions so hard to fight. It is difficult to design for human needs and for pro-life values when both the opportunities for design and the reinforcement contingencies for designers and their rich employers (clients) are determined by profit making in a competitive, growth-oriented economic system. In a sense, we might say that the guiding cognitive set is represented by the question, "How can available resources be used to maximize *my* profit?" rather than questions such as, "How can available resources be used to make life more pleasant for all of us?" The environmental results of the former orientation are all around us.

Another severe restriction on humane and sane design imposed by our economic system derives from our near worship of private property. As Shirley Passow (1973) has pointed out, it is in countries that practice public ownership of land, such as Sweden and Holland, that public-interest environmental planning has been most effective. (She noted in this regard that the sale of government-owned land to private enterprise—and, I might add, the frequent failure of the government to buy land when the price is still low—is a very poor planning policy. We thereby trade long-term planning capability for short-term gains in tax rates or government coffers.) Other instances of the harm wrought by the mystique of private property can be found in the violent Establishment response to the appropriation of an unused vacant lot for a "People's Park" in Berkeley some years ago (see Sommer, 1972), and in our willingness to tolerate the private ownership of vast quantities of shorelines and other potential park land. If we were not so devoted to private land ownership, we could easily make it a national policy to preserve virtually all land of certain types, such as shorelines, for public use. The resulting proliferation of parks could be a delight for *everyone*.

Still another highly restrictive aspect of our economic system is its tendency to channel design efforts toward serving only the wealthy. Papanek (1971) has made this point vividly with respect to the scale of world-wide needs, citing how American designers could (but generally do not) contribute a small portion of their efforts and expertise to helping underdeveloped nations. Similarly, within our society, architects are employed mainly by the wealthy. This may have the effect of giving us spots of secluded beauty and creativity tucked away here and there, but the environment at large goes wanting. It is fascinating, for instance, to compare our approach to middle- and lower-income suburban housing with what can be done when creative design is sought and employed on a large and public scale—as in the case of Tapiola, Finland (von Hertzen and Spreiregen, 1973). It is possible to make use of architectural talent on a broad basis, but our economic and value systems do not encourage it. Perhaps even more serious, our design and planning bias toward the wealthy all too easily works to make the lives of the poor that much harder. It is much more likely, for example, that a new highway will be built through a poor neighborhood than through a rich one, even though many more people may be affected and even though they may have far less ability to deal with the resulting disruption in their lives. The net result of the bias toward the wealthy, however, is that virtually everyone suffers, since this is but one more force that distracts us from issues of community design for total communal benefit.

Social forces against pro-life creativity in design. The cultural and economic context of our design decisions also generates societal forces that hinder creativity and communal concern. As numerous critics of our educational system have noted, far too little attention is paid to training for creativity. Indeed, the designer Papanek (1971) has provocatively argued that since creativity by its very nature challenges the status quo, it tends to be downplayed by education that seeks to pass along the dominant culture. He is joined by the architects Serge Chermayeff and Alexander Tzonis (1971, p. 175) as they charge that "architectural education in 'accredited schools' . . . has accepted almost exclusively in its curricula the framework of existing conditions."

But lack of creativity on the part of the designers is surely not the main problem, whatever the shortcomings of status-quo–oriented design education. Even the most innovative and creative American architects, planners, and other designers end up working in a society that has traditionally disparaged aesthetics, public amenity, and often even fun. For example, when costs (almost always meaning monetary, not human, costs) must be cut in a public architectural project, it will typically be the aesthetic or recreation-oriented "frills" that must go. John Zeisel and Mary Griffin (1975) detail a classic instance of this in the case of a public housing development where cost cutting resulted in the elimination of play equipment and various types of landscaping and fencing in an inner courtyard—thus rendering this area virtually useless to the tenants and thereby interfering with the development of community life, not to mention the enjoyability of looking out the windows. That this sort of thing is so typical in our society may in large part be the result of a general lack of public concern with beauty or creativity. It is instructive to recall Rokeach's (1973) findings that "a world of beauty" ranked near the bottom of his national sample's ordering of terminal values and that "imaginativeness" placed similarly on the ordering of instrumental values.

Furthermore, as Sommer (1974) and others have argued, a lack of exposure to creative and pro-life design can easily numb people into acceptance of environmental mediocrity and deterioration. The need for better environmental and design education for the general public seems clear (see also Colbert, 1966). It might be most helpful, also, if we could adopt John Dewey's (1934) position that art and aesthetics belong to all experience and should not be thought of as confined to museums. Bernard Rudofsky (1964, 1969), in his delightful studies of streets and of "vernacular" architecture, has pictured how numerous "underdeveloped" societies seem to have been much more successful at this than we have.

But there are of course still other social forces spawned by economics and culture that create problems for creative design. Banks, for instance, are notoriously conservative in lending money for innovative projects. Jane Jacobs (1961) angrily compared the ease of obtaining a loan for a standard suburban house with the difficulty of getting money for something more unusual, such as renovating an inner-city dwelling owned by the same applicant. The conservatism of our banks is doubtless also a problem for those who want to depart from the tried and true path in suburban developments (such as people favoring cluster designs). In the past at least, this has been true even in relatively publicly oriented societies such as Finland, where Tapiola got off to an uncertain start because of difficulties in obtaining loans (see von Hertzen and Spreiregen, 1973). Things may be changing now both abroad and here in the United States, but the environment we *have* has most certainly been shaped by highly conservative forces.

Unfortunately, other forces that tend to produce more of the same include governmental inertia and uncoordinated bureaucracy, tax laws that discourage slum renovation and make good architecture disproportionately more expensive than hack work (see, for example, Blake, 1964; Logue, 1966; Weitzman, 1973), lack of regional planning so essential for the development of vibrant new towns and good public transit, and the correlative entrenched and uncoordinated local and departmental interests (for example, highway departments *versus* transit authorities). These diverse forces have tended to combine to thwart any sort of communal rationality in either design or planning, and their links to our underlying economic and value systems should be clear.

Political processes in design decisions. There are of course many dimensions to how political or societal decision-making processes influence environmental design. It was just noted, for instance, that bureaucratic divisiveness and local power interests inhibit regional and new-town planning. In addition, the overrepresentation of the interests of large corporations and other rich power groups is evident in all aspects of political decision making, certainly including that pertaining directly to the physical environment. Just one example of political bias toward private profit and the wealthy may be gleaned from certain applications of the federal urban renewal program, in which many poor families were dispossessed of their homes to make way for new money-making housing and business projects that in no way benefited them (see, for example, Goodman, 1971). Clearly, the government often subsidizes the wealthy private developer instead of making the total life of the community better. This does seem an odd use of tax money, and would also seem to set a low moral tone for the design and planning decisions involved.

However, even where design really is intended for the benefit of the poor or other low-power public groups (which often include members of the middle class), there is frequently little or no effort to include the intended users in the design decisions. As Melvin Mogulof (1973) has pointed out, although some Model Cities programs do represent welcome exceptions, overall we still have a long way to go in the area of citizen participation. Of course, citizen involvement in design decisions could entail problems for the participants themselves. Donald Grant (1975) suggested, for instance, that having to worry about shaping one's own environment could lead to "information overload" and that untrained or uncreative participants might produce poor designs. However, there is considerable reason to be optimistic about the value of user input in design decisions. If people felt that they really did have a voice in designing their environment, they would have much more incentive than they do now to look into design alternatives and to choose the best obtainable quality. After all, it is the users who would have the most to gain or to lose in the final product. Furthermore, competence motivation is on the side of enjoying the chance to influence one's own environment (see Chapter 2).

As behavioral-science observers of design decisions have recently pointed out (for example, Zeisel, 1975; Sommer, 1974), there is often a gap between the designer and the user. The *client* may be a government agency or a private firm; the *users* may be a group of unknown future residents or workers. Increasingly, efforts are being made—or at least urged—to bring potential users or their representatives into the design process either through behavioral research or through direct participation (see, for example, Anderson, 1968; Sommer, 1972; Zeisel, 1975). But in the past such user input has often not been sought, and many design monstrosities have been built that could have been avoided (to name only a few, demolished or moribund public housing projects and virtually all of Sommer's [1974] examples of hard architecture).

Ways of thinking by designers and planners. It would hardly be fair to blame environmental designers and planners for the jobs that are given to them or for the cultural and economic constraints under which they work. A number of critics, sympathetic and otherwise, have nonetheless raised issues about the contributions of architects and planners to many of the environmental problems we have considered. Both friendly critics (for example, Sommer 1974) and more hostile ones (for example, Kurtz, 1973; Goodman, 1971; Colbert, 1966) have charged that too many architects are overly concerned with monumentality or indi-vidualistic aesthetic niceties and underconcerned with what happens to the people who live or work in the buildings they design. The need seems to be for more cooperative design efforts involving professional designers, behavioral scientists, and, one would hope, actual users. Cer-tainly Sommer (1972), Zeisel (1975), and many contributors to design-and-behavior conferences have been emphatic in calling for this sort of collaboration.[13] However, as many have pointed out (for example, Ostrander, 1975), there are problems in such joint ventures, even if only architects and behavioral scientists are involved. Issues of jargon, pro-fessional territoriality, credibility (of behavioral scientists mainly), time pressure (mainly on architects), and so on, often arise. Nonetheless, more and more collaborative efforts do seem to be emerging, and or-ganizations such as the Environmental Design Research Association augur well for the future (as do a few recent team evaluation studies, such as that reported by Zeisel and Griffin, 1975, concerning a public housing project).

Perhaps coordinate with the accusation that architects tend toward "prima donna-ism" is the charge that planners tend to oversimplify. Jane Jacobs (1961) and Christopher Alexander (1965), for instance, have complained that planners usually fail to realize how complex and organic an entity a city (or even a town) is. According to Alexander, planners and most other people have tended to conceive of a city as a "tree" structure of relatively independent and separate parts rather than as the "semi-lattice" replete with overlap and interconnection that it really is. If one agrees with William Whyte's (1968) critique of most planned new towns as relatively sterile environments, Alexander's mis-givings may be seen to receive some support. Similarly, Jacobs (1961) claimed that much (if not all) of both traditional planning theory and semi-utopian design has ignored the complexity of city functioning, the need for concentration of both people and mixed uses to create and preserve city vitality, the underlying liveliness of many apparently slum-like neighborhoods, and so on. I would not like to push such accusations too far, however. Planners often work under severe political and eco-nomic constraints, and in any case they appear to be increasingly sophis-ticated and concerned with complex social as well as physical features

of the environment (see, for example, Scott, 1969; Godschalk, 1974)—
not to mention that many planners seem to have taken Jane Jacobs's
ideas to heart!

However, probably the most serious problem of which architects,
planners, and other environmental designers have been accused is that
they tend to be too much oriented to the status quo. Here the chorus of
critics grows loud indeed. An architect, Eugene Raskin (1974), points
out that architects tend to express and reflect their own culture, to do
mainly what the Establishment wants, and to be among the "people" in
his statement (p. 105) that "the world is being built largely by people
who approve of it . . . who do not want it to change." A planning professor, Jerome Kaufman (1974), presents evidence that planning practice lags far behind much of the more innovative planning theory and
wishes of younger planners, in part because of the insecurity of planning agencies and the conservatism and "playing it safe" of the directors
of these agencies. These represent the milder criticisms. A more radical
note is sounded by critics such as Martin Kuenzlen (1972), Robert
Goodman (1971), and Murray Bookchin (1974), who see modern environmental design as occurring in a context of economic and political
oppression. Planners and architects, by accepting and working without
opposition to the existing economic system and its associated undemo-
cratic distribution of power, are seen as part of the problem rather than
as part of the solution.

As noted, there may be some question about whether environmental
designers really have an active role in producing environmental and
social difficulties or are simply the "tools" of an entrenched Establishment (or even of an unguided but non–pro-life system of social decision
making). However, there can be little doubt that many design professionals do indeed favor the status quo and that their thinking and design
solutions reflect this. When the status quo goes unquestioned, even relatively sophisticated approaches to planning and design, such as systems
analysis, will fail to be of much help—and can indeed bear out the fears
of critics such as Kuenzlen (1972), and do much harm. A noteworthy
example of status-quo systems analysis is evident in Jay Forrester's
(1969, 1972) suggestions for helping to "solve" the problem of deterioration in cities. As discussed in the next chapter, Forrester (1972) does
offer a helpful and insightful exposition of the counter-intuitive nature
of complex systems, but his actual suggestions for improving cities operate within a framework of acceptance of our current economic system

(see also Schwartz and Foin, 1972). If we are to deal with our environmental and social problems in a way that benefits everyone, we will almost certainly have to question many aspects of the sociocultural context within which environmental design occurs. Can there be much doubt that people who treat the existing context as sacrosanct will continue to be part of the problem, perhaps even in direct proportion to the power of their analytic devices?

ENVIRONMENTAL POTENTIALS

In the remainder of this chapter we shall examine criteria and possibilities for pro-life environmental design. As a foreword to this discussion, the following three points are offered.

First, the "good life" obviously requires more than even an ideal physical environment. As argued throughout this book, human happiness is a function of many different types of factors (social, cultural, psychological, and so on); it is the total human/environmental system that must ultimately be considered. Nevertheless, the physical aspects of the environment are important ingredients in this whole and can certainly be influenced to promote and reflect a pro-life existence.

Second, we will undoubtedly aim too low if we only consider how people have used space in the past or currently say they would like to use it in the future. As implicitly argued thus far, designing with users and for their needs is essential to a pro-life approach; but simply polling individuals to see what they want or even observing the way existing environments are used should be only part of the process. As Goodman (1971) and Altman (1975) have pointed out, there is a danger in designing only for people as they are now. People may be responding to stresses that themselves should be removed or they may lack the education (in the broadest sense) that would allow them to appreciate and make use of richer environments. Environmental design should be integrated with a total program to help all people advance up Maslow's hierarchy (see Chapter 2). This would mean designing for all universal human needs—that is, physiological, safety, belonging, esteem, and self-actualization needs, if Maslow is correct. Obviously, if design decisions were based mainly on how people who were stuck at, say, the safety level responded to questionnaires or environments, much would be left to be desired for people at higher levels. This of course is not meant to be an elitist plea to design only for what would appeal to self-actualizers. It is rather a plea to employ environmental design, along with everything else we can influence, to facilitate an expanded (and more ecological) consciousness and a better life for everyone. To do this we will have to design for human potentials as well as human actualities.

Finally, the following discussion of possible criteria for achieving this goal is arranged according to the scheme of the eight components linking cognition, environment, and affect given in Chapter 3. It will be recalled that the components of Complexity, Composition, Comprehension, Comparison, Competence, and Complications are essentially interlinked aspects of experience, while Comportment refers to behavior and Compatibility is a general evaluative concept. As developed in Chapter 3, this scheme was used to examine the effects of different cognitive sets, the notion being that the eight components collectively mediate the affective experience arising from the use of particular types of cognitive sets. As indicated by the overall model of environment/experience/behavior interrelations, the specific nature of the environment is obviously also a major influence on the eight components and hence on the affective quality of life. This same eight-part scheme can thus be used as a set of guidelines for designing environments that will increase the enjoyment of life. However, it should also be recalled that these eight components, while analytically distinct, are highly inrerrelated. For any truly pro-life design it seems absolutely essential to take account of all eight.[14]

Criteria for Pro-Life Design

Compatibility

Compatibility was originally defined as consistency with cooperative, ecological, and happiness-oriented values. At this stage, a more meaningful way to define it is consistency with pro-life values and the other aspects of ecological consciousness. It should be clear from the discussions in the previous two chapters that increasing Compatibility is no small order. To do so for our society as a whole would involve nothing less than a reversal of several major aspects of our culture's dominant value system and a substantial change in common patterns of thinking.

But temporarily holding in abeyance the question of how to achieve these fundamental social and cognitive shifts, what specific considerations would design for Compatibility entail? As the concept has been developed in this book, the list would include at least the following:

1. Promotion of happiness for all people. As the central element in pro-life values, the facilitation of general human well-being and happiness would obviously be a paramount concern. Architects such as Richard Neutra (1969) and Dolf Schnebli (1972) seem to have this idea in mind when they recommend such things as designing for the needs of the human nervous system (Neutra) or designing a world especially fit for *children*—which because of its resulting attention to basic human needs would also probably turn out to be a lively and pleasant place for everyone (Schnebli). To carry Schnebli's idea a little further, why not approach all design problems with the promotion of pleasure and fun at least in the back of our minds? As Lawrence Halprin (1972) pointed out, for example, it is important to make mass transit *fun* (as in the case of elevated monorails) if people are to be enticed to use it and if urban life is to be made truly pleasant. The same could of course be said for pedestrian environments (see Rudofsky, 1969) or indeed virtually any place or thing. This is not to say we should be unrestrained hedonists or let fun and pleasure be our *only* criteria (although it might be interesting to try), but rather that both immediate enjoyability and the promotion of long-lasting well-being should be important and even essential concerns in design.

But of course the issue of general human happiness and well-being goes far beyond simple questions of designing for fun and pleasure, even long-lasting fun and pleasure. Victor Papanek (1971) has argued for concern with the well-being of *all* people. In a truly humane and pro-life world, the needs of the Third World, the handicapped and infirm, the old, the very young, and all others, would necessarily be considered. And as noted above, all of the types of needs covered in Maslow's hierarchy—at both the deficiency and Being levels—must be considered in pro-life design. Furthermore, as was indicated above and in Chapter 3, it is necessary to enhance every one of the components linking cognition, affect, and the environment if long-term positive affect—happiness—is to be achieved. Compatibility would simply call for this to be done as much as possible for everyone rather than just for the privileged few.

2. *Promotion of cooperation and community.* It should be recalled from the discussion in Chapter 4 of the probable supporting values in a pro-life system that concern for human welfare would entail special attention to health; the flowering of intrinsic motivation and satisfaction; cooperation; minimal unpleasant experience and work; and high freedom, individuality, and diversity. All of these considerations are naturally relevant to the concept of Compatibility because of the focus on human happiness. However, the relatively individualistic items in the list (health, intrinsic motivation, freedom, and so on) are more specifically encompassed in the remaining seven components. The pro-life supporting value of most central concern here is *cooperation.*

Many architects (for example, Chermayeff and Tzonis, 1971) and urban commentators (for example, Mumford, 1968; Bookchin, 1974) have stressed the need for designing for more cooperative, communal contact and the delight that it can bring. Of course, others might question the desirability of too closely knit communities with their potential for invasion of privacy and pressures for conformity; but we have already considered some of these general issues and noted that healthy community involves *mutual* influence and can certainly allow a high degree of individuality and choice (see Chapter 4 and compare Jacobs, 1961). Additionally, as was previously discussed at length, cooperation would seem to be essential for dealing effectively with many of our complex social and environmental problems. And it would certainly be involved in promoting collective control over our lives and in equalizing the distribution of wealth and power—necessary prerequisites for universal optimization of the components involved in positive affect and self-actualization.

Here are a few design suggestions that have been offered for encouraging greater community (if not full cooperation, since that would also require basic value changes). Chermayeff and Tzonis (1971) have proposed using pleasant mass transit nodes as mixed-use pedestrian concourses that would encourage contact and casual communication as well as more formal meetings. Constance Perin (1970) has suggested making communication channels such as mail and telephones free, increasing the access of local groups to public TV, increasing meeting spaces, and providing more frequent holidays. Jane Jacobs (1961) has called for concentrated diversity of uses, widened sidewalks, and other environmental changes that increase opportunity for public contact. Certain new-town designs, especially (again) Tapiola, Finland, have been specifically structured to encourage the development of community—such as by containing town centers with high levels of amenity and mixed uses, and by providing pleasant recreational centers for the whole town. And, on a more radical level, communalists such as Bookchin (for example, 1974) have advocated interconnected houses; a profusion of people's parks, gardens, plazas, and markets; and a move toward decentralized communities that stress collective endeavors and ecological concern.

3. *Promoting and reflecting ecological consciousness.*   To "design with nature," as Ian McHarg (1969) put it, would certainly be a major aspect of high Compatibility. McHarg's specific technique for land use planning and large-scale environmental design derives from a value system stressing the fitness or suitability of an environment for a particular organism or use. This system relies on maintaining and using the characteristics and processes within an ecosystem to minimize the need for costly or damaging adaptation and to maximize such criteria for good design as negentropy (increase in the level of order, as in transforming raw materials into a computer or inert material into a complex living system), symbiosis (whereby living systems mutually benefit each other), and the overall health and "creativity" of ecosystems. (To facilitate such goals in land use planning, McHarg's approach uses overlay maps representing various ecological land characteristics and human values and employs the final overlay configuration to determine optimal placement of human constructions.)

It is increasingly easy, of course, to find suggestions for ecologically oriented environmental design. Since the environmental movement of the sixties and seventies awakened public concern, a steady stream of books and ideas has issued forth. Critics urge us to preserve natural diversity and not to dangerously simplify ecosystems, to use natural materials to avoid contaminating our environment with potentially biologically disruptive synthetics (see especially Commoner, 1971, on this), to recycle, to reduce our energy consumption and curb the production of waste heat and radioactivity, to design total "ecocommunities" (Bookchin, 1974) that are stably symbiotic with the surrounding natural environment, and so on. It is true, as René Dubos (1973b) has pointed out, that the fear of modifying ecosystems can be carried too far—we can still be good "stewards" of nature while we "humanize" the earth and shape it more to our liking. However, he and many others also note that we must be very careful in making these modifications, and that we should always remember that we are interdependent with the biosphere.

Furthermore, as discussed in the preceding chapters, we as well as the rest of nature stand to benefit from the exercise of an ecological conscience in our dealings with other living things. Compatibility thus also entails consideration of the effects on nonhuman well-being and experience in addition to that of humans. Just as one example, we might note Robert Sommer's (1974) analysis of the unnecessary cruelty of many zoo environments for the animals they incarcerate. He suggests more pro-life alternatives, including, for instance, locking the people into closed containers through which they can view the free-roaming creatures in an animal park. A less poignant example of how an ecological ethic might operate would be deliberate preservation of natural areas through the use of cluster development in new towns or suburbs (see, for example, Whyte, 1968).

High Compatibility would also call for design that encouraged as well as appealed to ecological consciousness. Design might thus aim to achieve a kind of educative function, helping to make people aware of underlying ecological interrelations and interdependencies. Perhaps as some types of functional architecture deliberately expose pipes and the other "innards" of structures, some environmental influences might make apparent the interdependence of people and nonhuman nature. More visible links between food production and the market, some way of making clearer the ultimate source of various materials or fuels, building in some indication of the side effects and long-range fate of various appliances or other material objects, and similar efforts to reveal the "world lines" (Payne, 1973; see also set WLL, Chapter 3) of the things we design might at least serve as small facilitators of ecological consciousness.

The key concern, however, is for design decisions themselves to reflect consideration of the full complexity and interrelatedness of things. This is the essence of truly ecological design. As Jane Jacobs (1961) put it in the case of cities (following Warren Weaver's terminology), we are dealing with "problems of organized complexity." That is, large-scale environmental and social design involves making changes in often counter-intuitive complex systems (Forrester, 1972). As noted, however, truly pro-life and ecologically sound design may require questioning virtually all aspects of these systems and even expanding our horizons to the world-wide scale (compare Falk, 1972, for instance). Often, even people such as Jacobs and Forrester who think in terms of complex interactions and systemic processes seem to fail to question such basic elements of our environmental problems as the underlying economic or educational system. Design that reflected ecological consciousness would take into account the potentials of the total sociocultural environment.

Let us now turn to the other seven components linking cognition, environment, and affect, and examine briefly how each could serve as a guide for furthering the values represented by the concept of Compatibility.

Complexity

The term *Complexity* has been used to refer to the arousal potential of the structural aspects of experience—in effect, the degree of novelty, surprisingness, intensity, complexity, and so on, of an ongoing experience. As many investigators and theorists have argued (see Chapters 2 and 3), Complexity seems to have important effects on aesthetic experience and general affective quality. In fact, Amos Rapoport and Robert Kantor (1967) wrote a widely cited article in the *Journal of the American Institute of Planners* in which they proposed that an appropriate level of ambiguity and complexity should be a major design goal. By adjusting the "intricacy in design" to produce an "optimal perceptual rate" Rapoport and Kantor argued that greater visual satisfaction could be afforded to people.[15]

Many others have also suggested attention to designing for optimal Complexity in order to enhance the quality of experience. For example, in one of the few studies of environmental preference that concentrated on a sense other than vision, Michael Southworth (1969) found that subjects on a guided trip through Boston liked sounds that were "novel, informative, responsive to personal action, and culturally approved" (p. 59). Overly stimulating sounds—such as loud and disorienting ones—were disliked, especially by blindfolded subjects. These findings, as well as some of Southworth's design suggestions for increasing the interestingness and manipulability or "responsiveness" of the sonic environment (for example, sculptures that emit sounds in response to viewers' movements), can be couched in terms of enhancing overall environmentally induced Complexity. Kaplan and Wendt's (1972) proposal that environmental complexity and "mystery" are key elements in landscape preference provides another recognition of the importance of Complexity. And seekers after more enjoyable parks and townscapes (for example, Whitaker and Browne, 1971; Cullen, 1961) often join in the praise for such Complexity enhancers as mystery, contrasting forms, multiple levels, enclosures, and so on.

On a less purely aesthetic level, however, environmental dimensions relating to variety, novelty, and other boosters of Complexity can serve valuable pro-life functions. For instance, Charles Jencks (1971) has pointed out the importance of pluralism in architectural design traditions as a source of *choice;* and Raymond Dasmann (1970) has argued similarly with reference to ecological and cultural diversity, even proposing that a *variety* of utopias would be a good idea in order to allow choice. It is also almost a truism in ecology, of course, that diversity tends to be associated with ecological stability and well-being. And Jacobs (1961) has offered convincing arguments, as have designers such as Carr (1967) and Chermayeff and Tzonis (1971), that concentrated diversity is essential for city vitality and also for people's ability to execute diverse Plans. Indeed, Jacobs's proposed "generators of diversity"— mixed primary uses, short blocks, mixtures of old and new buildings, and a relatively high concentration of people—would certainly tend to provide ample opportunity for heightening Complexity as well as generating urban diversity.

It is important in designing for Complexity, however, to provide for widely varying personal preferences—we need diversity even in levels of diversity! But most important, the environmental sources of pleasant arousal should also help to enhance the other seven components relating to environment and affect. Of all the design criteria we are discussing, Complexity can probably be promoted in the greatest variety of ways. Almost *any* change, for instance, can boost arousal. It is thus extremely important in seeking to "optimize" Complexity to consider interactions with the other design criteria. It is perhaps their failure to look beyond Complexity that has led some architects to be criticized for lacking concern for people (see, for example, Goodman, 1971; Kurtz, 1973). Failure to *consider* Complexity, however, can result in an overstimulating environment or in one that virtually ignores aesthetics, diversity, and choice.

Composition

In designing for enhanced *Composition,* the concern is to provide (or retain) environments that have pro-life content, meaning, and significance. Key considerations include the material, form, style, purpose, and implications of any human influence or artifact. The six criteria for good design set forth by Victor Papanek (1971) provide examples of what might be involved. Papanek's criteria, which he calls the "function complex" for design, are the following:

Method: The designed object should be produced by the most appropriate tools, processes, and materials, and should reflect honest and efficient use of materials.

Use: The object should do well what it is supposed to do (and without harmful side effects).

Need: The object should serve *real* human needs.

Telesis: The object should reflect the times and fit in with the culture in which it is to be used.

Association: The object should arouse feelings, ideas, and values that enrich the life of the user.

Aesthetics: The object should provide delight, beauty, excitement.

To this list Papanek also appends *elegance*—meaning a design solution "which reduces the complex to the simple" (p. 41), and which thus can serve as an added source of intellectual and aesthetic pleasure. Papanek also points out that good design requires fulfilling *all six* of his main criteria.

It should be clear that environmental constructions or other influences that did indeed meet these requirements would involve many key aspects of good Composition. Among these I might list connoting safety, pleasure, health, and satisfaction of desires; containing pleasing colors, forms, textures, smells, and other sensual elements (which of course can be considered independently of their effects on Complexity); eliciting pleasant associations or linking to pleasant cognitive and cultural networks; and embodying an imaginative solution to a problem. Other Compositional criteria might be provision of a sense of place, construction on a human scale, and giving a sense of individuality or perhaps privacy.

In looking over the various criteria for good design that are suggested by architects, planners, and design commentators, the role of such variables clearly stands out. To cite just a few examples: Designing for pleasant input to all the senses is stressed by architects such as Rasmussen (1962) and Neutra (1969) as well as social science observers such as Hall (1966). Giving advice on site planning, Kevin Lynch (1971) makes numerous suggestions about how to increase the pleasantness of the content of an environment, such as designing so that interesting visible activities by people will be encouraged, thus providing pleasure for participants and spectators alike (see also Lynch, 1976). Landscape architect Lawrence Halprin (1972) advises attention to detail (even doorknobs) as well as to overall layout and form, and—as mentioned earlier—notes the importance of making environments fun. Some of the fountains he has designed, for instance, combine beautiful visual display with an invitation to romp and get wet. Architects Chermayeff and Alexander (1963) carefully describe ways of pleasantly designing for privacy through the use of multiple interior courtyards in clustered houses. Finally, Burton Litton and his associates (1974) note that human artifacts often brutally intrude on natural scenery; they suggest designing for minimal contrast in natural areas, as by using local natural materials, employing flowing lines to match natural contours, and so on.

However, the most central aspect of environmental influence on Composition is probably the type of use to which the environment is put rather than the specific style of the construction. In short, it is what is being built—hospital, prison, park, ICBM, or whatever—that is centrally important to determining the experienced content, meaning, and significance of the specific environment or object. Compositional design variables might thus be said to operate on two levels: the level of the *category* of thing that is being designed, and the level of the *style* or specific content of the finished product. Thus, a well-designed prison might still be unpleasant just because it is a prison (notwithstanding that a hideous, uncomfortable one would be worse). It is here that Papanek's need criterion comes into play. Pleasant, pro-life environmental influences on Composition will involve constructing things designed to meet real human needs. Presumably examples of this sort of environmental design would include environmental content such as numerous public parks, places designed for friendly communal contact, schools designed for intrinsic motivation and cooperation, factories that produced items designed according to Papanek's full set of criteria, and so on.

Many more examples of design criteria for pleasing content, significance, and meaning could of course be offered, but it should be clear that Composition covers a lot of territory. Included are important aspects of environmental aesthetics (independent of Complexity; see Chapters 2 and 3); environmental impacts on feelings of safety, privacy, individuality, hope for the future, and virtually any other sentiment arising from perceived *implications* of the environment (compare Berlyne's ecological variables, discussed in Chapter 2); the whole domain of associations aroused by an environment; and indeed the very meaning (including uses, functions, purposes, and so on) of environments. Designing for pro-life Composition—or more precisely, designing environments that have an enhancing effect on the Composition of all users' experience—is clearly a difficult and complex task.

Comprehension

As noted in past chapters, both psychologists and design professionals (for example, Kaplan, 1973; Lynch, 1960; Carr, 1967) have postulated a basic human need for *understanding and clarity* in relation to the environment. Although the prerequisites for satisfying this need may of course at times conflict with human requirements for optimal Complexity (for example, mystery, ambiguity, and intricacy), it is clear that some degree of legibility is required for usable, not to mention enjoyable, environments. Carrying this theme one step further, it might be added that an environment should be even more enjoyable if it is not only itself reasonably legible but also in some way facilitates deeper understanding about things extending beyond the immediate vicinity.

Turning first to the issue of an environment's own legibility, it may be recalled from the appendix to Chapter 3 that research into mental mapping has uncovered considerable information about how people usually form functional representations of their everyday environments. Kevin Lynch (1960), notwithstanding possible criticisms of his heavy reliance on sketch maps for inferences (see Wood, 1973), still stands out as one of the most provocative and insightful experts on what contributes to high environmental clarity. He has also displayed a humanistic concern with making cities and other large-scale environments more livable and enjoyable. Based both on his research and on his intuitions as an environmental designer, Lynch (1960, pp. 105–108) has suggested ten general design guidelines for increasing the imageability (tendency to evoke vivid images) and the consequent delightfulness of urban areas or other large-scale environmental regions. In summary, they are:

1. Singularity: uniqueness, "figure-background clarity," high contrast, vividness, etc. (for example, a lone skyscraper amid low surrounding buildings)

2. Form simplicity: simple geometric forms such as straight lines and rectangular grids (which facilitate accurate comprehension and memory of areas since people tend cognitively to simplify and regularize anyway)

3. Continuity: "continuance of edge or surface"; clustering; repetition of similar forms, patterns, or materials; other qualities that bestow a "single identity" to "a complex physical reality"

4. Dominance: "dominance of one part over others by means of size, intensity, or interest, resulting in the reading of the whole as a principal feature with an associated cluster (as in the 'Harvard Square area')"

5. Clarity of joint: highly visible and clear nodes (for example, intersections) and interconnections (as between a subway station and the overhead street)

6. Directional differentiation: "asymmetries, gradients, and radial references which differentiate one end . . . or one side from another" (for example, a street going up a hill or having the two sides painted different colors)

7. Visual scope: "qualities which increase the range and penetration of vision" (for example, vistas, glass walls, open spaces)

8. Motion awareness: visual or kinesthetic cues to actual or potential motion (for example, salient slopes and curves)

9. Time series: environmental configurations that provide interesting temporal sequences of experiences (for example, a series of landmarks that together present a spatially rhythmic impression)

10. Names and meanings: "non-physical characteristics which may enhance the imageability of an element" (for example, sequential lettering or numbering of street names; meanings or associations that serve to reinforce the images evoked by the physical form).

Lynch also urged that guidelines such as these be used collectively and in relation to one another for optimal effects on imageability. He did point out, however, that whether people actually form vivid images of their surroundings depends on their own effort and sensitivity, as well as on the structure of the environment.

Environmental psychologists and designers alike, including writers such as Sommer, Carr, and Lynch himself, have gone on to suggest that people's environmental sensitivity can be enhanced both by socially initiated programs and by appropriate environmental design. An example of the first approach is Lynch's (1971) idea that user self-observation studies not only would provide feedback to designers but also would increase the users' environmental consciousness. Stephen Carr's (1967) design criteria seem especially enlightening as guides to the second approach. As I have interpreted and selected them, the gist of Carr's ideas is as follows:

1. Design for *exposure* to a wide variety of settings. Approaches might include concentration of mixed uses in a small space (à la Jane Jacobs's suggestion) or provision of readily available and inexpensive public transportation.

2. Design for ease and interestingness of *exploring* the environment. The "right level . . . of novelty and complexity to stimulate curiosity plus sufficient openness and connectedness to allow easy access" are the key design considerations for this.

3. Design for *clear mental representations* of the environment. All of Lynch's guidelines for increasing legibility would presumably apply here, and Carr offers other interesting suggestions (such as provision of strategically placed "information boards" programmed to indicate, say, "the quickest or most scenic route to any destination").[16]

4. Design in ways that emphasize *"the special character of places."* According to Carr, this both adds to the meaningfulness and attractiveness of places and helps to increase diversity. Interest in further understanding the environment should also be enhanced.

5. Design so that the environment is open to *manipulation* by people. (This point is at least as relevant to the enhancement of Competence as of Comprehension, but it is worth noting here that an environment open to individual or small-group personalization—a "soft" environment in Sommer's terminology—is also one that is likely to encourage environmental sensitivity and interest.)

6. Design to facilitate *"contrast, comparison, and the formation of new mental connections."* Carr suggests techniques such as providing al-

ternate routes of very disparate character linking the same places, and putting different types of settings next to each other. The net effect would again be to make the environment more interesting and to encourage environmental insight through comparison.

The suggestions presented above by Lynch and Carr are intended only as examples of considerations in environmental design that would contribute to enhanced Comprehension. Obviously, in a complete design effort along pro-life lines, such criteria would have to be integrated with—and perhaps in some cases balanced against—criteria for optimizing the other components.

Comparison

Comparison is the way that experience relates to or changes adaptation or comparison levels (ALs and CLs). The chief concerns of pro-life environmental design with respect to this variable would be (1) to decrease psychological adaptation (habituation) both to pleasant aspects of the environment and to ameliorable unpleasant aspects; (2) to encourage awareness of environmental alternatives (and hence to raise CLs); (3) to provide experiences as much above people's environmental CLs as possible; and (4) to facilitate psychological adaptation to truly uncorrectable environmental problems (if there are any totally uncorrectable ones). In past chapters we explored certain cognitive techniques for achieving such goals, but what can environmental design itself do?

First, decreasing habituation to pleasant aspects of the environment might be accomplished through such design approaches as providing many different types of vantage points or types of contact with the pleasant features. Enable people to obtain different views and different types of views of pleasant features, such as lakes, mountains, parks, outdoor sculptures, well-designed buildings, and so forth. Provide for different types of contacts as well—for example, easy access to climbing as well as looking at mountains, trees, sculptures, buildings, and so on. Also, provide so many good things in the environment that people do not have to rely on a small number of places or features for their pleasure. If there are a large number and variety of amenities, then when frequented ones begin to seem ordinary, people will have easy access to many others. And of course try to make each place or thing so rich and delightful that people will be slow to tire of it—or, even better, will grow fonder of it as their familiarity increases, as in the case of most great works of art. Still another approach to inhibiting psychological adaptation to good things is to frequently introduce small changes. Peter Smith (1973) has advocated this tactic and provided interesting everyday examples such as changes in shop windows. He also suggested such techniques as varying patterns of lighting and encouraging highly varied activities (festivals, protests, and so on). It is likely that environments that inherently contain much activity and change, such as busy shopping areas or mass transit lines and terminals, discourage psychological adaptation. And they can of course be deliberately designed to be pleasant and interesting places as well as active ones. This would imply that one approach could be to think of types of things to which people do not easily become habituated and then to design as many pleasant versions of these things as the environment could take. Finally, if people can themselves easily modify parts of the environment to suit their tastes, habituation should be decreased (and Competence enhanced as well).

The strategies for decreasing habituation to *unpleasant* but changeable environmental features might be a little different, however. It must be remembered that people will generally be at least somewhat motivated to reduce their psychological adaptation to pleasant things, since that increases enjoyment. Hence, for example, designers might be able to count on people to take time to try out new views of, or contacts with, an amenity. Not so for eyesores or other annoyances—most of us are normally motivated to tune them out unless some ulterior interest is involved (thinking of buying the property, using a new cognitive set, or the like). So what can be done? Just leaving the annoyances alone will not do much good, and deliberately introducing small changes in them to make sure they are noticed seems a rather unlikely design strategy for those who usually have control over such things as overhead telephone lines, slum buildings, hard architecture, oil storage tanks, or polluting factories.

Rather, the best general design strategy for decreasing psychological adaptation to eyesores or other problems is probably something like that suggested by Robert Sommer (1972, 1974). Basically, this strategy is to fight environmental numbness by exposing people to the high contrast between nice and lousy environmental features (for example, furnishing a slum with a few pleasant little parks or exciting outdoor sculptures) and by allowing and encouraging people to modify their own personal or local environments to suit their tastes (as noted above, this is also a good technique for decreasing habituation even to good environments). Fundamental to this type of strategy is Sommer's dictum that the only real cure for habituation to problems is awareness that something can actually be done about them. According to Sommer, simply knowing that a problem exists will not block psychological adaptation to it unless that knowledge is accompanied by the belief that one can take action to solve the problem. Hence, the same strategies of environmental design that will contribute to enhanced Competence (see below) should have the salutary side effect of helping to decrease habituation to solvable environmental problems. Additionally, each good thing done to the environment may help make the bad things stand out.

Rather parsimoniously, these same design strategies of giving people a sense of control over their environment and introducing good environmental examples wherever possible are precisely what is needed to satisfy the Comparison goal of elevating people's CLs (comparison levels) for environmental quality. As pointed out in Chapter 3, CLs tend to rise as a function of the *salience* of actual or potential outcomes. Salience, in turn, is positively related to feelings of control over the outcomes as well as to other factors (such as frequency of experience) that make an outcome easy to call to mind. If good environmental design examples are easy to call to mind *and* if people gain a sense of environmental competence by experience with reasonably malleable and responsive environments, these individuals' CLs should rise. The better the environmental examples to which people are exposed and the greater the sense of environmental competence they develop, the higher their CLs should go. In this way, for example, live "ecocommunities" (or even just ecologically benign new towns), together with dissemination of the story of how they came about, could further the widespread rise in CL that might go along with ecological consciousness development.

Of course, as indicated by the third Comparison goal, the idea is not simply to raise CLs but also to keep environmental outcomes well above the level of subjective neutrality. This naturally gets tougher as comparison levels rise, and we thus seem faced with a spiral of rising demands. As long as the demands are in a pro-life direction, however, people would be striving for a constantly more pleasant and ecologically sane environment. The designer's best strategy for keeping such people happy would seem to be to help them create ever-improving surroundings. This may sound a bit flippant, but it *is* the best way to provide experiences as much above people's environmental CLs as possible. If a point of diminishing returns began to set in—as might occur for reasons of ecological or technological limits—the best strategy would probably be to follow the procedures discussed earlier for decreasing habituation to pleasant environments.

Finally, if any genuinely intractable environmental problems are lying around, what can be done through design to help people become habituated to them? Examples of appropriate techniques might be camouflage, drawing people away from the problem with attractions elsewhere, blocking off public information about the problem, and trying to avoid any influence that would heighten contrast between the problem and its surroundings or that would involve attention-grabbing change in the problem. Unfortunately, many of these devices now seem used to promote habituation to environmental problems that *are* tractable (given certain social and economic changes, that is). Although perhaps some elements of nature (for example, climates or natural hazards) may presently be relatively unmalleable for human beings, it is hard to think of any human-induced environmental problem about which we can do nothing; and the natural problems are usually not the sort for which one could easily *design* habituation. Hence, the design techniques mentioned in this paragraph would generally be either low in Compatibility or impracticable.

Competence

The processes and products of environmental design are obviously powerful forces in determining the degree to which people experience feelings of personal (and collective) control and effectiveness in dealing with their environments. There are at least two major ways that environmental design can enhance Competence. First, the *actual environment* can facilitate people's execution of their existing Plans and encourage them to develop new pro-life Plans. Second, the *processes* of environmental design and construction can be carried out in ways that favor the development of enhanced Competence for all environmental users.

Let us turn first to the possible role of the actual environment. It should be clear that environmental design that helps enhance Comprehension will also tend to facilitate the execution of existing Plans. This was a major argument set forth by Carr (1967) and Lynch (1960) in defense of their proposals for increasing environmental legibility. You have to know where things are to use them. However, another of Carr's design criteria—not included in our Comprehension guidelines—was to "adapt the form of environmental settings to facilitate the predominant plans being executed within them" (Carr, 1967, p. 223). While admittedly rather general, this criterion captures a major intent of Carr's other suggestions and, if followed, it should certainly help people to feel more competent. As Carr stated, the way to achieve this sort of Plan-facilitating environment would be to discover exactly what people were trying to do (and in what order of preference), and then design to make these things as easy as possible.

Jacobs's (1961) generators of diversity (discussed under Complexity) may thus also constitute a design suggestion for aiding Competence by making it possible for people to execute many different types of Plans within a small space. This is a design policy favored by many architects and planners, including Carr. Besides advocating contiguous mixed uses, however, many writers have called for a generally more responsive environment—one that people can readily *shape* to fit their desires or Plans. Although it does not offer much acoustic flexibility, the traditional Japanese house with its movable walls and multi-use furnishings is frequently cited as an example (see, for example, Nelson, 1965). The overall goal, as expressed both by behavioral scientists and by environmental design professionals, is to design for maximum "environmental capabilities" (Altman, 1975) or to "maximize the possibilities" for users (Perin, 1974).

However, it is important to carry the theme of environmental aids to Competence a step further and ask what the environment might do to aid the development of skills and the generation of new and better Plans. This was in fact another major theme in Carr's (1967) rationale for such design suggestions as facilitating exposure to new places and encouraging exploration and manipulation. But besides making Plan execution *easy*, it may also be advisable to introduce enough challenge and potential difficulty to help people develop their coping abilities. Van Rensselaer Potter (1971) has even argued that an "optimum environment" would deliver an "optimum stress" level—one that facilitated the development of continually improving adaptive responses. The principal elements in environmental stimulation of new skills and Plans would seem to be those already mentioned for facilitating the execution of diverse existing Plans (reasonable legibility, concentrated diversity, responsiveness and flexibility, and so on) *combined with* (1) graduated stimuli to higher levels of Complexity, (2) a large pool of resources, and (3) the encouragement of exploration and creative manipulation of the environment. While most of these requirements can be designed *for* users, the encouragement of creative environmental manipulation may entail changes in the underlying design and construction processes such that they would have to be done *with* or even *by* users (compare Porteous, 1977).

Such an emphasis on how design *processes* can enhance Competence raises issues that can be sidestepped when only the effects of the finished product are considered (as above). Specifically, to provide the greatest opportunity for enhancing Competence through environmental design, it is necessary to regard users not simply as collectors, selectors, or even interactors with respect to the environment, but rather as potential environmental *creators* (compare Sommer, 1972; Kurtz, 1973). On the simplest level, this could mean just involving potential users directly in the initial stages of determining the requirements for an environmental design (usually referred to by architects as the "program"). Limited time and resources for social or psychological assessment often preclude including potential users in this phase, but it is increasingly recognized that such efforts not only can produce better designs but also can enliven users' concern and sensitivity to their environments (for example, Lynch, 1971; Sommer, 1972). If it genuinely affected the final design, it also seems likely that even this minimal sort of involvement by users in the design process would enhance their overall sense of power to influence their environments. Indeed, even in the case of "advocacy planning" (see, for example, Anderson, 1968)—whereby the interests of a low-power group are represented by a professional planner serving as advocate for the group—an enhanced sense of competence can arise (but is often illusory; see, for example, Goodman, 1971).

A more radical proposal is to involve potential users in the design processes more directly. Martin Kuenzlen (1972), for example, has called for "*participatory* planning," and pro-life activists like Robert Goodman (1971) have even recommended "guerrilla architecture" (for example, creating "squatter environments" in abandoned buildings or lots) and other forms of direct action outside the usual Establishment channels. Actually, as observers like Goodman and Kuenzlen see it, there is more than one advantage to taking direct action rather than simply begging (or even demanding) that Establishment powers respond to one's needs. First, direct action is a way of achieving real environmental change quickly; and such change, even if relatively small, can help to increase the felt competence and environmental awareness of the activists and the observing public. Second, direct action is often effective in eliciting positive Establishment response. Goodman (1971), for example, has cited cases where creating squatter environments has actually produced beneficial changes in housing policy. As Goodman sees it, guerrilla architecture tends to force officials either to acquiesce to the demands or to reveal "the oppressive nature of their control" (as in the case of Berkeley's People's Park). The first result increases the activists' sense of competence; the second can create public pressures for social and political change.

On a less radical level as well, active participation in designing and directly influencing the environment has many beneficial effects for Competence. Experiences provided by groups' constructing intentional communities (communes), by tenants' buying and renovating their buildings (see, for example, Kurtz, 1973; Jacobs, 1961), by local residents' helping to design and build their own recreation areas (see note 12, Chapter 2), or even by residents' painting their own rooms or helping to construct communal sculptures (see Farallones, 1971; Sommer, 1975) all help people gain a sense of effectiveness and control in being able to make pleasant changes in their surroundings. As Sommer (1974) put it, "small tangible goals" and resulting self-induced "improvements in a person's life situation" are extremely important paths to continued efforts to humanize the environment. Just as such efforts can contribute to rising CLs, they can also serve as a continuing source of rising Competence.

To conclude this section, however, two important provisos should be added about environmental design as a path to enhanced Competence. First, no matter how high the level of environmental richness and flexibility and no matter how much opportunity for involvement in design processes, people will benefit in their level of Competence only if they are successful in effectively using the environmental possibilities or in actually achieving environmental designs more to their liking. It is clear that such success will often require professional aid and special design and environmental education (see, for example, Altman, 1975; Sommer, 1972). Second, only when people are able to join actively and share power in the design of their social, economic, and political environments will they be able to gain control over their physical ones. (See Chapter 7.)

Complications

Complications was originally introduced as referring to the experience of strain or difficulty in the attempted execution of a cognitive or behavioral Plan. When applied as an environmental design criterion, Complications may be best conceived of as relating to constraints imposed by (1) the feasibility of a project, (2) the material and psychological costs entailed in producing an environmental change, and (3) the potential difficulties in achieving appropriate use of the actualized design. Before proceeding to a brief examination of each of these influences on Complications, let us again note that in principle any alleged complication might optimistically be regarded as simply a *challenge*. To whatever extent this is so (and to the extent the challenge is eventually overcome), problems that induce a high level of Complications might ultimately serve to enhance the other components (especially Competence, Comprehension, and Complexity). Essentially, then, an environmental design would rank unacceptably high on the criterion of Complications only if it entailed difficulties that would be truly insurmountable or that would require effort that interfered with more valuable endeavors.

Feasibility constraints. Quite obviously, regardless of how wonderful a proposed environmental design would be, it will rank unacceptably high on Complications if the material, technology, or skill needed to build it are unobtainable. We should be careful, however, to distinguish between real impossibility (for example, a time-travel machine) and mere difficulty. Of course, when a time limit is specified, such as "within the next two years," some designs that ultimately may only be difficult to achieve (for example, nuclear fusion as a major source of peaceful energy) might be forced into the "impossible" category. An additional problem in definition can arise when the political or economic context of design decisions is taken into account. Something, such as pleasant and efficient mass transit, may be perfectly feasible technologically but made nearly impossible by the economic or political systems. In such cases, it would be necessary to examine the feasibility (and the overall desirability) of changing the relevant economic, political, or perhaps cultural constraints on the project's realization. Assuming the desirability of the economic or political changes, the question would then become whether they are really impossible or just difficult.

Cost constraints.   Basically, feasibility constraints refer to the temporarily or permanently impossible, while cost constraints refer to the possible but difficult or dangerous. Environmental design projects that would require excessive expenditure of effort or resources (hence cutting into alternative endeavors deemed more valuable), or that would produce harmful side effects, would thus rank high on costs. A key question here is "cost to whom?" From the point of view of Compatibility, the main issue should be cost to virtually all people and other sentient creatures, so that questions of pollution, resource depletion, ecosystem disruption, and unequally spread hardship would loom large. Considering the way the environment has typically been abused in our society, it would appear that cost to the rich and powerful has been a more potent consideration than cost to the public at large or to future generations (and certainly than cost to other societies or to nonhuman creatures). When "economic" or "political" infeasibility is raised as an objection to some (usually pro-life) environmental proposal, usually what is meant is that the cost to powerful corporations or other wealthy minorities would be increased (or, alternatively, that these powerful minorities would simply force the cost onto the middle class). As Philip Slater (1974, pp. 140–141) has forcefully put it:

> It is said, for example, that we cannot afford better schools, communities, health care, and so on. But what we can afford least of all is to allow some people to become very rich. This is our most expensive social program: To make it possible, we have spent billions upon billions of dollars, allowed our air and water to become polluted, our environment to become ugly, our cities to deteriorate, our health care to become third-rate, created untold poverty, misery, sickness, suffering, chaos, disorder, and mass murder. We nonetheless managed to afford it.

It would thus seem imperative, for pro-life design, to redefine what is considered a "cost" and what is commonly experienced as Complications with respect to environmental design. Negative "externalities," as they are called by economists—the environmental degradation and other costs imposed on the public by environmentally and biologically damaging products and production techniques, but not included in the direct price of the product—are more and more being *talked* about as real costs; but water, air, land, and our bodies continue to pay for these side effects of selfish profit seeking by the few and of apathy by the many. Cost constraints, as a criterion for pro-life environmental design, would thrust such externalities into the spotlight, would apply much higher standards of reducing the ill effects (including the long-term ill effects) of environmental modifications, and would apply equal standards to everyone rather than favoring the rich.

User difficulties.   Finally, an environmental design might offer excellent potentials that simply exceed the users' abilities or that conflict with users' current dispositions, motivations, or tastes. For example, classrooms designed for egalitarian cooperative interactions and the development of intrinsic motivation might be experienced as highly stressful by teachers (or students) accustomed to traditional, authoritarian educational procedures (see, for example, Gump, 1975; Sommer, 1974). Of course, from a pro-life perspective, it might be argued that this particular source of Complications should be treated more as a challenge than as a deterrent to open classroom design. Nevertheless, it is clearly very important to consider the current characteristics of users as well as their potentials. The key would seem to be to design for growth, in the sense of providing aids to satisfying basic human needs and to educating people to function at a higher level of ecological insight, aesthetic and environmental sensitivity, and cooperative social concern. An environmental design that assumed that these traits existed in users but that did not contribute to their development might be as unusable and unappreciated as a slide rule would be to a chipmunk. Some high-Compatibility improvements in environmental design, then, might require either accompanying advances in the education of users or some sort of built-in aid to appropriate use (perhaps, for example, in the way many toy building sets contain inherent patterns of reinforcement that gradually lead children to more intricate and creative uses). Obviously, designers and design critics can play major roles in reducing Complications attendant upon good but unusual innovations by helping to educate potential users and by designing so that they will be tempted to discover the possibilities for themselves.

Comportment

Comportment has been our term for any pattern of behavior arising from an experience. It has also been pointed out that Comportment forms complex feedback relations with the components directly relating to the quality of experience (Complexity, Composition, and so on). Behavioral Plans arise from information processing, and their execution in turn affects the content and style of information processing. The environment, of course, is a major ingredient in the whole interplay. Comportment as a pro-life design criterion refers, then, to creating environments that encourage patterns of overt behavior that tend to enhance all the components of experience both for the actor and for other people. If we can go back to Churchill's dictum, we might say the idea is to shape our buildings (and other environmental artifacts) so that they will shape our behavior in ways that move everyone's experience toward optimal Complexity, Comprehension, Competence, and so forth (all consistent with the requirements of Compatibility, of course!). Although I certainly do not want to make any claims for simple architectural—or even environmental—determinism, I believe that some guidelines could be established for designing environments that would encourage pro-life behavior.

At the beginning of this chapter, several forces leading to environment/behavior congruence were discussed. Ignoring for the moment the various systemic complexities and social forces involved, we may recall that physical contingencies of reinforcement constituted a major category. The power of the physical environment to shape behavior was exemplified by such instances as pleasant, wide sidewalks encouraging walking, and properly arranged chairs encouraging talking. All that is required for generating a list of specific design suggestions based on the criterion of pro-life Comportment is to determine what specific types of behavior contribute to optimizing Compatibility and the other components in our scheme and what specific types of environmental design differentially elicit or reinforce those types of behavior. A few examples of relevant patterns of behavior would be friendly communication, cooperative play, collective and individual production of art works or other environmental amenities, behavior that increases the overall opportunity for others to execute diverse pro-life Plans (for example, increasing the sources of pleasant diversity in a neighborhood, as by opening up a good restaurant in an area that lacked one), contributing time or materials to community parks, and helping to pass on skills in environmental improvement to children or other people.

To design for such behavior patterns, especially in the context of a highly individualistic and competitive culture such as ours, is not necessarily easy. Nonetheless, many designers with pro-life values have offered both encouragement and suggestions for the task. Lawrence Halprin (1969, 1972), for instance, has called for urban environments that invite people to participate and become enjoyably involved in their surroundings. His designs for fountains and pedestrian-oriented public streets vividly reflect this concern and seem actually to elicit such behavior. As discussed earlier, architects Chermayeff and Tzonis (1971) have been especially concerned to design for community-fostering behavior. Their ideas for concentrated mixed uses and pedestrian-oriented sociopetal spaces (involving nodes in pleasantly designed mass transit systems) show one way the environment might be shaped to facilitate this. And the communities of Tapiola, Finland, and perhaps Reston, Virginia (see, for example, Whyte, 1968; Von Eckardt, 1967; von Hertzen and Spreiregen, 1973), show how it is possible to foster community spirit through appropriate design. As a final example, consider open classroom designs. Although, as Paul Gump (1975) has pointed out, open classrooms do not necessarily lead to nontraditional teaching techniques, it is clear that easy collective shaping of one's environment, sitting in circular arrangements that encourage equality and communication, and being able to choose among a variety of activities and facilities all create an environment far more conducive to cooperation and intrinsically motivated behavior than does the traditional classroom.

Unfortunately, there is no algorithm for generating designs that foster pro-life behavior. Indeed, while sociopetal spaces, soft architecture, pedestrian amenities, and all the rest, will certainly help, the best that even the most imaginative pro-life environmental design is likely to do is to *set the stage* for activities that will enhance life.

Summary Examples

To conclude, let us briefly apply the set of eight criteria to the evaluation of an anti-life type of designed environment and to a pro-life type. So that we can end on an upbeat note, the anti-life example will be considered first.

The traditional maximum security prison.   As analyzed by observers such as Sommer (1974, 1976) and Sykes (1958), there are few human-made environments any "harder" (in Sommer's sense) than the conventional maximum security prison with its barren cells, iron bars, isolation chambers, acres of bare concrete, and nearly universal depersonalization. But, just for "fun," let's see how this sort of place stacks up with respect to the criteria we have been examining:

Complexity
> provides extremely sub-optimal levels of variety; is low on Compatibility for sources of strong arousal that are present (for example, attacks or threats from other inmates; overcrowding).

Composition
> is associated with extremely negative meanings (incarceration, punishment, and so on); involves drab and harsh architecture and sparse interior decoration; has many threats and other unpleasant implications built into the everyday physical and social environment; may border on outright torture in some cases (see Footlick, 1976); fails miserably on Papanek's (1971) criteria of use, need, association, and aesthetics.

Comprehension
> may be relatively clear and understandable, but separates users (especially inmates) sharply from outside world; limits information; prohibits exploration; and (because of factors ranging from overcrowded cells and lights-out policies to general demoralization) can discourage reading and other Comprehension-boosting activities; may, however, help to increase insight into how to commit crimes (low-Compatibility knowledge).

Comparison
> presents situation usually well below CL; encourages numbness to environmental situation, but numbness and lack of change may help to make this situation easier to bear.

Competence
> severely limits possible Plans that can be executed; provides very little opportunity to manipulate environment and gain pro-life skills (although may facilitate development of criminal, aggressive, and other low-Compatibility abilities); fails to involve users in design decisions.

Complications
> exacts high indirect costs (even on society at large) through brutalization of both inmates and caretakers; creates grave difficulties in satisfying virtually all higher-level pro-life goals, including even rehabilitation of inmates.

Comportment
> encourages aggressive, antisocial behavior by inmates and often guards (see

Zimbardo et al., 1975); fails to facilitate cooperation and other pro-life behavior patterns.

Compatibility

egregiously fails to promote happiness for anyone except perhaps sadists, masochists, and bitter victims of crime; discourages cooperation and community, except perhaps on a small and antisocietal scale; discourages growth toward ecological consciousness because of all these other effects.

Admittedly, not all prisons—even maximum security ones—in our society come out so badly. Sommer (1974) points out that *some* prisons do indeed allow inmates to decorate their rooms with everything from rugs and TV sets to tropical fish; one prison he mentions is even made largely out of glass. But the haunting question remains, in view of the current tendency toward hardened public environments of all sorts (again, see Sommer, 1974), whether the prison environment analyzed above is or is not high on Papanek's criterion of "telesis"—a good fit with the culture and times.

The adventure playground.   Here is a pro-life type of environment at last—and this claim can even be backed up with a variety of behavioral research as well as subjective observation (see references below). Essentially, an adventure playground is simply a recreation area for children in which they have access to a variety of movable, manipulable materials (as well as some permanent structures) and in which they are free to create things for themselves. As Lady Allen of Hurtwood (1968, p. 55) put it, "Adventure playgrounds are places where children of all ages can develop their own ideas of play." As developed in the 1930s and 1940s by the Danish architect C. Th. Sørensen (see Allen of Hurtwood, 1968), the adventure playground was primarily designed around the use of junk (old car parts, tires, pieces of scrap wood, and so on); and that is the image that persists today. Although the use of often unsightly second-hand junk material is indeed the most common way of outfitting adventure playgrounds (perhaps in part because they usually seem to be constructed for children at lower socioeconomic levels), there is no inherent reason that the basic principles of the adventure playground could not be actualized by the use of the most exquisitely beautiful and expensive metals, plastics, and fine woods and cloth imaginable. But this sort of concern seems to be mainly a problem for adults; to most children, playing in a junkyard or well-strewn vacant lot is just fine. Adventure playgrounds, often supervised by adults, carry the joys of junk into the world of publicly sponsored fun. The simplicity of the whole thing, combined with its increasingly recognized accomplishments, may well make this design a candidate for Papanek's highest design accolade: elegance. Now, for some real fun, let us evaluate the adventure playground according to our eight components:

Complexity

provides a wide range of possibilities for experience in all sense modalities; allows for individual differences; encourages imaginative play (thus facilitating enhancement of Complexity via cognitive techniques as well as physical input); concentrates great diversity in a small space, and manipulability allows for almost unlimited increase in environmental complexity (but under players' control).

Composition

as noted, presents a possible problem here in terms of untidiness—does not usually have the overall pleasing form of many "contemporary" style playgrounds (see Hayward et al., 1974); but provides marvelous opportunity for enhanced meaning in play activities; connotes freedom to child; satisfies Papanek's criteria of method, use, need, association (for children at least), and even aesthetics at least potentially; plus contains elegance in the underlying concept.

Comprehension

facilitates increased understanding about a variety of areas—including play possibilities, environmental design, social relations, and anything else that derives from highly imaginative play with diverse materials; may require considerable exploration to understand its potentials, but has built-in rewards for learning how to use it (and models in the form of older children or adults are usually available); meets Carr's criteria very well (see Comprehension section earlier in this chapter).

Comparison

discourages habituation to pleasant aspects by providing constant change and opportunity for self-directed environmental manipulation; similarly can encourage awareness of environmental alternatives and help to raise CL by increasing sense of control over outcomes.

Competence

facilitates execution of a wide variety of Plans, both group and individual (see, for example, R. Moore, 1974; Hayward et al., 1974); encourages development of new skills by promoting interaction with intrinsically interesting materials and tasks and by facilitating learning from other people; allows users to have a hand in designing and constructing actual environments.

Complications

is a physically feasible, low-cost type of playground, but may face social or political opposition because of unsightliness and mistaken impressions of danger (accident rates actually tend to be low relative to other playground types and other play areas—see Whyte, 1968; Allen of Hurtwood, 1968); produces some need to replenish movable materials, but this is usually easy and inexpensive; contains some materials that are difficult to use, but this tends to be more a challenge than a contributor to an unpleasant level of Complications.

Comportment

seems to encourage cooperative play and much friendly communication on a wide variety of topics (see, for example, Hayward et al., 1974; R. Moore, 1974); encourages creative play activities; can aid in fostering community activities and direct involvement of adults in pro-life behavior (see R. Moore, 1974).

Compatibility

promotes happiness, fun, cooperation, community, and probably some growth in recognition of interrelationships and potentials of natural materials; reuses otherwise wasted materials (and might thereby also encourage users and observers of the playground to do this themselves); possibly can serve as a model for increasing people's pro-life interactions with their total environment.

Well, just as the evaluation of prisons made them sound pretty terrible, this little whirlwind tour through the world of adventure playgrounds made *them* sound pretty good. I think they are great in principle, even though some poor examples will probably turn up (just as there are some reasonably soft prisons). It is the underlying concept that I am really evaluating, however; and it does indeed look good by the criteria discussed in this chapter. In fact, it is this same underlying concept of providing freedom, manipulability, flexibility, communal and cooperative involvement among users, and an environment generally promoting fun in life that seems to underlie many other apparently delightful places. Open classrooms in a free school setting are another case in point, for example. Indeed, the California design group calling themselves Farallones have published a marvelous "scrapbook" (1971) in which they give detailed examples of how students can join in the process of reshaping their classrooms and playgrounds (and presumably homes) by using readily available, cheap materials. That just reading about this sort of thing can generate excitement is a good sign that Sommer (1974) was on the right track when he suggested that personal involvement in changing one's own environment could help to trigger Establishment-shattering pro-life social change. Today, a sandlot adventure playground; tomorrow, an "adventure world"?

This chapter has deliberately emphasized the *physical* environment in its discussion of issues in pro-life design. Even so, no effort has been made to detail exactly what an entire pro-life human environment would be like (adventure playgrounds and other examples cited in the account of design criteria are really only hints and bits and pieces). A pro-life environment would have to arise within the context of a pro-life society; it would be futile to try to describe a specific physical picture without a full account of the supporting cultural context. It is the integrated whole of culture/environment that is really the issue if we are to have the Good Life—or even *a* good collective life. Hence, it is time to pack up our components and head for that big question in the sky that has been waiting for us throughout this book: What is the *full* package of ingredients needed for a workable "utopia," and how can we at least narrow the gap between where we are and where such a vision would lead us? This question will be our concern in the next chapter.

NOTES

1. For general reviews of proxemics, see, for example, Altman (1975), Ball (1973), Pederson and Shears (1973), Watson (1972), Hall (1959, 1966), and Sommer (1969). See also Edney (1976) for an interesting brief review (and provocative theory) of human "territoriality."
2. See, for example, Fried and Gleicher (1961), Michelson (1970), and Brower and Williamson (1974).
3. Designers themselves tend to define "design" in terms of imposing or planning for *order* (see, for example, Bevlin, 1970; Papanek, 1971). I am using the term in the somewhat broader sense of any deliberate environmental modification; and I am lumping together the processes of planning or figuring out the modification and the actual execution or construction of it. I hope the reader will excuse this somewhat amorphous usage and bear in mind that our concern in this discussion is the whole domain of deliberate human modification of the environment, including everything from the cultural context in which design decisions are made to the unforeseen side effects of particular types of environmental alterations.
4. For general accounts of the effects of noise on human beings, see, for example, Baron (1970), Glass and Singer (1972), and especially Kryter (1970). Because of possible confounding factors, it is difficult to establish clear evidence that

long-term exposure to low- or moderate-intensity noise is by itself a cause of human psychological or physiological problems. However, a study by Cohen, Glass, and Singer (1973) has uncovered an intriguing relation between long-term exposure to traffic noises and reading difficulty for young children. (This effect seemed to be mediated by decrements in the children's auditory discrimination—in this case apparently the result of processes of psychological adaptation, not physiological impairment.) It also seems clear that even noise of low intensity, if it disrupts difficult tasks or important activities such as sleep, may indirectly produce considerable stress for the organism.

5. For example, see M. H. Jones (1972) for a laboratory study on the "pain thresholds for smog components." One might also consider historical incidents of killer smogs, such as the London air pollution disaster of 1952 (see, for example, Ehrlich and Ehrlich, 1970, p. 120).

6. Curiously, *ongoing* noise seems not to disrupt performance on many types of laboratory tasks. According to Glass and Singer (1972), people tend to adapt both psychophysiologically and behaviorally to even very loud, uncontrollable, and unpredictable noise (although such noise *can* cause decrements in the performance of ongoing tasks that are very complex or that require continuous attentional vigilance).

7. See, for example, Leavitt (1970), Buel (1972), and Schneider (1971).

8. See Freedman (1975), Fischer et al. (1975), Lawrence (1974), and Zlutnick and Altman (1972).

9. Also see Proshansky et al. (1970) for an excellent development of the idea that crowding arises from having one's freedom restricted by the presence of other people; and compare Altman's (1975) related treatment in terms of restriction on the regulation of "privacy" or "self/other boundaries." In addition, see Stokols (1976) for a succinct typological overview of certain major "theoretical perspectives on crowding."

10. The results of the research by Freedman and his associates indicated that crowding had little effect on task performance, but that it elevated the competitiveness and punitiveness of males (while having the *opposite* effect on female subjects). An experiment by Stokols et al. (1973) similarly detected a sex effect in the finding that males who were crowded together with other males in a small room rated themselves as more aggressive than did males who were spread out in a larger room. Again the opposite was true for females (who also found the situation in the small room more pleasant than the larger one, exactly the opposite of the males' preferences). However, Griffitt and Veitch (1971) reported no data on sex differences in their study, in which apparently both males and females in crowded (same-sex) groups evidenced more negative affect and less liking for an anonymous stranger than did subjects in less crowded (smaller) groups.

11. In addition to Barker (1968) and the various references cited there, see also Barker and Schoggen (1973), Wicker (1973), and Wicker and Kirmeyer (1976). It should be noted that Wicker's development of "manning" theory departs somewhat from Barker's original terminology and conceptualization. For the sake of simplicity, I am sticking more or less to Barker's approach; but the reader might note that according to Wicker's scheme, suboptimal levels of participation can be either below the actual "maintenance minimum" for the setting (truly "undermanned") or simply near this minimum ("poorly manned"), while "overmanning" is held to occur only when "applicants" actually exceed "capacity." The basic dynamics of "manning"-level effects, however, are fun-

damentally the same in Wicker's and Barker's theories. (I should also note, along with Wicker, that the sexist connotations of this terminology were unintentional.)

12. As a slightly fanciful example, consider Bertrand Russell's (1932) argument in his essay "In Praise of Idleness." Russell pointed out that if a new technique were suddenly discovered for producing twice as many pins with the same amount of human effort, the rational (and, I might add, the pro-life) thing to do would be to ask each pin worker to put in only half as much time for the same pay as before. Thus, in contrast to what might be the usual approach in our society (that is, to fire half the workers and "let" the other half labor full time for the old pay), "overmanning" could be easily avoided in this and the many types of similar situations.

13. See, for example, Küller (1973), Lang et al. (1974), and Honikman (1975).

14. The outcome for each of the eight components will, of course, be a function of the *interaction* between environment and cognitive set. To keep Complications arising from writing or reading this discussion to a reasonable level, our focus is here being limited mainly to the contribution of the (physical) environment. The idea is that some types of environmental design might in themselves either enhance the various components or at least stimulate cognitive sets that serve to enhance the quality of experience. It might be noted, however, that appropriate cognitive sets can be adopted in many cases to "compensate" for minor deficiencies in certain aspects of environments (for example, using ASF sets to augment Complexity in physically dull environments). It might be an interesting cognitive set, for some readers, to figure out other examples of such compensatory cognitive sets for each of the eight components in the following discussion.

15. Bear in mind, however, that the final *aesthetic* value of stimuli seems to depend more on "unity in diversity" (see, for example, Platt, 1961; Dewey, 1934) than on just diversity.

16. Also see Richard Wurman (1971) for a fine account, with graphic examples, of how to "make the city observable" by the use of special displays.

7
UTOPIA AND CHANGE

DESIGNING UTOPIA

The term *utopia* tends to stir up obfuscating passions and to connote impossibility, but a book on human potentials might as well go for broke. To cool things down just a bit, however, let us think of utopia as not necessarily the perfect society, but rather as any societal design that falls among the best possible for human beings to achieve. This definition assumes that a design for a society must in some sense be "achievable" in order to be considered utopian, and also that there may be more than one design that can qualify as "best." True, we are still left with the problems of determining what is best for people and how achievability is to be gauged—issues to be addressed shortly. But this somewhat unusual use of the term "utopia" saves us from having to compare the world as it is with visions of societies so perfect as to be forever beyond our grasp. In effect, our definition directs us to examine the intersection of what we as human beings really want with what we as human beings can really do.

All right, so how do we go about figuring out what the class of "best achievable societies" is? First, we should be forewarned that we'll probably never know for sure whether we have actually figured out the *best* possible guidelines for social designs, although we should be able to come up with guidelines that would at least suggest alternatives substantially better than any existing large-scale society. But now to the main issues facing us as would-be utopian designers: (1) What is actually "best" for us? (2) Based on existing utopian designs and real-life ventures, what appears to be "achievable"? (3) After assessing any differences between our actual society and our utopian designs, what can we *do* to narrow the gap? The third question is the toughest one (although the others are not easy), and will take up the entire latter part of this chapter. Let us now tackle—or should I say wrestle with—the other two.

What Is Best for Us (All of Us)?

If your ecological consciousness is up, you'll notice that right away we have problems in just delimiting "us," not to mention answering the question itself. To simplify the initial discussion, let's for the moment understand "us" to mean all human beings—but bear in mind that our fundamental interrelatedness in the web of life will probably require that any utopia give a valued place to other sentient creatures. Also, ecological consciousness and all that it entails may be part of what is best for people. Before turning to my views, however, let us see if we can discern any consistencies in what various utopian thinkers have considered ideal for human beings.

George Kateb (1963), in his aptly titled book *Utopia and its Enemies*, cited as standard utopian ends "peace, abundance, leisure, equality, untroubled virtue" (p. 83). Rosabeth Kanter (1972), in her analysis of utopian communes, noted the ideals of "human perfectibility," "order," "brotherhood," "unity of body and mind," "experimentation," and "coherence as a group." Those two brief lists are intended as distillations from the visions of a considerable number of utopians. To flesh out the picture just a little further, however, we might note the views of a few more or less contemporary utopian (or at least idealistic) writers.

B. F. Skinner (1948), for example, posited in *Walden Two* that the "Good Life" required in the main only health, minimal unpleasant work, "a chance to exercise talents and abilities," "intimate and satisfying personal contacts," and "relaxation and rest" (Chapter 20). The sociologist Amitai Etzioni (1968), in his moderately utopian book *The Active Society*, posited basic human needs for affection, recognition (self-esteem), and "context" (wholeness and meaning)—along with such requirements as repeated gratification and stability—as some of the things society should strive to optimize. But most important in Etzioni's view is the general "active" orientation according to which a society's members would broadly participate in self-consciously shaping the society's goals. Paul and Percival Goodman (1962), in *Communitas*, favored societal designs that would manage to unite production and consumption, thereby rendering virtually all work both useful and enjoyable. Erich Fromm (1955) defined "the sane society" as one that meets real human needs, and specified that such real human needs are "relatedness" (both with nature and other people), "creativeness," "rootedness," a "sense of identity," and a "frame of orientation." Furthermore, he argued that a society based on "humanistic communitarian socialism" would maximize people's chances to meet these needs. And finally, for two examples of environmentally oriented utopians: Kevin Lynch (1975), in a brief utopian sketch, posited that the biological "fitness," the "openness" (equal accessibility to all), and the "connection" (richness in meaning) of the environment are crucial to human well-being. Also echoing the ecological concerns of many current utopians, Rudolph Moos (1976) has argued that the world needs a stabilized population, a steady-state economy with egalitarian distribution, a united world order, and a new value system stressing partnership with nature.

The above array of utopian ideals is far from an exhaustive survey, but I think it illustrates some important points. (1) Utopian goals can be stated either in terms of the human *needs* that are to be fulfilled or in terms of social and environmental *structures* that are supposed to produce the good life. Sometimes, as in the case of peace or stability, it is difficult to draw a clear line; but for the sake of distinguishing between means and ends, and in keeping with the thesis that the quality of experience is the ultimate touchstone for determining value, it would seem best to consider human needs before proposing designs for social and environmental structure. (2) There is a surprising amount of consistency in what utopians consider to be good for people. Both Kateb (1963) and Kanter (1972) intimated this in their lists, which, though not identical, are certainly consistent with each other. Indeed, it is tempting to classify most utopian goals in terms of Maslow's proposed hierarchy of human needs (see Chapter 2). Thus, survival and safety needs would seem to encompass goals such as peace, health, abundance, and perhaps order. Belongingness seems to capture the spirit of utopian calls for brotherhood, coherence as a group, and intimate and satisfying personal contacts. Esteem would include such goals as recognition and a sense of identity. And that handy catchall, self-actualization, would certainly seem an apt category for creativeness, perfectibility, wholeness and meaning, and perhaps even the uniting of production and consumption; ecological consciousness could probably even be slipped in if we felt so inclined.

However, as you are no doubt aware, the scheme I most prefer for discussing what is best for us is that provided by the eight components linking cognition, environment, and affect. These components (henceforth to be referred to as the "Comps") have already been used to provide criteria for evaluating cognitive sets and physical environments. It is time now to turn them loose on the question of evaluating whole societies.

An Answer in Terms of the Comps

Throughout this book it has been argued that the quality of experience is the most important consideration for evaluating virtually anything, since indeed it is the quality of experience—especially its *affective* quality—that forms the basis for value itself. As the discussion in Chapter 4 attempted to show, however, optimizing the quality of everyone's experience is not a task to be solved by any simple algorithm. Both the range of individual differences and the inherent need for compromises between conflicting goods complicate the effort considerably. Furthermore, as Gardner Murphy (1958) forcefully argued, human potentialities are open—it is neither possible nor desirable for us to specify what will be fulfilling to future generations.

Nonetheless, the Comps scheme is intended to represent at least the beginnings of a general theory of happiness. While in most cases it is not possible to specify either the exact nature of the optimum level of a given component or the conditions under which such a level would be reached, I have attempted in previous discussions to demonstrate the utility of the scheme as a general guide for considering the effects of cognition and of environments on the affective quality of experience. Clearly, the most crucial evaluative element in the scheme is the concept of *Compatibility*—consistency with pro-life values and the other aspects of ecological consciousness. The previous discussions relating to this concept of course apply equally when it is used to evaluate whole societies. Rather than repeat those general points here, I will instead simply use the idea of Compatibility as the basis for pursuing the discussion of the other Comps. Together, I believe they give us a genuine start at figuring out what is "best" for all of us.[1]

Complexity. Just as it is important for cognitive sets or physical environments to yield an "optimal" level of experiential novelty, variety, and intensity, so this basic component in affective arousal provides a central touchstone for the effects of a whole social structure. Indeed, one of the major complaints about many utopian designs is that they are or would become boring (see Kateb, 1963). Hence, it would seem to be essential for a utopian society to incorporate enough diversity and change to allow all people to optimize their Complexity. As noted in the discussion of Complexity in relation to environmental design (Chapter 6), Raymond Dasmann (1970) has proposed that a diversity of utopias would be better than any single utopian design. Then people could sample different life styles and avoid whatever boredom might result from a lifetime in any single culture.

It is crucial to bear in mind, however, that Compatibility would put some constraints on the *type* of diversity or other sources of excitement. As Kateb (1963) pointed out, war is a way to stir things up and decrease boredom, but there are other ways that have far less dire consequences. A few examples would be technological innovations, education in Complexity-enhancing cognitive sets, public participation in sports and holidays, widespread artistic activity, and interesting work. Also, as Kateb noted, it is important to distinguish between the arousal value of a society for *participants* versus for *observers*. Happiness or cooperation may indeed be less interesting to contemplate than misery or conflict, but that does not mean that the active experience of being happy or of cooperating on a personally interesting task will provide a less optimal level of Complexity than will suffering or being in a fight. Often what is interesting to observe or read about is well beyond the optimum level to experience. Hence, utopian designs must be judged by how it would feel to live in them, not by how interesting it would be to observe or think about them.

Composition.   The effects of a society on the content, meaning, and significance of its members' experience constitute an extremely broad category. From the perspective of high Compatibility, at least all of the following would be included: (1) a physical environment that meets the design criteria set forth under Composition in Chapter 6 (for example, fulfillment of Papanek's [1971] "function complex" for all aspects of environmental and product design); (2) fulfillment of the lower-level needs of Maslow's hierarchy—which would almost certainly require relatively equal distribution of goods and services and the development of ecologically sound, pro-life technology (again, see Papanek's criteria for design); (3) the opportunity for all to fulfill the higher-level needs of Maslow's hierarchy—which would doubtless require reasonable material abundance, considerable leisure, a wide variety of interesting work opportunities, and education that promoted the development of interest, facility in B-cognition, and cooperation; (4) the facilitation of widespread ecological consciousness, and the opportunity for all to participate in the cooperative self-determination of the society's goals and operating procedures (compare Etzioni, 1968).

It might also be noted at this point that John Rawls's (1971) notions of "a theory of justice" seem applicable to considerations of utopian societal effects on Composition. Rawls asked what principles of justice a group of rational people would use in designing a societal structure starting completely from scratch, so that no invididual would know in advance where she or he would place in the final social structure. (Actually, this question of societal design under "the veil of ignorance," as Rawls termed it, is simply a philosophical device for looking at the question of human fairness in the most abstract way.) His answer was basically as follows: "All social primary goods—liberty and opportunity, income and wealth, and the bases of self-respect—are to be distributed equally unless an unequal distribution of any or all of these goods is to the advantage of the least favored" (p. 303). It is impossible to do justice here to the painstaking arguments Rawls developed to support this general proposition and the more detailed principles from which it derives, but his conclusion seems to represent a highly sophisticated and very utopian Equity 2 norm. If a society adopted it in practice, any departures from equality in the distribution of social goods (for example, special training or job rewards) would require common consent and would have to improve life for those who got less, as by providing them with creative inventions or special services. Otherwise, all would get (and perhaps suffer) the same. Such a system would almost certainly lead to a high level of cooperation, mutual caring, high self-esteem, and the most pleasant widespread Composition possible for the whole society. The important consideration in Rawls's theory is that it avoids asking *anyone* to make sacrifices for the "greater good of all" (that is, for everyone else). Such a system would thus present the least possible threat to all individuals, while maximizing everyone's chance for freedom and fulfillment. *That* would make for good Composition.

Comprehension. The satisfaction derivable from high-Compatibility clarity, understanding, and insight takes on special significance when related to the structure of a whole society. There is first the importance of everyone's being able to understand the norms and structure of the society (analogous to the importance of comprehending the physical environment so that Plans can be executed). This means that a utopian society must combine *clarity* with the diversity and excitement needed for optimal Complexity. The governmental structure, for example, should be clearly understandable so that all citizens can grasp how it operates, how they can influence decisions, and so on.

However, even more important than the clarity of the social structure would be the degree to which the society would foster the growth of each person's cognitive abilities and curiosity (compare Murphy, 1958).

Cognitive development would be especially important for any society that rested on collective decision making, mutual problem-solving approaches to conflict resolution, and striving for consensus on important issues. As discussed in Chapter 4, growth in the level of "moral development" may well be a function of the ability to understand progressively more sophisticated ways of thinking about ethical issues. Education in values clarification and related cognitive development would thus seem to be crucial. Indeed, the very possibility of a *participatory* utopia might well rest on whether most people achieved the level of insight suggested by Kohlberg's higher stages of moral development (see Chapter 4).

Additionally, the types of understanding required for ecological consciousness—and the educational and other cultural supports needed for their development (Chapter 5)—would also be part of what seems best for us (*all* of us, not just the human ones who would be doing the cognitive work). Again, if a utopian society were to be genuinely participatory, it would be essential for as many people as humanly possible to attain a high degree of insight into the interrelatedness of people with each other and the rest of the biosphere. Similarly, a systemic mode of understanding and some degree of transcendence of the cognitive limitations discussed by Slovic and his associates (1974; see Chapter 5) would be highly desirable. One aid to these developments might be the widespread use of cooperative, creative *groups* of people to generate insights into problems and possibilities. (Another important aid might be systematic attention to the insight-generating capacity of special cognitive sets.)

Comparison.   The discussion in Chapter 6 of high-Compatibility enhancement of Comparison with respect to the physical environment can easily be generalized to relate to the society as a whole. The goals discussed there under the heading of Comparison were (1) decreasing psychological adaptation (habituation) both to pleasant aspects of the environment and to changeable unpleasant aspects; (2) encouraging awareness of environmental alternatives (and hence raising CLs); (3) providing experiences as much above people's environmental CLs as possible; and (4) facilitating psychological adaptation to truly uncorrectable environmental problems. Any society that could meet these goals even for the physical environment would clearly be at least mildly utopian.

However, as Philip Brickman and Donald Campbell (1971) have argued, adaptation-level theory seems to imply a "hedonic treadmill," according to which happiness will fade as people's ALs and CLs rise with improving outcomes. As discussed in previous chapters, this problem can be countered by techniques such as (1) providing a very wide variety of good things; (2) introducing frequent changes; (3) constantly improving the social and physical environment; and (4) helping people to use cognitive techniques (remembering bad times, using special cognitive sets, and so on) that lower their CLs for things that cannot be improved. Also, as Brickman and Campbell point out, there are some sources of joy in life that seem to operate in self-renewing cycles (for example, eating and sex). Perhaps utopias could emphasize such sources of satisfaction in life. Indeed, many utopian writers (for example, Huxley, 1962; Wagar, 1971; Skinner, 1948) have taken pains to emphasize just these sorts of recurrent, nonhabituating pleasures.

The CL-theory terminology of "outcomes" perhaps tends to call to mind too much the image of getting *things* rather than stressing the idea of having a certain type of *experience*. Nonetheless, there are many good things in life—love, art, sport, natural beauty, various sensual pleasures, and so on—that can *increase* in attractiveness as one's experience of them deepens. A utopian society would certainly have to be concerned with the issue of habituation or boredom, but I think many people overestimate the problem. It seems to me that the main issues are to avoid sameness and stagnation and to alert people to sources of satisfaction (and to ways of experiencing them) that do not pale. Aside from an ever-improving social and physical environment, perhaps the best Comparison-enhancing tactic is that suggested by Gardner Murphy (1958): seek satisfactions that increase one's sensitivities to further and deeper satisfactions. A society that could help all people to do that would be utopian indeed.

Competence.   Closely related to the generation of increased Comprehension is the society's fostering of high-Compatibility Competence. The qualification of "high-Compatibility" becomes especially important with respect to Competence, since it is effectiveness in such domains as cooperating with others and working in harmony with ecological demands that would be required for a utopian society. Skills in communicating and in creative problem solving, for example, would appear to have much more utopian value than, say, skills in manipulating other people or winning in zero-sum games. As discussed under the heading of Competence in Chapter 6, however, a utopian society should facilitate people's general ability to execute their Plans and to form new and more interesting (and beneficial) Plans. Such notions as Potter's (1971) idea of an "optimum stress" level to aid continual development of adaptive responses would certainly seem to apply to the whole society as well as to the physical environment. A utopia should not make life so easy that people would become too "soft." (But self-governing people with ecological insight and a high level of competence would doubtless challenge themselves anyway.)

To slightly modify the summary statement from Chapter 6: A society that enhanced Competence would embody legibility, concentrated diversity, responsiveness, and flexibility, all *combined with* (1) graduated instigators to higher levels of Complexity; (2) a large pool of resources available to all; (3) the encouragement of exploration and creativity (through cooperative open education, for example); and (4) the opportunity for all people to participate meaningfully in decisions that affect them.

Complications.   Ideally, a utopia would have many challenges but very few sources of strain great enough to detract from the joy of life. As in the case of Rawls's (1971) principle of justice, the ideal would be for any source of strain always to have the ultimate effect of enhancing life for those experiencing the strain. But that is probably too much to hope for in any achievable society of human beings. So what can be said about "optimizing" Complications? Basically, only that (1) *some* strain is desirable to maintain an "optimal stress level" (see Competence); (2) every attempt should be made to overcome excessive difficulties connected with otherwise good things (as by improving educational techniques for teaching certain cognitive sets, systems thinking, difficult but enjoyable skills, and so on); and (3) wherever undesirable burdens cannot be eased, they should be shared as equally as possible.

It may also be asked whether there are any sources of Complications that might be specific to a utopian society. In fact, there probably are— although I would rather think of them as challenges. For instance, if participation in societal decision making is to be open and widespread, there may be extra strain for many people resulting from the social demands that might be made on everyone. Thus, all might be expected to be systems thinkers, to have achieved a high level of moral reasoning, to be ecologically aware, and so on. For many, this might be a considerable strain, even though they might eventually succeed. Problems such as this, however, can be met in several ways. First, improvements in teaching techniques may make learning the required cognitive skills relatively easy. Second, cooperative group problem-solving may allow sophisticated solutions and decisions to emerge from groups (and societies) that include intellectually handicapped, but nonetheless contributing, members. Finally, if all else fails, decisions might be made by an elite of sorts (all in accordance with Rawls's notions of benefit to the nonelite and with their consent) rather than by a more direct broad-based consensual process. This is one area where we seem far from an answer concerning what is actually possible for a large-scale society to accomplish. That is, the evidence as of now does not seem complete enough to judge whether most people would or could reach the level of cognitive sophistication probably needed for a participatory utopian society to function without putting great stress on many of its members. But the question in this form concerns more what is actually achievable than what is best in principle. Clearly, the best for all of us is for each of us to function with the requisite levels of competence and to enjoy it. Let us hope that this can be.

Comportment. For the actual promotion of high Compatibility, people's overt patterns of behavior are certainly the most directly important variables to consider. In a sense, then, evaluating the other Comps with respect to Compatibility mainly involves consideration of their resultant contribution to Comportment (although ultimately Comportment is only important because of its effects on experience—that is, on the other Comps). In any case, the types of behavior encouraged in a society will be critical for determining the overall quality of life. The orientation throughout this book has been to regard cooperative, friendly, mutually creative, playful, intrinsically satisfying, ecologically sound behavior—that is, pro-life Comportment—as the ideal.

Perhaps no other theoretical development in the recent history of psychology is of more importance for understanding how utopian patterns of behavior might differ from our current ones than Chris Argyris and Donald Schön's (1974; Argyris, 1975, 1976a,b) distinction between "Model 1" and "Model 2." Model 1 behavior involves the following goals ("governing variables"): (1) unilaterally "define goals and try to achieve them"; (2) "maximize winning and minimize losing"; (3) "minimize generating or expressing negative feelings"; and (4) "be rational" (meaning "intellectual" and unemotional). The behavioral strategies that these goals purportedly generate are to "design and manage the environment unilaterally," to "own and control the task," and to "unilaterally protect yourself and others" (which entails withholding and distorting information and engaging in other forms of deceptive behavior). Argyris and Schön argue that this overall pattern of behavior results in defensive, competitive, power-oriented, mistrustful social relations, and little chance for public testing or questioning of basic goals or even of techniques being used to reach them. The net effect is "decreased effectiveness" and a quality of life much lower than it need be. Argyris and Schön (1974) have also found that most behavior by the professional and managerial Americans they have tested tends toward Model 1.

Model 2 behavior, by contrast, operates according to the governing variables of (1) "valid information"; (2) "free and informed choice"; and (3) "internal commitment to the choice and constant monitoring of its implementation." Such goals are hypothesized to result in behavioral Plans to treat other participants as Origins; to allow tasks to be controlled jointly; and to use open, bilateral, growth-oriented techniques to protect yourself and others. This pattern of behavior would supposedly result in minimally defensive, maximally collaborative and trusting interpersonal relations and would encourage public testing and questioning of basic goals and techniques. It would also lead, according to Argyris and Schön, to "high authenticity and high freedom of choice" and to very effective decision making and problem solving (particularly for hard problems). Virtually everything claimed by Argyris and Schön is consistent with a tremendous variety of research and real-life experience concerning the effects of cooperation and of a mutual problem-solving approach to conflict resolution.[2] I think it is fair to say that Comportment in utopia would be Model 2 all the way.

Structural Requirements for Utopia

Now that we have examined how our eight-component scheme might help to indicate what would be best for enhancing human happiness, let us conclude by considering what would be needed in the basic structure of a society to facilitate maximal enhancement of all of the Comps. Although the list may well not be complete, my guess is that a utopian society defined in terms of optimizing the quality of everyone's experience would need to include at least the following:

1. *An economic and political system based mainly on an Equity 2 norm for the distribution of resources and power,* perhaps best operating in accordance with Rawls's (1971) notion of justifying any inequality only with the consent and for the benefit of those receiving less. Such a system would encourage maximal cooperation and the highest minimum level of development and need satisfaction for all members of the society. In addition, an Equity 2 system is most compatible with low levels of "throughput" and ecologically sound patterns of growth (see Daly, 1973, and the discussion in Chapter 2). All in all, this would seem critical both for enhancing Composition for everyone and for enabling everyone to achieve a reasonably high level of Comprehension and Competence.

2. *A high level of resources and ecologically sound practices relative to population level.* There is no need to repeat here the arguments against unlimited population growth, or even to discuss in detail that population past the point needed for efficient, nonstressful production will inevitably mean less per person. The important consideration for maintaining high Compatibility in both the ecological and the human-happiness sense is that population levels be appropriate to the level of natural and technological resources and to the environmental impact of the existing technology. Since excellent arguments can be made that leisure and a reasonably high level of resources are both vital to the realization of our highest potentials for creativity and happiness (see, for example, Skinner, 1948; Kateb, 1963), this requirement seems essential. Also, as we shall see, the absence of just this high relative level of resources has been perhaps the chief drawback of some of the world's otherwise most promising utopian ventures.

3. *A system of socialization, education, cultural norms, and everyday contingencies of reinforcement that promote full ecological consciousness and prepare and encourage all people for full participation in making central decisions that affect them.* This requirement would seemingly entail a general Model 2 approach to virtually all social interactions and institutional functioning. This is of course a huge order, but if a participatory utopian culture is to be self-maintaining and self-examining, nothing less will do. In short, if people are to experience real Competence in accordance with high Compatibility, they must

mature in a system that prepares and allows them to control and to improve their own utopian society.

4. *Societal commitment to pro-life rationality, diversity, and experimentation.* This requirement in a way is implicit in the preceding one, but since utopias are so often pictured or criticized as being static, it seems a good idea to accentuate the need for high-Compatibility (that is, "rational") diversity and experimentation. A truly utopian society would probably be best considered more as a set of *processes* than as a single structure. It would be a society of people with a self-conscious commitment to finding ever-better ways to enhance experience for themselves and for all other sentient creatures they affect (including posterity). Obviously, this would call for rich diversity and continual experimentation. Additionally, as Argyris and Schön (1974) stress, Model 2's "most significant property . . . is its ability not to be self-sealing, its tendency to permit progressively more effective testing of assumptions and progressively greater learning about one's effectiveness"(p. 86). Thus, a pro-life, high-Compatibility utopian society would have to be an open, constantly searching one. Is there any need to point out the beneficial implications for Complexity, Comparison, Comprehension, and Competence?

As mentioned, this list is not necessarily complete—and, in keeping with Model 2, I would encourage everyone to question all that underlies it for the sake of seeking truly valid information. But the main outline of this book's conception of what is best for people should by now be reasonably clear. So let us turn to the general issue of "achievability" in my definition of utopia, following which we can finally explore the tough question, "How do we get there?"

What Is Achievable?

First, the question of utopian achievability can be broken down into the two sub-issues of (1) whether there are any designs that would actually provide the above utopian structural requirements, and (2) whether any such design can be established, given the nature of the existing world. A very important consideration, however, is that determining whether something can be achieved depends to a large extent on one's time frame. Given an indefinitely long time, who knows what human beings may become or accomplish? Science fiction is full of varyingly wild imaginings about what the very long-range future might hold. Hence, to tie our discussion a bit more to the present, let us limit the focus of our consideration to what might conceivably be achieved within the next generation or so—recognizing that, even optimistically speaking, the best we might hope for is merely a movement *toward* a truly utopian society.

A Place to Start

Now to consider the first question: Is there any conceivable societal design that would be self-maintaining and that would come reasonably close to providing the utopian structural requirements proposed above? My answer may strike some as a bit surprising, given the antipathy sometimes evidenced by humanistic critics of the design I'm going to praise; but here it is: *With some essential modifications* (to be discussed shortly), I believe that the "deep structure" of B. F. Skinner's (1948) design for a utopian community ("Walden Two") captures most of the essential elements needed for a viable utopia.[3] Also, there is some empirical evidence that the underlying design is both feasible and consistent with pro-life values.

To keep this discussion brief I am not going to delve into the details and more superficial aspects of the novel *Walden Two*, nor am I going to deal with criticisms that seem to me based on (1) misunderstanding or distortion of what Skinner said (for example, that Walden Two members would be mere "puppets" or uncreative); (2) emotional distaste for Skinner's other work or derivatives of it (for example, objections that Skinner is "against" human dignity and freedom); or (3) points that Skinner himself quite adequately answered in the novel itself (for example, the danger of tyranny by power-hungry "Planners"). There are, I think, some quite valid criticisms to be made, mainly along the line suggested by George Kateb (1963), and these will be taken up shortly. For the beginning, though, let us look at what is good about the essence or "deep structure" of the design for Walden Two.

As I see it, the following characteristics are essential to Skinner's design, as presented in the novel:

1. The guiding *values* of the society—the criteria used in basic societal decisions and judgments of what is desirable—are equality, health, minimal unpleasant work, cooperative and satisfying interpersonal relationships, the opportunity for all to pursue interests and develop abili-

ties, and the provision of as much free time and "freedom of choice" [my term] as possible. This value system has the underlying goal of maximizing happiness in the most meaningful way for all community members.

2. There is a system of child rearing, education, and group pressure (but no punishment) to reinforce and operationalize this value system and to "shape" people to be cooperative, to be relatively free of personally debilitating negative emotions, to be creative, and to be self-directing. The chief means Skinner envisioned for this included group child rearing with stress on *cooperative* interpersonal relations (much like the child-rearing system actually used in Israeli kibbutzim), rather simplistic operant conditioning to promote moral development and the acquisition of self-control, a code of conduct (much like codified norms of etiquette) designed to promote cooperation and equality, and a system of education that is surprisingly similar to a combination of a "free school" and a "deschooled society" (compare Illich, 1971).

Both in this novel and elsewhere (for example, Skinner, 1953, 1971), Skinner perhaps overestimates the potential for "behavioral technology" based on operant conditioning to produce the sort of self-actualizers envisioned as inhabiting Walden Two. Furthermore, he has consistently neglected the importance of cognitive processes and cognitive development. But, paradoxically, the actual educational system envisioned in *Walden Two* combines "open education" elements, such as student choice of curriculum and a facilitator role for teachers, with an emphasis on people learning actively from each other and from the social environment (a "deschooling" of education, in Illich's terms). What a contrast with many a "behavior-modification" classroom!

Thus, despite certain serious weaknesses in Skinner's averred reliance on conditioning as a chief socializing device, the actual procedures suggested in *Walden Two* clearly leave room for (and in fact seem to call for) the use of cognitively sophisticated approaches to socialization, such as Origin training, values clarification, and a Kohlbergian style of moral education (see Chapters 2 and 4 and the discussion of "corrections" below). Of course, many of us do not like to think that we have been "shaped" by *anything* and rebel against the notion of a culture's being planned to turn out a certain sort of person. As any anthropologist could demonstrate, however, we are inevitably shaped by our culture (not totally determined, but certainly "shaped" in a certain direction). What Skinner has done—perhaps inadequately, but better than many critics acknowledge—is to suggest a concerted effort to design an integrated system of socialization that would help people to become cooperative, creative, self-directing, and prone to enjoy life. I believe it is the idea of a cultural commitment to such a concerted effort, and not the specific plan offered, that is a crucially valuable part of Walden Two's deep structure.

3. The economic system is based on an Equity 2 norm of distribution, allows freedom of choice in work, and utilizes technology and resources to allow for a minimal amount of unpleasant work for all people. A central point here, of course, is that Walden Two is assumed to have sufficient resources to enable the work expected of each person to be relatively low (about four hours per day) while still providing a reasonably high standard of living. Everyone is expected to accumulate a certain number of "labor credits," and the credit value for each type of job is empirically determined according to how much demand there is for being assigned the job. Thus, unpopular jobs will yield more labor credits per hour. However, all of the essential consumer resources of the community (food, building materials, health care, entertainment, and so on) are essentially open to equal use by all members.

As will be discussed further below, there are communities in existence that employ an economic system similar to this. But not one of these communities (certain communes in the United States and over two hundred kibbutzim in Israel) has achieved the level of resources or the safety necessary for a low amount of required work. I consider this point absolutely critical in evaluating such "utopian" experiments. As Skinner repeatedly illustrated in *Walden Two,* any flowering of human potentials is very likely to depend not only on equality and the meeting of basic survival needs but also on the availability of considerable free time and of resources for personal and social development during that time (indeed, I do not think even Walden Two went far enough in that direction).

It should also be borne in mind that Skinner envisioned this utopian society as functioning not only according to an Equity 2 norm of distribution but also according to a set of highly pro-life values. Unlike our current society, consumption was not considered an end in itself but rather only a means to promoting the happiness of all members of the society. Hence, technology, production, innovation, and resource use were to be geared to the satisfaction of real human needs and the stimulation of growth in intrinsically satisfying pursuits. While the specific activities that Skinner pictured for Walden Two's people may not strike many of us as especially exciting (Skinner's utopia is often criticized as too orderly—Harris [1971] has even likened its residents to "guests at an eternal Tupperware party"), this is *not* part of the deep structure. The basic economic design of Walden Two—combining high resources, low required work, and decision making according to pro-life values—would allow any number of life styles to emerge. Orgies, Eastern meditative exercises, complex games, artistic happenings, world-wide travel, new types of peak experiences—all of these and much more would be possible and perhaps likely, given the economic and value system embedded in the deep structure of Walden Two.

4. Finally, Walden Two is designed as a society devoted to experimentation in the pursuit of an ever more fulfilling life for its people. It is true that, in places, Skinner does waver a bit about the ultimate *goal* of the experimenting. Through his partial alter ego, Frazier, he seems at times to view experimentation as important more for increasing efficiency than for increasing happiness. Nonetheless, Walden Two is clearly highly pragmatic and experimental; and, as noted in the previous section on defining what is "best," an essential element in any pro-life utopia would be commitment to diversity and experimentation. Perhaps one other problem in *Walden Two* is that insufficient stress is placed on diversity at any given time; the experimentation seems to be done mainly sequentially. But that is easily corrected and should not detract from the point that open and pervasive experimentation is an essential feature in the design.

Suggested "Corrections"

I chose to cite Skinner's design not because I think it is a perfect blueprint for a viable utopian society, but simply to give us a place to start and to demonstrate that someone has indeed put together a reasonably self-consistent paradigm for a society that, even with its faults, would probably far surpass most (if not all) existing communities in providing a pleasant and creative life for its members. Nevertheless, there are flaws.

First and perhaps most central, Skinner fails to include a convincing picture of *how* culture could be counted on to facilitate everyone's becoming a cooperative self-actualizer. Indeed, my impression on repeated readings of *Walden Two* is that Skinner really seems to be assuming that meeting people's needs for survival, safety, belongingness, and esteem would almost automatically catapult them into the realm of Maslow's "metamotivation" (the self-actualization syndrome: see Chapter 2). Skinner and Maslow in the same camp! Of course, he did add a dash (actually, a surprisingly small dash if you read the book carefully) of operant conditioning, especially in early childhood (for example, moral training was to be completed by the age of six). Even allowing for a free school system of education, however, much more may be needed to help people reach their highest potentials.

The problem, it seems to me, is that Skinner expects both too much and too little of people: too much, because he does not provide a plan for the types of cognitive supports that would very likely be needed for people to develop self-actualization-type potentials even if the first four levels of Maslow's hierarchy were adequately met (as they *would* be in Skinner's design, even as is); but also too little (as Kateb, 1963, has pointed out), because he seems to have a limited vision of human potentials and little faith in most people's ability or desire to engage in collective self-government.

To correct the problem of expecting too much, it seems to me that what needs to be added to Skinner's basic design is a great deal more attention to helping people develop their cognitive abilities in such areas as systems thinking, B-cognition, creativity in generating and using a wide variety of cognitive sets, ability to consider a wide range of alternatives and to use "lateral" as well as "vertical" thinking (see Chapter 3), and so on. Indeed, it is interesting to speculate on how Aldous Huxley's (1962) ideas for a somewhat less structured but cognitively adroit utopia might be combined with Skinner's seemingly sounder basic social structure. In any case, it may be that Skinner's rather simplistic reliance on operant conditioning turns people off to the utopian power of his basic economic and value system, to the systemic interrelations in his design, and to the ease with which his overemphasis on conditioning might be corrected. Skinner really has integrated a lot of good points in his utopian design, and it seems a shame that they are so often overlooked.

But that Skinner appears to expect too little of people is a serious flaw, as Kateb (1963) has cogently argued. Especially with regard to government, it does seem essential for people to be able to have a meaningful say in any basic policy decisions that affect them. Skinner argued that basic political decisions were like basic technological decisions, and people wouldn't want just anybody fooling around with the community's diesel engines, would they? Hence, Skinner opted for a nondemocratic scheme of government by a board of highly qualified, prolife "Planners." Kateb, however, has aptly pointed out that political decisions are *not* the same as technological decisions, but rather relate to issues regarding basic societal goals and processes—questions that should indeed be open to consideration by all societal members if they are to achieve optimal levels of Competence. This open participation and collective decision making is also essential if Model 2 is to be the guiding pattern for social behavior: all people must be able to confront and question the basic goals so that "valid information, free choice, and internal commitment and constant monitoring" can all be maximized. In this respect, Israel's highly democratic kibbutzim, for example, would in fact be ahead of Walden Two. Consequently, Skinner's basic design needs to incorporate more than increased attention to cognitive education and cognitive growth. At least as important would be a consensual or other high-participation decision-making system allowing for self-government in accordance with Model 2 requirements. Such a system would of course be highly consistent with an emphasis on education for cognitive growth. This type of education would presumably help the society's members reach the higher stages of moral reasoning, thus assisting the attainment of pro-life consensus in making collective political decisions. (Also see the discussion of consensual decision making in Chapter 5.)

In addition to these changes, it has already been suggested that greater diversity would be needed and that more excitement and more exciting life styles might make Walden Two a more interesting place. But there is one other major area that we should consider: interrelations with the environment outside the community.

First, ecological values could be stressed more than they were in Skinner's scheme. This correction, however, is easily made, with virtually no change in the deep structure. After all, such basic Walden Two values as human happiness and health would depend on sound environmental relations.

And second, it is easily argued (see Kateb, 1963; Wagar, 1971; Brameld, 1976) that a real and long-lasting utopian design must include the whole world, not just an isolated community. In fairness to Skinner, it should be noted that he did present a plan whereby Walden Two could sprout new communities by a process reminiscent of cellular division and thus spread its way of life. Nevertheless, Skinner's basic conception of utopian design seems focused on individual communities acting rather independently (or even manipulatively) in relation to the surrounding world. Such a conception tends to ignore that the "outside" world eventually tends to intrude on the community. Indeed, Huxley's (1962) fictional utopia came to fictional grief for just that reason, and the Israeli kibbutzim face a constant real-life threat from international warfare (see Criden and Gelb, 1974). Also, Kanter (1972) has pointed out that the outside society presents various subtle threats to intentional communities, such as gradual erosion of basic values through compromises and economic transactions. On a less purely pragmatic level, however, it can also be argued that pro-life values and ecological consciousness require that the whole world be brought into the fold if we are to have a real utopia. It is not happiness for the few that is being sought, but the good life for everyone.

Utopian writers such as Warren Wagar (1971) have indeed tried to paint such a vision of a unified world-wide utopian society. Interestingly, however, even Wagar's vision involved a very high level of decentralization. Although some architectural—or should I say "architectonic" —utopians have called for giant "megastructures" to house the hordes of the future (see, for example, Burns, 1972), most utopian writers have gravitated toward decentralized social organization that stresses core communities on a scale small enough to allow a feeling of real community. Of course, even within large cities (or even megastructures) such organization is possible. Indeed, urban activists ranging from Jane Jacobs to Saul Alinsky have often looked to the neighborhood as the main base for people to gain collective self-governance. Additionally, *if* self-contained communities are taken as a viable model for large-scale societies, it is easy to imagine cooperative federations of relatively autonomous small communities spread across the land or in places even tightly clustered into large cities, sharing various central facilities. Such loose federation has not only been suggested by utopian analysts such as Rosabeth Kanter (1972), but has in fact been achieved on a rural level by the kibbutzim in Israel (Criden and Gelb, 1974; see below).

But notwithstanding certain environmental benefits of self-sufficient communities (see Goldsmith et al., 1972), Walden Two may be a bit too self-sufficient to provide the best model for an interrelated world. A correction in the direction of interdependent linkage into a "world community" (again, see Wagar, 1971; Brameld, 1976) would seem to be needed for a fully utopian design. At worst, however, this is only to blame Skinner for not thinking big enough. As the title of the previous section indicated, Walden Two can give us a place to *start* in thinking about what a utopian community structure—even for a world-wide "community" or system of communities—might be like.

To summarize this examination of the "essence" of Skinner's utopian design and how it might be improved, let us briefly relate this discussion to the utopian structural requirements outlined earlier.

1. Skinner's design for an economic system does indeed operate according to an Equity 2 norm. However, Skinner seems to deny the desirability of relatively equal distribution of political decision-making power. This form of equality may be essential for widespread Competence enhancement and would require a governmental system that encourages general participation as well as the fundamental cooperation Skinner did envision. (See Chapter 5 for a brief discussion of such systems.)

2. Skinner assumes a reasonably high level of material and technological resources. If it is not already implicit in his design, it would be a small step to incorporate the goal of ecologically sound practices as a basic guideline for production, consumption, and population levels.

3. Skinner goes to great pains to outline systems of collective child rearing, education, and even a "code of conduct" that are all specifically designed to promote equality, cooperation, a minimum of personally and socially damaging emotions (for example, jealousy), and a high ability to form and pursue interests. These goals are laudable, and Skinner is certainly on the right track in assuming that a culture should be designed to encourage the skills and dispositions needed for utopian functioning (that is, needed to optimize the eight Comps). But his lack of attention to the development of cognitive skills and his apparently low estimate of the average person's ability or inclination to engage in collective self-government seem to call for correction. Nevertheless, the appropriate changes could be made without violating the basic value system of Walden Two. In fact, since this value system is definitely pro-life, preparing children for full ecological consciousness and self-government would seem to be even more consistent with Skinner's basic goals than is the more limited system of socialization he outlines.

4. Finally, although Skinner seems to include too little diversity in his sketch of life in Walden Two, his utopian design does include an

inherent commitment to experimentation for constant improvement of the members' lives. I believe, in fact, that any society genuinely committed to the rationality, pro-life values, economic system, and experimental, exploratory approach represented by the "deep structure" of Walden Two would tend to correct the faults that I and others have pointed out.

Some Existing Utopian Ventures

Let us now turn briefly to an examination of some *existing* communities and societies to gauge the empirical evidence for the achievability of at least some utopian elements. We'll start small and move up to the most populous country in the world.

American communes.   As several reports in the early 1970s indicated, most of the intentional communities of the last decade or so have been short-lived and often troubled by internal conflicts, lack of leadership or ideology, repression and harassment from the outside environment, and a lack of material resources.[4] In addition, Kanter (1972) has pointed out that even the relatively long-lasting utopian ventures of the nineteenth century (for example, Oneida and the Harmony Society) ran into trouble from sources such as a changing environment, the aging of members, failure to retain a sufficient portion of the second generation, and the tension of trying to maintain the community's values while having to deal with the nonutopian outside world. Consequently, the feasibility of a truly utopian design is difficult to gauge from a random sampling (or possibly even a complete sampling) of communal enclaves in our society.

However, it is interesting that one of the most successful current communes is based explicitly on the design presented by Skinner in *Walden Two*. That commune is Twin Oaks, near Louisa, Virginia. Kathleen Kinkade, one of the founding members, has written an account of the first five years of the commune (Kinkade, 1973). This account amply illustrates the difficulties of starting and maintaining a small intentional community with low material and technological resources, no matter how utopian the intentions. Nonetheless, Twin Oaks has survived, and a telephone interview with a member (in the spring of 1976) assured me that the community was still alive and well. As Kinkade (1973) and Kanter (1972) wrote, and as my telephone informant reaffirmed, this particular commune operates according to an economic system similar to that described in Walden Two (that is, an Equity 2 norm, whereby work and resources are equally shared), stresses cooperation (even to the point of developing an extremely popular form of noncompetitive volleyball—see Kinkade, 1973, but still being played!), and is pleasant enough to continue to attract new members of a wide range of ages and backgrounds. The commune has also begun to include members with children and has never seemed dependent on a charismatic leader.

It must be pointed out, though, that as of 1976, members had to work more than four hours a day, membership stood at about 75 (as compared with Walden Two's fictional 1,000 and the 2,000 of some Israeli kibbutzim), and the per capita income was well below the national average for the United States. Nevertheless, Twin Oaks does seem to be surviving, growing, functioning according to a highly utopian economic system, and governing itself in a way similar to—but more democratic than—Walden Two. It also appears to be a reasonably happy place, according to the evidence I have been able to gather. The point, of course, is not that Twin Oaks is a *utopia* (it obviously does not measure up even to Skinner's fictional community), but rather that it provides living proof that at least self-selected Americans can function according to an Equity 2 norm, a pro-life value system, and a highly cooperative social structure.

Israeli kibbutzim. As both outside observers such as Bruno Bettelheim (1969) and long-term insiders such as Yosef Criden and Saadia Gelb (1974) agree, the 250 or so Israeli kibbutzim represent a long-term, generally quite successful experiment in cooperative social structure and Equity 2 living. In addition, these communities demonstrate the feasibility of a collective child-rearing system very similar to the basic structure suggested by Skinner (1948)—although here Criden and Gelb (1974) indicate a tendency toward having very young children live at home. (This shift is important, it seems to them and to me, not so much for revealing any failure in the collective approach as for demonstrating the experimental spirit with which kibbutz members try to direct their social structure.)

Furthermore, the kibbutzim are in general run very democratically, although somewhat informally (as one would hope and expect in small communities that stress equality). The kibbutzim average several hundred members apiece, have formed cooperative federations for economic and political purposes, tend to be extremely socially conscious and idealistic in their values (see Cantril, 1965), and contribute a disproportionately large number of Israel's leaders. And many kibbutzim have survived for decades (Criden and Gelb's is more than thirty years old). According to Criden and Gelb, between 60 and 70 percent of kibbutz children choose to live in the kibbutz as adults. As they point out, this is a high percentage compared with the proportion of rural children in many industrialized societies who move to cities as adults.

Even so, it would be hard to claim that kibbutzim are utopias. The work is very hard, leaving comparatively little time or energy for the flowering of self-actualization pursuits such as those pictured by Skinner in *Walden Two*. The Israeli-Arab conflict provides an ever-present threat of war. And although most kibbutzim are becoming better and better off materially and technologically, they still lack the abundance one would expect in utopia. Nevertheless, perhaps much more than the relatively young Twin Oaks, the kibbutzim's success as cooperative, totally socialistic, self-governing endeavors provides powerful evidence of the viability of these elements in utopian design.

China. It should of course be noted that American communes and even the Israeli kibbutzim are small-scale—nay, minuscule—in the context of the world as a whole. And, as argued earlier, it is the world as a whole that must ultimately be taken as the arena for utopia. Hence, the development of what appears to be a relatively egalitarian and highly cooperative and participatory society in modern China may turn out to be of greatest significance for gauging the possibility of a world-scale utopian venture. Judging from reports by Westerners as of the mid-1970s, in the course of less than twenty-five years the socialist system in China managed to overcome prodigious problems of disease, poverty, illiteracy, social disorganization, drug addiction, and the like.[5]

China, as these observers see it (and they include Asian scholars as well as at least one highly seasoned reporter on the Far East), is presently a society based largely on Equity 2 norms for distributing wealth and on local policies arising from a decision-making system that stresses consensus, constructive mutual criticism, cooperation, and community participation. While the national government is certainly highly centralized, most observers have noted that China actually functions in a highly decentralized way. Neighborhood, factory, and commune committees make the basic operating decisions and carry out essential services. This system allows virtually all citizens to have meaningful input into decisions and procedures affecting them. Furthermore, the country seems pervaded by a spirit of revolutionary fervor, with the main goal being to "serve the people" rather than to act in narrow self-interest.

All this certainly sounds rather utopian. Unfortunately, of course, it is not the whole story; and China is far from being a genuine utopia. First, even these glowing accounts of China give the impression that current Chinese culture is perhaps too puritanical and narrowly focused on required *work* to qualify as utopian. Like the kibbutzim, China seems to demand too much self-sacrifice of its people to truly optimize the quality of human experience. One of the main problems is doubtless its lack of sufficiently developed resources and technology to permit a more open choice of life styles. In addition, however, the pervasive propaganda and government-sponsored revolutionary fervor have perhaps tended to overpoliticize all aspects of life and to reduce intellectual freedom and creativity (see especially Salisbury, 1973). (It is difficult, however, to know whether this pattern will continue under Mao's successors.) From a distance, the result appears to be a lack of diversity and of openness to new ideas or alternative ways of living. Of course, in judging any foreign culture, it is important to remember that outsiders are less likely than natives to perceive subtle aspects of diversity and choice within the culture. Even so, modern China appears to be too doctrinaire and too lacking in diversity and resources to make it a living example of a pro-life utopia.

Nevertheless, compared with other relatively poor nations, or even compared with Russia or the slums of America, China does exceedingly well. Even though there is still a sizable income spread, China has virtually eliminated abject poverty. And, notwithstanding its heavy reliance on state-generated propaganda, it does stress equality, cooperation, local autonomy, and mass participation. Incidentally, China's intense pragmatism and concern for the well-being of all its people has also given rise to certain practices that are more ecologically sound than those in many other modern nations. Some examples are productive use of wastes, reliance on local input in environmental decisions and planning, symbiotic cooperation between city and countryside, and viewing the people's prosperity rather than corporate profitability as the chief guideline for economic development (see Whitney, 1973; but also note that environmental concerns per se are not part of current Chinese ideology). For providing evidence of the world-wide feasibility of utopian design, however, the most important consideration is China's demonstration that an Equity 2 oriented, genuinely cooperative, at least moderately participatory society can function on a large scale. Furthermore, the results in terms of human welfare have been outstandingly impressive when measured against conditions in other relatively poor, highly populated countries.

Comment on community and commitment.   One thing that the various successful intentional communities and current Chinese society have in common is a relatively high commitment to the group by most individual members. Rosabeth Kanter (1972), in her intriguing study of nineteenth-century American communes, found evidence that generators of such commitment may be essential to the long-term survival of highly communal groups (and presumably whole societies). Kanter pointed out that people orient to their social groups *instrumentally* through the rewards and costs provided by the group, *affectively* through each member's feelings for the group, and *morally* through the members' ethical commitment to the group. Kanter further held that for a group to generate a high degree of commitment on these three dimensions, at least some of the following *commitment-building processes* appear necessary: *sacrifice* (for example, abstinence, austerity), *investment* (for example, giving one's property to the group), *renunciation* (for example, separation from the outside world, separation of parents and children), *communion* (for example, homogeneity, communal sharing and labor, group meetings), *mortification* (for example, mutual criticism), and *transcendence* (for example, communal ideology, tradition).

Such mechanisms are indeed present in all of the communities and societies considered here, and I must admit that maintaining high communal commitment may produce Complications for those who value very high individuality, strong attachments between individuals, and other feelings that might weaken one's devotion to the whole group. In essence, there may be a serious conflict between the structure needed for community and the freedom and flexibility needed for self-actualization and intense interpersonal commitments. *If* this is the case, it may place an upper limit on the possibilities for universal human fulfillment. But for the moment, I would prefer to view it as a challenge rather than a complication. May some creative utopian thinkers find a solution—or at least a good compromise.

Concluding Comments on Utopian Achievability

The discussion to this point, to be sure, is not sufficient proof that it is actually possible to construct a utopian society incorporating all of the points listed in my account of what would seem to be best for us. It *is* clear that many of these elements (for example, functioning according to an Equity 2 norm; being mainly cooperative; and satisfying basic survival, belongingness, and perhaps even esteem needs for virtually everyone) can be realized in real-life societies. Many Israeli kibbutzim, for example, have at least managed to do that much. However, I would readily admit that the full utopian picture of a world-wide system that would fulfill all four of the structural requirements proposed earlier is more a hope than a proven possibility. Even so, there is reason to believe that we could produce and function in a world considerably better than the one we have, with results that at the very least would greatly enhance life for the least advantaged among us.

Before considering possible pathways to a better world, I would like to pass along Robert Boguslaw's (1965) tidy typology of different techniques for designing utopias. According to Boguslaw, there are at least four approaches: (1) the *formalist* approach, whereby a detailed blueprint is offered; (2) the *heuristic* approach, according to which general principles, guidelines, or goals are specified that the society would follow as creatively as it could; (3) the *operating unit* approach, where the idea is to shape the people who are to inhabit the utopian society and let them develop the best world they can; and (4) the *ad hoc* approach, according to which one starts with the existing world and attempts to solve problems as they arise in the hope of "muddling through" to an eventually ideal system.

It is perhaps less clear than implied by Boguslaw exactly how to classify any given utopian thinker. For instance, Boguslaw saw Skinner mainly as using the operating unit approach in his design for Walden Two: that is, make the operating units (people) cooperative, community-oriented, and so on, and everything else will take care of itself. However, Skinner's approach, it seems to me, also has elements of a formalistic blueprint (even the Walden Two code of conduct is spelled out), a heuristic plan (strive to maximize health, minimize unpleasant work, promote satisfying interpersonal relations, and so on), and even an ad hoc quality insofar as Walden Two was pictured as a very prag-

matic and experimental community, constantly looking for better ways
to solve its problems and make life more pleasant. But Boguslaw's
scheme does show that there are many ways to design a utopia and that
for the sake of maximizing achievability one might be well advised to
try all of them. With that thought in mind, let us turn to the issue of
how to get from here to there.

UTOPIAN CHANGE

Are We Already Utopian?

As Neil Postman and Charles Weingartner (1971) have pointed out,
"people sometimes prefer problems that are familiar to solutions that
are not" (p. 8). Thus in practice the status quo is often treated as if it
represented the best of all achievable worlds. One purpose of this book
has of course been to challenge this sort of thinking, and throughout I
have tried to point out areas where our sociocultural systems are falling
short of pro-life human potentials. The educational and economic procedures that fail to encourage or even to recognize important bases for
intrinsic motivation, the operative value system that stresses competitive individualism and material accumulation, the environmental design that fails to reflect ecological consciousness, and numerous related
aspects of our culture have all been discussed. Rather than rehash all of
that again, let me just pose the following complex rhetorical question:

Does our society (and the world at large) currently (1) distribute
goods, services, costs, and power according to an Equity 2 norm (especially one resembling Rawls's principle of justice? (2) possess a high
level of resources *and* ecologically sound practices relative to population
level? (3) use a system of socialization, education, cultural norms, and
everyday contingencies of reinforcement that promotes full ecological
consciousness and that prepares and encourages all people for full
participation in making central decisions that affect them (in accordance with a Model 2 pattern of interpersonal behavior)? *and* (4) have a
guiding commitment to pro-life rationality, diversity, and experimentation?

As noted earlier, there may well be still other structural requirements
for a workable pro-life utopian society. But if you agree that the four
proposed utopian prerequisites would enhance the overall quality of
human (and probably other sentient creatures') experience and that we

do now fall short in at least some respects, we can proceed to the main question of how to move closer to our shared goal. (If you *disagree*, you may still find some value in the following discussion for figuring out how to reach whatever other societal goals you would like.)

Pathways to Social/Environmental Change

Importance of a Systems Approach

As Jay Forrester (1972) has aptly pointed out, societies are definitely "complex systems"—"high order, multiple-loop, nonlinear, feedback structures" (p. 153). Consequently, according to Forrester, they have the following characteristics: (1) Social systems are "counter-intuitive." This resistance to ready human insight arises because our everyday experience leads us to think of causal relations in relatively short-term, simple ways; whereas in complex systems, cause-effect relations are much more complicated and spread out in time than we are used to thinking about. And to make matters even more difficult, correlations between symptoms within complex systems often mislead us into thinking we have found cause-effect relations when we have not. (2) Societies are "insensitive to change in many system parameters." That is, a lot of changes can be made in many aspects of a complex system with little systemic effect, mainly because the system tends to have internal dynamics that maintain stability. (3) Social systems are resistant to most policy changes. This characteristic derives directly from the insensitivity to changes in many system parameters just noted. (4) Societies are highly sensitive to a *few* types of changes. Thus, there exist what I like to call "soft spots" in the system, changes in which tend to ramify and change the whole structure. However, as Forrester notes, these spots are generally not self-evident. (5) Complex systems such as societies tend to exhibit a "delicate balance between the forces of growth and decline." (6) Finally, social systems are likely to "drift to a low level of performance," a tendency that results in part from policy errors arising from failure to understand the complexity of the system.

This seems to me an impressive and instructive list, although, as noted in Chapter 6, Forrester's own suggestions for treating urban problems seem to ignore the possibility of changes in the basic economic system. (For example, Forrester [1972] suggested a policy of systematic reduction in housing for "the underemployed"—thus presumably forcing these residents out of the city—along with new programs designed to "favor business" and to "attract managers and skilled labor" [p. 164].) In fairness to Forrester, however, I should note that his intention was simply to show that there may be relatively *easy*, though counter-intuitive, ways to improve society if we learn to understand the underlying processes of our complex system. And if we take a simplistic, short-term cause-effect view, we run a high risk of making things worse than they were to start with (just compare, for instance, the errors made in *providing* new but sterile urban public housing that disrupted the inhabitants' previous community structure and also made them ready prey for criminals [see Jacobs, 1961; Newman, 1973]).

I think we need to push the systems approach even further than Forrester seemed to have in mind. It would be a good idea to be open not only to small changes that will use existing structures in a more effective or humane way, but also to consideration of relatively massive systemic changes that would move us in a more pro-life direction. Russell Ackoff (1974) has proposed the beautifully appropriate term *mess* to refer to a *system of problems*. I of course agree with him that this is exactly what we face in our society and world today: our seemingly diverse problems of environmental deterioration, crime, poverty, stultifying education, meaningless work, and so on, are *interrelated;* they are in large part symptoms of societal failures to understand human potentials and especially to act according to pro-life values. But our failure to find solutions also seems to me to hinge very often on an unwillingness or inability to consider systemic alternatives. We debate jobs versus environmental quality instead of seeking a new economic system that would yield both; we worry over automobile emissions versus the price of cars and gasoline instead of considering whole new systems of transportation and urban development; we ask what kind of birth-control-plus-incentive system should be forced on the Third World (and the poor at home) instead of examining the relations between poverty and population growth—and between our own economic system and patterns of world poverty.

This is a list that is easy to extend. For virtually every problem we in the United States (and in much of the "developed" world) seem to be worried about—crime, pollution, lack of recreational space, television violence, inflation, political corruption, energy shortage, and on and on —it is possible to consider much more sweeping and potentially effective solutions than we do. The "choices" normally discussed in the popular press and by our elected politicians seem confined to an extremely narrow range of alternatives.

It is doubtless true, though, as Donald Michael (1973) has pointed out, that the "long range social planning" needed for considering and implementing massive change would itself entail several costs. Such costs would include increased uncertainty as changes were being planned, intensified role conflicts, and the restructuring of organizations. Also, people would need greater interpersonal competence and the ability to "embrace error" (learn from, rather than try to cover up, mistakes) and to "span boundaries" of disciplines and bureaucracies. Nonetheless, as William Boyer (1975) has cogently argued, we desperately need *reconstructive* planning in place of the usual "expansive" planning we have been engaging in. It would seem that our environmental problems, not to mention our dawning realization of what most of humanity is missing in the possible quality of experience, should by now be forcing a fairly widespread readiness to consider such reconstructive, systems-oriented questioning and planning. With this hopeful thought in mind, let us turn to a brief overview of some general techniques for achieving planned systemic change.

Paradigms for Changing

General theories of sociocultural change.   Since my main intent for the remainder of this chapter is to explore *action* strategies for achieving pro-life social change, I will make no attempt to review the classical literature in sociology and anthropology concerning theories of broad-scale historical processes of social change. Interested readers might refer to works such as Wilbert Moore's (1974) *Social Change,* Richard Appelbaum's (1970) *Theories of Social Change,* and Robert Lauer's (1973) *Perspectives on Social Change* for a general introduction. Before proceeding, however, I would like to note two myths about change that Lauer (1973) argues should be laid to rest. (1) Change is deviant or abnormal. Lauer maintains that to the contrary, change per se is an inherent aspect of life and society, although the rate and direction of change may vary within great limits and at times be relatively deviant or unusual. (2) Change is traumatic. Lauer admits that this is indeed sometimes true, but he points out that certain types of change (from war to peace, for example) can be less traumatic than the conditions changed. Also, Lauer (citing Spicer, 1952) insightfully notes that people may resist change or find it traumatic when they perceive it as threatening "basic securities," they do not understand it, or they feel it is being imposed on them. If change itself is to be approached in a pro-life way, these three sources of resistance or "trauma" will have to be taken very seriously.

Argyris and Schön's scheme.   As our first, and in many ways most important, paradigm for achieving social change, let us again consider the typology of social "theories of action" proposed by Chris Argyris and Donald Schön (1974). (A theory of action is defined by Argyris and Schön as a person's conception of what actions will produce what consequences under what conditions; but as they actually use the concept, it also includes commitment to a particular set of goals or "governing variables" such as those previously discussed in reference to Model 1 and Model 2.) Recall that *Model 1* refers to a way of relating to other people that is characterized by unilateral goal-setting, a win/lose orientation, repression of feelings, and actions designed to unilaterally control environments, tasks, and the "protection" of self and others. Such an approach to interpersonal behavior—and perhaps to social change—tends to result, according to Argyris and Schön, in highly defensive, information-withholding and distorting, mistrustful social relations. In addition, Argyris and Schön posit that it inhibits open public examination and testing of underlying goals and social attributions. Furthermore, they argue persuasively that Model 1 behavior is pervasive in our society, evidenced at times even by many of those (Ralph Nader, for example) who are trying to get the society to move in a pro-life direction. One need only consider the nearly ubiquitous use of coercive, competitive, unilateral techniques such as lawsuits and economic pressure.

Model 2, on the other hand, is an approach to social behavior characterized by the goals of maximizing "valid information," "free and informed choice," and "internal commitment to the choice" for *all* involved. It calls for actions oriented toward creating situations where all participants can be Origins (in deCharms's [1968] sense; see Chapter 2), where *all* participate in controlling the task, and where protecting oneself and others is also a joint and open operation. All of this results supposedly in minimal defensiveness, high trust, and open public confrontation and testing of basic goals and procedures.

In general, we might summarize and perhaps slightly oversimplify by thinking of Model 1 as a manipulative, competitive, secretive way of dealing with people—or of trying to change things—and by thinking of Model 2 as a collaborative, cooperative, *openly exploratory* way of relating to people or of trying to change things. I have already argued that a Model 2 approach is by far the more pro-life, utopian way for people to relate to each other and that it would indeed necessarily be the dominant mode of social behavior in a truly utopian society.

A key question to consider as we proceed to explore specific change techniques is the degree to which a Model 2 approach may perhaps also be necessary in the process of changing to a more utopian society. This is in part simply the old question of whether "bad" means can adulterate good ends. But it is also the question of whether it is even possible to *manipulate* people into forming a pro-life utopia. While Model 1 tactics may conceivably be necessary to overpower or outwit absolutely incorrigible enemies of widespread human well-being and happiness, I think the odds are that a Model 2 approach will turn out to be necessary to use with the intended beneficiaries of any pro-life visions. As Lauer (1973) implied, a change will tend to be resisted or disliked unless it is perceived as nonthreatening, is understood, and is seen as not being imposed. It is doubtless possible on occasion to manipulate people into viewing a change in this way (see, for example, Varela, 1971), but in the long run it seems much better to collaborate with them in seeking out good changes rather than to decide unilaterally in advance. Aside from the obvious implications for enhancing general Competence and Compatibility, such open collaboration would also maximize the generation of new ideas for change.

Chin and Benne's scheme.   Robert Chin and Kenneth Benne (1969) have proposed a three-part typology for social change strategies, which can be summarized as follows:

> 1. *empirical-rational approaches*—just present the facts and arguments and rely on human rationality and self-interest to do the rest (examples would be trying to induce change through utopian novels, basic research, television documentaries, Presidential Commissions' reports, or traditional educational lectures);
>
> 2. *normative–re-educative approaches*—bring the people to be changed into the change process; give attention to their attitudes, values, norms, and social relations (as well as to new information) as paths to change; work collaboratively with the people to help them define their problems,

clarify their values, increase their problem-solving ability, and remove blocks to changes they desire (examples would include encounter groups, Origin training, and values clarification; obviously this type of approach is very similar to Argyris and Schön's ideas of Model 2 behavior);

3. *power-coercive approaches*—use economic, political, physical, or even "moral" force to coerce the changes you want (examples would include lawsuits, violent revolutions, union strikes, consumer boycotts, civil disobedience, terrorism, sabotage, "pulling rank," spanking, using extrinsic motivators such as grades or pay, and even guilt- or fear-provoking attitude change techniques; all such tactics clearly fall within the Model 1 paradigm).

This tidy little typology does not necessarily exhaust all types of change strategies (see the discussion below of socio-technical innovation, for instance). Nevertheless, it provides a very useful classificatory scheme and serves as a helpful reminder of the range of possible approaches to social change. As we shall see, although the empirical-rational and normative–re-educative strategies are much more in keeping with Model 2, various types of power-coercive potential (at least) may be essential if one side in a conflict is to induce a reluctant opponent to resolve the conflict in a cooperative, information-seeking fashion.

Schein's scheme.   Edgar Schein (for example, 1972) has developed an extension of a change model first proposed by the famed social psychologist Kurt Lewin. Basically, Schein's notion is that personal or social change occurs in a three-stage process: "unfreezing," "changing," and "refreezing." *Unfreezing* is the generation of the initial motivation to change, and arises from such processes as the "disconfirmation of present beliefs, attitudes, values, or behavior patterns," the "induction of 'guilt-anxiety' by comparison of actual with ideal states," and the "creation of psychological safety by the reduction of threats or removal of barriers to change." *Changing* is the process of "developing new beliefs, attitudes, values, and behavior patterns" and proceeds either by "identification" with the views of a specific single source of information or by what Schein regards as the more desirable process of "scanning multiple sources of information" in search of the best match with one's current motivations and situation. Finally (and this process is often ignored in change attempts), *refreezing* is "stabilizing and integrating new beliefs, attitudes, values, and behavior patterns into the rest of the system." This is a process that occurs by "integrating new responses

into the total personality or culture" or "into ongoing significant relationships and into [the] total social system through reconfirmation by
significant others."[6]

Schein's scheme is thus intended as a general model of the change
process rather than as a typology of different specific types of strategies.
Thus, presumably a Model 1 *or* a Model 2 approach, or any one or more of
the strategies in Chin and Benne's typology, could conceivably be used at
the unfreezing, changing, or refreezing stages in the overall change
process. Nevertheless, the types of applications Schein suggests, and the
information/Origin-oriented tone of his model, make this scheme especially applicable to understanding Model 2 or normative–re-educative
change procedures. In essence, it is suggested that a good "change
agent" would try to help people (1) see the discrepancies between
things as they are and things as they could be; (2) overcome unwar-
ranted fear of change; (3) be creative and thorough in searching out
innovations that fit their situation and real needs; and (4) effectively integrate the chosen innovations into a new stable pattern of behavior (an
effect that follows readily *if* people themselves search out and freely
choose the change). It is interesting to note the similarity between
Schein's view of change and the procedures that deCharms (1971, 1976)
used in his Origin training program (see Chapter 2) or that David and
Roger Johnson (1975) recommended for teaching new skills (see Chapter 5).

Socio-technical techniques for social change.   Finally, an approach referred to by John Platt (1966) as social "seed operations" (or more
fully as "self-amplifying socio-technical inventions") can lead to substantial social/environmental change but does not seem to fall readily
into any of the above categories. Basically, the idea is to invent some
new device or procedure that provides reinforcement for new patterns
of behavior and that thereby promotes desirable social change. Some of
Platt's examples are the telephone, postage stamp, federal income tax,
modern contraceptives, and the Constitution of the United States.
G. Tyler Miller (1975) has further developed this idea and labelled it
the "tunnel effect" (after the image of "tunneling through" problems by
providing an innovation that undercuts the conditions that produced
the problem or conflict, thus allowing everyone to "win").

Although in principle this sort of change strategy seems very simple
and appealing, many people may find the specific examples offered by

Platt and Miller not entirely convincing. Most of the inventions cited have indeed solved problems, but as can be seen by the possible sexist and health problems associated with some modern contraceptives or the win/lose conflicts and "dirty tricks" generated by the United States political system, any particular invention may turn out to have undesirable effects as well as desirable ones. Nevertheless, authors such as Platt, Miller, and Papanek (see Chapter 6), by advocating such a "socio-technical" approach to pro-life social/environmental change, have thereby provided a very creative slant on how to produce such change by a relatively painless process. We might simply note that perhaps an addition (or safeguard) needed is for people to be more collectively and collaboratively involved in the process of choosing and evaluating exactly what socio-technical innovations they wish to have thrust upon themselves—and with what effects.

Comment on evaluating change tactics. To conclude this brief and selective look at change models, I would like to point out that the Comps scheme can be applied to an evaluation of the experiential consequences of change techniques themselves—just as it has been applied to evaluating experiential consequences of cognitive sets, environmental designs, and even utopian social systems. Since a change tactic is presumably intended merely as a transition from one state to another, it may seem odd to be concerned with how much a tactic itself enhances participants' experience by its effects on Complexity, Comprehension, and so on. However, as organizers such as Saul Alinsky (1971) have pointed out, change activities must themselves be interesting and satisfying if people are to remain long involved. And perhaps most important, change tactics that are inherently low in Compatibility (for example, power-coercive and other Model 1 approaches) should probably be viewed with extreme caution and with a constant search for high-Compatibility substitutes.

Of course, the Comps also point to important considerations relating to the *effectiveness* of potential change techniques. For instance, tactics directed at unfreezing would presumably have to affect Comparison by accentuating negative aspects of the status quo or by raising people's expectations of what they could or should get (that is, by increasing people's CLs; see, for example, Pettigrew, 1967). And increases in CLs are, as previous chapters have noted, facilitated by enhanced Competence, by Composition arising from focus on possible improvements in one's situation, by insight into one's full range of alternatives, by a low feeling of strain, by effective behavior (which increases Competence), and probably by the good feelings arising from enhanced Complexity. Similarly, clear comprehension of the likely effects of alternative courses of action would seem to be crucial for both changing and refreezing, especially if a Model 2 approach is being used.

Even for power-coercive tactics, however, it is helpful to consider the role of the eight Comps and of cognitive-set processes. For example, how opponents *interpret* each other's actions is critical to the success of threats. Following Alinsky's (1971) argument that it is what the opposition *thinks* you can do that is important, it seems clear that appropriate stimulation of your opponent's imagination can in itself sometimes force negotiation or prevent your defeat.

But the most critical consideration for low-power groups—that is, for those most likely to be seeking pro-life change in the United States—is to increase the number and commitment of people involved in working toward such change. To do this will require getting more and more people to activate cognitive sets that promote (1) comprehension of big problems and big alternatives; (2) insight into the great potential effectiveness of collective action; (3) ever-rising expectations and demands; (4) a sense of personal competence; and (5) an understanding of the benefits of a high-Compatibility existence for all people.

So What Can We Do?

I would argue that we need change strategies that effectively move our society—and indeed the whole world—toward a social system based on the previously suggested structural requirements for a pro-life utopia: (1) distribution of resources and power according to an Equity 2 norm; (2) both ecologically sound living and a high level of resources relative to population; (3) a system of socialization and other cultural supports conducive to full ecological consciousness and full participation by all citizens; and (4) commitment to pro-life rationality, diversity, and experimentation. Alas, I have no grand plan to offer that will irresistibly move us toward these admittedly utopian goals. Instead I will suggest three main areas of endeavor—each area itself multifaceted—that collectively would seem to hold out considerable hope.

My underlying idea is simply that there are many different types of actions that would bring us closer to a utopian world. As Charles Beitz and Michael Washburn (1974) have suggested, there may be a need for some "critical mass" of people working toward pro-life social change before the system will actually shift in that direction. These changes, however, may be in different areas of life—education, the media, business, religion, politics, and so forth. If the pressures for change are maintained long enough and are all aimed in the same general direction, the possibilities for synergistic combination and total system change are great indeed (see also G. T. Miller, 1975).

There are of course many specific areas where anyone seeking pro-life change could find something constructive to do (see Beitz and Washburn, 1974, for a good list). The three *general* areas of endeavor suggested below constitute merely one effort to organize these possibilities around a set of interrelated goals that, *taken together*, would appear to yield the utopian structural requirements discussed above. These three areas of endeavor are (1) spreading both wealth and decision-making power as equally as possible; (2) engaging in pro-life innovation, design, and research; (3) socializing for ecological consciousness and Model 2 behavior. We shall take these up in order, in each case first briefly examining the underlying goals of action and then exploring possible tactics.

Increasing Equality in Wealth and Power

Specific goals.   The basic rationale for a more nearly equal world-wide distribution of wealth and decision-making power was presented in Chapter 2. Included were considerations such as enabling far more people to satisfy basic needs, thus not only eliminating many sources of human misery and conflict but also enabling more people to reach self-actualization concerns for justice, beauty, environmental quality, understanding, and so on. Documentation of the extent of poverty and inequality in the world at large and even in the most affluent country in the world clearly reveals how far we have to go.[7]

And the problem is not only inequality in wealth and income, but also in public services, health care, self-esteem, education, status, and virtually every other facet of social existence. Such inequality does not merely create unhappiness for the less fortunate; as Herbert Gans (1973) and David and Frank Johnson (1975) have noted, inequality tends to create distrust and to inhibit cooperation and compromise.

This last problem, however, is especially true of inequality in power rather than simply in wealth (although the two tend to go together). It is on the inequality of power that I will concentrate, since it is both a source and consequence of unequal wealth and it has special significance for environmental deterioration. In addition, tactics for redistributing decision-making power tend to be the same as for redistributing wealth. Besides making trust, compromise, cooperation, and other aspects of Model 2 behavior less likely, inequality in people's ability to influence decisions that affect them may be seen as deeply implicated in our environmental problems. For example, the giant multinational corporations (see Barnet and Müller, 1974) and the mere 200,000 or so American households that control 60 to 70 percent of the corporate wealth in this country (Domhoff, 1970) possess not only great wealth but great decision-making *power*—power to push for corporate profits and growth instead of human and environmental welfare; power to lobby for favorable tax laws and subsidies for themselves and thus to reduce the level of public funds; power to deprive people of their jobs or to use such deprivation as a threat to block sound environmental policies; power to waste resources, plan obsolescence, and control regulatory agencies (all to the disadvantage of the consumer); power to pollute; power to shape the mass media and issue "ecopornography" through advertising; power to influence political campaigns through contributions (legal and otherwise); power to dominate foreign policy; power to siphon off vast chunks of the world's resources for the most wasteful and anti-life purpose of all (military expenditures)—a purpose in part made "necessary" by the very inequalities in wealth and power that these powerful people and corporations help to spawn in the first place.[8]

It is not that such people and organizations are "bad" or are actively against human happiness and a pleasant environment. It is simply that they are seeking their own self-interest as they see it in a social system that has prepared and allowed them to exert far more decision-making power than most other people or organizations. Indeed, as many have argued (see, for example, Weisberg, 1971; Commoner, 1976; Anderson, 1976; and earlier chapters), capitalism as an economic system has built-in reinforcements for growth and profit as the central values directing decision making. And social psychologists such as Morton Deutsch (1975) and Edward Sampson (1975) have pointed out that the modes of economic behavior tend to carry over into the rest of social life; a competitive, capitalistic system will tend to encourage treating people as means rather than ends and using differentials in power as a base for winning out over others.

Many specific subgoals have been suggested for increasing the equality with which wealth and power are distributed, both for our society and for the world at large. Before looking at possible action tactics, let us very briefly consider the following selected examples of such proposed subgoals:[9]

—Tax rich individuals and corporations more heavily (largely by closing existing tax loopholes, legislating high inheritance taxes, and reducing present subsidies to the rich), and redistribute the wealth to the poorer segments of the society by such means as (1) a relatively high guaranteed minimum income (as by use of a "credit income tax"— see Gans, 1973); (2) better public services, housing subsidies, public transportation, health care, and environmental amenities such as parks; (3) better education; and (4) aid to self-help community organizations (such as community development corporations—see below).

—Provide guaranteed employment for all who want it (but, as Boyer, 1975, noted, it is important to couple this with a high guaranteed minimum income to avoid forcing people into unpleasant jobs for relatively low pay).

—Distribute corporate wealth more widely, as by dispersing stock ownership or even by replacing profits taxes with public (governmental) ownership of a portion of corporate stock (a suggestion offered by Schumacher, 1973).

—In general, move toward a socialist economic system—but one devoted to low "throughput" of nonrenewable resources, to other ecologically sound practices, and to as much decentralized, worker/consumer control as feasible.

—Increase control of production facilities and environmental decisions by representatives of workers, consumers, and the general public—regardless of the specific type of economic system; in the United States, decrease the control of governmental regulatory agencies by the industries they are supposed to be regulating; also, increase input to regulatory and design commissions by the ultimate clients (for example, have students represented on school boards, welfare recipients on welfare boards, users of public housing on the design review boards; see Gans, 1973).

—Move toward "egalitarian" as opposed to "majoritarian" democracy, as by increasing proportional representation to take account of minority group interests, funding all political campaigns from public money, increasing communication between people and legislators, eliminating the seniority system in legislatures, and increasing community control (all recommended by Gans, 1973).

—Substitute an international "peace-keeping" system for our present "war-making" system (Boyer, 1975) and thereby free vast amounts of the world's effort and resources for alleviating problems of poverty and environmental deterioration, as well as eliminate the threat of thermonuclear holocaust (see also, for example, Brown, 1972; Falk, 1972).

—Reduce the power of the so-called multinational corporations (mainly giant United States corporations with a "global reach")—seemingly major current sources of great inequality between and within many nations, as well as promoters of unwise growth, pollution, waste of resources, and sustained poverty for many "underdeveloped" countries (see especially Barnet and Müller, 1974; but also such analysts as Weisberg, 1971, and Anderson, 1976). Barnet and Müller suggest, for example, decentralizing corporate control (especially passing a substantial measure of control to the host country or community), increasing international cooperation among governments to control the multinational corporations, promoting national development plans proposed by the people, passing special reforms in tax and banking laws, and instituting similar changes that would increase public and local control and thus help redistribute wealth and power (as well as enhance environments).

Power-coercive and power-gaining tactics. As even Morton Deutsch (1969) has acknowledged, it is often difficult for a low-power person or group to induce a high-power opponent in a conflict situation to resolve the conflict through a cooperative (Model 2, mutual problem-solving) approach. It is simply too tempting to *use* high power if you have it. Hence, a standard piece of advice for those without much wealth or power, even from many analysts who favor a cooperative approach, is to get power (and at least threaten to use it if the other side will not engage in mutual cooperation). This advice would apply not only to poor people but also to those in the higher socioeconomic classes who would "save the environment" or who simply want to have a greater say in what happens to them and to their world. As we explore these power-oriented, basically Model 1 techniques, however, we might keep in mind that even these tactics can be used with the ultimate goal of attaining Model 2 conflict resolution. The late Saul Alinsky (1971), one of this country's most ingenious designers of power-coercive strategies for the less-than-equal, realistically indicated that negotiation is brought about by the power to compel negotiation. And, indeed, for the creation of a more Model 2 oriented world, perhaps all that is needed is sufficient power not to be readily defeated: if you can bring the price of competitive conflict home to your opponent, it may be easy to argue for a cooperative resolution.

But Alinsky has had far more to say than just that negotiation may take a little power-coercive nudging. For example, Alinsky (1969) pointed out that labor unions have become relatively conservative forces committed to preserving the employer/employee relationship and that what is really needed instead are full-scale "People's Organizations" oriented toward a better life, not just better work contracts. And in his later and more complete primer for organizers (*Rules for Radicals*), Alinsky (1971) provided many insightful guidelines for helping low-power groups "get it together"—all based on actual experience in community organizing. The following are just a few examples of the advice Alinsky gives:

—Stay close to the experience and goals of the people being helped to organize (for example, tax reform or pollution abatement might be appropriate topics for the middle class, while an end to rent-gouging or rats might be more appropriate as a start with the very poor).

—In forming a citizens' organization, it is important to attract large numbers of people; this is helped by a multiplicity of goals (indeed, one might compare logrolling in Congress, whereby Congresspersons help each other with local bills in a mutual back-scratching arrangement).

—To arouse awareness of problems and perhaps stir up hope, ask Socratic questions (for example, "What would happen if *none* of you paid rent to that slumlord?"—this is of course an excellent way to induce change-oriented cognitive sets).

—A feeling of some power over a situation is essential if people are to feel motivated to come up with creative ideas for how to improve it (compare the discussion of IMG sets in Chapter 3).

—A good way for people to gain a sense of power is for them to have a successful experience in doing something constructive (compare Sommer's [1972, 1974] ideas on starting close to home in making environmental improvements; also, a personal communication from William Boyer [1976] recounted several instances in which students whom he had encouraged to do some small environmentally beneficial thing went on to bigger and bigger projects after the first taste of effectiveness). It is thus important to start with relatively small—but *realizable*—goals.

—Actual power tactics for low-power groups include such "mass ju-jitsu" activities as making the opponent (high-power) group live up to its own proclaimed rules, playing off one powerful group against another (as in the case of low-power countries' using conflicts between major world powers to benefit themselves), and using humor and ridicule not only to gain support from group members and third parties but also to goad opponents into making errors.

—The tactics themselves should be enjoyable to the membership of a citizens' organization. This point is obviously important for drawing in new members and retaining old ones, especially in view of Useem's (1975) observation that many potential members of such groups know that they will benefit from successful efforts of protest movements and citizens' organizations whether or not they themselves participate.

—New tactics must continually be generated, both to counter the Establishment's ability to learn how to defeat old ones and to maintain the interest and enthusiasm of members.

—One of the most effective power techniques is the implicit threat provided by letting one's opponent know of a workable plan that would be of low cost to one's group but expensive to the opposition. (This seemed to be Alinsky's favorite strategy, illustrated by such examples as a ghetto organization's threat to tie up all the toilets in Chicago's main airport unless the city came through on commitments it had previously made to the organization.)

One of Alinsky's main ideas was clearly that low-power people can gain power in large part because of their numbers and because of the vulnerability of a purportedly democratic Establishment to harassment, ridicule, and losing the support of important third parties (such as swing voters or large segments of the middle class). Certainly the central point that Alinsky makes, however, is that *organizing* is essential. Low-power people must join together if they are to achieve a better balance of power.

Once organized, though, there are many possible tactics other than those Alinsky has emphasized. This is especially evident in the environmental realm, where environmental action groups may be regarded as attempting to spread more equally the power to affect the physical environment. You might almost say that while corporations and many land developers are out to use resources and the general physical environment mainly for the sake of profit and growth, "the people" would rather make environmental decisions on the basis of what leads to a more fulfilling and pleasant life for themselves and their offspring. Well, that may be a bit idealized; but the conflict between environmental organizations and those they oppose often seems to take on this pro-people versus pro-profit aspect. Indeed, one problem, as pointed out by political analysts such as Lamb (1972) and David and Peterson (1973), is that special-interest groups (the usual lobbies in Congress and even in local politics; also see Boyarsky and Boyarsky, 1974) tend to predominate in political decision making, leaving the general public interest to wither for lack of sufficient representation.

Of course, environmental groups and certain other public-interest organizations are now starting to make a dent in this pattern (see, for example, Morrison et al., 1972, for a seemingly accurate projection that the environmental movement would shift to power strategies). And the tactics of such groups extend well beyond harassment and ridicule—although these are used on occasion at least by individuals, as illustrated by Love and Obst's (1971) book on "ecotage." Specifically, it is increasingly common to find such groups engaging in political campaigns, lobbying, lawsuits, administrative hearings, initiating citizen referenda, advertising, and related activities.[10]

It is true that for the most part even the more radical of such organizations have not actively sought radical changes in the underlying economic system that perpetually fuels many of our social and environmental problems (see the discussion of the environmental movement in Chapter 5). Nonetheless, as Lynton Caldwell (1975), among others, has noted, environmental problems are "inevitable consequences"—not "unfortunate accidents"—of our sociopolitical system. Thus, almost inevitably, attempts to deal with them effectively will have to call for transformations of that system. If people such as Alinsky, Boyer, and Sommer are correct in their notion that radical change is best approached through gradual accretion of success and power by citizens' groups, perhaps what we are now witnessing in the organizations of the environmental movement is the beginning of an effort wherein concerned citizens will soon be demanding truly radical transformations. Whether they will have the means to achieve such transformations may depend on the extent to which different types of "people's organizations" or "liberation" groups manage to form *coalitions* (see, for example, Kidder and Stewart, 1975; David and Peterson, 1973).

Before leaving the area of power-coercive strategies, perhaps a few words should be said about the more extreme forms of such endeavors. Mild harassment, lawsuits, working for the passage of new legislation, and even boycotts and strikes are one thing, but serious "ecotage" (compare Weisberg's [1971] suggestion that the most environmentally dangerous production facilities should be destroyed) and violent revolution are, of course, another. It is probably generally agreed that violent revolution is exceedingly unlikely in the United States (see, for example, Rejai, 1973). Still, William Gamson (1975) did find in his examination of various protest organizations in American history that "unruly" groups (those using violence, strikes, and other "constraints") tended to be more successful in gaining "acceptance" and "new advantages" than did the less unruly. (This was true mainly for unruly groups that had fairly high public support to start with.) Overall, though, it seems clear that except in the most dire circumstances—some of which may indeed occur from time to time at various places around the world—violence against people would be so low in Compatibility and so conducive to counter-violence that it would probably only be reasonable as a strategy of last resort or of self-defense. Unfortunately, however, powerful Establishment forces often react to even nonviolent efforts at change with violence.

Normative–re-educative (and empirical-rational) tactics.   In ideal form, a Model 2 or normative–re-educative approach to equalizing the distribution of wealth and power would consist of cooperative confrontation and reasoning with the existing "power structure" that would lead those in power to become unselfish, cooperative, and willing to share their wealth and power. Such conversions may in fact occur on rare occasions. Erich Fromm (1955) and E. F. Schumacher (1973) have recounted instances of factory owners freely sharing control and profits with the workers (see below), although in the cases reported the instigation seemed to originate with the owners themselves rather than with the workers.

One of my students, Kevin Martin, has indeed offered the intriguing suggestion of trying to persuade the heads of at least a few major corporations to try to achieve pro-life transformations in their corporations—with the hope that the transformed corporations would serve as models for comparison with the traditionally operated ones. Given the success of the Scott Bader Commonwealth (an example cited by Schumacher, 1973, of a British corporation virtually given to the workers by the owner), such an effort might not be so far-fetched as it might sound. Indeed, Schein (1972) has discussed institutional change in terms of finding an appropriate "point of entry"—a person or group who is accessible, suitably linked to the rest of the system, and likely to be changed. Certainly it does not seem unreasonable to hope to change at least *some* powerful people (politicians, teachers, principals, wealthy heirs, even corporation presidents) by normative–re-educative approaches. Key problems include, of course, access to the powerful person and, as Schein would put it, one's "leverage" on such a person and the "vulnerability" of the person to a change in the desired direction. Also, there does not now seem to be any magic formula for converting successful practitioners of Model 1 behavior to a Model 2 pattern, which of course would entail sharing power. Even working with a group of six people who actively wanted to shift toward Model 2, Argyris (1976a,b) found that they required several very intensive workshops over a three-year period in order to do so. But since each of these six was in fact the president of a company, there may indeed be hope yet! Also, the popularity of encounter groups and other consciousness-raising activities among many relatively wealthy and powerful people may give added evidence for a measure of vulnerability to pro-life change within the Establishment.

But the more "realistic" view, expressed by writers such as G. William Domhoff (1971, 1974), is that it is less effective to "debate with the power structure" than to engage in what Domhoff calls "psychic guerrilla warfare." With this colorful phrase Domhoff included a vast variety of basically information-oriented tactics, all designed to alert people to the oppression and injustice of the system under which they live. Domhoff actually proposed a three-part overall strategy for "committing revolution in corporate America": first, research the power structure; second, work with people to propose visions of a better society; and third, use a variety of political and informational techniques to educate people to their oppression and thus to undercut their support for the status quo. These techniques might include everything from staging guerrilla theatre to forming an "American Revolutionary Party" or using political primaries to run radical candidates (who could use the primary campaigns to raise searching questions and expose the electorate to the faults and injustices of the society).

As Rejai (1973) has noted, Americans tend to have a somewhat illusory sense of participation; and as the articles in Lerner (1975) reviewed, Americans also tend to have a sense that this is a "just world" and that all people get what they deserve. Now, these are very comforting beliefs, and any attempt to challenge them is likely to run into difficulty both from the Establishment and also from people's tendency to insulate themselves from threatening insights. Nevertheless, issues such as inequitable taxation, environmental degradation, and perhaps the grossest forms of poverty and inequality do seem to register even on many of the most defensive Americans. If one hope would be to raise the level of moral thinking of those in power so that they would both see themselves as largely responsible for these problems and also be motivated to take constructive actions, a more realistic hope might be to help the less powerful understand more fully the nature of their plight and to form cooperative organizations for the purpose of changing the basic socioeconomic structure that gives rise to the problems of poverty, environmental degradation, and unrealized human potentials.

How can this be done? On the face of it—with education, the media, government, labor, and business firmly behind the status quo—it might seem nearly impossible. There is, however, reason for optimism. Pro-life changes toward greater equality in wealth and power, environmental enhancement, Model 2 behavior, cooperation, and so on, would be for the benefit of the masses of people across the planet. It is not to the benefit of these people to keep the world (or even our society) as it now is. Hence, arguments for pro-life change can be made in a relatively straightforward way with appeals to people's ultimate self-interest as well as to any higher moral sense they may possess. Those who wish to maintain our current system of injustices and environmental degradation, on the other hand, must argue in a distorting, manipulative way— or else use some sort of direct power-coercion (threats about the loss of jobs, and so on).

A similar point has been made by Joseph Robertson and John Lewallen (1975) in their book *The Grass Roots Primer*. Along with over a score of other tips on how to form successful citizens' environmental organizations, they include advice to remember that exploiters must conceal and delude (standard Model 1 behavior), while environmentalists are really working for everyone's good (well, *some* environmentalists—

see Chapter 5). They also urge an effort to "debunk the economic claims" of exploiters—to ask, "Who benefits and who pays?" Such a strategy often reveals long-term costs of environmental exploitation usually hidden from public consciousness. As Alinsky (1971) pointed out, *leaders* want to get power for themselves, but *organizers* want to get power for others. This is part of the essence of the distinction between Model 1 and Model 2, and it reveals the difficulties that must ultimately be faced by the perpetrators of our existing problems concerning the environment and social justice.

Still, even if many people could be drawn into people's organizations devoted to pro-life change, what tactics could they use that would themselves be high in Compatibility? In keeping with Domhoff's notion of psychic guerrilla warfare, a major one would of course be continued enlightenment of the rest of the public. Relatively large and powerful environmental and public-interest organizations, for example, may be able to support research and produce exposés (compare Ralph Nader's work).[11] Such organizations can also use the mass media and even initiate educational programs in addition to the organizations' regular publications. Especially helpful might be dissemination of success stories of how citizens manage to organize and achieve specific goals (such as the cases presented in Robertson and Lewallen, 1975, or Fanning, 1975). Indeed, one of Alinsky's (1971) suggested tactics for helping people organize is to point out how others have been successful. But in addition to disseminating information and arousing the populace, tactics such as legislative lobbying, arguing cases in court, initiating and campaigning for referendum issues, appearing before administrative hearings, and serving as advocates for low-power groups *can* all be conducted in Model 2 fashion. True, none of these approaches in itself has yet made much of a dent in the overall system. But collectively they do seem to present considerable potential, especially if we keep in mind G. T. Miller's (1975) counsel to work for synergistic combination of pro-life forces and to keep the pressure up long enough for delayed effects to emerge.

In conclusion, let me reiterate the second step in Domhoff's (1971, 1974) advice on how to bring about a nonviolent revolution in America: work together with other people to form a viable vision of a better society. As Russell Ackoff (1974) insightfully pointed out, it is usually easier to obtain agreement on *ends* rather than means. Thus the very process of involving people in a collective effort to picture the future they want may help draw them together, in addition to providing a CL-raising, action-inducing goal. (Who knows, it might even provide a basis for collaboration between those in power and those not.)

Recently, John Anderson, an innovative architect in Burlington, Vermont, initiated a widespread effort by townspeople and schoolchildren to come up with visions of what they would like Burlington to become. What, if anything, will finally come of this effort is not yet known; but it has captured the imaginations of many people and provided a hint of the excitement and creativity that could arise from the public's involvement in generating social and environmental goals. As mentioned earlier with respect to the need for systems thinking and consideration of systemic alternatives, a major prerequisite for moving toward a utopian society seems to be for people to start contemplating alterations in underlying social systems and to form utopian conceptions. As Sherif and his colleagues (1961) demonstrated on a small scale, a key path to cooperation is the need to collaborate to reach a *superordinate goal*—a goal so exciting, big, and important that it transcends old conflicts. If people can be encouraged to generate *collective* plans and visions of this magnitude, it may be but a short step to the widespread realization that mass collaborative action could improve life for virtually everyone.

Engaging in Pro-Life Innovation, Design, and Research

Main goals. In contrast to the main task implied in the previous section—to organize with others for the purpose of either forcing or co-operatively arguing for greater equality and environmental quality—the primary goal of this second major area of pro-life ("utopian") endeavor is to generate new ideas, new inventions, new models and examples, and new slants on social research and interpretation. The spirit of this type of activity was hinted at in the earlier account of socio-technical approaches to social change. Based on the views of such ecologically oriented scientists as John Platt (for example, 1966) and G. Tyler Miller (1975), the main notion is to devise some new plan, invention, or idea that in itself facilitates progress toward a pro-life world and does so in a self-reinforcing way that allows virtually everyone to "win." There is obviously room for considerable overlap with the previously discussed goal of redistributing wealth and power, but the basic approach fits neither the power-oriented nor (in many cases) the direct normative-re-educative tactics discussed up to now. We shall examine three general areas where pro-life innovation seems especially promising as a technique for generating utopian social/environmental change: technical/social/ideational inventions; real-life models and examples; and new orientations in social science and other professional activities.

Technical/social/ideational inventions. Robert Lauer (1973) has pointed out that changes in technology can effect social change by (1) increasing available alternatives; (2) modifying patterns of social interactions; and (3) both creating and solving social problems. Similarly, he argued that ideologies can inhibit, aid, or direct change by (1) legitimizing new social directions or new behavior patterns; (2) forming a basis for social solidarity; (3) providing motivation for individuals (and groups); and (4) "confronting society with contradictions." The challenge, of course, is to come up with scientific, technical, and "ideological" inventions that move society in a pro-life direction. As examples of areas where more work is needed (and hence the potential for action exists), let us consider the following:

1. In recent years, some rather simplistic and linear suggestions have been made for arresting the exponential growth rate of the world's population. Obviously, uncontrolled population growth, with all that it implies for decreasing per capita resources and increasing international tensions, is an exceedingly serious problem. However, it is becoming increasingly clear that a far more profound and systemic strategy will be needed than simply inventing better contraceptives, easily reversible vasectomies, and legal or economic sanctions against having children. Systems thinkers such as Arthur Dyck (1971), Lester Brown (1972), and Allan Chase (1971), to name only a few, have convincingly argued that what is really needed to reduce world population growth (especially if this is to be done in a pro-life, nontotalitarian way) are *all* of the following: greatly decreased poverty, provision of security for old age, increased literacy and generally improved education, improved sanitation and general health care, decreased infant mortality, enhanced status for women, education in family planning techniques and in the implications of population growth, improved nutrition—and, *along with all these things,* the development of better contraceptive techniques and perhaps the introduction of external economic and legal sanctions that would encourage smaller families.

Obviously, the range of socio-technical inventions that would facilitate this varied package of goals is enormous. For instance, in the previous chapter Victor Papanek (1971) was cited as calling for designers to contribute a portion of their efforts to helping the poor across the world (and, indeed, virtually all people across the world) by working for the fulfillment of real human needs—needs that would best be served by inexpensive, ingenious devices for better education, health care, communication, sanitation, safety, housing, transportation, agriculture, and so on. One possibility would be for designers to follow the example and suggestion of Papanek and actually donate some of their work time to such design endeavors. Even better, of course, would be for our own overdeveloped society to make a concerted effort through corporate- and government-sponsored research to give the world exactly the sort of innovations that Papanek and his students have attempted and argued for.

2. In addition to easing population problems, technological innovations of service to our own poor and the poor of the Third World could also help these people to become more self-sufficient, thus fulfilling human needs for enhanced Competence as well as equalizing power and wealth. E. F. Schumacher (1973), for instance, has called for the development of an "intermediate technology" that would facilitate "production by the masses, rather than mass production" (see also Illich, 1973). The idea would be to invent tools and procedures that would allow universally accessible, small-scale production in a way that is compatible with people's need for creativity and community. Schumacher even coined the term "Buddhist economics" to apply to a system whose goal would be to "maximize happiness with minimum consumption" and that would view work itself as an activity that should be productive, enjoyable, and cooperative. (Not necessarily the most efficient possible way to maximize profit, growth, and consumption, but certainly utopian.) In any case, Schumacher's pro-life goals would clearly be aided by the sorts of inventions called for by Papanek. Remember, though, that the corporate structure of the United States, especially in its multinational branches, thrives by taking local natural resources, employing cheap foreign labor, supporting incredible inequalities in the socioeconomic structure of these countries (our own, too), and encouraging dependence by foreign and domestic labor alike (again, see the excellent work by Barnet and Müller, 1974). Hence, the effects of Schumacher's and Papanek's type of technological innovations—and their world-wide use— could be radical indeed.

3. Technological invention could also be a great help in environmen-

tal and resource enhancement. Examples would be new, efficient techniques for recycling materials; nonpolluting energy sources (but note that within our society short shrift has been given to development of promising energy sources, such as solar and wind power, that did not promise to line the pockets of the "energy Establishment"—see, for example, Commoner, 1976; Miller, 1975); effective ways of removing pollutants; pleasant and efficient mass transit; new forms of modular housing; and any number of other domains where we are doing so little relative to our society's efforts in military technology and environmentally irresponsible profit seeking. Also, it is encouraging to think of what highly trained synectics teams might be able to do with such pro-life design problems if given time and support.[12]

4. Finally, consider the innumerable problem areas in which new ideas or social procedures could move us closer to a utopian society. Platt (1973), for instance, has pointed out how what he calls "social traps" and "social fences" can be overcome by human ingenuity. A social trap is a situation in which the short-term reinforcement is positive, but the long-term consequences are negative. Cigarette smoking is one example, and Garrett Hardin's (1968) tragedy of the commons is both a social trap and a "group trap" (where positive outcomes to individuals lead to behavior that is harmful to the whole group). A social fence is a situation characterized by negative short-term consequences but positive long-term ones. For instance, the immediate costs of better schools or sewage treatment often deter communities from behavior that would be to their long-term gain.

According to Platt there are six types of solutions to such situations, and together they illustrate a sizable range of areas in which innovative pro-life ideas could induce social change. Briefly, they are as follows: (1) Find ways to make long-term consequences more immediate, as by educating people to imagine these effects. (2) Impose "counterreinforcers," such as fines or rewards. (3) Ameliorate long-term negative consequences, as in finding a cure for cancer induced by cigarette smoking or environmental contaminants. (4) Add positive reinforcers for alternative behaviors that do not have negative long-term effects. (5) Use outside consultants or "therapists." (6) Set up a "superordinate authority to prevent entrapments, to allocate resources, to mediate conflicts, and to redirect immediate reinforcement patterns to more rewarding long-range goals" (as in the case of regulatory agencies or planning commissions).

Perhaps the most important aspect of Platt's discussion is the basic idea of social traps itself. Once recognized for what they are, the types of situations he describes may become less lethal. Prisoners who *know* they are in a "Prisoners' Dilemma" or commons users who *know* they are about to face a "commons tragedy" have a much better chance to avoid the trap than do those who do not understand the structure of their situation. Of course, some considerable ingenuity will still be required to "solve" the trap. Since many of the world's current problems of environmental degradation can be characterized as social traps or fences, this would indeed seem an important domain for more ingenuity.

As noted, the number of areas in which innovative pro-life ideas are needed is virtually limitless. Platt's generalization of concepts such as the Prisoners' Dilemma and the tragedy of the commons into the notion of social traps is just one example. Other illustrations would include suggestions for noncompetitive games that foster environmental concern as well as communal fun (see Fluegelman, 1976); innovations in tax schemes in order to redistribute wealth (for example, the negative income tax and especially the credit income tax—see Gans, 1973); ideas on how to change voting procedures to increase the representation of minority views in government and on how to change corporate structure to allow reciprocal power between subordinates and supervisors (see Ackoff, 1974); plans for an international political party oriented toward world unity (for example, Wagar, 1971); changes in our paradigms for how to solve social problems (see Varela, 1971) or how to relate to each other (as in Argyris and Schön's concept of Model 2); and changes in our prevailing ideas about what is just (for example, Rawls, 1971; Lerner, 1975) or what we can rightfully expect of government (as in Christopher Jencks's [1972] notion that we should come to regard government regulation of income distribution as a proper federal function). Even innovations in how to innovate, such as Gordon's and Prince's work on synectics or de Bono's on lateral thinking (see Chapter 3), are examples of how ideational invention can facilitate pro-life social change.

Real-life models and examples.   Earlier in this chapter, several actual semiutopian ventures were briefly discussed. Included were a relatively successful commune (Twin Oaks) modeled after some of Skinner's ideas in *Walden Two*, the successful egalitarian kibbutzim in Israel, and the huge society of contemporary China (which it would not be an exaggeration to characterize as "the wonder of the 'underdeveloped' world"). As noted, these examples of alternative social structures do not demonstrate the absolute realizability of utopia, but they do demonstrate the feasibility of some important elements in utopian design, such as equality and cooperation without loss of viability or motivation to engage in productive work, communal child rearing without social dissolution or personal trauma, pro-life values as feasible guiding lights for a continuing society, participation and self-sufficiency on a large as well as a small scale, and federation of cooperating but autonomous communities.

Similarly, endeavors on a scale less grand than a whole society or even than an intact commune can point out real potentials and serve as models for other people, institutions, or communities to emulate (or to improve on). For instance, the Scott Bader Commonwealth discussed by Schumacher (1973) has already been offered as an example that proves the feasibility both of a pro-life worker-managed company and of finding owners with a value system prompting them to initiate such an enterprise. Erich Fromm (1955) recounted similar cases in his discussion of "community of work" corporations in Europe—worker-controlled organizations devoted to solidarity, consensus, continuing education, and recreation, as well as to production. Charles Hampden-Turner (1974) has provided examples and an extensive rationale for a related development in the United States, the community development corporation (CDC)—basically, a local community-owned business venture that has broad social purposes for benefiting the whole community. CDCs are intended not only to make a profit and thus bring resources into the community, but also to provide services for the community and, even more important, to facilitate the development of greater community competence, identity, political power, and so on. Even if Hampden-Turner's embrace of this idea is overly optimistic (it is difficult to know at this time), successful CDCs are one example of how poor communities can gain a measure of self-sufficiency and greater wealth. The idea of the CDC thus constitutes a social invention of considerable pro-life potential. Borrowing an observation from Beitz and Washburn (1974), we might note that an institution such as a CDC, free school, food co-op, legal aid group, or free clinic not only demonstrates the existence of alternatives and provides a potential model but also can form a nucleus for further community organizing.[13]

New orientations in social science and other professional activities. At the beginning of this book it was argued that American psychology has been disproportionately focused on the study of behavior per se to the relative neglect of experience. One possible reason mentioned for this behavioral bias was its congruence with our unremittingly materialistic and acquisition-oriented culture. In addition, it was hinted that oppression or manipulation of other people for one's own benefit hinges on the control of their behavior, since that is what most directly affects one's own experience. Unfortunately, this orientation in the study of human psychological processes would seem to maximize the chances for discovering how to oppress or manipulate but not how to help people increase their happiness. This book has tried to argue for (and from) this latter orientation. While I have no great hopes for an imminent, massive swing in this direction by psychology and the other behavioral sciences, there are a few promising signs on the horizon. Recent research on "the perceived quality of life" (Campbell et al., 1976), the resurgence of interest in imagery and other processes linking cognition and affect (see Chapter 3), and the pro-life value tone increasingly apparent in many criticisms of contemporary psychology (for example, Argyris, 1975, and a large portion of humanistic psychology as represented, say, in the *Journal of Humanistic Psychology*) all betoken a more experience-oriented concern in psychology.

Note also that the prevailing orientation in psychology and the various social sciences may in itself be a force for social change. Social *sciences,* after all, can lend status and acceptability to ideas that have ideological implications. Indeed, they do this willy-nilly. For instance, the writings of some economists (for example, Mishan, Daly, Galbraith, Theobald, and Schumacher) have certainly helped to legitimize socialistic ideas and concern for the interrelations of economic processes with human and environmental well-being. And, as George Miller (1969; see Chapter 2) pointed out, the conceptions of human nature and possibilities purveyed by psychology can have a profound effect on what people think and do—regardless of the actual "truth" of the conceptions. Also, the very questions asked by the social sciences reflect (and perhaps induce) areas of social concern. Witness the growth of "environmental" branches of virtually all of the social sciences within the last decade or so. Here especially it should be clear, considering the potential for environmental issues to force a re-examination of the consequences of our entire sociocultural system, that social science could indeed help to encourage demand for social change.

But let us return for a moment to the criticism of psychology's role in the status quo. In addition to the behavior bias, other and perhaps related problems have been exposed recently. Argyris's (1975) indictment of most experimental work on attitude change and certain other aspects of social psychology has already been mentioned (see Chapter 4). He pointed out that experimental paradigms that employ unilateral goal-setting, deception, secrecy, and other forms of manipulation tend to yield results that are applicable and applied mainly in situations calling for unilateral goal-setting, deception, secrecy, and other forms of manipulation. That is, both the research and its application have tended to be overwhelmingly Model 1.

A somewhat different problem has been identified by Nathan Caplan and Stephen Nelson (1973), who accused psychology of inadvertently supporting the status quo by stressing "person-centered" explanations and "cures" for social problems rather than challenging the underlying social system as the root cause. Thus, poverty and drug problems, for example, tend to be blamed on inadequacies in the victims; and linear treatment programs tend to be suggested (drug rehabilitation centers, special programs for delinquents, and so on). An alternative approach would be to explore and "treat" such underlying social forces as poverty, forced dependence, and bureaucratic harassment. As Caplan and Nelson argue, however, the person-blame approach serves a number of status-quo–maintaining functions (just as Gans, 1973, pointed out that poverty itself serves a number of functions, such as provision of cheap labor). Included, for example, are freeing the government and other social institutions of any blame for social problems, allowing these institutions to appear humane when they try to help, and legitimizing relatively cheap "person-change" treatments rather than expensive "system-change" treatments. As Caplan and Nelson put it, *"person-blame interpretations are in everyone's interests except those subjected to analysis"* (p. 210, italics in original).

It is interesting to speculate about whether there might be some relationship between such functions of person blaming in the areas of social problems and the more generalized effort at "person blaming" in the environmental realm. Thus, as noted in Chapter 4, polluting industries (along with even some well-meaning environmentalists, to be sure) have tended to stress the responsibility of the *individual* for environmental problems (the "pollution is everybody's business" idea). The self-serving nature of such generalized person-blaming attributions should be clear—the alternative would be to question the economic and decision-making *systems* that cough up profits as well as pollution (see, for example, Gale, 1972; Weisberg, 1971). Psychology's infatuation with and perhaps inherent bias toward such person-oriented causal attributions may help add legitimacy to them wherever they occur. (Note even my own tendency to approach long-term social change in terms of changing individual consciousness on a broad scale!)

Psychology is of course not alone among the human sciences in being criticized as a servant of the status quo. C. Wright Mills (1959), among others, has argued that "grand theory" in sociology has in many cases tended to "legitimate stable forms of domination" (p. 49). (See also, for example, Useem, 1975.) Sexism in sociology has been singled out for attack as well (Millman and Kanter, 1975). Economists such as Galbraith (1973) have attacked the conservative bias and ideological functions of traditional economic theory. Indeed, I am confident that every discipline in the social sciences has recently been criticized as supporting our current anti-life system in some way.

But it is easy to criticize. What do these critics advise social scientists to *do* about the situation? I have of course argued that we should concentrate more on understanding the ways—systemic and psychological—that we could optimize the long-term quality of experience. Presumably this would require greater attention to understanding the interrelations between cognitive processes and the affective tone of experience. If my theory is correct, we would benefit greatly by gaining more insight into the social/environmental/cognitive underpinnings of the eight Comps. Psychologists might also give more attention to the various elements of ecological consciousness, including systems thinking, B-cognition, a cooperative orientation, and so on. And, as Caplan and Nelson (1973) argue, a sizable shift in the direction of trying to understand the *systemic* interrelations and causes of social, psychological, and environmental problems would seem of the utmost importance. All of this would represent a major reorientation in psychology; but, as indicated earlier, there are some signs that this may be beginning to take place. Fortunately, social scientists can choose to reorient themselves if they are willing to take some risks.

Argyris has also called for a radical shift in psychology (and, by implication, in the other social sciences), especially with respect to experimental methodology. Namely, Argyris (1975) urged the adoption of a Model 2 strategy for carrying out research. This would mean such drastic changes as consulting and collaborating with subjects on research goals as well as techniques, an end to deception, and full disclosure of hypotheses at the start of research. The research experience would thus become a true learning situation for both the subjects and the experimenters (indeed, the distinction between them might begin to dissolve). At the very least, subjects would be encouraged to confront the goals of the research and not merely to be passively manipulated. Now all of this *is* radical. Indeed, it is difficult even to find examples of such research outside of Argyris's own work and the few additional instances he cites (see Argyris, 1975, 1976a,b; Argyris and Schön, 1974). Of the work I have cited in this book, perhaps deCharms's research on Origin training (see Chapter 2) comes closest, although I would hope that at least some of the research following more traditional paradigms will nonetheless have Model 2 applications. In any event, just as a shift toward Model 2 patterns of social behavior would be of decidedly pro-life value in such areas as education and parent/child interactions (see next section), so would such a shift in the social sciences generally yield a new force for utopian social change. At the very least, as Argyris has pointed out, we need to study *new* models of social behavior and not just assume that what Americans have been doing expresses "human nature." Indeed, the same could be said for alternative norms of equity (see Chapter 2 and also Lerner, 1975) and virtually every other aspect of our culture.

Finally, on the issue of how social science research and theory can aid pro-life social change, we might recall George Miller's (1969) idea of "giving psychology away." We have of course explored this before, but there are other considerations in addition to Miller's points about helping to expand people's views of human nature and potentials and providing them with useful techniques for solving their everyday problems. (See also Varela, 1971, but be alert to his rather manipulative applications.) For instance, speaking mainly as sociologists, but with equal application to nearly all the other human sciences, C. Wright Mills (1959) and Irving Tallman (1976) have pinpointed two very different ways of viewing social events—two very different cognitive sets, if you will. Tallman refers to the distinction as *particularistic* versus *universalistic* ways of interpretation, the former meaning viewing events mainly in terms of the immediate circumstances and individuals involved, the latter, interpreting events as representative instances or symptoms of broader social forces. The distinction in some ways parallels that between linear and systems thinking, and would be illustrated, say, by viewing a given polluter as a deviant who should be punished (particularistic interpretation) versus viewing the polluter as part of a general social problem calling for institutional or systemic change (universalistic perception).

This distinction is also implicit in Mills's (1959) notion of the *sociological imagination,* which corresponds to universalistic thinking and involves understanding how social forces interrelate with individual experience. Examples might be seeing one's economic difficulties as arising from inflationary forces spawned by corporate interests in a competitive capitalistic system, or interpreting one's lack of recreational space as indicating social forces geared to ends other than human well-being. The point I wish to emphasize is that social scientists can help people develop a "sociological imagination" or a "universalistic" way of perceiving their own everyday life situations. In this way, fundamental social change—and hence solutions involving corrections of the underlying causes of our problems—might be facilitated. Indeed, as Tallman might put it, the passion and moral indignation needed for radical reform will be aroused only when people come to see their problems in a universalistic way.

To conclude, let us look very briefly at the *action* side of social science and related professions. Various forms of "advocacy," for example, would seem to offer opportunities for social scientists, urban planners, architects, lawyers, and other professionals to speak out for low-power groups (often including the middle class as well as the poor). We have encountered this notion earlier in this chapter as well as in Chapter 6. It is based on a presumed pluralism in social decision making, according to which any group with an interest in important decisions is supposed to have an impact on the final outcome. As many critics have argued, however, important social and environmental decisions are often much less open to influence by advocates than the pluralist position would imply.[14]

Nevertheless, the more activist forms of professional aid to low-power groups can be of value even in the face of a recalcitrant Establishment. For instance, social scientists, architects, planners, lawyers, and so forth, can use their expertise to help communities organize and reach their *own* goals. Robert Goodman (1971), for example, argued that architects and other design professionals could function as technical advisers to low-power groups who were trying to take direct action such as constructing their own dwellings (see also John Anderson's work in Philadelphia cited in note 12, Chapter 2). Similarly, Ira Iscoe (1974) has urged community psychologists to strive to help communities become more competent—more able to use their resources and increase their "repertoire of possibilities." In the process, he cautions, such communities will be pursuing *their* goals and will probably come to expect more and more from the broader society. But this, of course, is exactly what is needed to generate a demand for structural social change. If community mental health efforts are indeed to become more than a "pacification program" (Statman, 1971), attempts at stimulating Iscoe's brand of community competence will certainly be necessary. It may be too much to ask that professionals, not to mention "pure academics," work collaboratively with the people they affect or study. However, for those who are so inclined, the possibilities for aiding pro-life social change would seem to be substantial, even if the risks of professional criticism are also.

Socializing for Ecological Consciousness and Model 2 Behavior

Main goals. The main goal of socializing for ecological consciousness and Model 2 behavior is somehow to facilitate each person's becoming adept at systems thinking and B-cognition, sensitive to ecological interrelations and human interdependence, oriented toward interpersonal openness and collaboration, and guided by a self-derived value system that stresses optimizing the quality of all sentient creatures' experience. Such people—who might be characterized as cooperative, self-actualizing, pro-life Origins—could presumably be counted on to collaborate in the production and continuation of a fairly utopian world. Since probably few of us now fully match this description, we have a fair way to go. Just to point out a few hurdles:

The predominance of a male sex role characterized by aggressiveness, orientation toward individualistic success and competitive achievement, inhibition of emotional expression and self-disclosure, and a general tendency to try to dominate others
An educational system that currently prepares people for comfortably fitting into a society dominated by the just-outlined male sex role

A typical pattern of parent-child relations characterized by decidedly
Model 1 behavior

Mass media that in general defend and promote the status quo even
while claiming to be "objective" and "pluralistic"[15]

Again, this sort of list is easy to extend. But my goal in this chapter is
not to stress how terrible things are or how hard it will be to change
them, but rather to point out that there are many lines of possible
action. As I have hinted from time to time, my own greatest hope for a
long-term shift (or drift) toward a more pro-life society lies in socialization procedures, perhaps most centrally in educational processes.
Thus, to conclude our survey of promising tactics for approaching a
more utopian existence, let us now turn very briefly to a few of the ways
in which those involved in socializing others (most of us) could do it in
a more utopian way.

Education.   Chapters 3, 4, and 5 have already presented discussions of
educational approaches to facilitating ecological consciousness, so we
need not attempt a complete review here. Some key points are to use a
cooperative goal structure (see especially David and Roger Johnson,
1975), to encourage the development and practice of a wide and ever-
growing repertoire of cognitive sets that enhance as many Comps as
possible (especially Compatibility), to ensure ecological understanding
and appreciation, to facilitate not only values clarification but actual
growth in moral and valuational development, to utilize intrinsic motivation and help people become Origins, to encourage creativity and
systems thinking, and to involve all participants (that is, learners and
teachers) in collaborative pro-life action.

Still other suggestions were given in those earlier discussions, but a
few additional notions may be presented here. First, Argyris and Schön
(1974) seemed to regard Model 2 behavior as best taught by instructors
who (1) present Model 2 behavior themselves; (2) lead students in
tasks that call for Model 2 patterns, such as special role playing, case
study anaylsis, and cooperative group activities; and (3) encourage students to analyze their own behavior in terms of the Model 1/Model 2
paradigm—an activity that Argyris and Schön have found tends to lead
people to see the predominance (and ineffectiveness) of Model 1 behavior in their lives. Argyris and Schön also recommended that a good
tactic to move faculty members toward an active Model 2 orientation

is to get them to compare what they teach with what they practice.

Second, in a provocative call for change in professional education, Edgar Schein (1972) argued that there is need for much more flexibility, interdisciplinary work, and concern for the ultimate clients (that is, the actual users of professional services). Examples of helpful innovations would be a learning-centered (as opposed to teaching-centered) appoach to education; the use of variable modular units in place of the usual rigid course structure; greater collaboration among faculty, students, and administrators; and continual system-wide self-diagnosis and evaluation. Schein of course also discussed such changes in terms of his model of social change processes—and pointed out that unfreezing is best achieved if those desiring others to change work *with* them rather than *at* them. A similar idea was put forth by Neil Postman and Charles Weingartner (1971) in their "soft" approach to gaining change in education. They advised students, for instance, to ask searching questions, to help teachers become better informed, to create new materials and suggest new courses, to put forth detailed alternatives, and to try to get teachers to see contradictions in their ideas or between their ideas and their lives (compare Argyris and Schön's suggestion).

Finally, however, the impassioned and shattering criticism of our educational system offered by Jonathan Kozol (1975) should force us all to take more seriously the need for *acting* on pro-life beliefs in our lives outside the school. Kozol's anger and his critical focus seemed to arise mainly from his personal experience in helping victims of the crushing poverty that our society allows—and, according to Kozol's view, is in fact built upon. He may overstate the degree to which affluence for some is built directly on poverty within *this* society, although there can be little doubt that the same system that generates affluent consumption also gives rise to poverty. That same competitive, individualistic, corporate-capitalistic, overconsumptive system, however, even more inevitably helps to maintain poverty, militarism, dictatorial regimes, and untold suffering on a *world* scale. And Kozol has pointed a finger shaking with outrage at our society's educational system for failing to get students upset about this, at least upset enough to take action.

An example Kozol gave for how the schools might move in this direction was the case of a social studies teacher who simply required each of her students to perform some potentially effective real-life action (outside the school) based on whatever belief the student arrived at after careful study. Kozol reported that this rule has led students to such actions as press campaigns, picketing, and planning a boycott—all in the interest of slum residents. At least one university professor (William Boyer, personal communication, 1976) has employed a similar action rule in an environmentally oriented course—with excellent results, it seems.

Parent/child interactions.   Just as it was argued in Chapter 5 that the cooperative goal structure approach put forth by David and Roger Johnson (1975) could easily revolutionize education in a pro-life direction, so I believe the approach to child rearing developed by Thomas Gordon (1975, 1976; see also Gordon, 1974) could, if widely adopted, radically alter family socialization practices in a Model 2 direction. Basically, Gordon advocates that parents do such things as the following:

1. Treat children as Origins and as equal to adults in importance and in basic human rights.

2. Employ Carl Rogers's style of "active listening" to help children with their problems. That is, help your child work through a personal problem by listening with the cognitive set to determine what the child's underlying feelings are and what situation the child sees as producing these feelings; and respond simply by reflecting this information to the child to demonstrate your understanding and acceptance and thus to encourage the child to clarify and deal with his or her problem.

3. Act as a consultant who offers advice, not as a dictator who orders, forces, or cajoles. (Also, be willing to accept that children will not always do what you want.)

4. Attempt to change children's behavior mainly by modifying the environment, by a combination of active listening and consulting, or by processes of mutual problem solving.

5. Resolve family conflicts by a mutual problem-solving approach, which removes the "win/lose" aspect and also, according to Gordon, enhances the quality of solutions, improves thinking skills, increases family warmth, and generally has all the other good consequences of Model 2 behavior.

This is a big order and a radical change from the usual pattern of punishment, extrinsic motivation, authoritarianism, and win/lose conflicts that characterizes most American child-rearing practices. What makes Gordon's scheme more than mere pie in the sky, however, is the consideration that he and numerous colleagues have spent a number of years actively teaching this approach in workshops on a nation-wide basis, apparently with great success both for themselves and for the parents who participate. Gordon's books have also been extremely popular. It almost seems, indeed, that his "effectiveness training" programs (for parents, teachers, and even "youth") are becoming something of a movement. If so, this might be a way of bringing Model 2 to a whole generation.

Of course, there is more to ecological consciousness than even Gordon's approach would guarantee. However, we have already touched on these issues in Chapter 5 (for example, the possibilities of group child rearing and increased adult-child contact; deliberate induction of pro-social behavior; home modeling of sound environmental practices; and parental encouragement of B-cognition, systems thinking, and pro-life values).

The media.   Again, this is a topic dealt with in past chapters, so only a few points will be added here. First, although media experts such as Peter Sandman (1974; see Chapter 4) and especially Herbert Schiller (1973) have cogently argued that the media generally support the status quo, we can find some hope in the tendency of the media at least to provide channels for the dissemination of new ideas and information about social happenings. At the very least, the book publishing industry and an apparently increasing number of "underground" newspapers and even "guerrilla" radio stations (see Beitz and Washburn, 1974) permit the expression of truly radical critiques and new ideas. And, as noted in Chapter 4, we can perhaps even take heart in the possibility of social eversion (Slater, 1974; Reich, 1970) arising as environmental and leisure-oriented advertising helps, perhaps inadvertently, to push pro-life values.

Still, there is obviously great need for change if the media are to function as socializing forces for ecological consciousness and Model 2 behavior (including seeking valid information as well as striving for mutual cooperation). Schiller (1973) himself has found hope in the increasing number of intelligent, well-educated, and critical people who are becoming involved with the media; and Beitz and Washburn (1974) have offered intriguing advice to those who might see the media as an avenue to social change (for example, the choice of what to report as "news" is often more important than any ideological bias in how it is reported). A few illustrative examples of areas where change is needed would be the following:

1. As pointed out by Zick Rubin and Letitia Anne Peplau (1975), the media have helped to promote the idea of a "just world" where all people get what they deserve (this is especially true in children's entertainment). Rubin and Peplau argue that this leads to blaming the victim—to regarding unfortunate or poor people as deserving their misfortune. The media could thus do a far greater service, if Rubin and Peplau's argument is correct, by promoting the view that people do not always get what they deserve and that justice is not immanent in the nature of reality. Similarly, William Samuel (1975) has cited experimental evidence implying that people are more likely to take action to help others if they perceive themselves as at least partly responsible for the others' plight. Kozol (1975) called for the schools to stimulate affluent students to have just such a sense of responsibility for the plight of poor people, and the mass media could conceivably help to extend such social consciousness to the general public.

2. Schiller (1973) has noted that public opinion polling is easily biased by the issues on which opinions are sought and by the very wording of the questions. (The spirit of the underlying problem is captured beautifully in a purported statement by Boss Tweed: "I don't care who does the electing, so long as I can do the nominating"—see Kozol, 1975, p. 139). Schiller indeed expressed concern that only illusory gains in citizen participation might arise even if technological advances make easy two-way communication possible between receivers and transmitters of media messages. For a genuine increase in citizen participation (and concomitant potential for Model 2 socialization), procedures and safeguards should be built in to ensure that the citizens will be able to generate the issues and questions and not just respond to the power structure. Perhaps the citizens' ballot initiative, as it exists in California and Colorado, could serve as a potential model. According to this procedure, any person or group could have an issue or a proposal placed on the agenda for public consideration simply by demonstrating that a required proportion of the audience wanted it considered. Indeed, the technological developments allowing two-way communications in the electronic media might greatly facilitate such citizens' initiatives by eliminating the need for time-consuming petition campaigns.

3. As a final example of how the media might be shifted toward pro-life socialization, consider that even advertising could conceivably be used constructively by citizens' and public interest groups. This of course has already been happening in the realms of health and of environment. A technique that could have substantial ramifications has been suggested by Hampden-Turner (1974) as a procedure specifically designed to aid community development corporations. He labelled the technique *social marketing* and defined it as "the offering of goods for sale . . . on the basis of the humanity, the community and social purposes behind the products" (p. 193). This form of advertising would thus appeal to social (or perhaps even ecological) consciousness rather than making the usual effort to manipulate the consumer to buy for reasons of status, egocentric advantage, fear, sexual association, or whatever. What I find exciting about Hampden-Turner's idea is clearly not that it is free from manipulative possibilities or even from competitive capitalism, but rather that it genuinely opens up possibilities for even commercial advertising to raise people's awareness of social (and environmental) problems and of the plight and self-help efforts of other people. And, as Hampden-Turner points out, it would encourage a cooperative joining together of sellers and buyers in a pro-life effort that would extend beyond the mere advertising or exchange of goods.

Other avenues of socialization.   Education, the family, and the media scarcely exhaust the socializing influences in our society. Law and politics in all their facets, religion, recreation, and casual conversations are but some of the other sources. In various places in this book, we have of course touched on these as both maintainers of the status quo and as potential paths to pro-life shifts in values and life styles. Obviously, some of the goals that I have presented under specific socialization headings could be pursued through changes in other socializing forces as well. As you are fully aware by now, I would argue for a broad-scale, systemic approach to pro-life change. Let us use all the paths we can, wherever we can, to lead ourselves and others to a more utopian state of being. If nothing else, we can turn our own lives into pro-life examples and perhaps also follow G. T. Miller's (1975) advice to try to convince at least two other people to do so—and to urge each of them to convince at least two new people. . . .

NOTES

1. The following discussion of each component is brief. The points raised in the more extended discussion in Chapter 6 also apply.
2. See, for example, D. Johnson and R. Johnson (1975), D. Johnson and F. Johnson (1975), Deutsch (1973), Bennis et al. (1969, 1976), T. Gordon (1974, 1975, 1976), Prince (1970), and the discussions presented in the earlier chapters of this book and in the account of change strategies later in this chapter.
3. With apologies, I am appropriating the term *deep structure* from transformational linguistics (see, for example, Chomsky, 1972), where it applies to underlying meaning, as opposed to the "surface structure," which refers to the particular way this meaning is expressed (for example, a specific sentence). My intention in referring to the deep structure of Skinner's design is to focus on the essential elements in the plan that are implicit in the novel's picture of "Walden Two," and thus to distinguish these elements from the more superficial aspects of the fictional community. Just as the underlying meaning of a sentence can often be expressed in many different ways, so the underlying plan for a utopia can be "expressed" by many different styles of life. The fictional community of Walden Two is too often criticized, I believe, merely for aspects of its surface structure (for example, the use of simplistic operant conditioning as a socializing device, a lackluster social atmosphere, the use of air cribs for infants, or the personalities of some of the book's characters).
4. See, for example, Roberts (1971; especially good on sources of communes' dissolution), Melville (1972), Kanter (1972), and Houriet (1971).
5. See Oksenberg (1973), Salisbury (1973), Sidel (1974), Committee of Concerned Asian Scholars (1972), and Mauger et al. (1974).
6. All quotations are from Schein's (1972) summary table (p. 76).
7. Brown (1972), Boyer (1975), and Barnet and Müller (1974), to name only a few, give incisive accounts of world-wide inequality. For the nature of socioeconomic inequality in the United States, see, for example, Miller and Roby (1970), Shostak et al. (1973), Gans (1973), Rainwater (1974), and Jencks (1972). Also see D. M. Smith (1973) for an interesting account of inequality between geographical areas within the United States.
8. A full list of supporting references for this array of examples of "power pollution" would be long indeed. The following are merely illustrative: Weisberg (1971), Galbraith (1973), Boyer (1975), Mills (1956), Domhoff (1967, 1970), Barnet and Müller (1974), Anderson (1976), Miller (1975), Falk (1972), Schiller (1973), Gamson (1975), and David and Peterson (1973). These works range from armchair argument to the presentation of research evidence and other reasonably "hard" facts. While neither I nor most of those cited would care to argue that we are being deliberately tyrannized by a conspiratorial power elite, the above works collectively provide substantial evidence and argument that (1) we do not currently have pluralism—whereby all interests are represented in political-economic-environmental decision making (as Gamson, 1975, argued, such pluralism may operate *within* the ruling circles, but not for the total population)—and that (2) those who have been exerting disproportionate power have acted in many ways very damaging to human and environmental well-being.

9. The sources for this list include the following works, although it should be noted that not all of these authors would agree with *all* of the suggestions (in fact, I do not necessarily agree with all of them): Miller and Roby (1970), Shostak et al. (1973), Gans (1973), Weisberg (1971), Boyer (1975), Samuel (1975), Brown (1972), Barnet and Müller (1974), Ackoff (1974), Schumacher (1973), Fromm (1955), Anderson (1976), Miller (1975), Falk (1972), Jencks (1972), and Theobald (1972).

10. Here an especially wide range of books is relevant. A few examples are the works by Mitchell and Stallings (1970), Sax (1970), Fanning (1975), Caldwell (1971, 1975), Robertson and Lewallen (1975), De Bell (1970a,b), Love (1971), and Swatek (1970).

11. Of special interest in this regard are the "Public Interest Research Groups" (PIRGs) initiated by Ralph Nader. According to Fanning (1975), by the early 1970s PIRGs were being sponsored by students at well over 100 colleges in 25 states. PIRG activities have included concerted efforts on behalf of energy conservation, consumer interests, and numerous other issues relating to environmental and public welfare. It is hard to say what the future holds for these organizations, but they obviously provide a ready channel for pro-life, action-oriented research, lobbying, and public education.

12. See Chapters 3 and 5 for a discussion of synectics. Also note that the ideal is probably for the technologically more advanced societies to help train creative designers in the poorer parts of the world, not simply to give away the finished products or designs.

13. However, as Seymour Sarason (1972) has spelled out in some depth, there are often-overlooked difficulties in creating a new "setting" (a goal-oriented enterprise involving two or more people; examples range from marriages to utopian societies). Some key problems, for instance, are conflicts with already established settings, conflicts between the leader and core group, competition among core group members, the "myth of unlimited resources," leaders' tendency to view the setting as *theirs,* and the danger of boredom as the setting lasts. Indeed, the last problem may be the crucial one for many utopian and social-change endeavors, for, as Sarason points out, in the early stages of a new setting, people tend to be selfless, group-centered, and happy; but maintaining this euphoric state of group commitment is no easy task (see also Kanter, 1972; and see Duberman, 1972, for a fascinating case study).

14. See, for instance, Mazziotti (1974; but see also the Davidoffs' commentary included with that article), Kuenzlen (1972), and Guskin and Ross (1971).

15. On the male sex role, see, for instance, David and Brannon (1976). Also, it is interesting that there is research evidence that American males are more likely than American females to use Equity 1 norms in experimental settings (with females tending toward Equity 2 norms, presumably for the sake of enhancing interpersonal harmony; see Walster and Walster, 1975; Sampson, 1975). For critiques of our educational system, see references in previous chapters and also Kozol (1975). On parent-child relations, see Gordon (1975); and for excellent critiques of the media, see Schiller (1973) and Sandman (1974).

REFERENCES

Ackoff, R. L. *Redesigning the future: A systems approach to societal problems.* New York: Wiley, 1974.

Adams, J. L. *Conceptual blockbusting: A guide to better ideas.* San Francisco: Freeman, 1974.

Adams, J. S. Inequity in social exchange. In L. Berkowitz (Ed.), *Advances in experimental social psychology* (Vol. 2). New York: Academic Press, 1965.

Agne, R. M., & Nash, R. J. Environmental education: A fraudulent revolution? *Teachers College Record,* 1974, *76,* 304–315.

Agne, R. M., & Nash, R. J. The teacher educator as environmental activist. *Journal of Teacher Education,* 1976, *27,* 141–146.

Albrecht, S. L. Legacy of the environmental movement. *Environment and Behavior,* 1976, *8,* 147–168.

Alexander, C. A city is not a tree. *Architectural Forum,* 1965, *122,* 58–62 (April), 58–61 (May).

Alinsky, S. D. *Reveille for radicals.* New York: Vintage Books, 1969.

Alinsky, S. D. *Rules for radicals.* New York: Vintage Books, 1971.

Allen of Hurtwood, Lady. *Planning for play.* Cambridge, Mass.: MIT Press, 1968.

Allport, F. H. *Theories of perception and the concept of structure: A review and critical analysis with an introduction to a dynamic-structural theory of behavior.* New York: Wiley, 1955.

Allport, G. W. *The nature of prejudice.* Reading, Mass.: Addison-Wesley, 1954.

Allport, G. W. *Becoming: Basic considerations for a psychology of personality.* New Haven: Yale University Press, 1955.

Altman, I. Some perspectives on the study of man-environment phenomena. *Representative Research in Social Psychology,* 1973, *4,* 109–126.

Altman, I. *The environment and social behavior: Privacy, personal space, territory, crowding.* Monterey, Calif.: Brooks/Cole, 1975.

Anderson, C. H. *The sociology of survival: Social problems of growth.* Homewood, Ill.: Dorsey, 1976.

Anderson, S. (Ed.). *Planning for diversity and choice: Possible futures and their relations to the man-controlled environment.* Cambridge, Mass.: MIT Press, 1968.

Angyal, A. *Foundations for a science of personality.* Cambridge, Mass.: Harvard University Press, 1941.

Appelbaum, R. P. *Theories of social change.* Chicago: Markham, 1970.

Appley, M. H., & Trumbull, R. *Psychological stress: Issues in research.* New York: Appleton-Century-Crofts, 1967.

Appleyard, D. Why buildings are known: A predictive tool for architects and planners. *Environment and Behavior,* 1969, *1,* 131–156.

Appleyard, D. Styles and methods of structuring a city. *Environment and Behavior,* 1970, *2,* 100–117.

Appleyard, D. Notes on urban perception and knowledge. In R. M. Downs & D. Stea (Eds.), *Image and environment: Cognitive mapping and spatial behavior.* Chicago: Aldine, 1973.

Apter, M. J. *The computer simulation of behavior.* New York: Harper & Row, 1970.

Argyris, C. Dangers in applying results from experimental social psychology. *American Psychologist,* 1975, *30,* 469–485.

Argyris, C. *Increasing leadership effectiveness.* New York: Wiley, 1976. (a)

Argyris, C. Theories of action that inhibit individual learning. *American Psychologist,* 1976, *31,* 638–654. (b)

Argyris, C., & Schön, D. A. *Theory in practice: Increasing professional effectiveness.* San Francisco: Jossey-Bass, 1974.

Arieti, S. *Creativity: The magic synthesis.* New York: Basic Books, 1976.

Arnheim, R. *Art and visual perception.* Berkeley: University of California Press, 1954 (rev. ed., 1974).

Arnheim, R. *Visual thinking.* Berkeley: University of California Press, 1969.

Arnold, M. (Ed.). *Feelings and emotions: The Loyola symposium.* New York: Academic Press, 1970.

Aronoff, J. *Psychological needs and cultural systems: A case study.* Princeton, N.J.: Van Nostrand, 1967.

Bach, R. *Jonathan Livingston Seagull.* New York: Avon, 1970.

Bachelard, G. *The poetics of space* (M. Jolas, trans.). Boston: Beacon Press, 1964.

Baird, J. C., Degerman, R., Paris, R., & Noma, E. Student planning of town configuration. *Environment and Behavior,* 1972, *4,* 159–188.

Bakan, D. *The duality of human existence.* Chicago: Rand McNally, 1966.

Ball, D. W. *Microecology: Social situations and intimate space.* Indianapolis: Bobbs-Merrill, 1973.

Barber, T. X., Spanos, N. P., & Chaves, J. F. *Hypnosis, imagination, and human potentialities.* New York: Pergamon, 1974.

Barbour, I. G. (Ed.). *Earth might be fair: Reflections on ethics, religion, and ecology.* Englewood Cliffs, N.J.: Prentice-Hall, 1972.

Barbour, I. G. (Ed.). *Western man and environmental ethics: Attitudes toward nature and technology.* Reading, Mass.: Addison-Wesley, 1973.

Barker, M. L. Information and complexity: The conceptualization of air pollution by specialist groups. *Environment and Behavior,* 1974, *6,* 346–377.

Barker, R. G. *Ecological psychology.* Stanford, Calif.: Stanford University Press, 1968.

Barker, R. G., & Schoggen, P. *Qualities of community life.* San Francisco: Jossey-Bass, 1973.

Barnet, R. J., & Müller, R. E. *Global reach: The power of the multinational corporations.* New York: Simon & Schuster, 1974.

Baron, R. A. *The tyranny of noise.* New York: Harper & Row, 1970.

Barron, F. *Creativity and personal freedom.* Princeton, N.J.: Van Nostrand, 1968.

Bartlett, F. C. *Remembering.* Cambridge, England: Cambridge University Press, 1932.

Bateson, G. *Steps to an ecology of mind.* New York: Ballantine Books, 1972.

Beal, J. B. The new biotechnology. In J. White (Ed.), *Frontiers of consciousness.* New York: Julian Press, 1974.

Bechtel, R. The undermanned future. In B. Honikman (Ed.), *Responding to social change.* Stroudsburg, Pa.: Dowden, Hutchinson & Ross, 1975.

Beck, A. T. *Depression: Clinical, experimental, and theoretical aspects.* New York: Harper & Row, 1967.

Beck, R. J., & Wood, D. Cognitive transformation of information from urban geographic fields to mental maps. *Environment and Behavior,* 1976, *8,* 199–238.

Beckmann, P. *Eco-hysterics and the technophobes.* Boulder, Colo.: Golem Press, 1973.

Beecher, H. K. *Measurement of subjective responses.* New York: Oxford University Press, 1959.

Beitz, C., & Washburn, M. *Creating the future: A guide to living and working for social change.* New York: Bantam Books, 1974.

Bender, T. *Environmental design primer.* New York: Schocken Books, 1973.

Benedict, R. Synergy: Some notes of Ruth Benedict. *American Anthropologist,*

1970, 72, 320–333. (Based on 1941 lectures; notes selected and edited by A. H. Maslow & J. J. Honigmann.)

Benello, C. G., & Roussopoulos, D. (Eds.). *The case for participatory democracy: Some prospects for a radical society.* New York: Grossman, 1971.

Bennis, W. G., Benne, K. D., & Chin, R. (Eds.). *The planning of change* (2nd ed.). New York: Holt, Rinehart and Winston, 1969.

Bennis, W. G., Benne, K. D., Chin, R., & Corey, K. E. *The planning of change* (3rd ed.). New York: Holt, Rinehart and Winston, 1976.

Berlyne, D. E. *Conflict, arousal, and curiosity.* New York: McGraw-Hill, 1960.

Berlyne, D. E. Arousal and reinforcement. In D. Levine (Ed.), *Nebraska symposium on motivation, 1967.* Lincoln, Neb: University of Nebraska Press, 1967.

Berlyne, D. E. *Aesthetics and psychobiology.* New York: Appleton-Century-Crofts, 1971.

Berlyne, D. E., & Madsen, K. B. (Eds.). *Pleasure, reward, preference: Their nature, determinants, and role in behavior.* New York: Academic Press, 1973.

Bettelheim, B. *The children of the dream: Communal child-rearing and American education.* New York: Macmillan, 1969.

Bevlin, M. E. *Design through discovery* (2nd ed.). New York: Holt, Rinehart and Winston, 1970.

Bissell, J., White, S., & Zivin, G. Sensory modalities in children's learning. In G. S. Lesser (Ed.), *Psychology and educational practice.* Glenview, Ill.: Scott, Foresman, 1971.

Blake, P. *God's own junkyard: The planned deterioration of America's landscape.* New York: Holt, Rinehart and Winston, 1964.

Blau, P. M. *Exchange and power in social life.* New York: Wiley, 1964.

Blaut, J. M. *Studies in developmental geography* (Place Perception Research Report No. 1). Worcester, Mass.: Clark University Graduate School of Geography, 1969.

Boguslaw, R. *The new utopians: A study of system design and social change.* Englewood Cliffs, N.J.: Prentice-Hall, 1965.

Bookchin, M. On spontaneity and organization. In R. Kostelanetz (Ed.), *The edge of adaptation: Man and the emerging society.* Englewood Cliffs, N.J.: Prentice-Hall, 1973.

Bookchin, M. *The limits of the city.* New York: Harper & Row, 1974.

Boring, E. G. *A history of experimental psychology* (2nd ed.). New York: Appleton, 1950.

Borton, T. *Reach, touch, and teach: Student concerns and process education.* New York: McGraw-Hill, 1970.

Boyarsky, B., & Boyarsky, N. *Backroom politics.* Los Angeles: Tarcher, 1974.

Boyer, W. H. *Alternative futures: Designing social change.* Dubuque, Iowa: Kendall/Hunt, 1975.

Brameld, T. *Education as power.* New York: Holt, Rinehart and Winston, 1965.

Brameld, T. *Patterns of educational philosophy: Divergence and convergence in culturological perspective.* New York: Holt, Rinehart and Winston, 1971.

Brameld, T. *The teacher as world citizen: A scenario of the 21st century.* Palm Springs, Calif.: ETC Publications, 1976.

Brehm, J. W. *A theory of psychological reactance.* New York: Academic Press, 1966.

Brickman, P., & Campbell, D. T. Hedonic relativism and planning the good society. In M. H. Appley (Ed.), *Adaptation-level theory.* New York: Academic Press, 1971.

Briggs, R. Urban cognitive distance. In R. M. Downs & D. Stea (Eds.), *Image and environment.* Chicago: Aldine, 1973.

Briggs, R. Methodologies for the measurement of cognitive distance. In G. T. Moore & R. G. Golledge (Eds.), *Environmental knowing: Theories, research, and methods.* Stroudsburg, Pa.: Dowden, Hutchinson & Ross, 1976.

Bronfenbrenner, U. *Two worlds of childhood: U.S. and U.S.S.R.* New York: Basic Books, 1970.

Brooks, C. V. W. *Sensory awareness: The rediscovery of experiencing.* New York: Viking Press, 1974.

Brower, S., & Williamson, P. Outdoor recreation as a function of the urban housing environment. *Environment and Behavior,* 1974, *6,* 295–345.

Brown, B. B. *New mind, new body: Biofeedback: new directions for the mind.* New York: Harper & Row, 1974.

Brown, G. I. *Human teaching for human learning: An introduction to confluent education.* New York: Viking Press, 1971.

Brown, L. R. *World without borders.* New York: Vintage Books, 1972.

Brown, R. *Social psychology.* New York: Free Press, 1965.

Bruner, J. S. *On knowing: Essays for the left hand.* Cambridge, Mass.: Harvard University Press, 1962.

Bruner, J. S. The course of cognitive growth. *American Psychologist,* 1964 *19,* 1–15.

Bruner, J. S. *Toward a theory of instruction.* New York: Norton, 1966.

Bruner, J. S., Olver, R. R., & Greenfield, P. M. *Studies in cognitive growth.* New York: Wiley, 1966.

Bruner, J. S., & Potter, M. C. Interference in visual recognition. *Science,* 1964, *144,* 424–425.

Buel, R. A. *Dead end: The automobile in mass transportation.* Baltimore: Penguin Books, 1972.

Burns, J. T., Jr. Social and psychological implications of megastructures. In G. Kepes (Ed.), *Arts of the environment.* New York: Braziller, 1972.

Burton, I. Cultural and personality variables in the perception of natural hazards. In J. F. Wohlwill & D. H. Carson (Eds.), *Environment and the social sciences: Perspectives and applications.* Washington, D.C.: American Psychological Association, 1972.

Burton, I., Kates, R. W., & White, G. F. *The environment as hazard.* New York: Oxford University Press, 1978.

Cadwallader, M. T. Cognitive distance in intraurban space. In G. T. Moore & R. G. Golledge (Eds.), *Environmental knowing: Theories, research, and methods.* Stroudsburg, Pa.: Dowden, Hutchinson & Ross, 1976.

Caldwell, L. K. *Environment: A challenge to modern society.* Garden City, N.Y.: Anchor, 1971.

Caldwell, L. K. *Man and his environment: Policy and administration.* New York: Harper & Row, 1975.

Calhoun, J. B. The role of space in animal sociology. *Journal of Social Issues,* 1966, *22,* 46–58.

Calhoun, J. B. Space and the strategy of life. In A. H. Esser (Ed.), *Behavior and environment: The use of space by animals and men.* New York: Plenum Press, 1971.

Calvin, J. S., Dearinger, J. A., & Curtin, M. E. An attempt at assessing preferences for natural landscape. *Environment and Behavior,* 1972, *4,* 447–470.

Campbell, A., Converse, P. E., & Rodgers, W. L. *The quality of American life:*

Perceptions, evaluations, and satisfactions. New York: Russell Sage Foundation, 1976.

Camus, A. *The myth of Sisyphus and other essays.* New York: Knopf, 1955.

Canter, D., & Tagg, S. K. Distance estimation in cities. *Environment and Behavior,* 1975, 7, 59–80.

Cantril, H. *The pattern of human concerns.* New Brunswick, N.J.: Rutgers University Press, 1965.

Caplan, N., & Nelson, S. D. On being useful: The nature and consequences of psychological research on social problems. *American Psychologist,* 1973, 28, 199–211.

Carr, S. The city of the mind. In W. R. Ewald (Ed.), *Environment for man.* Bloomington: Indiana University Press, 1967.

Carson, R. *The sense of wonder.* New York: Harper & Row, 1956.

Castillo, G. A. *Left-handed teaching: Lessons in affective education.* New York: Praeger, 1974.

Chase, A. *The biological imperatives: Health, politics, and human survival.* Baltimore: Penguin Books, 1971.

Chermayeff, S., & Alexander, C. *Community and privacy: Toward a new architecture of humanism.* Garden City, N.Y.: Doubleday, 1963.

Chermayeff, S., & Tzonis, A. *Shape of community.* Baltimore: Penguin Books, 1971.

Chin, R., & Benne, K. D. General strategies for effecting changes in human systems. In W. G. Bennis, K. D. Benne, & R. Chin (Eds.), *The planning of change* (2nd ed.). New York: Holt, Rinehart and Winston, 1969.

Chomsky, N. Review of *Verbal behavior* by B. F. Skinner. *Language,* 1959, 35, 26–58.

Chomsky, N. *Studies on semantics in generative grammar.* The Hague: Mouton, 1972.

Christian, J. J., Flyger, V., & Davis, D. C. Factors in the mass mortality of a herd of Sika deer (*Cervus nippon*). *Chesapeake Science,* 1960, 1, 79–95.

Clark, K. *Landscape into art.* Boston: Beacon Press, 1961.

Cobb, J. Ecology, ethics, and theology. In H. E. Daly (Ed.), *Toward a steady-state economy.* San Francisco: Freeman, 1973.

Cofer, C. N., & Appley, M. H. *Motivation: Theory and research.* New York: Wiley, 1964.

Cohen, A. R. *Attitude change and social influence.* New York: Basic Books, 1964.

Cohen, S., Glass, D. C., & Singer, J. E. Apartment noise, auditory discrimination, and reading ability in children. *Journal of Experimental Social Psychology,* 1973, 9, 407–422.

Colbert, C. Naked utility and visual chorea. In L. B. Holland (Ed.), *Who designs America?* Garden City, N.Y.: Doubleday, 1966.

Colby, A. Review of *Values and teaching* and *Values clarification. Harvard Educational Review,* February 1975, 45, 134–143.

Cole, H. S. D., Freeman, C., Jahoda, M., & Pavitt, K. L. R. (Eds.). *Models of doom: A critique of The Limits to Growth.* New York: Universe Books, 1973.

Cole, M., & Scribner, S. *Culture & thought.* New York: Wiley, 1974.

Committee of Concerned Asian Scholars. *China! Inside the People's Republic.* New York: Bantam Books, 1972.

Commoner, B. *Science and survival.* New York: Ballantine Books, 1966.

Commoner, B. *The closing circle: Nature, man, & technology.* New York: Bantam Books, 1971.

Commoner, B. *The poverty of power: Energy and economic crisis.* New York: Knopf, 1976.

Conrad, D. R. *Education for transformation: Implications in Lewis Mumford's ecohumanism.* Palm Springs, Calif.: ETC Publications, 1976.

Cook, H., & Davitz, J. *60 seconds to mind expansion.* New York: Random House, 1975.

Craik, K. H. Human responsiveness to landscape: An environmental psychological perspective. *Student Publication of the School of Design,* Vol. 18, Raleigh, N.C.: North Carolina State University, 1969, 168–193.

Craik, K. H. Environmental psychology. In *New directions in Psychology 4.* New York: Holt, Rinehart and Winston, 1970.

Craik, K. H. Environmental psychology. *Annual Review of Psychology,* 1973, *24,* 403–422.

Craik, K. H. The personality research paradigm in environmental psychology. In S. Wapner, S. B. Cohen, & B. Kaplan (Eds.), *Experiencing the environment.* New York: Plenum Press, 1976.

Craik, K. H., & Zube, E. H. *Issues in perceived environmental quality research.* Amherst, Mass.: Institute for Man and Environment, University of Massachusetts, 1975.

Criden, Y., & Gelb, S. *The kibbutz experience: Dialogue in Kfar Blum.* New York: Schocken, 1974.

Csikszentmihalyi, M. *Beyond boredom and anxiety: The experience of play in work and games.* San Francisco: Jossey-Bass, 1975.

Cullen, G. *The concise townscape.* New York: Van Nostrand Reinhold, 1961.

Cyert, R. M., & March, J. G. *A behavioral theory of the firm.* Englewood Cliffs, N.J.: Prentice-Hall, 1963.

Dahl, R. A. *After the revolution?* New Haven, Conn.: Yale University Press, 1970.

Daly, H. E. Toward a stationary-state economy. In J. Harte & R. H. Socolow (Eds.), *Patient earth.* New York: Holt, Rinehart and Winston, 1971.

Daly, H. E. (Ed.). *Toward a steady-state economy.* San Francisco: Freeman, 1973.

Dasmann, R. F. *A different kind of country.* New York: Macmillan, 1970.

David, D. S., & Brannon, R. (Eds.). *The forty-nine percent majority: The male sex role.* Reading, Mass.: Addison-Wesley, 1976.

David, S. M., & Peterson, P. E. (Eds.). *Urban politics and public policy: The city in crisis.* New York: Praeger, 1973.

Day, H. I., & Berlyne, D. E. Intrinsic motivation. In G. S. Lesser (Ed.), *Psychology and educational practice.* Glenview, Ill.: Scott, Foresman, 1971.

De Bell, G. (Ed.). *The environmental handbook.* New York: Ballantine, 1970. (a)

De Bell, G. (Ed.). *The voter's guide to environmental politics.* New York: Ballantine, 1970. (b)

de Bono, E. *The mechanism of mind.* New York: Simon and Schuster, 1969.

de Bono, E. *Lateral thinking: Creativity step by step.* New York: Harper & Row, 1970.

de Bono, E. *Practical thinking.* London: Jonathan Cape, 1971.

deCharms, R. *Personal causation: The internal affective determinants of behavior.* New York: Academic Press, 1968.

deCharms, R. From Pawns to Origins: Toward self-motivation. In G. S. Lesser (Ed.), *Psychology and educational practice.* Glenview, Ill.: Scott, Foresman, 1971.

deCharms, R. *Enhancing motivation: Change in the classroom.* New York: Irvington, 1976.

Deci, E. L. *Intrinsic motivation.* New York: Plenum Press, 1975.

de Jonge, D. Images of urban areas: Their structure and psychological foundation. *Journal of the American Institute of Planners*, 1962, *28*, 266–276.

de Mille, R. *Put your mother on the ceiling: Children's imagination games.* New York: Viking Press, 1973.

Desor, J. A. Toward a psychological theory of crowding. *Journal of Personality and Social Psychology*, 1972, *21*, 79–83.

Deutsch, M. Conflicts: Productive and destructive. *Journal of Social Issues*, 1969, *25* (1), 7–42.

Deutsch, M. *The resolution of conflict: Constructive and destructive processes.* New Haven: Yale University Press, 1973.

Deutsch, M. Equity, equality, and need: What determines which value will be used as the basis of distributive justice? *Journal of Social Issues*, 1975, *31* (3), 137–149.

Dewey, J. *Art as experience.* New York: Capricorn Books, 1934.

Dewey, J. *Theory of valuation.* Chicago: University of Chicago Press, 1939.

Dewey, J. *Experience and nature.* New York: Dover, 1958.

Dillard, A. *Pilgrim at Tinker Creek.* New York: Bantam Books, 1974.

Disch, R. (Ed.). *The ecological conscience: Values for survival.* Englewood Cliffs, N.J.: Prentice-Hall, 1970.

Dixon, N. F. *Subliminal perception: The nature of a controversy.* London: McGraw-Hill, 1971.

Domhoff, G. W. *Who rules America?* Englewood Cliffs, N.J.: Prentice-Hall, 1967.

Domhoff, G. W. *The higher circles: The governing class in America.* New York: Vintage Books, 1970.

Domhoff, G. W. How to commit revolution. In R. Buckhout (Ed.), *Toward social change.* New York: Harper & Row, 1971.

Domhoff, G. W. How to commit revolution in corporate America [plus Addenda]. In P. Brickman (Ed.), *Social conflict: Readings in rule structure and conflict relationships.* Lexington, Mass.: D. C. Heath, 1974.

Downs, R. M., & Stea, D. Cognitive maps and spatial behavior: Process and products. In R. M. Downs & D. Stea (Eds.), *Image and environment: Cognitive mapping and spatial behavior.* Chicago: Aldine, 1973. (a)

Downs, R. M., & Stea, D. (Eds.). *Image and environment: Cognitive mapping and spatial behavior.* Chicago: Aldine, 1973. (b)

Dreeben, R. American schooling: Patterns and processes of stability and change. In B. Barber and A. Inkeles (Eds.), *Stability and change.* Boston: Little, Brown, 1971.

Duberman, M. *Black Mountain: An exploration in community.* Garden City, N.Y.: Anchor Press, 1972.

Dubos, R. *Man adapting.* New Haven: Yale University Press, 1965.

Dubos, R. *So human an animal.* New York: Scribner's, 1968.

Dubos, R. *A god within.* New York: Scribner's, 1972. (a)

Dubos, R. The perils of adaptation. In G. Kepes (Ed.), *Arts of the environment.* New York: Braziller, 1972. (b)

Dubos, R. A theology of the earth. In I. G. Barbour (Ed.), *Western man and environmental ethics: Attitudes toward nature and technology.* Reading, Mass.: Addison-Wesley, 1973. (a)

Dubos, R. Humanizing the earth. *Science*, 1973, *179*, 769–772. (b)

Dyck, A. J. Ethical aspects of population policy. In R. Buckhout (Ed.), *Toward social change.* New York: Harper & Row, 1971.

Dye, T. R., & Zeigler, L. H. *The irony of democracy: An uncommon introduction to American politics* (3rd ed.). North Scituate, Mass.: Duxbury Press, 1975.

Easterbrook, J. A. The effect of emotion on cue utilization and the organization of behavior. *Psychological Review,* 1959, *66,* 183–201.

Ecology Action East. The power to destroy, the power to create. In I. G. Barbour (Ed.), *Western man and environmental ethics: Attitudes toward nature and technology.* Reading, Mass.: Addison-Wesley, 1973.

Edberg, R. *On the shred of a cloud.* New York: Harper & Row, 1969.

Edney, J. J. Human territories: Comment on functional properties. *Environment and Behavior,* 1976, *8,* 31–47.

Ehrlich, P. R. *The population bomb.* New York: Ballantine Books, 1968.

Ehrlich, P. R. Eco-catastrophe! *Ramparts,* September 1969, pp. 24–28.

Ehrlich, P. R., & Ehrlich, A. H. *Population, resources, environment: Issues in human ecology.* San Francisco: Freeman, 1970.

Eisemon, T. Simulations and requirements for citizen participation in public housing: The Truax technique. *Environment and Behavior,* 1975, *7,* 99–123.

Eiser, J. R., & Stroebe, W. *Categorization and social judgement.* New York: Academic Press, 1972.

Ellul, J. *The technological society* (J. Wilkinson, trans.). New York: Knopf, 1964.

Emery, F. E. (Ed.). *Systems thinking.* Baltimore: Penguin Books, 1969.

Emery, F. E., & Trist, E. L. *Towards a social ecology: Contextual appreciations of the future in the present.* New York: Plenum Press, 1973.

Eriksen, B. A., & Eriksen, C. W. *Perception and personality.* Morristown, N.J.: General Learning Press, 1972.

Esser, A. H. A biosocial perspective on crowding. In J. F. Wohlwill & D. H. Carson (Eds.), *Environment and the social sciences: Perspectives and applications.* Washington, D.C.: American Psychological Association, 1972.

Esser, A. H. Experiences of crowding: Illustration of a paradigm for man-environment relations. *Representative Research in Social Psychology,* 1973, *4,* 207–218.

Esser, A. H. Synergy and social pollution in the communal imagery of mankind. In J. White (Ed.), *Frontiers of consciousness: The meeting ground between inner and outer reality.* New York: Julian Press, 1974.

Etzioni, A. *The active society.* New York: Free Press, 1968.

Eysenck, H. J. Personality and the law of effect. In D. E. Berlyne & K. B. Madsen (Eds.), *Pleasure, reward, preference: Their nature, determinants, and role in behavior.* New York: Academic Press, 1973.

Falk, R. A. *This endangered planet.* New York: Vintage Books, 1972.

Fanning, O. *Man and his environment: Citizen action.* New York: Harper & Row, 1975.

Farallones. *Farallones scrapbook.* Point Reyes, Calif.: Farallones Designs, 1971. (Distributed by Random House, New York.)

Farber, J. *The student as nigger.* New York: Pocket Books, 1969.

Feigenbaum, E. A., & Feldman J. (Eds.). *Computers and thought.* New York: McGraw-Hill, 1963.

Festinger, L. *A theory of cognitive dissonance.* Evanston, Ill.: Row, Peterson & Co., 1957.

Festinger, L. *Conflict, decision, and dissonance.* Stanford, Calif.: Stanford University Press, 1964.

Fischer, C. S., Baldassare, M., & Ofshe, R. J. Crowding studies and urban life: A critical review. *Journal of the American Institute of Planners,* 1975, *41,* 406–418.

Fishbein, M., & Ajzen, I.   *Belief, attitude, intention and behavior: An introduction to theory and research.* Reading, Mass.: Addison-Wesley, 1975.

Fiske, D. W., & Maddi, S. R. (Eds.).   *Functions of varied experience.* Homewood, Ill.: Dorsey, 1961.

Flavell, J. H.   *The developmental psychology of Jean Piaget.* Princeton, N.J.: Van Nostrand, 1963.

Flavell, J. H.   *Cognitive development.* Englewood Cliffs, N.J.: Prentice-Hall, 1977.

Fluegelman, A. (Ed.).   *The new games book.* Garden City, N.Y.: Doubleday, 1976.

Footlick, J. K.   The snake pits. *Newsweek,* January 26, 1976, p. 43.

Forrester, J. W.   *Urban dynamics.* Cambridge, Mass.: MIT Press, 1969.

Forrester, J. W.   Planning under the dynamic influences of complex social systems. In G. Kepes (Ed.), *Arts of the environment.* New York: Braziller, 1972.

Fowler, H.   *Curiosity and exploratory behavior.* New York: Macmillan, 1965.

Fowler, H.   Implications of sensory reinforcement. In R. Glaser (Ed.), *The nature of reinforcement.* New York: Academic Press, 1971.

Franck, F.   *The Zen of seeing.* New York: Vintage Books, 1973.

Freedman, J. L.   *Crowding and behavior.* San Francisco: Freeman, 1975.

Freedman, J. L., Klevansky, S., & Ehrlich, P. R.   The effect of crowding on human task performance. *Journal of Applied Social Psychology,* 1971, *1,* 7–25.

Freedman, J. L., Levy, A. S., Buchanan, R. W., & Price, J.   Crowding and human aggressiveness. *Journal of Experimental Social Psychology,* 1972, *8,* 528–548.

Fried, M., & Gleicher, P.   Some sources of residential satisfaction in an urban slum. *Journal of the American Institute of Planners,* 1961, *27,* 305–315.

Fromm, E.   *The sane society.* New York: Holt, Rinehart and Winston, 1955.

Fuller, R. B.   *Utopia or oblivion: The prospects for humanity.* New York: Bantam Books, 1969.

Galbraith, J. K.   *Economics and the public purpose.* Boston: Houghton Mifflin, 1973.

Gale, R. P.   From sit-in to hike-in: A comparison of the civil rights and environmental movements. In W. R. Burch, Jr., N. H. Creek, Jr., & L. Taylor (Eds.), *Social behavior, natural resources, and the environment.* New York: Harper & Row, 1972.

Galle, O. R., Gove, W. R., & McPherson, J. M.   Population density and pathology: What are the relations for man? *Science,* 1972, *176,* 23–30.

Gamson, W. A.   *The strategy of social protest.* Homewood, Ill.: Dorsey, 1975.

Gans, H. J.   *More equality.* New York: Pantheon Books, 1973.

Gardiner, W. L.   *An invitation to cognitive psychology.* Monterey, Calif.: Brooks/Cole, 1973.

Gardner, R. W.   Cognitive controls of attention deployment as determinants of visual illusions. In P. Bakan (Ed.), *Attention.* Princeton, N.J.: Van Nostrand, 1966.

Gergen, K. J.   *The concept of self.* New York: Holt, Rinehart and Winston, 1971.

Gibson, E. J.   *Principles of perceptual learning and development.* New York: Appleton-Century-Crofts, 1969.

Gibson, J. J.   A critical review of the concept of set in contemporary experimental psychology. *Psychological Bulletin,* 1941, *38,* 781–817.

Gibson, J. J.   *The perception of the visual world.* Boston: Houghton Mifflin, 1950.

Gibson, J. J.   *The senses considered as perceptual systems.* Boston: Houghton Mifflin, 1966.

Glacken, C. J.   *Traces on the Rhodian shore: Nature and culture in Western thought from ancient times to the end of the eighteenth century.* Berkeley, Calif.: University of California Press, 1967.

Glaser, R. (Ed.).   *The nature of reinforcement.* New York: Academic Press, 1971.

Glass, D. C., & Singer, J. E.   *Urban stress: Experiments on noise and social stressors.* New York: Academic Press, 1972.

Glass, D. C., & Singer, J. E.   Responses to uncontrollable aversive events. *Representative Research in Social Psychology,* 1973, *4,* 165–183.

Globus, G. G., Maxwell, G., & Savodnik, I. (Eds.).   *Consciousness and the brain: A scientific and philosophical inquiry.* New York: Plenum Press, 1976.

Godschalk, D. R. (Ed.).   *Planning in America: Learning from turbulence.* Washington, D.C.: American Institute of Planners, 1974.

Goffman, E.   *Behavior in public places: Notes on the social organization of gatherings.* New York: Free Press, 1963.

Goffman, E.   *Frame analysis: An essay on the organization of experience.* New York: Harper & Row, 1974.

Goldsmith, E., Allen, R., Allaby, M., Davoll, J., & Lawrence, S.   *Blueprint for survival.* Boston: Houghton Mifflin, 1972.

Goldstein, K.   *The organism.* New York: American Book Co., 1939.

Goodman, P., & Goodman, P.   *Communitas: Means of livelihood and ways of life.* New York: Vintage, 1960.

Goodman, R.   *After the planners.* New York: Simon and Schuster, 1971.

Goodwin, R. N.   *The American condition.* Garden City, N.Y.: Doubleday, 1974.

Gordon, T.   *T.E.T.: Teacher effectiveness training.* New York: Wyden, 1974.

Gordon, T.   *P.E.T.: Parent effectiveness training.* New York: Plume Books, 1975.

Gordon, T.   *P.E.T. in action.* New York: Wyden, 1976.

Gordon, W. J. J.   *Synectics: The development of creative capacity.* New York: Macmillan, 1961.

Gordon, W. J. J.   *The metaphorical way of learning & knowing* (2nd ed.). Cambridge, Mass.: Porpoise Books, 1973.

Gould, P.   On mental maps. Michigan Inter-University Community of Mathematical Geographers, Discussion Paper No. 9, 1966. Reprinted in R. M. Downs & D. Stea (Eds.), *Image and environment: Cognitive mapping and spatial behavior.* Chicago: Aldine, 1973.

Gould, P.   The black boxes of Jönköping: Spatial information and preference. In R. M. Downs & D. Stea (Eds.), *Image and environment: Cognitive mapping and spatial behavior.* Chicago: Aldine, 1973.

Gould, P., & White, R.   *Mental maps.* Baltimore: Penguin Books, 1974.

Graham, H. D., & Gurr, T. R. (Eds.).   *Violence in America: Historical and comparative perspectives.* New York: New American Library, 1969.

Graham, W. K., & Balloun, J. L.   An empirical test of Maslow's need hierarchy. *Journal of Humanistic Psychology,* 1973, *13* (1), 97–108.

Grant, D. P.   Aims and potentials of design methodology. In B. Honikman (Ed.), *Responding to social change.* Stroudsburg, Pa.: Dowden, Hutchinson & Ross, 1975.

Griffitt, W., & Veitch, R.   Hot and crowded: Influences of population density and temperature on interpersonal affective behavior. *Journal of Personality and Social Psychology,* 1971, *17,* 92–98.

Gruen, V.   New forms of community. In L. B. Holland (Ed.), *Who designs America?* Garden City, N.Y.: Doubleday, 1966.

Guilford, J. P.   *The nature of human intelligence.* New York: McGraw-Hill, 1967.

Gump, P. V.   Environmental psychology and the behavior setting. In B. Honikman

(Ed.), *Responding to social change*. Stroudsburg, Pa.: Dowden, Hutchinson & Ross, 1975.

Gunther, B. *Sense relaxation*. New York: Macmillan, 1968.

Guskin, A. E., & Ross, R. Advocacy and democracy: The long view. *American Journal of Orthopsychiatry*, 1971, *41* (1), 43–57.

Gustaitis, R. *Turning on*. New York: Macmillan, 1969.

Gutman, R. (Ed.). *People and buildings*. New York: Basic Books, 1972.

Gutman, R., & Westergaard, B. Building evaluation, user satisfaction, and design. In J. Lang, C. Burnette, W. Moleski, & D. Vachon (Eds.), *Designing for human behavior*. Stroudsburg, Pa.: Dowden, Hutchinson & Ross, 1974.

Haber, R. N., & Hershenson, M. *The psychology of visual perception*. New York: Holt, Rinehart and Winston, 1973.

Hall, E. T. *The silent language*. Greenwich, Conn.: Fawcett Publications, 1959.

Hall, E. T. *The hidden dimension*. Garden City, N.Y.: Doubleday, 1966.

Hall, E. T. Meeting man's basic spatial needs in artificial environments. In J. Lang, C. Burnette, W. Moleski, & D. Vachon (Eds.), *Designing for human behavior*. Stroudsburg, Pa.: Dowden, Hutchinson & Ross, 1974.

Hall, R. T., & Davis, J. U. *Moral education in theory and practice*. Buffalo, N.Y.: Prometheus Books, 1975.

Halprin, L. *The RSVP cycles: Creative processes in the human environment*. New York: Braziller, 1969.

Halprin, L. *Cities*. Cambridge, Mass.: MIT Press, 1972.

Hampden-Turner, C. *From poverty to dignity*. Garden City, N.Y.: Anchor, 1974.

Hardin, G. The tragedy of the commons. *Science*, 1968, *162*, 1243–1248.

Hardin, G. *Exploring new ethics for survival: The voyage of the spaceship Beagle*. Baltimore: Penguin Books, 1972.

Harlow, H. F., Harlow, M. K., & Meyer, D. R. Learning motivated by a manipulation drive. *Journal of Experimental Psychology*, 1950, *40*, 228–234.

Harney, T. R., & Disch, R. (Eds.). *The dying generations*. New York: Dell, 1971.

Harrington, M. *The other America: Poverty in the United States*. Baltimore: Penguin Books, 1971.

Harris, T. G. All the world's a box. *Psychology Today*, 1971, 5 (8), 33–35.

Harrison, J. D., & Howard, W. A. The role of meaning in the urban image. *Environment and Behavior*, 1972, *4*, 389–411.

Harrison, J., & Sarre, P. Personal construct theory in the measurement of environmental images: Problems and methods. *Environment and Behavior*, 1971, *3*, 351–374.

Harrison, J., & Sarre, P. Personal construct theory in the measurement of environmental images. *Environment and Behavior*, 1975, *7*, 3–58.

Hart, R. A., & Moore, G. T. The development of spatial cognition: A review. In R. M. Downs & D. Stea (Eds.), *Image and environment: Cognitive mapping and spatial behavior*. Chicago: Aldine, 1973.

Hastorf, A. H., & Cantril, H. They saw a game: A case study. *The Journal of Abnormal and Social Psychology*, 1954, *49*, 129–134.

Hawley, R. C., & Hawley, I. L. *Human values in the classroom: A handbook for teachers*. New York: Hart, 1975.

Hayward, D. G., Rothenberg, M., & Beasley, R. R. Children's play and urban playground environments: A comparison of traditional, contemporary, and adventure playground types. *Environment and Behavior*, 1974, *6*, 131–168.

Hebb, D. O. Drive and the C.N.S. (conceptual nervous system). *Psychological Review*, 1955, *62*, 243–254.

Hebb, D. O.   Concerning imagery. *Psychological Review,* 1968, 75, 466–477.

Hedgepeth, W., & Stock, D.   *The alternative: Communal life in new America.* New York: Macmillan, 1970.

Heise, D. R.   Some methodological issues in semantic differential research. *Psychological Bulletin,* 1969, 72, 406–422.

Heilbroner, R. L.   *An inquiry into the human prospect.* New York: Norton, 1974.

Held, R.   Plasticity in sensory-motor systems. *Scientific American,* 1965, 213, 84–94.

Helson, H.   *Adaptation-level theory.* New York: Harper & Row, 1964.

Helson, H.   A common model for affectivity and perception: An adaptation-level approach. In D. E. Berlyne & K. B. Madsen (Eds.), *Pleasure, reward, preference: Their nature, determinants, and role in behavior.* New York: Academic Press, 1973.

Henry, J.   *Culture against man.* New York: Random House, 1963.

Herrigel, E.   *Zen in the art of archery.* New York: Pantheon, 1953.

Hershberger, R. G.   Toward a set of semantic scales to measure the meaning of architectural environments. In W. J. Mitchell (Ed.), *Environmental design: Research and practice. Proceedings of the EDRA 3/AR8 conference January 1972.* Los Angeles: University of California Press, 1972.

Herzberg, F.   *Work and the nature of man.* Cleveland: World Publishing Co., 1966.

Herzberg, F., Mausner, B., & Snyderman, B. B.   *The motivation to work* (2nd ed.). New York: Wiley, 1959.

Hess, R. D.   Social class and ethnic influences on socialization. In P. H. Mussen (Ed.), *Carmichael's manual of child psychology* (3rd ed., Vol. 2). New York: Wiley, 1970.

Higbee, K. L.   Fifteen years of fear arousal: Research on threat appeals: 1953–1968. *Psychological Bulletin,* 1969, 72, 426–444.

Hoffman, M. L.   Moral development. In P. H. Mussen (Ed.), *Carmichael's manual of child psychology* (3rd ed., Vol. 2). New York: Wiley, 1970.

Holmes, D. S., & Houston, B. K.   Effectiveness of situation redefinition and affective isolation in coping with stress. *Journal of Personality and Social Psychology,* 1974, 29, 212–218.

Holt, J.   *How children fail.* New York: Dell, 1964.

Homans, G.   *Social behavior: Its elementary forms.* New York: Harcourt, Brace & World, 1961.

Honikman, B. (Ed.).   *Responding to social change.* Stroudsburg, Pa.: Dowden, Hutchinson & Ross, 1975.

Houriet, R.   *Getting back together.* New York: Avon Books, 1971.

Howe, L. W., & Howe, M. M.   *Personalizing education: Values clarification and beyond.* New York: Hart, 1975.

Hsu, F. L. K.   *Americans and Chinese: Reflections on two cultures and their people.* Garden City, N.Y.: Doubleday Natural History Press, 1970.

Huxley, A.   *The doors of perception.* New York: Harper & Row, 1956.

Huxley, A.   *Island.* New York: Bantam Books, 1962.

Illich, I.   *Deschooling society.* New York: Harper & Row, 1971.

Illich, I.   *Tools for conviviality.* New York: Harper & Row, 1973.

Insel, P. M., & Moos, R. H.   Psychological environments: Expanding the scope of human ecology. *American Psychologist,* 1974, 29, 179–188.

Insko, C. A.   *Theories of attitude change.* New York: Appleton-Century-Crofts, 1967.

Iscoe, I.   Community psychology and the competent community. *American Psychologist,* 1974, 29, 607–613.

Ittelson, W. H. *Visual space perception.* New York: Springer, 1960.

Ittelson, W. H. Perception and transactional psychology. In S. Koch (Ed.), *Psychology: A study of a science* (Vol. 4). New York: McGraw-Hill, 1962.

Ittelson, W. H. (Ed.). *Environment and cognition.* New York: Seminar Press, 1973. (a)

Ittelson, W. H. Environment perception and contemporary perceptual theory. In W. H. Ittelson (Ed.), *Environment and cognition.* New York: Seminar Press, 1973. (b)

Ittelson, W. H., Franck, K. A., & O'Hanlon, T. J. The nature of environmental experience. In S. Wapner, S. B. Cohen, & B. Kaplan (Eds.), *Experiencing the environment.* New York: Plenum Press, 1976.

Ittelson, W. H., Proshansky, H. M., Rivlin, L. G., & Winkel, G. H. *An introduction to environmental psychology.* New York: Holt, Rinehart and Winston, 1974.

Jackson, E. L., & Mukerjee, T. Human adjustment to the earthquake hazard of San Francisco, California. In G. F. White (Ed.), *Natural hazards: Local, national, global.* New York: Oxford University Press, 1974.

Jackson, W. (Ed.). *Man and the environment* (2nd ed.). Dubuque, Iowa: Brown, 1973.

Jacobs, J. *The death and life of great American cities.* New York: Vintage Books, 1961.

Jahoda, M. *Current concepts of positive mental health.* New York: Basic Books, 1958.

James, W. *The principles of psychology.* New York: Holt, 1890.

Jencks, C. *Architecture 2000: Predictions and methods.* New York: Praeger, 1971.

Jencks, C. *Inequality: A reassessment of the effect of family and schooling in America.* New York: Basic Books, 1972.

Johnson, D. M. *Systematic introduction to the psychology of thinking.* New York: Harper & Row, 1972.

Johnson, D. W., & Johnson, F. P. *Joining together: Group theory and group skills.* Englewood Cliffs, N.J.: Prentice-Hall, 1975.

Johnson, D. W., & Johnson, R. T. *Learning together and alone: Cooperation, competition, and individualization.* Englewood Cliffs, N.J.: Prentice-Hall, 1975.

Jones, E. E., Kanouse, D. E., Kelley, H. H., Nisbett, R. E., Valins, S., & Weiner, B. *Attribution: Perceiving the causes of behavior.* New York: General Learning Press, 1972.

Jones, M. H. Pain thresholds for smog components. In J. F. Wohlwill & D. H. Carson (Eds.), *Environment and the social sciences: Perspectives and applications.* Washington, D.C.: American Psychological Association, 1972.

Jones, R. M. *Fantasy and feeling in education.* New York: Harper & Row, 1968.

Kagan, J., & Kogan, N. Individuality and cognitive performance. In P. H. Mussen (Ed.), *Carmichael's manual of child psychology* (3rd ed., Vol. 1). New York: Wiley, 1970.

Kahneman, D. *Attention and effort.* Englewood Cliffs, N.J.: Prentice-Hall, 1973.

Kahneman, D., & Tversky, A. Subjective probability: A judgment of representativeness. *Cognitive Psychology,* 1972, *3,* 430–454.

Kameron, J. Experimental studies of environment perception. In W. H. Ittelson (Ed.), *Environment and cognition.* New York: Seminar Press, 1973.

Kanter, R. M. *Commitment and community: Communes and utopias in sociological perspective.* Cambridge, Mass.: Harvard University Press, 1972.

Kaplan, B., Wapner, S., & Cohen, S. B. Exploratory applications of the organismic-developmental approach to transactions of men-in-environments. In S. Wapner,

S. B. Cohen, & B. Kaplan (Eds.), *Experiencing the environment*. New York: Plenum Press, 1976.

Kaplan, R. Some psychological benefits of gardening. *Environment and Behavior,* 1973, *5*, 145–162.

Kaplan, S. Cognitive maps in perception and thought. In R. M. Downs & D. Stea (Eds.), *Image and environment: Cognitive mapping and spatial behavior.* Chicago: Aldine, 1973.

Kaplan, S., Kaplan, R., & Wendt, J. S. Rated preference and complexity for natural and urban visual material. *Perception & Psychophysics,* 1972, *12*, 354–356.

Kaplan, S., & Wendt, J. S. Preference and the visual environment: Complexity and some alternatives. In W. J. Mitchell (Ed.), *Environmental design: Research and practice. Proceedings of the EDRA 3/AR 8 Conference January 1972.* Los Angeles: University of California Press, 1972.

Kasten, K. Toward a psychology of being: A masculine mystique. *Journal of Humanistic Psychology,* 1972, *12* (2), 23–43.

Kateb, G. *Utopia and its enemies.* New York: Schocken Books, 1963.

Kates, R. W. *Hazard and choice perception in flood plain management* (Research Paper No. 78). Chicago: University of Chicago, Department of Geography, 1962.

Kates, R. W. Experiencing the environment as hazard. In S. Wapner, S. B. Cohen, & B. Kaplan (Eds.), *Experiencing the environment.* New York: Plenum Press, 1976.

Katz, D. *Gestalt psychology: Its nature and significance* (R. Tyson, trans.). New York: Ronald Press, 1950.

Kaufman, J. L. Contemporary planning practice: State of the art. In D. R. Godschalk (Ed.), *Planning in America: Learning from turbulence.* Washington, D.C.: American Institute of Planners, 1974.

Kaufman, L. *Sight and mind: An introduction to visual perception.* New York: Oxford University Press, 1974.

Keasey, C. B. Implicators of cognitive development for moral reasoning. In D. J. DePalma & J. M. Foley (Eds.), *Moral development: Current theory and research.* Hillsdale, N.J.: Lawrence Erlbaum Associates, 1975.

Kelley, H. H., & Thibaut, J. W. Group problem solving. In G. Lindzey & E. Aronson (Eds.), *The handbook of social psychology* (2nd ed., Vol. 4). Reading, Mass.: Addison-Wesley, 1969.

Kelly, G. A. *The psychology of personal constructs.* New York: Norton, 1955.

Kelman, H. C. Attitudes are alive and well and gainfully employed in the sphere of action. *American Psychologist,* 1974, *29*, 310–324.

Keniston, K. *Young radicals.* New York: Harcourt, Brace & World, 1968.

Kidder, L. H., & Stewart, V. M. *The psychology of intergroup relations: Conflict and consciousness.* New York: McGraw-Hill, 1975.

Kilpatrick, F. P. (Ed.). *Explorations in transactional psychology.* New York: New York University Press, 1961.

Kinkade, K. *A Walden Two experiment: The first five years of Twin Oaks Community.* New York: Morrow, 1973.

Klatzky, R. L. *Human memory: Structures and processes.* San Francisco: Freeman, 1975.

Klausner, S. Z. *On man in his environment.* San Francisco: Jossey-Bass, 1971.

Klein, G. S. *Perception, motives, and personality.* New York: Knopf, 1970.

Kluckhohn, C. Values and value-orientations in the theory of action: An exploration in definition and classification. In T. Parsons & E. A. Shils (Eds.), *Toward a general theory of action.* Cambridge, Mass.: Harvard University Press, 1951.

Kluckhohn, F. R., & Strodtbeck, F. L. *Variations in value orientations.* Evanston, Ill.: Row, Peterson, 1961.

Koberg, D., & Bagnall, J. *The universal traveler: A soft-systems guide to: creativity, problem-solving, and the process of reaching goals.* Los Altos, Calif.: Kaufmann, 1974.

Koestler, A. *The act of creation.* New York: Dell, 1964.

Koffka, K. *Principles of Gestalt psychology.* New York: Harcourt Brace, 1935.

Kogan, N. Educational implications of cognitive styles. In G. S. Lesser (Ed.), *Psychology and educational practice.* Glenview, Ill.: Scott, Foresman, 1971.

Kohlberg, L. Stage and sequence: The cognitive-developmental approach to socialization. In D. A. Goslin (Ed.), *Handbook of socialization theory and research.* Chicago: Rand McNally, 1969.

Kohlberg, L. Continuities in childhood and adult moral development revisited. In P. B. Baltes & K. W. Schaie (Eds.), *Life-span development psychology: Personality and socialization.* New York: Academic Press, 1973.

Kohlberg, L., & Turiel, E. Moral development and moral education. In G. S. Lesser (Ed.), *Psychology and educational practice.* Glenview, Ill.: Scott, Foresman, 1971.

Konorski, J. *Integrative activity of the brain: An interdisciplinary approach.* Chicago: University of Chicago Press, 1967.

Korman, A. K. *The psychology of motivation.* Englewood Cliffs, N.J.: Prentice-Hall, 1974.

Kozol, J. *The night is dark and I am far from home.* Boston: Houghton Mifflin, 1975.

Kreitler, H., & Kreitler, S. *Psychology of the arts.* Durham, N.C.: Duke University Press, 1972.

Krueger, A. P. Preliminary consideration of the biological significance of air ions. *Scientia,* September-October 1969, *104,* 1–17.

Kryter, K. D. *The effects of noise on man.* New York: Academic Press, 1970.

Kuenzlen, M. *Playing urban games: The systems approach to planning.* Boston: i Press, 1972.

Kuhn, T. S. *The structure of scientific revolutions* (2nd ed.). Chicago: University of Chicago Press, 1970.

Küller, R. (Ed.). *Architectural psychology: Proceedings of the Lund conference.* Stroudsburg, Pa.: Dowden, Hutchinson & Ross, 1973.

Kurtines, W., & Greif, E. B. The development of moral thought: Review and evaluation of Kohlberg's approach. *Psychological Bulletin,* 1974, *81,* 453–470.

Kurtz, S. A. *Wasteland: Building the American dream.* New York: Praeger, 1973.

Ladd, F. Black youths view their environment: Neighborhood maps. *Environment and Behavior,* 1970, *2,* 74–99.

Lamb, K. A. *The people, maybe: Seeking democracy in America.* Belmont, Calif.: Wadsworth, 1971.

Lang, J., Burnette, C., Moleski, W., & Vachon, D. (Eds.). *Designing for human behavior: Architecture and the behavioral sciences.* Stroudsburg, Pa.: Dowden, Hutchinson & Ross, 1974.

Lauer, R. H. *Perspectives on social change.* Boston: Allyn and Bacon, 1973.

Lawrence, J. E. S. Science and sentiment: Overview of research on crowding and human behavior. *Psychological Bulletin,* 1974, *81,* 712–720.

Lazarus, R. S. *Psychological stress and the coping process.* New York: McGraw-Hill, 1966.

Lazarus, R. S. Emotions and adaptation: Conceptual and empirical relations. In

W. J. Arnold (Ed.), *Nebraska symposium on motivation, 1968.* Lincoln, Neb.: University of Nebraska Press, 1968.

Lazarus, R. S.   A cognitively oriented psychologist looks at biofeedback. *American Psychologist,* 1975, *30,* 553–561.

Lazarus, R. S., Averill, J. R., & Opton, E. M., Jr.   Towards a cognitive theory of emotion. In M. B. Arnold (Ed.), *Feelings and emotions.* New York: Academic Press, 1970.

Leavitt, H.   *Superhighway—superhoax.* New York: Ballantine Books, 1970.

Lee, A. M.   *Toward humanist sociology.* Englewood Cliffs, N.J.: Prentice-Hall, 1973.

Lee, S.   Cognitive mapping research. In B. Honikman (Ed.), *Responding to social change.* Stroudsburg, Pa.: Dowden, Hutchinson & Ross, 1975.

Lee, T.   Urban neighborhood as a socio-spatial schema. *Human Relations,* 1968, *21,* 241–268.

Lee, T.   Perceived distance as a function of direction in the city. *Environment and Behavior,* 1970, *2,* 40–51.

Lee, T.   Psychology and living space. In R. M. Downs & D. Stea (Eds.), *Image and environment: Cognitive mapping and spatial behavior.* Chicago: Aldine, 1973.

Leff, H. L.   Interest and radical education. In N. Shimahara (Ed.), *Radical education: Its pertinence to our time* (Proceedings of the 2nd Annual Convention of the Society for Educational Reconstruction). New Brunswick, N.J.: Graduate School of Education, Rutgers University, 1972.

Leff, H. L., Gordon, L. R., & Ferguson, J. G.   Cognitive set and environmental awareness. *Environment and Behavior,* 1974, *6,* 395–447.

Leiss, W.   *The domination of nature.* Boston: Beacon Press, 1974.

Leonard, G. B.   *Education and ecstasy.* New York: Dell, 1968.

Leonard, G. B.   *The transformation.* New York: Dell, 1972.

Leopold, A.   *A sand county almanac.* New York: Oxford University Press, 1949.

Lepper, M. R., Greene, D., & Nisbett, R. E.   Undermining children's intrinsic interest with extrinsic reward. *Journal of Personality and Social Psychology,* 1973, *28,* 129–137.

Lerner, M. J.   The desire for justice and reactions to victims. In J. Macaulay & L. Berkowitz (Eds.), *Altruism and helping behavior.* New York: Academic Press, 1970.

Lerner, M. J. (Ed.).   *The justice motive in social behavior. Journal of Social Issues,* 1975, *31* (3).

Lester, D. (Ed.).   *Explorations in exploration.* New York: Van Nostrand, 1969.

Leveson, D.   *A sense of the earth.* Garden City, N.Y.: Doubleday, 1971.

Lewis, H. R., & Streitfeld, H. S.   *Growth games.* New York: Bantam Books, 1970.

Li, V. H.   Law and penology: Systems of reform and correction. In M. Oksenberg (Ed.), *China's developmental experience.* New York: Praeger, 1973.

Lilly, J. C.   *The mind of the dolphin.* New York: Avon Books, 1967.

Lilly, J. C.   *The center of the cyclone: An autobiography of inner space.* New York: Julian Press, 1972.

Lindblom, C. E.   The science of muddling through. In W. J. Gore & J. W. Dyson (Eds.), *The making of decisions.* New York: Free Press, 1964.

Linderman, E. W., & Herberholz, D. W.   *Developing artistic and perceptual awareness.* Dubuque, Iowa: Brown, 1969.

Lindsay, P. H., & Norman, D. A.   *Human information processing: An Introduction to Psychology* (2nd ed.). New York: Academic Press, 1977.

Linville, J., Jr., & Davis, R.   *The political environment: An ecosystems approach to urban management.* Washington, D.C.: American Institute of Planners, 1976.

Little, B. R.   Specialization and the varieties of environmental experience: Empirical studies within the personality paradigm. In S. Wapner, S. B. Cohen, & B. Kaplan (Eds.), *Experiencing the environment.* New York: Plenum Press, 1976.

Litton, R. B., Jr., Tetlow, R. J., Sorensen, J., & Beatty, R. A.   *Water and landscape: An aesthetic overview of the role of water in the landscape.* Port Washington, N.Y.: Water Information Center, 1974.

Lodge, G. C.   *The new American ideology.* New York: Knopf, 1975.

Loevinger, J.   *Ego development.* San Francisco: Jossey-Bass, 1976.

Logue, E. J.   The impact of political and social forces on design in America. In L. B. Holland (Ed.), *Who designs America?* Garden City, N.Y.: Doubleday, 1966.

London, H., & Nisbett, R. E. (Eds.).   *Thought and feeling: Cognitive alteration of feeling states.* Chicago: Aldine, 1974.

Lorenz, K.   *On aggression.* New York: Harcourt, Brace & World, 1966.

Love, S. (Ed.).   *Earth tool kit: A field manual for citizen activists.* New York: Pocket Books, 1971.

Love, S., & Obst, D. (Eds.).   *Ecotage!* New York: Pocket Books, 1972.

Lowenfeld, V., & Brittain, W. L.   *Creative and mental growth* (5th ed.). New York: Macmillan, 1970.

Lowenthal, D. (Ed.).   *Environmental perception and behavior* (Department of Geography Research Paper No. 109). Chicago: Department of Geography, University of Chicago, 1967.

Lowenthal, D.   The American scene. *Geographical Review,* 1968, *58,* 61–88.

Lowenthal, D.   Criteria for natural beauty. In R. Nash (Ed.), *Environment and Americans.* New York: Holt, Rinehart and Winston, 1972.

Lowenthal, D., & Prince, H. C.   English landscape tastes. *Geographical Review,* 1965, *55,* 186–222.

Lowenthal, D., & Prince, H. C.   Transcendental experience. In S. Wapner, S. B. Cohen, & B. Kaplan (Eds.), *Experiencing the environment.* New York: Plenum Press, 1976.

Lowenthal, D., & Riel, M.   The nature of perceived and imagined environments. *Environment and Behavior,* 1972, *4,* 189–207.

Luce, G. G.   *Body time: Physiological rhythms and social stress.* New York: Pantheon Books, 1971.

Lynch, K.   *The image of the city.* Cambridge, Mass.: MIT Press, 1960.

Lynch, K.   *Site planning* (2nd ed.). Cambridge, Mass.: MIT Press, 1971.

Lynch, K.   *What time is this place?* Cambridge, Mass.: MIT Press, 1972.

Lynch, K.   Grounds for utopia. In B. Honikman (Ed.), *Responding to social change.* Stroudsburg, Pa.: Dowden, Hutchinson & Ross, 1975.

Lynch, K.   *Managing the sense of a region.* Cambridge, Mass.: MIT Press, 1976.

Lynch, K., & Rivkin, M.   A walk around the block. *Landscape,* 1959, *8,* 24–34.

Lynd, S.   The movement: A new beginning. In C. G. Benello & D. Roussopoulos (Eds.), *The case for participatory democracy: Some prospects for a radical society.* New York: Grossman, 1971.

Maier, N. R. F.   *Problem solving and creativity in individuals and groups.* Belmont, Calif.: Brooks/Cole, 1970.

Maloney, M. P., & Ward, M. P.   Ecology: Let's hear from the people: An objective scale for the measurement of ecological attitudes and knowledge. *American Psychologist,* 1973, *28,* 583–586.

Maloney, M. P., Ward, M. P., & Braucht, G. N. A revised scale for the measurement of ecological attitudes and knowledge. *American Psychologist*, 1975, *30*, 787–790.

Maltz, M. *Psycho-cybernetics.* Englewood Cliffs, N.J.: Prentice-Hall, 1960.

Manders, J. Advertising and environmental awareness. In T. R. Harney & R. Disch (Eds.), *The dying generations: Perspectives on the environmental crisis.* New York: Dell, 1971.

Mandler, G. *Mind and emotion.* New York: Wiley, 1975.

Marcuse, H. *One-dimensional man: Studies in the ideology of advanced industrial society.* Boston: Beacon Press, 1964.

Marcuse, H. *Counterrevolution and revolt.* Boston: Beacon Press, 1972.

Marsden, H. M. Crowding and animal behavior. In J. F. Wohlwill & D. H. Carson (Eds.), *Environment and the social sciences: Perspectives and applications.* Washington, D.C.: American Psychological Association, 1972.

Marx, L. *The machine in the garden: Technology and the pastoral ideal in America.* New York: Oxford University Press, 1964.

Maslow, A. H. The need to know and the fear of knowing. *The Journal of General Psychology*, 1963, *68*, 111–125.

Maslow, A. H. *Eupsychian management.* Homewood, Ill.: Irwin, 1965.

Maslow, A. H. *Toward a psychology of Being.* Princeton, N.J.: Van Nostrand, 1968.

Maslow, A. H. *Motivation and personality* (2nd ed.). New York: Harper & Row, 1970.

Maslow, A. H. *The farther reaches of human nature.* New York: Viking Press, 1971.

Maslow, A. H., & Mintz, N. L. Effects of esthetic surroundings: I. Initial effects of three esthetic conditions upon perceiving "energy" and "well-being" in faces. *The Journal of Psychology*, 1956, *41*, 247–254.

Masters, R. E. L., & Houston, J. *The varieties of psychedelic experience.* New York: Dell, 1966.

Masters, R., & Houston, J. *Mind games.* New York: Dell, 1972.

Mauger, P., Mauger, S., Edmonds, W., Bergner, R., Daly, P., & Marett, V. *Education in China.* London: Anglo-Chinese Educational Institute, 1974.

May, R. *Love and will.* New York: Dell, 1969.

Mazziotti, D. F. The underlying assumptions of advocacy planning: Pluralism and reform. *Journal of the American Institute of Planners*, 1974, *40*, 38, 40–47.

McClelland, D. C. *The achieving society.* Princeton, N.J.: Van Nostrand, 1961.

McClelland, D. C. Toward a theory of motive acquisition. *American Psychologist*, 1965, *20*, 321-333.

McEvoy, J. III. The American concern with the environment. In W. R. Burch, Jr., N. H. Creek, Jr., & L. Taylor (Eds.), *Social behavior, natural resources, and the environment.* New York: Harper & Row, 1972.

McGhie, A. *Pathology of attention.* Baltimore: Penguin Books, 1969.

McGrath, J. E. (Ed.). *Social and psychological factors in stress.* New York: Holt, Rinehart and Winston, 1970.

McGregor, D. *The human side of enterprise.* New York: McGraw-Hill, 1960.

McGuire, W. J. The nature of attitudes and attitude change. In G. Lindzey & E. Aronson (Eds.), *The handbook of social psychology* (2nd ed., Vol. 3). Reading, Mass.: Addison-Wesley, 1969.

McHarg, I. L. *Design with nature.* Garden City, N.Y.: Doubleday, 1969.

McInnis, N., & Albrecht, D. (Eds.). *What makes education environmental?* Louisville, Ky.: Data Courier, 1975. (Copublished with Environmental Educators, Washington, D.C.)

McKechnie, G. E. *Manual for the Environmental Response Inventory*. Palo Alto, Calif.: Consulting Psychologists Press, 1974.

McKechnie, G. E. Explorations in environmental dispositions. In P. McReynolds (Ed.), *Advances in psychological assessment* (Vol. 4). San Francisco: Jossey-Bass, 1977.

McKim, R. H. *Experiences in visual thinking*. Monterey, Calif.: Brooks/Cole, 1972.

McRae, R. *Involver and facilitator environments: A concept of environment with behavioral implications*. Unpublished masters thesis, Graduate School of Architecture, University of New Mexico, Albuquerque, New Mexico, 1972.

Mead, G. H. *Mind, self and society*. Chicago: University of Chicago Press, 1934.

Mead, M. (Ed.). *Cooperation and competition among primitive peoples*. New York: McGraw-Hill, 1937.

Meadows, D. H., Meadows, D. L., Randers, J., & Behrens, W. W. III. *The limits to growth*. New York: Universe Books, 1972.

Means, R. L. *The ethical imperative: The crisis in American values*. Garden City, N.Y.: Anchor, 1969.

Mehrabian, A., & Russell, J. A. *An approach to environmental psychology*. Cambridge, Mass.: MIT Press, 1974.

Melville, K. *Communes in the counter culture: Origins, theories, styles of life*. New York: Morrow, 1972.

Melzack, R. The perception of pain. *Scientific American*, 1961, *204*, 41–49.

Melzack, R. *The puzzle of pain*. Middlesex, England: Penguin Books, 1973.

Michael, D. N. *On learning to plan and planning to learn*. San Francisco: Jossey-Bass, 1973.

Michelson, W. *Man and his urban environment: A sociological approach*. Reading, Mass.: Addison-Wesley, 1970.

Milgram, S. The experience of living in cities. *Science*, 1970, *167*, 1461–1468.

Miller, G. A. The magical number seven, plus or minus two: Some limits on our capacity for processing information. *Psychological Review*, 1956, *63*, 81–96.

Miller, G. A. Psychology as a means of promoting human welfare. *American Psychologist*, 1969, *24*, 1063–1075.

Miller, G. A., Galanter, E., & Pribram, K. *Plans and the structure of behavior*. New York: Holt, Rinehart and Winston, 1960.

Miller, G. T., Jr. *Living in the environment: Concepts, problems, and alternatives*. Belmont, Calif.: Wadsworth, 1975.

Miller, J. G. The nature of living systems. *Behavioral Science*, 1971, *16*, 277–301.

Miller, S. M., & Roby, P. A. *The future of inequality*. New York: Basic Books, 1970.

Miller, W. M. Radical environmentalism. *Not Man Apart*, 1972, 2 (11), 14–15.

Millman, M., & Kanter, R. M. (Eds.). *Another voice: Feminist perspectives on social life and social science*. New York: Doubleday, 1975.

Mills, C. W. *The power elite*. New York: Oxford University Press, 1956.

Mills, C. W. *The sociological imagination*. New York: Oxford University Press, 1959.

Minsky, M. A framework for representing knowledge. In P. H. Winston (Ed.), *The psychology of computer vision*. New York: McGraw-Hill, 1975.

Mischel, W. *Personality and assessment*. New York: Wiley, 1968.

Mischel, W. Continuity and change in personality. *American Psychologist*, 1969, *24*, 1012–1018.

Mitchell, J. G., & Stallings, C. L. (Eds.): *Ecotactics: The Sierra Club handbook for environmental activists.* New York: Pocket Books, 1970.

Mitchell, J. K.   Natural hazard research. In I. R. Manners & M. W. Mikesell (Eds.), *Perspectives on environment.* Washington, D.C.: Association of American Geographers, 1974.

Mogulof, M. B.   Citizen participation: Federal policy. In M. I. Urofsky (Ed.), *Perspectives on urban America.* Garden City, N.Y.: Doubleday, 1973.

Moncrief, L. W.   The cultural basis of our environmental crisis. *Science,* 1970, *170,* 508–512.

Montagu, (M. F.) A.   *On being human.* New York: Schuman, 1950.

Montagu, (M. F.) A.   *The human revolution.* Cleveland: World, 1965.

Montagu, M. F. A. (Ed.).   *Man and aggression.* New York: Oxford University Press, 1968.

Moore, G. T. (Ed.).   *Emerging methods in environmental design and planning.* Cambridge, Mass.: MIT Press, 1970.

Moore, G. T.   The development of environmental knowing: An overview of an interactional-constructivist theory and some data on within-individual developmental variations. In D. Canter & T. Lee (Eds.), *Psychology and the built environment.* New York: Wiley, 1974.

Moore, G. T., & Golledge, R. G. (Eds.).   *Environmental knowing: Theories, research, and methods.* Stroudsburg, Pa.: Dowden, Hutchinson & Ross, 1976.

Moore, R. C.   Patterns of activity in time and space: The ecology of a neighborhood playground. In D. Canter & T. Lee (Eds.), *Psychology and the built environment.* New York: Wiley, 1974.

Moore, W. E.   *Social change* (2nd ed.). Englewood Cliffs, N.J.: Prentice-Hall, 1974.

Moos, R. H.   Conceptualizations of human environments. *American Psychologist,* 1973, *28,* 652–665.

Moos, R. H.   Synthesizing major perspectives on environmental impact: A social ecological approach. In B. Honikman (Ed.), *Responding to social change.* Stroudsburg, Pa.: Dowden, Hutchinson & Ross, 1975.

Moos, R. H.   *The human context: Environmental determinants of behavior.* New York: Wiley, 1976.

Morris, C.   *Varieties of human value.* Chicago: University of Chicago Press, 1956.

Morrison, D. E., Hornback, K. E., & Warner, W. K.   The environmental movement: Some preliminary observations and predictions. In W. R. Burch, Jr., N. H. Creek, Jr., & L. Taylor (Eds.), *Social behavior, natural resources, and the environment.* New York: Harper & Row, 1972.

Mountcastle, V. B.   Sleep, wakefulness, and the conscious state: Intrinsic regulatory mechanisms of the brain. In V. B. Mountcastle (Ed.), *Medical physiology* (Vol. 1, 13th ed.). St. Louis: Mosby, 1974.

Mumford, L.   *The urban prospect.* New York: Harcourt, Brace & World, 1968.

Mumford, L.   *The myth of the machine: The pentagon of power.* New York: Harcourt Brace Jovanovich, 1970.

Munsinger, H., & Kessen, W.   Uncertainty, structure, and preference. *Psychological Monographs: General and Applied,* 1964, 78 (9, Whole No. 586).

Murphy, G.   *Human potentialities.* New York: Basic Books, 1958.

Naranjo, C., & Ornstein, R. E.   *On the psychology of meditation.* New York: Viking Press, 1971.

Nash, R.   *Wilderness and the American mind* (2nd ed.). New Haven: Yale University Press, 1973.

Neill, A. S. *Summerhill: A radical approach to child rearing.* New York: Hart, 1960.

Neisser, U. *Cognitive psychology.* New York: Appleton-Century-Crofts, 1967.

Neisser, U. Visual imagery as process and as experience. In J. S. Antrobus (Ed.), *Cognition and affect.* Boston: Little, Brown, 1970.

Neisser, U. *Cognition and reality: Principles and implications of cognitive psychology.* San Francisco: Freeman, 1976.

Nelson, G. *Problems of design.* New York: Whitney Publications, 1965.

Neuhaus, R. *In defense of people: Ecology and the seduction of radicalism.* New York: Macmillan, 1971.

Neutra, R. *Survival through design.* New York: Oxford University Press, 1969.

Newell, A., & Simon, H. A. *Human problem solving.* Englewood Cliffs, N.J.: Prentice-Hall, 1972.

Newman, O. *Defensible space: Crime prevention through urban design.* New York: Collier Books, 1973.

Nisbett, R. E., & Valins, S. Perceiving the causes of one's own behavior. In E. E. Jones, D. E. Kanouse, H. H. Kelley, R. E. Nisbett, S. Valins, & B. Weiner, *Attribution: Perceiving the causes of behavior.* Morristown, N.J.: General Learning Press, 1972.

Nobile, P. (Ed.). *The Con III controversy: The critics look at The Greening of America.* New York: Pocket Books, 1971.

Norman, D. A. *Memory and attention: An introduction to human information processing* (2nd ed.). New York: Wiley, 1976.

Norman, D. A., & Bobrow, D. G. On the role of active memory processes in perception and cognition. In C. N. Cofer (Ed.), *The structure of human memory.* San Francisco: Freeman, 1976.

Norman, D. A., Rumelhart, D. E., & the LNR Research Group. *Explorations in cognition.* San Francisco: Freeman, 1975.

Notz, W. W. Work motivation and the negative effects of extrinsic rewards: A review with implications for theory and practice. *American Psychologist,* 1975, *30,* 884–891.

Nyquist, E. B., & Hawes, G. R. (Eds.). *Open education: A sourcebook for parents and teachers.* New York: Bantam Books, 1972.

Oksenberg, M. (Ed.). *China's developmental experience.* New York: Praeger, 1973.

Olds, J., & Olds, M. Drives, rewards and the brain. In *New directions in psychology, II.* New York: Holt, Rinehart and Winston, 1965.

Oltmans, W. L. (Ed.). *On Growth.* New York: Capricorn Books, 1974.

O'Riordan, T. *Environmentalism.* London: Pion, 1976.

Orleans, P. Differential cognition of urban residents: Effects of social scale on mapping. In R. M. Downs & D. Stea (Eds.), *Image and environment: Cognitive mapping and spatial behavior.* Chicago: Aldine, 1973.

Ornstein, R. E. *The psychology of consciousness.* San Francisco: Freeman, 1972.

Osborn, F. *Our plundered planet.* New York: Pyramid Books, 1948.

Osborne, H. *The art of appreciation.* New York: Oxford University Press, 1970.

Osgood, C. E., Suci, G. J., & Tannenbaum, P. H. *The measurement of meaning.* Urbana, Ill.: University of Illinois Press, 1957.

Osmond, H. Function as the basis of psychiatric ward design. *Mental Hospitals,* 1957, *8,* 23–29.

Osmond, H. Some psychiatric aspects of design. In L. B. Holland (Ed.), *Who designs America?* Garden City, N.Y.: Doubleday, 1966.

Ostrander, E. R.   Behavioral research for design application: On making the myth a reality. In B. Honikman (Ed.), *Responding to social change.* Stroudsburg, Pa.: Dowden, Hutchinson & Ross, 1975.

Otto, H. A., & Mann, J. (Eds.).   *Ways of growth: Approaches to expanding awareness.* New York: Viking Press, 1968.

Paivio, A.   *Imagery and verbal processes.* New York: Holt, Rinehart and Winston, 1971.

Papanek, V.   *Design for the real world: Human ecology and social change.* New York: Bantam Books, 1971.

Parkes, H. B.   *The American experience: An interpretation of the history and civilization of the American people.* New York: Knopf, 1947.

Parmenter, R.   *The awakened eye.* Middletown, Conn.: Wesleyan University Press, 1968.

Parsegian, V. L.   *This cybernetic world of men, machines, and earth systems.* Garden City, N.Y.: Anchor Books, 1973.

Partridge, P. H.   *Consent and consensus.* New York: Praeger, 1971.

Passmore, J.   *Man's responsibility for nature: Ecological problems and Western traditions.* New York: Scribner's, 1974.

Passow, S. S.   Urban planning: Old realities and new directions. In M. I. Urofsky (Ed.), *Perspectives on urban America.* Garden City, N.Y.: Doubleday, 1973.

Pateman, C.   *Participation and democratic theory.* Cambridge, England: Cambridge University Press, 1970.

Payne, B.   *Getting there without drugs: Techniques and theories for the expansion of consciousness.* New York: Viking Press, 1973.

Pedersen, D. M., & Shears, L. M.   A review of personal space research in the framework of general system theory. *Psychological Bulletin,* 1973, *80,* 367–388.

Pelletier, K. R., & Garfield, C.   *Consciousness: East and West.* New York: Harper & Row, 1976.

Perin, C.   *With man in mind: An interdisciplinary prospectus for environmental design.* Cambridge, Mass.: MIT Press, 1970.

Perin, C.   The social order of environmental design. In J. Lang, C. Burnette, W. Moleski, & D. Vachon (Eds.), *Designing for human behavior.* Stroudsburg, Pa.: Dowden, Hutchinson & Ross, 1974.

Peterson, C. R. (Ed.).   *Cascaded inference.* Special issue of *Organizational Behavior and Human Performance,* 1973, *10* (3).

Pettigrew, T. F.   Social evaluation theory: Convergences and applications. In D. Levine (Ed.), *Nebraska symposium on motivation 1967.* Lincoln, Neb.: University of Nebraska Press, 1967.

Piaget, J.   *The moral judgment of the child.* New York: Harcourt, Brace, 1932.

Piaget, J., & Inhelder, B.   *The child's conception of space.* New York: Norton, 1967.

Platt, J. R.   Beauty: Pattern and change. In D. W. Fiske & S. R. Maddi (Eds.), *Functions of varied experience.* Homewood, Ill.: Dorsey, 1961.

Platt, J. R.   *The step to man.* New York: Wiley, 1966.

Platt, J. R.   Social traps. *American Psychologist,* 1973, *28,* 641–651.

Polya, G.   *How to solve it.* Garden City, N.Y.: Doubleday Anchor Books, 1957.

Porteous, J. D.   *Environment & behavior: Planning and everyday urban life.* Reading, Mass.: Addison-Wesley, 1977.

Posner, M. I.   *Cognition: An introduction.* Glenview, Ill.: Scott, Foresman, 1973.

Postman, N., & Weingartner, C.   *The soft revolution.* New York: Dell, 1971.

Potter, V. R. *Bioethics: Bridge to the future.* Englewood Cliffs, N.J.: Prentice-Hall, 1971.

Prince, G. M. *The practice of creativity.* New York: Macmillan, 1970.

Proshansky, H. M., Ittelson, W. H., & Rivlin, L. G. Freedom of choice and behavior in a physical setting. In H. M. Proshansky, W. H. Ittelson, & L. G. Rivlin (Eds.), *Environmental psychology: Man and his physical setting.* New York: Holt, Rinehart and Winston, 1970.

Putney, S., & Putney, G. J. *The adjusted American.* New York: Harper & Row, 1964.

Pylyshyn, Z. W. What the mind's eye tells the mind's brain: A critique of mental imagery. *Psychological Bulletin,* 1973, *80,* 1–24.

Rainwater, L. (Ed.). *Social problems and public policy: Inequality and justice.* Chicago: Aldine, 1974.

Randers, J., & Meadows, D. The carrying capacity of our global environment: A look at the ethical alternatives. In I. G. Barbour (Ed.), *Western man and environmental ethics: Attitudes toward nature and technology.* Reading, Mass.: Addison-Wesley, 1973.

Raphael, B. *The thinking computer: Mind inside matter.* San Francisco: Freeman, 1976.

Rapoport, A. *House form and culture.* Englewood Cliffs, N.J.: Prentice-Hall, 1969.

Rapoport, A. Toward a redefinition of density. *Environment and Behavior,* 1975, *7,* 131–158.

Rapoport, A., & Kantor, R. E. Complexity and ambiguity in environmental design. *Journal of the American Institute of Planners,* 1967, *33,* 210–221.

Raskin, E. *Architecture and people.* Englewood Cliffs, N.J.: Prentice-Hall, 1974.

Raskin, M. G. *Being and doing.* New York: Random House, 1971.

Rasmussen, S. E. *Experiencing architecture.* Cambridge, Mass.: MIT Press, 1962.

Raths, L. E., Harmin, M., & Simon, S. B. *Values and teaching: Working with values in the classroom.* Columbus, Ohio: Merrill, 1966.

Rawls, J. *A theory of justice.* Cambridge, Mass.: Harvard University Press, 1971.

Reich, C. A. *The greening of America.* New York: Random House, 1970.

Rejai, M. *The strategy of political revolution.* Garden City, N.Y.: Anchor Press, 1973.

Restle, F. Critique of pure memory. In R. L. Solso (Ed.), *Theories in cognitive psychology: The Loyola symposium.* Potomac, Md.: Lawrence Erlbaum Associates, 1974.

Richardson, A. *Mental imagery.* New York: Springer, 1969.

Rienow, R., & Rienow, L. T. *Moment in the sun.* New York: Ballantine, 1967.

Robbins, J., & Fisher, D. *Tranquillity without pills: All about transcendental meditation.* New York: Wyden, 1972.

Roberts, R. E. *The new communes.* Englewood Cliffs, N.J.: Prentice-Hall, 1971.

Robertson, J., & Lewallen, J. (Eds.). *The grass roots primer.* San Francisco: Sierra Club Books, 1975.

Rogers, C. R. *On becoming a person.* Boston: Houghton Mifflin, 1961.

Rogers, C. R. *Freedom to learn.* Columbus, Ohio: Merrill, 1969.

Rokeach, M. *Beliefs, attitudes, and values: A theory of organization and change.* San Francisco: Jossey-Bass, 1968.

Rokeach, M. Long-range experimental modification of values, attitudes, and behavior. *American Psychologist,* 1971, *26,* 453–459.

Rokeach, M. *The nature of human values.* New York: Free Press, 1973.

Rossiter, C. M., Jr.   Maxims for humanizing education. *Journal of Humanistic Psychology*, 1976, *16* (1), 75–80.

Roszak, T.   *The making of a counter culture.* Garden City, N.Y.: Doubleday, 1969.

Rotter, J. B.   Generalized expectancies for internal versus external control of reinforcement. *Psychological Monographs*, 1966, *80* (1, Whole No. 609).

Rowland, K.   *Looking and seeing 1–4.* London: Ginn and Company, 1964–1966.

Rubin, L. J. (Ed.).   *Facts and feelings in the classroom.* New York: Viking Press, 1973.

Rubin, Z., & Peplau, L. A.   Who believes in a just world? *Journal of Social Issues,* 1975, *31* (3), 65–89.

Rudofsky, B.   *Architecture without architects.* Garden City, N.Y.: Doubleday, 1964.

Rudofsky, B.   *Streets for people: A primer for Americans.* Garden City, N.Y.: Doubleday, 1969.

Ruesch, J., & Kees, W.   *Nonverbal communication.* Berkeley: University of California Press, 1964.

Rusch, C. W.   On understanding awareness. *The Journal of Aesthetic Education,* 1970 *4* (4), 57–79.

Russell, B.   *Roads to freedom: Socialism, anarchism and syndicalism.* London: George Allen & Unwin, 1966.

Russell, B.   *In Praise of Idleness and other essays.* New York: Simon & Schuster, 1972. ("In Praise of Idleness" written in 1932.)

Saarinen, T. F.   *Perception of environment* (Resource Paper No. 5). Washington, D.C.: Association of American Geographers, 1969.

Saarinen, T. F.   Student views of the world. In R. M. Downs & D. Stea (Eds.), *Image and environment: Cognitive mapping and spatial behavior.* Chicago: Aldine, 1973.

Saarinen, T. F.   Environmental perception. In I. R. Manners & M. W. Mikesell (Eds.), *Perspectives on environment.* Washington, D.C.: Association of American Geographers, 1974.

Saarinen, T. F.   *Environmental planning: Perception and behavior.* Boston: Houghton Mifflin, 1976.

Sakitt, B.   Iconic memory. *Psychological Review,* 1976, *83,* 257–276.

Salisbury, H. E.   *To Peking and beyond: A report on the new Asia.* New York: Capricorn Books, 1973.

Sampson, E. E.   On justice as equality. *Journal of Social Issues,* 1975, *31* (3), 45–64.

Samuel, W.   *Contemporary social psychology: An introduction.* Englewood Cliffs, N.J.: Prentice-Hall, 1975.

Sandman, P. M.   Mass environmental education: Can the media do the job? In J. A. Swan & W. B. Stapp (Eds.), *Environmental education: Strategies toward a more livable future.* Beverly Hills, Calif.: Sage Publications, 1974.

Sanoff, H.   *Seeing the environment: An advocacy approach.* Raleigh, N.C.: Learning Environments, 1975.

Sanoff, H.   *Asheville environmental workbook.* Raleigh, N.C.: School of Design, North Carolina State University, 1976.

Sarason, S. B.   *The creation of settings and the future societies.* San Francisco: Jossey-Bass, 1972.

Sarbin, T. R., & Allen, V. L.   Role theory. In G. Lindzey & E. Aronson (Eds.), *The handbook of social psychology* (2nd ed., Vol. I). Reading, Mass.: Addison-Wesley, 1968.

Sax, J. L.   *Defending the environment: A handbook for citizen action.* New York: Vintage Books, 1970.

SCEP (Study of Critical Environmental Problems).   *Man's impact on the global environment: Assessment and recommendations for action.* Cambridge, Mass.: MIT Press, 1970.

Schachtel, E. G.   *Metamorphosis: On the development of affect, perception, attention, and memory.* New York: Basic Books, 1959.

Schachter, S.   The interaction of cognitive and physiological determinants of emotional state. In L. Berkowitz (Ed.), *Advances in experimental social psychology* (Vol. I). New York: Academic Press, 1964.

Schachter, S.   The assumption of identity and peripheralist-centralist controversies in motivation and emotion. In M. Arnold (Ed.), *Feelings and emotions: The Loyola symposium.* New York: Academic Press, 1970.

Schachter, S.   *Emotion, obesity, and crime.* New York: Academic Press, 1971.

Schachter, S., & Singer, J. E.   Cognitive, social, and physiological determinants of emotional state. *Psychological Review,* 1962, *69,* 379–399.

Schattschneider, E. E.   *The semisovereign people: A realist's view of democracy in America.* New York: Holt, Rinehart and Winston, 1960.

Scheibe, K. E.   *Beliefs and values.* New York: Holt, Rinehart and Winston, 1970.

Schein, E. H.   *Professional education: Some new directions.* New York: McGraw-Hill, 1972.

Scherer, K. R., Abeles, R. P., & Fischer, C. S.   *Human aggression and conflict: Interdisciplinary perspectives.* Englewood Cliffs, N.J.: Prentice-Hall, 1975.

Schiller, H. I.   *The mind managers.* Boston: Beacon Press, 1973.

Schnebli, D.   Environments for children. In G. Kepes (Ed.), *Arts of the environment.* New York: Braziller, 1972.

Schneider, D. J.   *Social psychology.* Reading, Mass.: Addison-Wesley, 1976.

Schneider, K. R.   *Autokind vs. mankind.* New York: Schocken Books, 1971.

Schroder, H. M., Driver, M. J., & Streufert, S.   *Human information processing.* New York: Holt, Rinehart and Winston, 1967.

Schumacher, E. F.   *Small is beautiful: Economics as if people mattered.* New York: Harper & Row, 1973.

Schwartz, S. I., & Foin, T. C.   A critical review of the social systems models of Jay Forrester. *Human Ecology,* 1972, *1,* 161–173.

Scott, M.   *American city planning since 1890.* Berkeley, Calif.: University of California Press, 1969.

Seamon, D.   Environmental imagery: An overview and tentative ordering. In W. J. Mitchell (Ed.), *Environmental design: Research and practice. Proceedings of the EDRA 3/AR 8 Conference January 1972.* Los Angeles: University of California Press, 1972.

Segal, S. J. (Ed.).   *Imagery: Current cognitive approaches.* New York: Academic Press, 1971. (a)

Segal, S. J.   Processing of the stimulus in imagery and perception. In S. J. Segal (Ed.), *Imagery: Current cognitive approaches.* New York: Academic Press, 1971. (b)

Segal, S. J.   Assimilation of a stimulus in the construction of an image: The Perky effect revisited. In P. W. Sheehan (Ed.), *The function and nature of imagery.* New York: Academic Press, 1972.

Selye, H.   *The stress of life.* New York: McGraw-Hill, 1956.

Sewell, W. R. D.   Environmental perceptions and attitudes of engineers and public health officials. *Environment and Behavior,* 1971, *3,* 23–59.

Sheehan, P. W. (Ed.). *The function and nature of imagery.* New York: Academic Press, 1972.

Shepard, P. *Man in the landscape.* New York: Ballantine, 1967.

Shepard, P. Introduction: Ecology and man—a viewpoint. In P. Shepard & D. Mc-Kinley (Eds.), *The subversive science: Essays toward an ecology of man.* Boston: Houghton Mifflin, 1969.

Shepard, P., & McKinley, D. (Eds.). *The subversive science: Essays toward an ecology of man.* Boston: Houghton Mifflin, 1969.

Shepard, R. N. Form, formation, and transformation of internal representations. In R. L. Solso (Ed.), *Information processing and cognition: The Loyola symposium.* New York: Wiley, 1975.

Sherif, M., Harvey, O. J., White, B. J., Hood, W. E., & Sherif, C. W. *Intergroup conflict and cooperation: The Robber's Cave experiment.* Norman, Okla.: University of Oklahoma Book Exchange, 1961.

Shostak, A. B., Van Til, J., & Van Til, S. B. *Privilege in America: An end to inequality?* Englewood Cliffs, N.J.: Prentice-Hall, 1973.

Sidel, R. *Families of Fensheng: Urban life in China.* Baltimore: Penguin Books, 1974.

Siegel, A. W., & White, S. H. The development of spatial representations of large-scale environments. In H. W. Reese (Ed.), *Advances in child development and behavior* (Vol. 10). New York: Academic Press, 1975.

Silberman, C. E. *Crisis in the classroom: The remaking of American education.* New York: Random House, 1970.

Sills, D. L. The environmental movement and its critics. *Human Ecology,* 1975, *3,* 1–41.

Simon, H. A. Rational choice and the structure of the environment. *Psychological Review,* 1956, *63,* 129–138.

Simon, H. A. *The sciences of the artificial.* Cambridge, Mass.: MIT Press, 1969.

Simon, S. B., Howe, L. W., & Kirschenbaum, H. *Values clarification: A handbook of practical strategies for teachers and students.* New York: Hart, 1972.

Singer, J. L. *Daydreaming.* New York: Random House, 1966.

Singer, J. L. Drives, affects, and daydreams: The adaptive role of spontaneous imagery or stimulus-independent mentation. In J. S. Antrobus (Ed.), *Cognition and affect.* Boston: Little, Brown, 1970.

Singer, J. L. *The child's world of make-believe: Experimental studies of imaginative play.* New York: Academic Press, 1973.

Singer, J. L. *Imagery and daydream methods in psychotherapy and behavior modification.* New York: Academic Press, 1974.

Singer, J. L. Navigating the stream of consciousness: Research in daydreaming and related inner experience. *American Psychologist,* 1975, *30,* 727–738.

Skinner, B. F. *Walden Two.* New York: Macmillan, 1948.

Skinner, B. F. *Science and human behavior.* New York: Macmillan, 1953.

Skinner, B. F. *Contingencies of reinforcement: A theoretical analysis.* New York: Appleton-Century-Crofts, 1969.

Skinner, B. F. *Beyond freedom and dignity.* New York: Bantam/Vintage Books, 1971.

Skinner, B. F. *About behaviorism.* New York: Knopf, 1974.

Slater, P. *The pursuit of loneliness.* Boston: Beacon Press, 1970.

Slater, P. *Earthwalk.* New York: Anchor Press/Doubleday, 1974.

Slovic, P., Kunreuther, H., & White, G. F. Decision processes, rationality, and adjustment to natural hazards. In G. F. White (Ed.), *Natural hazards: Local, national, global.* New York: Oxford University Press, 1974.

Smelser, N. J. *Theory of collective behavior.* New York: The Free Press of Glencoe, 1963.

Smets, G. *Aesthetic judgment and arousal.* Leuven, Belgium: Leuven University Press, 1973.

Smith, A. *Powers of mind.* New York: Random House, 1975.

Smith, D. M. *The geography of social well-being in the United States: An introduction to territorial social indicators.* New York: McGraw-Hill, 1973.

Smith, M. B. *Social psychology and human values: Selected essays.* Chicago: Aldine, 1969.

Smith, M. B. On self-actualization: A transambivalent examination of a focal theme in Maslow's psychology. *Journal of Humanistic Psychology,* 1973, *13* (2), 17–33.

Smith, M. B. Metapsychology, politics, and human needs. In R. Fitzgerald (Ed.), *Human needs and politics.* Rushcutters Bay, Australia: Pergamon, 1977.

Smith, P. F. Perceptual hazards and urban remedies. In R. Küller (Ed.), *Architectural psychology.* Stroudsburg, Pa.: Dowden, Hutchinson & Ross, 1973.

Smith, R. A., & Smith, C. M. Aesthetics and environmental education. *The Journal of Aesthetic Education,* 1970, *4* (4), 125–140.

Snider, J. G., & Osgood, C. E. (Eds.). *Semantic differential technique: A sourcebook.* Chicago: Aldine, 1969.

Solow, R. M. Is the end of the world at hand? *Challenge,* March–April 1973, pp. 39–50.

Sommer, R. *Personal space: The behavioral basis of design.* Englewood Cliffs, N.J.: Prentice-Hall, 1969.

Sommer, R. *Design awareness.* Corte Madera, Calif.: Rinehart, 1972.

Sommer, R. *Tight spaces: Hard architecture and how to humanize it.* Englewood Cliffs, N.J.: Prentice-Hall, 1974.

Sommer, R. *Street art.* New York: Links Books, 1975.

Sommer, R. *The end of imprisonment.* New York: Oxford University Press, 1976.

Sonnenfeld, J. Variable values in space and landscape: An inquiry into the nature of environmental necessity. *Journal of Social Issues,* 1966, *22,* 71–82.

Sonnenfeld, J. Environmental perception and adaptation level in the arctic. In D. Lowenthal (Ed.), *Environmental perception and behavior* (Department of Geography Research Paper No. 109). Chicago: Department of Geography, University of Chicago, 1967.

Southworth, M. The sonic environment of cities. *Environment and Behavior,* 1969, *1,* 49–70.

Spicer, E. H. (Ed.). *Human problems in technological change.* New York: Russell Sage Foundation, 1952.

Sprout, H., & Sprout, M. *The ecological perspective on human affairs with special reference to international politics.* Princeton, N.J.: Princeton University Press, 1965.

Statman, J. Community mental health as a pacification program. In J. Agel (Ed.), *The radical therapist.* New York: Ballantine, 1971.

Staub, E. To rear a prosocial child: Reasoning, learning by doing, and learning by teaching others. In D. J. DePalma & J. M. Foley (Eds.), *Moral development: Current theory and research.* Hillsdale, N.J.: Lawrence Erlbaum Associates, 1975.

Stavrianos, L. S. *The promise of the coming dark age.* San Francisco: Freeman, 1976.

496   Experience, Environment, and Human Potentials

Stea, D.   Environmental perception and cognition: Toward a model for "mental maps." In G. J. Coates & K. M. Moffett (Eds.), *Response to Environment*. Raleigh, N.C.: Student Publications of the School of Design, North Carolina State University, 1969.

Stea, D.   Architecture in the head: Cognitive mapping. In J. Lang, C. Burnette, W. Moleski, & D. Vachon (Eds.), *Designing for human behavior*. Stroudsburg, Pa.: Dowden, Hutchinson & Ross, 1974.

Stea, D., & Blaut, J. M.   Notes toward a developmental theory of spatial learning. In R. M. Downs & D. Stea (Eds.), *Image and environment: Cognitive mapping and spatial behavior*. Chicago: Aldine, 1973.

Stea, D., & Wood, D.   *A cognitive atlas: Explorations into the psychological geography of four Mexican cities*. Place Perception Research Report No. 10. Chicago: Environmental Research Group, 1971.

Stein, M. I.   *Stimulating creativity: Volume 1: Individual procedures*. New York: Academic Press, 1974.

Stein, M. I.   *Stimulating creativity: Volume 2: Group procedures*. New York: Academic Press, 1975.

Stokols, D.   On the distinction between density and crowding: Some implications for future research. *Psychological Review*, 1972, 79, 275–277.

Stokols, D.   The experience of crowding in primary and secondary environments. *Environment and Behavior*, 1976, 8, 49–86.

Stokols, D., Rall, M., Pinner, B., & Schopler, J.   Physical, social, and personal determinants of the perception of crowding. *Environment and Behavior*, 1973, 5, 87–115.

Stone, C. D.   *Should trees have standing?: Toward legal rights for natural objects*. Los Altos, Calif.: Kaufmann, 1974.

Stone, T. R.   *Beyond the automobile*. Englewood Cliffs, N.J.: Prentice-Hall, 1971.

Stotland, E.   Exploratory investigations of empathy. In L. Berkowitz (Ed.), *Advances in experimental social psychology* (Vol. 4). New York: Academic Press, 1969.

Stotland, E., & Canon, L. K.   *Social psychology: A cognitive approach*. Philadelphia: Saunders, 1972.

Stotland, E., Sherman, S. E., & Shaver, K. G.   *Empathy and birth order: Some experimental explorations*. Lincoln, Neb.: University of Nebraska Press, 1971.

Strauss, A.   *Images of the American city*. New York: Free Press, 1961.

Suedfeld, P. (Ed.).   *Attitude change: The competing views*. Chicago: Aldine/Atherton, 1971.

Swan, J. A.   Attitudes and values and environmental education. In T. R. Armstrong (Ed.), *Why do we still have an ecological crisis?* Englewood Cliffs, N.J.: Prentice-Hall, 1972.

Swan, J. A.   Some human objectives for environmental education. In J. A. Swan & W. B. Stapp (Eds.), *Environmental education: Strategies toward a more livable future*. Beverly Hills, Calif.: Sage Publications, 1974.

Swan, J. A.   Behavior: Practice vs. preach syndrome. In N. McInnis & D. Albrecht (Eds.), *What makes education environmental?* Louisville, Ky.: Data Courier, 1975.

Swan, J. A., & Stapp, W. B. (Eds.).   *Environmental education: Strategies toward a more livable future*. Beverly Hills, Calif.: Sage Publications, 1974.

Swatek, P.   *The user's guide to the protection of the environment*. New York: Ballantine, 1970.

Sykes, G. M. *The society of captives: A study of a maximum security prison.* Princeton, N.J.: Princeton University Press, 1958.
Tajfel, H.   Social and cultural factors in perception. In G. Lindzey & E. Aronson (Eds.), *The handbook of social psychology* (Vol. 3). Reading, Mass.: Addison-Wesley, 1969.
Tallman, I.   *Passion, action, and politics: A perspective on social problems and social-problem solving.* San Francisco: Freeman, 1976.
Tart, C. T. (Ed.).   *Altered states of consciousness.* Garden City, N.Y.: Anchor Books, 1972.
Tart, C. T.   *States of consciousness.* New York: Dutton, 1975.
Taylor, G. R.   *Rethink: A paraprimitive solution.* New York: Dutton, 1972.
Terry, M.   *Teaching for survival.* New York: Ballantine, 1971.
Theobald, R.   *Habit and habitat.* Englewood Cliffs, N.J.: Prentice-Hall, 1972.
Thibaut, J. W., & Kelley, H. H.   *The social psychology of groups.* New York: Wiley, 1959.
Thorndike, E. L.   *Educational psychology.* Vol. 2. *The psychology of learning.* New York: Teachers College, 1913.
Tilden, F.   *Interpreting our heritage* (rev. ed.). Chapel Hill, N.C.: University of North Carolina Press, 1967.
Toffler, A.   *Future shock.* New York: Random House, 1970.
Toffler, A. (Ed.).   *Learning for tomorrow: The role of the future in education.* New York: Vintage Books, 1974.
Tognacci, L. N., Weigel, R. H., Wideen, M. F., & Vernon, D. T. A.   Environmental quality: How universal is public concern? *Environment and Behavior,* 1972, *4,* 73–86.
Tomkins, S. S.   *Affect, imagery, consciousness* (Vol. 1). New York: Springer, 1962.
Torney, J. V., & Hess, R. D.   The development of political attitudes in children. In G. S. Lesser (Ed.), *Psychology and educational practice.* Glenview, Ill.: Scott, Foresman, 1971.
Torrance, E. P.   Creativity in the educational process. In G. S. Lesser (Ed.), *Psychology and educational practice.* Glenview, Ill.: Scott, Foresman, 1971.
Torrance, E. P.   *Torrance tests of creative thinking: Norms-technical manual.* Lexington, Mass.: Ginn, 1974.
Torrance, E. P., & Myers, R. E.   *Creative learning and teaching.* New York: Dodd, Mead, 1970.
Treisman, A. M.   Strategies and models of selective attention. *Psychological Review,* 1969, *76,* 282–299.
Triandis, H. C.   *Attitude and attitude change.* New York: Wiley, 1971.
Triandis, H. C.   *The analysis of subjective culture.* New York: Wiley, 1972.
Tuan, Y.   Discrepancies between environmental attitudes and behavior: Examples from Europe and China. *Canadian Geographer,* 1968, *12,* 176–191.
Tuan, Y.   *Topophilia: A study of environmental perception, attitudes, and values.* Englewood Cliffs, N.J.: Prentice-Hall, 1974.
Tversky, A., & Kahneman, D.   Belief in the law of small numbers. *Psychological Bulletin,* 1971, *76,* 105–110.
Tversky, A., & Kahneman, D.   Availability: A heuristic for judging frequency and probability. *Cognitive Psychology,* 1973, *5,* 207–232.
Tversky, A., & Kahneman, D.   Judgment under uncertainty: Heuristics and biases. *Science,* 1974, *185,* 1124–1131.
Tzonis, A.   *Towards a non-oppressive environment: An essay.* Boston: i Press, 1972.

Upshaw, H. The personal reference scale: An approach to social judgment. In L. Berkowitz (Ed.), *Advances in experimental social psychology* (Vol. 4). New York: Academic Press, 1969.

Useem, M. *Protest movements in America.* Indianapolis: Bobbs-Merrill, 1975.

Uznadze, D. N. *The psychology of set* (B. Haigh, trans.). New York: Consultants Bureau, 1966.

Van Matre, S. *Acclimatizing: A personal and reflective approach to a natural relationship.* Martinsville, Ind.: American Camping Association, 1974.

Varela, J. A. *Psychological solutions to social problems: An introduction to social technology.* New York: Academic Press, 1971.

Von Eckardt, W. *A place to live: The crisis of the cities.* New York: Dell, 1967.

von Hertzen, H., & Spreiregen, P. D. *Building a new town* (2nd ed.). Cambridge, Mass.: MIT Press, 1973.

Wachtel, P. L. Conceptions of broad and narrow attention. *Psychological Bulletin,* 1967, *68,* 417–429.

Wagar, W. W. *Building the city of man.* New York: Grossman, 1971.

Walker, E. L. Psychological complexity as a basis for a theory of motivation and choice. In D. Levine (Ed.), *Nebraska symposium on motivation 1964.* Lincoln, Neb.: University of Nebraska Press, 1964.

Walker, E. L. Psychological complexity and preference: A hedgehog theory of behavior. In D. E. Berlyne & K. B. Madsen (Eds.), *Pleasure, reward, preference: Their nature, determinants, and role in behavior.* New York: Academic Press, 1973.

Wallach, M. A. *The intelligence/creativity distinction.* Morristown, N.J.: General Learning Press, 1971.

Walster, E., Berscheid, E., & Walster, G. W. New directions in equity research. *Journal of Personality and Social Psychology,* 1973, *25,* 151–176.

Walster, E., & Walster, G. W. Equity and social justice. *Journal of Social Issues,* 1975, *31* (3), 21–43.

Walton, R. E., & McKersie, R. B. *A behavioral theory of labor negotiations.* New York: McGraw-Hill, 1965.

Wann, T. W. (Ed.). *Behaviorism and phenomenology.* Chicago: University of Chicago Press, 1964.

Wapner, S., Kaplan, B., & Cohen, S. B. An organismic-developmental perspective for understanding transactions of men in environments. *Environment and Behavior,* 1973, *5,* 255–289.

Watson, O. M. *Symbolic and expressive uses of space: An introduction to proxemic behavior.* Reading, Mass.: Addison-Wesley, 1972.

Watts, A. W. *Nature, man, and woman.* New York: Pantheon Books, 1958. (a)

Watts, A. W. *The spirit of Zen.* New York: Grove Press, 1958. (b)

Watts, A. W. *Psychotherapy East and West.* New York: Random House, 1961.

Watts, A. W. The individual as man/world. *The Psychedelic Review,* 1963, *1* (1), 55–65. (Reprinted in P. Shepard and D. McKinley [1969].)

Watts, A. W. *The book: On the taboo against knowing who you are.* New York: Collier Books, 1966.

Weber, M. *The Protestant ethic and the spirit of capitalism* (T. Parsons, trans.). New York: Scribner's, 1958.

Weick, K. E. Reduction of cognitive dissonance through task enhancement and effort expenditure. *Journal of Abnormal and Social Psychology,* 1964, *68,* 533–539.

Weimer, W. B., & Palermo, D. S. (Eds.). *Cognition and the symbolic processes.* Hillsdale, N. J.: Lawrence Erlbaum Associates, 1974.

Weinstein, G., & Fantini, M. D.   *Toward humanistic education: A curriculum of affect.* New York: Praeger, 1970.

Weisberg, B.   *Beyond repair: The ecology of capitalism.* Boston: Beacon Press, 1971.

Weisler, A., & McCall, R. B.   Exploration and play: Résumé and redirection. *American Psychologist,* 1976, *31,* 492–508.

Weitzman, P.   The wealth of cities: Scarcity amidst plenty. In M. I. Urofsky (Ed.), *Perspectives on urban America.* Garden City, N.Y.: Doubleday, 1973.

Werner, H., & Kaplan, B.   *Symbol formation: An organismic-developmental approach to language and the expression of thought.* New York: Wiley, 1963.

Whitaker, B., & Browne, K.   *Parks for people.* New York: Winchester Press, 1971.

White, G. F. (Ed.).   *Natural hazards: Local, national, global.* New York: Oxford University Press, 1974.

White, J. (Ed.).   *The highest state of consciousness.* Garden City, N.Y.: Doubleday, 1972.

White, J. (Ed.).   *Frontiers of consciousness.* New York: Julian Press, 1974. (a)

White, J.   Plants, polygraphs and paraphysics. In J. White (Ed.), *Frontiers of consciousness.* New York: Julian Press, 1974. (b)

White, L., Jr.   The historical roots of our ecologic crisis. *Science,* 1967, *155,* 1203–1207.

White, L., Jr.   Continuing the conversation. In I. G. Barbour (Ed.), *Western man and environmental ethics: Attitudes toward nature and technology.* Reading, Mass.: Addison-Wesley, 1973.

White, R. W.   Motivation reconsidered: The concept of competence. *Psychological Review,* 1959, *66,* 297–333.

White, R. W.   Competence and the psychosexual stages of development. In M. R. Jones (Ed.), *Nebraska symposium on motivation 1960.* Lincoln, Neb.: University of Nebraska Press, 1960.

Whiteside, T.   A reporter at large: Smoking still. *The New Yorker,* November 18, 1974, pp. 121–151.

Whitney, J. B. R.   Ecology and environmental control. In M. Oksenberg (Ed.), *China's developmental experience.* New York: Praeger, 1973.

Whorf, B. L.   *Language, thought, and reality: Selected writings of Benjamin Lee Whorf* (J. B. Carroll, Ed.). Cambridge, Mass.: MIT Press, 1956.

Whyte, W. H.   *The last landscape.* Garden City, N.Y.: Doubleday, 1968.

Wickelgren, W. A.   *How to solve problems: Elements of a theory of problems and problem solving.* San Francisco: Freeman, 1974.

Wicker, A. W.   Processes which mediate behavior-environment congruence. *Behavioral Science,* 1972, *17,* 265–277.

Wicker, A. W.   Undermanning theory and research: Implications for the study of psychological and behavioral effects of excess populations. *Representative Research in Social Psychology,* 1973, *4,* 185–206.

Wicker, A. W., & Kirmeyer, S.   From church to laboratory to national park: A program of research on excess and insufficient populations in behavior settings. In S. Wapner, S. B. Cohen, & B. Kaplan (Eds.), *Experiencing the environment.* New York: Plenum Press, 1976.

Wicklund, R. A.   *Freedom and reactance.* Potomac, Md.: Lawrence Erlbaum Associates, 1974.

Williams, R. M.   *American society: A sociological interpretation* (3rd ed.). New York: Knopf, 1970.

Williams, R. M.   Change and stability in values and value systems. In B. Barber & A. Inkeles (Eds.), *Stability and social change.* Boston: Little, Brown, 1971.

Wilson, E. O.   *Sociobiology: The new synthesis.* Cambridge, Mass.: Belknap Press of Harvard University Press, 1975.

Winkel, G. H., Malek, R., & Thiel, P.   The role of personality differences in judgments of roadside quality. *Environment and Behavior,* 1969, *1,* 199–223.

Wohlwill, J. F.   Amount of stimulus exploration and preference as differential functions of stimulus complexity. *Perception & Psychophysics,* 1968, *4,* 307–312.

Wohlwill, J. F.   Factors in the differential response to the natural and the man-made environment. Paper presented at the meeting of the American Psychological Association, Montreal, August, 1973.

Wohlwill, J. F.   Human adaptation to levels of environmental stimulation. *Human Ecology,* 1974, *2,* 127–147.

Wohlwill, J. F.   Environmental aesthetics: The environment as a source of affect. In I. Altman & J. F. Wohlwill (Eds.), *Human behavior and environment* (Vol. 1). New York: Plenum Press, 1976.

Wohlwill, J. F., & Kohn, I.   The environment as experienced by the migrant: An adaptation-level view. *Representative Research in Social Psychology,* 1973, *4,* 135–164.

Wohlwill, J. F., & Kohn, I.   Dimensionalizing the environmental manifold. In S. Wapner, S. B. Cohen, & B. Kaplan (Eds.), *Experiencing the environment.* New York: Plenum Press, 1976.

Wolf, M. G.   Need gratification theory: A theoretical reformulation of job satisfaction/dissatisfaction and job motivation. *Journal of Applied Psychology,* 1970, *54,* 87–94.

Wood, D.   *I don't want to, but I will: The genesis of geographic knowledge: A real-time developmental study of adolescent images of novel environments.* Worcester, Mass.: Clark University Cartographic Laboratory, 1973.

Wrightsman, L. S.   *Assumptions about human nature: A social-psychological approach.* Monterey, Calif.: Brooks/Cole, 1974.

Wrightsman, L. S.   *Social psychology* (2nd ed.). Monterey, Calif.: Brooks/Cole, 1977.

Wurman, R. S.   *Making the city observable.* Cambridge, Mass.: MIT Press, 1971.

Yambert, P.   Language and word power. In N. McInnis & C. Albrecht (Eds.), *What makes education environmental?* Louisville, Ky: Data Courier, 1975.

Yerkes, R. M., & Dodson, J. D.   The relation of strength of stimulus to rapidity of habit-formation. *Journal of Comparative and Neurological Psychology,* 1908, *18,* 459–482.

Young, L. B.   *Power over people.* New York: Oxford University Press, 1973.

Zeisel, J.   *Sociology and architectural design.* New York: Russell Sage Foundation, 1975.

Zeisel, J., & Griffin, M.   *Charlesview housing: A diagnostic evaluation.* Cambridge, Mass.: Graduate School of Design, Harvard University, 1975.

Zerner, C., & Hubka, T. C.   The alligator learning experience: Children's strategies and approaches to a design problem. In W. J. Mitchell (Ed.), *Environmental design: Research and practice. Proceedings of the EDRA 3/AR 8 Conference January 1972.* Los Angeles: University of California Press, 1972.

Zimbardo, P. G.   The human choice: Individuation, reason, and order versus de-individuation, impulse, and chaos. In W. J. Arnold & D. Levine (Eds.), *Nebraska symposium on motivation, 1969.* Lincoln, Neb.: University of Nebraska Press, 1970.

Zimbardo, P. G., Haney, C., & Banks, W. C.   A Pirandellian prison. In E. Krupat (Ed.), *Psychology is social: Readings and conversations in social psychology.* Glenview, Ill.: Scott, Foresman, 1975.

Zlutnick, S., & Altman, I.   Crowding and human behavior. In J. F. Wohlwill & D. H. Carson (Eds.), *Environment and the social sciences: Perspectives and applications.* Washington, D.C.: American Psychological Association, 1972.

Zubek, J. P. (Ed.). *Sensory deprivation: Fifteen years of research.* New York: Appleton-Century-Crofts, 1969.

NAME INDEX

Campbell, A., 452
Campbell, D. T., 404, 405
Camus, A., 121
Canon, L. K., 202 $n7$
Canter, D., 193
Cantril, H., 74 $n8$, 217, 227, 263, 421
Caplan, N., 135, 453, 454
Carr, S., 120, 370, 373, 375, 376, 379, 380, 390
Carson, R., 313, 314
Castillo, G. A., 206 $n36$, 312, 322 $n15$
Chase, A., 447
Chermayeff, S., 357–58, 366, 370, 372, 387
Chin, R., 430, 432
Chomsky, N., 21, 464 $n3$
Christian, J. J., 345
Churchill, W., 328, 335, 386
Clark, K., 319
Cobb, J., 251, 253
Cofer, C. N., 47, 48, 336, 337
Cohen, A. R., 276 $n5$
Cohen, S., 393 $n4$
Colbert, C., 358, 361
Colby, A., 269
Cole, H. S. D., 75 $n16$
Cole, M., 104
Committee of Concerned Asian Scholars, 464 $n5$
Commoner, B., 71, 74 $n7$, 214, 356, 367, 436, 449
Conrad, D. R., 312
Cook, H., 204 $n24$, 205 $n27$
Cote, M., 206 $n33$
Craik, K. H., 103, 134, 135, 204 $n23$, 206 $n35$, 321 $n1$
Criden, Y., 75 $n17$, 417, 420, 421
Csikszentmihalyi, M., 15 $n1$, 35
Cullen, G., 334, 370
Cyert, R. M., 301

Dahl, R. A., 316, 317, 323 $n18$, 323 $n19$
Daly, H. E., 65, 70, 75 $n16$, 409, 452
Dasmann, R. F., 370, 401
David, D. S., 465 $n15$
David, S. M., 441, 442, 464 $n8$
Davidoff, L., 465 $n14$
Davidoff, P., 465 $n14$
Davis, J. U., 271, 273, 274
Davis, R., 323 $n16$
Davitz, J., 204 $n24$, 205 $n27$
Day, H. I., 73 $n4$
De Bell, G., 465 $n10$
de Bono, E., 169, 205 $n28$, 205 $n31$, 450
deCharms, R., 25, 26, 27, 31, 36, 37, 38, 42, 43, 46, 51, 55, 58, 73 $n4$, 126, 298, 322 $n15$, 429, 432, 455

Deci, E. L., 26, 27, 28
de Jonge, D., 195
de Mille, R., 204 $n24$, 322 $n15$
Desor, J. A., 349
Deutsch, M., 52, 75 $n15$, 226, 231, 234, 257, 318, 436, 438, 464 $n2$
Dewey, J., 7, 118, 253, 358, 394 $n15$
Dillard, A., 146, 205 $n26$
Disch, R., 74 $n7$, 276 $n3$
Dixon, N. F., 108
Dodson, J. D., 34
Domhoff, G. W., 74 $n11$, 436, 443, 445, 464 $n8$
Downs, R. M., 191, 193, 206 $n35$
Dreeben, R., 247
Duberman, M., 465 $n13$
Dubos, R., 41, 82, 221, 222, 238, 291, 320, 367
Dyck, A. J., 447
Dye, T. R., 74 $n11$, 76 $n19$

Easterbrook, J. A., 74 $n6$
Ecology Action East, 236
Edberg, R., 74 $n7$
Edney, J. J., 392 $n1$
Ehrlich, A. H., 74 $n7$, 393 $n5$
Ehrlich, P. R., 74 $n7$, 344, 393 $n5$
Eisemon, T., 205 $n31$
Eiser, J. R., 202 $n8$
Ellul, J., 237
Emery, F. E., 15 $n2$, 289
Eriksen, B. A., 204 $n21$
Eriksen, C. W., 204 $n21$
Esser, A. H., 287, 348, 349
Etzioni, A., 323 $n16$, 399, 402
Eysenck, H. J., 73 $n4$

Falk, R. A., 72, 74 $n7$, 264, 369, 438, 464 $n8$, 465 $n9$
Fanning, O., 322 $n6$, 445, 465 $n10$, 465 $n11$
Fantini, M. D., 206 $n36$, 322 $n15$
Farallones, 382, 391
Farber, J., 38, 246
Fechner, G. T., 82
Feigenbaum, E. A., 201 $n2$
Feldman, J., 201 $n2$
Ferguson, J. G., 140
Festinger, L., 33
Fischer, C. S., 347, 393 $n8$
Fishbein, M., 276 $n1$, 277 $n5$
Fisher, D., 204 $n20$
Fiske, D. W., 31, 34, 73 $n4$
Flavell, J. H., 200, 269
Fluegelman, A., 450
Foin, T. C., 363
Footlick, J. K., 388

SUBJECT INDEX

"Model of the mind." *See* Model of environment/experience/behavior interrelations
Model 1, 407–8, 429–30, 458
  and leaders vs. organizers, 445
  and psychological research, 264, 453
  and social change, 429–30, 431, 438
Model 2, 407–8, 429–30
  and education, 311, 458–59
  and inequality, 436
  and psychological research, 265, 455
  and social change, 429–30, 431, 432, 438–39, 442–45, 450
  socializing for, 457–63
  and utopia, 407–8, 409, 410, 416, 430
Moral education, 13, 268–74, 298
  and consensus, 317
  and utopia, 404
  and Walden Two, 412
Moral reasoning, stages of, 269–71, 273, 297–98, 404
Motivation, 20. *See also* Achievement motivation; Effectance motivation; Extrinsic motivation; Intrinsic motivation; Maslow's hierarchy; Reinforcement; Synergy
  and attitudes and values, 214–215
Multinational corporation, 436, 438, 448

Nationalism, 232
Natural hazards, responses to, 299–306
Nature, orientation toward, 135, 220–23, 241, 288, 320
Nature hating, 220–23, 231, 242
Nature interpretation, 309
Nature loving, 290
NBG, 159, 160, 173
Need, as design criterion, 371, 372, 388, 390
Needs, and utopia, 399, 400. *See also* Maslow's hierarchy
Negative feedback, 8
Negative reinforcement, 21
Neighborhood, 195, 417
News reporting, 214, 249
New towns
  and community, 366–67
  and comparison level, 378
  criticized, 361
  and ecological ethic, 368
  planning, 359
NNA, 170
Node, 192, 194, 199
Noise, 339, 340–41, 392–93 n4, 393 n6
Normative–re-educative change strategy, 430–31, 432, 442–46
Norway, 69

Open classroom, 38, 385, 387, 391, 412
Operant conditioning, and Walden Two, 412, 415
Operative values, 213, 275
Opportunity surface, 199
Organizing, as cognitive process, 100, 101–2, 106
Organizing, as social change tactic, 439–40, 445, 456–57
Orientation surface, 199
Orienting response, 351
Origin, 26, 36–38
  and ecological consciousness, 295, 457
  and education, 38–39, 51, 255. *See also* Origin training
  environmental implications of, 39–43
  and Model 2, 408, 429
  and pro-life values, 255
  and self-actualization, 46
Origin training, 37–38, 298, 455
  collective, 42–43, 322 n15
  and social change, 431, 432
  and Walden Two, 412
Overload, and stress, 337, 347, 351

Pain, 133
Panic, 232
Papanek's design criteria, 371–72
  and adventure playground, 390
  and prison, 388, 389
  and utopia, 402
Paradigm, 137
Parent effectiveness training, 313–14, 460–61
Participation paradox, 322 n7
Participatory democracy, 316, 322–323 n16
Participatory planning, 381
Participatory socialism, 318
Particularistic interpretation, 455–56
Pastoralism, 135
Path, 192, 194, 199
Pawn, 26, 36–37, 295
Peace-keeping vs. war-making system, 438
Peak experience, 46, 56, 148, 153, 319
"Pentagon of power," 238
People's organization, 439, 442
People's Park, 357, 382
Perception. *See* Cognitive set; Experience; Percipience; Physiognomic perception; Relating; Scanning/focusing; Sensory reception
Perceptual learning, 102
Perceptual organizing, 101–2, 146
Percipience, 141–43, 145, 286